Adam Nathan

WPF 4

UNLEASHED

SAMS | 800 East 96th Street, Indianapolis, Indiana 46240 USA

WPF 4 Unleashed

ISBN-13: 978-0-672-33119-0
ISBN-10: 0-672-33119-5

Library of Congress Cataloging-in-Publication Data

Nathan, Adam.
WPF 4 unleashed / Adam Nathan.
p. cm.
Includes index.
ISBN 978-0-672-33119-0
1. Windows presentation foundation. 2. Application software. 3. Microsoft .NET Framework. I. Title.
QA76.76.A65N386 2010
006.7'882—dc22

2010017765

Printed in the United States on America

Second Printing August 2011

Trademarks

Warning and Disclaimer

Bulk Sales

Sams Publishing offers excellent discounts on this book when ordered in quantity for bulk purchases or special sales. For more information, please contact

U.S. Corporate and Government Sales

1-800-382-3419

corpsales@pearsontechgroup.com

For sales outside of the U.S., please contact

International Sales

international@pearsoned.com

Editor-in-Chief
Karen Gettman

Executive Editor
Neil Rowe

Development Editor
Mark Renfrow

Managing Editor
Kristy Hart

Project Editor
Betsy Harris

Copy Editor
Kitty Wilson

Indexer
Erika Millen

Proofreader
Kathy Ruiz

Technical Editors
Dwayne Need
Robert Hogue
Joe Castro
Jordan Parker

Publishing Coordinator
Cindy Teeters

Book Designer
Gary Adair

Composition
Bronkella Publishing LLC

Contents at a Glance

Table of Contents

About the Author

Adam Nathan is a principal software development engineer for Microsoft Visual Studio, the latest version of which has been transformed into a first-class WPF application. Adam was previously the founding developer and architect for Popfly, Microsoft's first product built on Silverlight, named one of the 25 most innovative products of 2007 by *PCWorld Magazine*. Having started his career on Microsoft's Common Language Runtime team, Adam has been at the core of .NET and WPF technologies since the very beginning.

Adam's books have been considered required reading by many inside Microsoft and throughout the industry. He is the author of the best-selling *WPF Unleashed* (Sams, 2006) that was nominated for a 2008 Jolt Award, *Silverlight 1.0 Unleashed* (Sams, 2008), and *.NET and COM: The Complete Interoperability Guide* (Sams, 2002); a coauthor of *ASP.NET: Tips, Tutorials, and Code* (Sams, 2001); and a contributor to books including *.NET Framework Standard Library Annotated Reference, Volume 2* (Addison-Wesley, 2005) and *Windows Developer Power Tools* (O'Reilly, 2006). Adam is also the creator of PINVOKE.NET and its Visual Studio add-in. You can find him online at www.adamnathan.net, or @adamnathan on Twitter.

Dedication

To Lindsay, Tyler, and Ryan.

Acknowledgments

As always, I'd like to thank my wonderful wife, Lindsay, for her incredible support and understanding. Our life is always heavily affected by the seemingly never-ending process of writing a book, and by now you think she would have run out of patience. However, she has never been more supportive than she has been for this book. Lindsay, I couldn't have done it without you.

Although most of the process of writing a book is very solitary, this book came together because of the work of many talented and hard-working people. I'd like to take a moment to thank some of them by name.

I'd like to sincerely thank Dwayne Need, senior development manager from the WPF team, for being a fantastic technical editor. His feedback on my drafts was so thorough and insightful, the book is far better because of him. I'd like to thank Robert Hogue, Joe Castro, and Jordan Parker for their helpful reviews. David Teitlebaum, 3D expert from the WPF team, deserves many thanks for agreeing to update the great 3D chapter originally written by Daniel Lehenbauer. Having Daniel's and David's perspectives and advice captured on paper is a huge benefit for any readers thinking about dabbling in 3D.

I'd also like to thank (in alphabetical order): Brian Chapman, Beatriz de Oliveira Costa, Ifeanyi Echeruo, Dan Glick, Neil Kronlage, Rico Mariani, Mike Mueller, Oleg Ovetchkine, Lori Pearce, S. Ramini, Rob Relyea, Tim Rice, Ben Ronco, Adam Smith, Tim Sneath, David Treadwell, and Paramesh Vaidyanathan.

I'd like to thank the folks at Sams—especially Neil Rowe and Betsy Harris, who are always a pleasure to work with. I couldn't have asked for a better publishing team. Never once was I told that my content was too long or too short or too different from a typical *Unleashed* title. They gave me the complete freedom to write the kind of book I wanted to write.

I'd like to thank my mom, dad, and brother for opening my eyes to the world of computer programming when I was in elementary school. If you have children, please expose them to the magic of writing software while they're still young enough to care about what you have to say! (WPF and Silverlight can even help you make the experience fun!)

Finally, I thank *you* for picking up a copy of this book and reading at least this far! I hope you continue reading and find the journey of exploring WPF 4 as fascinating as I have!

We Want to Hear from You!

As the reader of this book, *you* are our most important critic and commentator. We value your opinion and want to know what we're doing right, what we could do better, what areas you'd like to see us publish in, and any other words of wisdom you're willing to pass our way.

You can email or write me directly to let me know what you did or didn't like about this book—as well as what we can do to make our books stronger.

Please note that I cannot help you with technical problems related to the topic of this book, and that due to the high volume of mail I receive, I might not be able to reply to every message.

When you write, please be sure to include this book's title and author as well as your name and phone or email address. I will carefully review your comments and share them with the author and editors who worked on the book.

E-mail: feedback@samspublishing.com

Mail: Neil Rowe
Executive Editor
Sams Publishing
800 East 96th Street
Indianapolis, IN 46240 USA

Reader Services

Visit our website and register this book at informit.com/register for convenient access to any updates, downloads, or errata that might be available for this book.

Introduction

Thank you for picking up *WPF 4 Unleashed*! Windows Presentation Foundation (WPF) is Microsoft's premier technology for creating Windows graphical user interfaces, whether they consist of plain forms, document-centric windows, animated cartoons, videos, immersive 3D environments, or all of the above. WPF is a technology that makes it easier than ever to create a broad range of applications. It's also the basis for Silverlight, which has extended WPF technology onto the Web and into devices such as Windows phones.

Ever since WPF was publicly announced in 2003 (with the code name "Avalon"), it has gotten considerable attention for the ways in which it revolutionizes the process of creating software—especially for Windows programmers used to Windows Forms and GDI. It's relatively easy to create fun, useful, and shareable WPF samples that demonstrate all kinds of techniques that are difficult to accomplish in other technologies. WPF 4, released in April 2010, improves on previous versions of WPF in just about every dimension.

WPF is quite a departure from previous technologies in terms of its programming model, underlying concepts, and basic terminology. Even viewing the source code for WPF (by cracking open its components with a tool such as .NET Reflector) is a confusing experience because the code you're looking for often doesn't reside where you'd expect to find it. When you combine all this with the fact that there are often several ways to accomplish any task in WPF, you arrive at a conclusion shared by many: *WPF has a very steep learning curve*.

That's where this book comes in. As WPF was developed, it was obvious that there would be no shortage of WPF books in the marketplace. But it wasn't clear to me that the books would have the right balance to guide people through the technology and its unique concepts while showing practical ways to exploit it. Therefore, I wrote the first edition of this book, *Windows Presentation Foundation Unleashed*, with the following goals in mind:

- To provide a solid grounding in the underlying concepts, in a practical and approachable fashion
- To answer the questions most people have when learning the technology and to show how commonly desired tasks are accomplished
- To be an authoritative source, thanks to input from members of the WPF team who designed, implemented, and tested the technology
- To be clear about where the technology falls short rather than selling the technology as the answer to all problems
- To be an easily navigated reference that you can constantly come back to

The first edition of this book was far more successful than I ever imagined it would be. Now, almost four years later, I believe that this second edition accomplishes all the same goals but with even more depth. In addition to covering new features introduced in WPF 3.5, WPF 3.5 SP1, and WPF 4, it expands the coverage of the existing features from the first version of WPF. Whether you're new to WPF or a long-time WPF developer, I hope you find this book to exhibit all these attributes.

Who Should Read This Book?

This book is for software developers who are interested in creating user interfaces for Windows. Regardless of whether you're creating line-of-business applications, consumer-facing applications, or reusable controls, this book contains a lot of content that helps you get the most out of the platform. It's designed to be understandable even for folks who are new to the .NET Framework. And if you are already well versed in WPF, I'm confident that this book still has information for you. At the very least, it should be an invaluable reference for your bookshelf.

Because the technology and concepts behind WPF are the same ones behind Silverlight, reading this book can also make you a better developer for Windows Phone 7 and even a better web developer.

Although this book's content is not optimized for graphic designers, reading this book can be a great way to understand more of the "guts" behind a product like Microsoft Expression Blend.

To summarize, this book does the following:

- Covers everything you need to know about Extensible Application Markup Language (XAML), the XML-based language for creating declarative user interfaces that can be easily restyled
- Examines the WPF feature areas in incredible depth: controls, layout, resources, data binding, styling, graphics, animation, and more
- Highlights the latest features, such as multi-touch, text rendering improvements, new controls, XAML language enhancements, the Visual State Manager, easing functions, and much more
- Delves into topics that aren't covered by most books: 3D, speech, audio/video, documents, effects, and more
- Shows how to create popular user interface elements, such as galleries, ScreenTips, custom control layouts, and more
- Demonstrates how to create sophisticated user interface mechanisms, such as Visual Studio–like collapsible/dockable panes
- Explains how to develop and deploy all types of applications, including navigation-based applications, applications hosted in a web browser, and applications with great-looking nonrectangular windows
- Explains how to create first-class custom controls for WPF

- Demonstrates how to create hybrid WPF software that leverages Windows Forms, DirectX, ActiveX, or other non-WPF technologies
- Explains how to exploit new Windows 7 features in WPF applications, such as Jump Lists, and how to go beyond some of the limitations of WPF

This book doesn't cover every last bit of WPF. (In particular, XML Paper Specification [XPS] documents are given only a small bit of attention.) WPF's surface area is so large that I don't believe any single book can. But I think you'll be pleased with the breadth and depth achieved by this book.

Examples in this book appear in XAML and C#, plus C++/CLI for interoperability discussions. XAML is used heavily for a number of reasons: It's often the most concise way to express source code, it can often be pasted into lightweight tools to see instant results without any compilation, WPF-based tools generate XAML rather than procedural code, and XAML is applicable no matter what .NET language you use, such as Visual Basic instead of C#. Whenever the mapping between XAML and a language such as C# is not obvious, examples are shown in both representations.

Software Requirements

This book targets the final release of version 4.0 of Windows Presentation Foundation, the corresponding Windows SDK, and Visual Studio 2010.

The following software is required:

- A version of Windows that supports the .NET Framework 4.0. This can be Windows XP with Service Pack 2 (including Media Center, Tablet PC, and x64 editions), Windows Server 2003 with Service Pack 1 (including the R2 edition), Windows Vista, or later versions.
- The .NET Framework 4.0, which is installed by default starting with Windows Vista. For earlier versions of Windows, you can download the .NET Framework 4.0 for free from http://msdn.com.

In addition, the following software is recommended:

- The Windows Software Development Kit (SDK), specifically the .NET tools it includes. This is also a free download from http://msdn.com.
- Visual Studio 2010 or later, which can be a free Express edition downloaded from http://msdn.com.

If you want additional tool support for WPF-based graphic design, Microsoft Expression (specifically Expression Blend) can be extremely helpful.

A few examples are specific to Windows Vista, Windows 7, or a computer that supports multi-touch, but the rest of the book applies equally to all relevant versions of Windows.

Code Examples

The source code for examples in this book can be downloaded from http://informit.com/title/9780672331190 or http://adamnathan.net/wpf.

How This Book Is Organized

This book is arranged into six main parts, representing the progression of feature areas that you typically need to understand to use WPF effectively. But if you're dying to jump ahead and learn about a topic such as 3D or animation, the book is set up to allow for nonlinear journeys as well. The following sections provide a summary of each part.

Part I: Background

This part includes the following chapters:

- Chapter 1: Why WPF, and What About Silverlight?
- Chapter 2: XAML Demystified
- Chapter 3: WPF Fundamentals

Chapter 1 introduces WPF by comparing it to alternative technologies and helping you make decisions about when WPF is appropriate for your needs. Chapter 2 explores XAML in great depth, giving you the foundation to understand the XAML you'll encounter in the rest of the book and in real life. Chapter 3 highlights the most unique pieces of WPF's programming model above and beyond what .NET programmers already understand.

Part II: Building a WPF Application

This part includes the following chapters:

- Chapter 4: Sizing, Positioning, and Transforming Elements
- Chapter 5: Layout with Panels
- Chapter 6: Input Events: Keyboard, Mouse, Stylus, and Multi-Touch
- Chapter 7: Structuring and Deploying an Application
- Chapter 8: Exploiting Windows 7

Part II equips you with the knowledge to assemble and deploy a traditional-looking application (although some fancier effects, such as transforms, nonrectangular windows, and Aero Glass, are also covered). Chapters 4 and 5 discuss arranging controls (and other elements) in a user interface. Chapter 6 covers input events, including new support for engaging multi-touch user interfaces. Chapter 7 examines several different ways to package and deploy WPF-based user interfaces to make complete applications. Chapter 8 ends this part by showing slick ways to exploit features in Windows 7 that can help make your application look modern.

Part III: Controls

This part includes the following chapters:

- Chapter 9: Content Controls
- Chapter 10: Items Controls
- Chapter 11: Images, Text, and Other Controls

Part III provides a tour of controls built into WPF. There are many that you'd expect to have available, plus several that you might not expect. Two categories of controls—content controls (Chapter 9) and items controls (Chapter 10)—are important and deep enough topics to merit their own chapters. The rest of the controls are examined in Chapter 11.

Part IV: Features for Professional Developers

This part includes the following chapters:

- Chapter 12: Resources
- Chapter 13: Data Binding
- Chapter 14: Styles, Templates, Skins, and Themes

The features covered in Part IV are not always necessary to use in WPF applications, but they can greatly enhance the development process. Therefore, they are indispensable for professional developers who are serious about creating maintainable and robust applications or components. These topics are less about the results visible to end users than they are about the best practices for accomplishing these results.

Part V: Rich Media

This part includes the following chapters:

- Chapter 15: 2D Graphics
- Chapter 16: 3D Graphics
- Chapter 17: Animation
- Chapter 18: Audio, Video, and Speech

This part of the book covers the features in WPF that typically get the most attention. The support for 2D and 3D graphics, animation, video, and more enable you to create a stunning experience. These features—and the way they are exposed—set WPF apart from previous systems. WPF lowers the barrier to incorporating such content in your software, so you might try some of these features that you never would have dared to try in the past!

Part VI: Advanced Topics

This part includes the following chapters:

- Chapter 19: Interoperability with Non-WPF Technologies
- Chapter 20: User Controls and Custom Controls
- Chapter 21: Layout with Custom Panels

The topics covered in Part VI are relevant for advanced application developers, or developers of WPF-based controls. The fact that existing WPF controls can be radically restyled greatly reduces the need for creating custom controls.

Conventions Used in This Book

Various typefaces in this book identify new terms and other special items. These typefaces include the following:

Typeface	Meaning
Italic	Italic is used for new terms or phrases when they are initially defined and occasionally for emphasis.
`Monospace`	`Monospace` is used for screen messages, code listings, and command samples, as well as filenames. In code listings, *`italic monospace type`* is used for placeholder text.
	Code listings are colorized similar to the way they are colorized in Visual Studio. `Blue monospace type` is used for XML elements and C#/C++ keywords, `brown monospace type` is used for XML element names and C#/C++ strings, `green monospace type` is used for comments, `red monospace type` is used for XML attributes, and `teal monospace type` is used for type names in C# and C++.

Throughout this book, you'll find a number of sidebar elements:

FAQ

What is a FAQ sidebar?

A FAQ sidebar presents a question readers might have regarding the subject matter in a particular spot in the book—and then provides a concise answer.

DIGGING DEEPER

Digging Deeper Sidebars

A Digging Deeper sidebar presents advanced or more detailed information on a subject than is provided in the surrounding text. Think of Digging Deeper material as stuff you can look into if you're curious but can ignore if you're not.

TIP

A tip is a bit of information that can help you in a real-world situation. Tips often offer shortcuts or alternative approaches to produce better results or to make a task easier or quicker.

WARNING

A warning alerts you to an action or a condition that can lead to an unexpected or unpredictable result—and then tells you how to avoid it.

PART I

Background

IN THIS PART

CHAPTER 1

Why WPF, and What About Silverlight?

IN THIS CHAPTER

- A Look at the Past
- Enter WPF
- The Evolution of WPF
- What About Silverlight?

In movies and on TV, the main characters are typically an exaggeration of the people you encounter in real life. They're more attractive, they react more quickly, and they somehow always know exactly what to do. The same could be said about the software they use.

This first struck me back in 1994 when watching the movie *Disclosure*, starring Michael Douglas, Demi Moore, and an email program that looks nothing like Microsoft Outlook! Throughout the movie, we're treated to various visual features of the program: a spinning three-dimensional "e," messages that unfold when you open them and crumple when you delete them, hints of inking support, and slick animations when you print messages. (The email program isn't even the most unrealistic software in the movie. I'll just say "virtual reality database" and leave it at that.)

Usability issues aside, Hollywood has been telling us for a long time that software in the real world isn't as compelling as it should be. You can probably think of several examples on your own of TV shows and movies with comically unrealistic software. But lately, real-world software has been catching up to Hollywood's standards! You can already see it in traditional operating systems (yes, even in Windows), on the web, and in software for devices such as the iPhone, iPad, Zune, TiVo, Wii, Xbox, Windows phones, and many more. Users have increasing expectations for the experience of using software, and companies are spending a great deal of time and money on user interfaces that differentiate themselves from the competition. This isn't limited to consumer-facing software; even business applications and internal tools can greatly benefit from a polished user interface.

With higher demands placed on user interfaces, traditional software development processes and technologies often fall short. Modern software usually needs to support rapid iteration and major user interface changes throughout the process—whether such changes are driven by professional graphic designers, developers with a knack for designing user interfaces, or a boss who wants the product to be more "shiny" and animated. For this to be successful, you need technology and tools that make it natural to separate the user interface from the rest of the implementation as much as possible and to decouple visual behavior from the underlying program logic. Developers should be able to create a fully functional "ugly" application that designers can directly retheme without requiring developers to translate their artwork. The Win32 style of programming, in which controls directly contain code to paint and repaint themselves, makes rapid user interface iteration far too difficult for most projects.

In 2006, Microsoft released a technology to help people create 21st-century software that meets these high demands: Windows Presentation Foundation (WPF). With the release of WPF 4 in 2010, the technology is better than ever at delivering amazing results for just about any kind of software. Almost a decade after Tom Cruise helped popularize the idea of multi-touch computer input in the movie *Minority Report*, and after successful multi-touch implementations in a variety of devices (most notably the iPhone), WPF 4 and Windows 7 are bringing multi-touch to the masses. Hollywood better start coming up with some fresh ideas!

A Look at the Past

The primary technologies behind many Windows-based user interfaces—the graphics device interface (GDI) and USER subsystems—were introduced with Windows 1.0 in 1985. That's almost prehistoric in the world of technology! In the early 1990s, OpenGL (created by Silicon Graphics) became a popular graphics library for doing advanced two-dimensional (2D) and three-dimensional (3D) graphics on both Windows and non-Windows systems. This was leveraged by people creating computer-aided design (CAD) programs, scientific visualization programs, and games. DirectX, a Microsoft technology introduced in 1995, provided a new high-performance alternative for 2D graphics, input, communication, sound, and eventually 3D (introduced with DirectX 2 in 1996).

Over the years, many enhancements have been made to both GDI and DirectX. GDI+, introduced in the Windows XP time frame, tried to improve upon GDI by adding support for features such as alpha blending and gradient brushes. It ended up being slower than GDI due to its complexity and lack of hardware acceleration. DirectX (which, by the way, is the technology behind Xbox) continually comes out with new versions that push the limits of what can be done with computer graphics. With the introduction of .NET and managed code in 2002, developers were treated to a highly productive model for creating Windows (and web) applications. In this world, Windows Forms (built on top of GDI+) became the primary way a C#, Visual Basic, and (to a lesser degree) C++ developer started to create new user interfaces on Windows. Windows Forms has been a successful and productive technology, but it still has all the fundamental limitations of GDI+ and USER.

Starting with DirectX 9, Microsoft shipped a DirectX framework for managed code (much like it shipped libraries specifically for Visual Basic in the past), which eventually was supplanted by the XNA Framework. Although this enables C# developers to use DirectX without most of the complications of .NET/COM interoperability, these managed frameworks aren't significantly easier to use than their unmanaged counterparts unless you're writing a game. (The XNA Framework makes writing a game easier because it includes new libraries specifically for game development and works with compelling tools such as the XNA Framework Content Pipeline and XNA Game Studio Express.)

So although you could have developed a Windows-based email program with the 3D effects seen in *Disclosure* ever since the mid-1990s with non-GDI technologies (actually, probably mixing DirectX or OpenGL with GDI), such technologies are rarely used in mainstream Windows applications even more than a decade later. There are several reasons for this: The hardware required to get a decent experience hasn't been ubiquitous until recently, it has been at least an order of magnitude harder to use alternative technologies, and GDI-based experiences have been considered "good enough."

Graphics hardware continues to get better and cheaper and consumer expectations continue to rise, but until WPF, the difficulty of creating modern user experiences had not been addressed. Some developers would take matters into their own hands to get cooler-looking applications and controls on Windows. A simple example of this is using bitmaps for buttons instead of using the standard button control. These types of customizations can not only be expensive to develop, but they also often produce a flakier experience. Such applications often aren't as accessible as they should be, don't handle high dots-per-inch (DPI) settings very well, and have other visual glitches.

Enter WPF

Microsoft recognized that something brand new was needed that escaped the limitations of GDI+ and USER yet provided the kind of productivity that people enjoy with frameworks like Windows Forms. And with the continual rise of cross-platform applications based on HTML and JavaScript, Windows desperately needed a technology that's as fun and easy to use as these, yet with the power to exploit the capabilities of the local computer. Windows Presentation Foundation (WPF) is the answer for software developers and graphic designers who want to create modern user experiences without having to master several difficult technologies. Although "Presentation" sounds like a lofty term for what I would simply call a user interface, it's probably more appropriate for describing the higher level of visual polish that's expected of today's applications and the wide range of functionality included in WPF!

The highlights of WPF include the following:

- **Broad integration**—Prior to WPF, a Windows developer who wanted to use 3D, video, speech, and rich document viewing in addition to normal 2D graphics and controls would have to learn several independent technologies with a number of inconsistencies and attempt to blend them together without much built-in support. But WPF covers all these areas with a consistent programming model as well as tight integration when each type of media gets composited and rendered. You can apply the same kind of effects consistently across different media types, and many of the techniques you learn in one area apply to all the other areas.

- **Resolution independence**—Imagine a world in which moving to a higher resolution or DPI setting doesn't mean that everything gets smaller; instead, graphics and text simply get crisper! Envision user interfaces that look reasonable on a small netbook as well as on a 60-inch TV! WPF makes this easy and gives you the power to shrink or enlarge elements on the screen independently from the screen's resolution. A lot of this is possible because of WPF's emphasis on vector graphics.
- **Hardware acceleration**—WPF is built on Direct3D, so content in a WPF application—whether 2D or 3D, graphics, or text—is converted to 3D triangles, textures, and other Direct3D objects and then rendered by hardware. This means that WPF applications get the benefits of hardware acceleration for smoother graphics and all-around better performance (due to work being offloaded to graphics processing units [GPUs] instead of central processor units [CPUs]). It also ensures that all WPF applications (not just high-end games) receive benefits from new hardware and drivers, whose advances typically focus on 3D capabilities. But WPF doesn't *require* high-end graphics hardware; it has a software rendering pipeline as well. This enables features not yet supported by hardware, enables high-fidelity printing of any content on the screen, and is used as a fallback mechanism when encountering inadequate hardware resources (such as an outdated graphics card or even a high-end one that has simply run out of GPU resources such as video memory).
- **Declarative programming**—Declarative programming is not unique to WPF, as Win16/Win32 programs have used declarative resource scripts to define the layout of dialog boxes and menus for over 25 years. And .NET programs of all types often leverage declarative custom attributes plus configuration and resource files based on Extensible Markup Language (XML). But WPF takes declarative programming to the next level with Extensible *Application* Markup Language (XAML; pronounced "Zammel"). The combination of WPF and XAML is similar to using HTML to define a user interface—but with an incredible range of expressiveness. This expressiveness even extends beyond the bounds of user interfaces; WPF uses XAML as a document format, a representation of 3D models, and more. The result is that graphic designers are empowered to contribute directly to the look and feel of applications, as well as some behavior for which you'd typically expect to have to write code. The next chapter examines XAML in depth.
- **Rich composition and customization**—WPF controls can be composed in ways never before seen. You can create a `ComboBox` filled with animated `Buttons` or a `Menu` filled with live video clips! Although these particular customizations might sound horrible, it's important that you don't have to write a bunch of code (or any code!) to customize controls in ways that the control authors never imagined (unlike owner-draw in prior technologies). Along the same lines, WPF makes it quite easy to "skin" applications with radically different looks (covered in Chapter 14, "Styles, Templates, Skins, and Themes").

In short, WPF aims to combine the best attributes of systems such as DirectX (3D and hardware acceleration), Windows Forms (developer productivity), Adobe Flash (powerful animation support), and HTML (declarative markup). With the help of this book, I think you'll find that WPF gives you more productivity, power, and fun than any other technology you've worked with in the past!

DIGGING DEEPER

GDI and Hardware Acceleration

GDI is actually hardware accelerated on Windows XP. The video driver model explicitly supported accelerating common GDI operations. Windows Vista introduced a new video driver model that does not hardware accelerate GDI primitives. Instead, it uses a "canonical display device" software implementation of the legacy video driver for GDI. However, Windows 7 reintroduced partial hardware acceleration for GDI primitives.

FAQ

Does WPF enable me to do something that I couldn't have previously done?

Technically, the answer is "No," just like C# and the .NET Framework don't enable you to do something that you couldn't do in assembly code. It's just a question of how much work you want to do to get the desired results!

If you were to attempt to build a WPF-equivalent application from scratch without WPF, you'd not only have to worry about the drawing of pixels on the screen and interaction with input devices, you'd also need to do a ton of additional work to get the accessibility and localization support that's built in to WPF, and so on. WPF also provides the easiest way to take advantage of Windows 7 features, such as defining Jump List items with a small chunk of XAML (see Chapter 8, "Exploiting Windows 7").

So I think most people would agree that the answer is "Yes" when you factor time and money into the equation!

FAQ

When should I use DirectX instead of WPF?

DirectX is more appropriate than WPF for advanced developers writing hard-core "twitch games" or applications with complex 3D models where you need maximum performance. That said, it's easy to write a naive DirectX application that performs far worse than a similar WPF application.

DirectX is a low-level interface to the graphics hardware that exposes all the quirks of whatever GPU a particular computer has. DirectX can be thought of as assembly language in the world of graphics: You can do anything the GPU supports, but it's up to you (the application author) to support all the hardware variations. This is onerous, but such low-level hardware access enables skilled developers to make their own tradeoffs between fine-grained quality and speed. In addition, DirectX exposes cutting-edge features of GPUs as they emerge more quickly than they appear in WPF.

Continued

In contrast, WPF provides a high-level abstraction that takes a description of a scene and figures out the best way to render it, given the hardware resources available. (It's a *retained mode* system rather than an *immediate mode* system.) 2D is the primary focus of WPF; its 3D support is focused on data visualization scenarios and integration with 2D rather than supporting the full power of DirectX.

The downside of choosing DirectX over WPF is a potentially astronomical increase in development cost. A large part of this cost is the requirement to test an application on each driver/GPU combination you intend to support. One of the major benefits of building on top of the WPF is that Microsoft has already done this testing for you! You can instead focus your testing on low-end hardware for measuring performance. The fact that WPF applications can even leverage the client GPU in a partial-trust environment is also a compelling differentiator.

Note that you are able to use both DirectX and WPF in the same application. Chapter 19, "Interoperability with Non-WPF Technologies," shows how this can be done.

The Evolution of WPF

Oddly enough, WPF 4 is the fourth major release of WPF. It's odd because the first release had the version number 3.0! The first release in November 2006 was called WPF 3.0 because it shipped as part of the .NET Framework 3.0. The second release—WPF 3.5—came almost exactly a year later (one day shy, in fact). The third release, once again, came almost a year later (in August 2008). This release was a part of Service Pack 1 (SP1) for .NET 3.5, but this was no ordinary service pack as far as WPF was concerned—it contained many new features and improvements.

In addition to these major releases, Microsoft introduced a "WPF Toolkit" in August 2008 at http://wpf.codeplex.com that, along with miscellaneous tools and samples, gets updated several times a year. The WPF Toolkit has been used as a way to ship features more quickly and in an experimental form (often with full source code). Features introduced in the WPF Toolkit often "graduate" to get included in a future release of WPF, based on customer feedback about their desirability and readiness.

When the first version of WPF was released, tool support was almost nonexistent. The following months brought primitive WPF extensions for Visual Studio 2005 and the first public preview release of Expression Blend. Now, Visual Studio 2010 not only has first-class support for WPF development but has been substantially rewritten to be a WPF application itself! Expression Blend, an application built 100% with WPF, has also gained a lot of functionality for designing and prototyping great user interfaces. And in the past several years, numerous WPF-based applications have been released from companies such as Autodesk, SAP, Disney, Blockbuster, Roxio, AMD, Hewlett Packard, Lenovo, and many more. Microsoft itself, of course, has a long list of software built with WPF (Visual Studio, Expression, Test and Lab Manager, Deep Zoom Composer, Songsmith, Surface, Semblio, Robotics Studio, LifeCam, Amalga, Games for Windows LIVE Marketplace, Office

TIP

To inspect the WPF elements used in any WPF-based application, you can use the Snoop tool available from http://snoopwpf.codeplex.com.

Communicator Attendant, Active Directory Administrative Center, Dynamics NAV, Pivot, PowerShell ISE, and many more).

Let's take a closer look at how WPF has changed over time.

Enhancements in WPF 3.5 and WPF 3.5 SP1

The following notable changes were made to WPF in versions 3.5 and 3.5 SP1:

- **Interactive 3D**—The worlds of 2D and 3D were woven together even more seamlessly with the `UIElement3D` base class, which gives 3D elements input, focus, and events; the odd-sounding `Viewport2DVisual3D` class, which can place any interactive 2D controls inside a 3D scene; and more. See Chapter 16, "3D Graphics."
- **First-class interoperability with DirectX**—Previously, WPF applications could only interoperate with DirectX via the lowest common denominator of Win32. Now, WPF has functionality for interacting directly with Direct3D surfaces with the `D3DImage` class rather than being forced to interact with its host HWND. One benefit from this is the ability to place WPF content on top of DirectX content and vice versa. See Chapter 19.
- **Better data binding**—WPF gained support for XLINQ binding, better validation and debugging, and output string formatting in XAML that reduces the need for custom procedural code. See Chapter 13, "Data Binding."
- **Better special effects**—The first version of WPF shipped with a handful of bitmap effects (blur, drop shadow, outer glow, emboss, and bevel) but with a warning to not use them because their performance was so poor! This has changed, with a new set of hardware-accelerated effects and a whole new architecture that allows you to plug in your own custom hardware-accelerated effects via pixel shaders. See Chapter 15, "2D Graphics."
- **High-performance custom drawing**—WPF didn't previously have a good answer for custom drawings that involve thousands of points or shapes, as even the lowest-level drawing primitives have too much overhead to make such things perform well. The `WriteableBitmap` class was enhanced so you can now specify dirty regions when drawing on it rather than getting a whole new bitmap every frame! Because `WriteableBitmap` only lets you set pixels, it is a very primitive form of "drawing," however.
- **Text improvements**—There's now better performance, better international support (improved input method editor [IME] support and improved Indic script support), and enhancements to `TextBox` and `RichTextBox`. See Chapter 11, "Images, Text, and Other Controls."
- **Enhancements to partial-trust applications**—More functionality became available in the partial-trust sandbox for .NET applications, such as the ability to use Windows Communication Foundation (WCF) for web service calls (via `basicHttpBinding`) and the ability to read and write HTTP cookies. Also, support for XAML Browser Applications (XBAPs)—the primary mechanism for running partial-trust

WPF applications—was extended to the Firefox web browser instead of just Internet Explorer (In WPF, however, the add-on that enables this is no longer installed by default.)

- **Improved deployment for applications and the .NET Framework**—This arrived in many forms: a smaller and faster .NET Framework installation process thanks to the beginnings of a .NET Framework "client profile" that excludes server-only .NET pieces such as ASP.NET; a new "bootstrapper" component that handles all .NET Framework dependencies, installations, and upgrades for you as well as enabling setups with custom branding; and a variety of new ClickOnce features.
- **Improved performance**—WPF and the underlying common language runtime implemented several changes that significantly boosted the performance of WPF applications without any code changes needed. For example, the load time (especially first-time load) has been dramatically improved, animations (especially slow ones) are much smoother, data binding is faster in a number of scenarios, and layered windows (described in Chapter 8) are now hardware accelerated. Other performance improvements were made that you must opt into due to compatibility constraints, such as improved virtualization and deferred scrolling in items controls, described in Chapter 10, "Items Controls."

Enhancements in WPF 4

WPF 4 brings the following changes, on top of the changes from previous versions:

- **Multi-touch support**—When running on computers that support multi-touch and run Windows 7 or later, WPF elements can get a variety of input events, from low-level data, to easy-to-consume manipulations (such as rotation and scaling), to high-level—including custom—gestures. The built-in WPF controls have also been updated to be multi-touch aware. The WPF team leveraged the work previously done by the Microsoft Surface team (whose software is built on WPF). As a result, multi-touch in WPF 4 is compatible with version 2 of the Surface SDK, which is great news for anyone considering developing for both Windows and Surface. See Chapter 6, "Input Events: Keyboard, Mouse, Stylus, and Multi-Touch."
- **First-class support for other Windows 7 features**—Multi-touch is a cool new feature of Windows 7, but there are plenty of others that don't require special hardware—so many more users will appreciate their inclusion. WPF provides the best way to integrate with new taskbar features such as Jump Lists and icon overlays, integrate with the latest common dialogs, and more. See Chapter 8.
- **New controls**—WPF 4 includes controls such as `DataGrid`, `Calendar`, and `DatePicker`, which originally debuted in the WPF Toolkit. See Chapter 11.
- **Easing animation functions**—Eleven new animation classes such as `BounceEase`, `ElasticEase`, and `SineEase` enable sophisticated animations with custom rates of acceleration and deceleration to be performed completely declaratively. These "easing functions" and their infrastructure were first introduced in Silverlight 3 before being adopted by WPF 4.

- **Enhanced styling with Visual State Manager**—The Visual State Manager, originally introduced in Silverlight 2, provides a new way to organize visuals and their interactivity into "visual states" and "state transitions." This feature makes it easier for designers to work with controls in tools such as Expression Blend, but importantly also makes it easier to share templates between WPF and Silverlight.
- **Improved layout on pixel boundaries**—WPF straddles the line between being automatically DPI independent (which requires ignoring physical pixel boundaries) and having visual elements that look crisp (which, especially for small elements, requires being aligned on pixel boundaries). From the beginning, WPF has supported a property called `SnapsToDevicePixels` that forces "pixel snapping" on elements. But using `SnapsToDevicePixels` can be complex and doesn't help in some scenarios. Silverlight went back to the drawing board and created a property called `UseLayoutRounding` that works more naturally. WPF 4 now has this property. Just set it to `true` on a root element, and the positions of that element plus all of children will be rounded up or down to lie on pixel boundaries. The result is user interfaces that can scale *and* can easily be crisp!
- **Non-blurry text**—WPF's emphasis on DPI independence and a scalable user interface has been an issue for small text—the kind of text that occurs a lot in traditional user interfaces on 96-DPI screens. This has frustrated numerous users and developers. In fact, I've always claimed that I can spot a user interface created with WPF simply by looking at the blurriness of its text. WPF 4 has finally addressed this with an alternative way to render text that can make it look as crisp as GDI-based text yet with almost all the benefits that WPF brings. Visual Studio 2010, for example, uses this rendering mode for its text documents. Because there are some limitations to the new rendering approach, you must opt into it. See Chapter 11.
- **More deployment improvements**—The .NET Framework client profile can run side-by-side with the full .NET Framework, and it can be used in just about every scenario relevant for WPF applications. In fact, .NET 4.0 projects in Visual Studio 2010 target the smaller client profile by default.
- **More performance improvements**—In order to make vector graphics perform as well as possible, WPF can cache rendered results as bitmaps and reuse them. For advanced scenarios, you can control this behavior with the new `CacheMode` property. See Chapter 15. The heavy usage of WPF in Visual Studio 2010 drove a lot of miscellaneous performance improvements into WPF 4 across the board, but all WPF applications get to enjoy these improvements.

FAQ

What will be added to WPF after version 4?

Nothing has been announced at the time of writing, but I think it's safe to say that performance and increased synergy with Silverlight will continue to be two major themes of WPF's evolution. Plus, the WPF Toolkit provides some clues to future features that could be integrated into the core platform, such as chart controls, a `BreadcrumbBar` control, a `NumericUpDown` control, and more.

FAQ

Are there any differences with WPF, depending on the version of Windows?

WPF exposes APIs that are relevant only for Windows 7 and later, such as multi-touch functionality and various features described in Chapter 8. Besides that, WPF has a few behavioral differences when running on Windows XP (the oldest version of Windows that WPF supports). For example, 3D objects do not get antialiased.

And, of course, WPF controls have different default themes to match their host operating system (Aero on Windows Vista and Windows 7 versus Luna on Windows XP).

Windows XP also has an older driver model that can negatively impact WPF applications. The driver model in later versions of Windows virtualizes and schedules GPU resources, making a system perform better when multiple GPU-intensive programs are running. Running multiple WPF or DirectX applications might bog down a Windows XP system but shouldn't cause performance issues on more recent versions of Windows.

What About Silverlight?

Silverlight is a small, lightweight version of the .NET Framework targeted at rich web scenarios (as an alternative to Adobe Flash and Flex, for example). Silverlight chose to follow WPF's approach to creating user interfaces rather than creating yet another distinct technology—and this approach has some great benefits. It was first released in 2007 and, like WPF, is already in its fourth major version. Silverlight 4 was released in April 2010, a few days after the release of WPF 4.

The relationship between WPF and Silverlight is a bit complex, and there is some confusion about when to use one technology versus the other. This is further exacerbated by the fact that WPF applications can run inside a web browser (as XBAPs) and be just as "web based" as Silverlight applications, and Silverlight applications can run outside a web browser, even in an offline mode.

Silverlight is mostly a subset of WPF plus the most fundamental classes in the .NET Framework (core data types, collection classes, and so on). Each new version of Silverlight includes more and more WPF functionality. Although compatibility with WPF and the full .NET Framework is a goal for Silverlight, its creators have taken some opportunities to learn from mistakes made in WPF and the .NET Framework. They have made some changes and begun to support new features that don't yet exist in the full .NET Framework. Some of these changes or additions have been later adopted by WPF and the full .NET Framework (such as the Visual State Manager and layout rounding), but others have not (such as video brushes and perspective transforms). There are parts of WPF and the .NET Framework that Silverlight will probably never support.

The bottom line is that the question to ask yourself isn't "Should I use WPF or Silverlight?" but rather, "Should I use the full .NET Framework or the small .NET Framework?" If you will require functionality that exists only in the full .NET Framework, then the choice is pretty simple. And WPF is the recommended user interface technology to use with the full .NET Framework. Similarly, if the ability to run on a Mac or devices other than a standard PC is a requirement, then the choice is also clear. And Silverlight has only one user interface technology (although it interoperates with HTML nicely). Otherwise, the best choice depends greatly on the nature of the software and the target audience.

Ideally, you wouldn't have to make an up-front choice of which framework you want to target. Ideally, you could use the same codebase—even the same compiled binaries—and have an easy way to morph the application to exploit capabilities of the underlying device, whether your program is running on a mobile device, a full Windows PC, or a Mac. Maybe one day that will be true, but in the meantime, having a common codebase that can work for both WPF and Silverlight involves a bit of work. The most common approach has been to create a Silverlight-compatible codebase with `#ifdef` blocks for WPF-specific functionality, so you can compile separately for Silverlight versus WPF with minimal divergence in code.

It is my expectation (and hope) that the distinction between WPF and Silverlight will fade over time. While Silverlight is a much cooler name than Windows Presentation Foundation, the fact that these technologies have different names causes trouble and artificial distinctions. The way to think of Silverlight and WPF is as two implementations of the same basic technology. In fact, inside Microsoft, largely the same team works on both. Microsoft talks a lot about having a "client continuum" to target all platforms and devices with common skills (what you learn in this book), common tools (Visual Studio, Expression Blend, and others), and at least common *code* (a .NET language such as C# or VB along with XAML, for example) if not common *binaries*. While it would be overkill to call this book *WPF and Silverlight Unleashed*, it should be comforting to know that the knowledge you gain from this book can help you be an expert in both WPF and Silverlight.

Summary

As time passes, more software is delivering high-quality—sometimes *cinematic*—experiences, and software that doesn't risks looking old-fashioned. However, the effort involved in creating such user interfaces—especially ones that exploit Windows—has been far too difficult in the past.

WPF makes it easier than ever before to create all kinds of user interfaces, whether you want to create a traditional-looking Windows application or an immersive 3D experience worthy of a role in a summer blockbuster. Such a rich user interface can be evolved fairly independently from the rest of an application, allowing graphic designers to participate in the software development process much more effectively. But don't just take my word for it; read on to see for yourself how it's done!

CHAPTER 2
XAML Demystified

IN THIS CHAPTER

- XAML Defined
- Elements and Attributes
- Namespaces
- Property Elements
- Type Converters
- Markup Extensions
- Children of Object Elements
- Mixing XAML with Procedural Code
- Introducing XAML2009
- Fun with XAML Readers and Writers
- XAML Keywords

Throughout .NET technologies, XML is used to expose functionality in a transparent and declarative fashion. XAML, a dialect of XML, has been especially important since its introduction with the first version of WPF in 2006. It is often misunderstood to be just a way to specify user interfaces, much like HTML. By the end of this chapter, you will see that XAML is about much more than arranging controls on a computer screen.

In WPF and Silverlight, XAML *is* primarily used to describe user interfaces (although it is used to describe other things as well). In Windows Workflow Foundation (WF) and Windows Communication Foundation (WCF), XAML is used to express activities and configurations that have nothing to do with user interfaces.

The point of XAML is to make it easy for programmers to work together with experts in other fields. XAML becomes the common language spoken by all parties, most likely via development tools and field-specific design tools. But because XAML (and XML in general) is generally human readable, people can participate in this ecosystem armed with nothing more than a tool such as Notepad.

In WPF and Silverlight, the "field experts" are graphic designers, who can use a design tool such as Expression Blend to create a slick user interface while developers independently write code. What enables the developer/designer cooperation is not just the common language of XAML but the fact that great care went into making functionality exposed by the relevant APIs accessible declaratively. This gives design tools a wide range of expressiveness (such as specifying complex animations or state changes) without having to worry about generating procedural code.

Even if you have no plans to work with graphic designers, you should still become familiar with XAML for the following reasons:

- XAML can be a very concise way to represent user interfaces or other hierarchies of objects.
- The use of XAML encourages a separation of front-end appearance and back-end logic, which is helpful for maintenance even if you're only a team of one.
- XAML can often be easily pasted into tools such as Visual Studio, Expression Blend, or small standalone tools to see results without any compilation.
- XAML is the language that almost all WPF-related tools emit.

This chapter jumps right into the mechanics of XAML, examining its syntax in depth and showing how it relates to procedural code. Unlike the preceding chapter, this is a fairly deep dive! Having this background knowledge before proceeding with the rest of the book will not only help you understand the code examples but give you better insight into why the APIs in each feature area were designed the way they were. This perspective can be helpful whether you are building WPF applications or controls, designing class libraries that you want to be XAML friendly, or building tools that consume and/or produce XAML (such as validation tools, localization tools, file format converters, designers, and so on).

TIP

There are several ways to run the XAML examples in this chapter, which you can download in electronic form with the rest of this book's source code. For example, you can do the following:

- Save the content in a `.xaml` file and open it inside Internet Explorer (in Windows Vista or later, or in Windows XP with the .NET Framework 3.0 or later installed). Firefox can also work if you install an add-on. However, by default your web browser will use the version of WPF installed with the operating system rather than using WPF 4.
- Paste the content into a lightweight tool such as the XAMLPAD2009 sample included with this chapter's source code or Kaxaml (from `http://kaxaml.com`), although the latter has not been updated to use WPF 4 at the time of writing.
- Create a WPF Visual Studio project and replace the content of the main `Window` or `Page` element with the desired content, which might require some code changes.

Using the first two options gives you a couple great ways to get started and do some experimentation. Mixing XAML with other content in a Visual Studio project is covered at the end of this chapter.

FAQ

What happened to XamlPad?

Earlier versions of the Windows SDK shipped with a simple tool called XamlPad that allows you to type in (or paste) WPF-compatible XAML and see it rendered as a live user interface. Unfortunately, this tool is no longer being shipped due to lack of resources. (Yes, contrary to popular belief, Microsoft does not have unlimited resources!) Fortunately, there are several alternative lightweight tools for quickly experimenting with XAML, including the following:

- **XAMLPAD2009**—A sample in this book's source code. Although it lacks the bells and whistles of the other tools, it provides full source code. Plus, it's the only tool that supports XAML2009 (explained later in this chapter) at the time of writing.
- **Kaxaml**—A slick tool downloadable from http://kaxaml.com, created by Robby Ingebretsen, a former WPF team member.
- **XamlPadX**—A feature-filled tool downloadable from http://blogs.msdn.com/llobo/archive/2008/08/25/xamlpadx-4-0.aspx, created by Lester Lobo, a current WPF team member.
- **XAML Cruncher**—A ClickOnce application available at http://charlespetzold.com/wpf/XamlCruncher/XamlCruncher.application, created by Charles Petzold, prolific author and blogger.

XAML Defined

XAML is a relatively simple and general-purpose declarative programming language suitable for constructing and initializing objects. XAML is just XML, but with a set of rules about its elements and attributes and their mapping to objects, their properties, and the values of those properties (among other things).

Because XAML is just a mechanism for using .NET APIs, attempts to compare it to HTML, Scalable Vector Graphics (SVG), or other domain-specific formats/languages are misguided. XAML consists of rules for how parsers/compilers must treat XML and has some keywords, but it doesn't define any interesting elements by itself. So, talking about XAML without a framework like WPF is like talking about C# without the .NET Framework. That said, Microsoft has formalized the notion of "XAML vocabularies" that define the set of valid elements for a given domain, such as what it means to be a WPF XAML file versus a Silverlight XAML file versus any other type of XAML file.

DIGGING DEEPER

Specifications for XAML and XAML Vocabularies

You can find detailed specifications for XAML and two XAML vocabularies in the following places:

- XAML Object Mapping Specification 2006 (MS-XAML): http://go.microsoft.com/fwlink/?LinkId=130721
- WPF XAML Vocabulary Specification 2006 (MS-WPFXV): http://go.microsoft.com/fwlink/?LinkId=130722
- Silverlight XAML Vocabulary Specification 2008 (MS-SLXV): http://go.microsoft.com/fwlink/?LinkId=130707

The role XAML plays in relation to WPF is often confused, so it's important to reemphasize that WPF and XAML can be used independently from each other. Although XAML was originally designed for WPF, it is used by other technologies as well. Because of its general-purpose nature, XAML can be applied to just about any object-oriented technology if you really want it to be. Furthermore, using XAML in WPF projects is optional. Almost everything done with XAML can be done entirely in your favorite .NET procedural language instead. (But note that the reverse is not true.) However, because of the benefits listed at the beginning of the chapter, it's rare to see WPF used in the real world without XAML.

DIGGING DEEPER

XAML Functionality Unavailable in Procedural Code

There are a few things that can be done in XAML that can't be done with procedural code. These are all fairly obscure, and covered in Chapters 12 and 14:

- Creating the full range of templates. Procedural code can create templates using `FrameworkElementFactory`, but the expressiveness of this approach is limited.
- Using `x:Shared="False"` to instruct WPF to return a new instance each time an element is accessed from a resource dictionary.
- Deferred instantiation of items inside of a resource dictionary. This is an important performance optimization, and only available via compiled XAML.

Elements and Attributes

The XAML specification defines rules that map .NET namespaces, types, properties, and events into XML namespaces, elements, and attributes. You can see this by examining the following simple (but complete) XAML file that declares a WPF `Button` and comparing it to the equivalent C# code:

XAML:

```
<Button xmlns="http://schemas.microsoft.com/winfx/2006/xaml/presentation"
  Content="OK"/>
```

C#:

```
System.Windows.Controls.Button b = new System.Windows.Controls.Button();
b.Content = "OK";
```


Although these two snippets are equivalent, you can instantly view the XAML in Internet Explorer and see a live button fill the browser window, as pictured in Figure 2.1, whereas the C# code must be compiled with additional code to be usable.

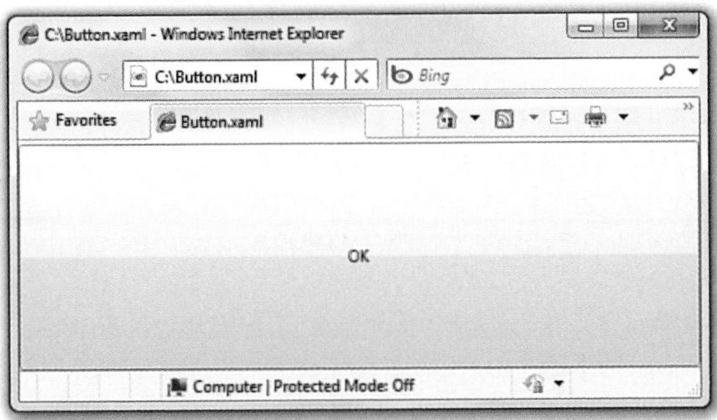

FIGURE 2.1 A simple WPF `Button` declared in a `.xaml` file.

Declaring an XML element in XAML (known as an *object element*) is equivalent to instantiating the corresponding .NET object via a default constructor. Setting an attribute on the object element is equivalent to setting a property of the same name (called a *property attribute*) or hooking up an event handler of the same name (called an *event attribute*). For example, here's an update to the `Button` that not only sets its `Content` property but also attaches an event handler to its `Click` event:

XAML:

```
<Button xmlns="http://schemas.microsoft.com/winfx/2006/xaml/presentation"
  Content="OK" Click="button_Click"/>
```

C#:

```
System.Windows.Controls.Button b = new System.Windows.Controls.Button();
b.Click += new System.Windows.RoutedEventHandler(button_Click);
b.Content = "OK";
```

This requires a method called `button_Click` to be defined somewhere, with the appropriate signature, which means that the XAML file can no longer be rendered standalone, as in Figure 2.1. The "Mixing XAML with Procedural Code" section at the end of this chapter explains how to work with XAML that requires additional code. Note that XAML, like C#, is a case-sensitive language.

DIGGING DEEPER

Order of Property and Event Processing

At runtime, event handlers are always attached *before* any properties are set for any object declared in XAML (excluding the `Name` property, described later in this chapter, which is set immediately after object construction). This enables appropriate events to be raised in response to properties being set without worrying about the order of attributes used in XAML.

The ordering of multiple property sets and multiple event handler attachments is usually performed in the relative order that property attributes and event attributes are specified on the object element. Fortunately, this ordering shouldn't matter in practice because .NET design guidelines dictate that classes should allow properties to be set in any order, and the same holds true for attaching event handlers.

Namespaces

The most mysterious part about comparing the previous XAML examples with the equivalent C# examples is how the XML namespace `http://schemas.microsoft.com/winfx/2006/xaml/presentation` maps to the .NET namespace `System.Windows.Controls`. It turns out that the mapping to this and other WPF namespaces is hard-coded inside the WPF assemblies with several instances of an `XmlnsDefinitionAttribute` custom attribute. (In case you're wondering, no web page exists at the `schemas.microsoft.com` URL—it's just an arbitrary string like any namespace.)

The root object element in a XAML file must specify at least one XML namespace that is used to qualify itself and any child elements. You can declare additional XML namespaces (on the root or on children), but each one must be given a distinct prefix to be used on any identifiers from that namespace. For example, WPF XAML files typically use a second namespace with the prefix `x` (denoted by using `xmlns:x` instead of just `xmlns`):

```
xmlns:x="http://schemas.microsoft.com/winfx/2006/xaml"
```

This is the XAML language namespace, which maps to types in the `System.Windows.Markup` namespace but also defines some special directives for the XAML compiler or parser. These directives often appear as attributes to XML elements, so they look like properties of the host element but actually are not. For a list of XAML keywords, see the "XAML Keywords" section later in this chapter.

DIGGING DEEPER

The Implicit .NET Namespaces

WPF maps all the following .NET namespaces from a handful of WPF assemblies to the WPF XML namespace (`http://schemas.microsoft.com/winfx/2006/xaml/presentation`) used throughout this book:

- `System.Windows`
- `System.Windows.Automation`
- `System.Windows.Controls`
- `System.Windows.Controls.Primitives`
- `System.Windows.Data`
- `System.Windows.Documents`
- `System.Windows.Forms.Integration`
- `System.Windows.Ink`
- `System.Windows.Input`
- `System.Windows.Media`
- `System.Windows.Media.Animation`
- `System.Windows.Media.Effects`
- `System.Windows.Media.Imaging`
- `System.Windows.Media.Media3D`
- `System.Windows.Media.TextFormatting`
- `System.Windows.Navigation`
- `System.Windows.Shapes`
- `System.Windows.Shell`

Because this is a many-to-one mapping, the designers of WPF needed to take care not to introduce two classes with the same name, despite the fact that the classes are in separate .NET namespaces.

TIP

Most of the standalone XAML examples in this chapter explicitly specify their namespaces, but in the remainder of the book, most examples assume that the WPF XML namespace (`http://schemas.microsoft.com/winfx/2006/xaml/presentation`) is declared as the primary namespace, and the XAML language namespace (`http://schemas.microsoft.com/winfx/2006/xaml`) is declared as a secondary namespace, with the prefix `x`. If you want to view such content in your web browser or copy it into a lightweight viewer such as the XAMLPAD2009 sample, be sure to add these explicitly.

Using the WPF XML namespace (`http://schemas.microsoft.com/winfx/2006/xaml/presentation`) as a default namespace and the XAML language namespace (`http://`

schemas.microsoft.com/winfx/2006/xaml) as a secondary namespace with the prefix x is just a convention, just like it's a convention to begin a C# file with a using System; directive. You could instead write the original XAML file as follows, and it would mean the same thing:

```
<WpfNamespace:Button
  xmlns:WpfNamespace="http://schemas.microsoft.com/winfx/2006/xaml/presentation"
  Content="OK"/>
```

Of course, for readability it makes sense for your most commonly used namespace (also known as the *primary* XML namespace) to be prefix free and to use short prefixes for any additional namespaces.

DIGGING DEEPER

WPF Has Accumulated Multiple WPF XML Namespaces over Time

It's practically a given that real-world WPF XAML will choose to use the WPF XML namespace as the default namespace, but it turns out that more than one XML namespace is mapped to the main WPF types in the various System.Windows namespaces.

WPF 3.0 shipped with support for http://schemas.microsoft.com/**winfx/2006**/xaml/presentation, but WPF 3.5 defined a new XML namespace— http://schemas.microsoft.com/**netfx/2007**/xaml/presentation—mapped to the same WPF types. (WinFX was the original name for a set of technologies introduced in the .NET Framework 3.0, including WPF, WCF, and WF. That term was abandoned, hence the change in namespace.) WPF 4 has once again defined a new XML namespace that is mapped to the same WPF types: http://schemas.microsoft.com/**netfx/2009**/xaml/presentation.

Despite all these options, it is best to stick with the original http://schemas.microsoft.com/winfx/2006/xaml/presentation namespace because it works in all versions of WPF. (Whether your *content* works with all versions of WPF is another story, as to do so it must stick to features present only in WPF 3.0.) Note that Silverlight also supports the http://schemas.microsoft.com/winfx/2006/xaml/presentation namespace to make it easier to use XAML meant for WPF inside a Silverlight project, although it also defines its own alternative namespace, http://schemas.microsoft.com/client/2007, which is not supported by WPF.

The XML namespaces are confusing. They are *not* schemas. They do *not* represent a closed set of types that were available when the namespace was introduced. Instead, each version of WPF retrofits all previous namespaces with any new assembly/namespace pairs introduced in the new version. Therefore, the winfx/2006 namespace effectively means "version 3.0 *or later*," the netfx/2007 namespace means "version 3.5 *or later*," and so on. However, WPF 4 accidentally excludes some namespace/assembly pairs from the netfx/2009 namespace, which makes using omitted types (like TextOptions) pretty challenging!

When loose XAML is loaded into Internet Explorer, it is loaded by PresentationHost.exe, which decides which version of the .NET Framework to load based on the XML namespaces on the root element. If the netfx/2009 namespace is present it will load version 4.0, otherwise it will load whichever 3.x version is present.

Property Elements

The preceding chapter mentioned that rich composition is one of the highlights of WPF. This can be demonstrated with the simple `Button` from Figure 2.1, because you can put arbitrary content inside it; you're not limited to just text! To demonstrate this, the following code embeds a simple square to make a Stop button like what might be found in a media player:

```
System.Windows.Controls.Button b = new System.Windows.Controls.Button();
System.Windows.Shapes.Rectangle r = new System.Windows.Shapes.Rectangle();
r.Width = 40;
r.Height = 40;
r.Fill = System.Windows.Media.Brushes.Black;
b.Content = r; // Make the square the content of the Button
```

`Button`'s `Content` property is of type `System.Object`, so it can easily be set to the 40x40 `Rectangle` object. The result is pictured in Figure 2.2.

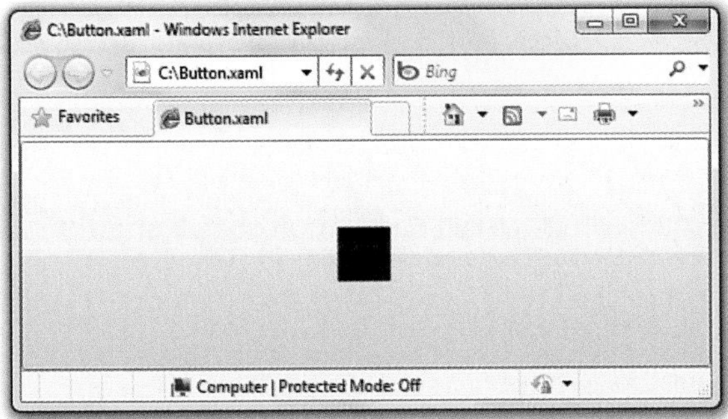

FIGURE 2.2 Updating the WPF `Button` with complex content.

That's pretty neat, but how can you do the same thing in XAML with property attribute syntax? What kind of string could you possibly set `Content` to that is equivalent to the preceding `Rectangle` declared in C#? There is no such string, but XAML fortunately provides an alternative (and more verbose) syntax for setting complex property values: *property elements*. It looks like the following:

```
<Button xmlns="http://schemas.microsoft.com/winfx/2006/xaml/presentation">
<Button.Content>
  <Rectangle Height="40" Width="40" Fill="Black"/>
</Button.Content>
</Button>
```

The `Content` property is now set with an XML element instead of an XML attribute, making it equivalent to the previous C# code. The period in `Button.Content` is what distinguishes property elements from object elements. Property elements always take the form *`TypeName.PropertyName`*, they are always contained inside a *`TypeName`* object element, and they can never have attributes of their own (with one exception—the `x:Uid` attribute used for localization).

Property element syntax can be used for simple property values as well. The following `Button` that sets two properties with attributes (`Content` and `Background`):

```
<Button xmlns="http://schemas.microsoft.com/winfx/2006/xaml/presentation"
  Content="OK" Background="White"/>
```

is equivalent to this `Button`, which sets the same two properties with elements:

```
<Button xmlns="http://schemas.microsoft.com/winfx/2006/xaml/presentation">
<Button.Content>
  OK
</Button.Content>
<Button.Background>
  White
</Button.Background>
</Button>
```

Of course, using attributes when you can is a nice shortcut when hand-typing XAML.

Type Converters

Let's look at the C# code equivalent to the preceding `Button` declaration that sets both `Content` and `Background` properties:

```
System.Windows.Controls.Button b = new System.Windows.Controls.Button();
b.Content = "OK";
b.Background = System.Windows.Media.Brushes.White;
```

Wait a minute. How can `"White"` in the previous XAML file be equivalent to the static `System.Windows.Media.Brushes.White` field (of type `System.Windows.Media.SolidColorBrush`) in the C# code? Indeed, this example exposes a subtlety with using strings to set properties in XAML that are a different data type than `System.String` or `System.Object`. In such cases, the XAML parser or compiler must look for a *type converter* that knows how to convert the string representation to the desired data type.

WPF provides type converters for many common data types: `Brush`, `Color`, `FontWeight`, `Point`, and so on. They are all classes deriving from `TypeConverter` (`BrushConverter`, `ColorConverter`, and so on). You can also write your own type converters for custom data types. Unlike the XAML language, type converters generally support case-insensitive strings.

Without a type converter for `Brush`, you would have to use property element syntax to set the `Background` in XAML, as follows:

```
<Button xmlns="http://schemas.microsoft.com/winfx/2006/xaml/presentation"
  Content="OK">
<Button.Background>
  <SolidColorBrush Color="White"/>
</Button.Background>
</Button>
```


And even that is only possible because of a type converter for `Color` that can make sense of the `"White"` string. If there were no `Color` type converter, you could still write the following:

```
<Button xmlns="http://schemas.microsoft.com/winfx/2006/xaml/presentation"
  Content="OK">
<Button.Background>
  <SolidColorBrush>
  <SolidColorBrush.Color>
    <Color A="255" R="255" G="255" B="255"/>
  </SolidColorBrush.Color>
  </SolidColorBrush>
</Button.Background>
</Button>
```

But *this* is only possible because of a type converter that can convert each `"255"` string into a `Byte` value expected by the `A`, `R`, `G`, and `B` properties of the `Color` type. Without this type converter, you would basically be stuck. Type converters don't just enhance the readability of XAML, they also enable values to be expressed that couldn't otherwise be expressed.

DIGGING DEEPER

Using Type Converters in Procedural Code

Although the C# code that sets `Background` to `System.Windows.Media.Brushes.White` produces the same result as the XAML declaration that assigns it to the `"White"` string, it doesn't actually use the same type conversion mechanism employed by the XAML parser or compiler. The following code more accurately represents the runtime retrieval and execution of the appropriate type converter for `Brush`:

```
System.Windows.Controls.Button b = new System.Windows.Controls.Button();
b.Content = "OK";
b.Background = (Brush)System.ComponentModel.TypeDescriptor.GetConverter(
  typeof(Brush)).ConvertFromInvariantString("White");
```

Unlike in the previous C# code, in this case, misspelling `White` would not cause a compilation error but would cause an exception at runtime, as with XAML. (Although Visual Studio does provide compile-time warnings for mistakes in XAML such as this.)

DIGGING DEEPER

Finding Type Converters

So how does a XAML parser or compiler find an appropriate type converter for a property value? By looking for a `System.ComponentModel.TypeConverterAttribute` custom attribute on the property definition or on the definition of the property's data type.

For example, the `BrushConverter` type converter is used when setting `Button`'s `Background` property in XAML because `Background` is of type `System.Windows.Media.Brush`, which has the following custom attribute:

```
[TypeConverter(typeof(BrushConverter)), …]
public abstract class Brush : …
{
  …
}
```

On the other hand, the `FontSizeConverter` type converter is used when setting `Button`'s `FontSize` property because the property (defined on the base `Control` class) has the following custom attribute:

```
[TypeConverter(typeof(FontSizeConverter)), …]
public double FontSize
{
  get { … }
  set { … }
}
```

In this case, marking the type converter on the property is necessary because its data type (`double`) is too generic to always be associated with `FontSizeConverter`. In fact, in WPF, `double` is often associated with another type converter, `LengthConverter`.

Markup Extensions

Markup extensions, like type converters, enable you to extend the expressiveness of XAML. Both can evaluate a string attribute value at runtime (except for a few built-in markup extensions that are currently evaluated at compile time for performance reasons) and produce an appropriate object based on the string. As with type converters, WPF ships with several markup extensions built in.

Unlike type converters, however, markup extensions are invoked from XAML with explicit and consistent syntax. For this reason, using markup extensions is a preferred approach for extending XAML. In addition, using markup extensions enables you to overcome potential limitations in existing type converters that you don't have the power to change. For example, if you want to set a control's background to a fancy gradient brush with a simple string value, you can write a custom markup extension that supports it even though the built-in `BrushConverter` does not.

Whenever an attribute value is enclosed in curly braces ({}), the XAML compiler/parser treats it as a markup extension value rather than a literal string (or something that needs to be type-converted). The following Button uses three different markup extension values with three different properties:

Markup extension class

```
<Button xmlns="http://schemas.microsoft.com/winfx/2006/xaml/presentation"
        xmlns:x="http://schemas.microsoft.com/winfx/2006/xaml"
        Background="{x:Null}"
        Height="{x:Static SystemParameters.IconHeight}"
        Content="{Binding Path=Height, RelativeSource={RelativeSource Self}}"/>
```

Positional parameter

Named parameters

The first identifier in each set of curly braces is the name of the markup extension class, which must derive from a class called MarkupExtension. By convention, such classes end with an Extension suffix, but you can leave it off when using it in XAML. In this example, NullExtension (seen as x:Null) and StaticExtension (seen as x:Static) are classes in the System.Windows.Markup namespace, so the x prefix must be used to locate them. Binding (which doesn't happen to have the Extension suffix) is in the System.Windows.Data namespace, so it can be found in the default XML namespace.

If a markup extension supports them, comma-delimited parameters can be specified. Positional parameters (such as SystemParameters.IconHeight in the example) are treated as string arguments for the extension class's appropriate constructor. Named parameters (Path and RelativeSource in the example) enable you to set properties with matching names on the constructed extension object. The values for these properties can be markup extension values themselves (using nested curly braces, as done with the value for RelativeSource) or literal values that can undergo the normal type conversion process. If you're familiar with .NET custom attributes (the .NET Framework's popular extensibility mechanism), you've probably noticed that the design and usage of markup extensions closely mirrors the design and usage of custom attributes. That is intentional.

In the preceding Button declaration, NullExtension enables the Background brush to be set to null, which isn't natively supported by BrushConverter (or many other type converters, for that matter). This is just done for demonstration purposes, as a null Background is not very useful. StaticExtension enables the use of static properties, fields, constants, and enumeration values rather than hard-coding literals in XAML. In this case, the Button's Height is set to the operating system's current height setting for icons, exposed by the static IconHeight property on a System.Windows.SystemParameters class. Binding, covered in depth in Chapter 13, "Data Binding," enables Content to be set to the same value as the Height property.

DIGGING DEEPER

Escaping the Curly Braces

If you ever want a property attribute value to be set to a literal string beginning with an open curly brace ({), you must escape it so it doesn't get treated as a markup extension. This can be done by preceding it with an empty pair of curly braces, as in the following example:

```
<Button xmlns="http://schemas.microsoft.com/winfx/2006/xaml/presentation"
        Content="{}{This is not a markup extension!}"/>
```

You can also use a backslash to escape characters such as an open curly brace, a single quote, or a double quote.

Alternatively, you could use property element syntax without any escaping because the curly braces do not have special meaning in this context. The preceding `Button` could be rewritten as follows:

```
<Button xmlns="http://schemas.microsoft.com/winfx/2006/xaml/presentation">
<Button.Content>
  {This is not a markup extension!}
</Button.Content>
</Button>
```

Data binding (covered in Chapter 13) takes advantage of this escaping with string formatting properties that use curly braces as part of their normal string syntax.

Because markup extensions are just classes with default constructors, they can be used with property element syntax. The following `Button` is identical to the preceding one:

```
<Button xmlns="http://schemas.microsoft.com/winfx/2006/xaml/presentation"
        xmlns:x="http://schemas.microsoft.com/winfx/2006/xaml">
<Button.Background>
  <x:Null/>
</Button.Background>
<Button.Height>
  <x:Static Member="SystemParameters.IconHeight"/>
</Button.Height>
<Button.Content>
  <Binding Path="Height">
  <Binding.RelativeSource>
    <RelativeSource Mode="Self"/>
  </Binding.RelativeSource>
  </Binding>
</Button.Content>
</Button>
```

This transformation works because these markup extensions all have properties corresponding to their parameterized constructor arguments (the positional parameters used with property attribute syntax). For example, `StaticExtension` has a `Member` property that has the same meaning as the argument that was previously passed to its parameterized constructor, and `RelativeSource` has a `Mode` property that corresponds to its constructor argument.

DIGGING DEEPER

Markup Extensions and Procedural Code

The actual work done by a markup extension is specific to each extension. For example, the following C# code is equivalent to the XAML-based `Button` that uses `NullExtension`, `StaticExtension`, and `Binding`:

```
System.Windows.Controls.Button b = new System.Windows.Controls.Button();
// Set Background:
b.Background = null;
// Set Height:
b.Height = System.Windows.SystemParameters.IconHeight;
// Set Content:
System.Windows.Data.Binding binding = new System.Windows.Data.Binding();
binding.Path = new System.Windows.PropertyPath("Height");
binding.RelativeSource = System.Windows.Data.RelativeSource.Self;
b.SetBinding(System.Windows.Controls.Button.ContentProperty, binding);
```

However, this code doesn't use the same mechanism as the XAML parser or compiler, which rely on each markup extension to set the appropriate values at runtime (essentially by invoking each one's `ProvideValue` method). The procedural code equivalent of this mechanism is often complex, sometimes requiring context that only a parser would have (such as how to resolve an XML namespace prefix that could be used in `StaticExtension`'s `Member`). Fortunately, there is no reason to use markup extensions this way in procedural code!

Children of Object Elements

A XAML file, like all XML files, must have a single root object element. Therefore, it should come as no surprise that object elements can support child object elements (not just property elements, which aren't children, as far as XAML is concerned). An object element can have three types of children: a value for a content property, collection items, or a value that can be type-converted to the object element.

The Content Property

Most WPF classes designate a property (via a custom attribute) that should be set to whatever content is inside the XML element. This property is called the *content property*, and it is really just a convenient shortcut to make the XAML representation more compact. In some ways, these content properties are like the (often-maligned) default properties in old versions of Visual Basic.

Button's Content property is (appropriately) given this special designation, so the following Button:

```
<Button xmlns="http://schemas.microsoft.com/winfx/2006/xaml/presentation"
  Content="OK"/>
```

could be rewritten as follows:

```
<Button xmlns="http://schemas.microsoft.com/winfx/2006/xaml/presentation">
  OK
</Button>
```

Or, more usefully, this Button with more complex content:

```
<Button xmlns="http://schemas.microsoft.com/winfx/2006/xaml/presentation">
<Button.Content>
  <Rectangle Height="40" Width="40" Fill="Black"/>
</Button.Content>
</Button>
```

could be rewritten as follows:

```
<Button xmlns="http://schemas.microsoft.com/winfx/2006/xaml/presentation">
  <Rectangle Height="40" Width="40" Fill="Black"/>
</Button>
```

There is no requirement that the content property must actually be called Content; classes such as ComboBox, ListBox, and TabControl (also in the System.Windows.Controls namespace) use their Items property as the content property.

Collection Items

XAML enables you to add items to the two main types of collections that support indexing: lists and dictionaries.

Lists

A *list* is any collection that implements System.Collections.IList, such as System.Collections.ArrayList or numerous collection classes defined by WPF. For example, the following XAML adds two items to a ListBox control whose Items property is an ItemCollection that implements IList:

```
<ListBox xmlns="http://schemas.microsoft.com/winfx/2006/xaml/presentation">
<ListBox.Items>
  <ListBoxItem Content="Item 1"/>
  <ListBoxItem Content="Item 2"/>
</ListBox.Items>
</ListBox>
```

This is equivalent to the following C# code:

```
System.Windows.Controls.ListBox listbox = new System.Windows.Controls.ListBox();
System.Windows.Controls.ListBoxItem item1 =
  new System.Windows.Controls.ListBoxItem();
System.Windows.Controls.ListBoxItem item2 =
  new System.Windows.Controls.ListBoxItem();
item1.Content = "Item 1";
item2.Content = "Item 2";
listbox.Items.Add(item1);
listbox.Items.Add(item2);
```

Furthermore, because `Items` is the content property for `ListBox`, you can shorten the XAML even further, as follows:

```
<ListBox xmlns="http://schemas.microsoft.com/winfx/2006/xaml/presentation">
  <ListBoxItem Content="Item 1"/>
  <ListBoxItem Content="Item 2"/>
</ListBox>
```

In all these cases, the code works because `ListBox`'s `Items` property is automatically initialized to any empty collection object. If a collection property is initially `null` instead (and is read/write, unlike `ListBox`'s read-only `Items` property), you need to wrap the items in an explicit element that instantiates the collection. WPF's built-in controls do not act this way, so an imaginary `OtherListBox` element demonstrates what this could look like:

```
<OtherListBox>
<OtherListBox.Items>
  <ItemCollection>
    <ListBoxItem Content="Item 1"/>
    <ListBoxItem Content="Item 2"/>
  </ItemCollection>
</OtherListBox.Items>
</OtherListBox>
```

Dictionaries

`System.Windows.ResourceDictionary` is a commonly used collection type in WPF that you'll see more of in Chapter 12, "Resources." It implements `System.Collections.IDictionary`, so it supports adding, removing, and enumerating key/value pairs in procedural code, as you would do with a typical hash table. In XAML, you can add key/value pairs to any collection that implements `IDictionary`. For example, the following XAML adds two `Colors` to a `ResourceDictionary`:

```
<ResourceDictionary
  xmlns="http://schemas.microsoft.com/winfx/2006/xaml/presentation"
  xmlns:x="http://schemas.microsoft.com/winfx/2006/xaml">
  <Color x:Key="1" A="255" R="255" G="255" B="255"/>
  <Color x:Key="2" A="0" R="0" G="0" B="0"/>
</ResourceDictionary>
```

This leverages the XAML Key keyword (defined in the secondary XML namespace), which is processed specially and enables us to attach a key to each Color value. (The Color type does not define a Key property.) Therefore, the XAML is equivalent to the following C# code:

```
System.Windows.ResourceDictionary d = new System.Windows.ResourceDictionary();
System.Windows.Media.Color color1 = new System.Windows.Media.Color();
System.Windows.Media.Color color2 = new System.Windows.Media.Color();
color1.A = 255; color1.R = 255; color1.G = 255; color1.B = 255;
color2.A = 0;   color2.R = 0;   color2.G = 0;   color2.B = 0;
d.Add("1", color1);
d.Add("2", color2);
```

Note that the value specified in XAML with x:Key is treated as a string unless a markup extension is used or the XAML2009 parser is used (see the later "Introducing XAML2009" section); no type conversion is attempted otherwise.

> **DIGGING DEEPER**
>
> **Lists, Dictionaries, and the XAML2009 Parser**
>
> Although the WPF XAML parser has historically only supported IList and IDictionary collections, the XAML2009 parser (described in the later "Introducing XAML2009" section) supports more. It first looks for IList and IDictionary, then for ICollection<T> and IDictionary<K,V>, then for the presence of both Add and GetEnumerator methods.

More Type Conversion

Plain text can often be used as the child of an object element, as in the following XAML declaration of SolidColorBrush:

```
<SolidColorBrush>White</SolidColorBrush>
```

This is equivalent to the following:

```
<SolidColorBrush Color="White"/>
```

even though Color has not been designated as a content property. In this case, the first XAML snippet works because a type converter exists that can convert strings such as "White" (or "white" or "#FFFFFF") into a SolidColorBrush object.

Although type converters play a huge role in making XAML readable, the downside is that they can make XAML appear a bit "magical," and it can be difficult to understand how it maps to instances of .NET objects. Using what you know so far, it would be reasonable to assume that you can't declare an abstract class element in XAML because there's no way to instantiate it. However, even though System.Windows.Media.Brush is an abstract base class for SolidColorBrush, GradientBrush, and other concrete brushes, you can express the preceding XAML snippets as simply:

```
<Brush>White</Brush>
```

because the type converter for Brushes understands that this is still SolidColorBrush. This may seem like an unusual feature, but it's important for supporting the ability to express primitive types in XAML, as demonstrated in "The Extensible Part of XAML."

DIGGING DEEPER

The Extensible Part of XAML

Because XAML was designed to work with the .NET type system, you can use it with just about any .NET object (or even COM objects, thanks to COM interoperability), including ones you define yourself. It doesn't matter whether these objects have anything to do with a user interface. However, the objects need to be designed in a "declarative-friendly" way. For example, if a class doesn't have a default constructor and doesn't expose useful instance properties, it's not going to be directly usable from XAML (unless you use the XAML2009 parser). A lot of care went into the design of the WPF APIs—above and beyond the usual .NET design guidelines—to fit XAML's declarative model.

The WPF assemblies are marked with `XmlnsDefinitionAttribute` to map their .NET namespaces to XML namespaces in a XAML file, but what about assemblies that weren't designed with XAML in mind and, therefore, don't use this attribute? Their types can still be used; you just need to use a special directive as the XML namespace. For example, here's some plain old C# code using .NET Framework APIs contained in `mscorlib.dll`:

```
System.Collections.Hashtable h = new System.Collections.Hashtable();
h.Add("key1", 7);
h.Add("key2", 23);
```

and here's how it can be represented in XAML:

```
<collections:Hashtable
  xmlns:collections="clr-namespace:System.Collections;assembly=mscorlib"
  xmlns:sys="clr-namespace:System;assembly=mscorlib"
  xmlns:x="http://schemas.microsoft.com/winfx/2006/xaml">
  <sys:Int32 x:Key="key1">7</sys:Int32>
  <sys:Int32 x:Key="key2">23</sys:Int32>
</collections:Hashtable>
```

The `clr-namespace` directive enables you to place a .NET namespace directly inside XAML. The assembly specification at the end is necessary only if the desired types don't reside in the same assembly that the XAML is compiled into. Typically the assembly's simple name is used (as with `mscorlib`), but you can use the canonical representation supported by `System.Reflection.Assembly.Load` (although with no spaces allowed), which includes additional information such as a version and/or public key token.

Two key points about this example really highlight the integration with not only the .NET type system but specific types in the .NET Framework:

- Child elements can be added to the parent `Hashtable` with the standard XAML `x:Key` syntax because `Hashtable` and other collection classes in the .NET Framework have implemented the `IDictionary` interface since version 1.0.
- `System.Int32` can be used in this simple fashion because a type converter already exists that supports converting strings to integers. This is because the type converters supported by XAML are simply classes that derive from `System.ComponentModel.TypeConverter`, a class that has also been around since version 1.0 of the .NET Framework. This is the same type conversion mechanism used by Windows Forms (enabling you to type strings into the Visual Studio property grid, for example, and have them converted to the appropriate type).

DIGGING DEEPER

XAML Processing Rules for Object Element Children

You've now seen the three types of children for object elements. To avoid ambiguity, any valid XAML parser or compiler follows these rules when encountering and interpreting child elements:

1. If the type implements `IList`, call `IList.Add` for each child.
2. Otherwise, if the type implements `IDictionary`, call `IDictionary.Add` for each child, using the `x:Key` attribute value for the key and the element for the value. (Although XAML2009 checks `IDictionary` *before* `IList` and supports other collection interfaces, as described earlier.)
3. Otherwise, if the parent supports a content property (indicated by `System.Windows.Markup.ContentPropertyAttribute`) and the type of the child is compatible with that property, treat the child as its value.
4. Otherwise, if the child is plain text and a type converter exists to transform the child into the parent type (*and* no properties are set on the parent element), treat the child as the input to the type converter and use the output as the parent object instance.
5. Otherwise, treat it as unknown content and potentially raise an error.

Rules 1 and 2 enable the behavior described in the earlier "Collection Items" section, rule 3 enables the behavior described in the section "The Content Property," and rule 4 explains the often-confusing behavior described in the "More Type Conversion" section.

Mixing XAML with Procedural Code

WPF applications can be written entirely in procedural code in any .NET language. In addition, certain types of simple applications can be written entirely in XAML, thanks to the data-binding features described in Chapter 13, the triggers introduced in the next chapter, and the fact that loose XAML pages can be rendered in a web browser. However, most WPF applications are a mix of XAML and procedural code. This section covers the two ways that XAML and code can be mixed together.

Loading and Parsing XAML at Runtime

WPF has a runtime XAML parser exposed as two classes in the `System.Windows.Markup` namespace: `XamlReader` and `XamlWriter`. And their APIs couldn't be much simpler. `XamlReader` contains a few overloads of a static `Load` method, and `XamlWriter` contains a few overloads of a static `Save` method. Therefore, programs written in any .NET language can leverage XAML at runtime without much effort. The .NET Framework 4.0 ships a new, separate set of XAML readers and writers but with a fair number of caveats. They are not important for this discussion but are covered later, in the "Fun with XAML Readers and Writers" section.

XamlReader

The set of `XamlReader.Load` methods parse XAML, create the appropriate .NET objects, and return an instance of the root element. So, if a XAML file named `MyWindow.xaml` in the current directory contains a `Window` object (explained in depth in Chapter 7,

"Structuring and Deploying an Application") as its root node, the following code could be used to load and retrieve the Window object:

```
Window window = null;
using (FileStream fs =
  new FileStream("MyWindow.xaml", FileMode.Open, FileAccess.Read))
{
  // Get the root element, which we know is a Window
  window = (Window)XamlReader.Load(fs);
}
```

In this case, Load is called with a FileStream (from the System.IO namespace). After Load returns, the entire hierarchy of objects in the XAML file is instantiated in memory, so the XAML file is no longer needed. In the preceding code, the FileStream is instantly closed by exiting the using block. Because XamlReader can be passed an arbitrary Stream (or System.Xml.XmlReader, via a different overload), you have a lot of flexibility in retrieving XAML content.

TIP

XamlReader also defines LoadAsync instance methods that load and parse XAML content asynchronously. You'll want to use LoadAsync to keep a responsive user interface during the loading of large files or files over the network, for example. Accompanying these methods are a CancelAsync method for halting the processing and a LoadCompleted event for knowing when the processing is complete.

The behavior of LoadAsync is a bit odd, however. The work is done on the UI thread via multiple Dispatcher.BeginInvoke calls. (WPF tries to break the work up into 200-millisecond chunks.) Furthermore, this asynchronous processing is only used if x:SynchronousMode="Async" is set on the root XAML node. If this attribute is not set, LoadAsync will silently load the XAML synchronously.

Now that an instance of the root element exists, you can retrieve child elements by making use of the appropriate content properties or collection properties. The following code assumes that the Window has a StackPanel object as its content, whose fifth child is an OK Button:

```
Window window = null;
using (FileStream fs =
  new FileStream("MyWindow.xaml", FileMode.Open, FileAccess.Read))
{
  // Get the root element, which we know is a Window
  window = (Window)XamlReader.Load(fs);
}
// Grab the OK button by walking the children (with hard-coded knowledge!)
StackPanel panel = (StackPanel)window.Content;
Button okButton = (Button)panel.Children[4];
```

With a reference to the Button, you can do whatever you want: Set additional properties (perhaps using logic that is hard or impossible to express in XAML), attach event handlers, or perform additional actions that you can't do from XAML, such as calling its methods.

Of course, the code that uses a hard-coded index and other assumptions about the user interface structure isn't very satisfying, as simple changes to the XAML can break it. Instead, you could write code to process the elements more generically and look for a Button element whose content is an "OK" string, but that would be a lot of work for such a simple task. In addition, if you want the Button to contain graphical content, how can you easily identify it in the presence of multiple Buttons?

Fortunately, XAML supports naming of elements so they can be found and used reliably from procedural code.

Naming XAML Elements

The XAML language namespace has a Name keyword that enables you to give any element a name. For the simple OK button that we're imagining is embedded somewhere inside a Window, the Name keyword can be used as follows:

```
<Button x:Name="okButton">OK</Button>
```

With this in place, you can update the preceding C# code to use Window's FindName method that searches its children (recursively) and returns the desired instance:

```
Window window = null;
using (FileStream fs =
  new FileStream("MyWindow.xaml", FileMode.Open, FileAccess.Read))
{
  // Get the root element, which we know is a Window
  window = (Window)XamlReader.Load(fs);
}
// Grab the OK button, knowing only its name
Button okButton = (Button)window.FindName("okButton");
```

FindName is not unique to Window; it is defined on FrameworkElement and FrameworkContentElement, which are base classes for many important classes in WPF.

DIGGING DEEPER

Naming Elements Without x:Name

The x:Name syntax can be used to name elements, but some classes define their own property that can be treated as the element's name (by marking themselves with System.Windows.Markup.RuntimeNamePropertyAttribute). For example, FrameworkElement and FrameworkContentElement have a Name property, so they mark themselves with RuntimeNameProperty("Name"). This means that on such elements you can simply set the Name property to a string rather than use the x:Name syntax. You can use either mechanism, but you can't use both simultaneously. Having two ways to set a name is a bit confusing, but it's handy for these classes to have a Name property for use by procedural code.

TIP

In all versions of WPF, the `Binding` markup extension can be used to reference a named element as a property value:

```
<StackPanel xmlns="http://schemas.microsoft.com/winfx/2006/xaml/presentation">
  <Label Target="{Binding ElementName=box}" Content="Enter _text:"/>
  <TextBox Name="box"/>
</StackPanel>
```

(In this case, assigning the `TextBox` as the `Target` of the `Label` gives it focus when the `Label`'s access key, Alt+T, is pressed.) WPF 4 includes a new, simpler markup extension (that finds the element at parse time rather than runtime): `System.Windows.Markup.Reference`. It can be used as follows:

```
<StackPanel xmlns="http://schemas.microsoft.com/winfx/2006/xaml/presentation"
            xmlns:x="http://schemas.microsoft.com/winfx/2006/xaml">
  <Label Target="{x:Reference box}" Content="Enter _text:"/>
  <TextBox Name="box"/>
</StackPanel>
```

Or, when a relevant property is marked with the `System.Windows.Markup.NameReferenceConverter` type converter (as in this case), a simple name string can be implicitly converted into the referenced instance:

```
<StackPanel xmlns="http://schemas.microsoft.com/winfx/2006/xaml/presentation">
  <Label Target="box" Content="Enter _text:"/>
  <TextBox Name="box"/>
</StackPanel>
```

Compiling XAML

Loading and parsing XAML at runtime is interesting for dynamic skinning scenarios or for .NET languages that don't have the necessary support for XAML compilation. Most WPF projects, however, leverage the XAML compilation supported by MSBuild and Visual Studio. XAML compilation involves three things: converting a XAML file into a special binary format, embedding the converted content as a binary resource in the assembly being built, and performing the plumbing that connects XAML with procedural code automatically. C# and Visual Basic are the two languages with the best support for XAML compilation.

DIGGING DEEPER

Supporting Compiled XAML with Any .NET Language

If you want to leverage XAML compilation with an arbitrary .NET language, there are two basic requirements for enabling this: having a corresponding CodeDom provider and having an MSBuild target file. In addition, language support for partial classes is helpful but not strictly required.

If you don't care about mixing procedural code with your XAML file, then all you need to do to compile it is add it to a WPF project in Visual Studio with a **Build Action** of **Page**. (Chapter 7 explains ways to make use of such content in the context of an application.) But for the typical case of compiling a XAML file *and* mixing it with procedural code, the first step is specifying a subclass for the root element in a XAML file. This can be done with the `Class` keyword defined in the XAML language namespace, for example:

```
<Window xmlns="http://schemas.microsoft.com/winfx/2006/xaml/presentation"
        xmlns:x="http://schemas.microsoft.com/winfx/2006/xaml"
        x:Class="MyNamespace.MyWindow">
  …
</Window>
```

In a separate source file (but in the same project), you can define the subclass and add whatever members you want:

```
namespace MyNamespace
{
  partial class MyWindow : Window
  {
    public MyWindow()
    {
      // Necessary to call in order to load XAML-defined content!
      InitializeComponent();
      …
    }
    Any other members can go here…
  }
}
```

This is often referred to as the *code-behind file*. If you reference any event handlers in XAML (via event attributes such as `Click` on `Button`), this is where they should be defined.

The `partial` keyword in the class definition is important, as the class's implementation is spread across more than one file. If the .NET language doesn't support partial classes (for example, C++/CLI and J#), the XAML file must also use a `Subclass` keyword in the root element, as follows:

```
<Window xmlns="http://schemas.microsoft.com/winfx/2006/xaml/presentation"
        xmlns:x="http://schemas.microsoft.com/winfx/2006/xaml"
        x:Class="MyNamespace.MyWindow" x:Subclass="MyNamespace.MyWindow2">
  …
</Window>
```

With this change, the XAML file completely defines the `Subclass` (`MyWindow2` in this case) but uses the `Class` in the code-behind file (`MyWindow`) as its base class. Therefore, this simulates the ability to split the implementation across two files by relying on inheritance.

When creating a WPF-based C# or Visual Basic project in Visual Studio, or when you use **Add New Item...** to add certain WPF items to a project, Visual Studio automatically creates a XAML file with `x:Class` on its root, creates the code-behind source file with the partial class definition, and links the two together so they are built properly.

If you're an MSBuild user and want to understand the contents of the project file that enables code-behind, you can open any of the C# project files included with this book's source code in a simple text editor such as Notepad. The relevant part of a typical project is as follows:

```
<ItemGroup>
  <Page Include="MyWindow.xaml"/>
</ItemGroup>
<ItemGroup>
  <Compile Include="MyWindow.xaml.cs">
    <DependentUpon>MyWindow.xaml</DependentUpon>
    <SubType>Code</SubType>
  </Compile>
</ItemGroup>
```

For such a project, the build system generates several items when processing `MyWindow.xaml`, including these:

- A BAML file (`MyWindow.baml`), which gets embedded in the assembly as a binary resource by default.
- A C# source file (`MyWindow.g.cs`), which gets compiled into the assembly like all other source code.

TIP

`x:Class` can only be used in a XAML file that gets compiled. But you can sometimes compile a XAML file with no `x:Class` just fine. This simply means that there is no corresponding code-behind file, so you can't use any features that rely on the presence of procedural code. Therefore, adding a XAML file to a Visual Studio project without an `x:Class` directive can be a handy way to get the deployment and performance benefits of compiled XAML without having to create an unnecessary code-behind file.

BAML

BAML, which stands for Binary Application Markup Language, is simply XAML that has been parsed, tokenized, and converted into binary form. Although almost any chunk of XAML can be represented by procedural code, the XAML-to-BAML compilation process *does not* generate procedural source code. So, BAML is not like Microsoft intermediate language (MSIL); it is a compressed declarative format that is faster to load and parse (and smaller in size) than plain XAML. BAML is basically an implementation detail of the XAML compilation process. Nevertheless, it's interesting to be aware of its existence. In fact, WPF 4 contains a public BAML reader class (see the "Fun with XAML Readers and Writers" section).

DIGGING DEEPER

There Once Was a CAML...

Prerelease versions of WPF had the ability to compile XAML into BAML *or* MSIL. This MSIL output was called CAML, which stood for *Compiled* Application Markup Language. The idea was to enable the choice of optimizing for size (BAML) or speed (CAML). But the team decided not to burden the WPF codebase with these two independent implementations that did essentially the same thing. BAML won out over CAML because it has several advantages: It's less of a security threat than MSIL, it's more compact (resulting in smaller download sizes for web scenarios), and it can be localized postcompilation. Furthermore, using CAML was not appreciably faster than using BAML, as people had theorized it would be. It generated a lot of code that would only ever run once. This is inefficient, it bloats DLLs, it doesn't take advantage of caches, and so on.

Generated Source Code

Some procedural code does get generated in the XAML compilation process (if you use `x:Class`), but it's just some "glue code" similar to what had to be written to load and parse a loose XAML file at runtime. Such files are given a suffix such as `.g.cs` (or `.g.vb`), where the `g` stands for *generated.*

Each generated source file contains a partial class definition for the class specified with `x:Class` on the root object element. This partial class contains a field (internal by default) for every named element in the XAML file, using the element name as the field name. It also contains an `InitializeComponent` method that does the grunt work of loading the embedded BAML resource, assigning the fields to the appropriate instances originally declared in XAML, and hooking up any event handlers (if any event handlers were specified in the XAML file).

Because the glue code tucked away in the generated source file is part of the same class you've defined in the code-behind file (and because BAML gets embedded as a resource), you often don't need to be aware of the existence of BAML or the process of loading and parsing it. You simply write code that references named elements just like any other class member, and you let the build system worry about hooking things together. The only thing you need to remember is to call `InitializeComponent` in your code-behind class's constructor.

WARNING

Don't forget to call `InitializeComponent` in the constructor of your code-behind class!

If you fail to do so, your root element won't contain any of the content you defined in XAML (because the corresponding BAML doesn't get loaded), and all the fields representing named object elements will be `null`.

DIGGING DEEPER

Procedural Code Inside XAML

XAML actually supports an obscure "code-inside" feature in addition to code-behind (somewhat like in ASP.NET). This can be done with the `Code` keyword in the XAML language namespace, as follows:

```
<Window xmlns="http://schemas.microsoft.com/winfx/2006/xaml/presentation"
        xmlns:x="http://schemas.microsoft.com/winfx/2006/xaml"
        x:Class="MyNamespace.MyWindow">
  <Button Click="button_Click">OK</Button>
  <x:Code><![CDATA[
    void button_Click(object sender, RoutedEventArgs e)
    {
        this.Close();
    }
  ]]></x:Code>
</Window>
```

When such a XAML file is compiled, the contents inside the `x:Code` element get plopped inside the partial class in the `.g.cs` file. Note that the procedural language is not specified in the XAML file; it is determined by the project containing this file.

Wrapping the code in `<![CDATA[…]]>` isn't required, but it avoids the need to escape less-than signs as `<` and ampersands as `&`. That's because CDATA sections are ignored by XML parsers, whereas anything else is processed as XML. (The tradeoff is that you must avoid using `]]>` anywhere in the code, because that terminates the CDATA section!)

Of course, there's no good reason to pollute your XAML files with this "code-inside" feature. Besides making the division between user interface and logic messier, loose XAML pages don't support it, and Visual Studio doesn't support any of its typical code features, such as IntelliSense and syntax coloring.

FAQ

Can BAML be decompiled back into XAML?

Sure, because BAML can be converted into a graph of live object instances, and these instances can be serialized as XAML, regardless of how they were originally declared.

The first step is to retrieve an instance that you want to be the root of the XAML. If you don't already have this object, you can call the static `System.Windows.Application.LoadComponent` method to load it from BAML, as follows:

```
System.Uri uri = new System.Uri("/WpfApplication1;component/MyWindow.xaml",
  System.UriKind.Relative);
Window window = (Window)Application.LoadComponent(uri);
```

Continued

Yes, that code is loading BAML despite the `.xaml` suffix. This differs from previous code that uses `FileStream` to load a `.xaml` file because with `LoadComponent`, the name specified as the uniform resource identifier (URI) does not have to physically exist as a standalone `.xaml` file. `LoadComponent` can automatically retrieve BAML embedded as a resource when given the appropriate URI (which, by MSBuild convention, is the name of the original XAML source file). In fact, Visual Studio's autogenerated `InitializeComponent` method calls `Application.LoadComponent` to load embedded BAML, although it uses a different overload. Chapter 12 provides more details about this mechanism of retrieving embedded resources with URIs.

After you've gotten a hold of the root element instance, you can use the `System.Windows.Markup.XamlWriter` class to get a XAML representation of the root element (and, therefore, all its children). `XamlWriter` contains five overloads of a static `Save` method, the simplest of which accepts an object instance and returns appropriate XAML as a string:

```
string xaml = XamlWriter.Save(window);
```

It might sound a little troubling that BAML can be so easily "cracked open," but it's really no different from any other software running locally or displaying a user interface locally. (For example, you can easily dig into a website's HTML, JavaScript, and Cascading Style Sheets [CSS] files.) The popular .NET Reflector tool has a BamlViewer add-in (see http://codeplex.com/reflectoraddins) that displays BAML embedded in any assembly as XAML.

Introducing XAML2009

Although XAML is a general-purpose language whose use is broader than that of WPF, WPF's XAML compiler and parsers are architecturally tied to WPF. Therefore, they are not usable by other technologies without taking a dependency on WPF. The .NET Framework 4.0 fixes this by introducing a new `System.Xaml` assembly that contains a bunch of functionality for processing XAML. WPF (and WCF and WF) take a dependency on `System.Xaml`—not the other way around.

At the same time, the .NET Framework 4.0 introduces a handful of new features for the XAML language. This second generation of the XAML language is referred to as XAML2009. (To differentiate, the first generation is sometimes referred to as XAML2006.) The `System.Xaml` assembly supports XAML2009, unlike the older APIs (`System.Windows.Markup.XamlReader` and `System.Windows.Markup.XamlWriter` from the previous section), which only support XAML2006.

The new XAML2009 features, outlined in this section, are nothing revolutionary but represent a nice set of incremental improvements to XAML. However, don't get too excited; for the most part, these features are not usable in WPF projects because XAML compilation still uses the XAML2006-based APIs, as do Visual Studio's WPF designer and editor, due to schedule constraints.

At the time of writing, it is unclear when WPF will completely switch over to XAML2009. (Note that Silverlight doesn't support XAML2009 either; it doesn't even support the entire XAML2006 specification!) In WPF 4, however, you can take advantage of these features when using loose XAML with a host that processes the XAML with the XAML2009-based APIs, such as the XAMLPAD2009 sample from this book's source code or Internet Explorer when the `netfx/2009` XML namespace is used.

Therefore, the XAML2009 features are interesting to learn about, even if they are not yet terribly useful. Most of them revolve around the idea of making a wider range of types directly usable from XAML. This is good news for class library authors, as XAML2009 imposes fewer restrictions for making class libraries XAML friendly. On its own, each feature provides a small improvement in expressiveness, but many of the features work together to solve real-world problems.

Full Generics Support

In XAML2006, the root element can be an instantiation of a generic class, thanks to the `x:TypeArguments` keyword. `x:TypeArguments` can be set to a type name or a comma-delimited list of type names. But because `x:TypeArguments` can only be used on the root element, generic classes generally have not been XAML friendly.

A common workaround for this limitation is to derive a non-generic class from a generic one simply so it can be referenced from XAML, as in the following example:

C#:

```
public class PhotoCollection : ObservableCollection<Photo> {}
```

XAML:

```
<custom:PhotoCollection>
  <custom:Photo …/>
  <custom:Photo …/>
</custom:PhotoCollection>
```

In XAML2009, however, `x:TypeArguments` can be used on *any* element, so a class like `ObservableCollection<Photo>` can be instantiated directly from XAML:

```
<collections:ObservableCollection TypeArguments="custom:Photo">
  <custom:Photo …/>
  <custom:Photo …/>
</collections:ObservableCollection>
```

In this case, `collections` is assumed to map to the `System.Collections.ObjectModel` namespace that contains `ObservableCollection`.

Dictionary Keys of Any Type

In XAML2009, type conversion is now attempted with `x:Key` values, so you can successfully add items to a dictionary with non-string keys without using a markup extension. Here's an example:

```
<collections:Dictionary x:TypeArguments="x:Int32, x:String">
  <x:String x:Key="1">One</x:String>
  <x:String x:Key="2">Two</x:String>
</collections:Dictionary>
```

Here, `collections` is assumed to map to the `System.Collections.Generic` namespace.

DIGGING DEEPER

Turning Off the Type Conversion of Non-String Dictionary Keys

For backwards compatibility, the XAML2009 `XamlObjectWriter` has a setting for turning off the new automatic type conversion. This is controlled by the `XamlObjectWriterSettings.PreferUnconvertedDictionaryKeys` property. When set to `true`, `System.Xaml` won't convert keys if the dictionary implements the non-generic `IDictionary` interface, unless:

- `System.Xaml` has already failed calling `IDictionary.Add` on this same instance, or
- The dictionary is a well-known type from the .NET Framework that `System.Xaml` knows requires conversion.

Built-In System Data Types

In XAML2006, using core .NET data types such as `String` or `Int32` is awkward due to the need to reference the `System` namespace from the `mscorlib` assembly, as seen previously in this chapter:

```
<sys:Int32 xmlns:sys="clr-namespace:System;assembly=mscorlib">7</sys:Int32>
```

In XAML2009, 13 .NET data types have been added to the XAML language namespace that most XAML is already referencing. With a namespace prefix of `x`, these data types are `x:Byte`, `x:Boolean`, `x:Int16`, `x:Int32`, `x:Int64`, `x:Single`, `x:Double`, `x:Decimal`, `x:Char`, `x:String`, `x:Object`, `x:Uri`, and `x:TimeSpan`. Therefore, the previous snippet can be rewritten as follows:

```
<x:Int32 xmlns:x="http://schemas.microsoft.com/winfx/2006/xaml">7</x:Int32>
```

But it is typically seen as follows in a XAML file already referencing the XAML language namespace:

```
<x:Int32>7</x:Int32>
```

Instantiating Objects with Non-Default Constructors

XAML2009 introduces an `x:Arguments` keyword that enables you to specify one or more arguments to pass to a class's constructor. Consider, for example, the `System.Version` class, which has a default constructor and four parameterized constructors. You could not construct an instance of this class in XAML2006 unless someone provided an appropriate type converter (or unless you were happy with the behavior of the default constructor, which produces a version number of `0.0`).

In XAML2009, you can instantiate this class with its constructor that accepts a single string as follows:

```
<sys:Version x:Arguments="4.0.30319.1"/>
```

The constructor argument doesn't have to be a string; the attribute value undergoes type conversion as necessary.

Unlike `x:TypeArguments`, `x:Arguments` does not allow you to specify multiple arguments in the attribute value with a comma-delimited string. Instead, you can use the element form of `x:Arguments` to specify any number of arguments. For example, calling `System.Version`'s constructor that accepts four integers can be done as follows:

```
<sys:Version>
<x:Arguments>
  <x:Int32>4</x:Int32>
  <x:Int32>0</x:Int32>
  <x:Int32>30319</x:Int32>
  <x:Int32>1</x:Int32>
</x:Arguments>
</sys:Version>
```

Getting Instances via Factory Methods

With the new `x:FactoryMethod` keyword in XAML2009, you can now get an instance of a class that doesn't have *any* public constructors. `x:FactoryMethod` enables you to specify any public static method that returns an instance of the desired type. For example, the following XAML uses a `Guid` instance returned by the static `Guid.NewGuid` method:

```
<Label xmlns=http://schemas.microsoft.com/winfx/2006/xaml/presentation
       xmlns:x=http://schemas.microsoft.com/winfx/2006/xaml
       xmlns:sys="clr-namespace:System;assembly=mscorlib">
  <sys:Guid x:FactoryMethod="sys:Guid.NewGuid"/>
</Label>
```

When `x:FactoryMethod` is used with `x:Arguments`, the arguments are passed to the static factory method rather than to a constructor. Therefore, the following XAML calls the static `Marshal.GetExceptionForHR` method, which accepts an `HRESULT` error code as input and returns the corresponding .NET exception that would be thrown by the common language runtime interoperability layer when encountering such an error:

```
<Label xmlns=http://schemas.microsoft.com/winfx/2006/xaml/presentation
       xmlns:x=http://schemas.microsoft.com/winfx/2006/xaml
       xmlns:sys="clr-namespace:System;assembly=mscorlib"
       xmlns:interop=
         "clr-namespace:System.Runtime.InteropServices;assembly=mscorlib">
  <sys:Exception x:FactoryMethod="interop:Marshal.GetExceptionForHR">
  <x:Arguments>
    <x:Int32>0x80004001</x:Int32>
  </x:Arguments>
  </sys:Exception>
</Label>
```

Figure 2.3 shows the result of the previous two `Labels` stacked in the same XAML content, as rendered by the XAMLPAD2009 sample.

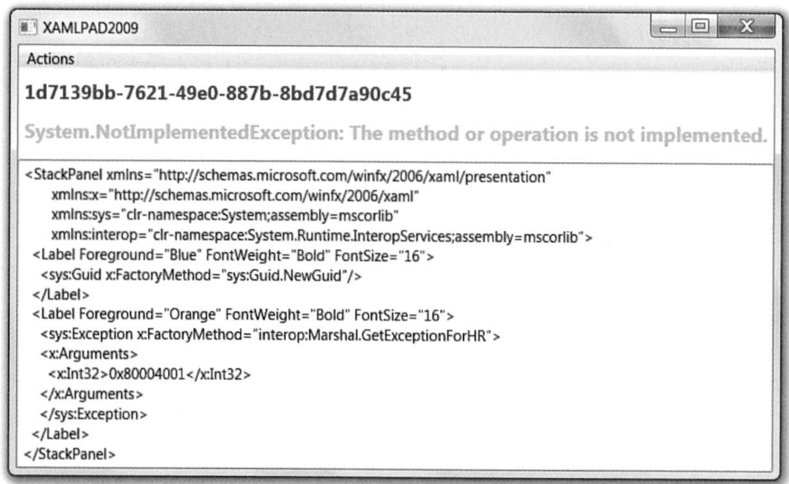

FIGURE 2.3 Displaying two instances retrieved via static factory methods.

Event Handler Flexibility

Event handlers can't be assigned in a loose XAML2006 file, but they can be assigned in a loose XAML2009 file as long as the root instance can be located and it has a method with a matching name and appropriate signature. In addition, in XAML2009, the value of an event attribute can be any markup extension that returns an appropriate delegate:

```
<Button Click="{custom:DelegateFinder Click}"/>
```

As with any markup extension, it can accept arbitrary input and perform arbitrary logic to look up the delegate.

Defining New Properties

XAML is primarily focused on instantiating existing classes and setting values of their predefined properties. Two new elements in XAML2009—`x:Members` and the corresponding `x:Property`—enable the *definition* of additional properties directly inside XAML. This functionality doesn't apply to WPF, however. You can see it used in Windows Workflow Foundation XAML, as in the following example:

```
<Activity x:Class="ActivityLibrary1.Activity1" …>
<x:Members>
  <x:Property Name="argument1" Type="InArgument(x:Int32)"/>
  <x:Property Name="argument2" Type="OutArgument(x:String)"/>
</x:Members>
…
</Activity>
```

Fun with XAML Readers and Writers

You have already seen how to read and write XAML with `XamlReader.Load` and `XamlWriter.Save` from the `System.Windows.Markup` namespace. These APIs have been around since the first version of WPF and still work just fine on WPF content—as long as that content stays within the XAML2006 subset.

The new `System.Xaml` assembly contains `System.Xaml.XamlReader` and `System.Xaml.XamlWriter` abstract base classes (not to be confused with the aforementioned reader/writer classes) that are the foundation of a new way to read and write XAML. The classes in `System.Xaml` are much more flexible than the "black box" conversion done by the older classes, and they support XAML2009.

Overview

`XamlReader` is designed to generate a stream of logical XAML nodes from an arbitrary source (dictated by the concrete derived implementation), and `XamlWriter` is designed to consume such a stream of XAML nodes and write them out in an arbitrary way. The following derived readers and writers are currently shipped as public classes:

Readers (derived from `System.Xaml.XamlReader`):

- **`System.Xaml.XamlXmlReader`**—Reads XML (by working with a `System.Xml.XmlReader`, `System.IO.TextReader`, `System.IO.Stream`, or filename string)
- **`System.Xaml.XamlObjectReader`**—Reads a live object graph
- **`System.Windows.Baml2006.Baml2006Reader`**—Reads BAML (the 2006 form still used by WPF)
- **`System.Xaml.XamlBackgroundReader`**—Wraps another `XamlReader`, implementing double-buffering so the reader can do its work on a separate thread from a writer

Writers (derived from `System.Xaml.XamlWriter`):

- **`System.Xaml.XamlXmlWriter`**—Writes XML (using either a `System.Xml.XmlWriter`, `System.IO.TextWriter`, or `Stream`)
- **`System.Xaml.XamlObjectWriter`**—Produces a live graph of objects

XAML readers and XAML writers work together much like the readers and writers elsewhere in the .NET Framework, such as ones in the `System.IO` and `System.Xml` namespaces. The result is an ecosystem in which many different readers and writers can be mixed and matched, where the notion of logical XAML nodes becomes the common connection. This is pictured in Figure 2.4, with the readers and writers that ship with the .NET Framework. The XAML node stream is not tightly associated with the XML text representation but rather the logical notion of a hierarchy of objects with various members set to various values.

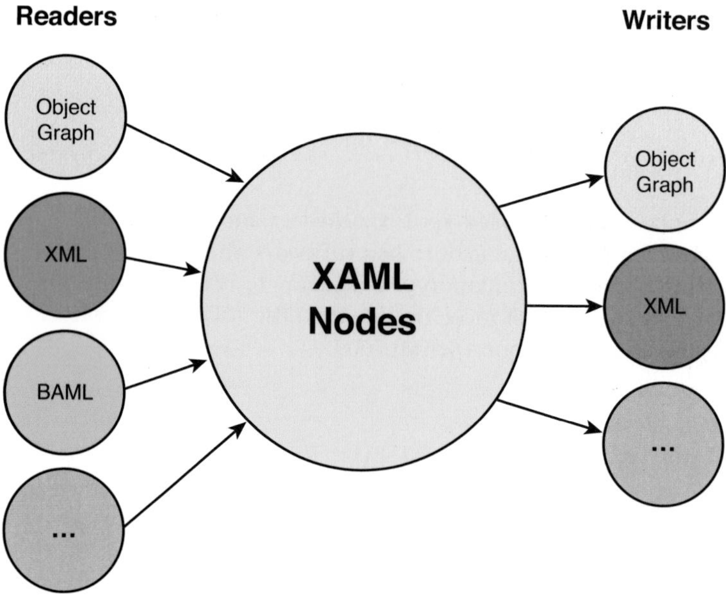

FIGURE 2.4 Readers and writers working together to enable all sorts of transformations.

The ... parts of Figure 2.4 are important, as there can be a rich set of third-party readers and writers that enable a wide variety of transformations. Over the past few years, people have shared a number of converters that transform XAML to and from other file formats (although not yet based on these new APIs at the time of writing). These formats include more than 40 3D formats (Autodesk 3ds Max and Maya, AutoCAD DXF, NewTek LightWave, and so on), Adobe Illustrator/Photoshop/Flash/Fireworks, SVG, HTML 5 Canvas, Visio, PowerPoint, Windows Metafile (WMF), Enhanced Metafile (EMF), and even Visual Basic 6 forms!

WARNING

The functionality in this section works best with non-WPF XAML!

There's a reason this section is called "*Fun* with XAML Readers and Writers." Sure, these classes are fun to work with, but you might have to limit your use of them to experimental tinkering for now. The current version of `XamlObjectReader` doesn't support several aspects of WPF objects, so for WPF XAML serialization, you'll have to stick with `System.Windows.Markup.XamlWriter`. If you're using XAML for non-WPF purposes, then it should work great for you.

FAQ

Why is `XamlXmlReader` better at reading a XAML file than a simple `XmlReader`? Isn't XAML just XML?

`XamlXmlReader` does use `XmlReader` to do its work, but it provides two important features on top of the reading of XML:

- It abstracts away differences in XML representations that have equivalent meanings in XAML.
- It produces a XAML node stream that is compatible with any XAML writer and contains rich information not even present in the source XML.

The first point is crucial for reducing the amount of work needed to consume XAML. The following three chunks of XAML all express the same concept—a `Button` whose content property called `Content` is set to the string `"OK"`:

```
<!-- Implicit setting of the content property: -->
<Button xmlns="http://schemas.microsoft.com/winfx/2006/xaml/presentation">
  OK
</Button>
<!-- Setting the property via property element syntax: -->
<Button xmlns="http://schemas.microsoft.com/winfx/2006/xaml/presentation">
<Button.Content>
  OK
</Button.Content>
</Button>
<!-- Setting the property via property attribute syntax: -->
<Button xmlns="http://schemas.microsoft.com/winfx/2006/xaml/presentation"
  Content="OK"/>
```

These three snippets look very different to `XmlReader` but are made to look the same by `XamlXmlReader`. This is exactly what a XAML-consumption tool wants (unless the tool is doing something like enforcing style guidelines on the textual representation of XAML), and it takes considerable extra work. For example, `XamlXmlReader` can only know that that the first snippet is equivalent to the other two by examining the definition of `Button` and discovering that it has a content property named `Content`.

Continued

As for the second point, the rich information present in the XAML node stream provided by `XamlXmlReader` (or any XAML reader) is a result of combining the input data with the definitions of the types being referenced. For example, through `XamlXmlReader`, you can discover that `Content` is a content property, and its type is `System.Object`.

The Node Loop

Performing a transformation from one format to another involves reading XAML nodes from an appropriate reader and sending them to an appropriate writer. `XamlReader` and `XamlWriter` are designed to make this easy, enabling you to write a simple "node loop" that performs the necessary reading and writing from beginning to end. With a XAML reader called `reader` and a XAML writer called `writer`, here is what a simple node loop looks like:

```
// Simple node loop
while (reader.Read())
{
  writer.WriteNode(reader);
}
```

What actually happens in this loop depends on the type of the reader and writer. The XAMLPAD2009 sample has the goal of reading XAML in XML format (stored in a string) and producing a live object graph that can be attached (and therefore rendered) inside its own user interface. Therefore, Listing 2.1 uses the simple node loop with `XamlXmlReader` and `XamlObjectWriter` to accomplish this. Most of the effort involves getting `XamlXmlReader` to read an XML string. The easiest way to do this is to create a `System.IO.StringReader` for the string which can be passed to `XamlXmlReader` (because `StringReader` is a `TextReader`).

LISTING 2.1 A Simple Node Loop That Converts a XAML XML String to a Live Object Graph

```
public static object ConvertXmlStringToObjectGraph(string xmlString)
{
  // String -> TextReader -> XamlXmlReader
  using (TextReader textReader = new StringReader(xmlString))
  using (XamlXmlReader reader = new XamlXmlReader(textReader,
           System.Windows.Markup.XamlReader.GetWpfSchemaContext()))
  using (XamlObjectWriter writer = new XamlObjectWriter(reader.SchemaContext))
  {
    // Simple node loop
    while (reader.Read())
    {
      writer.WriteNode(reader);
    }
```

LISTING 2.1 Continued

```
    // When XamlObjectWriter is done, this is the root object instance
    return writer.Result;
  }
}
```


The WPF schema context is passed to `XamlObjectWriter` to make it work better with WPF XAML. It enables a number of features and compatibility quirks that aren't appropriate for general-purpose XAML processing.

Reading XAML

XAML readers expose a lot of useful information about the resultant XAML node stream, so you can do a whole lot more than just blindly write the nodes into some other form, such as morphing the content during the transformation.

The most important `XamlReader` property to inspect when writing a custom node loop is `NodeType`, which can be one of eight enumeration values:

- **`StartObject`**—The reader is positioned at the start of an explicit object, such as an element's start tag in XML or the beginning of a markup extension in a property value.
- **`GetObject`**—The reader is positioned at the start of an *implicit* object, such as a collection whose items appear in XAML but not the collection itself (as seen with `ListBox` in the earlier "Collection Items" section).
- **`EndObject`**—The reader is positioned at the end of an object (which was previously discovered via `StartObject` or `GetObject`). Every `StartObject` and `GetObject` node is matched with a corresponding `EndObject` node later in the stream.
- **`StartMember`**—The reader is positioned at the start of an object's member: a property (attached or not), an event (attached or not), or a XAML directive such as `x:Key`. Every member belongs to a parent object, so you won't encounter a `StartMember` node without first encountering a `StartObject` or `GetObject` node. Note that in XML, it doesn't matter whether the member is specified using property attribute syntax or property element syntax—it still shows up as a member, not an object.
- **`EndMember`**—The reader is positioned at the end of a member (which was previously discovered via `StartMember`). Every `StartMember` node is matched with a corresponding `EndMember` node later in the stream.
- **`Value`**—The reader is positioned at the start of a member's value. Every value is associated with a member, so you won't encounter a `Value` node without first encountering a `StartMember` node (and a `StartObject` or `GetObject` node before that).
- **`NamespaceDeclaration`**—The reader is positioned at the declaration of an XML namespace (which associates the namespace value with a prefix). Note that these appear in the XAML node stream immediately before the `StartObject` node that

"contains" these declarations. This might sounds surprising, but given that the namespace declarations provide context to even the root element, it's valuable to have that context first.

- **None**—The reader is positioned at something that is not a real node, such as the end of a file. This `NodeType` can be safely ignored.

`XamlReader` defines four important properties that enable you to extract the relevant data about any node: `Type`, `Member`, `Value`, and `Namespace`. The data that you can retrieve from these properties depends on the node type of its current position. For example, when `NodeType` is `StartObject`, `Type` is set to a `XamlType` instance, and the other three properties are `null`. When `NodeType` is `StartMember`, `Member` is set to a `XamlMember` instance, and the other three properties are `null`. When `NodeType` is `Value`, the `Value` property is the only one that is non-`null`, and when `NodeType` is `NamespaceDeclaration`, `Namespace` is the only non-`null` property.

In addition, all the XAML readers in the .NET Framework 4.0 (except for `XamlObjectReader`) implement an `IXamlLineInfo` interface that produces line number information when available. When the `HasLineInfo` property is `true`, you can retrieve row and column data from `LineNumber` and `LinePosition` properties, respectively.

FAQ

What are these `XamlType` and `XamlMember` instances exposed by XAML readers?

These classes expose a XAML-specific form of .NET reflection.

`XamlType` wraps `System.Type` (which is available from `XamlType`'s `UnderlyingType` property), adding XAML-specific concepts such as content properties, attached properties, and much more. This layer of abstraction also enables `XamlType` to represent non-.NET types, if desired.

`XamlMember` effectively wraps `System.Reflection.MemberInfo` (which is available from `XamlMember`'s `UnderlyingMember` property when there actually is an underlying `MemberInfo`). It also adds XAML-specific concepts such as `IsDirective` and `PreferredXamlNamespace` properties.

To demonstrate what working with a XAML reader looks like in depth, Table 2.1 traces through the node stream produced by `XamlXmlReader` when reading the XAML content in Listing 2.2. The indenting of the `XamlNodeType` values illustrates the nesting of objects, members, and values.

LISTING 2.2 Sample XAML Content to Demonstrate the Behavior of `XamlXmlReader`

```
<StackPanel xmlns="http://schemas.microsoft.com/winfx/2006/xaml/presentation"
            xmlns:x="http://schemas.microsoft.com/winfx/2006/xaml">
  <!-- Set names two different ways -->
  <Button Name="okButton" Click="okButton_Click">OK</Button>
```

LISTING 2.2 Continued

```
  <Button x:Name="cancelButton">Cancel</Button>
  <ListBox>
    <!-- Set content three different ways -->
    <ListBoxItem Content="Item 1"/>
    <ListBoxItem>Item 2</ListBoxItem>
    <ListBoxItem>
    <ListBoxItem.Content>
      Item 3
    </ListBoxItem.Content>
    </ListBoxItem>
  </ListBox>
</StackPanel>
```


TABLE 2.1 The XAML Node Stream Produced by `XamlXmlReader` When Reading Listing 2.2

`XamlNodeType`	**Data**	**Line Number**	**Line Position**
`NamespaceDeclaration`	Namespace="…/xaml/presentation", Prefix=""	1	13
`NamespaceDeclaration`	Namespace="…/xaml", Prefix="x"	2	13
`StartObject`	Type=StackPanel	1	2
`StartMember`	Member=Children of type UIElementCollection	4	4
`GetObject`	null	4	4
`StartMember`	Member=_Items, a XamlDirective of type List<Object>	4	4
`StartObject`	Type=Button	4	4
`StartMember`	Member=Name of type String	4	11
`Value`	Value="okButton"	4	11
`EndMember`	null	4	11
`StartMember`	Member=Click of type RoutedEventHander (IsEvent=true)	4	27
`Value`	Value="okButton_Click"	4	27
`EndMember`	null	4	27
`StartMember`	Member=Content of type Object	4	54
`Value`	Value="OK"	4	54
`EndMember`	null	4	54
`EndObject`	null	4	54
`StartObject`	Type=Button	5	4
`StartMember`	Member=Name, a XamlDirective of type String	5	11
`Value`	Value="cancelButton"	5	11

TABLE 2.1 Continued

XamlNodeType	Data	Line Number	Line Position
EndMember	null	5	11
StartMember	Member=Content of type Object	5	41
Value	Value="Cancel"	5	41
EndMember	null	5	41
EndObject	null	5	41
StartObject	Type=ListBox	6	4
StartMember	Member=Items of type ItemCollection	8	6
GetObject	null	8	6
StartMember	Member=_Items, a XamlDirective of type List<Object>	8	6
StartObject	Type=ListBoxItem	8	6
StartMember	Member=Content of type Object	8	18
Value	Value="Item 1"	8	18
EndMember	null	8	18
EndObject	null	9	6
StartObject	Type=ListBoxItem	9	6
StartMember	Member=Content of type Object	9	26
Value	Value="Item 2"	9	26
EndMember	null	9	26
EndObject	null	9	26
StartObject	Type=ListBoxItem	10	6
StartMember	Member=Content of type Object	11	6
Value	Value="Item 3"	13	7
EndMember	null	13	7
EndObject	null	14	7
EndMember	null	15	5
EndObject	null	15	5
EndMember	null	15	5
EndObject	null	15	5
EndMember	null	16	3
EndObject	null	16	3
EndMember	null	16	3
EndObject	null	16	3

Notice that all three `ListBoxItem` elements are represented identically in Table 2.1, as are the two `Button` elements, although it is possible to tell the difference between the use of `Button`'s `Name` property and the use of the `x:Name` XAML directive. (In the latter case, `XamlMember` is a derived `XamlDirective` type whose `IsDirective` property returns `true`.)

Also notice that `GetObject`, `EndMember`, and `EndObject` are not accompanied with any additional information; relevant information must be derived from the rest of the node stream. Because of this, interesting transformations to XAML often involve maintaining your own stack with data related to objects and/or members.

DIGGING DEEPER

Markup Compatibility

The markup compatibility XML namespace (`http://schemas.openxmlformats.org/markup-compatibility/2006`, typically used with an `mc` prefix) contains an `Ignorable` attribute that instructs XAML processors to ignore all elements/attributes in specified namespaces if they can't be resolved to their .NET types/members. (The namespace also has a `ProcessContent` attribute that overrides `Ignorable` for specific types inside the ignored namespaces.)

Expression Blend takes advantage of this feature to do things like add design-time properties to XAML content that can be ignored at runtime. Here's an example:

```
<StackPanel xmlns="http://schemas.microsoft.com/client/2007"
  xmlns:d="http://schemas.microsoft.com/expression/blend/2008"
  xmlns:mc="http://schemas.openxmlformats.org/markup-compatibility/2006"
  mc:Ignorable="d" d:DesignWidth="100" d:DesignHeight="100">
…
</StackPanel>
```

`mc:Ignorable` can be given a space-delimited list of namespaces, and `mc:ProcessContent` can be given a space-delimited list of elements.

When `XamlXmlReader` encounters ignorable content that can't be resolved, it doesn't report any nodes for it. If the ignorable content *can* be resolved, it will be reported normally. So consumers don't need to do anything special to handle markup compatibility correctly.

Writing to Live Objects

The XAMLPAD2009 sample doesn't convert XAML to live objects as-is; it makes a few modifications to the XAML content to ensure that a wider range of WPF XAML can be rendered successfully. Specifically, it makes two modifications to the content:

- It removes all event members, because unless the handler can be located, `XamlObjectWriter` would fail with an exception explaining, for example, "Failed to create a 'Click' from the text 'button_Click'." Note that `XamlObjectWriter` has a `RootObjectInstance` property that could be set to an object with appropriate event handlers, but stripping out the events is the easiest approach, and usually just fine for a XAML experimentation tool. It also removes `x:Class` because it's not valid for loose XAML.
- It converts any `Window` element into a `Page` element instead. Chapter 7 covers these elements in depth, but the bottom line is that a `Window` element cannot be a child of another element, and XAMLPAD2009 always attempts to attach the root instance as a child of its own user interface. There are other ways to handle this (such as

detecting when the root is a `Window` element and launching it on its own), but swapping one XAML node with another makes for an instructive sample.

Listing 2.3 shows the custom node loop that makes these two customizations while transforming the content from an XML string to live objects.

LISTING 2.3 A Custom Node Loop That Converts a XAML XML String to a Live Object Graph with Modifications

```
public static object ConvertXmlStringToMorphedObjectGraph(string xmlString)
{
  // String -> TextReader -> XamlXmlReader
  using (TextReader textReader = new StringReader(xmlString))
  using (XamlXmlReader reader = new XamlXmlReader(textReader,
           System.Windows.Markup.XamlReader.GetWpfSchemaContext()))
  using (XamlObjectWriter writer = new XamlObjectWriter(reader.SchemaContext))
  {
    // Node loop
    while (reader.Read())
    {
      // Skip events and x:Class
      if (reader.NodeType == XamlNodeType.StartMember &&
          reader.Member.IsEvent || reader.Member == XamlLanguage.Class)
      {
        reader.Skip();
      }

      if (reader.NodeType == XamlNodeType.StartObject &&
          reader.Type.UnderlyingType == typeof(Window))
      {
        // Turn a Window into a Page
        writer.WriteStartObject(new XamlType(typeof(Page),
          reader.SchemaContext));
      }
      else
      {
        // Otherwise, just write the node as-is
        writer.WriteNode(reader);
      }
    }

    // When XamlObjectWriter is done, this is the root object instance
    return writer.Result;
  }
}
```

Listing 2.3 leverages XamlReader's Skip method to skip event members (IsEvent = true) and any x:Class members. (The latter is checked with help from the handy System.Xaml.XamlLanguage static class, which exposes all XamlDirectives and the built-in system XamlTypes as read-only properties for easy comparison.) When the reader is on a StartObject or StartMember node, Skip advances the stream to the node *after* the matching EndObject/EndMember (skipping any nested objects/members, which is exactly what we want). When the reader is on any other node type, calling Skip is equivalent to calling Read again: It advances to the next node.

For the Window/Page replacement, only the StartObject node needs to be swapped out. Recall that an EndObject node doesn't have any data associated with it; its meaning depends on the rest of the node stream. So an EndObject node for Window can happily become an EndObject node for Page. This replacement doesn't properly transfer Window's members to the Page, however, because they are resolved on the Window by the reader before the node loop begins. The source code accompanying this book does the extra work of creating a new member on the Page for each applicable member set on the Window.

You've seen from Listings 2.1 and 2.3 that XamlObjectWriter.Result is set to the root object instance when the node loop is finished. More specifically, every time an EndObject node is successfully written, XamlObjectWriter.Result is set to the live object instance corresponding to that object. Because the last EndObject written to the node stream belongs to the root node, the final value of Result is the root.

Writing to XML

Writing WPF objects to XAML in XML form is a common activity. Because XamlObjectReader doesn't currently support WPF objects, Listing 2.4 demonstrates converting from XML to XML by pairing up XamlXmlReader with XamlXmlWriter. This may sound nonsensical, but the combination produces a simple "XAML scrubber" that normalizes the input XML to produce consistently represented, consistently spaced XML with comments removed.

LISTING 2.4 A "XAML Scrubber" That Normalizes the Input XML

```
public static string RewriteXaml(string xmlString)
{
  // String -> TextReader -> XamlXmlReader
  using (TextReader textReader = new StringReader(xmlString))
  using (XamlXmlReader reader = new XamlXmlReader(textReader))
  // TextWriter -> XmlWriter -> XamlXmlWriter
  using (StringWriter textWriter = new StringWriter())
  using (XmlWriter xmlWriter = XmlWriter.Create(textWriter,
          new XmlWriterSettings { Indent = true, OmitXmlDeclaration = true }))
  using (XamlXmlWriter writer = new XamlXmlWriter(xmlWriter,
          reader.SchemaContext))
  {
```

LISTING 2.4 Continued

```
    // Simple node loop
    while (reader.Read())
    {
      writer.WriteNode(reader);
    }

    return textWriter.ToString();
  }
}
```

Just about all the work is setting up the reader and writer. `XamlXmlReader` is constructed the same way as in the previous listing. `XamlXmlWriter` is constructed from an `XmlWriter`, which is constructed from a `System.IO.StringWriter`. (`XmlWriter` could alternatively be constructed with a `StringBuilder`.) The use of `XmlWriter` enables pretty printing (each element on a separate line with appropriate indenting) as well as the removal of an unnecessary XML declaration (`<?xml version="1.0" encoding="utf-16"?>`). If you don't care about these things and are fine with all the content being emitted on the same line, you could directly give `XamlXmlWriter` the `StringWriter` (because it's a `TextWriter`) rather than wrap it in the `XmlWriter`:

```
// TextWriter -> XamlXmlWriter
using (StringWriter textWriter = new StringWriter())
using (XamlXmlWriter writer = new XamlXmlWriter(textWriter,
      reader.SchemaContext))
{
  …
}
```

XamlServices

To minimize the amount of code you need to write, the most common uses for XAML readers and writers are packaged in a set of easy-to-use static methods in a class called `System.Xaml.XamlServices`. It has the following methods:

- **Load**—Depending on the overload, you can give it a filename string, a `Stream`, a `TextReader`, an `XmlReader`, or a `XamlReader`, and it returns the root of the corresponding live object graph, like the older `XamlReader.Load` API. Internally, `Load` uses `XamlXmlReader` and `XamlObjectWriter` to do its work, as in Listing 2.1.
- **Parse**—Like `Load`, `Parse` returns the root of a live object graph, but it accepts XAML content as a string for input. Internally, it creates a `StringReader` for the string, creates an `XmlReader` and then a `XamlXmlReader` so it can call `Load`. This makes `Parse` just like the `ConvertXmlStringToObjectGraph` method in Listing 2.1.
- **Save**—`Save` takes an object as input and, depending on the overload, returns the content as a string, `Stream`, `TextWriter`, `XmlWriter`, or `XamlWriter`, or even saves the

contents directly to a text file. Internally, Save uses XamlObjectReader and XamlXmlWriter (unless you pass in a different XamlWriter). It sets the XmlWriter's Indent and OmitXmlDeclaration properties to true, just like in Listing 2.4.

- **Transform**—Transform performs a basic node loop with whatever reader and writer are passed in.

XamlServices.Transform is actually slightly more sophisticated than the simple node loop presented earlier. It preserves line number and line position information if both the reader and the writer support the appropriate interfaces to produce and consume it (IXamlLineInfo for the reader and IXamlLineInfoConsumer for the writer). Therefore, Transform effectively does the following:

```
public static void Transform(XamlReader reader, XamlWriter writer)
{
  IXamlLineInfo producer = reader as IXamlLineInfo;
  IXamlLineInfoConsumer consumer = writer as IXamlLineInfoConsumer;
  bool transferLineInfo = (producer != null && producer.HasLineInfo &&
                           consumer != null && consumer.ShouldProvideLineInfo);

  // Better node loop
  while (reader.Read())
  {
    // Transfer line info
    if (transferLineInfo && producer.LineNumber > 0)
      consumer.SetLineInfo(producer.LineNumber, producer.LinePosition);

    writer.WriteNode(reader);
  }
}
```

Therefore, the node loop from Listing 2.1 could be replaced (and slightly enhanced) by replacing the node loop with a call to XamlServices.Transform, as shown in Listing 2.5. Of course, the whole ConvertXmlStringToObjectGraph method is unnecessary, as it is a duplication of XamlServices.Parse.

LISTING 2.5 A Minor Simplification to Listing 2.1

```
public static object ConvertXmlStringToObjectGraph(string xmlString)
{
  // String -> TextReader -> XamlXmlReader
  using (TextReader textReader = new StringReader(xmlString))
  using (XamlXmlReader reader = new XamlXmlReader(textReader,
           System.Windows.Markup.XamlReader.GetWpfSchemaContext()))
  using (XamlObjectWriter writer = new XamlObjectWriter(reader.SchemaContext))
  {
    // The node loop
```

LISTING 2.5 Continued

```
    XamlServices.Transform(reader, writer);

    // When XamlObjectWriter is done, this is the root object instance
    return writer.Result;
  }
}
```

WARNING

Beware of `XamlServices` gotchas with WPF XAML!

You might expect that you could combine `XamlServices.Parse` and `XamlServices.Save` to implement the XAML scrubber from Listing 2.4 in an easy, albeit inefficient, manner:

```
public static string RewriteXaml(string xmlString)
{
  return XamlServices.Save(XamlServices.Parse(xmlString));
}
```

This would be inefficient because internally the string goes through a `XamlXmlReader` to be written to live objects with a `XamlObjectWriter` (the root of which is returned by `XamlServices.Parse`), and then the hierarchy of objects is read by a `XamlObjectReader` before being written by a `XamlXmlWriter` into an `XmlWriter` to produce the final string. The intermediate step of transferring to live objects is problematic for more than just performance reasons; it requires special treatment in the face of certain XAML such as event handlers that need to be attached or an `x:Class` directive that needs to be resolved.

Even worse than these limitations, the code simply doesn't work because `XamlObjectWriter` doesn't currently support WPF objects. Instead, you could use the older `XamlReader` and `XamlWriter`:

```
return System.Windows.Markup.XamlWriter.Save(
  System.Windows.Markup.XamlReader.Parse(xmlString));
```

Or, if you care about pretty printing:

```
using (StringWriter textWriter = new StringWriter())
using (XmlWriter xmlWriter = XmlWriter.Create(textWriter,
         new XmlWriterSettings { Indent = true, OmitXmlDeclaration = true }))
{
  System.Windows.Markup.XamlWriter.Save(
    System.Windows.Markup.XamlReader.Parse(xmlString), xmlWriter);
  return textWriter.ToString();
}
```

But these approaches still suffer from the problems inherent to converting the XAML to live objects as an intermediate step.

TIP

The Microsoft XAML Toolkit, available from http://code.msdn.microsoft.com/XAML, builds on `System.Xaml` and provides several compelling features, such as XAML integration into the FxCop tool and a XAML Document Object Model (DOM). The XAML DOM is a LINQ-friendly set of APIs that enables even easier inspection and modification of XAML content compared what the readers and writers in this chapter enable. The toolkit also includes additional schema contexts—`SilverlightSchemaContext` for Silverlight XAML and `UISchemaContext` that provides a common abstraction for WPF XAML and Silverlight XAML.

XAML Keywords

The XAML language namespace (`http://schemas.microsoft.com/winfx/2006/xaml`) defines a handful of keywords that must be treated specially by any XAML compiler or parser. They mostly control aspects of how elements get exposed to procedural code, but several are useful even without any procedural code. You've already seen some of them (such as `Key`, `Name`, `Class`, `Subclass`, and `Code`), but Table 2.2 lists them all. They are listed with the conventional `x` prefix because that is how they usually appear in XAML and in documentation.

DIGGING DEEPER

Special Attributes Defined by the W3C

In addition to keywords in the XAML language namespace, XAML also supports two special attributes defined for XML by the World Wide Web Consortium (W3C): `xml:space` for controlling whitespace parsing and `xml:lang` for declaring the document's language and culture. The `xml` prefix is implicitly mapped to the standard XML namespace: `http://www.w3.org/XML/1998/namespace`.

TABLE 2.2 Keywords in the XAML Language Namespace, Assuming the Conventional x Namespace Prefix

Keyword	Valid As	Version	Meaning
`x:AsyncRecords`	Attribute on root element	2006+	Controls the size of asynchronous XAML-loading chunks.
`x:Arguments`	Attribute on or element inside any element	2009	Specifies an argument (or multiple arguments in the element syntax) to be passed to the element's constructor. When used with `x:FactoryMethod`, specifies argument(s) for the factory method.
`x:Boolean`	An element	2009	Represents a `System.Boolean`.
`x:Byte`	An element	2009	Represents a `System.Byte`.
`x:Char`	An element	2009	Represents a `System.Char`.
`x:Class`	Attribute on root element	2006+	Defines a class for the root element that derives from the element type, optionally prefixed with a .NET namespace.

TABLE 2.2 Continued

Keyword	Valid As	Version	Meaning
`x:ClassAttributes`	Attribute on root element and must be used with `x:Class`	2009	Not used by WPF; contains attributes relevant for Windows Workflow Foundation activities.
`x:ClassModifier`	Attribute on root element and must be used with `x:Class`	2006+	Defines the visibility of the class specified by `x:Class` (which is public by default). The attribute value must be specified in terms of the procedural language being used (for example, `public` or `internal` for C#).
`x:Code`	Element anywhere in XAML, but must be used with `x:Class`	2006+	Embeds procedural code to be inserted into the class specified by `x:Class`.
`x:ConnectionId`	Attribute	2006+	Not for public use.
`x:Decimal`	An element	2009	Represents a `System.Decimal`.
`x:Double`	An element	2009	Represents a `System.Double`.
`x:FactoryMethod`	Attribute on any element	2009	Specifies a static method to be called to retrieve the element instance instead of its constructor.
`x:FieldModifier`	Attribute on any nonroot element but must be used with `x:Name` (or equivalent)	2006+	Defines the visibility of the field to be generated for the element (which is internal by default). As with `x:ClassModifier`, the value must be specified in terms of the procedural language (for example, `public`, `private`, ... for C#).
`x:Int16`	An element	2009	Represents a `System.Int16`.
`x:Int32`	An element	2009	Represents a `System.Int32`.
`x:Int64`	An element	2009	Represents a `System.Int64`.
`x:Key`	Attribute on an element whose parent implements `IDictionary`	2006+	Specifies the key for the item when added to the parent dictionary.
`x:Members`	Not valid in WPF XAML	2009	Defines additional members for the root class specified by `x:Class`.
`x:Name`	Attribute on any nonroot element but must be used with `x:Class`	2006+	Chooses a name for the field to be generated for the element, so it can be referenced from procedural code.
`x:Object`	An element	2009	Represents a `System.Object`.
`x:Property`	Not valid in WPF XAML	2009	Defines a property inside an `x:Members` element.

TABLE 2.2 Continued

Keyword	Valid As	Version	Meaning
x:Shared	Attribute on any element in a ResourceDictionary, but only works if XAML is compiled	2006+	Can be set to false to avoid sharing the same resource instance in multiple places, as explained in Chapter 12.
x:Single	An element	2009	Represents a System.Single.
x:String	An element	2009	Represents a System.String.
x:Subclass	Attribute on root element and must be used with x:Class	2006+	Specifies a subclass of the x:Class class that holds the content defined in XAML, optionally prefixed with a .NET namespace (used with languages without support for partial classes).
x:SynchronousMode	Attribute on root element	2006+	Specifies whether the XAML content is allowed to be loaded asynchronously.
x:TimeSpan	An element	2009	Represents a System.TimeSpan.
x:TypeArguments	Attribute on any element in XAML2009, or attribute on root element that must be used with x:Class in XAML2006	2006+	Makes the class generic (for example, List<T>) with the specified generic argument instantiations (for example, List<Int32> or List<String>). Can be set to a comma-delimited list of generic arguments, with XML namespace prefixes for any types not in the default namespace.
x:Uid	Attribute on any element	2006+	Marks an element with an identifier used for localization, as described in Chapter 12.
x:Uri	An element	2009	Represents a System.Uri.
x:XData	Element used as the value for any property of type IXmlSerializable	2006+	An arbitrary XML data island that remains opaque to the XAML parser, as explained in Chapter 13.

Table 2.3 contains additional items in the XAML language namespace that can be confused as keywords but are actually just markup extensions (real .NET classes in the System.Windows.Markup namespace). Each class's Extension suffix is omitted from the table because the classes are typically used without the suffix.

TABLE 2.3 Markup Extensions in the XAML Language Namespace, Assuming the Conventional x Namespace Prefix

Extension	Meaning
`x:Array`	Represents a .NET array. An `x:Array` element's children are the elements of the array. It must be used with `x:Type` to define the type of the array.
`x:Null`	Represents a `null` reference.
`x:Reference`	A reference to a named element. It has a single positional parameter, which is the name of the referenced element.
`x:Static`	References any static property, field, constant, or enumeration value defined in procedural code. This can even be a nonpublic member in the same assembly, when XAML is compiled. Its `Member` string must be qualified with an XML namespace prefix if the type is not in the default namespace.
`x:Type`	Represents an instance of `System.Type`, just like the `typeof` operator in C#. Its `TypeName` string must be qualified with an XML namespace prefix if the type is not in the default namespace.

Summary

You have now seen how XAML fits in with WPF and, most importantly, you now have the information needed to translate most XAML examples into a language such as C# and vice versa. However, because type converters and markup extensions are "black boxes," a straightforward translation is not always going to be obvious. That said, invoking a type converter directly from procedural code is always an option if you can't figure out the conversion that the type converter is doing internally! (Many classes with corresponding type converters even expose a static `Parse` method that does the same work, for the sake of simpler procedural code.)

I love the fact that simple concepts that could have been treated specially by XAML (such as `null` or a named reference) are expressed using the same markup extension mechanism used by third parties. This keeps the XAML language as simple as possible, and it ensures that the extensibility mechanism works really well.

As you proceed further with WPF, you might find that some WPF APIs can be a little clunky from procedural code because their design is often optimized for XAML use. For example, WPF exposes many small building blocks (enabling the rich composition described in the previous chapter), so a WPF application generally must create far more objects manually than, say, a Windows Forms application. Besides the fact the XAML excels at expressing deep hierarchies of objects concisely, the WPF team spent more time implementing features to effectively hide intermediate objects in XAML (such as type converters) rather than features to hide them from procedural code (such as constructors that create inner objects on your behalf).

Most people understand the benefit of WPF having the separate declarative model provided by XAML, but some lament XML as the choice of format. The following sections are two common complaints and my attempt to debunk them.

Complaint 1: XML Is Too Verbose to Type

This is true: Almost nobody enjoys typing lots of XML, but that's where tools come in. Tools such as IntelliSense and visual designers can spare you from typing a single angle bracket! The transparent and well-specified nature of XML enables you to easily integrate new tools into the development process (creating a XAML exporter for your favorite tool, for example) and also enables easy hand-tweaking or troubleshooting.

In some areas of WPF—complicated paths and shapes, 3D models, and so on—typing XAML by hand isn't even practical. In fact, the trend from when XAML was first introduced in beta form has been to remove some of the handy human-typable shortcuts in favor of a more robust and extensible format that can be supported well by tools. But I still believe that being familiar with XAML and seeing the WPF APIs through both procedural and declarative perspectives is the best way to learn the technology. It's like understanding how HTML works without relying on a visual tool.

Complaint 2: XML-Based Systems Have Poor Performance

XML is about interoperability, not about an efficient representation of data. So, why should most WPF applications be saddled with a bunch of data that is relatively large and slow to parse?

The good news is that in a normal WPF scenario, XAML is compiled into BAML, so you don't pay the full penalties of size and parsing performance at runtime. BAML is both smaller in size than the original XAML and optimized for efficient use at runtime. Performance pitfalls from XML are therefore limited to development time, which is when the benefits of XML are needed the most.

CHAPTER 3

WPF Fundamentals

IN THIS CHAPTER

- A Tour of the Class Hierarchy
- Logical and Visual Trees
- Dependency Properties

To finish Part I, "Background," and before moving on to the *really* fun topics, it's helpful to examine some of the main concepts that WPF introduces above and beyond what .NET programmers are already familiar with. The topics in this chapter are some of the main culprits responsible for WPF's notoriously steep learning curve. By familiarizing yourself with these concepts now, you'll be able to approach the rest of this book (or any other WPF documentation) with confidence.

Some of this chapter's concepts are brand new (such as logical and visual trees), but others are just extensions of concepts that should be quite familiar (such as properties). As you learn about each one, you'll see how to apply it to a very simple piece of user interface that most programs need—an *About dialog*.

A Tour of the Class Hierarchy

WPF's classes have a very deep inheritance hierarchy, so it can be hard to get your head wrapped around the significance of various classes and their relationships. A handful of classes are fundamental to the inner workings of WPF and deserve a quick explanation before we get any further in the book. Figure 3.1 shows these important classes and their relationships.

These 12 classes have the following significance:

- **`Object`**—The base class for all .NET classes and the only class in the figure that isn't WPF specific.

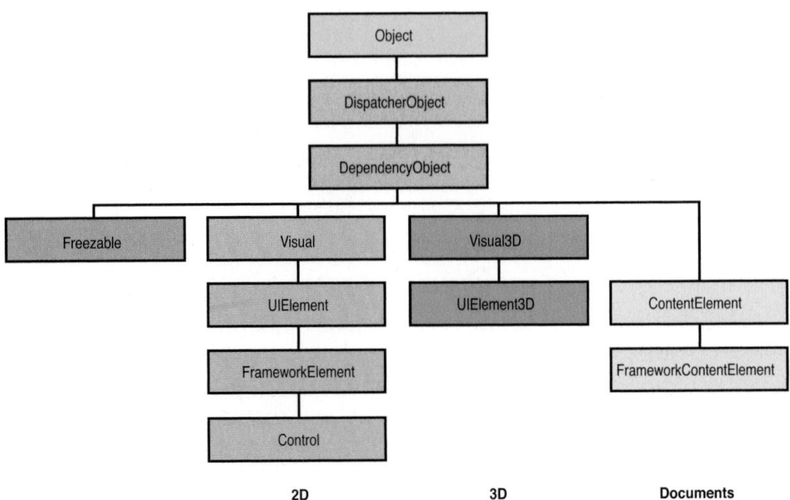

FIGURE 3.1 The core classes that form the foundation of WPF.

- **`DispatcherObject`**—The base class meant for any object that wishes to be accessed only on the thread that created it. Most WPF classes derive from `DispatcherObject` and are therefore inherently thread-unsafe. The `Dispatcher` part of the name refers to WPF's version of a Win32-like message loop, discussed further in Chapter 7, "Structuring and Deploying an Application."
- **`DependencyObject`**—The base class for any object that can support dependency properties, one of the main topics in this chapter.
- **`Freezable`**—The base class for objects that can be "frozen" into a read-only state for performance reasons. `Freezable`s, once frozen, can be safely shared among multiple threads, unlike all other `DispatcherObject`s. Frozen objects can never be unfrozen, but you can clone them to create unfrozen copies. Most `Freezable`s are graphics primitives such as brushes, pens, and geometries or animation classes.
- **`Visual`**—The base class for all objects that have their own 2D visual representation. `Visual`s are discussed in depth in Chapter 15, "2D Graphics."
- **`UIElement`**—The base class for all 2D visual objects with support for routed events, command binding, layout, and focus. These features are discussed in Chapter 5, "Layout with Panels," and Chapter 6, "Input Events: Keyboard, Mouse, Stylus, and Multi-Touch."
- **`Visual3D`**—The base class for all objects that have their own 3D visual representation. `Visual3D`s are discussed in depth in Chapter 16, "3D Graphics."
- **`UIElement3D`**—The base class for all 3D visual objects with support for routed events, command binding, and focus, also discussed in Chapter 16.
- **`ContentElement`**—A base class similar to `UIElement` but for document-related pieces of content that don't have rendering behavior on their own. Instead,

ContentElements are hosted in a Visual-derived class to be rendered on the screen. Each ContentElement often requires multiple Visuals to render correctly (spanning lines, columns, and pages).

- **FrameworkElement**—The base class that adds support for styles, data binding, resources, and a few common mechanisms for Windows-based controls, such as tooltips and context menus.
- **FrameworkContentElement**—The analog to FrameworkElement for content. Chapter 11, "Images, Text, and Other Controls," examines the FrameworkContentElements in WPF.
- **Control**—The base class for familiar controls such as Button, ListBox, and StatusBar. Control adds many properties to its FrameworkElement base class, such as Foreground, Background, and FontSize, as well as the ability to be completely restyled. Part III, "Controls," examines WPF's controls in depth.

Throughout the book, the simple term *element* is used to refer to an object that derives from UIElement or FrameworkElement, and sometimes ContentElement or FrameworkContentElement. The distinction between UIElement and FrameworkElement or between ContentElement and FrameworkContentElement is not important because WPF doesn't ship any other public subclasses of UIElement and ContentElement.

Logical and Visual Trees

XAML is natural for representing a user interface because of its hierarchical nature. In WPF, user interfaces are constructed from a tree of objects known as a *logical tree*.

Listing 3.1 defines the beginnings of a hypothetical About dialog, using a Window as the root of the logical tree. The Window has a StackPanel child element (described in Chapter 5) containing a few simple controls plus another StackPanel that contains Buttons.

LISTING 3.1 A Simple About Dialog in XAML

```
<Window xmlns="http://schemas.microsoft.com/winfx/2006/xaml/presentation"
  Title="About WPF 4 Unleashed" SizeToContent="WidthAndHeight"
  Background="OrangeRed">
  <StackPanel>
    <Label FontWeight="Bold" FontSize="20" Foreground="White">
      WPF 4 Unleashed
    </Label>
    <Label>© 2010 SAMS Publishing</Label>
    <Label>Installed Chapters:</Label>
    <ListBox>
      <ListBoxItem>Chapter 1</ListBoxItem>
      <ListBoxItem>Chapter 2</ListBoxItem>
    </ListBox>
```

LISTING 3.1 Continued

```
    <StackPanel Orientation="Horizontal" HorizontalAlignment="Center">
      <Button MinWidth="75" Margin="10">Help</Button>
      <Button MinWidth="75" Margin="10">OK</Button>
    </StackPanel>
    <StatusBar>You have successfully registered this product.</StatusBar>
  </StackPanel>
</Window>
```

Figure 3.2 shows the rendered dialog (which you can easily produce by pasting the content of Listing 3.1 into a tool such as the XAMLPAD2009 sample from the previous chapter), and Figure 3.3 illustrates the logical tree for this dialog.

Note that a logical tree exists even for WPF user interfaces that aren't created in XAML. Listing 3.1 could be implemented entirely in procedural code, and the logical tree would be identical.

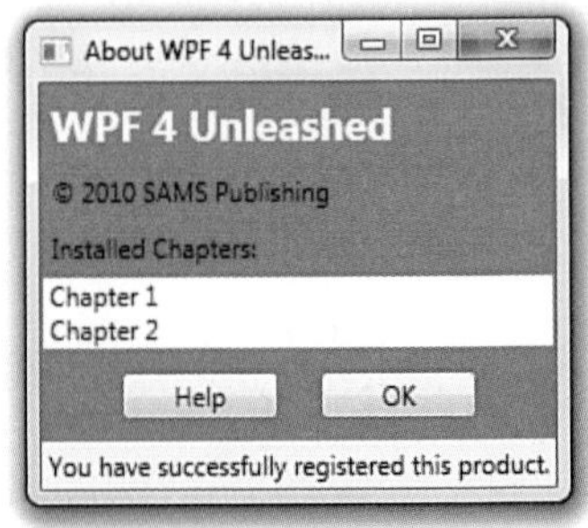

FIGURE 3.2 The rendered dialog from Listing 3.1.

The logical tree concept is straightforward, but why should you care about it? Because just about every aspect of WPF (properties, events, resources, and so on) has behavior tied to the logical tree. For example, property values are sometimes propagated down the tree to child elements automatically, and raised events can travel up or down the tree. This behavior of property values is discussed later in this chapter, and this behavior of events is discussed in Chapter 6.

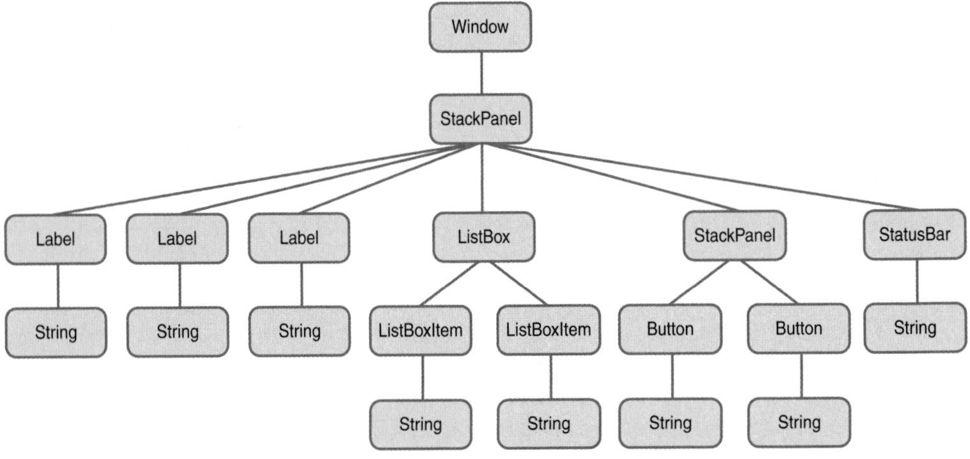

FIGURE 3.3 The logical tree for Listing 3.1.

The logical tree exposed by WPF is a simplification of what is actually going on when the elements are rendered. The entire tree of elements actually being rendered is called the *visual tree*. You can think of the visual tree as an expansion of a logical tree, in which nodes are broken down into their core visual components. Rather than leaving each element as a "black box," a visual tree exposes the visual implementation details. For example, although a `ListBox` is logically a single control, its default visual representation is composed of more primitive WPF elements: a `Border`, two `ScrollBars`, and more.

Not all logical tree nodes appear in the visual tree; only the elements that derive from `System.Windows.Media.Visual` or `System.Windows.Media.Visual3D` are included. Other elements (and simple string content, as in Listing 3.1) are not included because they don't have inherent rendering behavior of their own.

> **TIP**
>
> Some lightweight XAML viewers, such as the XamlPadX tool mentioned in the preceding chapter, have functionality for exploring the visual tree (and property values) for the objects that it renders from XAML.

Figure 3.4 illustrates the default visual tree for Listing 3.1 when running on Windows 7 with the Aero theme. This diagram exposes some inner components of the user interface that are currently invisible, such as the `ListBox`'s two `ScrollBars` and each `Label`'s `Border`. It also reveals that `Button`, `Label`, and `ListBoxItem` are all composed of the same elements, except `Button` uses an obscure `ButtonChrome` element rather than `Border`. (These controls have other visual differences as the result of different default property values. For example, `Button` has a default `Margin` of `10` on all sides, whereas `Label` has a default `Margin` of `0`.)

Because they enable you to peer inside the deep composition of WPF elements, visual trees can be surprisingly complex. Fortunately, although visual trees are an essential part of the WPF infrastructure, you often don't need to worry about them unless you're radically restyling controls (covered in Chapter 14, "Styles, Templates, Skins, and Themes") or doing low-level drawing (covered in Chapter 15). Writing code that depends on a specific visual tree for a `Button`, for example, breaks one of WPF's core tenets—the separation of look and logic. When someone restyles a control such as `Button` using the techniques described in Chapter 14, its entire visual tree is replaced with something that could be completely different.

> **WARNING**
>
> **Avoid writing code that depends on a specific visual tree!**
>
> Whereas a logical tree is static without programmer intervention (such as dynamically adding/removing elements), a visual tree can change simply because a user switches to a different Windows theme!

However, you can easily traverse both the logical and visual trees using the somewhat symmetrical `System.Windows.LogicalTreeHelper` and `System.Windows.Media.VisualTreeHelper` classes. Listing 3.2 contains a code-behind file for Listing 3.1 that, when run under a debugger, outputs a simple depth-first representation of both the logical and visual trees for the About dialog. (This requires adding `x:Class="AboutDialog"` and the corresponding `xmlns:x` directive to Listing 3.1 in order to hook it up to this procedural code.)

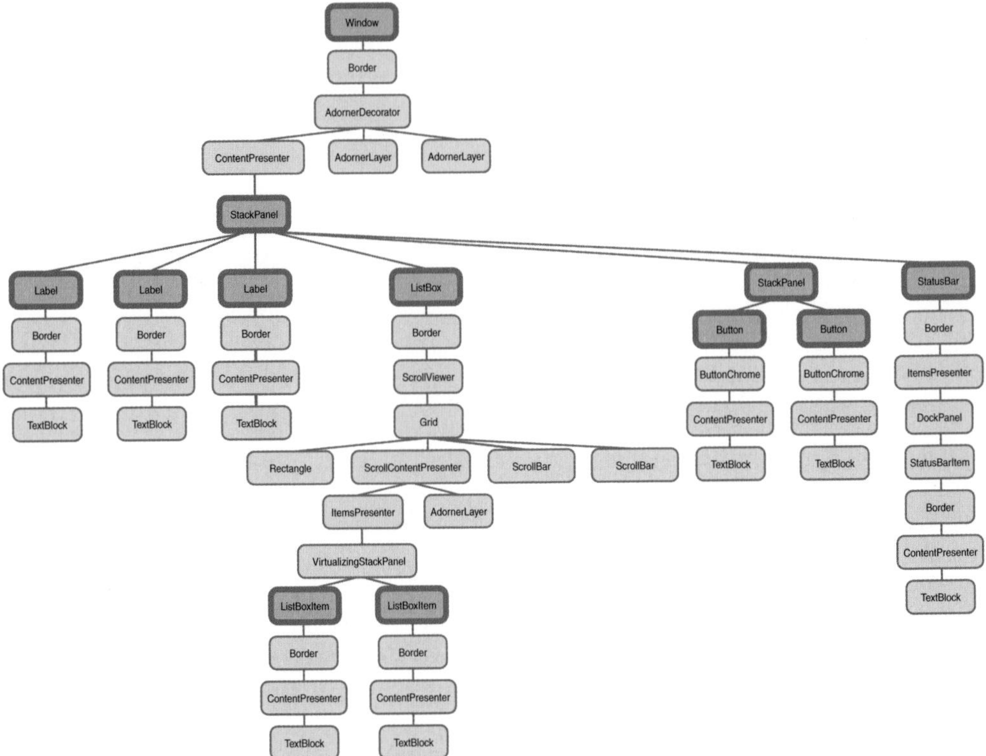

FIGURE 3.4 The visual tree for Listing 3.1, with logical tree nodes emphasized.

LISTING 3.2 Walking and Printing the Logical and Visual Trees

```
using System;
using System.Diagnostics;
using System.Windows;
using System.Windows.Media;

public partial class AboutDialog : Window
{
  public AboutDialog()
  {
    InitializeComponent();
    PrintLogicalTree(0, this);
  }

  protected override void OnContentRendered(EventArgs e)
  {
    base.OnContentRendered(e);
    PrintVisualTree(0, this);
```

LISTING 3.2 Continued

```
  }

  void PrintLogicalTree(int depth, object obj)
  {
    // Print the object with preceding spaces that represent its depth
    Debug.WriteLine(new string(' ', depth) + obj);

    // Sometimes leaf nodes aren't DependencyObjects (e.g. strings)
    if (!(obj is DependencyObject)) return;

    // Recursive call for each logical child
    foreach (object child in LogicalTreeHelper.GetChildren(
      obj as DependencyObject))
      PrintLogicalTree(depth + 1, child);
  }

  void PrintVisualTree(int depth, DependencyObject obj)
  {
    // Print the object with preceding spaces that represent its depth
    Debug.WriteLine(new string(' ', depth) + obj);

    // Recursive call for each visual child
    for (int i = 0; i < VisualTreeHelper.GetChildrenCount(obj); i++)
      PrintVisualTree(depth + 1, VisualTreeHelper.GetChild(obj, i));
  }
}
```

When calling these methods with a depth of 0 and the current `Window` instance, the result is a text-based tree with exactly the same nodes shown in Figures 3.2 and 3.3. Although the logical tree can be traversed within `Window`'s constructor, the visual tree is empty until the `Window` undergoes layout at least once. That is why `PrintVisualTree` is called within `OnContentRendered`, which doesn't get called until after layout occurs.

TIP

Visual trees like the one represented in Figure 3.4 are often referred to simply as *element trees*, because they encompass both elements in the logical tree and elements specific to the visual tree. The term *visual tree* is then used to describe any subtree that contains visual-only (illogical?) elements. For example, most people would say that `Window`'s default visual tree consists of a `Border`, an `AdornerDecorator`, two `AdornerLayers`, a `ContentPresenter`, and nothing more. In Figure 3.4, the top-most `StackPanel` is generally *not* considered to be the visual child of the `ContentPresenter`, despite the fact that `VisualTreeHelper` presents it as one.

> **TIP**
>
> In the Visual Studio 2010 debugger, you can click the little magnifying glass next to an instance of a `Visual`-derived variable to navigate and visualize the visual tree.

Navigating either tree can sometimes be done with instance methods on the elements themselves. For example, the `Visual` class contains three protected members (`VisualParent`, `VisualChildrenCount`, and `GetVisualChild`) for examining its visual parent and children. `FrameworkElement`, the common base class for controls such as `Button` and `Label`, and its peer `FrameworkContentElement` both define a public `Parent` property representing the logical parent and a protected `LogicalChildren` property for the logical children. Subclasses of these two classes often publicly expose their logical children in a variety of ways, such as in a public `Children` collection. Some classes, such as `Button` and `Label`, expose a `Content` property and enforce that the element can have only one logical child.

Dependency Properties

WPF introduces a new type of property called a *dependency property* that is used throughout the platform to enable styling, automatic data binding, animation, and more. You might first meet this concept with skepticism, as it complicates the picture of .NET types having simple fields, properties, methods, and events. But when you understand the problems that dependency properties solve, you will likely accept them as a welcome addition.

A dependency property *depends* on multiple providers for determining its value at any point in time. These providers could be an animation continuously changing its value, a parent element whose property value propagates down to its children, and so on. Arguably the biggest feature of a dependency property is its built-in ability to provide change notification.

The motivation for adding such intelligence to properties is to enable rich functionality directly from declarative markup. The key to WPF's declarative-friendly design is its heavy use of properties. `Button`, for example, has 111 public properties (98 of which are inherited from `Control` and its base classes)! Properties can be easily set in XAML (directly or by using a design tool) without any procedural code. But without the extra plumbing in dependency properties, it would be hard for the simple action of setting properties to get the desired results without the need to write additional code.

In this section, we briefly look at the implementation of a dependency property to make this discussion more concrete, and then we dig deeper into some of the ways that dependency properties add value on top of plain .NET properties:

- Change notification
- Property value inheritance
- Support for multiple providers

Understanding most of the nuances of dependency properties is usually important only for custom control authors. However, even casual users of WPF need to be aware of what dependency properties are and how they work. For example, you can only style and animate dependency properties. After working with WPF for a while, you might find yourself wishing that *all* properties would be dependency properties!

A Dependency Property Implementation

In practice, dependency properties are just normal .NET properties hooked into some extra WPF infrastructure. This is all accomplished via WPF APIs; no .NET languages (other than XAML) have an intrinsic understanding of a dependency property.

Listing 3.3 demonstrates how `Button` effectively implements one of its dependency properties, called `IsDefault`.

LISTING 3.3 A Standard Dependency Property Implementation

```
public class Button : ButtonBase
{
  // The dependency property
  public static readonly DependencyProperty IsDefaultProperty;

  static Button()
  {
    // Register the property
    Button.IsDefaultProperty = DependencyProperty.Register("IsDefault",
      typeof(bool), typeof(Button),
      new FrameworkPropertyMetadata(false,
      new PropertyChangedCallback(OnIsDefaultChanged)));
    …
  }

  // A .NET property wrapper (optional)
  public bool IsDefault
  {
    get { return (bool)GetValue(Button.IsDefaultProperty); }
    set { SetValue(Button.IsDefaultProperty, value); }
  }

  // A property changed callback (optional)
  private static void OnIsDefaultChanged(
    DependencyObject o, DependencyPropertyChangedEventArgs e) { … }
  …
}
```

The static `IsDefaultProperty` field is the actual dependency property, represented by the `System.Windows.DependencyProperty` class. By convention, all `DependencyProperty` fields are public, static, and have a `Property` suffix. Several pieces of infrastructure require that you follow this convention: localization tools, XAML loading, and more.

Dependency properties are usually created by calling the static `DependencyProperty.Register` method, which requires a name (`IsDefault`), a property type (`bool`), and the type of the class claiming to own the property (`Button`). Optionally (via different overloads of `Register`), you can pass metadata that customizes how the property is treated by WPF, as well as callbacks for handling property value changes, coercing values, and validating values. `Button` calls an overload of `Register` in its static constructor to give the dependency property a default value of `false` and to attach a delegate for change notifications.

Finally, the traditional .NET property called `IsDefault` implements its accessors by calling `GetValue` and `SetValue` methods inherited from `System.Windows.DependencyObject`, the low-level base class from which all classes with dependency properties must derive. `GetValue` returns the last value passed to `SetValue` or, if `SetValue` has never been called, the default value registered with the property. The `IsDefault` .NET property (sometimes called a *property wrapper* in this context) is not strictly necessary; consumers of `Button` could directly call the `GetValue`/`SetValue` methods because they are exposed publicly. But the .NET property makes programmatic reading and writing of the property much more natural for consumers, and it enables the property to be set via XAML. WPF should, but does not, provide generic overloads of `GetValue` and `SetValue`. This is primarily because dependency properties were invented before .NET generics were widely used.

TIP

Visual Studio has a snippet called `propdp` that automatically expands into a definition of a dependency property, which makes defining one much faster than doing all the typing yourself!

WARNING

.NET property wrappers are bypassed at runtime when setting dependency properties in XAML!

Although the XAML compiler depends on the property wrapper at compile time, WPF calls the underlying `GetValue` and `SetValue` methods directly at runtime! Therefore, to maintain parity between setting a property in XAML and procedural code, it's crucial that property wrappers not contain any logic in addition to the `GetValue`/`SetValue` calls. If you want to add custom logic, that's what the registered callbacks are for. All of WPF's built-in property wrappers abide by this rule, so this warning is for anyone writing a custom class with its own dependency properties.

On the surface, Listing 3.3 looks like an overly verbose way of representing a simple Boolean property. However, because `GetValue` and `SetValue` internally use an efficient sparse storage system and because `IsDefaultProperty` is a static field (rather than an instance field), the dependency property implementation saves per-instance memory compared to a typical .NET property. If all the properties on WPF controls were wrappers around instance fields (as most .NET properties are), they would consume a significant amount of memory because of all the local data attached to each instance. Having 111 fields for each `Button`, 104 fields for each `Label`, and so forth would add up quickly! Instead, 89 out of `Button`'s 111 public properties are dependency properties, and 82 out of `Label`'s 104 public properties are dependency properties.

The benefits of the dependency property implementation extend to more than just memory usage, however. The implementation centralizes and standardizes a fair amount of code that property implementers would have to write to check thread access, prompt the containing element to be re-rendered, and so on. For example, if a property requires its element to be re-rendered when its value changes (such as `Button`'s `Background` property), it can simply pass the `FrameworkPropertyMetadataOptions.AffectsRender` flag to an overload of `DependencyProperty.Register`. In addition, this implementation enables the three features listed earlier that we'll now examine one-by-one, starting with change notification.

Change Notification

Whenever the value of a dependency property changes, WPF can automatically trigger a number of actions, depending on the property's metadata. These actions can be re-rendering the appropriate elements, updating the current layout, refreshing data bindings, and much more. One of the most interesting features enabled by this built-in change notification is *property triggers*, which enable you to perform your own custom actions when a property value changes, without writing any procedural code.

For example, imagine that you want the text in each `Button` from the About dialog in Listing 3.1 to turn blue when the mouse pointer hovers over it. Without property triggers, you can attach two event handlers to each `Button`, one for its `MouseEnter` event and one for its `MouseLeave` event:

```
<Button MouseEnter="Button_MouseEnter" MouseLeave="Button_MouseLeave"
        MinWidth="75" Margin="10">Help</Button>
<Button MouseEnter="Button_MouseEnter" MouseLeave="Button_MouseLeave"
        MinWidth="75" Margin="10">OK</Button>
```

These two handlers could be implemented in a C# code-behind file as follows:

```
// Change the foreground to blue when the mouse enters the button
void Button_MouseEnter(object sender, MouseEventArgs e)
{
  Button b = sender as Button;
  if (b != null) b.Foreground = Brushes.Blue;
}

// Restore the foreground to black when the mouse exits the button
void Button_MouseLeave(object sender, MouseEventArgs e)
{
```

```
  Button b = sender as Button;
  if (b != null) b.Foreground = Brushes.Black;
}
```

With a property trigger, however, you can accomplish this same behavior purely in XAML. The following concise `Trigger` object is just about all you need:

```
<Trigger Property="IsMouseOver" Value="True">
  <Setter Property="Foreground" Value="Blue"/>
</Trigger>
```

This trigger can act on `Button`'s `IsMouseOver` property, which becomes `true` at the same time the `MouseEnter` event is raised and `false` at the same time the `MouseLeave` event is raised. Note that you don't have to worry about reverting `Foreground` to black when `IsMouseOver` changes to `false`. This is automatically done by WPF!

The only trick is assigning this `Trigger` to each `Button`. Unfortunately, because of a confusing limitation, you can't apply property triggers directly to elements such as `Button`. You can apply them only inside a `Style` object, so an in-depth examination of property triggers is saved for Chapter 14. In the meantime, to experiment with property triggers, you can apply the preceding `Trigger` to a `Button` by wrapping it in a few intermediate XML elements, as follows:

```
<Button MinWidth="75" Margin="10">
<Button.Style>
  <Style TargetType="{x:Type Button}">
  <Style.Triggers>
    <Trigger Property="IsMouseOver" Value="True">
      <Setter Property="Foreground" Value="Blue"/>
    </Trigger>
  </Style.Triggers>
  </Style>
</Button.Style>
  OK
</Button>
```

Property triggers are just one of three types of triggers supported by WPF. A *data trigger* is a form of property trigger that works for all .NET properties (not just dependency properties), also covered in Chapter 14. An *event trigger* enables you to declaratively specify actions to take when a routed event (covered in Chapter 6) is raised. Event triggers always involve working with animations or sounds, so they aren't covered until Chapter 17, "Animation."

WARNING

Don't be fooled by an element's `Triggers` collection!

`FrameworkElement`'s `Triggers` property is a read/write collection of `TriggerBase` items (the common base class for all three types of triggers), so it looks like an easy way to attach property triggers to controls such as `Button`. Unfortunately, this collection can only contain event triggers, so its name and type are misleading. Attempting to add a property trigger (or data trigger) to the collection causes an exception to be thrown at runtime.

Property Value Inheritance

The term *property value inheritance* (or *property inheritance* for short) doesn't refer to traditional object-oriented class-based inheritance but rather the flowing of property values down the element tree. A simple example of this can be seen in Listing 3.4, which updates the `Window` from Listing 3.1 by explicitly setting its `FontSize` and `FontStyle` dependency properties. Figure 3.5 shows the result of this change. (Notice that the `Window` automatically resizes to fit all the content thanks to its slick `SizeToContent` setting!)

FIGURE 3.5 The About dialog with `FontSize` and `FontStyle` set on the root `Window`.

LISTING 3.4 The About Dialog with Font Properties Set on the Root Window

```
<Window xmlns="http://schemas.microsoft.com/winfx/2006/xaml/presentation"
  Title="About WPF 4 Unleashed" SizeToContent="WidthAndHeight"
  FontSize="30" FontStyle="Italic"
  Background="OrangeRed">
  <StackPanel>
    <Label FontWeight="Bold" FontSize="20" Foreground="White">
      WPF 4 Unleashed
    </Label>
    <Label>© 2010 SAMS Publishing</Label>
    <Label>Installed Chapters:</Label>
    <ListBox>
      <ListBoxItem>Chapter 1</ListBoxItem>
      <ListBoxItem>Chapter 2</ListBoxItem>
    </ListBox>
    <StackPanel Orientation="Horizontal" HorizontalAlignment="Center">
      <Button MinWidth="75" Margin="10">Help</Button>
      <Button MinWidth="75" Margin="10">OK</Button>
    </StackPanel>
```

LISTING 3.4 Continued

```
    <StatusBar>You have successfully registered this product.</StatusBar>
  </StackPanel>
</Window>
```

For the most part, these two settings flow all the way down the tree and are inherited by children. This affects even the `Buttons` and `ListBoxItems`, which are three levels down the logical tree. The first `Label`'s `FontSize` does not change because it is explicitly marked with a `FontSize` of `20`, overriding the inherited value of `30`. The inherited `FontStyle` setting of `Italic` affects all `Labels`, `ListBoxItems`, and `Buttons`, however, because none of them have this set explicitly.

Notice that the text in the `StatusBar` is unaffected by either of these values, despite the fact that it supports these two properties just like the other controls. The behavior of property value inheritance can be subtle in cases like this for two reasons:

- Not every dependency property participates in property value inheritance. (Internally, dependency properties can opt in to inheritance by passing `FrameworkPropertyMetadataOptions.Inherits` to `DependencyProperty.Register`.)
- There may be other higher-priority sources setting the property value, as explained in the next section.

In this case, the latter reason is to blame. A few controls, such as `StatusBar`, `Menu`, and `ToolTip`, internally set their font properties to match current system settings. This way, users get the familiar experience of controlling their font via Control Panel. The result can be confusing, however, because such controls end up "swallowing" any inheritance from proceeding further down the element tree. For example, if you add a `Button` as a logical child of the `StatusBar` in Listing 3.4, its `FontSize` and `FontStyle` would be the default values of `12` and `Normal`, respectively, unlike the other `Buttons` outside of the `StatusBar`.

DIGGING DEEPER

Property Value Inheritance in Additional Places

Property value inheritance was originally designed to operate on the element tree, but it has been extended to work in a few other contexts as well. For example, values can be passed down to certain elements that *look like* children in the XML sense (because of XAML's property element syntax) but *are not* children in terms of the logical or visual trees. These pseudochildren can be an element's triggers or the value of *any* property (not just `Content` or `Children`), as long as it is an object deriving from `Freezable`. This may sound arbitrary and isn't well documented, but the intention is that several XAML-based scenarios "just work" as you would expect, without requiring you to think about it.

Support for Multiple Providers

WPF contains many powerful mechanisms that independently attempt to set the value of dependency properties. Without a well-defined mechanism for handling these disparate property value providers, the system would be a bit chaotic, and property values could be unstable. Of course, as their name indicates, dependency properties were designed to depend on these providers in a consistent and orderly manner.

Figure 3.6 illustrates the five-step process that WPF runs each dependency property through in order to calculate its final value. This process happens automatically, thanks to the built-in change notification in dependency properties.

FIGURE 3.6 The pipeline for calculating the value of a dependency property.

Step 1: Determine the Base Value

Most of the property value providers factor into the base value calculation. The following list reveals the ten providers that can set the value of most dependency properties, in order from highest to lowest precedence:

1. Local value
2. Parent template trigger
3. Parent template
4. Style triggers
5. Template triggers
6. Style setters
7. Theme style triggers
8. Theme style setters
9. Property value inheritance
10. Default value

You've already seen some of the property value providers, such as property value inheritance (#9). *Local value* (#1) technically means any call to `DependencyObject.SetValue`, but this is typically seen with a simple property assignment in XAML or procedural code (because of the way dependency properties are implemented, as shown previously with `Button.IsDefault`). *Default value* (#10) refers to the initial value registered with the dependency property, which naturally has the lowest precedence. The other providers, which all involve styles and templates, are explained further in Chapter 14.

This order of precedence explains why `StatusBar`'s `FontSize` and `FontStyle` were not impacted by property value inheritance in Listing 3.4. The setting of `StatusBar`'s font properties to match system settings is done via theme style setters (#8). Although this has precedence over property value inheritance (#9), you can still override these font settings using any mechanism with a higher precedence, such as simply setting local values on `StatusBar`.

TIP

If you can't figure out where a given dependency property is getting its current value, you can use the static `DependencyPropertyHelper.GetValueSource` method as a debugging aid. This returns a `ValueSource` structure that contains a few pieces of data: a `BaseValueSource` enumeration that reveals where the base value came from (step 1 in the process) and Boolean `IsExpression`, `IsAnimated`, and `IsCoerced` properties that reveal information about steps 2 through 4.

When calling this method on the `StatusBar` instance from Listing 3.1 or 3.4 with the `FontSize` or `FontStyle` property, the returned `BaseValueSource` is `DefaultStyle`, revealing that the value comes from a theme style setter. (Theme styles are sometimes referred to as *default styles*. The enumeration value for a theme style trigger is `DefaultStyleTrigger`.)

Do *not* use this method in production code! Future versions of WPF could break assumptions you've made about the value calculation. In addition, treating a property value differently, depending on its source, goes against the way things are supposed to work in WPF applications.

DIGGING DEEPER

Clearing a Local Value

The earlier "Change Notification" section demonstrates the use of procedural code to change a `Button`'s `Foreground` to blue in response to the `MouseEnter` event and then changing it back to black in response to the `MouseLeave` event. The problem with this approach is that black is set as a local value inside `MouseLeave`, which is much different from the `Button`'s initial state, in which its black `Foreground` comes from a setter in its theme style. If the theme is changed and the new theme tries to change the default `Foreground` color (or if other providers with higher precedence try to do the same), this change is trumped by the local setting of black.

What you likely want to do instead is *clear* the local value and let WPF set the value from the relevant provider with the next-highest precedence. Fortunately, `DependencyObject` provides exactly this kind of mechanism with its `ClearValue` method. This can be called on a `Button` b as follows in C#:

```
b.ClearValue(Button.ForegroundProperty);
```

(`Button.ForegroundProperty` is the static `DependencyProperty` field.) After calling `ClearValue`, the local value is simply removed from the equation when WPF recalculates the base value.

Note that the trigger on the `IsMouseOver` property from the "Change Notification" section does not have the same problem as the implementation with event handlers. A trigger is either active or inactive, and when it is inactive, it is simply ignored in the property value calculation.

Step 2: Evaluate

If the value from step one is an *expression* (an object deriving from `System.Windows.Expression`), WPF performs a special evaluation step to convert the expression into a concrete result. Expressions mostly appear in data binding (the topic of Chapter 13, "Data Binding").

Step 3: Apply Animations

If one or more animations are running, they have the power to alter the current property value (using the value after step 2 as input) or completely replace it. Therefore, animations (the topic of Chapter 17) can trump all other property value providers—even local values! This is often a stumbling block for people who are new to WPF.

Step 4: Coerce

After all the property value providers have had their say, WPF passes the almost-final property value to a `CoerceValueCallback` delegate, if one was registered with the dependency property. The callback is responsible for returning a new value, based on custom logic. For example, built-in WPF controls such as `ProgressBar` use this callback to constrain its `Value` dependency property to a value between its `Minimum` and `Maximum` values, returning `Minimum` if the input value is less than `Minimum` and `Maximum` if the input value is greater than `Maximum`. If you change your coercion logic at runtime, you can call `CoerceValue` to make WPF run the new coercion and validation logic again.

Step 5: Validate

Finally, the potentially coerced value is passed to a `ValidateValueCallback` delegate, if one was registered with the dependency property. This callback must return `true` if the input value is valid and `false` otherwise. Returning `false` causes an exception to be thrown, canceling the entire process.

TIP

WPF 4 adds a new method to `DependencyObject` called `SetCurrentValue`. It directly updates the current value of a property without changing its value source. (The value is still subject to coercion and validation.) This is meant for controls that set values in response to user interaction. For example, the `RadioButton` control modifies the value of the `IsChecked` property on other `RadioButton`s in the same group, based on user interaction. In prior versions of WPF, it sets a local value, which overrides all of the other value sources and can break things like data binding. In WPF 4, `RadioButton` has been changed to use `SetCurrentValue` instead.

Attached Properties

An *attached property* is a special form of dependency property that can effectively be *attached* to arbitrary objects. This may sound strange at first, but this mechanism has several applications in WPF.

DIGGING DEEPER

Understanding the Attached Property Provider

The most confusing part about the FontSize and FontStyle attached properties used in Listing 3.5 is that they aren't defined by Button or even Control, the base class that defines the normal FontSize and FontStyle dependency properties! Instead, they are defined by the seemingly unrelated TextElement class (and also by the TextBlock class, which could alternatively be used in the preceding examples).

How can this possibly work when TextElement.FontSizeProperty is a separate DependencyProperty field from Control.FontSizeProperty (and TextElement.FontStyleProperty is separate from Control.FontStyleProperty)? The key is the way these dependency properties are internally registered. If you were to look at the source code for TextElement, you would see something like the following:

```
TextElement.FontSizeProperty = DependencyProperty.RegisterAttached(
  "FontSize", typeof(double), typeof(TextElement), new FrameworkPropertyMetadata(
  SystemFonts.MessageFontSize, FrameworkPropertyMetadataOptions.Inherits |
  FrameworkPropertyMetadataOptions.AffectsRender |
  FrameworkPropertyMetadataOptions.AffectsMeasure),
  new ValidateValueCallback(TextElement.IsValidFontSize));
```

This is similar to the earlier example of registering Button's IsDefault dependency property, except that the RegisterAttached method optimizes the handling of property metadata for attached property scenarios.

Control, on the other hand, doesn't register its FontSize dependency property! Instead, it calls AddOwner on TextElement's already-registered property, getting a reference to exactly the same instance:

```
Control.FontSizeProperty = TextElement.FontSizeProperty.AddOwner(
  typeof(Control), new FrameworkPropertyMetadata(SystemFonts.MessageFontSize,
  FrameworkPropertyMetadataOptions.Inherits));
```

Therefore, the FontSize, FontStyle, and other font-related dependency properties inherited by all controls *are* the same properties exposed by TextElement!

Fortunately, in most cases, the class that exposes an attached property (the Get*XXX* and Set*XXX* methods) is the same class that defines the normal dependency property, avoiding this confusion.

DIGGING DEEPER

Attached Properties as an Extensibility Mechanism

As in previous technologies such as Windows Forms, many classes in WPF define a Tag property (of type System.Object) intended for storing arbitrary custom data with each instance. But attached properties are a more powerful and flexible mechanism for attaching custom data to any object deriving from DependencyObject. It's often overlooked that attached properties even enable you to effectively add custom data to instances of sealed classes (and WPF has plenty of them)!

Continued

A further twist to the story of attached properties is that although setting them in XAML relies on the presence of the static Set*XXX* method, you can bypass this method in procedural code and call DependencyObject.SetValue directly. This means that you can use *any* dependency property as an attached property in procedural code. For example, the following code attaches ItemsControl's IsTextSearchEnabled property to a Button and assigns it a value:

```
// Attach an unrelated property to a Button and set its value to true:
okButton.SetValue(ItemsControl.IsTextSearchEnabledProperty, true);
```

Although this seems nonsensical, and it certainly doesn't magically enable new functionality on this Button, you have the freedom to consume this property value in a way that makes sense to your application or component.

There are more interesting ways to extend elements in this manner. For example, FrameworkElement's Tag property is a dependency property, so you can attach it to an instance of GeometryModel3D (a class you'll see again in Chapter 16, that is sealed and does *not* have a Tag property), as follows:

```
GeometryModel3D model = new GeometryModel3D();
model.SetValue(FrameworkElement.TagProperty, "my custom data");
```

This is just one of the ways in which WPF provides extensibility without the need for traditional inheritance.

3

Although the About dialog example uses attached properties for advanced property value inheritance, attached properties are most commonly used for layout of user interface elements. (In fact, attached properties were originally designed for WPF's layout system.) Various Panel-derived classes define attached properties designed to be attached to their children for controlling how they are arranged. This way, each Panel can apply its own custom behavior to arbitrary children without requiring all possible child elements to be burdened with their own set of relevant properties. It also enables systems such as layout to be easily extensible, because anyone can write a new Panel with custom attached properties. Chapter 5, "Layout with Panels," and Chapter 21, "Layout with Custom Panels," have all the details.

Summary

In this chapter and the preceding two chapters, you've learned about all the major ways that WPF builds on top of the foundation of the .NET Framework. The WPF team could have exposed its features via typical .NET APIs, as in Windows Forms, and still have created an interesting technology. Instead, the team added several fundamental concepts that enable a wide range of features to be exposed in a way that can provide great productivity for developers and designers.

Indeed, when you focus on these core concepts, as this chapter does, you can see that the landscape isn't quite as simple as it used to be: There are multiple types of properties, multiple trees, and multiple ways of achieving the same results (such as writing declarative versus procedural code)! Hopefully you can now appreciate some of the value of these new mechanisms. Throughout the rest of the book, these concepts generally fade into the background as we focus on accomplishing specific development tasks.

PART II

Building a WPF Application

IN THIS PART

CHAPTER 4

Sizing, Positioning, and Transforming Elements

IN THIS CHAPTER

- Controlling Size
- Controlling Position
- Applying Transforms

When building a WPF application, one of the first things you must do is arrange a bunch of controls on the application's surface. This sizing and positioning of controls (and other elements) is called *layout*, and WPF contains a lot of infrastructure to provide a feature-rich layout system.

Layout in WPF boils down to interactions between parent elements and their child elements. Parents and their children work together to determine their final sizes and positions. Although parents ultimately tell their children where to render and how much space they get, they are more like collaborators than dictators; parents also *ask* their children how much space they would like before making their final decision.

Parent elements that support the arrangement of multiple children are known as *panels*, and they derive from the abstract `System.Windows.Controls.Panel` class. All the elements involved in the layout process (both parents and children) derive from `System.Windows.UIElement`.

Because layout in WPF is such a big and important topic, this book dedicates three chapters to it:

- Chapter 4, "Sizing, Positioning, and Transforming Elements"
- Chapter 5, "Layout with Panels"
- Chapter 21, "Layout with Custom Panels"

This chapter focuses on the children, examining the common ways that you can control layout on a child-by-child basis. Several properties control these aspects, most of which are summarized in Figure 4.1 for an arbitrary element inside an arbitrary panel. Size-related properties are shown in blue, and position-related properties are shown in red. In addition, elements can have transforms applied to them (shown in green) that can affect both size and position.

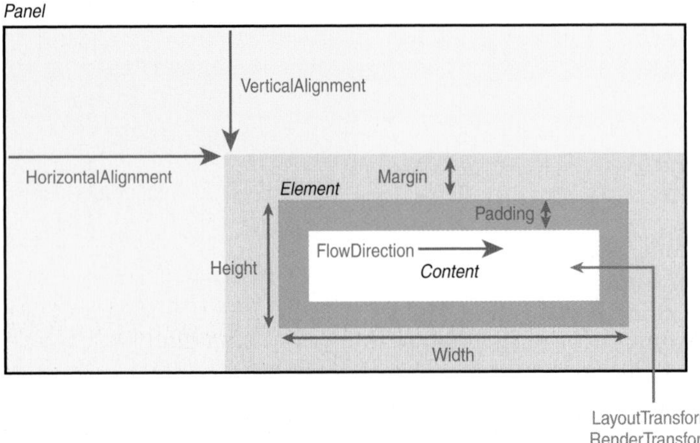

FIGURE 4.1 The main child layout properties examined in this chapter.

The next chapter continues the layout story by examining the variety of parent panels built in to WPF, each of which arranges its children in unique ways. Creating custom panels is an advanced topic reserved for the final part of the book.

Controlling Size

Every time layout occurs (such as when a window is resized), child elements tell their parent panel their desired size. WPF elements tend to *size to their content*, meaning that they try to be large enough to fit their content and no larger. (Even `Window` does this, but only when you explicitly set its `SizeToContent` property as done in the preceding chapter.) This size can be influenced on individual instances of children via several straightforward properties.

`Height` and `Width`

All `FrameworkElements` have simple `Height` and `Width` properties (of type `double`), and they also have `MinHeight`, `MaxHeight`, `MinWidth`, and `MaxWidth` properties that can be used to specify a range of acceptable values. Any or all of these can be easily set on elements in procedural code or in XAML.

An element naturally stays as small as possible, so if you use `MinHeight` or `MinWidth`, it is rendered at that height/width unless its content forces it to grow. In addition, that growth can be limited by using MaxHeight and MaxWidth (as long as these values are larger than their Min counterparts). When using an explicit Height and Width at the same time as their Min and Max counterparts, Height and Width take precedence as long as they are in the range from Min to Max. The default value of MinHeight and MinWidth is 0, and the default value of MaxHeight and MaxWidth is Double.PositiveInfinity (which can be set in XAML as simply "Infinity").

WARNING

Avoid setting explicit sizes!

Giving controls explicit sizes, especially ContentControls such as Button and Label, opens up the risk of cutting off text when users change system font settings or if the text gets translated into other languages. Therefore, you should avoid setting explicit sizes unless absolutely necessary. Fortunately, setting explicit sizes is rarely necessary, thanks to the panels described in the next chapter.

DIGGING DEEPER

The Special "Auto" Length

FrameworkElement's Height and Width have a default value of Double.NaN (where NaN stands for *not a number*), meaning that the element will be only as large as its content needs it to be. This setting can also be explicitly specified in XAML using "NaN" (which is case sensitive) or the preferred "Auto" (which is not case sensitive), thanks to the LengthConverter type converter associated with these properties. To check if one of these properties is autosized, you can use the static Double.IsNaN method.

To complicate matters, FrameworkElement also contains a few more size-related properties:

- DesiredSize (inherited from UIElement)
- RenderSize (inherited from UIElement)
- ActualHeight and ActualWidth

Unlike the other six properties that are *input* to the layout process, these are read-only properties representing *output* from the layout process. An element's DesiredSize is calculated during layout, based on other property values (such as the aforementioned Width, Height, Min*XXX*, and Max*XXX* properties) and the amount of space its parent is currently giving it. It is used internally by panels.

RenderSize represents the final size of an element after layout is complete, and ActualHeight and ActualWidth are exactly the same as RenderSize.Height and RenderSize.Width, respectively. That's right: Whether an element specified an explicit size, specified a range of acceptable sizes, or didn't specify anything at all, the behavior of the parent can alter an element's final size on the screen. These three properties are, therefore, useful for advanced scenarios in which you need to programmatically act on an element's size. The values of all the other size-related properties, on the other hand, aren't very interesting to base logic on. For example, when not set explicitly, the value of Height and Width are Double.NaN, regardless of the element's true size.

All these properties are put into context in Chapter 21.

WARNING

Be careful when writing code that uses `ActualHeight` and `ActualWidth` (or `RenderSize`)!

Every time the layout process occurs, it updates the values of each element's `RenderSize` (and, therefore, `ActualHeight` and `ActualWidth` as well). However, layout occurs asynchronously, so you can't rely on the values of these properties at all times. It's safe to access them only within an event handler for the `LayoutUpdated` event defined on `UIElement`.

Alternatively, `UIElement` defines an `UpdateLayout` method to force any pending layout updates to finish synchronously, but you should avoid using this method. Besides the fact that frequent calls to `UpdateLayout` can harm performance because of the excess layout processing, there's no guarantee that the elements you're using properly handle the potential reentrancy in their layout-related methods.

Margin and Padding

`Margin` and `Padding` are two very similar properties that are also related to an element's size. All `FrameworkElements` have a `Margin` property, and all `Controls` (plus `Border`) have a `Padding` property. Their only difference is that `Margin` controls how much extra space gets placed around the *outside* edges of the element, whereas `Padding` controls how much extra space gets placed around the *inside* edges of the element.

Both `Margin` and `Padding` are of type `System.Windows.Thickness`, an interesting class that can represent one, two, or four `double` values. The meaning of these values is demonstrated in Listing 4.1, which applies various `Padding` and `Margin` settings to `Label` controls. The second set of `Labels` is wrapped in `Borders` because the margin settings would not be noticeable otherwise. Figure 4.2 shows the rendered result for each `Label` if each one is individually placed in a `Canvas` (a panel covered in the next chapter). Although not shown in this figure, `Margin` permits negative values. `Padding` does not.

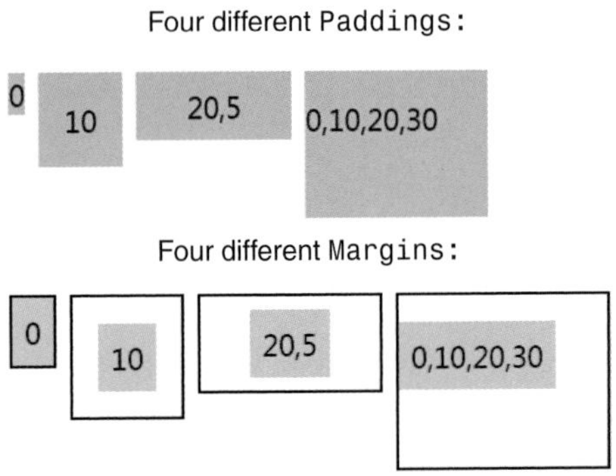

FIGURE 4.2 The effects of `Padding` and `Margin`.

LISTING 4.1 Applying Padding and Margin Values with One, Two, or Four Digits

```
<!-- PADDING: -->

<!-- 1 value: The same padding on all four sides: -->
<Label Padding="0" Background="Orange">0</Label>
<Label Padding="10" Background="Orange">10</Label>

<!-- 2 values: Left & Right get the 1st value,
              Top & Bottom get the 2nd value: -->
<Label Padding="20,5" Background="Orange">20,5</Label>

<!-- 4 values: Left,Top,Right,Bottom: -->
<Label Padding="0,10,20,30" Background="Orange">0,10,20,30</Label>

<!-- MARGIN: -->

<Border BorderBrush="Black" BorderThickness="1">
  <!-- No margin: -->
  <Label Background="Aqua">0</Label>
</Border>

<Border BorderBrush="Black" BorderThickness="1">
  <!-- 1 value: The same margin on all four sides: -->
  <Label Margin="10" Background="Aqua">10</Label>
</Border>

<Border BorderBrush="Black" BorderThickness="1">
  <!-- 2 values: Left & Right get the 1st value,
                Top & Bottom get the 2nd value: -->
  <Label Margin="20,5" Background="Aqua">20,5</Label>
</Border>

<Border BorderBrush="Black" BorderThickness="1">
  <!-- 4 values: Left,Top,Right,Bottom: -->
  <Label Margin="0,10,20,30" Background="Aqua">0,10,20,30</Label>
</Border>
```

`Label` has a default `Padding` of `5`, but it can be overridden to any valid value. That is why Listing 4.1 explicitly sets the first `Label`'s `Padding` to `0`. Without the explicit setting, it would look like the fifth `Label` (the one demonstrating the implicit `Margin` of `0`), and the visual comparison to the other `Padding` values would be confusing.

DIGGING DEEPER

The Syntax for `Thickness`

The comma-delimited syntax supported by `Margin` and `Padding` are enabled by (what else?) a type converter. `System.Windows.ThicknessConverter` constructs a `Thickness` object based on the input string. `Thickness` has two constructors, one that accepts a single `double`, and one that expects four. Therefore, it can be used in C# as follows:

```
myLabel.Margin = new Thickness(10);          // Same as Margin="10" in XAML
myLabel.Margin = new Thickness(20,5,20,5);   // Same as Margin="20,5" in XAML
myLabel.Margin = new Thickness(0,10,20,30); // Same as Margin="0,10,20,30" in XAML
```

Note that the handy two-number syntax is a shortcut only available through the type converter!

FAQ

What unit of measurement does WPF use?

The `LengthConverter` type converter associated with the various length properties supports specifying explicit units of `cm`, `pt`, `in`, or `px` (the default).

By default, all absolute measurements, such as the numbers used in this section's size-related properties, are specified in *device-independent pixels*. These "logical pixels" are meant to represent 1/96 inch, regardless of the screen's DPI setting. Note that device-independent pixels are always specified as double values, so they can be fractional.

The exact measurement of 1/96 inch isn't important, although it was chosen because on a typical 96-DPI display, 1 device-independent pixel is identical to 1 physical pixel. Of course, the notion of a true "inch" depends on the physical display device. If an application draws a 1-inch line on my laptop screen, that line will certainly be longer than 1 inch if I hook up my laptop to a projector!

What *is* important is that all such measurements are DPI independent. But this functionality alone doesn't prevent items from shrinking when you increase the screen resolution. To get resolution independence, you need the automatic scaling functionality discussed in the next chapter.

`Visibility`

`Visibility` (defined on `UIElement`) might sound like a strange property to talk about in the context of layout, but it is indeed relevant. An element's `Visibility` property actually isn't Boolean but rather a three-state `System.Windows.Visibility` enumeration. Its values and meanings are as follows:

- **`Visible`**—The element is rendered and participates in layout.
- **`Collapsed`**—The element is invisible and does not participate in layout.
- **`Hidden`**—The element is invisible *yet still participates in layout.*

A `Collapsed` element effectively has a size of zero, whereas a `Hidden` element retains its original size. (Its `ActualHeight` and `ActualWidth` values don't change, for example.) The difference between `Collapsed` and `Hidden` is demonstrated in Figure 4.3, which compares the following `StackPanel` with a `Collapsed` `Button`:

```
<StackPanel Height="100" Background="Aqua">
  <Button Visibility="Collapsed">Collapsed Button</Button>
  <Button>Below a Collapsed Button</Button>
</StackPanel>
```

to the following `StackPanel` with a `Hidden` `Button`:

```
<StackPanel Height="100" Background="Aqua">
  <Button Visibility="Hidden">Hidden Button</Button>
  <Button>Below a Hidden Button</Button>
</StackPanel>
```


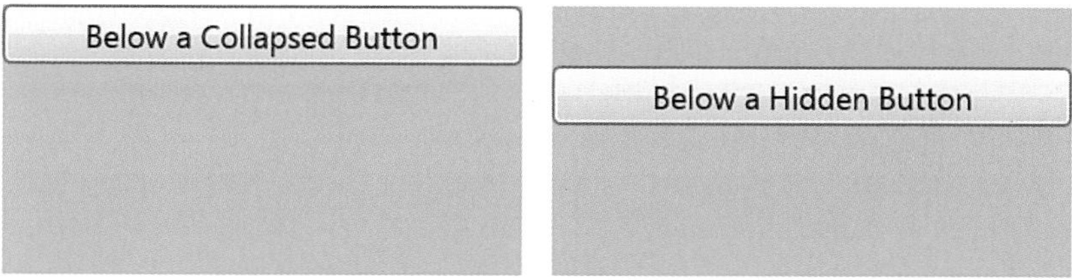

FIGURE 4.3 A `Hidden` `Button` still occupies space, unlike a `Collapsed` `Button`.

Controlling Position

This section doesn't discuss positioning elements with (X,Y) coordinates, as you might expect. Parent panels define their own unique mechanisms for enabling children to position themselves (via attached properties or simply the order in which children are added to the parent). A few mechanisms are common to all `FrameworkElement` children, however, and that's what this section examines. These mechanisms are related to alignment and a concept called *flow direction*.

Alignment

The `HorizontalAlignment` and `VerticalAlignment` properties enable an element to control what it does with any extra space that its parent panel gives it. Each property has a corresponding enumeration with the same name in the `System.Windows` namespace, giving the following options:

- **`HorizontalAlignment`**—`Left`, `Center`, `Right`, and `Stretch`
- **`VerticalAlignment`**—`Top`, `Center`, `Bottom`, and `Stretch`

Stretch is the default value for both properties, although various controls override the setting in their theme styles. The effects of HorizontalAlignment can easily be seen by placing a few Buttons in a StackPanel and marking them with each value from the enumeration:

```
<StackPanel>
  <Button HorizontalAlignment="Left" Background="Red">Left</Button>
  <Button HorizontalAlignment="Center" Background="Orange">Center</Button>
  <Button HorizontalAlignment="Right" Background="Yellow">Right</Button>
  <Button HorizontalAlignment="Stretch" Background="Lime">Stretch</Button>
</StackPanel>
```

The rendered result appears in Figure 4.4.

These two properties are useful only when a parent panel gives the child element more space than it needs. For example, adding VerticalAlignment values to elements in the StackPanel used in Figure 4.4 would make no difference, as each element is already given the exact amount of height it needs (no more, no less).

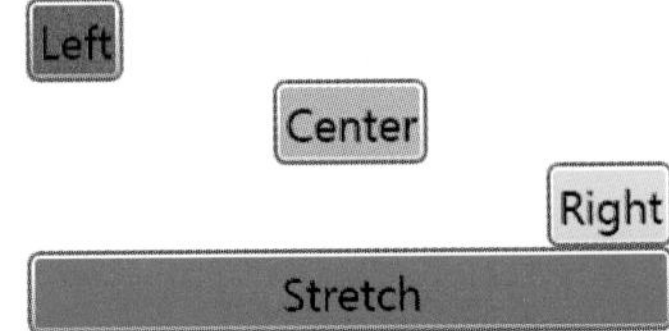

FIGURE 4.4 The effects of HorizontalAlignment on Buttons in a StackPanel.

DIGGING DEEPER

Interaction Between Stretch Alignment and Explicit Element Size

When an element uses Stretch alignment (horizontally or vertically), an explicit Height or Width setting still takes precedence. MaxHeight and MaxWidth also take precedence, but only when their values are smaller than the natural stretched size. Similarly, MinHeight and MinWidth take precedence only when their values are *larger* than the natural stretched size. When Stretch is used in a context that constrains the element's size, it acts like an alignment of Center (or Left if the element is too large to be centered in its parent).

Content Alignment

In addition to HorizontalAlignment and VerticalAlignment properties, the Control class also has HorizontalContentAlignment and VerticalContentAlignment properties. These properties determine how a control's content fills the space *within* the control. (Therefore, the relationship between alignment and content alignment is somewhat like the relationship between Margin and Padding.)

The content alignment properties are of the same enumeration types as the corresponding alignment properties, so they provide the same options. However, the default value for HorizontalContentAlignment is Left, and the default value for VerticalContentAlignment is Top. This wasn't the case for the previous Buttons, however, because their theme style overrides these settings. (Recall the order of precedence for dependency property value providers in the preceding chapter. Default values have the lowest priority and are trumped by styles.)

Figure 4.5 demonstrates the effects of HorizontalContentAlignment, simply by taking the previous XAML snippet and changing the property name as follows:

```
<StackPanel>
  <Button HorizontalContentAlignment="Left" Background="Red">Left</Button>
  <Button HorizontalContentAlignment="Center" Background="Orange">Center</Button>
  <Button HorizontalContentAlignment="Right" Background="Yellow">Right</Button>
  <Button HorizontalContentAlignment="Stretch" Background="Lime">Stretch</Button>
</StackPanel>
```

In Figure 4.5, the Button with HorizontalContentAlignment="Stretch" might not appear as you expected. Its inner TextBlock is indeed stretched, but TextBlock is not a true Control (rather just a FrameworkElement) and, therefore, doesn't have the same notion for stretching its inner text.

FIGURE 4.5 The effects of HorizontalContentAlignment on Buttons in a StackPanel.

FlowDirection

FlowDirection is a property on FrameworkElement (and several other classes) that can reverse the way an element's inner content flows. It applies to some panels and their arrangement of children, and it also applies to the way content is aligned inside child controls. The property is of type System.Windows.FlowDirection, with two values: LeftToRight (FrameworkElement's default) and RightToLeft.

The idea of FlowDirection is that it should be set to RightToLeft when the current culture corresponds to a language that is read from right to left. This reverses the meaning of left and right for settings such as content alignment. The following XAML demonstrates this, with Buttons that force their content alignment to Top and Left but then apply each of the two FlowDirection values:

```
<StackPanel>
  <Button FlowDirection="LeftToRight"
          HorizontalContentAlignment="Left" VerticalContentAlignment="Top"
          Height="40" Background="Red">LeftToRight</Button>
  <Button FlowDirection="RightToLeft"
          HorizontalContentAlignment="Left" VerticalContentAlignment="Top"
          Height="40" Background="Orange">RightToLeft</Button>
</StackPanel>
```

The result is shown in Figure 4.6.

Notice that FlowDirection does not affect the flow of letters within these Buttons. English letters always flow left to right, and Arabic letters always flow right to left, for example. But FlowDirection reverses the notion of left and right for other pieces of the user interface, which typically need to match the flow direction of letters.

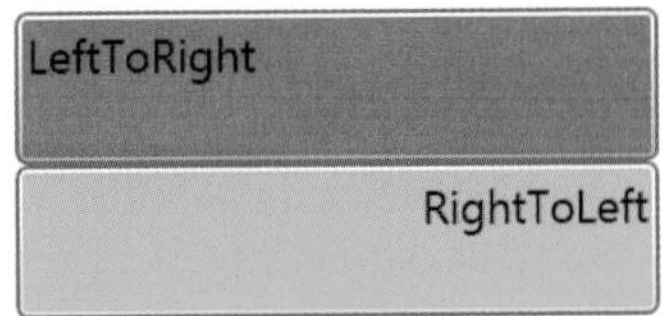

FIGURE 4.6 The effects of FlowDirection on Buttons with Top and Left content alignment.

FlowDirection must be explicitly set to match the current culture (and can be done on a single, top-level element). This should be part of your localization process.

Applying Transforms

WPF contains a handful of built-in 2D transform classes (derived from System.Windows.Media.Transform) that enable you to change the size and position of elements independently from the previously discussed properties. Some also enable you to alter elements in more exotic ways, such as by rotating or skewing them.

All FrameworkElements have two properties of type Transform that can be used to apply such transforms:

- LayoutTransform, which is applied *before* the element is laid out
- RenderTransform (inherited from UIElement), which is applied *after* the layout process has finished (immediately before the element is rendered)

Figure 4.7 demonstrates the difference between applying a transform called RotateTransform as a LayoutTransform versus a RenderTransform. In both cases, the transform is applied to the second of three consecutive Buttons in a StackPanel. When applied as a LayoutTransform, the third Button is pushed out of the way. But when applied as a RenderTransform, the third Button is placed as if the second Button weren't rotated.

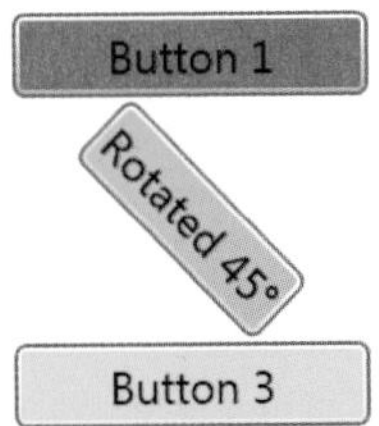

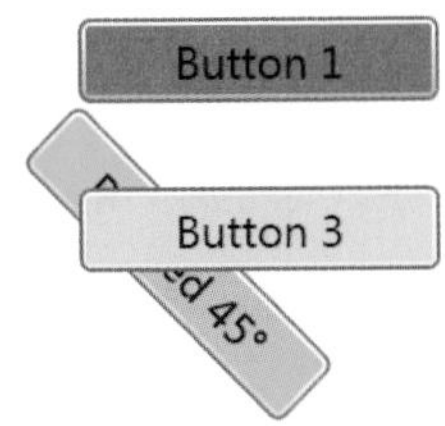

Rotation as a LayoutTransform Rotation as a RenderTransform

FIGURE 4.7 The difference between LayoutTransform and RenderTransform on the middle of three Buttons in a StackPanel.

UIElements also have a handy RenderTransformOrigin property that represents the starting point of the transform (the point that remains stationary). For the RotateTransform used in Figure 4.7, the origin is the Button's top-left corner, which the rest of the Button pivots around. LayoutTransforms, on the other hand, don't have the notion of an origin because the positioning of the transformed element is completely dictated by the parent panel's layout rules.

RenderTransformOrigin can be set to a System.Windows.Point, with (0,0) being the default value. This represents the top-left corner, as in Figure 4.7. An origin of (0,1) represents the bottom-left corner, (1,0) is the top-right corner, and (1,1) is the bottom-right corner. You can use numbers greater than 1 to set the origin to a point outside the bounds of an element, and you can use fractional values. Therefore, (0.5,0.5) represents the middle of the object. Figure 4.8 demonstrates the five origins most commonly used with the RenderTransform from Figure 4.7.

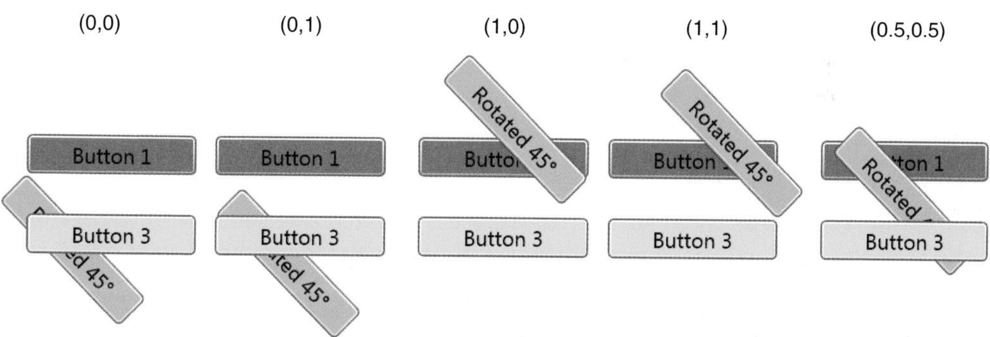

FIGURE 4.8 Five common RenderTransformOrigins used on the rotated Button from Figure 4.7.

Thanks to System.Windows.PointConverter, the value for RenderTransformOrigin can be specified in XAML with two comma-delimited numbers (and no parentheses). For example, the Button rotated around its center at the far right of Figure 4.8 can be created as follows:

```
<Button RenderTransformOrigin="0.5,0.5" Background="Orange">
<Button.RenderTransform>
  <RotateTransform Angle="45"/>
</Button.RenderTransform>
  Rotated 45°
</Button>
```

At this point, you might be wondering why you would ever want to have a rotated Button in an application! Indeed, such transforms look silly on standard controls with their default style. They often make more sense in a heavily themed application, but even with default-styled controls, transforms can add a nice touch when used within animations.

This section looks at the five built-in 2D transforms, all in the `System.Windows.Media` namespace:

- `RotateTransform`
- `ScaleTransform`
- `SkewTransform`
- `TranslateTransform`
- `MatrixTransform`

RotateTransform

`RotateTransform`, demonstrated in the preceding section, rotates an element according to the values of three `double` properties:

- **`Angle`**—Angle of rotation, specified in degrees (default value = `0`)
- **`CenterX`**—Horizontal center of rotation (default value = `0`)
- **`CenterY`**—Vertical center of rotation (default value = `0`)

The default (`CenterX`,`CenterY`) point of (0,0) represents the top-left corner. `CenterX` and `CenterY` are only useful when `RotateTransform` is applied as a `RenderTransform` because when `LayoutTransform`s are applied, the position is still dictated by the parent panel.

FAQ

What's the difference between using the `CenterX` and `CenterY` properties on transforms such as `RotateTransform` versus using the `RenderTransformOrigin` property on `UIElement`?

When a transform is applied to a `UIElement`, the `CenterX` and `CenterY` properties at first appear to be redundant with `RenderTransformOrigin`. Both mechanisms control the origin of the transform, and both mechanisms work only when the transform is applied as a `RenderTransform`.

However, `CenterX` and `CenterY` enable absolute positioning of the origin rather than the relative positioning of `RenderTransformOrigin`. Their values are specified as device-independent pixels, so the top-right corner of an element with a `Width` of `20` would be specified with `CenterX` set to `20` and `CenterY` set to `0` rather than the point (1,0). Also, when multiple `RenderTransform`s are grouped together (described later in the chapter), `CenterX` and `CenterY` on individual transforms enables more fine-grained control. Finally, the individual `double` values of `CenterX` and `CenterY` are easier to use with data binding than the `Point` value of `RenderTransformOrigin`.

That said, `RenderTransformOrigin` is generally more useful than `CenterX` and `CenterY`. For the common case of transforming an element around its middle, the relative (0.5,0.5) `RenderTransformOrigin` is easy to specify in XAML, whereas accomplishing the same thing with `CenterX` and `CenterY` would require writing some procedural code to calculate the absolute offsets.

Continued

Note that you can use `RenderTransformOrigin` on an element simultaneously with using `CenterX` and `CenterY` on its transform. In this case, the two `X` values and two `Y` values are combined to calculate the final origin point.

Whereas Figures 4.7 and 4.8 show rotated `Buttons`, Figure 4.9 demonstrates what happens when `RotateTransform` is applied as a `RenderTransform` *to the inner content* of `Buttons`, with two different values of `RenderTransformOrigin`. To achieve this, the simple string inside each `Button` is replaced with an explicit `TextBlock` as follows:

```
<Button Background="Orange">
  <TextBlock RenderTransformOrigin="0.5,0.5">
  <TextBlock.RenderTransform>
    <RotateTransform Angle="45"/>
  </TextBlock.RenderTransform>
    45°
  </TextBlock>
</Button>
```

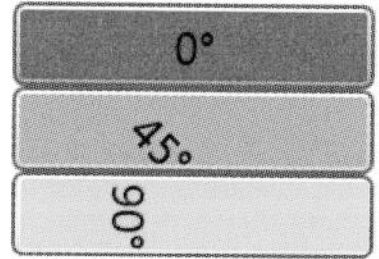

Text rotation around the top-left corner

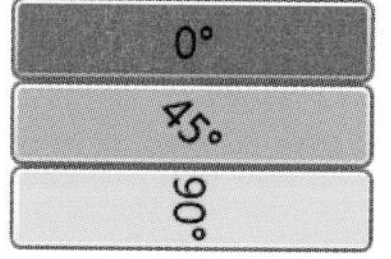

Text rotation around the middle

FIGURE 4.9 Using `RotateTransform` on the content of `Buttons` in a `StackPanel`.

The `TextBlocks` in the `Buttons` on the left side of Figure 4.9 might not seem to be rotated around their top-left corners, but that's because the `TextBlocks` are slightly larger than the text. When you give the `TextBlocks` an explicit aqua `Background`, the rotation makes more sense. Figure 4.10 demonstrates this.

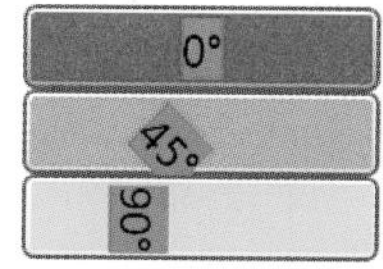

FIGURE 4.10 Inner `TextBlocks` rotated around their top-left corner, with an explicit background.

`RotateTransform` has parameterized constructors that accept an angle or both angle and center values, for the convenience of creating the transform from procedural code.

ScaleTransform

`ScaleTransform` enlarges or shrinks an element horizontally, vertically, or in both directions. This transform has four straightforward `double` properties:

- **`ScaleX`**—Multiplier for the element's width (default value = 1)
- **`ScaleY`**—Multiplier for the element's height (default value = 1)

- **CenterX**—Origin for horizontal scaling (default value = 0)
- **CenterY**—Origin for vertical scaling (default value = 0)

A ScaleX value of 0.5 shrinks an element's rendered width in half, whereas a ScaleX value of 2 doubles the width. CenterX and CenterY work the same way as with RotateTransform.

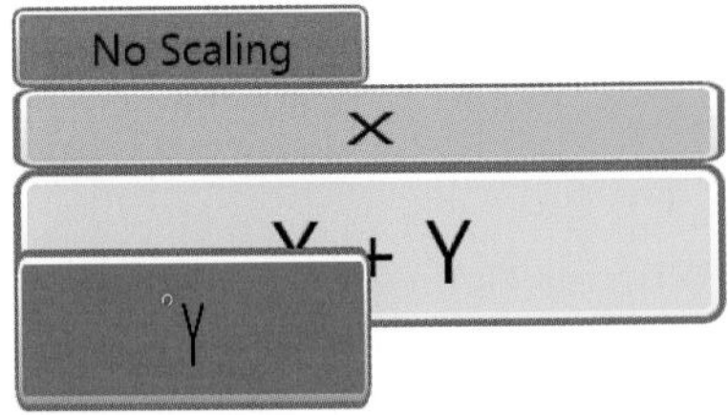

FIGURE 4.11 The scaled Buttons from Listing 4.2.

Listing 4.2 applies ScaleTransform to three Buttons in a StackPanel, demonstrating the ability to stretch them independently in height or in width. Figure 4.11 shows the result.

LISTING 4.2 Applying ScaleTransform to Buttons in a StackPanel

```
<StackPanel Width="100">
  <Button Background="Red">No Scaling</Button>
  <Button Background="Orange">
  <Button.RenderTransform>
    <ScaleTransform ScaleX="2"/>
  </Button.RenderTransform>
    X</Button>
  <Button Background="Yellow">
  <Button.RenderTransform>
    <ScaleTransform ScaleX="2" ScaleY="2"/>
  </Button.RenderTransform>
    X + Y</Button>
  <Button Background="Lime">
  <Button.RenderTransform>
    <ScaleTransform ScaleY="2"/>
  </Button.RenderTransform>
    Y</Button>
</StackPanel>
```

Figure 4.12 displays the same Buttons from Listing 4.2 (and Figure 4.11) but with explicit CenterX and CenterY values set. The point represented by each pair of these values is displayed in each Button's text. Notice that the lime Button isn't moved to the left like the orange Button, despite being marked with the same CenterX of 70. That's because CenterX is relevant only when ScaleX is a value other than 1, and CenterY is relevant only when ScaleY is a value other than 1.

As with other transforms, ScaleTransform has a few parameterized constructors for the convenience of creating it from procedural code.

No Scaling

X (70,0)

Y (70,0)

X + Y (-10,-60)

FIGURE 4.12 The `Buttons` from Listing 4.2 but with explicit scaling centers.

DIGGING DEEPER

Interaction Between `ScaleTransform` and `Stretch` Alignment

When you apply `ScaleTransform` as a `LayoutTransform` on an element that is already stretching in the dimension of scaling, it has an effect only if the amount of scaling is greater than the amount the natural-sized element is already being stretched.

FAQ

How do transforms such as `ScaleTransform` affect `FrameworkElement`'s `ActualHeight` and `ActualWidth` properties or `UIElement`'s `RenderSize` property?

Applying a transform to `FrameworkElement` never changes the values of these properties. This is true whether it is applied as a `RenderTransform` or `LayoutTransform`. Therefore, because of transforms, these properties can "lie" about the size of an element on the screen. For example, all the `Buttons` in Figures 4.11 and 4.12 have the same `ActualHeight`, `ActualWidth`, and `RenderSize`.

Such "lies" might surprise you, but they're for the best. First, it's debatable how such values should even be expressed for some transforms. More importantly, the point of transforms is to alter an element's appearance without the element's knowledge. Giving elements the illusion that they are being rendered normally enables arbitrary controls to be plugged in and transformed without special handling.

FAQ

How does `ScaleTransform` affect `Margin` and `Padding`?

`Padding` is scaled along with the rest of the content (because `Padding` is internal to the element), but `Margin` does not get scaled. As with `ActualHeight` and `ActualWidth`, the numeric `Padding` property value does not change, despite the visual scaling.

SkewTransform

SkewTransform slants an element according to the values of four double properties:

- **AngleX**—Amount of horizontal skew (default value = 0)
- **AngleY**—Amount of vertical skew (default value = 0)
- **CenterX**—Origin for horizontal skew (default value = 0)
- **CenterY**—Origin for vertical skew (default value = 0)

These properties behave much like the properties of the previous transforms. Figure 4.13 demonstrates SkewTransform applied as a RenderTransform on several Buttons, using the default center of the top-left corner.

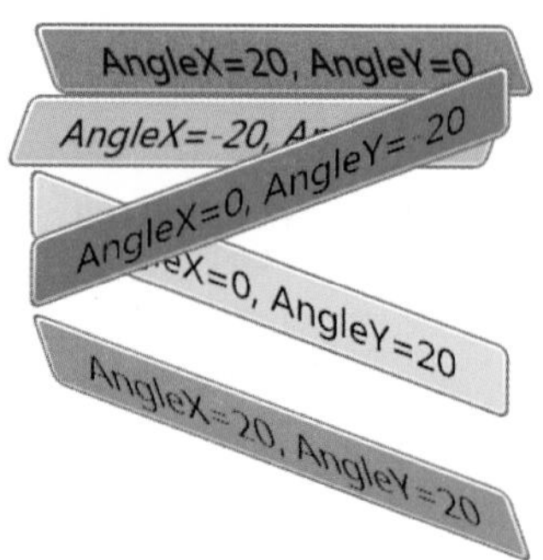

FIGURE 4.13
SkewTransform applied to Buttons in a StackPanel.

TranslateTransform

TranslateTransform simply moves an element according to two double properties:

- **X**—Amount to move horizontally (default value = 0)
- **Y**—Amount to move vertically (default value = 0)

TranslateTransform has no effect when you apply it as a LayoutTransform, but applying it as a RenderTransform is an easy way to "nudge" elements one way or another. Most likely, you'd do this dynamically based on user actions (and perhaps in an animation). With all the panels described in the next chapter, it's unlikely that you'd need to use TranslateTransform to arrange a static user interface.

MatrixTransform

MatrixTransform is a low-level mechanism that can be used to create custom 2D transforms. MatrixTransform has a single Matrix property (of type System.Windows.Media.Matrix) representing a 3x3 affine transformation matrix. In case you're not a linear algebra buff, this basically means that all the previous transforms (or any combination of them) can also be expressed using MatrixTransform.

The 3x3 matrix has the following values:

$$\begin{bmatrix} \texttt{M11} & \texttt{M12} & 0 \\ \texttt{M21} & \texttt{M22} & 0 \\ \texttt{OffsetX} & \texttt{OffsetY} & 1 \end{bmatrix}$$

The final column's values are fixed, but the other six values can be set as properties of the Matrix type (with the same names as shown) or via a constructor that accepts the six values in row-major order.

DIGGING DEEPER

MatrixTransform's Type Converter

MatrixTransform is the only transform that has a type converter to enable its use as a simple string in XAML. (The type converter is called TransformConverter, and it is actually associated with the abstract Transform class, but it only supports MatrixTransform.) For example, you can translate a Button 10 units to the right and 20 units down with the following syntax:

```
<Button RenderTransform="1,0,0,1,10,20" />
```

The comma-delimited list represents the M11, M12, M21, M22, OffsetX, and OffsetY values, respectively. The values 1, 0, 0, 1, 0, 0 give you the identity matrix (meaning no transform is done), so making MatrixTransform act like TranslateTransform is as simple as starting with the identity matrix and then using OffsetX and OffsetY as TranslateTransform's X and Y values. Scaling can be done by treating the first and fourth values (the 1s in the identity matrix) as ScaleX and ScaleY, respectively. Rotation and skewing are more complicated because they involve sin, cos, and angles specified in radians.

If you're comfortable with the matrix notation, representing transforms with this concise (and less-readable) syntax can be a time saver when you're writing XAML by hand.

Combining Transforms

A few different options exist for combining multiple transforms, such as rotating an element while simultaneously scaling it. You can apply both a LayoutTransform and a RenderTransform simultaneously. Or, you could figure out the correct MatrixTransform representation to get the combined effect. Most likely, however, you would take advantage of the TransformGroup class.

TransformGroup is just another Transform-derived class (so it can be used wherever the previous classes are used), and its purpose is to combine child Transform objects. From procedural code, you can add transforms to its Children collection, or from XAML, you can use it as follows:

```
<Button>
<Button.RenderTransform>
  <TransformGroup>
    <RotateTransform Angle="45"/>
    <ScaleTransform ScaleX="5" ScaleY="1"/>
    <SkewTransform AngleX="30"/>
  </TransformGroup>
</Button.RenderTransform>
  OK
</Button>
```

Figure 4.14 shows the result of all three transforms being applied to the Button.

For maximum performance, WPF calculates a combined transform out of a TransformGroup's children and applies it as a single transform (much as if you had used

MatrixTransform). Note that you can apply multiple instances of the same transform to a TransformGroup. For example, applying two separate 45° RotateTransforms would result in a 90° rotation.

FIGURE 4.14 A Button that has been thoroughly tortured by being rotated, scaled, and skewed.

WARNING

Not all FrameworkElements support transforms!

Elements hosting content that isn't native to WPF do not support transforms, despite inheriting the LayoutTransform and RenderTransform properties. For example, HwndHost, used to host GDI-based content and discussed in Chapter 19, "Interoperability with Non-WPF Technologies," does not support them. Frame, a control that can host HTML (described in Chapter 9, "Content Controls"), supports them completely only when it is not hosting HTML. Otherwise, ScaleTransform can still be applied to scale its size, but the inner content won't scale.

Figure 4.15 demonstrates this with a StackPanel containing some Buttons and a Frame containing a webpage (constrained to be 100x100). When the entire StackPanel is rotated and scaled, the Frame does its best to scale but doesn't rotate at all. It ends up hiding most of the rotated Buttons.

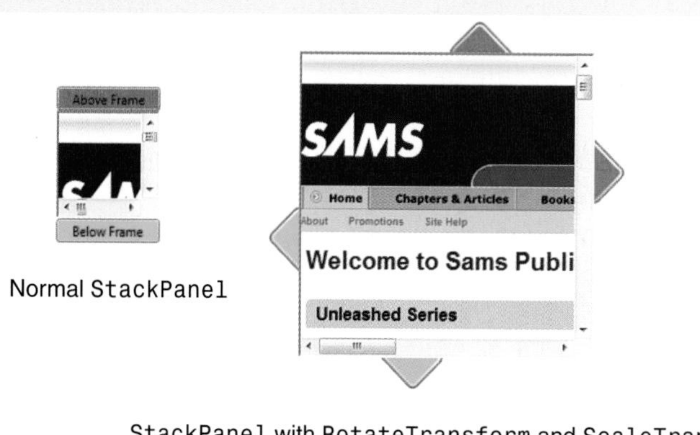

FIGURE 4.15 A Frame with HTML content responds somewhat to ScaleTransform but no other transforms.

Summary

That concludes our tour of the layout properties that child elements can use to influence the way they appear on the screen. In this chapter, you also got some first glimpses into user-visible features unlike anything you'd see in Win32 or Windows Forms: rotated and skewed controls!

But the most important part of layout is the parent panels. This chapter repeatedly uses a StackPanel for simplicity, but the next chapter formally introduces this panel and all the other panels as well.

CHAPTER 5

Layout with Panels

IN THIS CHAPTER

- Canvas
- StackPanel
- WrapPanel
- DockPanel
- Grid
- Primitive Panels
- Handling Content Overflow
- Putting It All Together: Creating a Visual Studio–Like Collapsible, Dockable, Resizable Pane

Layout is a critical component of an application's usability on a wide range of devices, but without good platform support, getting it right can be extremely difficult. Arranging the pieces of a user interface simply with static pixel-based coordinates and static pixel-based sizes can work in limited environments, but these types of interfaces start to crumble under the influence of many varying factors: different screen resolutions and dimensions, user settings such as font sizes, or content that changes in unpredictable ways (such as text being translated into different languages). Plus, applications that don't allow users to resize various pieces of them (and take advantage of the extra space intelligently) frustrate most users.

On my 1024x600 netbook screen, Outlook 2010 adapts nicely, but many programs, such as Visual Studio 2010, do not fare so well. If I change the screen to portrait mode (600x1024), Outlook 2010 does an admirable job of using the space intelligently, but the experience of other programs (such as Visual Studio 2010) gets far worse. (This is especially ironic because Visual Studio is at least partially a WPF application, whereas Outlook does not use WPF. However, this specific outcome is not really a result of the technologies being used, but rather the priority that the teams placed on handling small or unusual screen sizes.)

WPF contains built-in panels that can make it easy to avoid layout pitfalls. This chapter begins by examining the five main built-in panels, all in the `System.Windows.Controls` namespace, in increasing order of complexity (and general usefulness):

- `Canvas`
- `StackPanel`
- `WrapPanel`

- DockPanel
- Grid

For completeness, this chapter also looks at a few rarely used "primitive panels." Then, after a section on content overflow (which happens when parents and children can't agree on the use of available space), this chapter ends with a large example. This example applies a variety of layout techniques to make a relatively sophisticated user interface found in applications such as Visual Studio that would be hard to construct without the help of WPF's layout features.

Canvas

Canvas is the most basic panel. It's so basic, in fact, that you probably should never bother using it for arranging typical user interfaces. Canvas only supports the "classic" notion of positioning elements with explicit coordinates, although at least those coordinates are device-independent pixels, unlike in older user interface systems. Canvas also enables you to specify coordinates relative to *any* corner, not just the top-left corner.

You can position elements in a Canvas by using its attached properties: Left, Top, Right, and Bottom. By setting a value for Left or Right, you're stating that the closest edge of the element should remain a fixed distance from that edge of the Canvas. And the same goes for setting a value for Top or Bottom. In essence, you choose the corner in which to "dock" each element, and the attached property values serve as margins (to which the element's own Margin values are added). If an element doesn't use any of these attached properties (leaving them with their default value of Double.NaN), it is placed in the top-left corner of the Canvas (the equivalent of setting Left and Top to 0). This is demonstrated in Listing 5.1, and the result is shown in Figure 5.1.

LISTING 5.1 Buttons Arranged in a Canvas

```
<Window xmlns="http://schemas.microsoft.com/winfx/2006/xaml/presentation"
        Title="Buttons in a Canvas">
  <Canvas>
    <Button Background="Red">Left=0, Top=0</Button>
    <Button Canvas.Left="18" Canvas.Top="18"
            Background="Orange">Left=18, Top=18</Button>
    <Button Canvas.Right="18" Canvas.Bottom="18"
            Background="Yellow">Right=18, Bottom=18</Button>
    <Button Canvas.Right="0" Canvas.Bottom="0"
            Background="Lime">Right=0, Bottom=0</Button>
    <Button Canvas.Right="0" Canvas.Top="0"
            Background="Aqua">Right=0, Top=0</Button>
    <Button Canvas.Left="0" Canvas.Bottom="0"
            Background="Magenta">Left=0, Bottom=0</Button>
  </Canvas>
</Window>
```

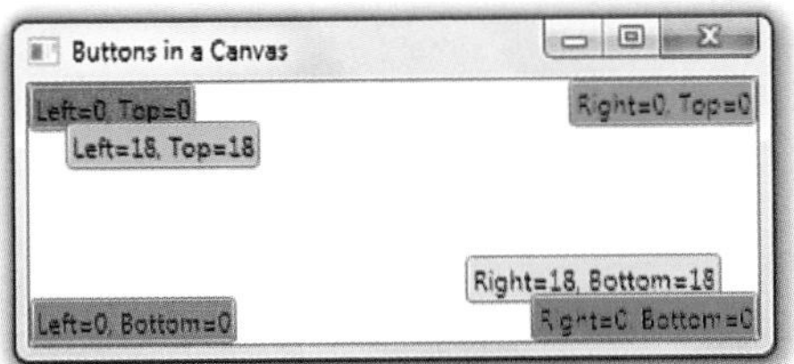

FIGURE 5.1 The Buttons in a Canvas from Listing 5.1.

WARNING

Elements can't use more than two of the Canvas attached properties!

If you attempt to set Canvas.Left and Canvas.Right simultaneously, Canvas.Right gets ignored. And if you attempt to set Canvas.Top and Canvas.Bottom simultaneously, Canvas.Bottom gets ignored. Therefore, you can't dock an element to more than one corner of a Canvas at a time.

Table 5.1 evaluates the way that some of the child layout properties discussed in the preceding chapter apply to elements inside a Canvas.

TABLE 5.1 Canvas's Interaction with Child Layout Properties

Property	Usable Inside Canvas?
Margin	Partially. On the two sides used to position the element (Top and Left by default), the relevant two out of four margin values are added to the attached property values.
HorizontalAlignment and VerticalAlignment	No. Elements are given only the exact space they need.
LayoutTransform	Yes. Differs from RenderTransform because when LayoutTransform is used, elements always remain the specified distance from the selected corner of the Canvas.

TIP

The default Z order (defining which elements are "on top of" other elements) is determined by the order in which the children are added to the parent. In XAML, this is the order in which children are listed in the file. Elements added later are placed on top of elements added earlier. So in Figure 5.1, the orange Button is on top of the red Button, and the green Button is on top of the yellow Button. This is relevant not just for the built-in panels that enable elements to overlap (such as Canvas) but whenever a RenderTransform causes an element to overlap another (as shown in Figures 4.7, 4.8, 4.11, 4.12, and 4.13 in the preceding chapter).

However, you can customize the Z order of any child element by marking it with the ZIndex attached property that is defined on Panel (so it is inherited by all panels). ZIndex is an integer with a default value of 0 that you can set to any number (positive or negative). Elements with larger ZIndex values are rendered on top of elements with smaller ZIndex values, so the element with the smallest value is in the back, and the element with the largest value is in the front. In the following example, ZIndex causes the red button to be on top of the orange button, despite being an earlier child of the Canvas:

Continued

```
<Canvas>
  <Button Canvas.ZIndex="1" Background="Red">On Top!</Button>
  <Button Background="Orange">On Bottom with a Default ZIndex=0</Button>
</Canvas>
```

If multiple children have the same `ZIndex` value, the order is determined by their order in the panel's `Children` collection, as in the default case.

Therefore, programmatically manipulating Z order is as simple as adjusting the `ZIndex` value. To cause the preceding red button to be rendered behind the orange button, you can set the attached property value to any number less than or equal to zero. The following line of C# does just that (assuming that the red button's name is `redButton`):

```
Panel.SetZIndex(redButton, 0);
```

Although `Canvas` is too primitive a panel for creating flexible user interfaces, it is the most lightweight panel. So, you should keep it in mind for maximum performance when you need precise control over the placement of elements. For example, `Canvas` is very handy for precise positioning of primitive shapes in vector-based drawings, discussed in Chapter 15, "2D Graphics."

StackPanel

`StackPanel` is a popular panel because of its simplicity and usefulness. As its name suggests, it simply stacks its children sequentially. Examples in previous chapters use `StackPanel` because it doesn't require the use of any attached properties to get a reasonable-looking user interface. In fact, `StackPanel` is one of the few panels that doesn't even define any of its own attached properties!

With no attached properties for arranging children, you just have one way to customize the behavior of `StackPanel`—setting its `Orientation` property (of type `System.Windows.Controls.Orientation`) to `Horizontal` or `Vertical`. `Vertical` is the default `Orientation`. Figure 5.2 shows simple `Buttons`, with no properties set other than `Background` and `Content`, in two `StackPanels` with only their `Orientation` set.

Table 5.2 evaluates the way that some of the child layout properties apply to elements inside a `StackPanel`.

DIGGING DEEPER

`StackPanel` and Right-to-Left Environments

When `FlowDirection` is set to `RightToLeft`, stacking occurs right to left for a `StackPanel` with `Horizontal` `Orientation`, rather than the default left-to-right behavior.

`Vertical` stacks elements from top to bottom.

1
2
3
4
5
6

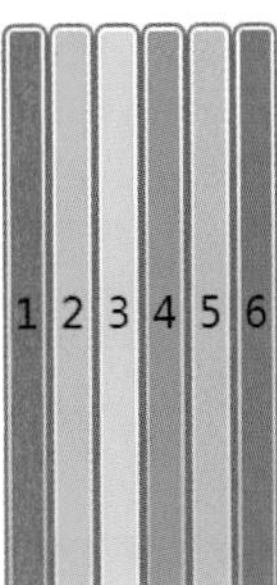

FIGURE 5.2 Buttons in a `StackPanel`, using both `Orientation`s.

TABLE 5.2 `StackPanel`'s Interaction with Child Layout Properties

Property	Usable Inside `StackPanel`?
`Margin`	Yes. `Margin` controls the space between an element and the `StackPanel`'s edges as well as space between elements.
`HorizontalAlignment` and `VerticalAlignment`	Partially, because alignment is effectively ignored in the direction of stacking (because children get the exact amount of space they need). For `Orientation="Vertical"`, `VerticalAlignment` is meaningless. For `Orientation="Horizontal"`, `HorizontalAlignment` is meaningless.
`LayoutTransform`	Yes. This differs from `RenderTransform` because when `LayoutTransform` is used, the remaining elements in the stack are pushed out further to make room. When combining `Stretch` layout with `RotateTransform` or `SkewTransform` as a `LayoutTransform`, the stretching only occurs for angles that are multiples of 90°.

The final sentence discussing `LayoutTransform` in Table 5.2 needs a little more explanation. Figure 5.3 reveals that when an element that normally would be stretched is rotated, the stretching occurs only when edges of the element are parallel or perpendicular to the direction of stretching. This behavior isn't specific to `StackPanel` but can be seen whenever an element is stretched in only one direction. This odd-looking behavior only applies to `LayoutTransform`; it doesn't happen with `RenderTransform`.

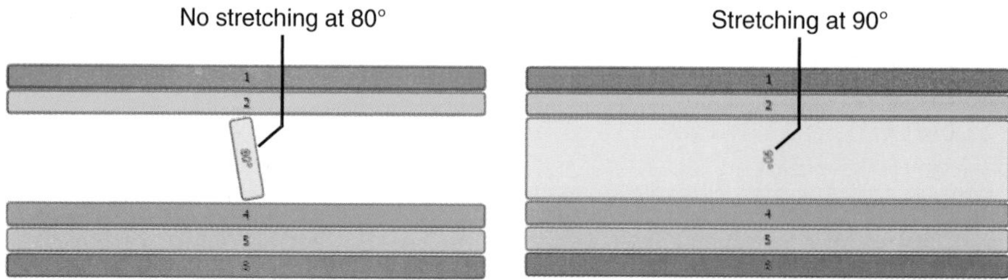

FIGURE 5.3 The yellow `Button` is rotated 80° then 90° using `LayoutTransform`.

DIGGING DEEPER

Virtualizing Panels

Panels that derive from the abstract `System.Windows.Controls.VirtualizingPanel` class are important implementation details of several controls. The most notable one is `VirtualizingStackPanel`, which acts just like `StackPanel` but temporarily discards any items offscreen to optimize performance (only when data binding). Therefore, `VirtualizingStackPanel` is the best panel for data binding to a *really* large number of child elements, and `ListBox` uses it internally by default. It can also be used in `TreeView`, as discussed in Chapter 10, "Items Controls." `DataGridCellsPanel` and `DataGridRowsPresenter` are two other virtualizing panels, and they are leveraged by `DataGrid` and its associated types, discussed in Chapter 11, "Images, Text, and Other Controls."

WrapPanel

`WrapPanel` is similar to `StackPanel`. But in addition to stacking its child elements, it wraps them to additional rows or columns when there's not enough space for a single stack. This is useful for displaying an indeterminate number of items with a more interesting layout than a simple list, much like what Windows Explorer does.

Like `StackPanel`, `WrapPanel` has no attached properties for controlling element positions. It defines three properties for controlling its behavior:

- **`Orientation`**—This is just like `StackPanel`'s property, except `Horizontal` is the default. `Horizontal` `Orientation` is like Windows Explorer's Thumbnails view: Elements are stacked left to right and then wrap top to bottom. `Vertical` `Orientation` is like Windows Explorer's List view: Elements are stacked top to bottom and then wrap left to right.
- **`ItemHeight`**—A uniform height for all child elements. The way each child fills that height depends on its own `VerticalAlignment`, `Height`, and so forth. Any elements taller than `ItemHeight` get clipped.
- **`ItemWidth`**—A uniform width for all child elements. The way each child fills that width depends on its own `HorizontalAlignment`, `Width`, and so forth. Any elements wider than `ItemWidth` get clipped.

By default, ItemHeight and ItemWidth are not set (or, rather, they are set to Double.NaN). In this case, a WrapPanel with Vertical Orientation gives each column the width of its widest element, whereas a WrapPanel with Horizontal Orientation gives each row the height of its tallest element. So no intra-WrapPanel clipping occurs by default.

> **TIP**
>
> You can force WrapPanel to arrange elements in a single row or column by setting its Width (for Horizontal Orientation) or Height (for Vertical Orientation) to Double.MaxValue or Double.PositiveInfinity. In XAML, this must be done with the x:Static markup extension because neither of these values is supported by the type converter for System.Double.

Figure 5.4 shows four snapshots of a WrapPanel with Horizontal Orientation in action, because it is inside a Window that is being resized. Figure 5.5 shows the same thing for a WrapPanel with Vertical Orientation. When a WrapPanel has plenty of space and ItemHeight/ItemWidth aren't set, WrapPanel looks just like StackPanel.

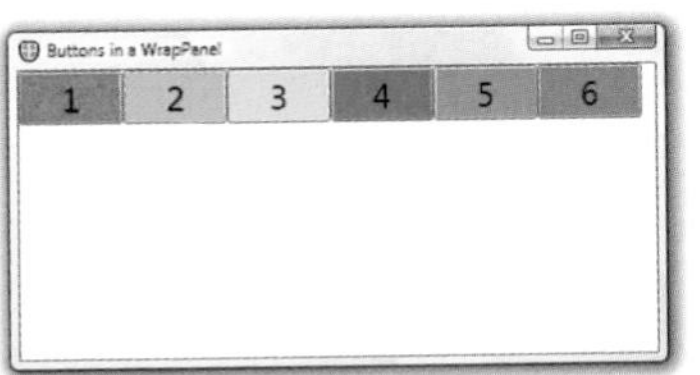

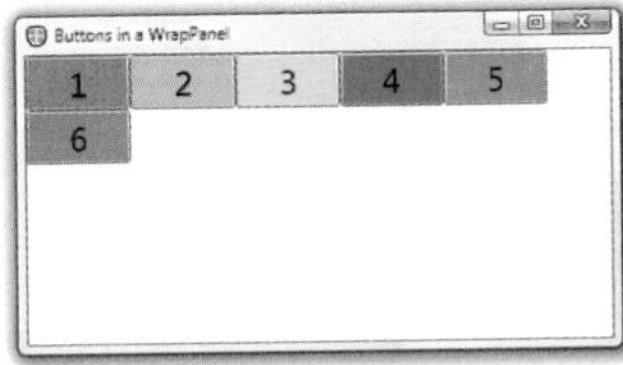

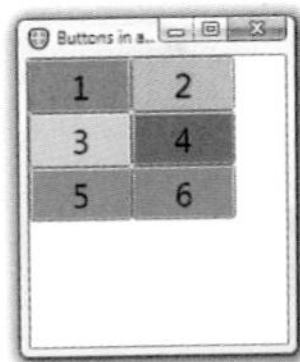

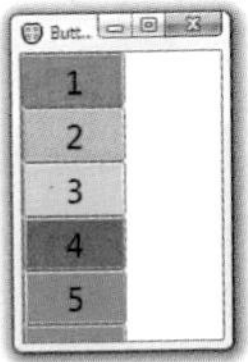

FIGURE 5.4 Buttons arranged in a WrapPanel with its default Horizontal Orientation, as the Window width shrinks.

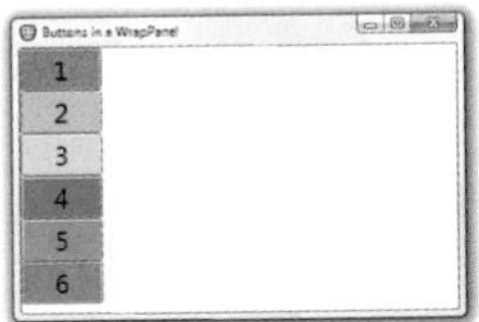

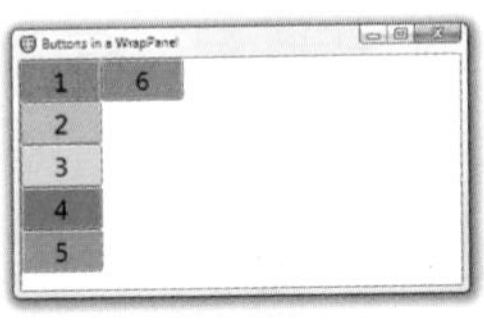

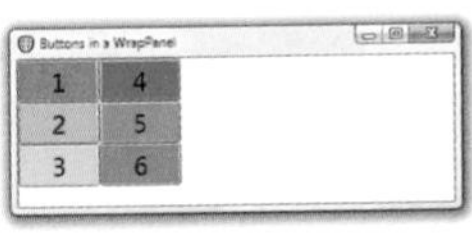

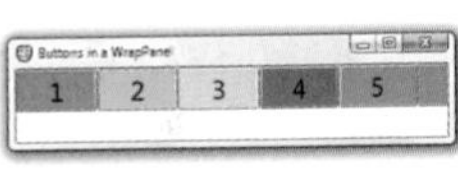

FIGURE 5.5 Buttons arranged in a WrapPanel with Vertical Orientation, as the Window height shrinks.

> **DIGGING DEEPER**
>
> **WrapPanel and Right-to-Left Environments**
>
> When FlowDirection is set to RightToLeft, wrapping occurs right to left for a WrapPanel with Vertical Orientation, and stacking occurs right to left for a WrapPanel with Horizontal Orientation.

Table 5.3 evaluates the way that some of the child layout properties apply to elements inside a WrapPanel.

TABLE 5.3 WrapPanel's Interaction with Child Layout Properties

Property	Usable Inside WrapPanel?
Margin	Yes. Margins are included when WrapPanel calculates the size of each item for determining default stack widths or heights.
HorizontalAlignment and VerticalAlignment	Partially. Alignment can be used in the opposite direction of stacking, just like with StackPanel. But alignment can also be useful in the direction of stacking when WrapPanel's ItemHeight or ItemWidth gives an element extra space to align within.
LayoutTransform	Yes. It differs from RenderTransform because when LayoutTransform is used, the remaining elements are pushed out further to make room, but only if WrapPanel's ItemHeight or ItemWidth (depending on the Orientation) is not set. When combining Stretch layout with RotateTransform or SkewTransform as a LayoutTransform, the stretching only occurs for angles that are multiples of 90°, as with StackPanel.

WrapPanel is typically not used for laying out controls in a Window, but rather for controlling layout *inside* controls. Chapter 10 explains how this is done.

DockPanel

DockPanel enables easy docking of elements to an entire side of the panel, stretching it to fill the entire width or height. (This is unlike Canvas, which enables you to dock elements to a corner only.) DockPanel also enables a single element to fill all the remaining space unused by the docked elements.

DockPanel has a Dock attached property (of type System.Windows.Controls.Dock), so children can control their docking with one of four possible values: Left (the default when Dock isn't applied), Top, Right, and Bottom. Note that there is no Fill value for Dock. Instead, the last child added to a DockPanel fills the remaining space unless DockPanel's LastChildFill property is set to false. With LastChildFill set to true (the default), the last child's Dock setting is ignored. With it set to false, it can be docked in any direction (Left by default).

Figure 5.6 displays the following five Buttons in a DockPanel (with LastChildFill left as true), each marked with its Dock setting:

```
<DockPanel>
  <Button DockPanel.Dock="Top" Background="Red">1 (Top)</Button>
  <Button DockPanel.Dock="Left" Background="Orange">2 (Left)</Button>
  <Button DockPanel.Dock="Right" Background="Yellow">3 (Right)</Button>
```

```
  <Button DockPanel.Dock="Bottom" Background="Lime">4 (Bottom)</Button>
  <Button Background="Aqua">5</Button>
</DockPanel>
```

The order in which these controls are added to the `DockPanel` is indicated by their number (and color).

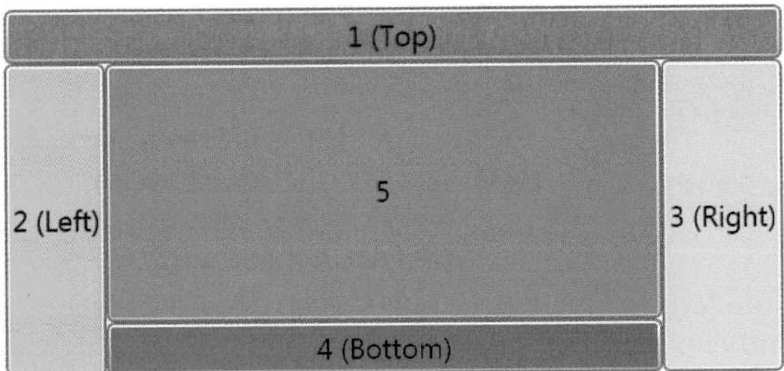

FIGURE 5.6 `Buttons` arranged in a `DockPanel`.

As with `StackPanel`, any stretching of elements is due to their default `HorizontalAlignment` or `VerticalAlignment` values of `Stretch`. Individual elements can choose different alignments if they don't want to fill the entire space that `DockPanel` gives them. Figure 5.7 demonstrates this with explicit `HorizontalAlignment` and `VerticalAlignment` values added to all but one `Button` rendered in Figure 5.6:

```
<DockPanel>
  <Button DockPanel.Dock="Top" HorizontalAlignment="Right"
    Background="Red">1 (Top, Align=Right)</Button>
  <Button DockPanel.Dock="Left" VerticalAlignment="Bottom"
    Background="Orange">2 (Left, Align=Bottom)</Button>
  <Button DockPanel.Dock="Right" VerticalAlignment="Bottom"
    Background="Yellow">3 (Right, Align=Bottom)</Button>
  <Button DockPanel.Dock="Bottom" HorizontalAlignment="Right"
    Background="Lime">4 (Bottom, Align=Right)</Button>
  <Button Background="Aqua">5</Button>
</DockPanel>
```

Notice that although four of the elements have chosen not to occupy all the space given to them, the space is not reclaimed for use by other elements.

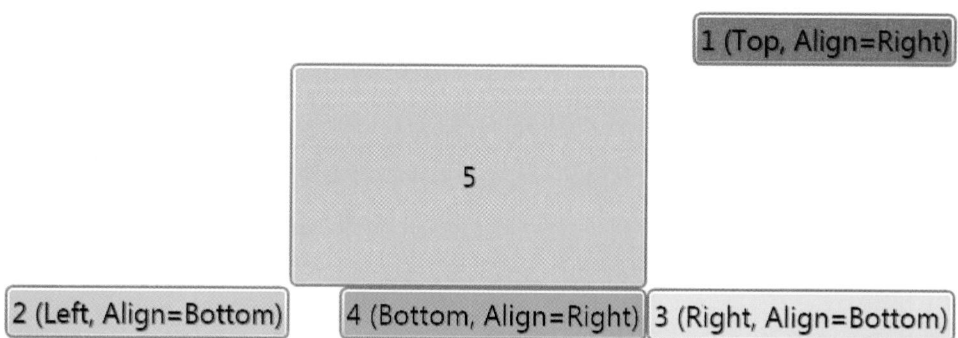

FIGURE 5.7 Buttons arranged in a DockPanel that don't occupy all the space given to them.

DockPanel is useful for arranging a top-level user interface in a Window or Page, where most docked elements are actually other panels containing the real meat. For example, applications typically dock a Menu on top, perhaps a panel on the side, and a StatusBar on the bottom, and then fill the remaining space with the main content.

The order in which children are added to DockPanel matters because each child is given all the space remaining on the docking edge. (This is somewhat like people selfishly claiming both armrests when they're the first to sit down in an airplane or auditorium.)

Figure 5.8 displays five Buttons in a DockPanel as in Figure 5.6, but added in a different order (indicated by their number and color). Notice how the layout differs from that in the preceding figure.

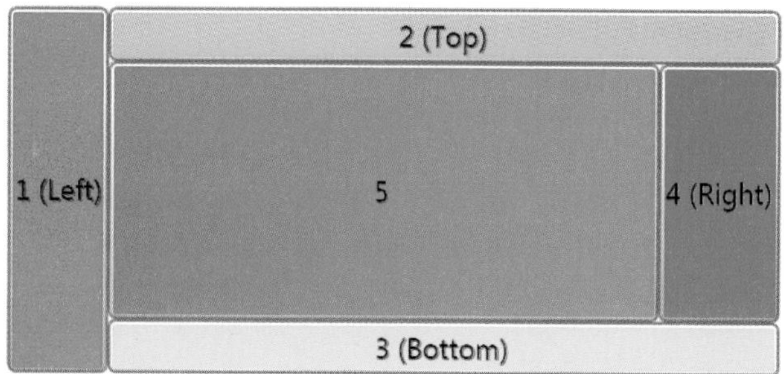

FIGURE 5.8 Buttons arranged in a DockPanel in a different order than Figure 5.6.

DockPanel supports an indefinite number of children—not just five. When multiple elements are docked in the same direction, they are simply stacked in the appropriate direction. Figure 5.9 shows a DockPanel with eight elements—three docked on the left, two docked on the top, two docked on the bottom, and one filling the remaining space.

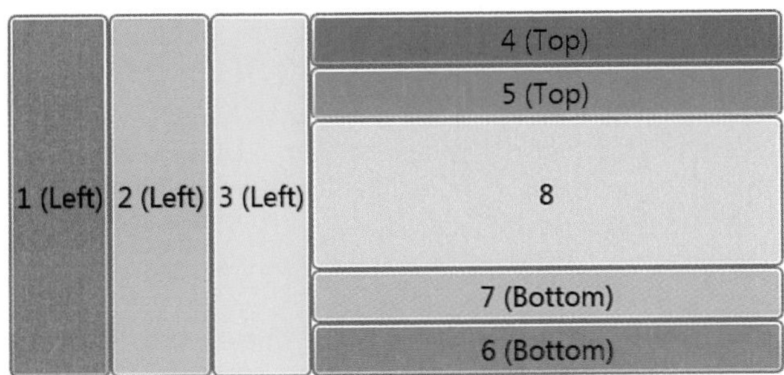

FIGURE 5.9 Multiple elements can be docked in all directions.

Therefore, `DockPanel`'s functionality is actually a superset of `StackPanel`'s functionality. With `LastChildFill` set to `false`, `DockPanel` behaves like a horizontal `StackPanel` when all children are docked to the left, and it behaves like a vertical `StackPanel` when all children are docked to the top.

Table 5.4 evaluates the way that some of the child layout properties apply to elements inside a `DockPanel`.

TABLE 5.4 `DockPanel`'s Interaction with Child Layout Properties

Property	Usable Inside DockPanel?
`Margin`	Yes. `Margin` controls the space between an element and the `DockPanel`'s edges as well as space between elements.
`HorizontalAlignment` and `VerticalAlignment`	Partially. As with `StackPanel`, alignment is effectively ignored in the direction of docking. For `Left` or `Right`, `HorizontalAlignment` is meaningless. For `Top` or `Bottom`, `VerticalAlignment` is meaningless. For the element filling the remaining space, however, both `HorizontalAlignment` and `VerticalAlignment` can be useful.
`LayoutTransform`	Yes. Differs from `RenderTransform` because when `LayoutTransform` is used, the remaining elements are pushed out further to make room. When combining `Stretch` layout with `RotateTransform` or `SkewTransform` as a `LayoutTransform`, the stretching occurs only for angles that are multiples of 90°, except for the element filling the remaining space (because it can stretch in both directions).

Grid

`Grid` is the most versatile panel and probably the one you'll use most often. (Visual Studio and Expression Blend use `Grid` by default for their projects.) It enables you to arrange its children in a multirow and multicolumn fashion, without relying on wrapping (like `WrapPanel`), and it provides a number of features to control the rows and columns in interesting ways. Working with `Grid` is a lot like working with a `TABLE` in HTML.

TIP

WPF also contains a class called `Table` in the `System.Windows.Documents` namespace that exposes similar features to `Grid`. However, `Table` is not a `Panel` (or even a `UIElement`). It is a `FrameworkContentElement` designed for the display of document content, whereas `Grid` is a `Panel`. `Table` is covered in Chapter 11.

Rather than continue to use simple colored buttons to demonstrate layout, Listing 5.2 uses `Grid` to build a user interface somewhat like Visual Studio's start page in older versions. It defines a 4x2 `Grid` and arranges a `Label` and four `GroupBoxes` in some of its cells.

LISTING 5.2 A First Attempt at a Visual Studio–Like Start Page with a `Grid`

```
<Grid Background="LightBlue">

<!-- Define four rows: -->
<Grid.RowDefinitions>
  <RowDefinition/>
  <RowDefinition/>
  <RowDefinition/>
  <RowDefinition/>
</Grid.RowDefinitions>

<!-- Define two columns: -->
<Grid.ColumnDefinitions>
  <ColumnDefinition/>
  <ColumnDefinition/>
</Grid.ColumnDefinitions>

<!-- Arrange the children: -->
  <Label    Grid.Row="0" Grid.Column="0" Background="Blue" Foreground="White"
            HorizontalContentAlignment="Center">Start Page</Label>
  <GroupBox Grid.Row="1" Grid.Column="0" Background="White"
            Header="Recent Projects">…</GroupBox>
  <GroupBox Grid.Row="2" Grid.Column="0" Background="White"
            Header="Getting Started">…</GroupBox>
  <GroupBox Grid.Row="3" Grid.Column="0" Background="White"
    Header="Headlines">…</GroupBox>
  <GroupBox Grid.Row="1" Grid.Column="1" Background="White"
    Header="Online Articles">
    <ListBox>
      <ListBoxItem>Article #1</ListBoxItem>
      <ListBoxItem>Article #2</ListBoxItem>
      <ListBoxItem>Article #3</ListBoxItem>
      <ListBoxItem>Article #4</ListBoxItem>
    </ListBox>
```

LISTING 5.2 Continued

```
  </GroupBox>
</Grid>
```

For the basic usage of `Grid`, you define the number of rows and columns by adding that number of `RowDefinition` and `ColumnDefinition` elements to its `RowDefinitions` and `ColumnDefinitions` properties. (This is a little verbose but handy for giving individual rows and columns distinct sizes.) You can then position child elements in the `Grid` using its `Row` and `Column` attached properties, which are zero-based integers. When you don't explicitly specify any rows or columns, a `Grid` is implicitly given a single cell. And when you don't explicitly set `Grid.Row` or `Grid.Column` on child elements, the value `0` is used for each.

`Grid` cells can be left empty, and multiple elements can appear in the same `Grid` cell. In this case, elements are simply rendered on top of one another according to their Z order. As with `Canvas`, child elements in the same cell don't interact with each other in terms of layout; they simply overlap.

Figure 5.10 shows the rendered result of Listing 5.2.

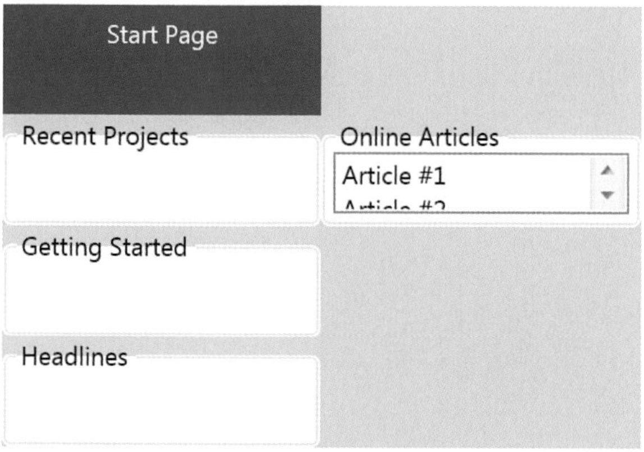

FIGURE 5.10 The first attempt at a Visual Studio–like start page is not very satisfactory.

The most noticeable problem with Figure 5.10 is that the list of online articles is too small. Also, it would probably look better if the "Start Page" label spanned the entire width of the `Grid`. Fortunately, we can solve both of these problems with two more attached properties defined by `Grid`: `RowSpan` and `ColumnSpan`.

`RowSpan` and `ColumnSpan` are set to `1` by default and can be set to any number greater than `1` to make an element span that many rows or columns. (If a value greater than the number of rows or columns is given, the element simply spans the maximum number that it can.) Therefore, by simply adding this to the last `GroupBox` in Listing 5.2:

```
Grid.RowSpan="3"
```

and adding this to the `Label` in Listing 5.2, you get a much better result, shown in Figure 5.11:

```
Grid.ColumnSpan="2"
```

FIGURE 5.11 Using `RowSpan` and `ColumnSpan` improves the Visual Studio–like start page.

The `Grid` in Figure 5.11 still looks a little strange, however, because by default the heights of all rows and the widths of all columns are equal. Ideally, we'd make more room for the list of online articles, and we wouldn't let the `Label` on top take up so much space. We can easily fix this by making the first row and first column size to their content. This *autosizing* can be done by setting the appropriate `RowDefinition`'s `Height` and `ColumnDefinition`'s `Width` to the case-insensitive string `Auto`. Therefore, updating the definitions in Listing 5.2 as follows gives the result shown in Figure 5.12:

```
<!-- Define four rows: -->
<Grid.RowDefinitions>
  <RowDefinition Height="Auto"/>
  <RowDefinition/>
  <RowDefinition/>
  <RowDefinition/>
</Grid.RowDefinitions>

<!-- Define two columns: -->
<Grid.ColumnDefinitions>
  <ColumnDefinition Width="Auto"/>
  <ColumnDefinition/>
</Grid.ColumnDefinitions>
```

FAQ

How can I give `Grid` cells background colors, padding, and borders, as with cells of an HTML TABLE?

There is no intrinsic mechanism to give `Grid` cells such properties, but you can simulate them pretty easily, thanks to the fact that multiple elements can appear in any `Grid` cell. To give a cell a background color, you can simply plop in a `Rectangle` with the appropriate `Fill`, which stretches to fill the cell by default. To give a cell padding, you can use autosizing and set the `Margin` on the appropriate child element. For borders, you can again use a `Rectangle` but give it an explicit `Stroke` of the appropriate color, or you can use a `Border` element instead.

Continued

Just be sure to add such `Rectangles` or `Borders` to the `Grid` *before* adding any of the other children (or explicitly mark them with the `ZIndex` attached property), so their Z order puts them behind the main content.

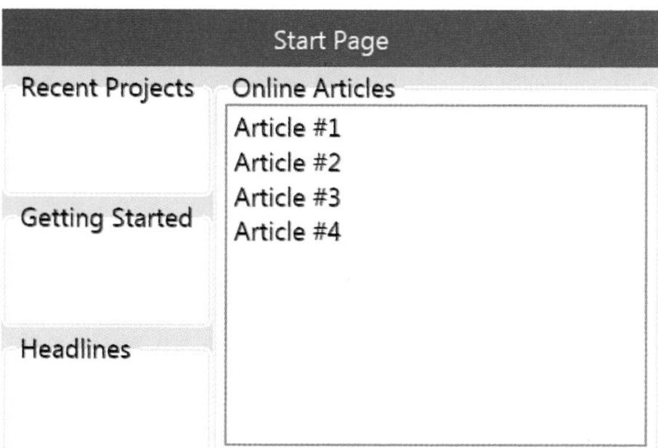

FIGURE 5.12 The final Visual Studio–like start page uses autosizing in the first row and first column.

TIP

`Grid` has a simple `ShowGridLines` property that can be set to `true` to highlight the edges of cells with blue and yellow dashed lines. Applications in production have no use for this, but this feature can be a helpful aid to "debug" the layout of a `Grid`. Figure 5.13 shows the result of setting `ShowGridLines="True"` on the `Grid` used in Figure 5.12.

FIGURE 5.13 Using `ShowGridLines` on a `Grid`.

Sizing the Rows and Columns

Unlike FrameworkElement's Height and Width properties, RowDefinition's and ColumnDefinition's corresponding properties do not default to Auto (or Double.NaN). And unlike almost all other Height and Width properties in WPF, theirs are of type System.Windows.GridLength rather than double. This way, Grid can uniquely support three different types of RowDefinition and ColumnDefinition sizing:

- **Absolute sizing**—Setting Height or Width to a numeric value representing device-independent pixels (like all other Height and Width values in WPF). Unlike the other types of sizing, an absolute-sized row or column does not grow or shrink as the size of the Grid or size of the elements changes.
- **Autosizing**—Setting Height or Width to Auto (seen previously), which gives child elements the space they need and no more (like the default setting for other Height and Width values in WPF). For a row, this is the height of the tallest element, and for a column, this is the width of the widest element. This is a better choice than absolute sizing whenever text is involved to be sure it doesn't get cut off because of different font settings or localization.
- **Proportional sizing (sometimes called star sizing)**—Setting Height or Width to special syntax to divide available space into equal-sized regions or regions based on fixed ratios. A proportional-sized row or column grows and shrinks as the Grid is resized.

Absolute sizing and autosizing are straightforward, but proportional sizing needs more explanation. It is done with *star syntax* that works as follows:

- When a row's height or column's width is set to *, it occupies all the remaining space.
- When multiple rows or columns use *, the remaining space is divided equally between them.
- Rows and columns can place a coefficient in front of the asterisk (like 2* or 5.5*) to take proportionately more space than other columns using the asterisk notation. A column with width 2* is always twice the width of a column with width * (which is shorthand for 1*) *in the same* Grid. A column with width 5.5* is always twice the width of a column with width 2.75* *in the same* Grid.

The "remaining space" is the height or width of the Grid minus any rows or columns that use absolute sizing or autosizing. Figure 5.14 demonstrates these different scenarios with simple columns in a Grid.

The default height and width for Grid rows and columns is *. That's why the rows and columns are evenly distributed in Figures 5.10 and 5.11.

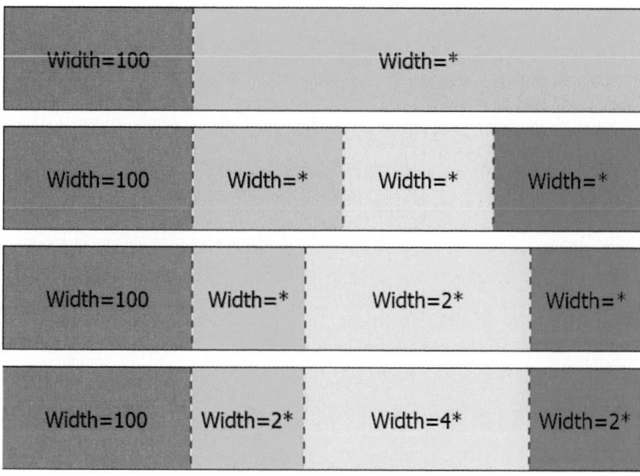

FIGURE 5.14 Proportional-sized `Grid` columns in action.

FAQ

Why doesn't WPF, like HTML, provide built-in support for percentage sizing?

The most common use of percentage sizing in HTML—setting the width or height of an item to 100%—is handled by setting an element's `HorizontalAlignment` or `VerticalAlignment` property to `Stretch` inside most panels. For more complicated scenarios, `Grid`'s proportional sizing effectively provides percentage sizing, but with a syntax that takes a little getting used to. For example, to have a column always occupy 25% of a `Grid`'s width, you can mark it with `*` and ensure that the remaining columns have a total width of `3*`.

The WPF team chose this syntax so developers wouldn't have to worry about keeping the sum of percentages equal to 100 as rows or columns are dynamically added or removed. In addition, the fact that proportional sizing is specified relative to the remaining space (as opposed to the entire `Grid`) makes its behavior more understandable than an HTML table when mixing proportional rows or columns with fixed-size rows or columns.

DIGGING DEEPER

Using `GridLength` from Procedural Code

`System.Windows.GridLengthConverter` is the type converter that converts strings like `"100"`, `"auto"`, and `"2*"` to `GridLength` structures. From C#, you can use one of two constructors to construct the appropriate `GridLength`. The key is a `GridUnitType` enumeration that identifies which of the three types of values you're creating.

For absolute sizing, you can use the constructor that takes a simple `double` value (such as `100`):

```
GridLength length = new GridLength(100);
```

Continued

or you can use another constructor that accepts a GridUnitType value:

```
GridLength length = new GridLength(100, GridUnitType.Pixel);
```

In both examples, the length is 100 device-independent pixels.

Double.NaN isn't a supported value for the GridLength constructors, so for autosizing you must use GridUnitType.Auto:

```
GridLength length = new GridLength(0, GridUnitType.Auto);
```

The number passed as the first parameter is ignored. However, the preferred approach is to simply use the static GridLength.Auto property, which returns an instance of GridLength just like the one created by the preceding line of code. For proportional sizing, you can pass a number along with GridUnitType.Star:

```
GridLength length = new GridLength(2, GridUnitType.Star);
```

This example is equivalent to specifying 2* in XAML. You can pass 1 with GridUnitType.Star to get the equivalent of *.

Interactive Sizing with GridSplitter

Another attractive feature of Grid is its support for interactive resizing of rows and columns using a mouse or keyboard (or stylus or finger, depending on your hardware). This is accomplished with the GridSplitter class from the same namespace. You can add any number of GridSplitter children to a Grid and give them Grid.Row, Grid.Column, Grid.RowSpan, and/or Grid.ColumnSpan attached property values like any other children. Dragging a GridSplitter resizes at least one cell. Whether the other cells resize or simply move depends on whether they use proportional or nonproportional sizing.

By default, which cells are directly affected by the resizing depends on GridSplitter's alignment values. Table 5.5 summarizes the behavior and also indicates in blue what the GridSplitter looks like with the various settings, treating the cells of the table as cells of a Grid.

TIP

Although GridSplitter fits in one cell by default, its resizing behavior always affects the entire column (when dragging horizontally) or the entire row (when dragging vertically). Therefore, it's best to give it a ColumnSpan or RowSpan value to ensure that it stretches across the entire height or width of the Grid.

GridSplitter has a default HorizontalAlignment of Right and a default VerticalAlignment of Stretch, so it docks to the right side of the specified cell by default. Any reasonable use of GridSplitter should set Stretch alignment in at least one direction. Otherwise, it ends up looking like a small dot, as seen in Table 5.5.

TABLE 5.5 The Cells Directly Affected When Dragging a GridSplitter with Various Alignment Settings

HorizontalAlignment

VerticalAlignment	Left	Right	Center	Stretch
Top	Current cell and cell to the left	Current cell and cell to the right	Cells to the left and right	Current cell and cell above
Bottom	Current cell and cell to the left	Current cell and cell to the right	Cells to the left and right	Current cell and cell below
Center	Current cell and cell to the left	Current cell and cell to the right	Cells to the left and right	Cells above and below
Stretch	Current cell and cell to the left	Current cell and cell to the right	Cells to the left and right	Cells to the left and right if GridSplitter is taller than it is wide, *or* cells to the top and bottom if GridSplitter is wider than it is tall

When all rows or columns are proportionally sized, dragging GridSplitter changes the coefficients for the two affected rows or columns accordingly. When all rows or columns are absolutely sized, dragging GridSplitter only changes the size of the topmost or left-most of the two affected cells (depending on the resize direction). The remaining cells get pushed down or to the right to make room. This same behavior applies for autosized rows and columns, although the row or column that gets resized is switched to absolute sizing on the fly.

Although you can control all aspects of the resizing behavior and direction with GridSplitter's alignment properties, GridSplitter also has two properties for explicitly and independently controlling these aspects: ResizeDirection (of type GridResizeDirection) and ResizeBehavior (of type GridResizeBehavior). ResizeDirection defaults to Auto and can be changed to Rows or Columns, but this has an effect only when GridSplitter is stretching in both directions (the bottom-right cell in Table 5.5). ResizeBehavior defaults to BasedOnAlignment to get the behavior in Table 5.5 but can be set to PreviousAndCurrent, CurrentAndNext, or PreviousAndNext to control which two rows or columns should be directly affected by the resizing.

TIP

The best way to use GridSplitter is to place it in its own autosized row or column. That way, it doesn't overlap the existing content in the adjacent cells. If you do place it in a cell with other elements, however, be sure to add it last (or choose an appropriate ZIndex value) so it has the topmost Z order!

5

Sharing Row and Column Sizes

RowDefinitions and ColumnDefinitions have a property called SharedSizeGroup that enables multiple rows and/or columns to remain the same length as each other, even as any of them change length at runtime (via GridSplitter, for example). SharedSizeGroup can be set to a simple case-sensitive string value representing an arbitrary group name, and any rows or columns with that same group name are kept in sync.

For a simple example, consider the following three-column Grid shown in Figure 5.15 that doesn't use SharedSizeGroup:

```
<Grid>
<Grid.ColumnDefinitions>
  <ColumnDefinition Width="Auto"/>
  <ColumnDefinition/>
  <ColumnDefinition/>
</Grid.ColumnDefinitions>

  <Label Grid.Column="0" Background="Red"
    HorizontalContentAlignment="Center" VerticalContentAlignment="Center">1
  </Label>
  <GridSplitter Grid.Column="0" Width="5"/>
  <Label Grid.Column="1" Background="Orange"
    HorizontalContentAlignment="Center" VerticalContentAlignment="Center">2
  </Label>
  <Label Grid.Column="2" Background="Yellow"
    HorizontalContentAlignment="Center" VerticalContentAlignment="Center">3
  </Label>
</Grid>
```

The first column is autosized and has both a Label and a GridSplitter. The two remaining columns are both *-sized and contain only a Label. As the first column is enlarged, the remaining two *-sized columns split the shrunken space evenly.

TIP

GridSplitter must be given an explicit Width (or Height, depending on orientation) in order to be seen and usable.

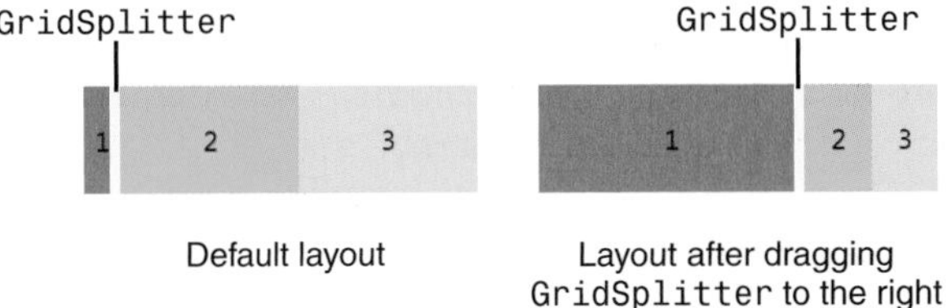

FIGURE 5.15 A simple Grid that doesn't use SharedSizeGroup.

In contrast, Figure 5.16 shows what happens with the same `Grid` when the first and last columns are marked with the same `SharedSizeGroup`. First, all members in the `SharedSizeGroup` are initialized to the largest auto or absolute size. Then, as the first column is enlarged, the last column is enlarged to match. The middle column is now effectively the only *-sized column, and it fills whatever space remains.

The XAML for the `Grid` shown in Figure 5.16 is as follows:

```
<Grid IsSharedSizeScope="True">
<Grid.ColumnDefinitions>
  <ColumnDefinition Width="Auto" SharedSizeGroup="myGroup"/>
  <ColumnDefinition/>
  <ColumnDefinition SharedSizeGroup="myGroup"/>
</Grid.ColumnDefinitions>
  <Label Grid.Column="0" Background="Red"
    HorizontalContentAlignment="Center" VerticalContentAlignment="Center">1
  </Label>
  <GridSplitter Grid.Column="0" Width="5"/>
  <Label Grid.Column="1" Background="Orange"
    HorizontalContentAlignment="Center" VerticalContentAlignment="Center">2
  </Label>
  <Label Grid.Column="2" Background="Yellow"
    HorizontalContentAlignment="Center" VerticalContentAlignment="Center">3
  </Label>
</Grid>
```

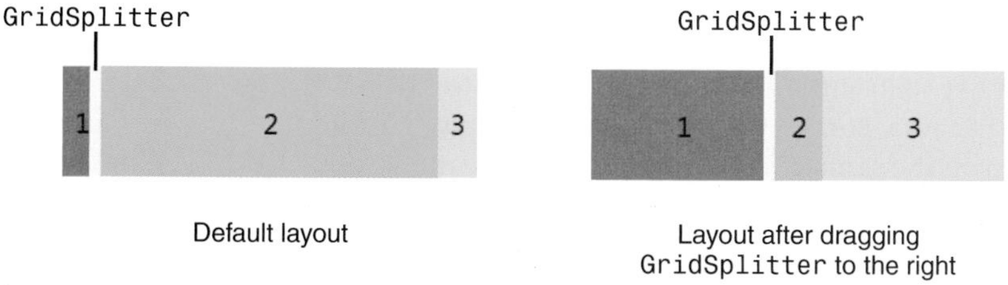

FIGURE 5.16 The `Grid` from Figure 5.15, but with the first and last columns in the same `SharedSizeGroup`.

The reason that the `IsSharedSizeScope` property needs to be set is that size groups can be shared *across multiple grids*! To avoid potential name collisions (and to cut down on the amount of logical tree walking that needs to be done), all uses of the same `SharedSizeGroup` must be under a common parent, with `IsSharedSizeScope` set to `true`. Besides being a dependency property of `Grid`, it's also an attached property that can be used on non-`Grid` parents. Here's an example:

```
<StackPanel Grid.IsSharedSizeScope="True">
  <Grid>…can use SharedSizeGroup…</Grid>
  <Grid>…can use SharedSizeGroup…</Grid>
```

```
  <WrapPanel>
    <Grid>...can use SharedSizeGroup...</Grid>
  </WrapPanel>
</StackPanel>
```

The "Putting It All Together: Creating a Visual Studio–Like Collapsible, Dockable, Resizable Pane" section at the end this chapter leverages `SharedSizeGroup` across multiple `Grid`s to create a useful user interface.

Comparing `Grid` to Other Panels

`Grid` is the best choice for most complex layout scenarios because it can do everything done by the previous panels and more, except for the wrapping feature of `WrapPanel`. `Grid` can also accomplish layout that would otherwise require multiple panels. For example, the start page displayed in Figure 5.12 could have been created with a `DockPanel` and a `StackPanel`. The `DockPanel` would be the outermost element, with the `Label` docked on top, the `StackPanel` docked to the left (which would contain the first three `GroupBox`es). The last `GroupBox` would be left to fill the `DockPanel`'s remaining space.

To prove that `Grid` is usually the best choice, it's interesting to see how to mimic the behavior of the other panels with `Grid`, knowing that you can take advantage of `Grid`'s extra features at any time.

Mimicking `Canvas` with `Grid`

If you leave `Grid` with a single row and column and set the `HorizontalAlignment` and `VerticalAlignment` of all children to values other than `Stretch`, the children get added to the single cell just as they do in a `Canvas`. Setting `HorizontalAlignment` to `Left` and `VerticalAlignment` to `Top` is like setting `Canvas.Left` and `Canvas.Top` to `0`. Setting `HorizontalAlignment` to `Right` and `VerticalAlignment` to `Bottom` is like setting `Canvas.Right` and `Canvas.Bottom` to `0`. Furthermore, applying `Margin` values to each element can give you the same effect as setting `Canvas`'s attached properties to the same values. This is what the Visual Studio designer does when the user places and moves items on the design surface.

Mimicking `StackPanel` with `Grid`

A single-column `Grid` with autosized rows looks just like a vertical `StackPanel` when each element is manually placed in consecutive rows. Similarly, a single-row `Grid` with autosized columns looks just like a horizontal `StackPanel` when each element is manually placed in consecutive columns.

Mimicking `DockPanel` with `Grid`

With `RowSpan` and `ColumnSpan`, you can easily arrange the outermost elements to be docked and stretched against a `Grid`'s edges just like what you would see with `DockPanel`. In Figure 5.12, the start page's `Label` is effectively docked along the top.

As with the previous panels, Table 5.6 evaluates the way that some of the child layout properties apply to elements inside a `Grid`.

TABLE 5.6 Grid's Interaction with Child Layout Properties

Property	Usable Inside Grid?
Margin	Yes. Margin controls the space between an element and the edges of its cell.
HorizontalAlignment and VerticalAlignment	Yes. Unlike with the previous panels, both directions are completely usable unless an autosized cell causes an element to have no extra room. Therefore, by default, most elements completely stretch to fill their cells.
LayoutTransform	Yes. Differs from RenderTransform because when LayoutTransform is used, elements remain inside their cells (when they can) and respect their Margin. Unlike with RenderTransform, an element scaled outside the bounds of a cell gets clipped.

TIP

Although Grid looks like it can practically do it all, StackPanel and WrapPanel are better choices when dealing with an indeterminate number of child elements (typically as an items panel for an items control, described in Chapter 10. Also, a DockPanel with complicated subpanels is sometimes a better choice than a single Grid panel because the isolation provided by subpanels is more manageable when the user interface changes. With a single Grid, you might need to adjust RowSpan and ColumnSpan values to keep the docking illusion while rows and columns are added to the Grid.

Primitive Panels

The previous panels are generally useful for both application layout and control layout. But WPF also ships a few lightweight panels that are likely to be useful only inside controls, whether you're simply restyling a built-in control (covered in Chapter 14, "Styles, Templates, Skins, and Themes") or creating a custom control (covered in Chapter 20, "User Controls and Custom Controls"). They aren't nearly as general purpose as the previous panels but are worth a quick look. All these panels are in the System.Windows.Controls.Primitives namespace, except for ToolBarTray, which is in System.Windows.Controls.

TabPanel

TabPanel is a lot like WrapPanel, but with limitations in some areas and extra features in other areas. As its name indicates, it is used in the default style for TabControl to arrange its tabs. Unlike WrapPanel, it supports only horizontal stacking and vertical wrapping. When wrapping occurs, it evenly stretches elements so that all rows consume the entire width of the panel. TabControl is covered in Chapter 10.

ToolBarPanel

ToolBarPanel, used by the default style of ToolBar, is like StackPanel. However, it works in conjunction with an overflow panel (covered next) to arrange items that don't fit in its own bounds (the ToolBar's main area). ToolBar is covered in Chapter 10.

ToolBarOverflowPanel

ToolBarOverflowPanel is a simplified WrapPanel that supports only horizontal stacking and vertical wrapping, used by the default style of ToolBar to display the extra elements in the overflow area. Above and beyond WrapPanel's functionality, it adds a WrapWidth property that acts like a Padding property. But there's no compelling reason to use this panel over WrapPanel.

ToolBarTray

ToolBarTray supports only ToolBar children (and throws an InvalidOperationException if you try to add children of any other type). It arranges the ToolBars sequentially (horizontally by default), and it also enables you to drag them around to form additional rows or compress/expand neighboring ToolBars.

UniformGrid

UniformGrid is an interesting primitive panel, although its usefulness is questionable. It's a simplified form of Grid in which all rows and columns are of size * and can't be changed. Because of this, UniformGrid has two simple double properties to set the number of rows and columns rather than the more verbose RowDefinitions and ColumnDefinitions collections. It also has no attached properties; children are added in row-major order, and there can be only one child per cell.

Furthermore, if you don't explicitly set the number of rows and columns (or if the number of children exceeds the explicit number of cells), UniformGrid automatically chooses suitable values. For example, it automatically places 2–4 elements in a 2x2 arrangement, 5–9 elements in a 3x3 arrangement, 10–16 elements in a 4x4 arrangement, and so on. Figure 5.17 demonstrates UniformGrid's default layout when eight Buttons are added to it.

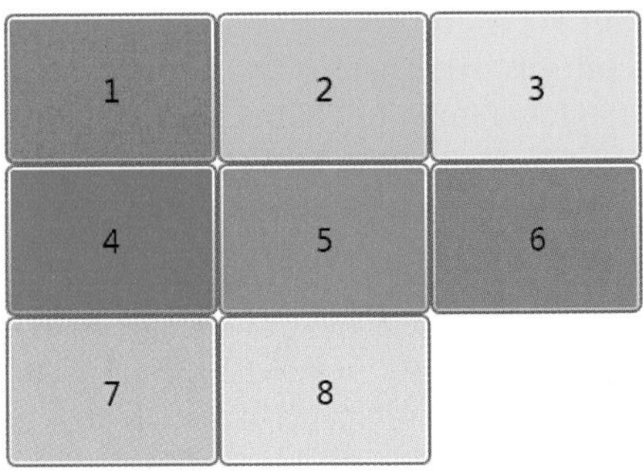

FIGURE 5.17 Eight Buttons added to a UniformGrid.

SelectiveScrollingGrid

SelectiveScrollingGrid is a Grid subclass used by the default style of the DataGridRow control. On top of Grid's functionality, it adds the ability to "freeze" cells while the rest of them scroll. This behavior is controlled by the SelectiveScrollingOrientation property, which can be set to one of the following values:

- **None**—The cells will not scroll in either direction.
- **Horizontal**—The cells can scroll only horizontally.
- **Vertical**—The cells can scroll only vertically.
- **Both**—The cells can scroll in any direction. This is the default value.

Handling Content Overflow

The built-in panels make their best effort to accommodate the size needs of their children. But sometimes they are forced to give children smaller space than they would like, and sometimes children refuse to render completely within that smaller space. For example, perhaps an element is marked with an explicit width that's wider than the containing panel. Or perhaps a control such as ListBox contains so many items that they can't all fit within the containing Window. In such cases, a content overflow problem exists.

You can deal with content overflow by using several different strategies:

- Clipping
- Scrolling
- Scaling
- Wrapping
- Trimming

The first three strategies are examined in this section. You've already seen examples of wrapping with WrapPanel (plus TabPanel and ToolBarOverflowPanel). This is the only built-in way to get wrapping behavior for content other than text (the layout of which is covered in Chapter 11).

Trimming refers to a more intelligent form of clipping. It is only supported for text by the TextBlock and AccessText elements. They have a TextTrimming property (of type System.Windows.TextTrimming) that can be set to None (the default), CharacterEllipsis, or WordEllipsis. With the latter two values, text gets trimmed with ellipses (...) rather than simply being truncated at an arbitrary place.

Clipping

Clipping (that is, truncating or cropping) children is the default way that panels handle them when they are too large. Clipping can happen at the edges of a panel or within a panel (such as at the edges of a Grid cell or the fill area of a DockPanel). This behavior can be controlled to some degree, however.

All `UIElements` have a Boolean `ClipToBounds` property that controls whether child elements can be rendered outside its bounds. If an outer element's edge coincides with the outer `Window`'s or `Page`'s edge, however, clipping still occurs. This mechanism is *not* a means to draw outside the bounds of a `Window`. (However, nonrectangular windows are discussed in Chapter 7, "Structuring and Deploying an Application.")

Despite the fact that all panels inherit a `ClipToBounds` property, most panels automatically clip their children regardless of this property's value. `Canvas` and `UniformGrid` do *not* clip their children by default, and they both support setting `ClipToBounds` to `true` to force clipping.

Figure 5.18 shows the difference that `ClipToBounds` makes with a `Button` that isn't entirely contained within its parent `Canvas` (which has a tan background).

This behavior means that unless you set `ClipToBounds` to `true`, the size of `Canvas` is irrelevant; it can be given a `Height` and `Width` of `0`, yet all its contents will be rendered as if the `Canvas` occupied the whole screen!

`ClipToBounds="False"` `ClipToBounds="True"`

FIGURE 5.18 `ClipToBounds` determines whether children can be rendered outside their panel.

Controls can also control the clipping of their own content with `ClipToBounds`. For example, `Button` has `ClipToBounds` set to `false` by default. Figure 5.19 demonstrates the effect of setting it to `true` when its text is scaled with `ScaleTransform` (applied as a `RenderTransform`).

`ClipToBounds="False"` `ClipToBounds="True"`

FIGURE 5.19 `ClipToBounds` can be used on a control such as `Button` to affect the rendering of its inner content.

TIP

`Canvas` can be used as an intermediate element to prevent clipping in other panels. For example, if a large `Button` gets clipped at the edge of a `Grid`, you can make it render past the edge of the `Grid` if you instead place a `Canvas` in that cell (which gets sized to fit the cell) and then place the `Button` inside that `Canvas`. Of course, you need to write some code if you want the `Button` to get the same stretching behavior it would have gotten by being a direct child of the `Grid`.

Continued

You can use the same approach to work around clipping within *inner* cells of a `Grid`, but increasing an element's `RowSpan` and/or `ColumnSpan` is usually the best way to enable it to "bleed" into adjacent cells.

WARNING

Clipping occurs before `RenderTransforms` are applied!

When enlarging an element with `ScaleTransform` as a `RenderTransform`, the element can easily surpass the bounds of the parent panel yet doesn't get clipped (unless it reaches the edge of the `Window` or `Page`). *Shrinking* an element with `ScaleTransform` as a `RenderTransform` is more subtle. If the unscaled element would have been clipped because it exceeds its parent's bounds, the scaled element is still clipped exactly the same way, even if the entire element can fit! That's because clipping is part of the layout process and already determined by the time `RenderTransform` is applied. If you need to shrink a large element by using `ScaleTransform`, applying it as a `LayoutTransform` might suit your needs better.

Scrolling

For many applications, the ability to scroll through content that is too large to view all at once is critical. WPF makes this easy because all you need to do is wrap an element in a `System.Windows.Controls.ScrollViewer` control, and the element instantly becomes scrollable. `ScrollViewer` makes use of `ScrollBar` controls and hooks them up to your content automatically.

`ScrollViewer` has a `Content` property that can be set to a single item, typically an entire panel. Because `Content` is `ScrollViewer`'s content property in the XAML sense, you can place the item requiring scrolling as its child element:

```
<Window Title="Using ScrollViewer"
  xmlns="http://schemas.microsoft.com/winfx/2006/xaml/presentation">
  <ScrollViewer>
    <StackPanel>
      …
    </StackPanel>
  </ScrollViewer>
</Window>
```

Figure 5.20 shows the `Window` containing the simple `StackPanel`, with and without a `ScrollViewer`.

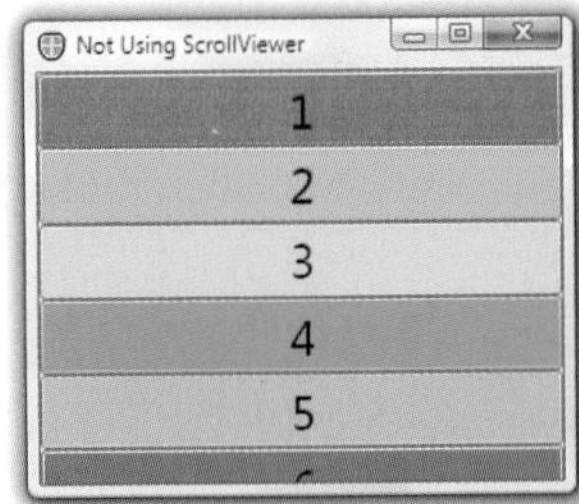

Not using ScrollViewer

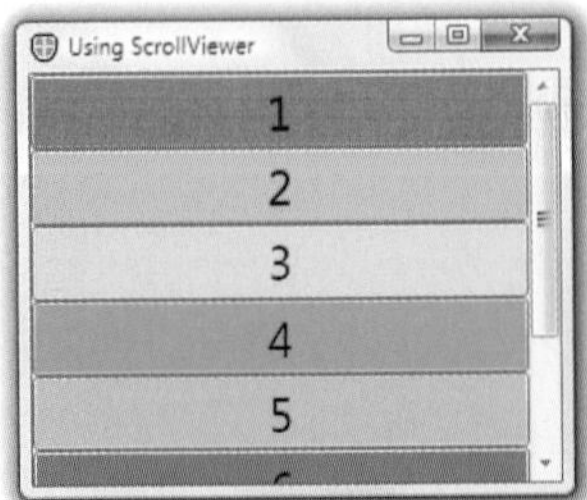

Using ScrollViewer

FIGURE 5.20 ScrollViewer enables scrolling of an element that is larger than the space given to it.

The ScrollBar controls respond to a variety of input, such as arrow keys for fine-grained scrolling, Page Up and Page Down for coarser scrolling, and Ctrl+Home or Ctrl+End to jump to the beginning or end, respectively.

ScrollViewer exposes several properties and methods for more advanced or programmatic manipulation of scrolling, but its two most important properties are VerticalScrollBarVisibility and HorizontalScrollBarVisibility. Both of these properties are of type ScrollBarVisibility, an enumeration that defines four distinct states specific to its two ScrollBars:

- **Visible**—The ScrollBar is always visible, regardless of whether it's needed. When it's not needed, it has a disabled look and doesn't respond to input. (But this is different from the ScrollBarVisibility value called Disabled.)
- **Auto**—The ScrollBar is visible if the content is big enough to require scrolling in that dimension. Otherwise, the ScrollBar disappears.
- **Hidden**—The ScrollBar is always invisible but still logically exists, in that scrolling can still be done with arrow keys. Therefore, the content is still given all the length it wants in that dimension.
- **Disabled**—The ScrollBar is not only invisible but doesn't exist, so scrolling is not possible via mouse or keyboard. In this case, the content is only given the length of its parent rather than all the length it wants.

The default value for VerticalScrollBarVisibility is Visible, and the default value for HorizontalScrollBarVisibility is Auto, to match the scrolling behavior used by most applications.

Depending on the content inside ScrollViewer, the subtle difference between Hidden and Disabled can be not so subtle. For example, Figure 5.21 shows two different Windows containing a ScrollViewer with exactly the same WrapPanel. The only difference is that in one Window the ScrollViewer has HorizontalScrollBarVisibility set to Hidden, and in the other Window the ScrollViewer has it set to Disabled.

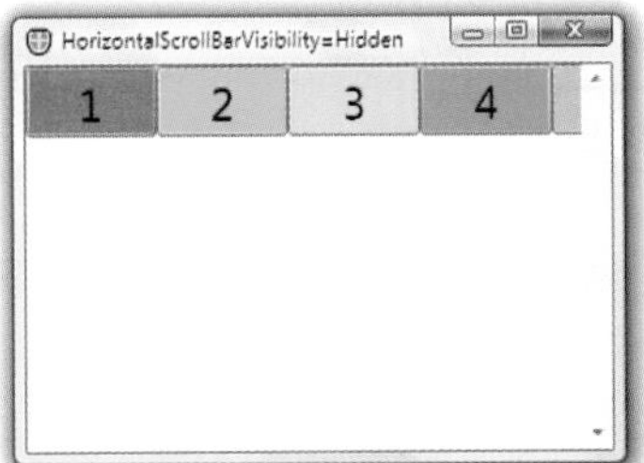

`HorizontalScrollBarVisibility="Hidden"`

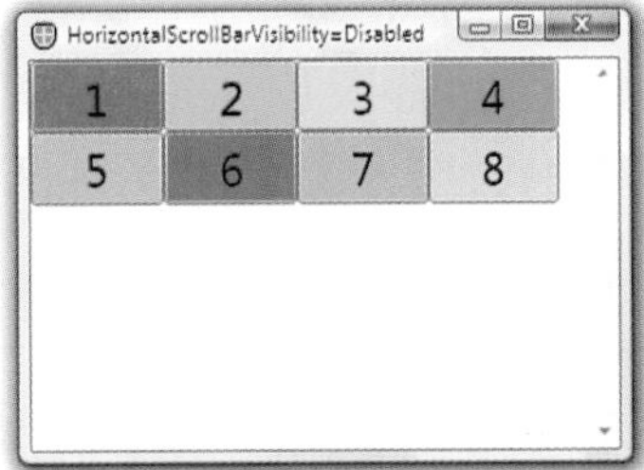

`HorizontalScrollBarVisibility="Disabled"`

FIGURE 5.21 Although the horizontal `ScrollBar` is invisible in both cases, the different values for `HorizontalScrollBarVisibility` drastically alter the layout of the `WrapPanel`.

In the `Hidden` case, the `WrapPanel` is given as much width as it desires (the same as if `HorizontalScrollBarVisibility` were set to `Visible` or `Auto`), so it makes use of it and arranges all children on the same row. In the `Disabled` case, the `WrapPanel` is only given the width of the parent `Window`, so wrapping occurs as if no `ScrollViewer` existed.

5

TIP

Chapter 3, "WPF Fundamentals," reveals that the default visual tree for `ListBox` contains a `ScrollViewer`. You can set its `VerticalScrollBarVisibility` and `HorizontalScrollBarVisibility` properties as attached properties on the `ListBox` to impact the behavior of the implicit `ScrollViewer`:

```
<ListBox ScrollViewer.HorizontalScrollBarVisibility="Disabled">
  …
</ListBox>
```

Scaling

Although scrolling is a popular and long-standing way to deal with large content, dynamically shrinking or enlarging content to "just fit" in a given space is more appropriate for several scenarios. As a simple example, imagine that you want to create a card game. You need some playing cards, and you probably want them to scale proportionally with the game's `Window`.

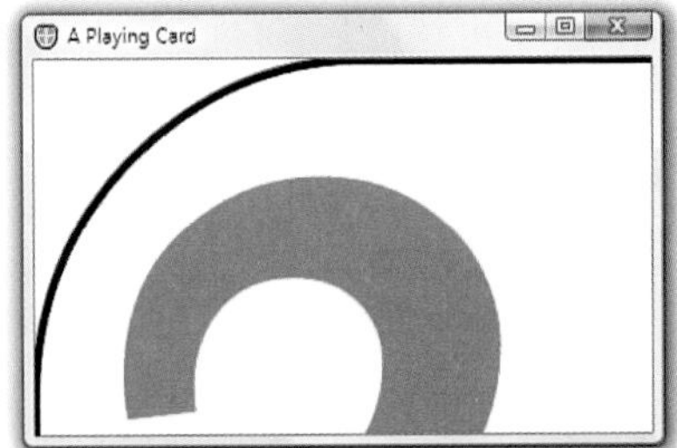

FIGURE 5.22 The shapes representing the playing card do not scale with the `Window`.

Figure 5.22 displays some shapes that form a vector representation of a playing card (shown with its source XAML in Chapter 20). These shapes are placed inside a `Canvas`, which is inside a `Window`. Because of their explicit sizes, they do not change size as the `Window` gets resized (even if they were placed in a `Grid` rather than a `Canvas`), and, obviously, the shapes are currently far too big.

`ScaleTransform` can scale elements *relative to their own size* (and easily help with the size of the playing card), but it doesn't provide a mechanism to scale elements *relative to their available space* without writing some custom code. Fortunately, `System.Windows.Controls.Viewbox` provides an easy mechanism to scale arbitrary content within a given space.

`Viewbox` is a type of class known as a *decorator*, a panel-like class that can have only one child element. It derives from `System.Windows.Controls.Decorator`, along with classes such as `Border`. By default, `Viewbox` (like most controls) stretches in both dimensions to fill the space given to it. But it also has a `Stretch` property to control how its single child gets scaled within its bounds. The property is a `System.Windows.Media.Stretch` enumeration, which has the following values (demonstrated in Figure 5.23 by wrapping the `Canvas` inside a `Viewbox`):

- **`None`**—No scaling is done. This is the same as not using `Viewbox` at all.
- **`Fill`**—The child's dimensions are set to equal the `Viewbox`'s dimensions. Therefore, the child's aspect ratio is not necessarily preserved.
- **`Uniform`**—The child is scaled as large as it can be while still fitting entirely within the `Viewbox` and preserving its aspect ratio. Therefore, there will be extra space in one dimension if its aspect ratio doesn't match. This is the default value.
- **`UniformToFill`**—The child is scaled to entirely fill the `Viewbox` while preserving its aspect ratio. Therefore, the content will be cropped in one dimension if its aspect ratio doesn't match.

Although it's unrealistic for a card game to want its cards to be the size of the `Window`, the same techniques apply for making the cards occupy a certain fraction of the `Window`'s size. In Figure 5.23, `Viewbox` is the child element of the `Window`, but in a real application, you would likely place the `Viewbox` inside an appropriately sized `Grid` cell.

A second property of `Viewbox` controls whether you want to use it only to shrink content or enlarge content (as opposed to doing either). This property is called `StretchDirection`, and it is a `System.Windows.Controls.StretchDirection` enumeration with the following values:

- **`UpOnly`**—Enlarges the content, if appropriate. If the content is already too big, `Viewbox` leaves the current content size as is.
- **`DownOnly`**—Shrinks the content, if appropriate. If the content is already small enough, `Viewbox` leaves the current content size as is.
- **`Both`**—Enlarges or shrinks the content, whichever is needed to get the stretching described earlier. This is the default value.

Stretch="None"

Stretch="Fill"

Stretch="Uniform"

Stretch="UniformToFill"

FIGURE 5.23 Each of the four values for `Viewbox`'s `Stretch` property changes the playing card's layout.

It's pretty amazing how easy it is to choose between a scrolling strategy and a scaling strategy for dealing with large content. Consider the following `Window` that is shown in Figure 5.20:

```
<Window Title="Using ScrollViewer"
  xmlns="http://schemas.microsoft.com/winfx/2006/xaml/presentation">
  <ScrollViewer>
    <StackPanel>
      …
    </StackPanel>
  </ScrollViewer>
</Window>
```

Simply changing the `ScrollViewer` element to `Viewbox` (and updating the `Window`'s `Title`) produces the result in Figure 5.24:

```
<Window Title="Using Viewbox"
  xmlns="http://schemas.microsoft.com/winfx/2006/xaml/presentation">
  <Viewbox>
    <StackPanel>
      …
    </StackPanel>
  </Viewbox>
</Window>
```

Just like that, you can now see all eight buttons, regardless of the `Window` size!

FIGURE 5.24 The `StackPanel` used in Figure 5.20, but now wrapped in a `Viewbox` instead of `ScrollViewer`.

WARNING

`Viewbox` removes all wrapping!

`Viewbox` is very handy for many situations, but it's not a good choice for content you'd normally like to wrap, such as a paragraph of text or any content in a `WrapPanel`. That's because the content is given as much space as it needs in both directions before it is potentially scaled. Figure 5.25 demonstrates this by using the `WrapPanel` with eight `Buttons` from Figure 5.21, but replacing `ScrollViewer` with `Viewbox`.

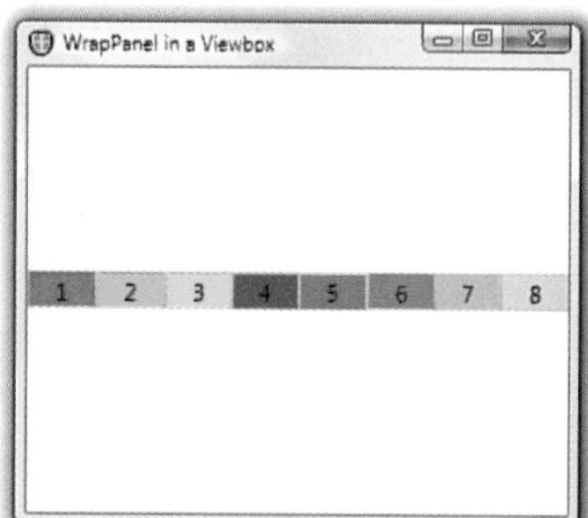

FIGURE 5.25 The `WrapPanel` used in Figure 5.21 has no need to wrap when placed in a `Viewbox` instead of a `ScrollViewer`.

The result is a single line of content that could potentially be much smaller than you would have liked. Giving `Viewbox` a `StretchDirection` of `UpOnly` rather than the default of `Both` doesn't help either. The layout of `Viewbox`'s content happens before any potential scaling. Therefore, `UpOnly` prevents the `Buttons` from shrinking, but they are still arranged in a single line, as shown in Figure 5.26.

Continued

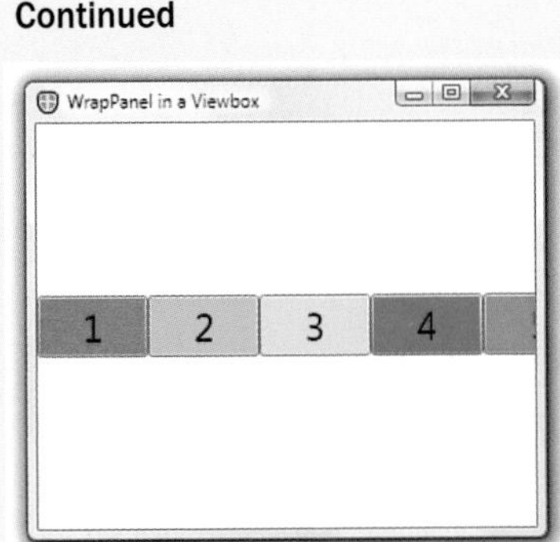

FIGURE 5.26 Giving the `Viewbox` from Figure 2.25 a `StretchDirection="UpOnly"` prevents the `Buttons` from shrinking but doesn't affect the inner `WrapPanel`'s layout.

The result of this is similar to the use of `HorizontalScrollBarVisibility="Hidden"` in Figure 5.21, except that there's no way to scroll to the remaining content, even with the keyboard.

Putting It All Together: Creating a Visual Studio–Like Collapsible, Dockable, Resizable Pane

Let's put WPF's layout features to the test and create a more complex piece of user interface. In this section, we create some Visual Studio–like panes that can be docked next to the window's main content or collapsed to a button along the edge of the window. In this collapsed form, hovering over the button shows the pane, but rather than being docked, it overlaps on top of the main content. Whether it is docked or undocked, each pane is resizable using a splitter. Figures 5.27 through 5.33 walk through several sequential states of the user interface as it is being used.

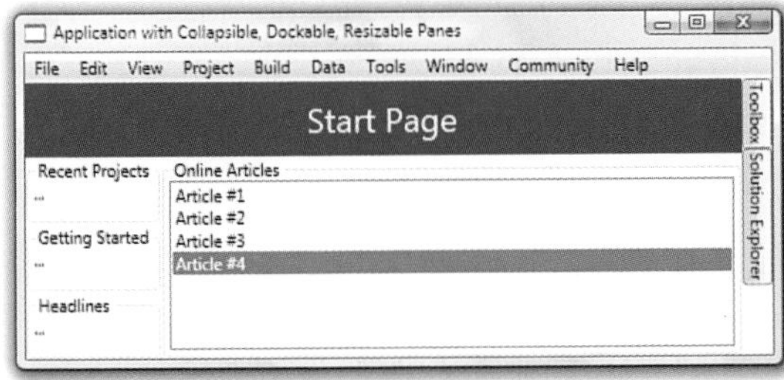

FIGURE 5.27 Both panes start out hidden, so you see only their buttons docked on the right.

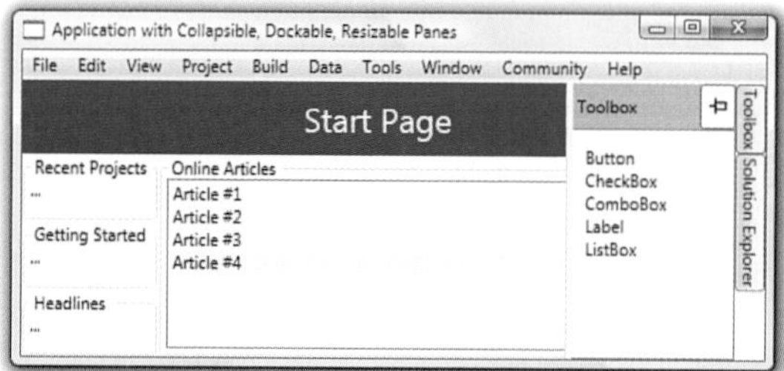

FIGURE 5.28 Hovering over the Toolbox button presents the undocked Toolbox pane, which stays open unless the mouse wanders onto the main content or a different pane's button.

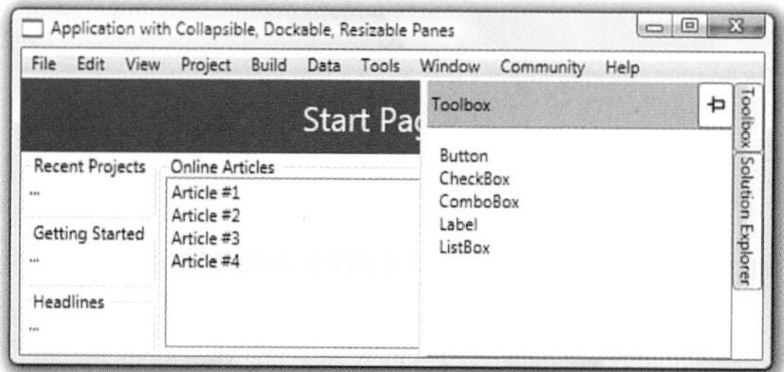

FIGURE 5.29 An undocked pane can be resized, and it still overlaps the main content.

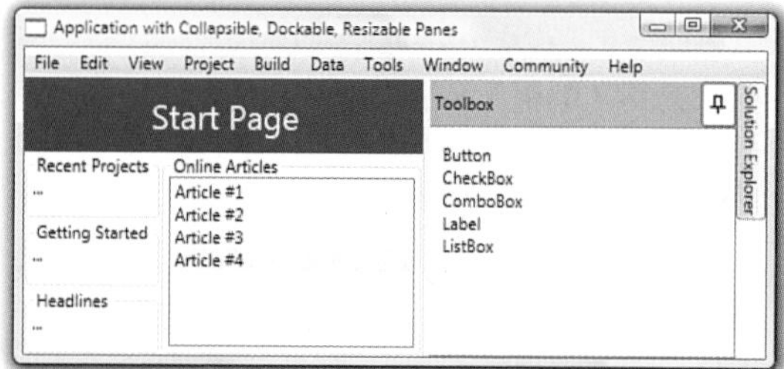

FIGURE 5.30 The Toolbox pane is docked by clicking the pushpin, making the main content shrink to fit beside it and making the Toolbox button on the right disappear.

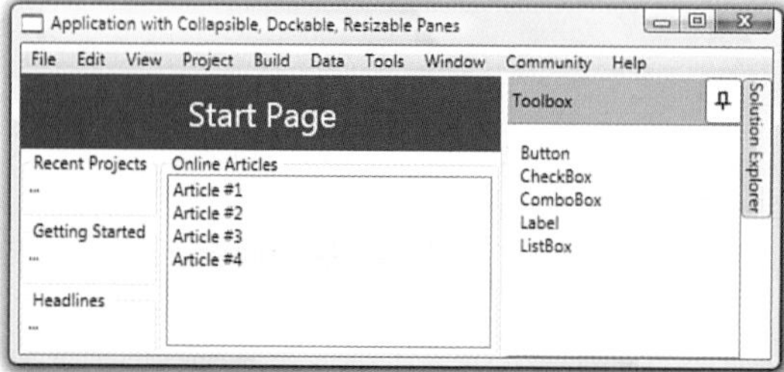

FIGURE 5.31 The docked pane can still be resized with the `GridSplitter`, but this time the main content stretches and shrinks in unison.

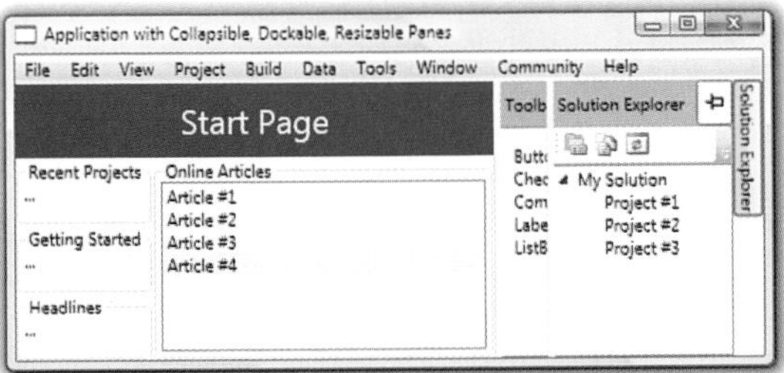

FIGURE 5.32 Hovering over the Solution Explorer button presents the undocked Solution Explorer pane, which overlaps all other content (including the docked Toolbox pane). The undocked pane can be resized independently to overlap more or less of the other content.

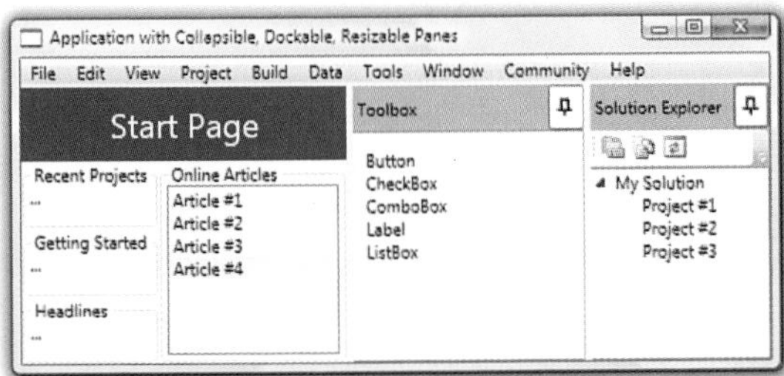

FIGURE 5.33 The Solution Explorer pane is docked by clicking the pushpin, pushing the Toolbox pane over, and making the entire rightmost bar disappear because there are no more undocked pane buttons to show.

When both panes are undocked, they resize independently from the main content and each other. When both panes are docked (as in Figure 5.33), the user interface behaves like a single `Grid` with three cells that can be resized but never overlap.

So, how do you go about implementing such a user interface? Because splitters are needed for interactive resizing, using `Grid` with `GridSplitters` is a natural choice. No other built-in panels provide an interactive splitter. But because undocked panes need to overlap and resize independently from one another, a single `Grid` won't do. Instead, this example uses three independent `Grids`—one for the main content and one for each pane—layered on top of each other. `SharedSizeGroup` is then used to keep these three independent `Grids` in sync when they need to be (that is, the docked case). Figure 5.34 illustrates the structure of these three `Grids` and how they are tied together.

The bottom layer (Layer 0) contains the main content that stretches to fill the `Grid` when both panes are collapsed. Hovering over either pane's button switches the appropriate pane's visibility in Layers 1 or 2 from `Collapsed` to `Visible`. Each pane's splitter can be used to adjust the space between itself and the column to the left (which is empty, revealing the content from Layer 0 behind it).

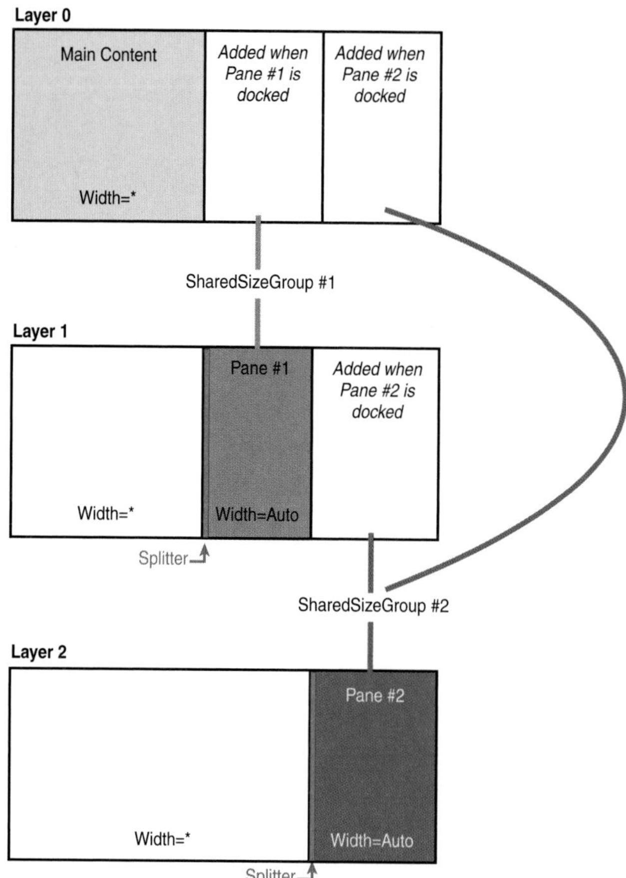

FIGURE 5.34 The three independent `Grid`s used to implement two collapsible, dockable, resizable panes.

The main trickery occurs when it's time to dock a panel. When docking Pane 1, the main content needs to be squeezed to match the width of the empty 0th column in Layer 1. Therefore, an empty column is dynamically added to Layer 0 and given the same width as Pane 1. Because a `SharedSizeGroup` is used rather than a hard-coded width, the bottom layer stays up to date as the splitter in Layer 1 is used.

The same technique is used when docking Pane 2, except that the dummy column needs to be added to all layers underneath (both Layers 0 and 1). This enables both docked panes to be seen simultaneously with no overlap, and it enables the main content on Layer 0 to be sized appropriately in the presence of zero, one, or two docked panes. Note that the ordering of the panes when both are docked is predetermined.

These three `Grid`s are placed in (what else?) a `Grid` with a single row and column, so they can completely overlap each other while stretching to completely fill the space given to them. Although Layer 0 always has the bottommost Z order, the Z order between the other layers can get swapped so the current undocked pane is always on top.

Listing 5.3 contains the XAML for the application shown in Figures 5.27 to 5.33, with some of the irrelevant parts removed for brevity. The entire project appears with this book's source code (available on the book's website, http://informit.com/title/9780672331190).

LISTING 5.3 VisualStudioLikePanes.xaml—The XAML Implementation of the Application in Figures 5.27 to 5.33

```
<Window x:Class="MainWindow"
        xmlns="http://schemas.microsoft.com/winfx/2006/xaml/presentation"
        xmlns:x="http://schemas.microsoft.com/winfx/2006/xaml"
        Title="Application with Collapsible, Dockable, Resizable Panes">
  <DockPanel>
    <Menu DockPanel.Dock="Top">
      …
    </Menu>

    <!-- The bar of buttons docked along the right edge: -->
    <StackPanel Name="buttonBar" Orientation="Horizontal" DockPanel.Dock="Right">
    <StackPanel.LayoutTransform>
      <RotateTransform Angle="90"/>
    </StackPanel.LayoutTransform>
      <Button Name="pane1Button" MouseEnter="pane1Button_MouseEnter">
        Toolbox
      </Button>
      <Button Name="pane2Button" MouseEnter="pane2Button_MouseEnter">
        Solution Explorer
      </Button>
    </StackPanel>

    <!-- The Grid containing the three child Grids fills the DockPanel: -->
    <Grid Name="parentGrid" Grid.IsSharedSizeScope="True">

      <!-- Layer 0: -->
      <Grid Name="layer0" MouseEnter="layer0_MouseEnter">
        … (content of this Grid is similar to Listing 5.2)
      </Grid>

      <!-- Layer 1: -->
      <Grid Name="layer1" Visibility="Collapsed">
      <Grid.ColumnDefinitions>
        <ColumnDefinition/>
        <ColumnDefinition SharedSizeGroup="column1" Width="auto"/>
      </Grid.ColumnDefinitions>
        <!-- Column 0 is empty,
             but column 1 contains a Grid and a GridSplitter: -->
```

5

LISTING 5.3 Continued

```
    <Grid Grid.Column="1" MouseEnter="pane1_MouseEnter"
          Background="{DynamicResource
                       {x:Static SystemColors.ActiveCaptionBrushKey}}">
    <Grid.RowDefinitions>
      <RowDefinition Height="auto"/>
      <RowDefinition/>
    </Grid.RowDefinitions>
      <!-- Row 0 contains a header,
           and row 1 contains pane-specific content: -->
      <DockPanel Grid.Row="0">
        <Button Name="pane1Pin" Width="26" DockPanel.Dock="Right"
                Click="pane1Pin_Click" Background="White">
          <Image Name="pane1PinImage" Source="pinHorizontal.gif"/>
        </Button>
        <TextBlock Padding="8" TextTrimming="CharacterEllipsis"
          Foreground="{DynamicResource
                       {x:Static SystemColors.ActiveCaptionTextBrushKey}}"
          DockPanel.Dock="Left">Toolbox</TextBlock>
      </DockPanel>
      … (pane-specific content fills row 1)
    </Grid>
    <GridSplitter Width="5" Grid.Column="1" HorizontalAlignment="Left"/>
  </Grid>

  <!-- Layer 2: -->
  <Grid Name="layer2" Visibility="Collapsed">
  <Grid.ColumnDefinitions>
    <ColumnDefinition/>
    <ColumnDefinition SharedSizeGroup="column2" Width="auto"/>
  </Grid.ColumnDefinitions>
    <!-- Column 0 is empty,
         but column 1 contains a Grid and a GridSplitter: -->
    <Grid Grid.Column="1" MouseEnter="pane2_MouseEnter"
          Background="{DynamicResource
                       {x:Static SystemColors.ActiveCaptionBrushKey}}">
    <Grid.RowDefinitions>
      <RowDefinition Height="auto"/>
      <RowDefinition Height="auto"/>
      <RowDefinition/>
    </Grid.RowDefinitions>
      <!-- Row 0 contains a header,
           and rows 1 & 2 contain pane-specific content: -->
      <DockPanel Grid.Row="0">
        <Button Name="pane2Pin" Width="26" DockPanel.Dock="Right"
```

LISTING 5.3 Continued

```
                Click="pane2Pin_Click" Background="White">
          <Image Name="pane2PinImage" Source="pinHorizontal.gif"/>
        </Button>
        <TextBlock Padding="8" TextTrimming="CharacterEllipsis"
          Foreground="{DynamicResource
                       {x:Static SystemColors.ActiveCaptionTextBrushKey}}"
          DockPanel.Dock="Left">Solution Explorer</TextBlock>
      </DockPanel>
      … (pane-specific content fills rows 1 & 2)
    </Grid>
    <GridSplitter Width="5" Grid.Column="1" HorizontalAlignment="Left"/>
  </Grid>
 </Grid>
</DockPanel>
</Window>
```

The Window's top-level panel is a DockPanel, which arranges a Menu, the "button bar" StackPanel (rotated 90° with a RotateTransform), and a single-cell grid containing the three "layer" Grids. Notice that the Menu is added to the DockPanel before the StackPanel so it stretches all the way across the top.

Each layer Grid has only one column containing any content, and that content happens to be encased in a Grid in all three cases. Each GridSplitter is docked on the left inside the column with the content, so it doesn't overlap any content from the other layers. One subtlety is that a TextBlock is used for each pane's header instead of a Label so that TextTrimming="CharacterEllipsis" can be set to get a more polished effect than simply clipping the text when the pane is resized.

Listing 5.4 contains the C# code-behind file for Listing 5.3.

LISTING 5.4 VisualStudioLikePanes.xaml.cs—The C# Implementation of the Application in Figures 5.27 to 5.33

```
using System;
using System.Windows;
using System.Windows.Controls;
using System.Windows.Media.Imaging;

public partial class MainWindow : Window
{
  // Dummy columns for layers 0 and 1:
  ColumnDefinition column1CloneForLayer0;
  ColumnDefinition column2CloneForLayer0;
  ColumnDefinition column2CloneForLayer1;
```

LISTING 5.4 Continued

```
public MainWindow()
{
  InitializeComponent();

  // Initialize the dummy columns used when docking:
  column1CloneForLayer0 = new ColumnDefinition();
  column1CloneForLayer0.SharedSizeGroup = "column1";
  column2CloneForLayer0 = new ColumnDefinition();
  column2CloneForLayer0.SharedSizeGroup = "column2";
  column2CloneForLayer1 = new ColumnDefinition();
  column2CloneForLayer1.SharedSizeGroup = "column2";
}

// Toggle between docked and undocked states (Pane 1)
public void pane1Pin_Click(object sender, RoutedEventArgs e)
{
  if (pane1Button.Visibility == Visibility.Collapsed)
    UndockPane(1);
  else
    DockPane(1);
}

// Toggle between docked and undocked states (Pane 2)
public void pane2Pin_Click(object sender, RoutedEventArgs e)
{
  if (pane2Button.Visibility == Visibility.Collapsed)
    UndockPane(2);
  else
    DockPane(2);
}

// Show Pane 1 when hovering over its button
public void pane1Button_MouseEnter(object sender, RoutedEventArgs e)
{
  layer1.Visibility = Visibility.Visible;

  // Adjust Z order to ensure the pane is on top:
  Grid.SetZIndex(layer1, 1);
  Grid.SetZIndex(layer2, 0);

  // Ensure the other pane is hidden if it is undocked
  if (pane2Button.Visibility == Visibility.Visible)
```

LISTING 5.4 Continued

```
    layer2.Visibility = Visibility.Collapsed;
}

// Show Pane 2 when hovering over its button
public void pane2Button_MouseEnter(object sender, RoutedEventArgs e)
{
  layer2.Visibility = Visibility.Visible;

  // Adjust Z order to ensure the pane is on top:
  Grid.SetZIndex(layer2, 1);
  Grid.SetZIndex(layer1, 0);

  // Ensure the other pane is hidden if it is undocked
  if (pane1Button.Visibility == Visibility.Visible)
    layer1.Visibility = Visibility.Collapsed;
}

// Hide any undocked panes when the mouse enters Layer 0
public void layer0_MouseEnter(object sender, RoutedEventArgs e)
{
  if (pane1Button.Visibility == Visibility.Visible)
    layer1.Visibility = Visibility.Collapsed;
  if (pane2Button.Visibility == Visibility.Visible)
    layer2.Visibility = Visibility.Collapsed;
}

// Hide the other pane if undocked when the mouse enters Pane 1
public void pane1_MouseEnter(object sender, RoutedEventArgs e)
{
  // Ensure the other pane is hidden if it is undocked
  if (pane2Button.Visibility == Visibility.Visible)
    layer2.Visibility = Visibility.Collapsed;
}

// Hide the other pane if undocked when the mouse enters Pane 2
public void pane2_MouseEnter(object sender, RoutedEventArgs e)
{
  // Ensure the other pane is hidden if it is undocked
  if (pane1Button.Visibility == Visibility.Visible)
    layer1.Visibility = Visibility.Collapsed;
}

// Docks a pane, which hides the corresponding pane button
public void DockPane(int paneNumber)
```

LISTING 5.4 Continued

```
{
  if (paneNumber == 1)
  {
    pane1Button.Visibility = Visibility.Collapsed;
    pane1PinImage.Source = new BitmapImage(new Uri("pin.gif", UriKind.Relative));

    // Add the cloned column to layer 0:
    layer0.ColumnDefinitions.Add(column1CloneForLayer0);
    // Add the cloned column to layer 1, but only if pane 2 is docked:
    if (pane2Button.Visibility == Visibility.Collapsed)
      layer1.ColumnDefinitions.Add(column2CloneForLayer1);
  }
  else if (paneNumber == 2)
  {
    pane2Button.Visibility = Visibility.Collapsed;
    pane2PinImage.Source = new BitmapImage(new Uri("pin.gif", UriKind.Relative));

    // Add the cloned column to layer 0:
    layer0.ColumnDefinitions.Add(column2CloneForLayer0);
    // Add the cloned column to layer 1, but only if pane 1 is docked:
    if (pane1Button.Visibility == Visibility.Collapsed)
      layer1.ColumnDefinitions.Add(column2CloneForLayer1);
  }
}

// Undocks a pane, which reveals the corresponding pane button
public void UndockPane(int paneNumber)
{
  if (paneNumber == 1)
  {
    layer1.Visibility = Visibility.Visible;
    pane1Button.Visibility = Visibility.Visible;
    pane1PinImage.Source = new BitmapImage
      (new Uri("pinHorizontal.gif", UriKind.Relative));

    // Remove the cloned columns from layers 0 and 1:
    layer0.ColumnDefinitions.Remove(column1CloneForLayer0);
    // This won't always be present, but Remove silently ignores bad columns:
    layer1.ColumnDefinitions.Remove(column2CloneForLayer1);
  }
  else if (paneNumber == 2)
  {
    layer2.Visibility = Visibility.Visible;
    pane2Button.Visibility = Visibility.Visible;
```

LISTING 5.4 Continued

```
      pane2PinImage.Source = new BitmapImage
        (new Uri("pinHorizontal.gif", UriKind.Relative));

      // Remove the cloned columns from layers 0 and 1:
      layer0.ColumnDefinitions.Remove(column2CloneForLayer0);
      // This won't always be present, but Remove silently ignores bad columns:
      layer1.ColumnDefinitions.Remove(column2CloneForLayer1);
    }
  }
}
```

The C# code is hard-coded to work with exactly two panes. You would be more likely to generalize the code and abstract it into a custom control, but as far as layout goes, the concepts are the same.

Notice that there is no code to hide the "button bar" when all panes have been docked or to reveal it when at least one pane is undocked. This happens automatically because the `StackPanel` sizes to its content by default, so collapsing both `Buttons` ends up collapsing the `StackPanel`.

Although Listing 5.4 doesn't contain very much code (or any complex code), it achieves a relatively sophisticated user interface.

Summary

With all the features described in this chapter and the preceding chapter, you can control layout in many interesting ways. This isn't like the old days, where your only options were pretty much just choosing a size and choosing an (X,Y) point on the screen.

The built-in panels—notably `Grid`—are a key part of WPF's capability to enable rapid application development. But one of the most powerful aspects of WPF's layout is that parent panels can themselves be children of other panels. Although each panel was examined in isolation in this chapter, panels can be nested to provide impressive versatility.

CHAPTER 6

Input Events: Keyboard, Mouse, Stylus, and Multi-Touch

IN THIS CHAPTER

- Routed Events
- Keyboard Events
- Mouse Events
- Stylus Events
- Multi-Touch Events
- Commands

Now that you know how to arrange a WPF user interface, it's time see how to make it interactive. This chapter covers two pieces of important plumbing in WPF—routed events and commands. It also examines the events you can handle for each category of input device: keyboard, mouse, stylus, and multi-touch.

Routed Events

Chapter 3, "WPF Fundamentals," demonstrates how WPF adds more infrastructure on top of the simple notion of .NET properties with its dependency properties. WPF also adds more infrastructure on top of the simple notion of .NET events. *Routed events* are events that are designed to work well with a tree of elements. When a routed event is raised, it can travel up or down the visual and logical tree, getting raised on each element in a simple and consistent fashion, without the need for any custom code.

Event routing helps most applications remain oblivious to details of the visual tree (which is good for restyling) and is crucial to the success of WPF's element composition. For example, `Button` exposes a `Click` event based on handling lower-level `MouseLeftButtonDown` and `KeyDown` events. When a user presses the left mouse button with the mouse pointer over a standard `Button`, however, he or she is really interacting with its `ButtonChrome` or `TextBlock` visual child. Because the event travels up the *visual* tree, the `Button` eventually sees the event and can handle it. Similarly, for the media-player-style Stop Button in Chapter 2, "XAML Demystified," a user might press the left mouse button directly over the Rectangle logical child. Because the event travels up the *logical* tree, the Button still sees the event and can handle it as well. (Yet if you really wish to distinguish between an event on the Rectangle and the outer Button, you have the freedom to do so.)

Therefore, you can embed arbitrarily complex content inside an element such as a Button or give it an arbitrarily complex visual tree (using the techniques in Chapter 14, "Styles, Templates, Skins, and Themes"), and a mouse left-click on any of the internal elements still results in a Click event raised by the parent Button. Without routed events, producers of the inner content or consumers of the Button would have to write code to patch everything together.

The implementation and behavior of routed events have many parallels to dependency properties. As with the dependency property discussion, we'll first look at how a simple routed event is implemented to make things more concrete. Then we'll examine some of the features of routed events and apply them to the About dialog from Chapter 3.

A Routed Event Implementation

In most cases, routed events don't look very different from normal .NET events. As with dependency properties, no .NET languages (other than XAML) have an intrinsic understanding of the *routed* designation. The extra support is based on a handful of WPF APIs.

Listing 6.1 demonstrates how Button effectively implements its Click routed event. (Click is actually implemented by Button's base class, but that's not important for this discussion.)

Just as dependency properties are represented as public static DependencyProperty fields with a conventional Property suffix, routed events are represented as public static RoutedEvent fields with a conventional Event suffix. The routed event is registered much like a dependency property in the static constructor, and a normal .NET event—or *event wrapper*—is defined to enable more familiar use from procedural code and adding a handler in XAML with event attribute syntax. As with a property wrapper, an event wrapper must not do anything in its accessors other than call AddHandler and RemoveHandler.

LISTING 6.1 A Standard Routed Event Implementation

```
public class Button : ButtonBase
{
  // The routed event
  public static readonly RoutedEvent ClickEvent;

  static Button()
  {
    // Register the event
    Button.ClickEvent = EventManager.RegisterRoutedEvent("Click",
```

LISTING 6.1 Continued

```
      RoutingStrategy.Bubble, typeof(RoutedEventHandler), typeof(Button));
    …
  }

  // A .NET event wrapper (optional)
  public event RoutedEventHandler Click
  {
    add { AddHandler(Button.ClickEvent, value); }
    remove { RemoveHandler(Button.ClickEvent, value); }
  }

  protected override void OnMouseLeftButtonDown(MouseButtonEventArgs e)
  {
    …
    // Raise the event
    RaiseEvent(new RoutedEventArgs(Button.ClickEvent, this));
    …
  }
  …
}
```


These `AddHandler` and `RemoveHandler` methods are not inherited from `DependencyObject` but rather `UIElement`. These methods attach and remove a delegate to the appropriate routed event. Inside `OnMouseLeftButtonDown`, `RaiseEvent` (also defined on the base `UIElement` class) is called with the appropriate `RoutedEvent` field to raise the `Click` event. The current `Button` instance (`this`) is passed as the source element of the event. It's not shown in this listing, but `Button`'s `Click` event is also raised in response to a `KeyDown` event to support clicking with the spacebar or sometimes the Enter key.

Routing Strategies and Event Handlers

When registered, every routed event chooses one of three *routing strategies*—the way in which the event raising travels through the element tree. These strategies are exposed as values of a `RoutingStrategy` enumeration:

- **`Tunneling`**—The event is first raised on the root, then on each element down the tree until the source element is reached (or until a handler halts the tunneling by marking the event as handled).

- **`Bubbling`**—The event is first raised on the source element and then on each element up the tree until the root is reached (or until a handler halts the bubbling by marking the event as handled).

- **`Direct`**—The event is raised only on the source element. This is the same behavior as a plain .NET event, except that such events can still participate in mechanisms specific to routed events such as event triggers.

Handlers for routed events have a signature matching the pattern for general .NET event handlers: The first parameter is a `System.Object` typically named `sender`, and the second parameter (typically named `e`) is a class that derives from `System.EventArgs`. The `sender` parameter passed to a handler is always the element to which the handler was attached. The `e` parameter is (or derives from) an instance of `RoutedEventArgs`, a subclass of `EventArgs` that exposes four useful properties:

- **`Source`**—The element in the logical tree that originally raised the event.
- **`OriginalSource`**—The element in the visual tree that originally raised the event (for example, the `TextBlock` or `ButtonChrome` child of a standard `Button`).
- **`Handled`**—A Boolean that can be set to `true` to mark the event as handled. This is precisely what halts any tunneling or bubbling.
- **`RoutedEvent`**—The actual routed event object (such as `Button.ClickEvent`), which can be helpful for identifying the raised event when the same handler is used for multiple routed events.

The presence of both `Source` and `OriginalSource` enable you to work with the higher-level logical tree or the lower-level visual tree. This distinction applies only to physical events such as mouse events, however. For more abstract events that don't necessarily have a direct relationship with an element in the visual tree (for example, `Click` due to its keyboard support), the same object is passed for both `Source` and `OriginalSource`.

Routed Events in Action

The `UIElement` class defines many routed events for keyboard, mouse, multi-touch, and stylus input. Most of these are bubbling events, but many of them are paired with a tunneling event. Tunneling events can be easily identified because, by convention, they are named with a `Preview` prefix. These events, also by convention, are raised immediately before their bubbling counterpart. For example, `PreviewMouseMove` is a tunneling event raised before the `MouseMove` bubbling event.

The idea behind having a pair of events for various activities is to give elements a chance to effectively cancel or otherwise modify an event that's about to occur. By convention, WPF's built-in elements take action only in response to a bubbling event (when a bubbling and tunneling pair is defined), ensuring that the tunneling event lives up to its "preview" name. For example, imagine that you want to implement a `TextBox` that restricts its input to a certain pattern or regular expression (such as a phone number or zip code). If you handle `TextBox`'s `KeyDown` event, the best you can do is remove text that has already been displayed inside the `TextBox`. But if you handle `TextBox`'s `PreviewKeyDown` event instead, you can mark it as "handled" to not only stop the tunneling but also stop the bubbling `KeyDown` event from being raised. In this case, the `TextBox` will never receive the `KeyDown` notification, and the current character will not get displayed.

To demonstrate the use of a simple bubbling event, Listing 6.2 updates the original About dialog from Chapter 3 by attaching an event handler to `Window`'s `MouseRightButtonDown` event. Listing 6.3 contains the C# code-behind file with the event handler implementation.

LISTING 6.2 The About Dialog with an Event Handler on the Root Window

```
<Window xmlns="http://schemas.microsoft.com/winfx/2006/xaml/presentation"
  xmlns:x="http://schemas.microsoft.com/winfx/2006/xaml"
  x:Class="AboutDialog" MouseRightButtonDown="AboutDialog_MouseRightButtonDown"
  Title="About WPF 4 Unleashed" SizeToContent="WidthAndHeight"
  Background="OrangeRed">
  <StackPanel>
    <Label FontWeight="Bold" FontSize="20" Foreground="White">
      WPF 4 Unleashed
    </Label>
    <Label>© 2010 SAMS Publishing</Label>
    <Label>Installed Chapters:</Label>
    <ListBox>
      <ListBoxItem>Chapter 1</ListBoxItem>
      <ListBoxItem>Chapter 2</ListBoxItem>
    </ListBox>
    <StackPanel Orientation="Horizontal" HorizontalAlignment="Center">
      <Button MinWidth="75" Margin="10">Help</Button>
      <Button MinWidth="75" Margin="10">OK</Button>
    </StackPanel>
    <StatusBar>You have successfully registered this product.</StatusBar>
  </StackPanel>
</Window>
```

6

LISTING 6.3 The Code-Behind File for Listing 6.2

```
using System.Windows;
using System.Windows.Input;
using System.Windows.Media;
using System.Windows.Controls;

public partial class AboutDialog : Window
{
  public AboutDialog()
  {
    InitializeComponent();
  }

  void AboutDialog_MouseRightButtonDown(object sender, MouseButtonEventArgs e)
  {
    // Display information about this event
    this.Title = "Source = " + e.Source.GetType().Name + ", OriginalSource = " +
```

LISTING 6.3 Continued

```
      e.OriginalSource.GetType().Name + " @ " + e.Timestamp;

    // In this example, all possible sources derive from Control
    Control source = e.Source as Control;

    // Toggle the border on the source control
    if (source.BorderThickness != new Thickness(5))
    {
      source.BorderThickness = new Thickness(5);
      source.BorderBrush = Brushes.Black;
    }
    else
      source.BorderThickness = new Thickness(0);
  }
}
```

The `AboutDialog_MouseRightButtonDown` handler performs two actions whenever a right-click bubbles up to the `Window`: It prints information about the event to the `Window`'s title bar, and it adds (then subsequently removes) a thick black border around the specific element in the logical tree that was right-clicked. Figure 6.1 shows the result. Notice that right-clicking the `Label` reveals `Source` set to the `Label` but `OriginalSource` set to its `TextBlock` visual child.

FIGURE 6.1 The modified About dialog, after the first `Label` control is right-clicked.

If you run this example and right-click everything, you'll notice two interesting behaviors:

- `Window` never receives the `MouseRightButtonDown` event when you right-click on either `ListBoxItem`. That's because `ListBoxItem` internally handles this event as well as the `MouseLeftButtonDown` event (halting the bubbling) to implement item selection.
- `Window` receives the `MouseRightButtonDown` event when you right-click on a `Button`, but setting `Button`'s `Border` property has no visual effect. This is due to `Button`'s default visual tree, which was shown back in Figure 3.3. Unlike `Window`, `Label`, `ListBox`, `ListBoxItem`, and `StatusBar`, the visual tree for `Button` has no `Border` element.

DIGGING DEEPER

Halting a Routed Event Is an Illusion

Although setting the `RoutedEventArgs` parameter's `Handled` property to `true` in a routed event handler appears to stop the tunneling or bubbling, individual handlers further up or down the tree can opt to receive the events anyway! This can only be done from procedural code, using an overload of `AddHandler` that adds a Boolean `handledEventsToo` parameter.

For example, the event attribute could be removed from Listing 6.2 and replaced with the following `AddHandler` call in `AboutDialog`'s constructor:

```
public AboutDialog()
{
  InitializeComponent();
  this.AddHandler(Window.MouseRightButtonDownEvent,
    new MouseButtonEventHandler(AboutDialog_MouseRightButtonDown), true);
}
```

With `true` passed as a third parameter, `AboutDialog_MouseRightButtonDown` now receives events when you right-click a `ListBoxItem` and adds the black border!

You should avoid processing handled events whenever possible, because there is likely a reason the event is handled in the first place. Attaching a handler to the `Preview` version of an event is the preferred alternative.

The bottom line, however, is that the halting of tunneling or bubbling is really just an illusion. Tunneling and bubbling still continue when a routed event is marked as handled, but event handlers see only unhandled events by default.

6

Attached Events

The tunneling and bubbling of a routed event is natural when every element in the tree exposes that event. But WPF supports tunneling and bubbling of routed events through elements that don't even define that event! This is possible thanks to the notion of *attached events*.

Attached events operate much like attached properties (and their use with tunneling or bubbling is very similar to using attached properties with property value inheritance). Listing 6.4 changes the About dialog again by handing the bubbling `SelectionChanged` event raised by its `ListBox` and the bubbling `Click` event raised by both of its `Buttons` directly on the root `Window`. Because `Window` doesn't define its own `SelectionChanged` or `Click` events, the event attribute names must be prefixed with the class name defining these events. Listing 6.5 contains the corresponding code-behind file that implements the two event handlers. Both event handlers simply show a `MessageBox` with information about what just happened.

LISTING 6.4 The About Dialog with Two Attached Event Handlers on the Root Window

```
<Window xmlns="http://schemas.microsoft.com/winfx/2006/xaml/presentation"
  xmlns:x="http://schemas.microsoft.com/winfx/2006/xaml"
  x:Class="AboutDialog" ListBox.SelectionChanged="ListBox_SelectionChanged"
  Button.Click="Button_Click"
  Title="About WPF Unleashed" SizeToContent="WidthAndHeight"
  Background="OrangeRed">
  <StackPanel>
    <Label FontWeight="Bold" FontSize="20" Foreground="White">
      WPF 4 Unleashed
    </Label>
    <Label>© 2010 SAMS Publishing</Label>
    <Label>Installed Chapters:</Label>
    <ListBox>
      <ListBoxItem>Chapter 1</ListBoxItem>
      <ListBoxItem>Chapter 2</ListBoxItem>
    </ListBox>
    <StackPanel Orientation="Horizontal" HorizontalAlignment="Center">
      <Button MinWidth="75" Margin="10">Help</Button>
      <Button MinWidth="75" Margin="10">OK</Button>
    </StackPanel>
    <StatusBar>You have successfully registered this product.</StatusBar>
  </StackPanel>
</Window>
```

LISTING 6.5 The Code-Behind File for Listing 6.4

```
using System.Windows;
using System.Windows.Controls;

public partial class AboutDialog : Window
{
  public AboutDialog()
  {
    InitializeComponent();
  }

  void ListBox_SelectionChanged(object sender, SelectionChangedEventArgs e)
  {
    if (e.AddedItems.Count > 0)
      MessageBox.Show("You just selected " + e.AddedItems[0]);
  }

  void Button_Click(object sender, RoutedEventArgs e)
  {
```

LISTING 6.5 Continued

```
      MessageBox.Show("You just clicked " + e.Source);
  }
}
```

Every routed event can be used as an attached event. The attached event syntax used in Listing 6.4 is valid because the XAML compiler sees the `SelectionChanged` .NET event defined on `ListBox` and the `Click` .NET event defined on `Button`. At runtime, however, `AddHandler` is directly called to attach these two events to the `Window`. Therefore, the two event attributes are equivalent to placing the following code inside the `Window`'s constructor:

```
public AboutDialog()
{
  InitializeComponent();
  this.AddHandler(ListBox.SelectionChangedEvent,
    new SelectionChangedEventHandler(ListBox_SelectionChanged));
  this.AddHandler(Button.ClickEvent, new RoutedEventHandler(Button_Click));
}
```

DIGGING DEEPER

Consolidating Routed Event Handlers

Because of the rich information passed to routed events, you could handle every event that tunnels or bubbles with one top-level "megahandler" if you really wanted to. This handler could examine the `RoutedEvent` object to determine which event got raised, cast the `RoutedEventArgs` parameter to an appropriate subclass (such as `KeyEventArgs`, `MouseButtonEventArgs`, and so on), and go from there.

For example, Listing 6.5 could be changed to assign both `ListBox.SelectionChanged` and `Button.Click` to the same `GenericHandler` method, defined as follows:

```
void GenericHandler(object sender, RoutedEventArgs e)
{
  if (e.RoutedEvent == Button.ClickEvent)
  {
    MessageBox.Show("You just clicked " + e.Source);
  }
  else if (e.RoutedEvent == ListBox.SelectionChangedEvent)
  {
    SelectionChangedEventArgs sce = (SelectionChangedEventArgs)e;
    if (sce.AddedItems.Count > 0)
      MessageBox.Show("You just selected " + sce.AddedItems[0]);
  }
}
```

Continued

This is also made possible by the *delegate contravariance* feature in the .NET Framework, enabling a delegate to be used with a method whose signature uses a base class of an expected parameter (for example, RoutedEventArgs instead of SelectionChangedEventArgs). GenericHandler simply casts the RoutedEventArgs parameter when necessary to get the extra information specific to the SelectionChanged event.

Keyboard Events

The basic keyboard events supported by all UIElements are the bubbling KeyDown and KeyUp events and their tunneling counterparts, PreviewKeyDown and PreviewKeyUp. The EventArgs parameter passed to keyboard event handlers is a KeyEventArgs that contains a number of properties, such as the following:

- **Key, ImeProcessedKey, DeadCharProcessedKey, and SystemKey**—Four properties of type Key, a large enumeration of every possible key. The Key property identifies what key the event is about. If the key is or will be processed by an Input Method Editor (IME), you can check the value of ImeProcessedKey. If the key is part of a *dead key composition*, the value of Key will be DeadCharProcessed, with the actual key revealed by the DeadCharProcessedKey property. When a *system key* is pressed, such as Alt, the value of Key will be System, with the key pressed with it revealed by the SystemKey property.
- **IsUp, IsDown, and IsToggled**—Boolean properties that reveal more information about the key event, although in some cases this information is redundant. (If you're handling a KeyDown event, you know the key is down!) IsToggled pertains to keys with toggle states, such as Caps Lock and Scroll Lock.
- **KeyStates**—A property of type KeyStates, a bit-flags enumeration whose value is the combination of None, Down, or Toggled. These values map to IsUp, IsDown, and IsToggled, respectively. Because Toggled will sometimes be combined with Down, you need to be careful not to check the value of KeyStates with a simple equality expression. It's easiest just to use the Is*XXX* methods instead.
- **IsRepeat**—A Boolean property that is true when the key is being repeated. This is the case of holding down the spacebar, for example, and getting a flurry of KeyDown events. IsRepeat would be true for all but the first KeyDown event.
- **KeyboardDevice**—A property of type KeyboardDevice that enables you to interact with the keyboard in more depth, such as asking about what keys are down or requesting focus to be moved to a specific element.

TIP

The static System.Windows.Input.Keyboard class and its PrimaryDevice property (of type KeyboardDevice) can be used to obtain information about the keyboard at any time, not just inside keyboard event handlers.

One important reason to access KeyboardDevice is for its Modifiers property of type ModifierKeys, another enumeration. It reveals whether certain keys are pressed in combination with the primary key. Its values are None, Alt, Control, Shift, and Windows. This is a bit-flags enumeration, so you won't want to check for equality unless you care about the state of every modifier key. For example, the following code checks whether Alt and A are being pressed but doesn't rule out Alt+Shift+A or Alt+Ctrl+A, and so on:

```
protected override void OnKeyDown(KeyEventArgs e)
{
  if ((e.KeyboardDevice.Modifiers & ModifierKeys.Alt) == ModifierKeys.Alt
      && (e.Key == Key.A || e.SystemKey == Key.A))
  {
    // Alt+A has been pressed, potentially also with Ctrl, Shift, and/or Windows
  }
  base.OnKeyDown(e);
}
```

On the other hand, the following code checks for Alt+A and nothing else:

```
protected override void OnKeyDown(KeyEventArgs e)
{
  if (e.KeyboardDevice.Modifiers == ModifierKeys.Alt
      && (e.Key == Key.A || e.SystemKey == Key.A))
  {
    // Alt+A and only Alt+A has been pressed
  }
  base.OnKeyDown(e);
}
```

FAQ

How do I find out whether the left or right Alt, Ctrl, or Shift key was pressed?

The Key enumeration has separate values for LeftAlt versus RightAlt, LeftCtrl versus RightCtrl, and LeftShift versus RightShift. However, because the Alt key is usually the "system key," it can show up as System, hiding which Alt key was actually pressed. Fortunately, you can use KeyboardDevice's IsKeyDown method (or IsKeyUp or IsKeyToggled) to ask about specific keys, such as LeftAlt or RightAlt. For example, the following code checks specifically for LeftAlt+A being pressed:

```
protected override void OnKeyDown(KeyEventArgs e)
{
  if (e.KeyboardDevice.Modifiers == ModifierKeys.Alt
      && (e.Key == Key.A || e.SystemKey == Key.A)
      && e.KeyboardDevice.IsKeyDown(Key.LeftAlt))
  {
```

Continued

```
    // LeftAlt+A has been pressed
  }
  base.OnKeyDown(e);
}
```

These keyboard events can get a little bit complicated in certain scenarios, but usually the most difficulty anybody has with keyboard handling revolves around keyboard *focus*. (This is further complicated when interoperating with non-WPF technologies, covered in Chapter 19, "Interoperability with Non-WPF Technologies.") A `UIElement` receives keyboard events only if it has keyboard focus. You can control whether an element is eligible for focus by setting its Boolean `Focusable` property, which is `true` by default. A `FocusableChanged` event is raised whenever its value changes.

`UIElements` define many more properties and events related to keyboard focus. The relevant properties are `IsKeyboardFocused`, which reports whether the current element has keyboard focus, and `IsKeyboardFocusWithin`, which reports the same thing but for the current element and any child elements. (These properties are read-only; to attempt to set keyboard focus, you can call the `Focus` or `MoveFocus` methods.) The events that report changes in these properties are `IsKeyboardFocusedChanged`, `IsKeyboardFocusWithinChanged`, `GotKeyboardFocus`, `LostKeyboardFocus`, `PreviewGotKeyboardFocus`, and `PreviewLostKeyboardFocus`.

Mouse Events

All `UIElements` support the following basic mouse events:

- `MouseEnter` and `MouseLeave`
- `MouseMove` and `PreviewMouseMove`
- `MouseLeftButtonDown`, `MouseRightButtonDown`, `MouseLeftButtonUp`, `MouseRightButtonUp`, and the more generic `MouseDown` and `MouseUp`, as well as the `Preview`*`XXX`* versions of all six of these events
- `MouseWheel` and `PreviewMouseWheel`

The `MouseEnter` and `MouseLeave` events can be used to create "rollover" effects, although the preferred approach is to use a trigger with the `IsMouseOver` property.

FAQ

Where is the event for handling the pressing of a mouse's middle button?

This information can be retrieved via the generic `MouseDown` and `MouseUp` events (or their `Preview` counterparts). The `EventArgs` object passed to such event handlers include properties that reveal which of the following buttons have been pressed or released: `LeftButton`, `RightButton`, `MiddleButton`, `XButton1`, or `XButton2`.

UIElements also have an IsMouseDirectlyOver property (and corresponding IsMouseDirectlyOverChanged event) that exclude child elements, for advanced scenarios in which you know exactly what visual tree you are working with.

TIP

If you don't want an element to raise any mouse events (or block mouse events underneath), you can set its IsHitTestVisible property to false.

WARNING

Transparent regions raise mouse events, but null regions do not!

Although you can count on IsHitTestVisible suppressing mouse events when set to false, the conditions for raising mouse events in the first place are a bit subtle. Setting an element's Visibility to Collapsed suppresses its mouse events, whereas setting an element's Opacity to 0 does not affect its event-related behavior. One more subtlety is that areas with a null Background, Fill, or Stroke produce areas that don't raise mouse events. However, explicitly setting the Background, Fill, or Stroke to Transparent (or any other color) produces areas that *do* raise mouse events. (A null brush looks like a Transparent brush but differs in its hit-testability.)

MouseEventArgs

The handlers for all of the previously mentioned mouse events (other than IsMouseDirectlyOverChanged) are passed an instance of MouseEventArgs. This object exposes five properties of type MouseButtonState that provide information about each potential mouse button: LeftButton, RightButton, MiddleButton, XButton1, and XButton2. MouseButtonState is an enumeration whose values are Pressed and Released. It also defines a GetPosition function that returns a Point with X and Y properties, revealing the exact coordinates of the mouse pointer.

GetPosition is a function rather than a simple property because it enables you to get the mouse pointer position in more than one way. You can get the position relative to the top-left corner of the screen, or you can get the position relative to the top-left corner of any rendered UIElement. To get the screen-relative position, you can pass null as the single parameter to GetPosition. To get an element-relative position, you pass the desired element as the parameter.

Handlers for MouseWheel and PreviewMouseWheel are given an instance of Mouse**Wheel**EventArgs, which derives from MouseEventArgs and adds an integer Delta property that indicates how much the wheel has moved since the last event. Handlers for the 12 events in the MouseUp/MouseDown family are given an instance of Mouse**Button**EventArgs, another subclass of MouseEventArgs. MouseButtonEventArgs adds a ChangedButton property that tells exactly which button changed (a value from the MouseButton enumeration), a ButtonState property that tells whether ChangedButton was pressed or released, and a ClickCount property.

ClickCount reveals the number of consecutive clicks of the relevant mouse button, where the time between each click is less than or equal to the system's double-click speed (configurable in Control Panel). The same way Button raises a Click event by handling MouseLeftButtonDown, its base Control class raises a MouseDoubleClick event by checking for a ClickCount of 2 inside MouseLeftButtonDown and raises a PreviewMouseDoubleClick event by doing the same thing inside PreviewMouseLeftButtonDown. With this support, you could easily react to other gestures, such as a triple-click, double-middle-button-click, and so on.

WARNING

Canvas raises its own mouse events only within the area defined by its Width and Height!

It's easy to forget that Canvas has a Width and Height of 0 by default because its children get rendered outside the Canvas's bounds. But mouse events for Canvas itself (ignoring events bubbled up from any children) get raised only within the bounding box defined by its Width and Height (and only then when it has a non-null Background). Therefore, by default, Canvas-level mouse events are raised only for its children.

Drag and Drop

UIElements expose events for working with drag-and-drop:

- DragEnter, DragOver, DragLeave, with PreviewDragEnter, PreviewDragOver, and PreviewDragLeave
- Drop and PreviewDrop
- QueryContinueDrag and PreviewQueryContinueDrag

This is Win32-style dragging and dropping of clipboard content to/from elements, *not* dragging/dropping of elements themselves. Elements can opt in to participating in drag-and-drop by setting their AllowDrop property to true.

The first two sets of events give their handlers an instance of DragEventArgs, which contains the following:

- **GetPosition**—The same method exposed by MouseEventArgs
- **Data**—A property of type IDataObject that represents the Win32 clipboard object being dragged or dropped
- **Effects** and **AllowedEffects**— Bit-flags DragDropEffects enumeration values that can be any combination of Copy, Move, Link, Scroll, All, or None
- **KeyStates**—Another bit-flags enumeration (DragDropKeyStates) that reveals which of the following are pressed during the drag or drop: LeftMouseButton, RightMouseButton, MiddleMouseButton, ShiftKey, ControlKey, AltKey, or None

The QueryContinueDrag and PreviewQueryContinueDrag events are raised when the keyboard state or the state of a mouse button has changed during a drag. They allow handlers to easily cancel the whole operation. Their handlers are given an instance of QueryContinueDragEventArgs, which contains the following:

- **KeyStates**—The same property that DragEventArgs exposes
- **EscapePressed**—A separate Boolean property that tells whether the Esc key has been pressed
- **Action**—A property that handlers can set to determine the fate of the drag-and-drop operation; it can be set to a value from the DragAction enumeration: Continue, Drop, or Cancel

TIP

The static System.Windows.Input.Mouse class can be used to obtain information about the mouse at *almost* any time, not just inside mouse event handlers. What you can't do is get the correct position of the mouse from the static Mouse.GetPosition during drag-and-drop. Instead, you must either call GetPosition from the DragEventArgs instance passed to the relevant event handler or, if you must do this outside the context of an event handler, make a PInvoke call to the GetCursorPos Win32 API, which will give you the correct location.

Capturing the Mouse

Suppose you wanted to support dragging and dropping of UIElements rather than clipboard objects. It's easy to imagine using the MouseLeftButtonDown, MouseMove, and MouseLeftButtonUp events to implement drag-and-drop. You could start a drag action by setting a Boolean variable inside an element's MouseLeftButtonDown handler, move the element to remain under the mouse pointer if the Boolean is true inside its MouseMove handler, and then clear the Boolean inside its MouseLeftButtonUp event to end the dragging. It turns out that this simple scheme isn't quite good enough, however, because it's easy to move the mouse too fast or under another element, causing the mouse pointer to separate from the element you're trying to drag.

Fortunately, WPF enables any UIElement to *capture* and *release* the mouse at any time. When an element captures the mouse, it receives all mouse events, even if the mouse pointer is not within its bounds. When an element releases the mouse, the event behavior returns to normal. Capture and release can be done with two functions defined on UIElements—CaptureMouse and ReleaseMouseCapture. (And of course, there are a number of corresponding properties and events that reveal the state of mouse capture. The properties are IsMouseCaptured and IsMouseCaptureWithin, and the events are GotMouseCapture, LostMouseCapture, IsMouseCaptureChanged, and IsMouseCaptureWithinChanged.)

Therefore, for a drag-and-drop implementation, you should capture the mouse inside MouseLeftButtonDown and release it inside MouseLeftButtonUp. The only tricky thing, then, is deciding the best way to actually move the element inside MouseMove. The best approach depends on the layout being used in the application, but this likely involves applying a `RenderTransform` or `LayoutTransform` to the element being dragged.

Stylus Events

WPF has special support for a pen digitizer, also known as a stylus, found on devices such as a Tablet PC. (This is sometimes referred to as "ink" support.) If you don't add any special support for a stylus in your application, it appears to act just like a mouse, raising all the relevant mouse events, such as `MouseDown`, `MouseMove`, and `MouseUp`. This behavior is essential for a stylus to be usable with programs that aren't designed specifically for a Tablet PC.

However, if you want to provide an experience that is *optimized* for a stylus, you can interact with an instance of `System.Windows.Input.StylusDevice`. There are three ways to get an instance of `StylusDevice`:

- You can use a `StylusDevice` property on `MouseEventArgs` to get an instance inside mouse event handlers. (This property will be `null` if there is no stylus.)
- You can use the static `System.Windows.Input.Stylus` class and its `CurrentStylusDevice` property to interact with the stylus at any time. (This will also be `null` if there is no stylus.)
- You can handle a number of events specific to the stylus.

This support also applies to devices with a *touch digitizer* rather than a pen digitizer.

FAQ

I can already get stylus data by pretending it is a mouse, so what good is the stylus-specific information?

A pen digitizer or touch digitizer can give you two things that a normal mouse cannot (ignoring multi-touch, which is covered in the next section): pressure sensitivity and higher resolution. For a handwriting or drawing application, both of these things can make the writing or drawing much more natural than the result you would get with a mouse. A stylus can also do more "tricks" than a mouse, as evidenced by some of the properties and events discussed in this section. In addition, because multiple styluses can be detected at the same time, this support provides a way to write multi-touch-capable code with only WPF 3.5 SP1 on Windows 7.

`StylusDevice`

`StylusDevice` contains a number of properties, including the following:

- **`Inverted`**—A Boolean that reveals whether the stylus is being used as an eraser (with its back end against the screen).
- **`InAir`**—A Boolean that indicates whether the stylus is in contact with the screen, because on some devices its movement can still be registered as long as it is close enough.

- **StylusButtons**—A collection of StylusButton objects. Unlike with a mouse, there is no fixed list of possible buttons. Each StylusButton has a string Name and a Guid identifier, along with a StylusButtonState of Up or Down.
- **TabletDevice**—A property of type System.Windows.Input.TabletDevice that provides detailed information about the current hardware and which stylus capabilities it provides (such as pressure-sensitivity or in-air movement). Its Type property is Stylus for a pen digitizer or Touch for a touch digitizer.

StylusDevice has a GetPosition method that acts like the version for the mouse, but it also has a richer GetStylusPoints method that returns a collection of StylusPoint objects. Each StylusPoint object has properties such as the following:

- **X**—The horizontal coordinate of the stylus point relative to the passed-in element.
- **Y**—The vertical coordinate of the stylus point relative to the passed-in element.
- **PressureFactor**—A value between 0 and 1 that indicates how much pressure was applied to the stylus when the point was registered. The higher the value, the more pressure was applied, if the hardware supports pressure sensitivity. If pressure sensitivity is not supported, PressureFactor is set to 0.5.

The high resolution of a stylus explains why GetStylusPoints returns a *collection* of points (and pressures). In the time between two MouseMove events, for example, a lot of rich motion might have been detected and recorded.

Events

The stylus-specific events are as follows:

- StylusEnter and StylusLeave
- StylusMove and PreviewStylusMove
- StylusInAirMove and PreviewStylusInAirMove
- StylusDown, StylusUp, PreviewStylusDown, and PreviewStylusUp
- StylusButtonDown, StylusButtonUp, PreviewStylusButtonDown, and PreviewStylusButtonUp
- StylusSystemGesture and PreviewStylusSystemGesture
- StylusInRange, StylusOutOfRange, PreviewStylusInRange, and PreviewStylusOutOfRange
- GotStylusCapture and LostStylusCapture

The handlers for these events are given a StylusEventArgs instance that gives you access to the StylusDevice via a StylusDevice property. For convenience, it also defines InAir, Inverted, GetPosition, and GetStylusPoints members that wrap the same members from the StylusDevice.

Some handlers are given a `StylusEventArgs` subclass:

- **`StylusDownEventArgs`**—`StylusDown` and `PreviewStylusDown` are given a `StylusDownEventArgs` instance, which adds an integer `TapCount` property that is analogous to `ClickCount` for mouse events.
- **`StylusButtonEventArgs`**—`StylusButtonDown`, `StylusButtonUp`, and the corresponding `Preview` events are given a `StylusButtonEventArgs` instance, which adds a `StylusButton` property set to the relevant button.
- **`StylusSystemGestureEventArgs`**—`StylusSystemGesture` and `PreviewStylusSystemGesture` are given a `StylusSystemGestureEventArgs` instance, which adds a `SystemGesture` property set to one of the values from the `SystemGesture` enumeration: `Tap`, `RightTap`, `TwoFingerTap`, `Drag`, `RightDrag`, `Flick`, `HoldEnter`, `HoldLeave`, `HoverEnter`, `HoverLeave`, or `None`.

TIP

WPF defines a `Stroke` object that can be used to visually represent the information in a collection of `StylusPoints`, and an `InkPresenter` element that holds a collection of `Strokes`. For many drawing and handwriting scenarios, you could alternatively use the `InkCanvas` element, described in Chapter 11, "Images, Text, and Other Controls," that internally uses an `InkPresenter`. `InkCanvas` has built-in support for exploiting a stylus, if one is present, and collecting/displaying strokes. With this, you don't need to handle any `Stylus` events yourself!

Multi-Touch Events

When running on Windows 7 or later with hardware that supports multi-touch, you can take advantage of rich events introduced in WPF 4. These events can be separated into two categories—basic touch events and higher-level manipulation events.

Although multi-touch events, like stylus events, are exposed as mouse events, the reverse is not true. You cannot receive single-point touch events from the mouse, as if it were a finger on a touch device, without doing extra work to simulate a touch device.

TIP

If you want to simulate multi-touch (or even single-touch) on a "normal" computer, you can leverage the MultiPoint Mouse SDK (http://microsoft.com/multipoint/mouse-sdk), which enables up to 25 mice to be used simultaneously on the same computer! But that's not enough; you need to expose MultiPoint's functionality as a custom *touch device* by using the techniques described at http://blogs.msdn.com/ansont/archive/2010/01/30/custom-touch-devices.aspx.

Basic Touch Events

The basic touch events look and act a lot like mouse events:

- `TouchEnter` and `TouchLeave`
- `TouchMove` and `PreviewTouchMove`
- `TouchDown`, `TouchUp`, `PreviewTouchDown` and `PreviewTouchUp`
- `GotTouchCapture` and `LostTouchCapture`

When multiple fingers are touching simultaneously, these events get raised for each finger independently. Equivalent mouse events get raised as well for the *first* finger, thanks to the stylus support described earlier.

Handlers for the touch events are given an instance of `TouchEventArgs`, which contains the following:

- **`GetTouchPoint`**—A method that returns a `TouchPoint` instance relative to the passed-in element. This is analogous to the `GetPosition` method for mouse events.
- **`GetIntermediateTouchPoints`**—A method that returns a collection of `TouchPoint` instances relative to the passed-in element that got accumulated between the current and previous touch events. This is analogous to the `GetStylusPoints` method for stylus events.
- **`TouchDevice`**—A property that returns an instance of `TouchDevice`.

`TouchPoint` has not only a `Position` property but a `Size` property that reveals how much of the finger is in contact with the screen and a `Bounds` property that gives the exact contact area. It also exposes information that you already know in the context of one of these event handlers but can be handy at other times: the `TouchDevice` and an `Action` whose value can be `Down`, `Move`, or `Up` (from the `TouchAction` enumeration).

Each finger press is associated with its own `TouchDevice`, identified by an integer `Id` property. You can use this `Id` (or the `TouchDevice` instance itself) to keep track of which finger is which when handling events.

Listing 6.6 leverages `TouchDown`, `TouchMove`, and `TouchUp` to show fingerprint clipart images (not actual fingerprints!) whenever and wherever a finger is in contact with the screen. It is the code-behind file for the following simple `Window` that contains a `Canvas` named `canvas`:

```
<Window x:Class="TouchEvents.MainWindow"
        xmlns="http://schemas.microsoft.com/winfx/2006/xaml/presentation"
        xmlns:x="http://schemas.microsoft.com/winfx/2006/xaml"
        Title="Touch Events">
  <Canvas Name="canvas">
  <Canvas.Background>
    <LinearGradientBrush>
```

```
        <GradientStop Color="Black"/>
        <GradientStop Color="Red" Offset="1"/>
      </LinearGradientBrush>
    </Canvas.Background>
    </Canvas>
</Window>
```

The result is shown in Figure 6.2.

LISTING 6.6 MainWindow.xaml.cs—Handling TouchDown, TouchMove, and TouchUp

```
using System;
using System.Collections.Generic;
using System.Windows;
using System.Windows.Controls;
using System.Windows.Input;
using System.Windows.Media;
using System.Windows.Media.Imaging;

namespace TouchEvents
{
  public partial class MainWindow : Window
  {
    // Keep track of which images are used for which TouchDevices
    Dictionary<TouchDevice, Image> fingerprints =
      new Dictionary<TouchDevice, Image>();


    public MainWindow()
    {
      InitializeComponent();
    }

    protected override void OnTouchDown(TouchEventArgs e)
    {
      base.OnTouchDown(e);

      // Capture this touch device
      canvas.CaptureTouch(e.TouchDevice);

      // Create a new image for this new touch
      Image fingerprint = new Image { Source = new BitmapImage(
        new Uri("pack://application:,,,/fingerprint.png")) };

      // Move the image to the touch point
      TouchPoint point = e.GetTouchPoint(canvas);
```

LISTING 6.6 Continued

```
      fingerprint.RenderTransform = new TranslateTransform(
        point.Position.X, point.Position.Y);

      // Keep track of the image and add it to the canvas
      fingerprints[e.TouchDevice] = fingerprint;
      canvas.Children.Add(fingerprint);
    }

    protected override void OnTouchMove(TouchEventArgs e)
    {
      base.OnTouchMove(e);

      if (e.TouchDevice.Captured == canvas)
      {
        // Retrieve the right image
        Image fingerprint = fingerprints[e.TouchDevice];
        TranslateTransform transform =
          fingerprint.RenderTransform as TranslateTransform;

        // Move it to the new location
        TouchPoint point = e.GetTouchPoint(canvas);
        transform.X = point.Position.X;
        transform.Y = point.Position.Y;
      }
    }

    protected override void OnTouchUp(TouchEventArgs e)
    {
      base.OnTouchUp(e);

      // Release capture
      canvas.ReleaseTouchCapture(e.TouchDevice);

      // Remove the image from the canvas and the dictionary
      canvas.Children.Remove(fingerprints[e.TouchDevice]);
      fingerprints.Remove(e.TouchDevice);
    }
  }
}
```

This scheme works very much like dragging and dropping elements, as described in the "Mouse Events" section, except that the element is created on `TouchDown` and removed on `TouchUp`. Rather than attaching event handlers directly to the three events, this listing overrides the corresponding On*XXX* methods on Window.

In OnTouchDown, the code captures the touch device to make the dragging operation work reliably. Unlike with the keyboard, mouse, or stylus, a single element can capture multiple touch devices. In this case, the same Canvas captures each device. The Image is created from an embedded resource using syntax covered in Chapter 12, "Resources," placed appropriately using a TranslateTransform, then added to the Canvas and a dictionary used by the other events. In this dictionary, the TouchDevice itself is used as the key.

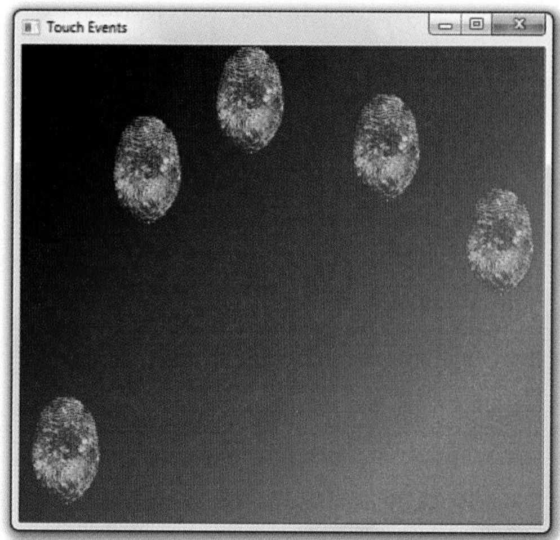

FIGURE 6.2 Pressing five fingers on the screen shows five fingerprint images at the right locations.

OnTouchMove retrieves the appropriate Image for the current TouchDevice and then moves it to the current TouchPoint. It makes sure that the event belongs to one of the TouchDevices captured by the Canvas. OnTouchUp releases touch capture then removes the Image from the Canvas and the dictionary.

How well this sample runs depends on your hardware. My multi-touch netbook supports only two simultaneous touch points, so I can't get any more than two fingerprints to appear at once.

TIP

As of version 4, Silverlight does not have any of these touch events. If you want to write multi-touch code that works with both WPF and Silverlight, you can use a lower-level FrameReported event supported by both. FrameReported is defined on a static System.Windows.Input.Touch class and reports TouchPoints for the entire application. This is not a routed event; you're responsible for doing hit-testing and figuring out which elements are being touched.

Manipulation Events for Panning, Rotating, and Zooming

Often, people want to leverage multi-touch for panning, rotating, and zooming elements. These actions are straightforward, as these concepts map exactly to applying a TranslateTransform, RotateTransform, and/or ScaleTransform. Detecting *when* you should apply these transforms and with *what values* is an entirely different story.

The one-finger swipe typically used for panning is a relatively simple gesture to detect, but trying to figure out if the user performed the two-finger rotation or zoom gesture would be difficult with the previously discussed events. Furthermore, the lack of consistency that would result in developers performing their own gesture recognition would result in frustrating user interfaces.

Fortunately, WPF provides higher-level *manipulation* events that make it easy to support panning, rotating, and zooming. These are the main manipulation events:

- `ManipulationStarting` and `ManipulationStarted`
- `ManipulationDelta`
- `ManipulationCompleted`

These events combine the information from independent touch devices updating simultaneously and package the data in an easy-to-consume form. For an element to receive these events, the `IsManipulationEnabled` property must be set to `true` on itself or a parent, and the relevant basic touch events must be left unhandled.

Using Manipulation Events

`ManipulationStarting`, followed by `ManipulationStarted`, gets raised when `TouchDown` happens for the first finger. `ManipulationDelta` gets raised for each `TouchMove`, and `ManipulationCompleted` gets raised after `TouchUp` is raised for *all* fingers. `ManipulationStarting` and `ManipulationStarted` give you the opportunity to customize aspects of the manipulation, restrict which manipulations are allowed, or cancel it.

The `ManipulationDelta` event gives you rich information about how the element is expected to be translated/rotated/scaled that can be applied directly to the relevant transforms. It gives you this data in a `ManipulationDelta` class that has the following properties:

- **`Translation`**—A `Vector` property with `X` and `Y` values
- **`Scale`**—Another `Vector` property
- **`Rotation`**—A `double` property that specifies the angle in degrees
- **`Expansion`**—A `Vector` property that is redundant with `Scale` but reports the size difference in terms of absolute device-independent pixels rather than in terms of a multiplier

Furthermore, the `ManipulationDeltaEventArgs` instance passed to handlers of the `ManipulationDelta` event has *two* properties of type `ManipulationDelta`—`DeltaManipulation`, which reports the changes compared to the last time the event was raised, and `CumulativeManipulation`, which reports the changes compared to when `ManipulationStarted` was raised. So no matter how you prefer to consume the data, there should be a way that pleases you!

Listing 6.7 contains the code-behind file for the following `Window`, making it possible to move, rotate, and zoom the contained photo with standard swipe, spin, and pinch gestures:

```
<Window x:Class="ManipulationEvents.MainWindow"
        xmlns="http://schemas.microsoft.com/winfx/2006/xaml/presentation"
        xmlns:x="http://schemas.microsoft.com/winfx/2006/xaml"
        Title="Manipulation Events">
  <Canvas Name="canvas" IsManipulationEnabled="True">
    <Image Name="photo" Source="photo.jpg">
    <Image.RenderTransform>
      <MatrixTransform/>
    </Image.RenderTransform>
    </Image>
  </Canvas>
</Window>
```

The result is shown in Figure 6.3.

LISTING 6.7 `MainWindow.xaml.cs`—Handling `ManipulationDelta` to Enable Panning, Rotating, and Zooming

```
using System;
using System.Windows;
using System.Windows.Input;
using System.Windows.Media;

namespace ManipulationEvents
{
  public partial class MainWindow : Window
  {
    public MainWindow()
    {
      InitializeComponent();
      canvas.ManipulationDelta += Canvas_ManipulationDelta;
    }

    void Canvas_ManipulationDelta(object sender, ManipulationDeltaEventArgs e)
    {
      MatrixTransform transform = photo.RenderTransform as MatrixTransform;
      if (transform != null)
      {
        // Apply any deltas to the matrix,
        // then apply the new Matrix as the MatrixTransform data:
        Matrix matrix = transform.Matrix;
        matrix.Translate(e.DeltaManipulation.Translation.X,
                         e.DeltaManipulation.Translation.Y);
```

LISTING 6.7 Continued

```
                matrix.RotateAt(e.DeltaManipulation.Rotation,
                                e.ManipulationOrigin.X, e.ManipulationOrigin.Y);
                matrix.ScaleAt(e.DeltaManipulation.Scale.X, e.DeltaManipulation.Scale.Y,
                               e.ManipulationOrigin.X, e.ManipulationOrigin.Y);
                transform.Matrix = matrix;
                e.Handled = true;
            }
        }
    }
}
```

The Image named photo conveniently has a MatrixTransform applied as its RenderTransform, so all the code inside the ManipulationDelta handler needs to do is update the transform's Matrix with data from the ManipulationDeltaEventArgs instance. The RotateAt and ScaleAt methods are used so the proper origin of rotation and scaling can be applied (e.ManipulationOrigin).

FIGURE 6.3 Enabling panning, rotating, and zooming on an Image by handling the ManipulationDelta event.

Manipulations are always done relative to a *manipulation container*. By default, this is the element marked with IsManipulationEnabled=True, which is why the XAML for this example sets it on the Canvas rather than the Image. You can set any element as the manipulation container by handling the ManipulationStarting event and setting ManipulationStartingEventArgs.ManipulationContainer to the element.

Adding Inertia

Manipulation events include support for giving objects inertia, so they can gradually slow to a stop when a gesture is done rather than stopping instantly. This makes the gestures feel more realistic and make it easy to support things like "flicking" an object to make it move a distance based on the speed of the flick.

To enable inertia, you can handle the ManipulationInertiaStarting event in addition to any other manipulation events. ManipulationInertiaStarting—not ManipulationCompleted—is actually the first manipulation event raised after all fingers lose contact with the screen. In the handler for ManipulationInertiaStarting, you can opt in to the support by setting properties on ManipulationInertiaStartingEventArgs.TranslationBehavior, ManipulationInertiaStartingEventArgs.RotationBehavior, and/or ManipulationInertiaStartingEventArgs.ExpansionBehavior. This causes the ManipulationDelta event to continue getting raised (with ManipulationDeltaEventArgs.IsInertial set to true) until friction causes it to stop, at which point

ManipulationCompleted is raised. (If you do nothing inside the ManipulationInertiaStarting event, ManipulationCompleted will get raised right after.)

Here are the properties you can set to enable inertia on position, rotation, and/or scale:

- **TranslationBehavior**—DesiredDisplacement, DesiredDeceleration, and InitialVelocity
- **RotationBehavior**—DesiredRotation, DesiredDeceleration, and InitialVelocity
- **ExpansionBehavior**—DesiredExpansion, DesiredDeceleration, InitialRadius, and InitialVelocity

Typically you only need to set DesiredDeceleration *or* the behavior-specific DesiredDisplacement, DesiredRotation, or DesiredExpansion. The latter properties are useful for ensuring that the element doesn't go too far. By default, InitialVelocity and InitialRadius are initialized with the current values to ensure a smooth transition. You can get the various velocities at the time of the ManipulationInertiaStarting event by checking ManipulationInertiaStartingEventArgs.InitialVelocities, which has LinearVelocity, AngularVelocity, and ExpansionVelocity properties.

Listing 6.8 updates Listing 6.7 with support for inertia.

LISTING 6.8 MainWindow.xaml.cs—Handling ManipulationDelta and ManipulationInertiaStarting to Enable Panning, Rotating, and Zooming with Inertia

```
using System;
using System.Windows;
using System.Windows.Input;
using System.Windows.Media;

namespace ManipulationEvents
{
  public partial class MainWindow : Window
  {
    public MainWindow()
    {
      InitializeComponent();
      canvas.ManipulationDelta += Canvas_ManipulationDelta;
      canvas.ManipulationInertiaStarting += Canvas_ManipulationInertiaStarting;
    }

    void Canvas_ManipulationInertiaStarting(object sender,
          ManipulationInertiaStartingEventArgs e)
    {
      e.TranslationBehavior.DesiredDeceleration = 0.01;
      e.RotationBehavior.DesiredDeceleration = 0.01;
      e.ExpansionBehavior.DesiredDeceleration = 0.01;
    }
```

LISTING 6.8 Continued

```
    void Canvas_ManipulationDelta(object sender, ManipulationDeltaEventArgs e)
    {
      MatrixTransform transform = photo.RenderTransform as MatrixTransform;
      if (transform != null)
      {
        // Apply any deltas to the matrix,
        // then apply the new Matrix as the MatrixTransform data:
        Matrix matrix = transform.Matrix;
        matrix.Translate(e.DeltaManipulation.Translation.X,
                         e.DeltaManipulation.Translation.Y);
        matrix.RotateAt(e.DeltaManipulation.Rotation,
                        e.ManipulationOrigin.X, e.ManipulationOrigin.Y);
        matrix.ScaleAt(e.DeltaManipulation.Scale.X, e.DeltaManipulation.Scale.Y,
                       e.ManipulationOrigin.X, e.ManipulationOrigin.Y);
        transform.Matrix = matrix;
        e.Handled = true;
      }
    }
  }
}
```


You need to be careful about elements getting moved completely offscreen, especially when inertia is involved. You can use the `ManipulationBoundaryFeedback` event to be notified when an element reaches the boundary of the manipulation container so that you can take steps to prevent its escape.

TIP

WPF provides an easy way to make your application's window bounce when something has been pushed past a boundary, similar to the scroll-past-the-end-of-a-list effect made popular by iPhone. Inside a `ManipulationDelta` event handler, you can call the `ReportBoundaryFeedback` method on the passed-in `ManipulationDeltaEventArgs` instance to make this happen. This raises the `ManipulationBoundaryFeedback` event, which is handled by WPF's `Window` in order to provide this effect.

FAQ

`ManipulationDeltaEventArgs` contains a `Complete` method and a `Cancel` method. What's the difference between them?

`Complete` halts the manipulation (both direct and inertial). `Cancel` also halts the manipulation, but it promotes the touch input data to mouse events, where some of the behavior can continue for elements that are mouse aware but not touch aware.

Listing 6.9 leverages rotation inertia to provide the "spin the prize wheel" user interface pictured in Figure 6.4. This listing is the code-behind file for the following `Window`:

```
<Window x:Class="SpinThePrizeWheel.MainWindow"
        xmlns="http://schemas.microsoft.com/winfx/2006/xaml/presentation"
        xmlns:x="http://schemas.microsoft.com/winfx/2006/xaml"
        Title="Spin the Prize Wheel">
<Window.Background>
  <LinearGradientBrush>
    <GradientStop Color="White"/>
    <GradientStop Color="Orange" Offset="1"/>
  </LinearGradientBrush>
</Window.Background>
  <Grid Name="grid" IsManipulationEnabled="True">
    <Image Name="prizeWheel" RenderTransformOrigin="0.5,0.5"
           Source="prizeWheel.png" Margin="0 30 0 0">
    <Image.RenderTransform>
      <RotateTransform/>
    </Image.RenderTransform>
    </Image>
    <Image Source="arrow.png" VerticalAlignment="Top" Stretch="None"/>
  </Grid>
</Window>
```

LISTING 6.9 `MainWindow.xaml.cs`—Implementation of a Spinning Prize Wheel with Inertia

```
using System;
using System.Windows;
using System.Windows.Input;
using System.Windows.Media;

namespace SpinThePrizeWheel
{
  public partial class MainWindow : Window
  {
    public MainWindow()
    {
      InitializeComponent();
      grid.ManipulationStarting        += Grid_ManipulationStarting;
      grid.ManipulationDelta           += Grid_ManipulationDelta;
      grid.ManipulationInertiaStarting += Grid_ManipulationInertiaStarting;
      grid.ManipulationCompleted       += Grid_ManipulationCompleted;
    }

    void Grid_ManipulationStarting(object sender,
                                   ManipulationStartingEventArgs e)
```

LISTING 6.9 Continued

```
    {
      e.Mode = ManipulationModes.Rotate; // Only allow rotation
    }

    void Grid_ManipulationDelta(object sender, ManipulationDeltaEventArgs e)
    {
      (prizeWheel.RenderTransform as RotateTransform).Angle +=
        e.DeltaManipulation.Rotation;
    }

    void Grid_ManipulationInertiaStarting(object sender,
                                          ManipulationInertiaStartingEventArgs e)
    {
      e.RotationBehavior.DesiredDeceleration = 0.001;
    }

    void Grid_ManipulationCompleted(object sender,
                                    ManipulationCompletedEventArgs e)
    {
      // Now that the wheel has stopped, tell the user what s/he won!
    }
  }
}
```


Listing 6.9 handles the `ManipulationStarting` event to tell the manipulation processing that it only cares about rotation. This is optional because it only pays attention to the rotation data inside the `ManipulationDelta` event handler, but it's good practice (and good for performance). The `ManipulationDelta` handler updates the `Image`'s `RotateTransform`, incrementing its `Angle` by `e.DeltaManipulation.Rotation`. Alternatively, it could just assign the value `e.CumulativeManipulation.Rotation` to the `Angle` property, but then any subsequent spins would cause the wheel to jump back to 0° at the beginning of the spin, which would be jarring and unnatural.

FIGURE 6.4 Rotation inertia enables the wheel to keep spinning after you let go, as on some game shows.

The handler for `ManipulationInertiaStarting` gives the wheel a very small deceleration, so it spins for a while after contact has ended. Finally, the handler for ManipulationCompleted is the perfect spot to determine the final state of the wheel and award the user a prize.

TIP

You can take advantage of panning support built into ScrollViewer by setting its PanningMode property to HorizontalOnly, VerticalOnly, HorizontalFirst, VerticalFirst, or Both. ScrollViewer also exposes PanningDeceleration and PanningRatio properties. The latter is used as a multiplier when applying the manipulation distance to the underlying TranslateTransform.

Although the default value for PanningMode is None, several WPF controls set their internal ScrollViewer to a different, appropriate value in their default styles to make them multi-touch aware without any explicit work for developers.

TIP

You can download the Surface Toolkit for Windows Touch to get numerous slick Microsoft Surface WPF controls that are optimized for multi-touch. This includes "surface versions" of most common controls (such as SurfaceButton and SurfaceCheckBox) and brand-new controls (such as ScatterView and LibraryStack).

Commands

Although this chapter focuses on events, it's important to be aware of WPF's built-in support for *commands*, a more abstract and loosely coupled version of events. Whereas events are tied to details about specific user actions (such as a Button being clicked or a ListBoxItem being selected), commands represent actions independent from their user interface exposure. Canonical examples of commands are Cut, Copy, and Paste. Applications often expose these actions through many mechanisms simultaneously: MenuItems in a Menu, MenuItems on a ContextMenu, Buttons on a ToolBar, keyboard shortcuts, and so on.

You could handle the multiple exposures of commands such as Cut, Copy, and Paste with events fairly well. For example, you could define a generic event handler for each of the three actions and then attach each handler to the appropriate events on the relevant elements (the Click event on a Button, the KeyDown event on the main Window, and so on). In addition, you'd probably want to enable and disable the appropriate controls whenever the corresponding actions are invalid (for example, disabling any user interface for Paste when there is nothing on the clipboard). This two-way communication gets a bit more cumbersome, especially if you don't want to hard-code a list of controls that need to be updated.

Fortunately, WPF's support for commands is designed to make such scenarios very easy. The support reduces the amount of code you need to write (and in some cases eliminates all procedural code), and it gives you more flexibility to change your user interface without breaking the underlying logic. Commands are not a new invention of WPF; older technologies such as the Microsoft Foundation Class Library (MFC) have a similar mechanism. Of course, even if you're familiar with MFC, you need to learn about the unique traits of commands in WPF.

Much of the power of commands comes from the following three features:

- WPF defines a number of built-in commands.
- Commands have automatic support for input gestures (such as keyboard shortcuts).
- Some of WPF's controls have built-in behavior tied to various commands.

Built-In Commands

A *command* is any object implementing the `ICommand` interface (from `System.Windows.Input`), which defines three simple members:

- **`Execute`**—The method that executes the command-specific logic
- **`CanExecute`**—A method that returns `true` if the command is enabled or `false` if it is disabled
- **`CanExecuteChanged`**—An event that is raised whenever the value of `CanExecute` changes

If you wanted to create `Cut`, `Copy`, and `Paste` commands, you could define and implement three classes implementing `ICommand`, find a place to store them (perhaps as static fields of the main `Window`), call `Execute` from relevant event handlers (when `CanExecute` returns `true`), and handle the `CanExecuteChanged` event to toggle the `IsEnabled` property on the relevant pieces of user interface. This doesn't sound much better than simply using events, however.

Fortunately, controls such as `Button`, `CheckBox`, and `MenuItem` have logic to interact with any command on your behalf. They expose a simple `Command` property (of type `ICommand`). When set, these controls automatically call the command's `Execute` method (when `CanExecute` returns `true`) whenever their `Click` event is raised. In addition, they automatically keep their value for `IsEnabled` synchronized with the value of `CanExecute` by leveraging the `CanExecuteChanged` event. By supporting all this via a simple property assignment, all this logic is available from XAML.

Even more fortunately, WPF defines a bunch of commands, so you don't have to implement `ICommand` objects for commands such as `Cut`, `Copy`, and `Paste` and worry about where to store them. WPF's built-in commands are exposed as static properties of five different classes:

- **`ApplicationCommands`**—`Close`, `Copy`, `Cut`, `Delete`, `Find`, `Help`, `New`, `Open`, `Paste`, `Print`, `PrintPreview`, `Properties`, `Redo`, `Replace`, `Save`, `SaveAs`, `SelectAll`, `Stop`, `Undo`, and more

- **ComponentCommands**—MoveDown, MoveLeft, MoveRight, MoveUp, ScrollByLine, ScrollPageDown, ScrollPageLeft, ScrollPageRight, ScrollPageUp, SelectToEnd, SelectToHome, SelectToPageDown, SelectToPageUp, and more
- **MediaCommands**—ChannelDown, ChannelUp, DecreaseVolume, FastForward, IncreaseVolume, MuteVolume, NextTrack, Pause, Play, PreviousTrack, Record, Rewind, Select, Stop, and more
- **NavigationCommands**—BrowseBack, BrowseForward, BrowseHome, BrowseStop, Favorites, FirstPage, GoToPage, LastPage, NextPage, PreviousPage, Refresh, Search, Zoom, and more
- **EditingCommands**—AlignCenter, AlignJustify, AlignLeft, AlignRight, CorrectSpellingError, DecreaseFontSize, DecreaseIndentation, EnterLineBreak, EnterParagraphBreak, IgnoreSpellingError, IncreaseFontSize, IncreaseIndentation, MoveDownByLine, MoveDownByPage, MoveDownByParagraph, MoveLeftByCharacter, MoveLeftByWord, MoveRightByCharacter, MoveRightByWord, and more

Each of these properties does not return a unique type implementing ICommand. Instead, they are all instances of RoutedUICommand, a class that not only implements ICommand but supports bubbling just like a routed event.

The About dialog revisited earlier in this chapter has a Help Button that currently does nothing, so let's demonstrate how these built-in commands work by attaching some logic with the Help command defined in ApplicationCommands. Assuming that the Button is named helpButton, you can associate it with the Help command in C# as follows:

```
helpButton.Command = ApplicationCommands.Help;
```

All RoutedUICommand objects define a Text property that contains a name for the command that's appropriate to show in a user interface. (This property is the only difference between RoutedUICommand and its base RoutedCommand class.) For example, the Help command's Text property is (unsurprisingly) set to the string Help. The hard-coded Content on this Button could therefore be replaced as follows:

```
helpButton.Content = ApplicationCommands.Help.Text;
```

TIP

The Text string defined by all RoutedUICommands is automatically localized into every language supported by WPF! This means that a Button whose Content is assigned to ApplicationCommands.Help.Text automatically displays "Ayuda" rather than "Help" when the thread's current user interface culture represents Spanish rather than English. Even in a context where you want to expose images rather than text (perhaps on a ToolBar), you can still leverage this localized string elsewhere, such as in a ToolTip.

Of course, you're still responsible for localizing any of your own strings that get displayed in your user interface. Leveraging Text on commands can simply cut down on the number of terms you need to translate.

If you were to run the About dialog with this change, you would see that the `Button` is now permanently disabled. That's because the built-in commands can't possibly know when they should be enabled or disabled, or even what action to take when they are executed. They delegate this logic to consumers of the commands.

To plug in custom logic, you need to add a `CommandBinding` to the element that will execute the command *or any parent element* (thanks to the bubbling behavior of routed commands). All classes deriving from `UIElement` (and `ContentElement`) contain a `CommandBindings` collection that can hold one or more `CommandBinding` objects. Therefore, you can add a `CommandBinding` for `Help` to the About dialog's root `Window` as follows in its code-behind file:

```
this.CommandBindings.Add(new CommandBinding(ApplicationCommands.Help,
  HelpExecuted, HelpCanExecute));
```

This assumes that methods called `HelpExecuted` and `HelpCanExecute` have been defined. These methods will be called back at appropriate times in order to plug in an implementation for the `Help` command's `CanExecute` and `Execute` methods.

Listings 6.10 and 6.11 change the About dialog again, binding the Help `Button` to the `Help` command entirely in XAML (although the two handlers must be defined in the code-behind file).

LISTING 6.10 The About Dialog Supporting the Help Command

```
<Window xmlns="http://schemas.microsoft.com/winfx/2006/xaml/presentation"
  xmlns:x="http://schemas.microsoft.com/winfx/2006/xaml"
  x:Class="AboutDialog"
  Title="About WPF Unleashed" SizeToContent="WidthAndHeight"
  Background="OrangeRed">
<Window.CommandBindings>
  <CommandBinding Command="Help"
    CanExecute="HelpCanExecute" Executed="HelpExecuted"/>
</Window.CommandBindings>
  <StackPanel>
    <Label FontWeight="Bold" FontSize="20" Foreground="White">
      WPF 4 Unleashed
    </Label>
    <Label>© 2010 SAMS Publishing</Label>
    <Label>Installed Chapters:</Label>
    <ListBox>
      <ListBoxItem>Chapter 1</ListBoxItem>
      <ListBoxItem>Chapter 2</ListBoxItem>
    </ListBox>
    <StackPanel Orientation="Horizontal" HorizontalAlignment="Center">
      <Button MinWidth="75" Margin="10" Command="Help" Content=
        "{Binding RelativeSource={RelativeSource Self}, Path=Command.Text}"/>
      <Button MinWidth="75" Margin="10">OK</Button>
```

LISTING 6.10 Continued

```
    </StackPanel>
    <StatusBar>You have successfully registered this product.</StatusBar>
  </StackPanel>
</Window>
```

LISTING 6.11 The Code-Behind File for Listing 6.10

```
using System.Windows;
using System.Windows.Input;

public partial class AboutDialog : Window
{
  public AboutDialog()
  {
    InitializeComponent();
  }

  void HelpCanExecute(object sender, CanExecuteRoutedEventArgs e)
  {
    e.CanExecute = true;
  }

  void HelpExecuted(object sender, ExecutedRoutedEventArgs e)
  {
    System.Diagnostics.Process.Start("http://www.adamnathan.net/wpf");
  }
}
```

The Window's CommandBinding can be set in XAML because it defines a default constructor and enables its data to be set with properties. The Button's Content can even be set to the chosen command's Text property in XAML, thanks to a popular data binding technique discussed in Chapter 13, "Data Binding." In addition, notice that a type converter simplifies specifying the Help command in XAML. A CommandConverter class knows about all the built-in commands, so the Command property can be set to Help in both places rather than using the more verbose {x:Static ApplicationCommands.Help}. (Custom commands don't get the same special treatment.) In the code-behind file, HelpCanExecute keeps the command enabled at all times, and HelpExecuted launches a web browser with an appropriate help URL.

Executing Commands with Input Gestures

Using the Help command in a simple About dialog might seem like overkill when a simple event handler for Click would do, but the command has provided an extra benefit besides localized text: automatic binding to a keyboard shortcut.

Applications typically invoke their version of help when the user presses the F1 key. Sure enough, if you press F1 while displaying the dialog defined in Listing 6.10, the `Help` command is automatically launched, as if you clicked the Help `Button`! That's because commands such as `Help` define a default *input gesture* that executes the command. You can bind your own input gestures to a command by adding `KeyBinding` and/or `MouseBinding` objects to the relevant element's `InputBindings` collection. (There's no support for stylus or touch bindings.) For example, to assign F2 as a keyboard shortcut that executes `Help`, you could add the following statement to `AboutDialog`'s constructor:

```
this.InputBindings.Add(
  new KeyBinding(ApplicationCommands.Help, new KeyGesture(Key.F2)));
```

This would make *both* F1 and F2 execute `Help`, however. You could additionally suppress the default F1 behavior by binding F1 to a special `NotACommand` command as follows:

```
this.InputBindings.Add(
  new KeyBinding(ApplicationCommands.NotACommand, new KeyGesture(Key.F1)));
```

Both of these statements could alternatively be represented in XAML as follows:

```
<Window.InputBindings>
  <KeyBinding Command="Help" Key="F2"/>
  <KeyBinding Command="NotACommand" Key="F1"/>
</Window.InputBindings>
```


Controls with Built-In Command Bindings

It can seem almost magical when you encounter it, but some controls in WPF contain their own command bindings. The simplest example of this is the `TextBox` control, which has its own built-in bindings for the `Cut`, `Copy`, and `Paste` commands that interact with the clipboard, as well as `Undo` and `Redo` commands. This not only means that `TextBox` responds to the standard Ctrl+X, Ctrl+C, Ctrl+V, Ctrl+Z, and Ctrl+Y keyboard shortcuts but that it's easy for additional elements to participate in these actions.

The following standalone XAML demonstrates the power of these built-in command bindings:

```
<StackPanel xmlns="http://schemas.microsoft.com/winfx/2006/xaml/presentation"
  xmlns:x="http://schemas.microsoft.com/winfx/2006/xaml"
  Orientation="Horizontal" Height="25">
  <Button Command="Cut" CommandTarget="{Binding ElementName=textBox}"
    Content="{Binding RelativeSource={RelativeSource Self}, Path=Command.Text}"/>
  <Button Command="Copy" CommandTarget="{Binding ElementName=textBox}"
    Content="{Binding RelativeSource={RelativeSource Self}, Path=Command.Text}"/>
  <Button Command="Paste" CommandTarget="{Binding ElementName=textBox}"
    Content="{Binding RelativeSource={RelativeSource Self}, Path=Command.Text}"/>
  <Button Command="Undo" CommandTarget="{Binding ElementName=textBox}"
    Content="{Binding RelativeSource={RelativeSource Self}, Path=Command.Text}"/>
```

```
  <Button Command="Redo" CommandTarget="{Binding ElementName=textBox}"
    Content="{Binding RelativeSource={RelativeSource Self}, Path=Command.Text}"/>
  <TextBox x:Name="textBox" Width="200"/>
</StackPanel>
```

You can paste this content into a XAML viewer or save it as a .xaml file to view in Internet Explorer, because no procedural code is necessary. Each of the five Buttons is associated with one of the commands and sets its Content to the string returned by each command's Text property. The only new thing here is the setting of each Button's CommandTarget property to the instance of the TextBox (using data binding rather than x:Reference to make this work with all versions of WPF). This causes the command to be executed from the TextBox rather than the Button, which is necessary in order for it to react to the commands.

This XAML produces the result in Figure 6.5. The first two Buttons are automatically disabled when no text in the TextBox is selected, and they are automatically enabled when there is a selection. Similarly, the Paste Button is automatically enabled whenever there is text content on the clipboard, and it is disabled otherwise.

FIGURE 6.5 The five Buttons work as expected without any procedural code, thanks to TextBox's built-in bindings.

Button and TextBox have no direct knowledge of each other, but through commands they can achieve rich interaction. This is why WPF's long list of built-in commands is so important. The more that third-party controls standardize on WPF's built-in commands, the more seamless (and declarative) interaction can be achieved among controls that have no direct knowledge of each other.

Summary

WPF's input events make it possible to create interactive content that leverages the full richness of any input device. Although routed events and commands are more complex than simple .NET events, they provide a great deal of functionality and make otherwise-difficult tasks much easier.

This chapter focuses on UIElement, but the same input events can also be used with ContentElement, described in Chapter 11, and UIElement3D, discussed in Chapter 16, "3D Graphics."

CHAPTER 7

Structuring and Deploying an Application

IN THIS CHAPTER

- Standard Windows Applications
- Navigation-Based Windows Applications
- Gadget-Style Applications
- XAML Browser Applications
- Loose XAML Pages

We've covered all the basics of arranging a WPF-based user interface and hooking it up to logic. Now it's time to see how to package it up as an application. There's no single canonical way to structure a WPF application. WPF supports standard Windows applications that take full advantage of the local computer, web-based applications that can still provide a compelling experience despite being restricted by Internet zone security, and a lot of other variations on these themes.

To help you explore the differences between each type of application (rather than just read about them), this book's source code contains a collection of sample "Photo Gallery" applications that are inspired by the Windows Live Photo Gallery. Each variation of the Photo Gallery corresponds to each application type covered here.

Standard Windows Applications

A standard Windows application runs locally on your computer and displays its user interface in one or more windows. Figure 7.1 shows the "standard" version of the Photo Gallery application.

When you create a new WPF Application project in Visual Studio, several files are generated for you. Most of them are familiar to .NET developers, such as `AssemblyInfo.*`, `Resources.*`, and `Settings.*`. But the WPF-specific meat of the project can be found in `App.xaml` and `MainWindow.xaml` (along with their corresponding code-behind files). These contain the Application and Window objects that are central to this type of application. (In older versions of Visual Studio, the MainWindow.xaml file is called Window1.xaml instead.)

FIGURE 7.1 Using the Photo Gallery application to browse local photos.

The Window Class

Window is the main element that traditional applications use to contain their content. A WPF Window is really just a Win32 window under the covers. The operating system doesn't distinguish between windows with WPF content and windows with Win32 content; it renders the chrome the same way for both, both appear in the Windows taskbar in the same manner, and so on. (*Chrome* is another name for the nonclient area, which contains the Minimize, Maximize, and Close buttons, among other things.)

Therefore, Window provides a straightforward abstraction for a Win32 window (like the Form class in Windows Forms), with a handful of simple methods and properties. After instantiating a Window, you can call Show to make it appear, Hide to make it disappear (which is the same as setting Visibility to Hidden or Collapsed), and Close to make it disappear for good. Despite being a Control, Window's Win32 dependency means that you cannot do certain advanced things like apply a transform to it.

Window's appearance can be controlled with properties such as Icon, Title (which is used as its caption), and WindowStyle. Its position can be controlled via the Left and Top properties, or you can set WindowStartupLocation to CenterScreen or CenterOwner to get more sophisticated behavior. In short, you can do just about everything you'd expect with Window by setting properties: Set Topmost to true to give it "always on top" behavior, set ShowInTaskbar to false if you don't want the typical item to appear in the taskbar, and so on.

A Window can spawn any number of additional Windows by instantiating a Window-derived class and calling Show. But it can also designate any of these additional Windows as child Windows. A child Window is just like any other top-level Window, but it automatically gets closed when the parent is closed and minimized when the parent is minimized. Such a Window is sometimes called a *modeless dialog*.

For a Window to make another Window its child, it must set the child Window's Owner property (of type Window) to a reference to itself, but only after the parent has been shown. It can enumerate its children via a read-only OwnedWindows property.

Every time a Window becomes active or inactive (for example, from the user flipping between windows), a corresponding Activated and Deactivated event is raised. You can also attempt to force a Window to become active by calling Window's Activate method (which behaves like the Win32 SetForegroundWindow API). You can *prevent* a Window from automatically being activated when it is first shown by setting its ShowActivated property to false.

Listing 7.1 contains portions of the MainWindow class defined by the Photo Gallery application.

LISTING 7.1 Portions of MainWindow.xaml.cs Related to Window Management

```
public partial class MainWindow : Window
{
  public MainWindow()
  {
    InitializeComponent();
  }

  protected override void OnClosing(CancelEventArgs e)
  {
    base.OnClosing(e);

    if (MessageBox.Show("Are you sure you want to close Photo Gallery?",
      "Annoying Prompt", MessageBoxButton.YesNo, MessageBoxImage.Question)
      == MessageBoxResult.No)
        e.Cancel = true;
  }

  protected override void OnClosed(EventArgs e)
  {
    base.OnClosed(e);

    // Persist the list of favorites
    …
  }

  protected override void OnInitialized(EventArgs e)
  {
    base.OnInitialized(e);

    // Retrieve the persisted list of favorites
    …
```

LISTING 7.1 Continued

```
  }
...
  void exitMenu_Click(object sender, RoutedEventArgs e)
  {
    this.Close();
  }
...
}
```

MainWindow calls InitializeComponent in its constructor to initialize the part of the Window defined in XAML. It then takes action on the Closing, Closed, and Initialized events. But it does this by overriding Window's On*EventName* methods rather than attaching event handlers to each event. It's conventional for managed classes to expose protected On*EventName* methods corresponding to each event, and WPF classes follow this convention. The end result is the same whether you override the method or attach an event handler, but the overriding mechanism tends to be a bit faster. The .NET Framework designers also felt that the override approach is a more natural way for a subclass to handle base class events.

WARNING

Don't forget to call InitializeComponent!

This was mentioned in Chapter 2, "XAML Demystified," but it's worth repeating: If you don't call InitializeComponent in the constructor of any class that has corresponding compiled XAML, the object will not get constructed correctly. That's because all the runtime processing of the compiled XAML happens inside this method. Fortunately, Visual Studio automatically generates calls to InitializeComponent, so it should be hard to accidentally omit.

The Closing event is raised when someone attempts to close the Window, whether it's done programmatically or via the user clicking the Close button, pressing Alt+F4, and so on. Any event handler can veto the closure, however, if it sets the Cancel property in the passed-in CancelEventArgs object (the same one used by Windows Forms for the same purpose) to true. Inside this listing's OnClosing method, the user is presented with a confirmation dialog, and the closing is canceled if the user clicks the No button. In this example, the dialog is just an annoyance because there's no data for the user to potentially save. But a typical usage of this event is to prompt the user to save some data that he or she hasn't already saved. If the closing process is not vetoed, the Window is closed, and the Closed event (which can't be canceled) gets raised.

In Listing 7.1, MainWindow handles Closed to persist the list of favorite folders that the user might have designated while running the application. It also handles the Initialized event to retrieve that persisted list and update the user interface appropriately. (The upcoming "Persisting and Restoring Application State" section shows the code that does this.) The listing ends with an event handler for the File, Exit menu, which closes the Window when selected.

The Application Class

Now, the application simply needs an entry point to create and show the `Window`. You might expect to write a `Main` method as follows, given a `MainWindow` class as defined in Listing 7.1:

```
public static void Main()
{
  MainWindow window = new MainWindow();
  window.Show();
}
```

This is incorrect for two reasons. First, the main thread in a WPF application must run in a single-threaded apartment (STA). Therefore, `Main` must be marked with an `STAThread` attribute. More importantly, `Show` is a nonblocking call; it shows the `Window` (by calling the Win32 `ShowWindow` API) and then immediately returns. But the call to `Show` is the last line of `Main`, so the application then exits. The result is `MainWindow` flashing on the screen for a fraction of a second!

FAQ

Please tell me that I did not just read the words *single-threaded apartment*! Isn't that a legacy COM thing?

Yes, apartments are a COM mechanism. And like previous Win32-based user interface frameworks (including Windows Forms), WPF requires the main thread to live in a single-threaded apartment. This is mainly the case to enable seamless interoperability with non-WPF technologies (the topic of Chapter 19, "Interoperability with Non-WPF Technologies"). But even without the interoperability requirement, the STA model—in which developers don't need to worry about correctly handling calls from arbitrary threads—is valuable for making programming with WPF easier. When an object is created on an STA thread, it can be called only on that same thread.

WPF enforces that many of its APIs (on `DispatcherObject`-derived classes) are called from the correct thread by throwing an exception if the call comes from any other thread. That way, there's no chance of accidentally calling such members from the wrong thread and only seeing intermittent failures (which can be incredibly hard to debug). At the same time, WPF provides an easy mechanism for multiple threads to communicate with the UI thread, as discussed in a later sidebar.

If you don't know anything about COM and don't want to deal with threading, don't worry. Simply mark your `Main` method with `STAThread` and forget about these rules!

To prevent `Main` from instantly exiting after showing `MainWindow`, you need to tell the application to dispatch messages from the operating system to `MainWindow` indefinitely until it has been closed. These messages are the same Windows messages that Win32 applications are built on: WM_PAINT, WM_MOUSEMOVE, and so on. Internally, WPF must handle these messages to run on Windows. In Win32, you would write a loop (called a *message loop* or *message pump*) that processes incoming messages and sends them to the appropriate window procedure. In WPF, the easiest way to accomplish the same task is by using the System.Windows.Application class.

Using Application.Run

Application defines a Run method that keeps the application alive and dispatches messages appropriately. So the previous Main implementation can be corrected as follows:

```
[STAThread]
public static void Main()
{
  Application app = new Application();
  MainWindow window = new MainWindow();
  window.Show();
  app.Run(window);
}
```

Application also defines a StartupUri property that provides an alternative means of showing the application's first Window. It can be used as follows:

```
[STAThread]
public static void Main()
{
  Application app = new Application();
  app.StartupUri = new Uri("MainWindow.xaml", UriKind.Relative);
  app.Run();
}
```

This implementation of Main is equivalent to the previous one because the instantiation of MainWindow and the call to Show is done implicitly by Application. Notice that MainWindow is identified only by the name of the XAML source file as a uniform resource identifier (URI) and that an overload of Run is called that doesn't need an instance of Window. WPF's use of URIs is explained in Chapter 12, "Resources."

The reason for having the StartupUri property is to enable this common initialization to be done in XAML instead. Indeed, the Visual Studio template for WPF Application projects defines an Application-derived class called App in XAML and sets the StartupUri property to the project's main Window. For the Photo Gallery application, the content of App.xaml is as follows:

```
<Application x:Class="PhotoGallery.App"
  xmlns="http://schemas.microsoft.com/winfx/2006/xaml/presentation"
  xmlns:x="http://schemas.microsoft.com/winfx/2006/xaml"
  StartupUri="MainWindow.xaml"/>
```

StartupUri can be set with a simple string, thanks to a type converter for Uri.

The corresponding code-behind file—App.xaml.cs—simply has the InitializeComponent call:

```
using System.Windows;

namespace PhotoGallery
{
  public partial class App : Application
  {
    public App()
    {
      InitializeComponent();
    }
  }
}
```

This is the most common approach for structuring a standard WPF application and showing its main Window. Note, however, that if you have nothing custom to add to the Application code-behind file, you can omit it altogether.

FAQ

Where's the Main method in my WPF application?

When you create a WPF Application project in Visual Studio, the generated project has no Main method, yet it still runs as expected! In fact, if you attempt to add a Main method, you get a compilation error telling you that it is already defined.

Application is special-cased when it is compiled from XAML, because Visual Studio assigns the XAML file the build action ApplicationDefinition. This causes a Main method to be autogenerated. For the Photo Gallery application, this entry point can be found inside App.g.cs:

```
[System.STAThreadAttribute()]
public static void Main() {
  PhotoGallery.App app = new PhotoGallery.App();
  app.InitializeComponent();
  app.Run();
}
```

The App.g.cs file is hidden by Visual Studio unless you select Show All Files in the Solution Explorer.

FAQ

How do I retrieve command-line arguments in my WPF application?

Command-line arguments are typically retrieved via a string array parameter passed to `Main`, but the common way to define WPF applications doesn't allow you to implement the `Main` method. You can get around this in two different ways. One way is to forgo defining an `Application`-derived class in XAML, so you can manually define the `Main` method with a string array parameter. The easier way, however, is to simply call `System.Environment.GetCommandLineArgs` at any point in your application, which returns the same string array you'd get inside `Main`.

Another option for doing custom startup logic (whether command-line processing, custom splash screen behavior, and so on) is to change the build action of your `Application`-derived class from `ApplicationDefinition` to `Page`. This enables you to provide your own `Main` method. After you perform your custom logic inside `Main`, you can create and run the `Application` instance with the same three lines of code that would have been generated inside `App.g.cs`.

Other Uses for `Application`

The `Application` class is more than a simple entry point and message dispatcher. It contains a handful of events, properties, and methods for managing common application-level tasks. The events, which are typically handled by overriding the `On`*`EventName`* methods in an `Application`-derived class (such as the Visual Studio–generated `App` class), include `Startup` and `Exit`, `Activated` and `Deactivated` (which behave like `Window`'s events of the same names but apply to any of `Application`'s `Windows`), and even `SessionEnding`, a cancellable event that occurs when the user logs off or shuts down the computer. The data passed with this event tells you whether it was raised due to logging off or shutting down, via a `ReasonSessionEnding` enumeration.

Because applications often have multiple windows, `Application` defines a read-only `Windows` collection to give you access to all open `Windows`. The initial `Window` is given a special designation and can be accessed via the `MainWindow` property. This property is read/write, however, so you can give any window the special designation at any time.

WARNING

Don't rely on a fixed index in the `Windows` collection!

`Windows` are added to `Application.Windows` in the order in which they are initially shown, and they are removed from the collection when they are closed. Therefore, the index of a given `Window` inside the collection can change over the lifetime of an application. You should not assume that `Windows[2]`, for example, is always going to reference the same `Window`!

By default, `Application` exits (that is, the `Run` method finally returns) when all `Windows` have been closed. But this behavior can be modified by setting the `ShutdownMode` property to various values of the `ShutdownMode` enumeration. For example, you can make `Application` exit when the main `Window` (designated by the `MainWindow` property) exits, regardless of the state of other `Windows`. Or, you could make `Application` continue to run until its Shutdown method is explicitly called, even if all Windows have been closed. This behavior is handy for applications that want to "minimize" to the Windows notification area (a practice that has thankfully fallen out of favor due to enhancements to the Windows taskbar).

One very handy property on the Application class is the Properties collection. Properties, much like application state or session state in ASP.NET, is a dictionary for conveniently storing data (as key/value pairs) that can easily be shared among Windows or other objects. Rather than define public fields or properties on your Application-derived class, you might want to simply store such data in the Properties collection. For example, Photo Gallery stores the filename of the currently selected photo in Properties as follows:

```
myApplication.Properties["CurrentPhotoFilename"] = filename;
```

and it retrieves the filename as follows:

```
string filename = myApplication.Properties["CurrentPhotoFilename"] as string;
```

Note that both the key and value are of type Object, so they are not constrained to be strings.

TIP

Application-level tasks are usually performed from code within Windows, requiring various Windows in an application to obtain a reference to the current Application instance. Fortunately, you can easily get access to this instance with the static Application.Current property. So the myApplication variable in the preceding code snippets can be replaced with Application.Current:

```
Application.Current.Properties["CurrentPhotoFilename"] = filename;
```

FAQ

How can I create a multiple-document interface (MDI) application using WPF?

The WPF classes don't have built-in support for creating MDI user interfaces, but Windows Forms classes do. Therefore, you can use the interoperability techniques discussed in Chapter 19 to get MDI in a WPF application. But please don't! MDI interfaces don't get to take full advantage of multiple monitors or window management features such as Aero Snap introduced Windows 7 and Flip 3D introduced in Windows Vista. If you want to avoid multiple top-level Windows, you could consider creating a tabbed interface (really just this century's version of MDI), for which WPF has built-in support.

FAQ

How can I create a single-instance application using WPF?

The classic approach to implementing single-instance behavior still applies to WPF applications: Use a named (and, therefore, operating system-wide) mutex. The following code shows how you can do this in C#:

```
bool mutexIsNew;
using (System.Threading.Mutex m =
  new System.Threading.Mutex(true, uniqueName, out mutexIsNew))
{
  if (mutexIsNew)
    // This is the first instance. Run the application.
  else
    // There is already an instance running. Exit!
}
```

Just be sure that *uniqueName* won't be chosen by other applications! It's common to generate a globally unique identifier (GUID) at development time and use that as your identifier. Of course, nothing prevents a malicious application from creating a semaphore with the same name to prevent such an application from running!

It is often desirable to communicate the command-line arguments to the running instance rather than silently exiting the duplicate instance. The only functionality in the .NET Framework for this is provided by the `Microsoft.VisualBasic.ApplicationServices.WindowsFormsApplicationBase` class which, despite its name, is usable from any .NET language and with WPF. Alternatively, the first instance could open an RPC channel and then any new instances can try to connect to it in order to communicate this information.

DIGGING DEEPER

Creating an Application Without `Application`

Although using an `Application` object is the recommended way to structure a WPF application, it's not an absolute requirement. Showing `Windows` without `Application` is easy, but you need to at least handle message dispatching to avoid the "instant exit" problem described at the beginning of this section.

This can be done using Win32 techniques, but WPF also defines a low-level `Dispatcher` class in the `System.Windows.Threading` namespace that enables you to perform dispatching without resorting to calling Win32 APIs.

For example, your `Main` method could call `Dispatcher.Run` rather than `Application.Run` after showing your main `Window`. (In fact, `Application.Run` internally calls `Dispatcher.Run` to get the message dispatching functionality!) But such an application still lacks other important application-management functionality. For example, `Dispatcher.Run` never returns unless you explicitly call `Dispatcher.ExitAllFrames` somewhere (such as in a handler for the main `Window`'s `Closed` event).

DIGGING DEEPER

Multithreaded Applications

A typical WPF application has a single UI thread and a render thread. (The render thread is an implementation detail that is never directly exposed to developers. It runs in the background and handles low-level tasks such as composition.) You can spawn additional threads to perform background work, but you must not directly communicate from such threads with any `DispatcherObject`-derived objects created on the UI thread. (There are some exceptions to this, such as a `Freezable` object that has been frozen.)

Fortunately, WPF makes it easy for an arbitrary thread to schedule code to be run on the UI thread. `DispatcherObject` defines a `Dispatcher` property (of type `Dispatcher`) that contains several overloads of `Invoke` (a synchronous call) and `BeginInvoke` (an asynchronous call). These methods enable you to pass a delegate to be invoked on the dispatcher's corresponding UI thread. All overloads of `Invoke` and `BeginInvoke` require a `DispatcherPriority` enumeration value. `DispatcherPriority` defines 10 active priorities, ranging from the highest-priority `Send` (meaning execute immediately) to the lowest-priority `SystemIdle` (meaning execute only when the dispatcher's queue is otherwise empty).

You can even give an application multiple UI threads by calling `Dispatcher.Run` in any new thread that you spawn. Therefore, you can make each `Window` run on a separate thread if your application has more than one top-level `Window`. Doing this is certainly not necessary for most applications, but such a scheme could improve your application's responsiveness if it's likely that one `Window` could start activities that would dominate the thread. The `Application` abstraction starts to break down in this case, however, because it is tied to a single `Dispatcher`. For example, the `Application.Windows` collection contains only `Window` instances created on the same thread as the `Application`.

Showing a Splash Screen

Ideally there would be no need for a splash screen, but sometimes an application takes a bit of time to show its main window after being launched—especially the first time it is launched in a user's session (called *cold start time*). WPF includes special functionality for adding a splash screen to an application.

The splash screen that is enabled by this support is an image that appears instantly when the application is launched and fades out when the main window appears. Although you are able to use a PNG file with transparency to achieve non-rectangular shapes or effects such as shadows, you can't use animated content (such as an animated GIF). You can't use any kind of dynamic content or WPF elements, as the splash screen is shown before WPF has even finished loading. (Otherwise, it could take as long to display the splash screen as it would have taken to display the main window!) Therefore, you can't produce fancy Office 2010–style splash screens with animations and updating status text with this support. However, you can produce a nice experience with almost no effort.

To take advantage of this support in Visual Studio 2010, simply select Splash Screen (WPF) in your WPF project's Add New Item dialog. (You can download the same item template for Visual Studio 2008 SP1 from http://codeplex.com.) This adds an image to your project with the build action `SplashScreen` that you can customize as desired. That's all there is to it! Figure 7.2 shows the splash screen for the Photo Gallery example application.

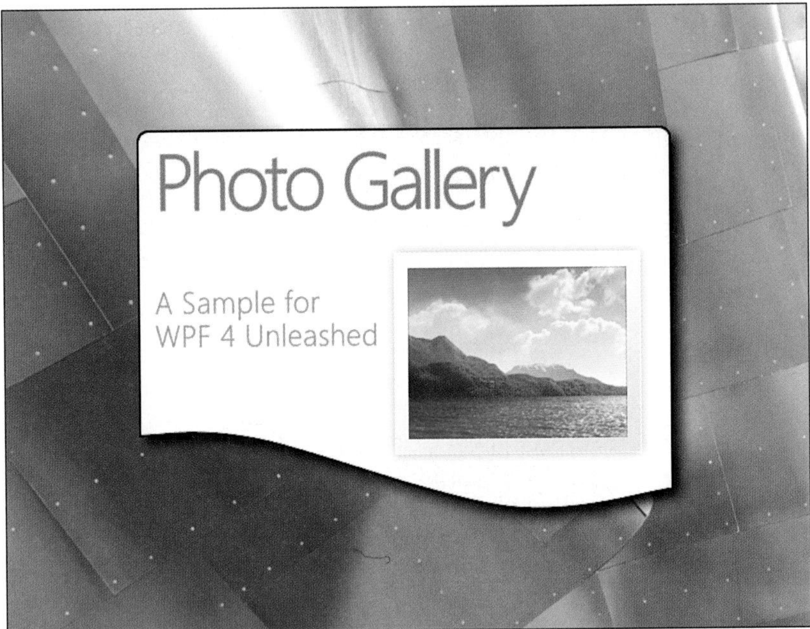

FIGURE 7.2 The splash screen for Photo Gallery takes advantage of transparency in the PNG image.

Another way to accomplish this is to simply add the desired image to your project and then set its build action to `SplashScreen`. This is the easiest approach in Visual Studio 2008 SP1, as it doesn't require any additional download. Or, to have a little more control over the splash screen, such as dynamically selecting the image or setting a maximum amount of time for the splash screen to show, you could use the `System.Windows.SplashScreen` class. This class contains a few simple APIs for creating, showing, and hiding the splash screen.

Creating and Showing Dialogs

Windows provides a set of common *dialogs* (modal subwindows) that you can leverage to handle common tasks such as opening/saving files, browsing folders, choosing fonts or colors, and printing. You can also create your own custom dialogs with the same modal behavior. (In other words, the dialog doesn't let you return to the current `Window` until you've dismissed it.)

Common Dialogs

WPF provides built-in exposure to a few of the common dialogs with classes that expose their functionality in a handful of straightforward methods and properties. Note that

WPF does not natively render these dialogs; it internally calls Win32 APIs to show them and communicate with them. This is good, however, because it means that the dialogs remain consistent with the version of the operating system on which your application is running.

> **TIP**
>
> Both Windows Forms and WPF define managed classes that wrap Windows common dialogs. But in the current version of WPF, not all the dialogs have corresponding classes in the WPF assemblies. (Windows Forms has `ColorDialog`, `FontDialog`, and `FolderBrowser`, whereas WPF still does not.) Therefore, the easiest way to use these omitted dialogs is to reference `System.Windows.Forms.dll` and use the managed classes defined by Windows Forms.

Using a built-in common dialog is often just a matter of instantiating it, calling its `ShowDialog` method, and then processing the result. For example, Photo Gallery uses `PrintDialog` to print photos as follows:

```
void printMenu_Click(object sender, RoutedEventArgs e)
{
  string filename = (pictureBox.SelectedItem as ListBoxItem).Tag as string;
  Image image = new Image();
  image.Source = new BitmapImage(new Uri(filename, UriKind.RelativeOrAbsolute));

  PrintDialog pd = new PrintDialog();
  if (pd.ShowDialog() == true) // Result could be true, false, or null
    pd.PrintVisual(image, Path.GetFileName(filename) + " from Photo Gallery");
}
```

If you ever find yourself considering writing your own custom dialog for which a common dialog is already provided by Windows, please abandon those thoughts immediately. Besides being inconsistent with most Windows applications, your dialog would undoubtedly lack features that certain users expect and would fall further behind with each new version of Windows. Just look at all the features that the built-in File Open dialog has in Windows 7: searching; special support for things like favorite places, libraries, and HomeGroup; multiple views with a rich set of columns to display/sort/filter; a preview pane; and much more. It also has features that are not directly visible, such as tracking what file(s) it opens to help populate recent and frequent file lists used in places such as Windows 7 Jump Lists.

Custom Dialogs

Although writing your own *common* dialog is a bad idea, applications often have good reasons to show their own *custom* dialogs, such as the simple Rename Photo dialog used by Photo Gallery, pictured in Figure 7.3.

FIGURE 7.3 A custom dialog enables the user to rename a photo.

In WPF, creating and using such a dialog is almost the same as creating and using a `Window`. In fact, such dialogs *are* just `Windows`, typically with a little extra handling for returning what's known as a *dialog result*.

To show a `Window` as a modal dialog rather than a modeless window, simply call its `ShowDialog` <$IShowDialog method>method instead of `Show`. Unlike `Show`, `ShowDialog` is a blocking call (so it doesn't exit until the `Window` is closed), and it returns a nullable Boolean (`bool?` in C#). Here is how Photo Gallery consumes its custom `RenameDialog`:

```
void renameMenu_Click(object sender, RoutedEventArgs e)
{
  string filename = (pictureBox.SelectedItem as ListBoxItem).Tag as string;
  RenameDialog dialog = new RenameDialog(
    Path.GetFileNameWithoutExtension(filename));
  if (dialog.ShowDialog() == true) // Result could be true, false, or null
  {
    // Attempt to rename the file
    try
    {
      File.Move(filename, Path.Combine(Path.GetDirectoryName(filename),
        dialog.NewFilename) + Path.GetExtension(filename));
    }
    catch (Exception ex)
    {
      MessageBox.Show(ex.Message, "Cannot Rename File", MessageBoxButton.OK,
        MessageBoxImage.Error);
    }
  }
}
```

When you develop a `Window` that you know will be used as a dialog (such as `RenameDialog`), you typically want the `ShowDialog` method to return `true` if the action enabled by a dialog is successful and `false` if it is unsuccessful or canceled. To control what gets returned by this method, simply set `Window`'s `DialogResult` property (of type `bool?`) to the desired value. Setting `DialogResult` implicitly closes the `Window`. Therefore, `RenameDialog`'s OK button could have an event handler like the following:

```
void okButton_Click(object sender, RoutedEventArgs e)
{
  this.DialogResult = true;
}
```

Or it could simply have its `IsDefault` property set to `true`, which accomplishes the same behavior without any procedural code.

DIGGING DEEPER

Another Use for `ShowDialog`

To get its blocking behavior while still allowing message dispatching, `Window`'s `ShowDialog` method effectively calls `Dispatcher.Run` just like `Application.Run` does. So, the following trick could be used to properly launch a WPF `Window` without using the `Application` class:

```
[STAThread]
public static void Main()
{
  MainWindow window = new MainWindow();
  window.ShowDialog();
}
```

Persisting and Restoring Application State

A standard Windows application can have full access to the computer (depending on user security settings), so there are many options for storing data, such as using the Windows Registry or the local file system. But an attractive alternative to these classic approaches is to use the .NET Framework's *isolated storage* technology. Besides being easy to use, the same techniques work in all environments in which managed code can run, such as in a Silverlight application or a XAML Browser Application (covered later in this chapter).

Photo Gallery uses the code in Listing 7.2 to persist and retrieve the user's favorites data to and from isolated storage.

LISTING 7.2 Portions of `MainWindow.xaml.cs` Related to Isolated Storage

```
protected override void OnClosed(EventArgs e)
{
  base.OnClosed(e);

  // Write each favorites item when the application is about to close
  IsolatedStorageFile f = IsolatedStorageFile.GetUserStoreForAssembly();
  using (IsolatedStorageFileStream stream =
    new IsolatedStorageFileStream("myFile", FileMode.Create, f))
  using (StreamWriter writer = new StreamWriter(stream))
  {
    foreach (TreeViewItem item in favoritesItem.Items)
      writer.WriteLine(item.Tag as string);
  }
}

protected override void OnInitialized(EventArgs e)
{
  base.OnInitialized(e);
```

LISTING 7.2 Continued

```
  // Read each favorites item when the application is initialized
  IsolatedStorageFile f = IsolatedStorageFile.GetUserStoreForAssembly();
  using (IsolatedStorageFileStream stream =
    new IsolatedStorageFileStream("myFile", FileMode.OpenOrCreate, f))
  using (StreamReader reader = new StreamReader(stream))
  {
    string line = reader.ReadLine();
    while (line != null)
    {
      AddFavorite(line);
      line = reader.ReadLine();
    }
  }
  ...
}
```

The `IsolatedStorageFile` and `IsolatedStorageFileStream` classes are in the `System.IO.IsolatedStorage` namespace. All data stored in isolated storage is physically located in a hidden folder under the current user's Documents folder.

> **TIP**
>
> For an even simpler way to persist and retrieve application settings, check out the Visual Studio–generated `Settings` class (under `Properties\Settings.settings`). This mechanism stores data in an application configuration file and provides strongly typed access.

Deployment: ClickOnce Versus Windows Installer

When you think of deploying standard Windows applications, you probably think of a setup program that places the relevant files in the Program Files directory (or a user-chosen directory), registers the necessary components, adds itself to the installed programs list under Control Panel, and perhaps adds Start menu or desktop shortcuts. You can do all these things with a WPF application by using Windows Installer technology. Visual Studio contains several "Setup and Deployment" project types for doing just that.

ClickOnce, however, is a more recent and simpler installation technology (introduced with the .NET Framework 2.0). It's an attractive option for installations that don't need the full power of Windows Installer. Visual Studio exposes ClickOnce functionality via a wizard accessed from the Build, Publish menu. If you don't have Visual Studio, you can use the Windows SDK, which has two tools for using ClickOnce: the `mage.exe` command-line tool and the `mageUI.exe` graphical tool.

In short, Windows Installer has the following benefits over ClickOnce:

- Supports customized setup user interfaces, such as showing an end user license agreement (EULA)

- Can give control over where the files are installed
- Supports arbitrary code at setup time via custom actions
- Supports installing shared assemblies in the Global Assembly Cache
- Supports registration of COM components and file associations
- Supports machine-wide installation (that is, the program is available for all users)
- Supports offline installation from a CD/DVD

ClickOnce has the following benefits over Windows Installer:

- Contains built-in support for automatic updates and rolling back to previous versions.
- Provides two installation models: a web-like experience where the application is addressed via a URL in a web browser and appears to "go away" when it is closed (although it is still cached for future use) and a more traditional experience where the application can have a Start menu shortcut and show up in Control Panel's list of installed programs.
- Guarantees that installation doesn't affect other applications because all files are placed in an isolated area, and no custom registration can be done.
- Practically guarantees a clean uninstallation because no custom code could be run during installation. (Full-trust applications still have the power to leave artifacts on the computer while they run.)
- Integrates with .NET code access security, enabling users to run applications without having to trust them completely.

TIP

Many people don't realize that ClickOnce can still be used even if an application contains unmanaged code, as long as the main executable isn't entirely unmanaged. You might need to alter some aspects of the unmanaged code, however, for this to work. For example, if COM objects are registered, you would need to set up registration-free COM instead.

Navigation-Based Windows Applications

Although the concept of navigation is usually associated with web browsers, many Windows applications implement some sort of navigation scheme: Windows Explorer, Windows Media Player, and, of course, the Windows Live Photo Gallery application that this chapter's Photo Gallery application is based on.

The first version of Photo Gallery, represented in Figure 7.1, has hand-crafted and primitive navigation functionality for traversing photos and returning to the main gallery screen. It turns out, however, that WPF has a lot of built-in infrastructure for adding rich navigation to an application with minimal effort. With these features, it becomes trivial to implement an application that can browse and navigate content like a web browser.

Although the title of this section makes it sound like the choice of using navigation impacts the design of your entire application, the truth is that navigation support can be integrated into an otherwise-traditional application as little or as much as you want. And even if you don't want to expose a browser-style user interface, you can still use the navigation support to structure your application more like you would structure a website. For example, you can organize various pieces of user interface in separate pages identifiable via URIs and use hyperlinks to navigate from one to another. Or you can just use navigation simply for a small chunk of an application or component, such as a wizard.

This section examines these features and highlights some of the changes made to the "standard" version of Photo Gallery to leverage them. Adding navigation to a WPF application doesn't change the discussions in the previous section about deployment, persisting data, and so on. Instead, it involves becoming familiar with a few additional elements, such as `NavigationWindow` and `Page`.

Pages and Their Navigation Containers

Whenusing navigation in WPF, content is typically organized in `Page` elements. (`Page` is basically a simpler version of the `Window` class.) `Page` elements can then be hosted in one of two built-in navigation containers: `NavigationWindow` or `Frame`. These containers provide a way to navigate from one page to another, a "journal" that keeps track of navigation history, and a series of navigation-related events.

FAQ

What's the difference between `NavigationWindow` and `Frame`?

They have almost identical functionality, except that `NavigationWindow` functions more like a top-level browser, whereas `Frame` functions more like an HTML `FRAME` or `IFRAME`. Whereas `NavigationWindow` is a top-level window, `Frame` can fill an arbitrary (but rectangular) region of its parent element. A `Frame` can be nested inside a `NavigationWindow` or inside another `Frame`. By default, `NavigationWindow` has a bar along the top with Back/Forward buttons and `Frame` does not, but you can add or remove this bar on either element by setting the `ShowsNavigationUI` property on the `Page` it contains. In addition, `NavigationWindow` has a `ShowsNavigationUI` property and `Frame` has a `NavigationUIVisibility` property for enabling or disabling this bar, regardless of `Page` settings.

The navigation-enabled version of Photo Gallery changes `Application`'s `StartupUri` to point to the following `NavigationWindow`:

```
<NavigationWindow x:Class="PhotoGallery.Container"
  xmlns="http://schemas.microsoft.com/winfx/2006/xaml/presentation"
  xmlns:x="http://schemas.microsoft.com/winfx/2006/xaml"
  Title="Photo Gallery" Source="MainPage.xaml">
</NavigationWindow>
```

The `MainPage.xaml` referenced by the `NavigationWindow` has a `Page` root that contains all the content that the original `MainWindow.xaml` previously had:

```
<Page x:Class="PhotoGallery.MainPage"
  xmlns="http://schemas.microsoft.com/winfx/2006/xaml/presentation"
  xmlns:x="http://schemas.microsoft.com/winfx/2006/xaml"
  Title="Photo Gallery" Loaded="Page_Loaded">
  …Application-specific content…
</Page>
```

Similarly, the code-behind in `MainPage.xaml.cs` corresponds to the code-behind that was previously in `MainWindow.xaml.cs`. The main code difference in `MainPage.xaml.cs` is that the `OnClosing` and `OnClosed` logic has been moved back to the `Window` level because `Page` doesn't have these methods (nor would it be appropriate to invoke them every time the `Page` goes away).

As seen in Figure 7.4, the introduction of `NavigationWindow` and `Page` into Photo Gallery doesn't appear to add much—just a new bar at the top of the window with (disabled) Back and Forward buttons. But it sets up the application to navigate to other content within the same container, which is covered next.

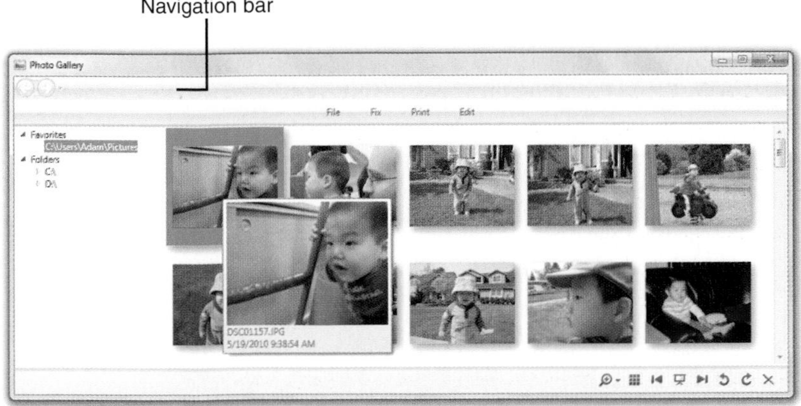

FIGURE 7.4 When Photo Gallery is hosted in a `NavigationWindow`, an extra bar appears at the top.

Of course, having an extra bar along the top of this application looks a bit ridiculous. An application such as Photo Gallery would be better served by implementing custom Back and Forward buttons that hook into `NavigationWindow`'s built-in navigation functionality. For example, the `Click` handler for the Back button could call

> **TIP**
>
> WPF's navigation containers can hold more than `Page`s; they can also hold HTML files (from the file system or from the Internet)! You can even navigate back and forth between WPF content and HTML content, using techniques described in the next section.

NavigationWindow.GoBack, and the Click handler for the Forward button could call NavigationWindow.GoForward.

A Page can interact with its navigation container by using the NavigationService class, which exposes relevant functionality regardless of whether the container is a NavigationWindow or a Frame. You can get an instance of NavigationService by calling the static NavigationService.GetNavigationService method and passing the instance of the Page. But even more easily, you can simply use Page's NavigationService property. For example, you can set a title that is used in the drop-down menu associated with the Back and Forward buttons as follows:

```
this.NavigationService.Title = "Main Photo Gallery Page";
```

Or you can refresh the current Page as follows:

```
this.NavigationService.Refresh();
```

But Page also contains a few of its own properties that control the behavior of the parent container, such as WindowHeight, WindowWidth, and WindowTitle. These are handy because you can easily set them within the XAML for the Page.

Navigating from Page to Page

The purpose of using navigation is to progress from one page to another, whether in a predetermined linear sequence (as with a simple wizard), a user-driven path through a hierarchy (as with most websites), or a dynamically generated path.

You can perform navigation in three main ways:

- Calling the Navigate method
- Using Hyperlinks
- Using the journal

Calling the Navigate Method

Navigation containers support a Navigate method that enables the current page to be changed. You can call Navigate with an instance of the target page or a URI that points to it:

```
// Navigate to a page instance
PhotoPage nextPage = new PhotoPage();
this.NavigationService.Navigate(nextPage);
// Or navigate to a page via a URI
this.NavigationService.Navigate(new Uri("PhotoPage.xaml", UriKind.Relative));
```

The Page specified by a URI could be a loose XAML file or a compiled resource. (Chapter 12 explains how such URIs work in WPF.) The root element of this XAML file must be a Page.

If you want to navigate to an HTML page, you must use the overload of `Navigate` that accepts a URI. Here's an example:

```
this.NavigationService.Navigate(new Uri("http://www.adamnathan.net/wpf"));
```

DIGGING DEEPER

`Navigate` Exposed as Two Properties

Navigation containers have two properties that behave identically to these two overloads of the `Navigate` method. You can navigate to a `Page` instance by setting the `Content` property:

```
this.NavigationService.Content = nextPage;
```

or you can navigate via a URI by setting the `Source` property:

```
this.NavigationService.Source = new Uri("PhotoPage.xaml", UriKind.Relative);
```

Other than their ability to be set declaratively, there's no reason to use these properties instead of the `Navigate` method.

Using `Hyperlink`

For simple navigation schemes, WPF provides a `Hyperlink` element that acts much like hyperlinks in HTML. You can embed `Hyperlinks` inside a `TextBlock` element and, as with the HTML `AREA` (or `A`) tag, the content is automatically rendered as a clickable hyperlink that navigates the current page to the desired target page. This target page is specified via `Hyperlink`'s `NavigateUri` property (the analog to the `href` attribute in HTML). For example, the following XAML gets rendered as shown in Figure 7.5:

Click here to view the photo.

FIGURE 7.5 A rendered `Hyperlink` element looks like an HTML hyperlink.

```
<TextBlock>
Click <Hyperlink NavigateUri="PhotoPage.xaml">here</Hyperlink> to view the photo.
</TextBlock>
```

`Hyperlink`, therefore, is really just a more-wordy version of the HTML `A` tag. Although it can be used programmatically like any other WPF element, its purpose is for simple HTML-like links where the target page is known in advance.

TIP

If you want to combine the flexibility of programmatic navigation with the convenience of `Hyperlink`'s automatic text formatting, you can use `Hyperlink` with a dummy `NavigateUri` value, then handle `Hyperlink`'s `Click` event and call `Navigate` however you desire inside this handler.

FAQ

How can I have a link in an HTML page that navigates to a WPF `Page`?

Hyperlinks in HTML work automatically, but there's no way to give an `HREF` value that points to a compiled WPF `Page`. Instead, you can use a technique similar to the previous tip to achieve HTML-to-WPF navigation: Use a sentinel value as the `HREF` value, listen to the `Navigating` event, and then dynamically change the target by calling `Navigate` yourself. (`Navigating` and other events are examined in the next section.) Depending on the nature of the desired HTML and WPF interaction, you might also want to consider creating a XAML Browser Application or a loose XAML page (or think about using Silverlight instead). These options are discussed at the end of this chapter.

TIP

`Hyperlink` supports more complex functionality, similar to HTML hyperlinks. For example, to navigate a single `Frame` in the presence of multiple `Frames`, set `Hyperlink`'s `TargetName` property to the name of the desired `Frame`. To navigate to a section of a `Page` (like using # anchors in HTML), simply append a # and a name to the URI. The name can be the name of any element on the target page.

Using the Journal

Both navigation containers have a *journal* that records navigation history, just like a web browser. This journal provides the logic behind the Back and Forward buttons shown in Figure 7.4. Internally, it maintains two stacks—a back stack and a forward stack—and uses them as shown in Table 7.1.

TABLE 7.1 Navigation Effects on the Journal

Action	Result
Back	Pushes the current page onto the forward stack, pops a page off the back stack, and navigates to it
Forward	Pushes the current page onto the back stack, pops a page off the forward stack, and navigates to it
Any other navigation	Pushes the current page onto the back stack and empties the forward stack

The Back and Forward actions can be initiated by the user or invoked programmatically by calling the navigation container's `GoBack` and `GoForward` methods (after calling `CanGoBack` or `CanGoForward` to avoid an exception by trying to pop an empty stack).

`NavigationWindow` always has a journal, but `Frame` might not have its own journal, depending on the value of its `JournalOwnership` property. It has the following settings:

- **OwnsJournal**—The Frame has its own journal.
- **UsesParentJournal**—The history is stored in the parent container's journal or not at all if the parent doesn't have a journal.
- **Automatic**—Equivalent to UsesParentJournal if the Frame is hosted in either of the two navigation containers (NavigationWindow or Frame), or OwnsJournal otherwise. This is the default value.

When Frame gets its own journal, it also gets the built-in navigation buttons. But if you don't want them, you can set NavigationUIVisibility to Hidden.

TIP

When navigating to a Page via a URI (whether done by calling the Navigate method or by using Hyperlink), a new instance of Page is created, even if you've already visited it. Therefore, you need to maintain your own state (via static variables or Application.Properties, for example) if you want a page to "remember" its data. (When calling an overload of Navigate that accepts a Page instance, of course, you're in control of whether a new or old instance is used.)

In the case of journal navigation, however, you can force a Page to reuse the same instance by setting its JournalEntry.KeepAlive attached property to true.

TIP

A Page can opt out of the journal by setting its RemoveFromJournal property to true. This can be appropriate for pages representing a sequence of steps that shouldn't be randomly visited after the transaction is complete.

FAQ

Web browser–like Back and Forward actions are handled by the journal, but how do I implement Stop and Refresh?

There's no built-in user interface for Stop and Refresh buttons, but navigation containers have ways to easily accomplish these actions.

To stop a pending navigation at any time, you can call the navigation container's StopLoading method.

To refresh a page, simply call the navigation container's parameterless Refresh method. This acts identically to calling Navigate with the URI or instance for the current page, except that the data passed to the Navigating event contains the NavigationMode.Refresh value, in case any event handlers want to customize their behavior in this situation.

DIGGING DEEPER

Using the Journal for Purposes Other Than Navigation

You can add custom entries to the journal that have nothing to do with built-in navigation. For example, you could build an application-specific undo/redo scheme on top of the journal and get most of the functionality for free.

To do this, call the navigation container's `AddBackEntry` method with an instance of a `CustomContentState` object. `CustomContentState` is an abstract class, so you must create a derived class that implements a method called `Replay`. `Replay` is called whenever going back or forward makes the action the current state. You can optionally override the `JournalEntryName` property to give the entry a label in the drop-down list.

Photo Gallery uses this technique to implement a simple undoable image rotation, as follows:

```
[Serializable]
class RotateState : CustomContentState
{
  FrameworkElement element;
  double rotation;

  public RotateState(FrameworkElement element, double rotation)
  {
    this.element = element;
    this.rotation = rotation;
  }
  public override string JournalEntryName
  {
    get { return "Rotate " + rotation + "°"; }
  }

  public override void Replay(NavigationService navigationService,
                              NavigationMode mode)
  {
    // Rotate the element by the specified amount
    element.LayoutTransform = new RotateTransform(rotation);
  }
}
```

Navigation Events

Regardless of whether navigation occurs via `Navigate`, `Hyperlinks`, or the journal, it is performed asynchronously. A number of events are raised during the navigation process that enable you to display a rich user interface or even cancel navigation.

Figures 7.6 and 7.7 show the progression of navigation-related events when the first page is loaded and when navigation occurs from one page to another.

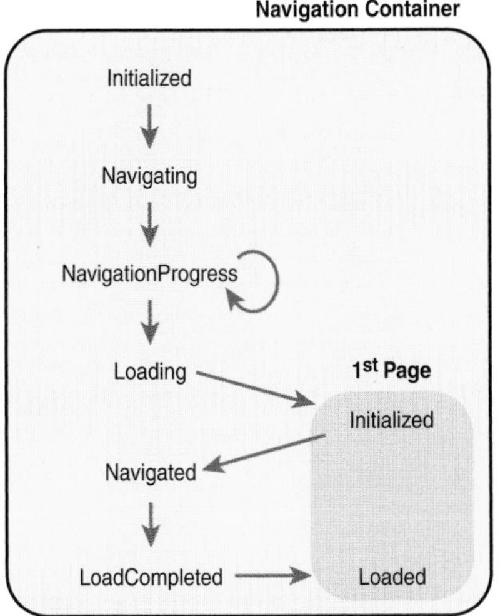

FIGURE 7.6 Navigation events that are raised when the first page is loaded.

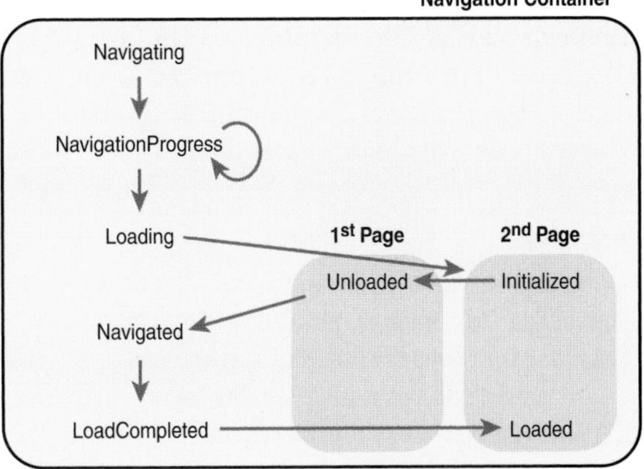

FIGURE 7.7 Navigation events that are raised when navigation occurs between two pages.

`NavigationProgress` is raised periodically until `Navigated` is raised. One event that isn't shown is `NavigationStopped`. This event is raised instead of `LoadCompleted` if the navigation is canceled or if an error occurs.

TIP

A navigation container raises the events shown in Figures 7.6 and 7.7 when navigation occurs within itself (including child containers). But `Application` also defines these events, enabling you to handle them in one place for all navigation containers within the `Application`.

7

WARNING

Navigation events aren't raised when navigating from one HTML page to another!

The WPF navigation events are raised when navigating from one WPF `Page` to another, from a WPF `Page` to an HTML page, and from an HTML page to a WPF `Page`. However, these events are not raised when navigating from one HTML page to another HTML page. Such HTML-to-HTML navigation also doesn't appear in the journal.

Passing Data Between Pages

When an application employs navigation for more than just document browsing, it likely needs to pass data from one page to another. HTML-based web applications might encode such data as URL parameters or use server-side variables. In WPF, you can use a variety of techniques for sending or returning data.

Sending Data to Pages

WPF supports a scheme similar to URL parameters via overloads of the Navigate method that accept an extra object parameter. There's an overload for the version that accepts a Page instance and an overload for the version that accepts a Uri. You can pass anything you want via this object parameter (a simple data type, an array, a custom data structure, and so on), and it is sent to the target page. Here's an example:

```
int photoId = 10;
// Navigate to a page instance
PhotoPage nextPage = new PhotoPage();
this.NavigationService.Navigate(nextPage, photoId);
// Or navigate to a page via a URI
this.NavigationService.Navigate(
  new Uri("PhotoPage.xaml", UriKind.Relative), photoId);
```

For the target page to receive this data, it must handle the navigation container's LoadCompleted event and check the ExtraData parameter of the event argument:

```
this.NavigationService.LoadCompleted += new
  LoadCompletedEventHandler(container_LoadCompleted);
…
void container_LoadCompleted(object sender, NavigationEventArgs e)
{
  if (e.ExtraData != null)
    LoadPhoto((int)e.ExtraData);
}
```

A simpler scheme of passing data, however, is to use the basic version of Navigate that accepts a Page instance and define a constructor on the target page that accepts the custom data (using as many parameters as you want). This looks like the following for the Photo Gallery example:

```
int photoId = 10;
// Navigate to a page instance
PhotoPage nextPage = new PhotoPage(photoId);
this.NavigationService.Navigate(nextPage);
```

For this to work, PhotoPage has a constructor defined as follows:

```
public PhotoPage(int id)
{
  LoadPhoto(id);
}
```

An advantage of this approach is that the parameters can be strongly typed, so PhotoPage doesn't need to check that the passed-in data is non-null or an integer. The type system guarantees it!

A third approach is to globally share the data in the `Application` object's `Properties` collection, discussed earlier in the chapter. Here's an example:

```
// Navigate to a page by instance or URI
Application.Properties["PhotoId"] = 10;
this.NavigationService.Navigate(…);
```

The target page can then check the value from anywhere in code that gets executed after `Navigate` is called:

```
if (Application.Properties["PhotoId"] != null)
  LoadPhoto((int)Application.Properties["PhotoId"]);
```

This might be the desired approach if you want to share the data between multiple pages (rather than explicitly pass it from page to page). However, just like the first scheme, it lacks the convenience of type safety.

Returning Data from Pages with `PageFunction`

Perhaps you want the user to navigate to a page, take some action, and then automatically return to a previous page that can act on the action (and, therefore, must receive data from the latter page). A classic example for this is a settings or options page. You could simulate this behavior by navigating forward to the old page and passing the data using the first two of the three schemes just discussed. This process is illustrated in Figure 7.8.

FIGURE 7.8 Simulating the return of data by navigating forward to the page on the back stack.

This can be awkward, however. If you're navigating via URI, you'd need to manually reconstruct the state of the new instance of `MainPage` to match the old instance. Furthermore, navigating forward to simulate the action of navigating back causes undesirable effects in the journal without manually manipulating it.

Instead, you could share the data globally (via `Application.Properties`) and have the target page call the navigation container's `GoBack` method to return to the previous page. This works but is a bit sloppy because of the global (and typeless) sharing of data that might be relevant to only two pages rather than to the entire application.

Therefore, WPF provides yet another mechanism to "return" data to the previous page in a type-safe manner and automatically navigate back to it, as illustrated in Figure 7.9.

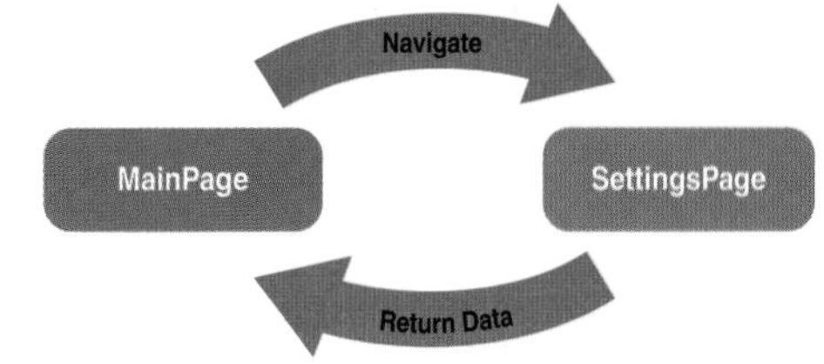

FIGURE 7.9 The commonsense navigation flow can be achieved with `PageFunction`.

This can be accomplished with a funny-named class called PageFunction. A PageFunction is really just a Page (because it derives from Page), but it acts like a function because of its mechanism for returning data.

Visual Studio has a template for creating a new PageFunction just like it does for Page. Here's what you get when you choose Page Function (WPF) via Visual Studio's Add New Item dialog:

```
<PageFunction
    xmlns="http://schemas.microsoft.com/winfx/2006/xaml/presentation"
    xmlns:x="http://schemas.microsoft.com/winfx/2006/xaml"
    xmlns:sys="clr-namespace:System;assembly=mscorlib"
    x:Class="MyProject.PageFunction1"
    x:TypeArguments="sys:String"
    Title="PageFunction1">
  <Grid>
  </Grid>
</PageFunction>
```

Notice the use of the TypeArguments keyword. PageFunction is actually a generic class (as in PageFunction<T>), where the type argument represents the type of the return value. For the PageFunction shown, the returned value must be a string. Although the use of generics makes defining a PageFunction a little trickier, the benefit is the type safety that is lacking from some of the earlier schemes.

Because PageFunction derives from Page, you can navigate to it just as you would with any other page:

```
PageFunction1 nextPage = new PageFunction1<string>();
this.NavigationService.Navigate(nextPage);
```

To receive the return value, the source page must handle PageFunction's Return event:

```
nextPage.Return += new ReturnEventHandler<string>(nextPage_Return);
…
void nextPage_Return(object sender, ReturnEventArgs<string> e)
{
  string returnValue = e.Result;
}
```

Notice that the same generic argument also applies to the ReturnEventHandler and ReturnEventArgs types. This enables the event argument's Result property to be the same type as the data returned by the PageFunction (a string in this case).

The PageFunction can return data by wrapping it in the ReturnEventArgs type and calling OnReturn, which it inherits from the base PageFunction class:

```
OnReturn(new ReturnEventArgs<string>("the data"));
```

Gadget-Style Applications

WPF makes it easier than ever to create nonrectangular top-level windows. With this support, you could give an otherwise-standard application custom chrome with a more fun shape. Or you could create a smaller gadget-style application that looks like a custom object "floating" on the desktop.

To take advantage of this support, just do the following:

1. On the `Window`, set `AllowsTransparency` to `true`. (If you're doing this programmatically, it must be set before the `Window` has been shown. Otherwise, you'll get an `InvalidOperationException`.)
2. Set the `Window`'s `WindowStyle` to `None`, which removes all the chrome. (Any other setting combined with `AllowsTransparency="True"` results in an `InvalidOperationException`.)
3. Set the `Window`'s `Background` to `Transparent`. This prevents the content from being surrounded by an opaque rectangle.
4. Decide how you want the user to move the `Window` around and call `Window`'s `DragMove` method at the appropriate place to enable it. Technically, this is not a requirement, but an application that can't be moved is not going to please users.
5. Consider adding a custom Close `Button` so the user doesn't have to right-click the Windows taskbar in order to close the application. This is especially important if you set `ShowInTaskbar` to `false`!

Here is a XAML file for such a `Window`, which contains a translucent red circle and a Close `Button`:

```
<Window x:Class="GadgetWindow"
  xmlns="http://schemas.microsoft.com/winfx/2006/xaml/presentation"
  xmlns:x="http://schemas.microsoft.com/winfx/2006/xaml"
  Height="300" Width="300"
  AllowsTransparency="True" WindowStyle="None" Background="Transparent"
  MouseLeftButtonDown="Window_MouseLeftButtonDown">
  <Grid>
    <Ellipse Fill="Red" Opacity="0.5" Margin="20">
    <Ellipse.Effect>
      <DropShadowEffect/>
    </Ellipse.Effect>
    </Ellipse>
    <Button Margin="100" Click="Button_Click">Close</Button>
  </Grid>
</Window>
```

DropShadowEffect, covered in Chapter 15, "2D Graphics," is added to give the circle a bit more visual polish. This Window uses the following code-behind file:

```
using System.Windows;
using System.Windows.Input;

public partial class GadgetWindow : Window
{
  public GadgetWindow()
  {
    InitializeComponent();
  }
  void Window_MouseLeftButtonDown(object sender, MouseButtonEventArgs e)
  {
    this.DragMove();
  }
  void Button_Click(object sender, RoutedEventArgs e)
  {
    this.Close();
  }
}
```

To enable the Window to be moved, the handler for MouseLeftButtonDown simply calls Window.DragMove. DragMove handles the rest of the logic automatically. Figure 7.10 shows this little application in action.

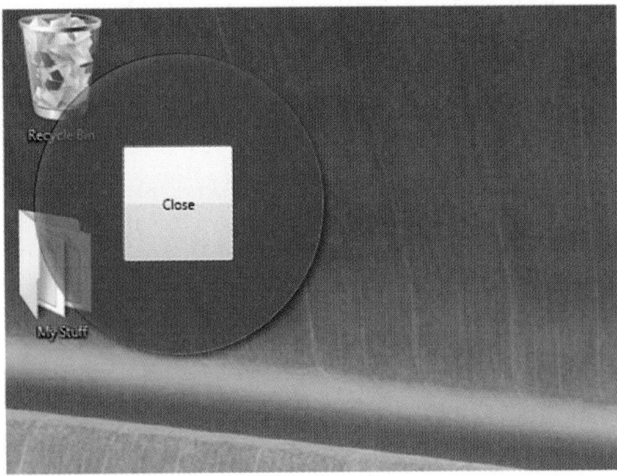

FIGURE 7.10 An invisible Window that contains nonrectangular (and half-transparent) content.

XAML Browser Applications

WPF supports the creation of applications that run directly in a web browser. They are called XAML Browser Applications (XBAPs), but WPF Browser Applications would be a more appropriate name. XBAPs have become less attractive over time as Silverlight has gained more of WPF's power, but they still serve a purpose of delivering partial-trust WPF content in a browser, without any prompts getting in the way.

Creating an XBAP isn't much different from creating a standard Windows application, as long as you stay within the subset of the .NET Framework available from partial-trust code. The main differences are as follows:

- Not all features in WPF or the .NET Framework are accessible (by default).
- Navigation is integrated into the browser.
- Deployment is handled differently.

FAQ

Do XAML Browser Applications work on any operating system or in any web browser?

No. Unlike Silverlight applications, XBAPs require the full .NET Framework (3.0 or later) and therefore run only on Windows. They are also only supported in Internet Explorer (or any program that hosts the Microsoft `WebBrowser` ActiveX control) and Firefox (with the .NET Framework 3.5 or later). With the .NET Framework 4.0, Firefox support requires an add-on to be explicitly downloaded and installed. (Version 3.5 installed the add-on automatically.)

This section drills into these three aspects of XAML Browser Applications.

So how do you create a XAML Browser Application? If you have Visual Studio, you simply follow these steps:

1. Create a new XAML Browser Application project in Visual Studio. (Visual Studio appropriately calls it a WPF Browser Application instead.)
2. Create the user interface inside a `Page` and add the appropriate code-behind logic.
3. Compile and run the project.

If you don't have Visual Studio, you can still use MSBuild on project files with the appropriate settings, as described in the Digging Deeper sidebar.

DIGGING DEEPER

How XAML Browser Applications Work

There's nothing XBAP-specific about the source files generated by Visual Studio. The key is in a handful of settings in the project file, such as these:

```
<HostInBrowser>True</HostInBrowser>
<Install>False</Install>
<TargetZone>Internet</TargetZone>
```

Continued

The project file also contains a few settings to make the debugger launch `PresentationHost.exe` rather than the output of the compilation.

A standard executable is generated, but it does nothing if it is run directly because the infrastructure quits if it detects that it's not hosted in a web browser. In addition to the EXE file, two XML files are generated:

- A `.manifest` file, which is a ClickOnce application manifest
- An `.xbap` file, which is simply a ClickOnce deployment manifest (typically seen with the `.application` extension for non-XBAPs)

And that's it. XBAPs are really just online-only ClickOnce applications, but with some special handling by WPF for the browser-integrated experience.

WARNING

Beware of ClickOnce caching!

XBAPs are based on ClickOnce technology, which has caching behavior that can be confusing during development. For maximum performance, a ClickOnce application is stored in a cache when first run. Subsequent requests to run the application go to the cache unless the application's version number changes. (As with isolated storage, the ClickOnce cache is implemented as a hidden folder under the current user's Documents folder.)

Therefore, if you make a change to an application, recompile it, and then run it, you won't see the result of your changes if you don't also change the version number! The default Visual Studio settings increment your version number each time you recompile (because of the `AssemblyVersion("1.0.*")` marking in the `AssemblyInfo` source file), so you won't encounter this issue unless you give your application a fixed version number.

If you find incrementing the version number on recompilation to be unacceptable, you can clear the cache at any time, using the `mage.exe` tool in the Windows SDK. Just run `mage -cc` at a command prompt. Or you can execute the following command without requiring the SDK to be installed:

```
rundll32 %windir%\system32\dfshim.dll CleanOnlineAppCache
```

Limited Feature Set

For a simple WPF application, you can change a few project settings, recompile, and run it just fine as a XAML browser application. But WPF applications usually aren't so simple. What complicates developing a XAML browser application is that XBAPs run as partially trusted in the Internet zone, so not all APIs work in this context. For example, if you try to convert the standard Photo Gallery application to an XBAP, you'll quickly find that a call such as the following throws a (very verbose) security exception:

```
// Whoops! Partially trusted code is not allowed to get this data!
AddFavorite(Environment.GetFolderPath(Environment.SpecialFolder.MyPictures));
```

The .NET Framework's code access security blocks the call because it requires `FileIOPermission`, which is not granted to the Internet zone by default. (Note that individual users could expand the set of allowed permissions in their Internet zone, but they are not likely to do so, nor should they do so, because of the security risks.)

For most people, figuring out what works and what doesn't in the Internet zone is a process of trial and error. Some features don't work because of their inherently insecure nature—for example, arbitrary access to the local file system or Registry, interoperability with unmanaged code, or launching new `Windows`. (You can use `Popup` elements, but they won't extend past the `Page`'s bounds.) But some other features that aren't allowed in the Internet zone aren't obvious because the restriction is a result of implementation details. Other features may be restricted depending on the host browser. For example, WPF does not allow its `WebBrowser` control to be used in an XBAP *when the XBAP is hosted in Firefox*.

TIP

If you want to share the same code between a full-trust standard application and a partial-trust XBAP, it's helpful to be able to determine which state you're in at runtime so you can adapt to your environment. This can be done with the static `BrowserInteropHelper.IsBrowserHosted` Boolean property in the `System.Windows.Interop` namespace.

Despite the limitations, there is still a lot of functionality to take advantage of in the Internet zone. You still can display rich text and media, read/write to isolated storage (up to 512 KB), and open arbitrary files on the host web server. You can even launch the browser's standard File, Open dialog to interact with local files (with the user's explicit permission). This is done with `Microsoft.Win32.OpenFileDialog` as follows:

```
string fileContents = null;
OpenFileDialog ofd = new OpenFileDialog();
if (ofd.ShowDialog() == true) // Result could be true, false, or null
{
  using (Stream s = ofd.OpenFile())
  using (StreamReader sr = new StreamReader(s))
  {
    fileContents = sr.ReadToEnd();
  }
}
```

TIP

Another difference between a XAML Browser Application and a standard Windows application is the way in which parameters (or, really, any external data) are passed in. One simple approach is to send URL parameters to the HTML page hosting an XBAP and then have the XBAP call `BrowserInteropHelper.Source` to retrieve the complete URL (including parameters). Another approach is to store the information in a browser cookie and then retrieve the cookie by using the `Application.GetCookie` method.

FAQ

How do I enable my own components to run in the Internet zone?

You use the same mechanism that applies to all .NET components: If you mark an assembly with the `AllowPartiallyTrustedCallers` attribute and install it into the Global Assembly Cache (which can be done only if the user trusts your code and decides to run it), any of the assembly's public APIs can be called by any XBAP.

Note that marking an assembly with `AllowPartiallyTrustedCallers` should never be taken lightly. Any security bug or design flaw that makes it inappropriate for the Internet zone could open up your users to a severe security hole. And if that happens, they might never trust code from you again!

FAQ

How do I create a full-trust XAML Browser Application?

If you want to take advantage of functionality that requires a higher level of trust yet still want to be integrated into a browser, you can configure an XBAP to require full trust. The two actions to enable this are a bit convoluted, however:

1. In the ClickOnce application manifest (`app.manifest`), add `Unrestricted="true"` to the `PermissionSet` XML element, as in the following example:

```
<PermissionSet class="System.Security.PermissionSet" version="1"
 ID="Custom" SameSite="site" Unrestricted="true"/>
```

2. In the project file (with the `.csproj` or `.vbproj` extension), change this:

```
<TargetZone>Internet</TargetZone>
```

to this:

```
<TargetZone>Custom</TargetZone>
```

You can also make this change inside Visual Studio's project properties user interface on the Security tab.

After you do this, deploying and running your XBAP in the Local Computer zone should work just fine. It's also possible to run such a full-trust application in the Internet zone, but only if users list you (or, more specifically, the certificate used to sign the manifest) as a trusted publisher.

Integrated Navigation

All `Pages` in XBAPs are implicitly hosted in a `NavigationWindow`. In Internet Explorer 6 and Firefox, you see the typical bar with Back and Forward buttons. This is usually not desirable because many XBAPs don't take advantage of navigation. And if they do, having separate Back and Forward buttons right below the browser's Back and Forward buttons is clumsy. To disable this unwanted navigation bar, you can set `ShowsNavigationUI` to `false` on your `Page`.

Fortunately, versions 7 and later of Internet Explorer merge the `NavigationWindow`'s journal with the browser's own journal, providing a much slicker experience. The separate navigation bar is not shown, and WPF journal entries automatically appear in the browser's Back/Forward list, right along with web pages.

TIP

The journal integration in Internet Explorer 7 and later applies only to the top-level `Page`. If you host an XBAP in an HTML `IFRAME`, you still get the navigation bar unless you set `ShowsNavigationUI` to `false` on the WPF `Page`.

Deployment

Deploying an XBAP is as easy as deploying any other ClickOnce application. It's a matter of using Visual Studio's publishing wizard (or the Mage tool in the Windows SDK) and copying the files to a web server or file share. (The web server must also be configured to serve the content correctly.)

The most compelling thing about XBAPs is the fact that users can install and run them simply by navigating to a URL, with no plug-in required (in the case of Internet Explorer). In addition, unlike with other ClickOnce applications, no security prompts get in the way, assuming that you don't create an XBAP that needs nonstandard permissions. (So you don't even have to "click once" to view such an application!)

FAQ

There are no security prompts when running an XBAP? Isn't that a huge security issue?

As with any other software features, there is some risk of enabling a security breach just by being enabled. But with the multiple layers of security from Windows, Internet Explorer, and the .NET Framework, the WPF team is confident that users are safe from hackers who would try to use the XBAP mechanism to circumvent security. For example, the .NET Framework enforces a sandbox on top of the sandbox already enforced by Internet Explorer. And although this amount of security should be enough in theory, WPF goes one step further and removes additional operating system–level privileges from the host process token (such as the ability to load device drivers), just in case all the other layers of security are somehow breached.

TIP

Similar to Silverlight, XBAPs are the key to using WPF content in diverse environments. For example, Windows Media Center and Windows desktop gadgets enable developers to plug in HTML. By hosting an XBAP in an HTML page, you can create a WPF Media Center application or a WPF desktop gadget simply by creating an appropriate XBAP!

Downloading Files on Demand

ClickOnce provides support for on-demand downloading of files in an application, so you can design a small application that loads quickly and then downloads additional content as needed, based on arbitrary logic. This support is a great remedy for large XBAPs that would otherwise be slow to load, and it can apply to other types of applications as well.

To take advantage of this support, you can assign a set of loose files in a project to a *download group* in Visual Studio. This functionality can be found under Publish, Application Files in the project's Properties page. You can then programmatically prompt the download and be notified when it completes by using a few APIs in the `System.Deployment.Application` namespace (in `System.Deployment.dll`).

Listing 7.3 demonstrates how this might be done to display a custom progress user interface while the application's main content loads. The application is assumed to start by loading `Page1`, whose code-behind file is the content of Listing 7.3. (The specific user interface presumed to be defined in XAML is irrelevant.) `Page1` initiates the download of any files assigned to a download group called MyGroup and then navigates to `Page2` (which presumably uses some of these downloaded files) when the download is complete.

LISTING 7.3 Using ClickOnce Support for On-Demand Download

```
using System;
using System.Windows.Controls;
using System.Windows.Threading;
using System.Deployment.Application;

public partial class Page1 : Page
{
  public Page1()
  {
    InitializeComponent();
  }

  protected override void OnInitialized(EventArgs e)
  {
    base.OnInitialized(e);

    if (ApplicationDeployment.IsNetworkDeployed)
    {
      // Handle the event that is raised when the download of files
      // in MyGroup is complete.
      ApplicationDeployment.CurrentDeployment.DownloadFileGroupCompleted +=
      delegate {
        // We're on a different thread, so invoke GotoPage2 on the UI thread
        Dispatcher.BeginInvoke(DispatcherPriority.Send,
          new DispatcherOperationCallback(GotoPage2), null);
      };
```

LISTING 7.3 Continued

```
      ApplicationDeployment.CurrentDeployment.DownloadFileGroupAsync("MyGroup");
    }
    else
    {
      // We're not running in the context of ClickOnce (perhaps because
      // we're being debugged), so just go directly to Page2.
      GotoPage2(null);
    }
  }

  // Navigates to Page2 when ready. Accepts and returns an object simply
  // to match the signature of DispatcherOperationCallback
  private object GotoPage2(object o)
  {
    return NavigationService.Navigate(new Uri("Page2.xaml", UriKind.Relative));
  }
}
```

The download support applies only when the application is run over the network (not locally under a debugger), so the listing first calls `ApplicationDeployment.IsNetworkDeployed` to determine whether to rely on it. If the application is not network deployed, all files are present locally, so the code immediately navigates to `Page2`. Otherwise, the download is prompted by calling `DownloadFileGroupAsync`. Before that call, however, an anonymous delegate is attached to the `DownloadFileGroupCompleted` event so the navigation can be initiated as soon as the download finishes. `ApplicationDeployment` defines additional events, in case you want to expose more fine-grained progress during the download process.

Loose XAML Pages

If the .NET Framework 3.0 or later is installed, Internet Explorer can navigate to a loose `.xaml` file just like a `.html` file and render it with WPF. Therefore, in certain environments, XAML can be used as a richer form of HTML, with better support for layout, text, graphics, and so on. It's a bit limiting in that you can't use any procedural code in loose XAML and such pages can be rendered only on Windows. Still, this support can be interesting for experimentation.

Despite the lack of procedural code, you can still create pretty powerful dynamic user interfaces in loose XAML, thanks to data binding (covered in Chapter 13, "Data Binding"). Figure 7.11 shows the loose XAML version of Photo Gallery, which displays a static set of pictures from the web server but uses data binding to keep the snazzy zoom feature.

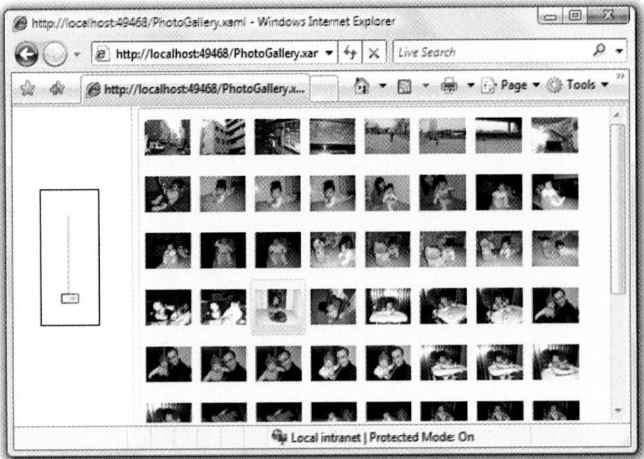

FIGURE 7.11 Photo Gallery can still be very functional as a loose XAML page.

> **TIP**
>
> If you want your website to take advantage of the richness of loose XAML but still want to show HTML to users who aren't able to view XAML, you can maintain two versions of your content and adaptively pick the appropriate one. This is easy to do by checking the user agent string for content such as ".NET CLR 3.0." That said, I've never seen a website go through the hassle of doing this. Adaptively adding Silverlight to your website would be a much better choice.

> **TIP**
>
> To mix HTML and loose XAML content, simply host one or more `.xaml` files in `IFRAME`s on an HTML page.

Summary

WPF's rich support for building applications covers all the basics needed by a Windows application and extends into areas such as web browser–like navigation and web browser–hosted content. As demonstrated by the Photo Gallery source code that accompanies this book (available from the website, http://informit.com/title/9780672331190), you can sometimes apply the same user interface implementation to everything from a traditional Windows application to a code-less "rich web page."

The deployment of an application can be fast and easy in each case examined in this chapter. The only wrinkle is the prerequisite of having the right version of the .NET Framework installed. Fortunately, with WPF 3.0 installed by default with Windows Vista, WPF 3.5 installed by default with Windows 7, and WPF 4 or later likely to be installed by default on the next version of Windows, this prerequisite is less of an issue if you don't require the most recent version of the .NET Framework.

CHAPTER 8

Exploiting Windows 7

IN THIS CHAPTER

With every new version of Windows comes a vast amount of new functionality for developers to exploit, and Windows 7 is no exception. Windows 7, like Windows Vista, introduced a number of new user interface concepts for applications to leverage. An application can appear much more modern and provide users some extra delight by exploiting these features.

This chapter begins by examining how to leverage two common features that make a WPF application feel more at home on Windows 7:

- Jump Lists
- Taskbar item customizations

After that, it demonstrates two features introduced in Windows Vista that are still just as relevant for Windows 7:

- Aero Glass
- `TaskDialog`

Jump Lists

One of the most prominent new user interface features in Windows 7 is Jump Lists on taskbar items. A Jump List contains handy shortcuts and can be seen when you right-click or swipe upward on a taskbar item. Figure 8.1 shows the Jump List for Internet Explorer.

Even if an application doesn't do anything to take advantage of Jump Lists, it still gets a default one. Figure 8.2 shows the default Jump List for the previous chapter's Photo Gallery application, when the application is open and when it is closed. (You can see a Jump List for a closed application only if it has been pinned to the taskbar.)

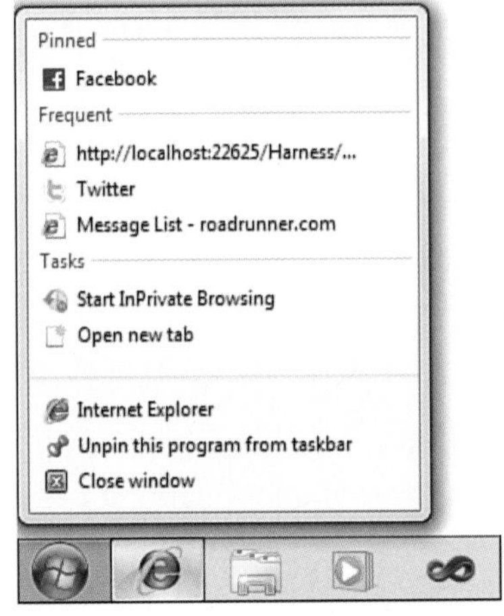

FIGURE 8.1 The Jump List for Internet Explorer can contain items in several categories.

In WPF 4, the `System.Windows.Shell.JumpList` class enables you to define a custom Jump List for an application in simple managed code—or even in XAML! This doesn't mean that you can use WPF visual elements inside the Jump List, just that the available functionality is exposed via managed objects with simple properties.

To associate a custom Jump List with an application, you set the silly-sounding `JumpList.JumpList` attached property on the `Application` instance to a `JumpList` instance or call the corresponding `JumpList.SetJumpList` method from procedural code. If you create or modify a `JumpList` from procedural code, you must call `JumpList`'s `Apply` method to send the updates to the Windows shell.

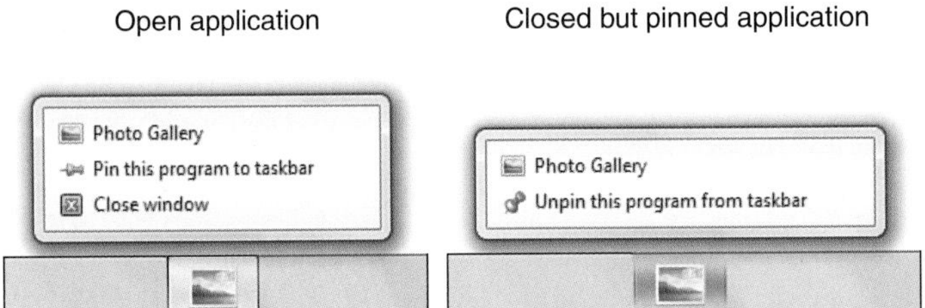

FIGURE 8.2 The default Jump List for Photo Gallery.

`JumpList` has a `JumpItems` content property that can contain two types of items, `JumpTasks` and `JumpPaths`, both of which derive from a common abstract `JumpItem` class.

JumpTask

To a user, `JumpTasks` represent actions to perform, such as the Start InPrivate Browsing and Open new tab tasks from Figure 8.1. To a developer, `JumpTasks` represent programs to be launched (operating system tasks). These are typically used to launch the host program with command-line arguments that indicate which task was selected.

Listing 8.1 demonstrates the use of a few `JumpTasks` by updating the `App.xaml` file from the last chapter's Photo Gallery example. The resulting Jump List is shown in Figure 8.3. Notice that the bottom three items (two, if the application is pinned and closed) are always present, so a custom Jump List only affects what items are presented on top of these standard ones.

LISTING 8.1 App.xaml—Applying a Custom JumpList with Simple JumpTasks

```
<Application x:Class="PhotoGallery.App"
             xmlns="http://schemas.microsoft.com/winfx/2006/xaml/presentation"
             xmlns:x="http://schemas.microsoft.com/winfx/2006/xaml"
             StartupUri="MainWindow.xaml">
<JumpList.JumpList>
  <JumpList>
    <JumpTask Title="Launch another instance"
              Description="Launches another instance of this program."/>
    <JumpTask Title="Task #1" Arguments="-task1"
              Description="Performs task #1."/>
    <JumpTask Title="Task #2" Arguments="-task2"
              Description="Performs task #2."/>
  </JumpList>
</JumpList.JumpList>
</Application>
```

Each `JumpTask` has a `Title` shown inside the Jump List and an optional `Description` used as its tooltip. Because no other properties are specified, the first `JumpTask` simply relaunches the host Photo Gallery application. This duplicates the functionality of the standard Photo Gallery item in the bottom section of the Jump List, so it doesn't make sense for a real application to do this. The next two `JumpTasks`, however, pass command-line arguments so the new instance of Photo Gallery that gets launched can take some arbitrary action. Photo Gallery can use `Environment.CommandLine` at some point in its initialization to respond appropriately.

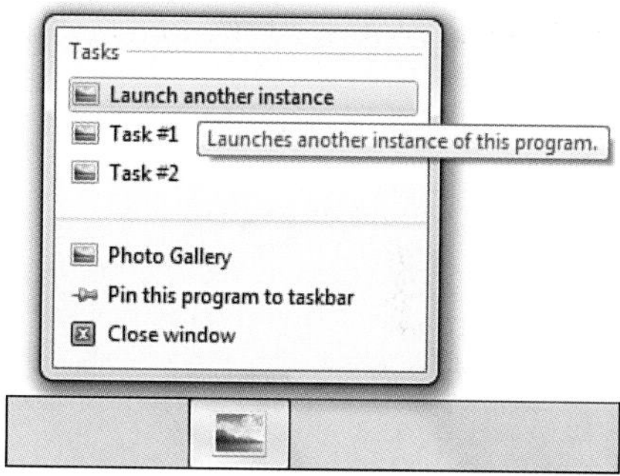

FIGURE 8.3 A custom Jump List with three simple `JumpTasks`.

TIP

From the user's perspective, a typical task from a Jump List doesn't launch a new instance of the program but rather causes something to happen inside the already-running instance. To accomplish this behavior, you can make an application a single-instance application (discussed in the preceding chapter) and communicate the action back to the running instance.

Whenever an application has a custom Jump List, its items also appear in the Start menu when the application is selected. Figure 8.4 shows how the Jump List from Listing 8.1 automatically enhances the Start menu.

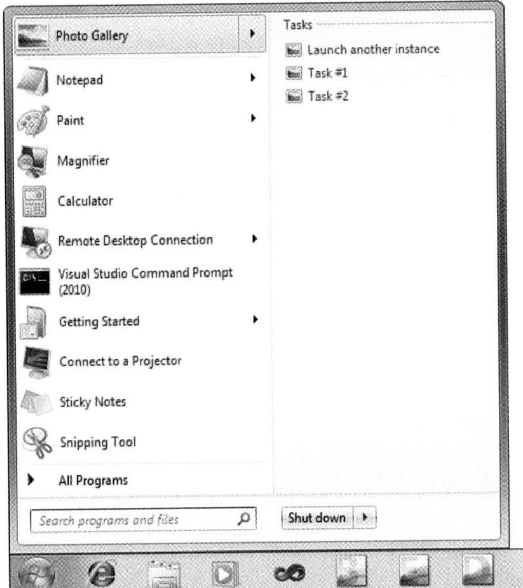

FIGURE 8.4 The same Jump List from Figure 8.3 automatically appears in the Start menu.

WARNING

Visual Studio's debugger interferes with Jump Lists!

When you run an application under the Visual Studio debugger, the application appears as `vshost32.exe`, as shown in Figure 8.5. You still see the custom `JumpTasks`, but their icons might be different, and clicking on them won't work (because it causes `vshost32.exe`, rather than your application, to be launched). The situation is even worse for `JumpPaths`, described in the next section, which don't appear at all. To avoid this problem, you can uncheck "Enable the Visual Studio hosting process" in the Debug section of the project's properties.

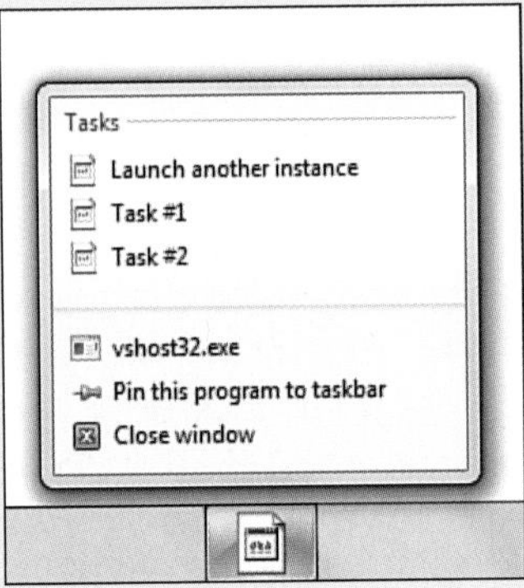

FIGURE 8.5 The Jump List is affected by Visual Studio's debugger host process.

WARNING

Jump Lists are shared by all instances of an application!

Jump Lists are associated with an application—not a specific window or running instance. Any items placed in a Jump List are persisted when the application isn't running. If a second instance of an application starts and places different items in its Jump List, those items replace the items that the first instance previously placed.

Customizing `JumpTask` Behavior

`JumpTask` has a number of properties for customizing each item's icon and for launching other applications besides the host. Listing 8.2 demonstrates these properties, and Figure 8.6 shows the results.

LISTING 8.2 `App.xaml`—Demonstrating Additional `JumpTask` Properties

```
<Application x:Class="PhotoGallery.App"
             xmlns="http://schemas.microsoft.com/winfx/2006/xaml/presentation"
             xmlns:x="http://schemas.microsoft.com/winfx/2006/xaml"
             StartupUri="MainWindow.xaml">
<JumpList.JumpList>
  <JumpList>
    <JumpTask Title="Magnifier"
              Description="Open the Windows Magnifier."
              ApplicationPath="%WINDIR%\system32\magnify.exe"/>
    <JumpTask Title="Calculator"
              Description="Open the Windows Calculator."
              ApplicationPath="%WINDIR%\system32\calc.exe"
              IconResourcePath="%WINDIR%\system32\calc.exe"/>
    <JumpTask Title="Notepad"
              Description="Open Notepad."
              ApplicationPath="%WINDIR%\system32\notepad.exe"
              IconResourcePath="%WINDIR%\system32\notepad.exe"
              WorkingDirectory="%HOMEDRIVE%%HOMEPATH%"/>
    <JumpTask Title="Internet Explorer (No Add-Ons)"
              Description="Start without ActiveX controls or extensions."
              ApplicationPath="%PROGRAMFILES%\Internet Explorer\iexplore.exe"
              IconResourcePath="%PROGRAMFILES%\Internet Explorer\iexplore.exe"
              WorkingDirectory="%HOMEDRIVE%%HOMEPATH%"
              IconResourceIndex="6" Arguments="-extoff"/>
  </JumpList>
</JumpList.JumpList>
</Application>
```

8

Each JumpTask sets an additional property to customize the experience above and beyond the previous one. The first item leverages ApplicationPath to invoke magnify.exe. Notice that ApplicationPath happily accepts environment variable syntax, so you can reliably set certain paths in XAML rather than build up the path in procedural code.

The second JumpTask sets IconResourcePath to customize the icon. The icon should be a Win32 resource embedded inside an EXE or DLL file. (You can specify a loose .ico file instead, but this requires a full path that doesn't use environment variables, so it's not reasonable to set this inside XAML.) By setting the path to an EXE file, you can easily get the default icon for that program. When IconResourcePath is null, as with the first JumpTask, the host executable is used. That's why the first JumpTask picks up Photo Gallery's icon.

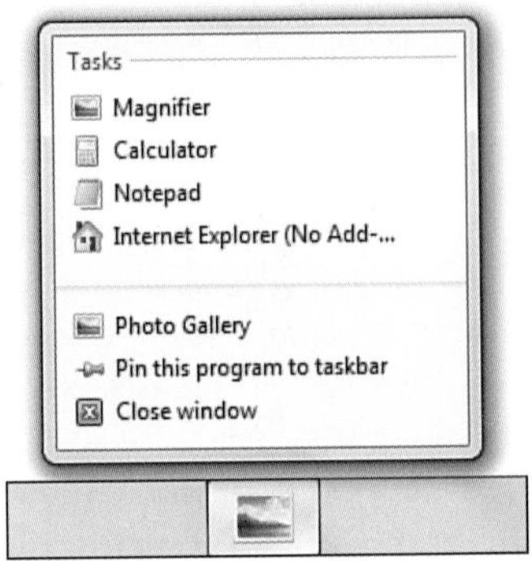

FIGURE 8.6 Launching other programs with customized JumpTasks.

TIP

%WINDIR%\System32\shell32.dll and %WINDIR%\System32\imageres.dll have many stock icons that can useful for JumpTasks. They are not guaranteed to be the same across different versions of Windows, but they can be helpful.

The third JumpTask sets WorkingDirectory to affect how the program (Notepad, in this case) is launched. As with ApplicationPath and IconResourcePath, you can use environment variable syntax inside the string.

The last JumpTask not only sets Arguments to invoke Internet Explorer in its "no add-ons" mode but sets IconResourceIndex to customize the icon. This is why the icon in Figure 8.6 is a house rather than the blue "e" logo. An EXE or DLL file might have a long list of icon resources embedded inside. When IconResourceIndex is left at its default value of zero, the first icon (the one also used by the Windows shell) is used. But if the EXE or DLL file has more, you simply set IconResourceIndex to a higher index to leverage it. If you specify an invalid index, you get a generic icon, like the one shown in Figure 8.5.

TIP

If you don't want any icon next to a JumpTask, set its IconResourceIndex to -1. This works whether or not you explicitly set IconResourcePath.

TIP

If you want to separate JumpTasks with a horizontal line, just add a JumpTask at the appropriate spot, with no properties set. Figure 8.7 shows the result of adding <JumpTask/> between the first two JumpTasks and again adding <JumpTask/> between the last two JumpTasks from Listing 8.2.

FIGURE 8.7 Adding two horizontal line separators with empty JumpTask elements.

Custom Categories

You can use one more property to customize the behavior of a JumpTask, although this one is inherited from the base JumpItem class. You can set the CustomCategory property to any non-empty string to place an item in a separate section with a heading other than the "Tasks" default.

Listing 8.3 updates Listing 8.2 by placing one item in a category called One and two items in a category called Two. Figure 8.8 shows the results.

LISTING 8.3 App.xaml—Using the CustomCategory Property

```
<Application x:Class="PhotoGallery.App"
             xmlns="http://schemas.microsoft.com/winfx/2006/xaml/presentation"
             xmlns:x="http://schemas.microsoft.com/winfx/2006/xaml"
             StartupUri="MainWindow.xaml">
<JumpList.JumpList>
  <JumpList>
    <JumpTask Title="Magnifier" CustomCategory="One"
              Description="Open the Windows Magnifier."
              ApplicationPath="%WINDIR%\system32\magnify.exe"/>
```

LISTING 8.3 Continued

```
    <JumpTask Title="Calculator" CustomCategory="Two"
              Description="Open the Windows Calculator."
              ApplicationPath="%WINDIR%\system32\calc.exe"
              IconResourcePath="%WINDIR%\system32\calc.exe"/>
    <JumpTask Title="Notepad" CustomCategory="Two"
              Description="Open Notepad."
              ApplicationPath="%WINDIR%\system32\notepad.exe"
              IconResourcePath="%WINDIR%\system32\notepad.exe"
              WorkingDirectory="%HOMEDRIVE%%HOMEPATH%"/>
    <JumpTask Title="Internet Explorer (No Add-Ons)"
              Description="Start without ActiveX controls or extensions."
              ApplicationPath="%PROGRAMFILES%\Internet Explorer\iexplore.exe"
              IconResourcePath="%PROGRAMFILES%\Internet Explorer\iexplore.exe"
              WorkingDirectory="%HOMEDRIVE%%HOMEPATH%"
              IconResourceIndex="6" Arguments="-extoff"/>
  </JumpList>
</JumpList.JumpList>
</Application>
```

Items in custom categories automatically support user pinning and user removal. (The latter is available via a context menu.) When an item is pinned, it moves into a Pinned category. The user can later unpin the item, as shown in Figure 8.9.

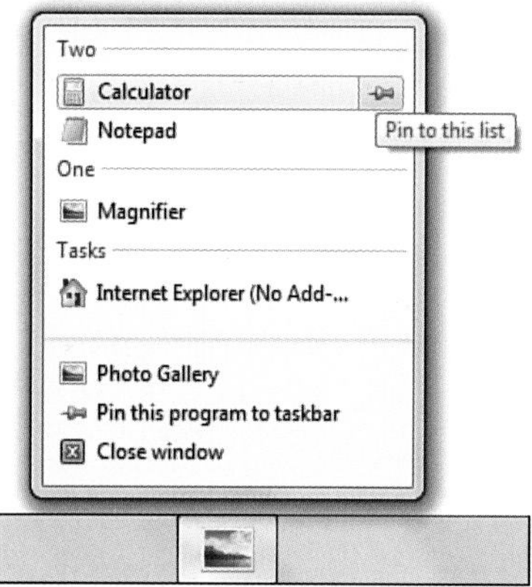

FIGURE 8.8 Applying custom categories to a Jump List.

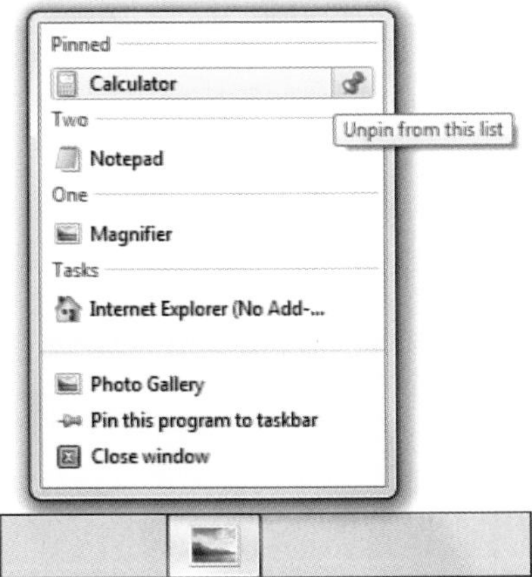

FIGURE 8.9 Pinning a `JumpTask` from a custom category.

> **WARNING**
>
> **Pinning a `JumpTask` doesn't work when it its `Arguments` property is not set!**
>
> Due to a bug in Windows 7, argument-free tasks cannot be pinned. The pin button still appears, but nothing happens when the user clicks on it. Fortunately, most tasks use at least one argument. If you want to launch a program that doesn't need any arguments, and if you are not able to pass a dummy argument, you can work around this by using an intermediary program that accepts and ignores the argument.

> **WARNING**
>
> **Custom categories appear in order from the bottom up!**
>
> Both `JumpTask`s and custom categories appear in the order in which they appear inside the `JumpItems` collection. However, whereas the list of `JumpTask`s grows from top to bottom, the list of categories grows from bottom to top! That is why Two appears above One in Figures 8.8 and 8.9.

JumpPath

Whereas `JumpTask`s represent programs, `JumpPath`s represent files that can be opened by the host application. In fact, an application can use `JumpPath`s only if it is registered with Windows to handle the relevant file extension(s). To run the examples in this section, you can temporarily register the sample application as a handler for `.JPG` files. (For experimentation, you probably want to do this via Windows Explorer's Open With, Choose Default Program context menu item rather than doing this programmatically.)

Listing 8.4 updates Listing 8.3 by adding a `JumpPath` to the existing collection of `JumpTask`s. (`JumpPath`s and `JumpTask`s can be intermingled because they share the common JumpItem base class.) Because this file exists on the current C: drive, and because the application is registered to handle .JPG files, the Jump List now appears as shown in Figure 8.10. If either of these conditions were false, the Jump List would appear the same as it did in Figure 8.8.

LISTING 8.4 App.xaml—Adding a JumpPath to Listing 8.3

```
<Application x:Class="PhotoGallery.App"
             xmlns="http://schemas.microsoft.com/winfx/2006/xaml/presentation"
             xmlns:x="http://schemas.microsoft.com/winfx/2006/xaml"
             StartupUri="MainWindow.xaml">
<JumpList.JumpList>
  <JumpList>
    <JumpPath Path="C:\Users\Adam\Pictures\DSC06397.jpg"
              CustomCategory="Photos"/>
    <JumpTask Title="Magnifier" CustomCategory="One"
              Description="Open the Windows Magnifier."
              ApplicationPath="%WINDIR%\system32\magnify.exe"/>
    …
  </JumpList>
</JumpList.JumpList>
</Application>
```

FIGURE 8.10 A JumpPath added to the Jump List from Figure 8.8 in its own Photos custom category.

By default, JumpPaths are placed in the Tasks category, which is a bit odd. But you can set CustomCategory (inherited from JumpItem) to move them to different categories. This approach has the advantage of making each item automatically pinnable.

When the user clicks the DSC06397.jpg item, a new instance of the host application is launched, with Path passed as the one and only command-line argument. Therefore, except for its icon and context menu, the JumpPath in Listing 8.4 is somewhat like the following JumpTask:

```
<JumpTask Title="DSC06397.jpg"
          Arguments="C:\Users\Adam\Pictures\DSC06397.jpg"
          Description="DSC06397 (C:\Users\Adam\My Pictures)"
          CustomCategory="Photos"/>
```

It is the responsibility of the application to respect the command-line argument and do whatever it means to "open" the file, just as with any other JumpTasks you may define.

WARNING

JumpPath's Path property does not support environment variable syntax!

That is why Listing 8.4 uses a hard-coded path to the .JPG file. In practice, however, this should not be a big problem. Applications typically add JumpPaths dynamically from procedural code, which can use arbitrary logic (including environment variables) to compose each path.

Recent and Frequent JumpPaths

Most applications—even ones that are registered handlers for certain file types—will have no reason to do anything explicit with JumpPaths. That's because Jump Lists automatically provide end-to-end functionality for the two most common types of categories—*recent items* and *frequent items*.

To get either one of these categories added to a Jump List, you simply set JumpList's ShowRecentCategory and/or ShowFrequentCategory properties to true. These categories will automatically appear and be populated if appropriate files have been recently and/or frequently opened. Windows tracks the opening of a file whenever it is done through the common File Open dialog or whenever the file type association is leveraged (for example, by double-clicking the file in Windows Explorer or by clicking a JumpPath).

If you want to force items onto these lists (for example, if an application opens files in a way that doesn't go through these mechanisms), you can call the JumpList.AddToRecentCategory method. It has overloads that accept either a path string, a JumpPath instance, or even a JumpTask instance. There is no AddToFrequentCategory method; you would only be able to force an item to show up as frequent by adding it to the recent category enough times.

Adding both categories to the JumpList from Listing 8.4 gives the result in Figure 8.11:

```
<JumpList ShowFrequentCategory="True" ShowRecentCategory="True">
  <JumpPath Path="C:\Users\Adam\Pictures\DSC06397.jpg"
            CustomCategory="Photos"/>
  <JumpTask Title="Magnifier" CustomCategory="One"
            Description="Open the Windows Magnifier."
```

```
        ApplicationPath="%WINDIR%\system32\magnify.exe"/>
  …
</JumpList>
```

Of course, using both categories simultaneously is not typical due to the high amount of overlap that is likely between the two lists. As seen in Figure 8.1, Internet Explorer chooses to show Frequent, whereas a lot of applications choose Recent. (Windows 7 provides the Recent category automatically for apps not built to specifically take advantage of Jump Lists.)

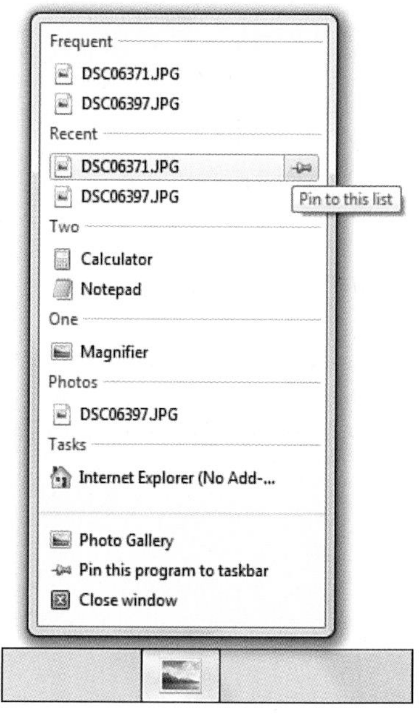

FIGURE 8.11 Leveraging the built-in Recent and Frequent categories.

Responding to Rejected or Removed Items

Because `JumpPath`s added to `JumpList`'s `JumpItems` property might be rejected by Windows if the application isn't registered to handle the file type or if the file doesn't exist, items are sometimes automatically removed from the `JumpItems` collection. If you want to react to such automatic removal, you can handle `JumpList`'s `JumpItemsRejected` event.

`JumpItemsRejected` is raised *once* if one or more items are removed, although not until the next time a `JumpList` is applied, such as the next launch of the application. To handle the event for a XAML-defined `JumpList`, you should attach the handler in XAML. For a `JumpList` created in procedural code, be sure to attach the handler before calling `Apply`.

The `JumpItemsRejectedEventArgs` instance passed to event handlers contains a list of the rejected `JumpItem`s as well as a list of `JumpItemRejectionReason` enumeration values. Each value can be one of the following:

- **`NoRegisteredHandler`**—The application is not registered to handle the file type.
- **`InvalidItem`**—The file does not exist (or you're running a version of Windows prior to Windows 7).
- **`RemovedByUser`**—The item was manually removed by the user.
- **`None`**—The item was rejected for an unknown reason.

If you only care about handling items removed by the user, you could alternatively handle the `JumpItemsRemovedByUser` event, which simply presents the list of removed `JumpItem`s. It makes sense to handle this, for example, to see if the user has removed one of your `JumpTask`s. That way, you know to stop including it in the Jump List on future launches.

DIGGING DEEPER

The Timing of the `JumpItemsRejected` and `JumpItemsRemovedByUser` Events

The fact that these events only get raised the next time `JumpList.Apply` is called is confusing, but WPF is limited by the behavior of underlying Shell Win32 APIs. The Windows Shell doesn't enable querying the current contents of a Jump List, nor does it provide a way to determine in advance whether an item will be accepted into a Jump List. Consumers (such as WPF) must try to atomically commit an entire category. Windows will then either accept or reject it, sometimes giving a decent error code and sometimes not. Windows also has heuristics for rejecting an item if the user previously removed it, but only if it was removed between the current attempt to update the list and the previous attempt.

`JumpList`'s `Apply` method exists to avoid trying to commit a `JumpTask` or `JumpPath` with only some of its properties set. The partial set of properties might cause an item to be invalid, or the partial set might make it valid but the full set might cause it to be rejected. After calling `Apply`, the contents of the WPF `JumpList` object reflect what the Shell reports as the accepted list. The one or two events get raised (if appropriate) within the `Apply` call because that is when WPF finds out what the user did since the last time the program updated the Jump List.

Taskbar Item Customizations

Starting with WPF 4, `Window` has a `TaskbarItemInfo` property (of type `System.Windows.Shell.TaskbarItemInfo`) that enables several customizations to an application's taskbar item or its corresponding thumbnail preview. For example, you can add a custom tooltip to the taskbar item's thumbnail preview by setting `TaskbarItemInfo`'s `Description` property as follows:

```
<Window ...>
<Window.TaskbarItemInfo>
  <TaskbarItemInfo Description="Custom tooltip"/>
</Window.TaskbarItemInfo>
  ...
</Window>
```

Or, in C# you can set it this way:

```
public MainWindow()
{
  ...
  this.TaskbarItemInfo = new TaskbarItemInfo();
  this.TaskbarItemInfo.Description = "Custom tooltip";
}
```

8

Figure 8.12 shows the result of doing this.

Of course, you can do much more with `TaskbarItemInfo` besides setting a tooltip.

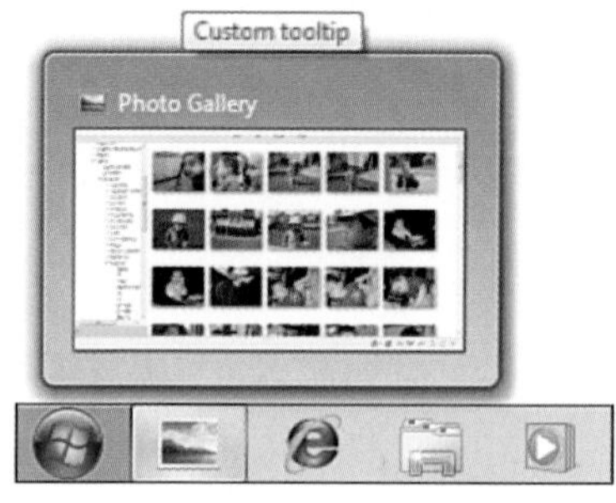

FIGURE 8.12 The tooltip supplied by `TaskbarItemInfo.Description`.

Using a Taskbar Item Progress Bar

Taskbar items support a built-in progress bar, which is useful for displaying the status of long-running tasks in a low-impact fashion. Windows Explorer and Internet Explorer take advantage of this functionality, which is especially nice for keeping an eye on progress while you're working inside another program.

Showing a progress bar is as simple as setting two properties on `TaskbarItemInfo`: `ProgressValue` and `ProgressState`. `ProgressValue` can be set to a `double` between `0` (0%) and `1` (100%) to affect how "filled" the progress bar is. `ProgressState` can be set to one of the following values from the `TaskbarItemProgressState` enumeration:

- **`Normal`**—Show a green progress bar.
- **`Paused`**—Show a yellow progress bar.
- **`Error`**—Show a red progress bar.
- **`Indeterminate`**—Show a green progress bar that constantly animates rather than showing the standard fill that reveals the value of `ProgressValue`.
- **`None`**—Don't show a progress bar. This is the default value.

The first three values all result in a "normal" progress bar; the choice only affects the color. Yellow is meant to be used when progress is paused, and red is meant to be used when an error has occurred, but this is entirely in your control. For instance, you're not prevented from reporting progress even when `ProgressState` is `Paused`.

The `Indeterminate` `ProgressState` is perfect for situations in which you are unable to report ongoing progress values. In this state, the progress bar animation ignores the value of `ProgressValue` and simply shows a standard animation.

You can update `ProgressState` and `ProgressValue` at any time, and you can see the change reflected in the progress bar. Figure 8.13 demonstrates all five values of `ProgressState` with `ProgressValue` set to `.85`.

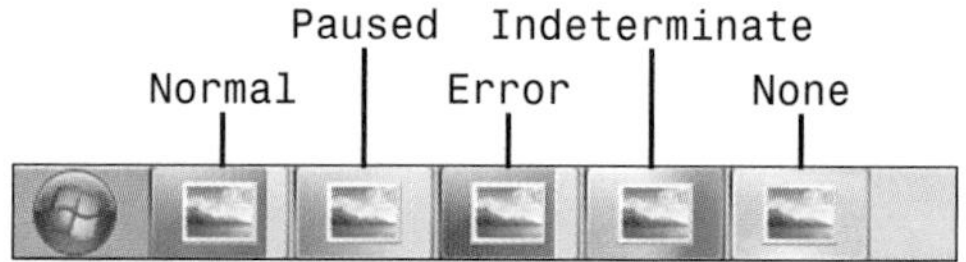

FIGURE 8.13 The five `ProgressState` settings supported by a taskbar item progress bar.

Adding an Overlay to the Taskbar Item

In addition to a progress bar, taskbar items support displaying a little image overlay on top of its icon to communicate additional status. `TaskbarItemInfo` exposes this as an `Overlay` property of type `ImageSource` (a class examined in later chapters).

Figure 8.14 shows what happens when setting an overlay as follows:

```
<Window …>
<Window.TaskbarItemInfo>
  <TaskbarItemInfo Overlay="overlay.png"/>
</Window.TaskbarItemInfo>
  …
</Window>
```

overlay.png The overlay in action

FIGURE 8.14 An overlay image and its use on a taskbar item.

If the user has changed the taskbar to use small icons, overlay images are not supported, so setting this property does nothing. Similarly, using *any* of the `TaskbarItemInfo` functionality does nothing when the application runs on a version of Windows earlier than Windows 7.

When the overlay image is applied, it is placed in the lower-right corner and smoothly fades in. Similarly, removing the overlay by later setting `Overlay` to `null` smoothly fades it out.

> **TIP**
>
> Changing `Overlay` from one image to another does not trigger the fade effect. Therefore, you can rapidly update `Overlay` with a series of images to produce an animated result!

Customizing the Thumbnail Content

By default, the thumbnail shown when hovering over a taskbar item is a live preview of the entire window. `TaskbarItemInfo` provides one small way to customize this. By setting the `ThumbnailClipMargin` property (of type `Thickness`), you can crop the default thumbnail.

Figure 8.15 demonstrates one potential use of this feature. Photo Gallery could set `ThumbnailClipMargin` (and adjust its value when the window is resized) whenever viewing a single photo, in order to crop out the chrome and focus on the main content.

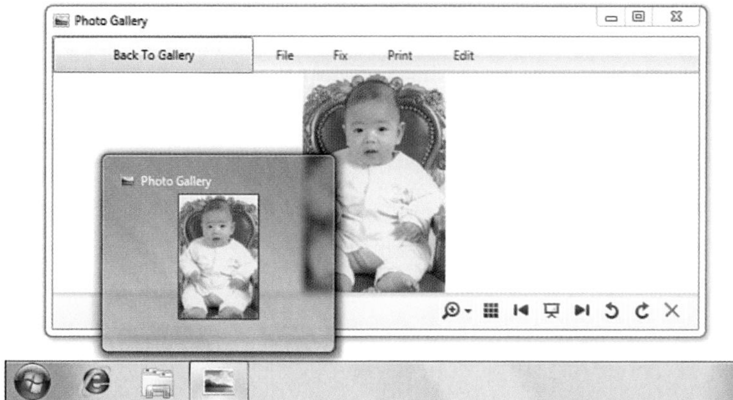

FIGURE 8.15 Clipping the taskbar thumbnail to a photo rather than the entire window.

Adding Thumb Buttons to the Taskbar Thumbnail

The last customization exposed by `TaskbarItemInfo` is the ability to place buttons at the bottom of the thumbnail preview, to provide a user interface like Windows Media Player's miniature Play/Pause, Previous, and Next buttons. This is exposed as `TaskbarItemInfo`'s `ThumbButtonInfos` property, a collection of `ThumbButtonInfo` objects.

Although `ThumbButtonInfo` is not a WPF `UIElement`, it exposes the basic properties you would expect for a button, considering the limitation that its content can only be an `ImageSource`. Each `ThumbButtonInfo` has an `ImageSource` property for its content, a `Description` property for its tooltip, and a `Click` event. (However, unlike `Button`, its `Click` event is not a routed event. It works with plain event handlers.) `ThumbButtonInfo` also has a `Command` property with corresponding `CommandTarget` and `CommandParameter` properties, so these buttons can participate nicely in commands used by your application.

`ThumbButtonInfo` has a standard `Visibility` property, with all three possible values doing what you would expect. (This is a neat trick, considering that WPF layout is not involved here.) It also has a handful of Boolean properties that are all `true` by default except for the last one: `IsEnabled`, `IsInteractive`, `IsBackgroundVisible`, and `DismissWhenClicked`. The "background" referred to by `IsBackgroundVisible` is the button chrome; there actually is no customizable background for these buttons.

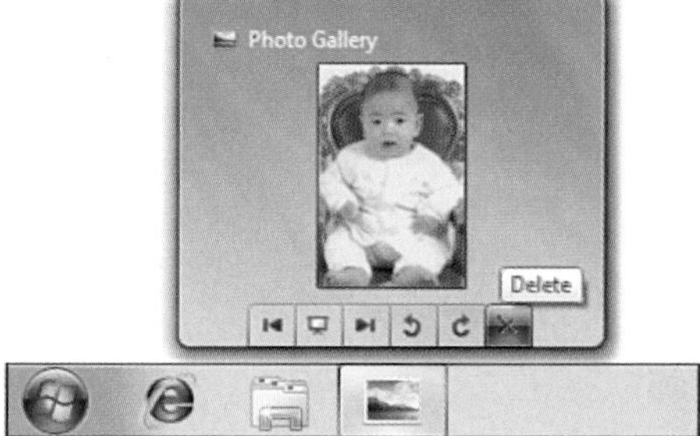

FIGURE 8.16 Thumb buttons can be placed inside the thumbnail preview popup.

Figure 8.16 demonstrates the following `ThumbButtonInfos` applied to Photo Gallery:

```
<Window ...>
<Window.TaskbarItemInfo>
  <TaskbarItemInfo>
  <TaskbarItemInfo.ThumbButtonInfos>
    <ThumbButtonInfo Description="Previous" Click="..."
                     ImageSource="Images\previousSmall.gif"/>
    <ThumbButtonInfo Description="Slideshow" Click="..."
                     ImageSource="Images\slideshowSmall.gif"/>
    <ThumbButtonInfo Description="Next" Click="..."
                     ImageSource="Images\nextSmall.gif"/>
    <ThumbButtonInfo Description="Undo" Click="..."
                     ImageSource="Images\counterclockwiseSmall.gif"/>
    <ThumbButtonInfo Description="Redo" Click="..."
                     ImageSource="Images\clockwiseSmall.gif"/>
    <ThumbButtonInfo Description="Delete" Click="..."
                     ImageSource="Images\deleteSmall.gif"/>
    </TaskbarItemInfo.ThumbButtonInfos>
  </TaskbarItemInfo>
</Window.TaskbarItemInfo>
  ...
</Window>
```

WARNING

Only the first seven `ThumbButtonInfos` matter!

Because there is room for only seven thumb buttons on the thumbnail preview popup, only the first seven `ThumbButtonInfos` in the collection are respected. What's subtle is that this is true even if some of the first seven buttons are marked with `Visibility` set to `Collapsed` (leaving room for later buttons to appear). Therefore, to dynamically swap between more than seven buttons, you actually need to add/remove items from the collection rather than simply toggle their `Visibility`.

FAQ

How can I customize the hover color of my taskbar item?

You can't customize this color, other than changing the colors in your icon. Windows picks up the dominant color of the icon and bases the glow color on that.

Aero Glass

Aero Glass is the blurry, transparent window chrome that can be extended into the client area, introduced with Windows Vista. The easiest way to use it in a WPF application is to call the Win32 `DwmExtendFrameIntoClientArea` API. (The `Dwm` stands for Desktop Window

Manager.) With this method, you can make an entire `Window` a sheet of glass (as shown in Figure 8.17) or choose to extend the glass a specified amount from any of the `Window's` four edges (as shown in Figure 8.18). Either way, you can add WPF content on top of the glass, just as you would if the `Window` background were a simple solid color.

FIGURE 8.17 A glass background for the entire `Window`.

FIGURE 8.18 Extending glass on the bottom of the `Window` only.

If you're using Visual C++, you can call the `DwmExtendFrameIntoClientArea` API directly. But in a language like C# or Visual Basic, `PInvoke` (that is, using the `DllImport` attribute) enables you to call it. `PInvoke` is the key to calling all the Desktop Window Manager APIs from C#. Listing 8.5 contains `PInvoke` signatures and a simple reusable utility method that wraps the `PInvoke` calls.

LISTING 8.5 Using Glass in C#

```
[StructLayout(LayoutKind.Sequential)]
public struct MARGINS
{
  public MARGINS(Thickness t)
  {
    Left = (int)t.Left;
    Right = (int)t.Right;
    Top = (int)t.Top;
    Bottom = (int)t.Bottom;
  }
  public int Left;
  public int Right;
  public int Top;
  public int Bottom;
}

public class GlassHelper
{
  [DllImport("dwmapi.dll", PreserveSig=false)]
  static extern void DwmExtendFrameIntoClientArea(
    IntPtr hWnd, ref MARGINS pMarInset);

  [DllImport("dwmapi.dll", PreserveSig=false)]
  static extern bool DwmIsCompositionEnabled();

  public static bool ExtendGlassFrame(Window window, Thickness margin)
  {
    if (!DwmIsCompositionEnabled())
      return false;

    IntPtr hwnd = new WindowInteropHelper(window).Handle;
    if (hwnd == IntPtr.Zero)
      throw new InvalidOperationException(
        "The Window must be shown before extending glass.");

    // Set the background to transparent from both the WPF and Win32 perspectives
    window.Background = Brushes.Transparent;
    HwndSource.FromHwnd(hwnd).CompositionTarget.BackgroundColor =
```

LISTING 8.5 Continued

```
            Colors.Transparent;

        MARGINS margins = new MARGINS(margin);
        DwmExtendFrameIntoClientArea(hwnd, ref margins);
        return true;
    }
}
```

The `GlassHelper.ExtendGlassFrame` method accepts a `Window` and a familiar `Thickness` object for representing how much glass should be extended on all four edges. (To get the "sheet of glass" effect, you can pass `-1` for all four sides.) After checking that desktop composition is enabled (a prerequisite for glass), the code maps the `Thickness` object to the `MARGINS` type expected by `DwmExtendFrameIntoClientArea` and calls this API with the appropriate `HWND`. The `Window`'s `Background` is also set to `Transparent` so the glass is able to show through. For more information about the techniques used here, consult Chapter 19, "Interoperability with Non-WPF Technologies."

Any WPF `Window` can use `GlassHelper.ExtendGlassFrame` as follows:

```
protected override void OnSourceInitialized(EventArgs e)
{
  base.OnSourceInitialized(e);
  // This can't be done any earlier than the SourceInitialized event:
  GlassHelper.ExtendGlassFrame(this, new Thickness(-1));

  // Attach a window procedure in order to detect later enabling of desktop
  // composition
  IntPtr hwnd = new WindowInteropHelper(this).Handle;
  HwndSource.FromHwnd(hwnd).AddHook(new HwndSourceHook(WndProc));
}

private IntPtr WndProc(IntPtr hwnd, int msg, IntPtr wParam, IntPtr lParam, ref bool
  handled)
{
  if (msg == WM_DWMCOMPOSITIONCHANGED)
  {
    // Reenable glass:
    GlassHelper.ExtendGlassFrame(this, new Thickness(-1));
    handled = true;
  }
  return IntPtr.Zero;
}

private const int WM_DWMCOMPOSITIONCHANGED = 0x031E;
```

The method must not only be called during initialization but whenever desktop composition is disabled and then reenabled. This could happen because of explicit user action, or it could be triggered from something like Remote Desktop. To be notified of changes to desktop composition, you need to intercept a Win32 message (`WM_DWMCOMPOSITIONCHANGED`). See Chapter 19 to get a better understanding of how the preceding code works.

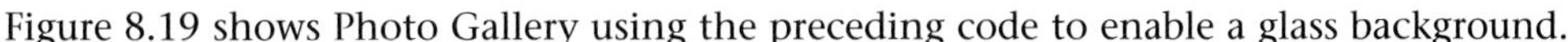

Figure 8.19 shows Photo Gallery using the preceding code to enable a glass background.

FIGURE 8.19 A glass-enabled Photo Gallery.

TaskDialog

It's often tempting for a developer to use `MessageBox` where it might be more appropriate to craft a custom dialog. But laziness is a fact of life, so Windows Vista introduced a new and improved `MessageBox`—called `TaskDialog`—that gives such developers better results and more flexibility. It matches the more modern look and feel of Windows and even enables deep customization of the dialog with additional controls.

You can take advantage of this new functionality by calling a Win32 API called `TaskDialog`. As with working with Aero Glass, `PInvoke` is the key to calling the `TaskDialog` API. Listing 8.6 shows a `PInvoke` signature for `TaskDialog` and its associated types.

LISTING 8.6 `TaskDialog` Signature and Types in C#

```
[DllImport("comctl32.dll", PreserveSig=false, CharSet=CharSet.Unicode)]
static extern TaskDialogResult TaskDialog(IntPtr hwndParent, IntPtr hInstance,
  string title, string mainInstruction, string content,
```

LISTING 8.6 Continued

```
  TaskDialogButtons buttons, TaskDialogIcon icon);

enum TaskDialogResult
{
  Ok=1,
  Cancel=2,
  Retry=4,
  Yes=6,
  No=7,
  Close=8
}
[Flags]
enum TaskDialogButtons
{
  Ok = 0x0001,
  Yes = 0x0002,
  No = 0x0004,
  Cancel = 0x0008,
  Retry = 0x0010,
  Close = 0x0020
}
enum TaskDialogIcon
{
  Warning = 65535,
  Error = 65534,
  Information = 65533,
  Shield = 65532
}
```

Unlike `MessageBox`, the `TaskDialog` API enables you to specify a main instruction that is visually separated from the rest of the content. It also enables you to choose an arbitrary mix of buttons. Figures 8.20 and 8.21 illustrate the difference between `MessageBox` and `TaskDialog`, based on the following code:

```
// Using MessageBox
result = MessageBox.Show("Are you sure you want to delete '" + filename + "'?",
  "Delete Picture", MessageBoxButton.YesNo, MessageBoxImage.Warning);

// Using TaskDialog
result = TaskDialog(new System.Windows.Interop.WindowInteropHelper(this).Handle,
  IntPtr.Zero, "Delete Picture",
  "Are you sure you want to delete '" + filename + "'?",
  "This will delete the picture permanently, rather than sending it
   ➥to the Recycle Bin.",
  TaskDialogButtons.Yes | TaskDialogButtons.No, TaskDialogIcon.Warning);
```

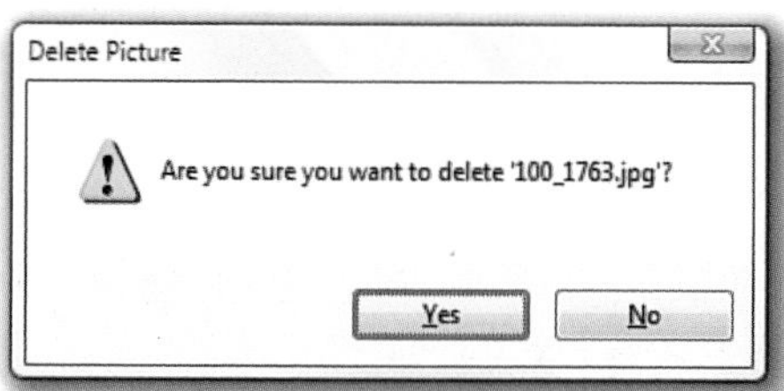

FIGURE 8.20 A `MessageBox` looks a little old-fashioned and lazy on Windows 7.

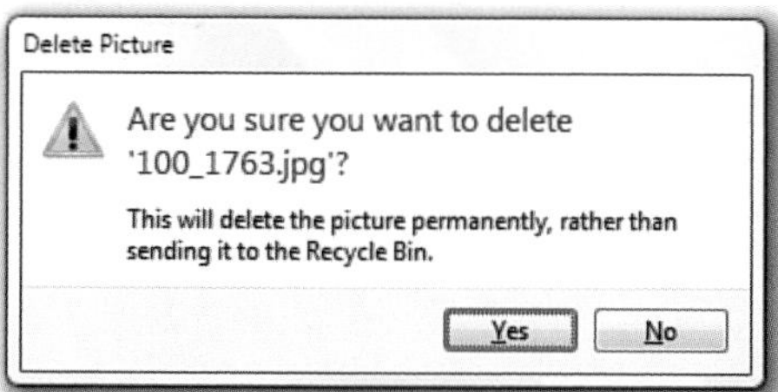

FIGURE 8.21 A similar `TaskDialog` looks more user friendly.

WARNING

The use of `TaskDialog` requires version 6 of the Windows Common Controls DLL (`ComCtl32.dll`)!

For compatibility reasons, applications don't bind to this version by default. One way to bind to version 6 is to place a manifest file alongside your executable (named *`YourAppName`*`.exe.manifest`), with the following content:

```
<?xml version="1.0" encoding="UTF-8" standalone="yes"?>
<assembly xmlns="urn:schemas-microsoft-com:asm.v1" manifestVersion="1.0">
  <assemblyIdentity version="1.0.0.0"
      processorArchitecture="X86" name="YourAppName" type="win32" />
  <description>Your description</description>
  <dependency>
    <dependentAssembly>
      <assemblyIdentity
          type="win32" name="Microsoft.Windows.Common-Controls"
          version="6.0.0.0" processorArchitecture="X86"
          publicKeyToken="6595b64144ccf1df" language="*" />
    </dependentAssembly>
  </dependency>
</assembly>
```

This manifest can also be embedded as a Win32 resource inside your executable (with the name `RT_MANIFEST` and `ID` set to 1), if you don't want to have the extra standalone file. Visual Studio can do this work for you, if you associate your manifest file in your project's properties.

8

Continued

If you fail to bind to this version, calling `TaskDialog` results in an `EntryPointNotFoundException` with the message `"Unable to find an entry point named 'TaskDialog' in DLL 'comctl32.dll'."`

It is a good idea to bind to this version of the Windows Common Controls DLL even if you don't use `TaskDialog`. If you don't do this, *any* Win32 control that might get displayed, such as `MessageBox`, is given an older visual style that might look out of place.

TIP

To customize `TaskDialog` further, you can use a more complicated `TaskDialogIndirect` API. The Windows SDK contains samples for using this and other Win32 features in .NET applications. You can also check `http://pinvoke.net` for `PInvoke` signatures and types for just about any popular Win32 API.

Summary

This chapter examines the newest Windows user interface enhancements introduced in Windows 7 and some of the interesting enhancements introduced in Windows Vista. Fortunately, WPF provides first-class support for consuming these Windows 7 features in XAML or the procedural .NET language of your choice. Leveraging the Windows Vista features requires the use of PInvoke to call the unmanaged Win32 APIs. However, the basic functionality is still pretty easy to use from managed code.

Although this chapter covers all the Windows 7 features that WPF exposes for easy consumption, it only scratches the surface of new functionality available as Win32 APIs in Windows 7 (and Windows Vista). Rather than start from scratch and attempt to do all sorts of unmanaged interoperability wizardry to consume some of these other features, you should download the Windows API Code Pack from http://code.msdn.microsoft.com/WindowsAPICodePack. The Windows API Code Pack contains a bunch of classes and samples that make it easy to consume a lot of Windows 7 and Windows Vista functionality from managed code. It covers a wide variety of functionality, from more advanced shell and taskbar customizations to areas such as sensors, linguistic services, and power management.

TIP

If you are not yet ready to migrate an application to WPF 4, you can still take advantage of the Windows 7 features in this chapter by using the WPF Shell Integration Library available at http://code.msdn.microsoft.com/WPFShell.

This library is a .NET Framework 3.5-compatible version of the `System.Windows.Shell` APIs from WPF 4. There are a few minor incompatibilities between the two sets of APIs (for example, in the 3.5 library, `TaskbarItemInfo` is an attached property rather than a regular dependency property), but it provides a nice migration path for moving to a newer version of WPF at a later date.

TIP

Whenever you exploit features in a specific version of Windows, you need to think about your fallback plans for running on earlier versions of Windows—if you want to support them.

For the Jump List and taskbar item features exposed through the `System.Windows.Shell` namespace, WPF gracefully handles older versions of Windows for you. If you run the related samples in this chapter on Windows Vista, your code that interacts with `JumpList`, `TaskbarItemInfo`, and so on will still execute without errors but will do nothing.

For the features that you consume directly via unmanaged interoperability, you must explicitly check for the version of Windows and adjust your behavior accordingly. .NET code can easily check the operating system version using `System.Environment.OSVersion`. Here's an example:

```
if (System.Environment.OSVersion.Version.Major >= 6)
  // Windows Vista or later, so use TaskDialog
else
  // Earlier than Windows Vista, so just use MessageBox
```

The major/minor version of Windows 7 is 6.1, and the major/minor version of Windows Vista is 6.0.

PART III

Controls

IN THIS PART

CHAPTER 9

Content Controls

IN THIS CHAPTER

- Buttons
- Simple Containers
- Containers with Headers

No modern presentation framework would be complete without a standard set of controls that enables you to quickly assemble traditional user interfaces. And Windows Presentation Foundation has plenty of such controls included "in the box." You've seen a few of them in previous chapters. This part of the book takes you on a tour of the major built-in controls, highlighting some of what makes each control unique.

The figures in this book show WPF controls under the Aero theme from Windows 7 and Windows Vista. Most WPF controls contain several distinct default appearances, however. That's because WPF ships with theme DLLs that contain control templates for the following Windows themes:

- Aero (the default Windows 7 and Windows Vista theme)
- Luna (the default Windows XP theme)
- Royale (the somewhat-obscure theme from Windows XP Media Center Edition 2005 and Windows XP Tablet PC Edition 2005)
- Classic (the theme available in Windows 2000 and later)

For example, Figure 9.1 displays the default appearance of a WPF `Button` control under each of the supported Windows themes. If WPF encounters an unsupported theme, such as the Zune theme released by Microsoft in 2006, it defaults to Classic.

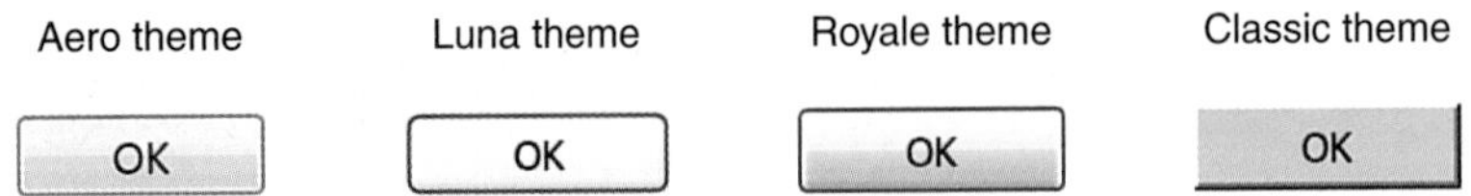

FIGURE 9.1 The WPF `Button`'s theme-specific default appearances.

In most cases, the difference in appearance is very subtle. Of course, you can give controls a radically different look (based on the current theme or theme-independent) by using custom control templates, as discussed in Chapter 14, "Styles, Templates, Skins, and Themes."

WPF's built-in controls can be grouped roughly into the following categories, which coincide with their inheritance hierarchy:

- Content controls (this chapter)
- Items controls (Chapter 10, "Items Controls")
- Range controls (Chapter 11, "Images, Text, and Other Controls")
- Everything else (Chapter 11)

This chapter covers *content controls*, which are simply controls that are constrained to contain a single item. Content controls all derive from `System.Windows.Controls.ContentControl`, which has a `Content` property of type `Object` that contains the single item (first shown with `Button` in Chapter 2, "XAML Demystified").

Because a content control's single item can be any arbitrary object, the control can contain a potentially large tree of objects. There just can be only one *direct* child. Besides `Content`, the other interesting member of the `ContentControl` class is the Boolean `HasContent` property. This simply returns `false` if `Content` is `null`, and it returns `true` otherwise.

FAQ

Why does `ContentControl` define a `HasContent` property? Checking for `Content==null` is just as easy as checking for `HasContent==false`!

Welcome to the world of WPF APIs, which don't always look like your typical .NET APIs! From a C# perspective, the `HasContent` property is redundant. But from a XAML perspective, the property is useful. For example, it makes it easy to use a property trigger to set various property values when `HasContent` becomes `true`.

DIGGING DEEPER

`Content` and Arbitrary Objects

Given that a content control's `Content` can be set to any managed object, it's natural to wonder what happens if you set the content to a non-visual object, such as an instance of `Hashtable` or `TimeZone`. The way it works is fairly simple: If the content derives from WPF's `UIElement` class, it gets rendered via `UIElement`'s `OnRender` method. Otherwise, if a data template is applied to the item (as described in Chapter 13, "Data Binding"), that template can provide the rendering behavior on behalf of the object. Otherwise, the content's `ToString` method is called, and the returned text is rendered inside a `TextBlock` control.

The built-in content controls come in three major varieties:

- Buttons
- Simple containers
- Containers with headers

The `Window` class, already examined in Chapter 7, "Structuring and Deploying an Application," is also a content control. Its `Content` is usually set to a `Panel` such as `Grid`, so it can contain an arbitrarily complex user interface.

Buttons

Buttons are probably the most familiar and essential user interface elements. WPF's `Button`, pictured in Figure 9.1, has already made several appearances in this book.

Although everyone intuitively knows what a button is, its precise definition (at least in WPF) might not be obvious. A basic button is a content control that can be clicked but not double-clicked. This behavior is actually captured by an abstract class called `ButtonBase`, from which a few different controls are derived.

The `ButtonBase` class contains the `Click` event and contains the logic that defines what it means to be clicked. As with typical Windows buttons, a click can occur from a mouse's left button being pressed down and then let up or from the keyboard with Enter or spacebar, if the button has focus.

`ButtonBase` also defines a Boolean `IsPressed` property, in case you want to act on the pressed state (when the left mouse button or spacebar is held down but not yet released).

The most interesting feature of `ButtonBase`, however, is its `ClickMode` property. This can be set to a value of a `ClickMode` enumeration to control exactly when the `Click` event gets raised. Its values are `Release` (the default), `Press`, and `Hover`. Although changing the `ClickMode` setting on standard buttons would likely confuse users, this capability is very handy for buttons that have been restyled to look like something completely different. In these cases, it's a common expectation that *pressing* an object should be the same as *clicking* it.

DIGGING DEEPER

`Click`'s Effect on Other Events

To raise the `Click` event, `ButtonBase` listens to more primitive events, such as `MouseLeftButtonDown` and `MouseLeftButtonUp`. For a `ClickMode` of `Release` or `Press`, neither of these primitive events bubbles up from a `ButtonBase`-derived element because `ButtonBase` sets the `MouseButtonEventArgs.Handled` field to `true`. For a `ClickMode` of `Hover`, the `MouseEnter` and `MouseLeave` events don't bubble up for the same reason. If you want to handle the primitive mouse events on a `ButtonBase`-derived element, you must either handle the preview version of these events (`PreviewMouseLeftButtonDown`, `PreviewMouseLeftButtonUp`, and so on) or attach your event handler(s) in procedural code with the `AddHandler` overload that ignores whether an event has been marked as handled.

Several controls ultimately derive from `ButtonBase`, and the following sections examine each of them in turn:

- `Button`
- `RepeatButton`
- `ToggleButton`
- `CheckBox`
- `RadioButton`

Additional `ButtonBase`-derived controls exist, but they were designed to be used inside specific complex controls, such as `Calendar` and `DataGrid`.

`Button`

The WPF `Button` class adds two simple concepts on top of what `ButtonBase` already provides: being a *cancel button* or a *default button*. These two mechanisms are handy shortcuts for dialogs. If `Button.IsCancel` is set to `true` on a `Button` inside a dialog (that is, a `Window` shown via its `ShowDialog` method), the `Window` is automatically closed with a `DialogResult` of `false`. If `Button.IsDefault` is set to `true`, pressing Enter causes the `Button` to be clicked unless focus is explicitly taken away from it.

FAQ

What's the difference between `Button`'s `IsDefault` and `IsDefaulted` properties?

`IsDefault` is a read/write property that enables you to decide whether a `Button` should be the default one. The poorly named `IsDefaulted` property, on the other hand, is read-only. It indicates when a default button is in a state such that pressing Enter causes it to be clicked. In other words, `IsDefaulted` can be `true` only when `IsDefault` is `true` *and* either the default button or a `TextBox` (with `AcceptsReturn` set to `false`) has focus. The latter condition enables the Enter key to click the default button without tabbing out of a `TextBox`.

FAQ

How can I programmatically click a `Button`?

`Button`, like many other WPF controls, has a peer class in the `System.Windows.Automation.Peers` namespace to support UI Automation: `ButtonAutomationPeer`. It can be used as follows with a `Button` called `myButton`:

```
ButtonAutomationPeer bap = new ButtonAutomationPeer(myButton);
IInvokeProvider iip = bap.GetPattern(PatternInterface.Invoke)
  as IInvokeProvider;
iip.Invoke(); // This clicks the Button
```

These UI Automation classes have several members that are extremely useful for automated testing and accessibility.

RepeatButton

`RepeatButton` acts just like `Button` except that it continually raises the `Click` event as long as the button is being pressed. (It also doesn't have `Button`'s cancel and default behaviors because it derives directly from `ButtonBase`.) The frequency of the raised `Click` events depends on the values of `RepeatButton`'s `Delay` and `Interval` properties, whose default values are `SystemParameters.KeyboardDelay` and `SystemParameters.KeyboardSpeed`, respectively. The default look of a `RepeatButton` is exactly the same as that of `Button` (shown in Figure 9.1).

The behavior of `RepeatButton` might sound strange at first, but it is useful (and standard) for buttons that increment or decrement a value each time they are pressed. For example, the buttons at the ends of a scrollbar exhibit the repeat-press behavior when you click them and hold the mouse button down. Or, if you were to build a numeric "up-down" control (which WPF still does not have built in), you would likely want to use two `RepeatButton`s to control the numeric value. `RepeatButton` is in the `System.Windows.Controls.Primitives` namespace because it is likely that you would use this control only as part of a more sophisticated control rather than use it directly.

ToggleButton

`ToggleButton` is a "sticky" button that holds its state when it is clicked (again without `Button`'s cancel and default behaviors). Clicking it the first time sets its `IsChecked` property to `true`, and clicking it again sets `IsChecked` to `false`. The default appearance of `ToggleButton` is exactly the same as that of `Button` and `RepeatButton`.

`ToggleButton` also has an `IsThreeState` property that, if set to `true`, gives `IsChecked` three possible values: `true`, `false`, or `null`. In fact, `IsChecked` is of type `Nullable<Boolean>` (`bool?` in C#). In the three-state case, the first click sets `IsChecked` to `true`, the second click sets it to `null`, the third click sets it to `false`, and so on. To vary the order of these state changes, you could either intercept the clicks by handling the preview versions of the mouse events and manually set `IsChecked` to the value you desire, or you could create your own subclass and override `ToggleButton`'s `OnToggle` method to perform your custom logic.

In addition to the IsChecked property, ToggleButton defines a separate event for each value of IsChecked: Checked for true, Unchecked for false, and Indeterminate for null. It might seem odd that ToggleButton doesn't have a single IsCheckedChanged event, but the three separate events are handy for declarative scenarios.

As with RepeatButton, ToggleButton is in the System.Windows.Controls.Primitives namespace, which essentially means that the WPF designers don't expect people to use ToggleButtons directly or without additional customizations. It is quite natural, however, to use ToggleButtons directly inside a ToolBar control, as described in Chapter 10.

CheckBox

CheckBox, shown in Figure 9.2, is a familiar control. But wait a minute...isn't this section supposed to be about buttons? Yes, but consider the characteristics of a WPF CheckBox:

- It has a single piece of *externally supplied* content (so the standard check box doesn't count).
- It has a notion of being clicked by mouse or keyboard.
- It retains a state of being checked or unchecked when clicked.
- It supports a three-state mode, where the state toggles from checked to indeterminate to unchecked.

FIGURE 9.2 The WPF CheckBox control, with all three IsChecked states shown.

Does this sound familiar? It should, because a CheckBox is nothing more than a ToggleButton with a different appearance! CheckBox is a simple class deriving from ToggleButton that does little more than override its default style to the visuals shown in Figure 9.2.

> **DIGGING DEEPER**
>
> **CheckBox Keyboard Support**
>
> CheckBox supports one additional behavior that ToggleButton does not, for parity with a little-known feature of Win32 check boxes. When a CheckBox has focus, pressing the plus (+) key checks the control and pressing the minus (–) key unchecks the control! Note that this works only if IsThreeState hasn't been set to true.

RadioButton

RadioButton is another control that derives from ToggleButton, but it is unique because it has built-in support for mutual exclusion. When multiple RadioButton controls are grouped together, only one can be checked at a time. Checking one RadioButton—even programmatically—automatically unchecks all others in the same group. In fact, users can't even directly uncheck a RadioButton by clicking it; unchecking can only be done programmatically. Therefore, `RadioButton` is designed for multiple-choice questions. Figure 9.3 shows the default appearance of a `RadioButton`.

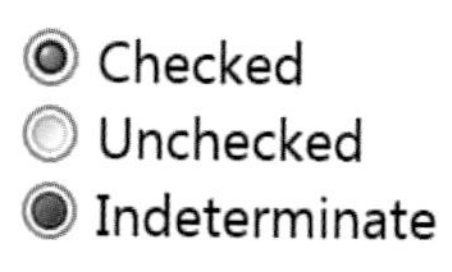

FIGURE 9.3 The WPF `RadioButton`, with all three `IsChecked` states shown.

The rarely used indeterminate state of a `RadioButton` control (`IsThreeState=true` and `IsChecked=null`) is similar to the unchecked state in that a user cannot enable this state by clicking on it; it must be set programmatically. If the `RadioButton` is clicked, it changes to the checked state, but if another `RadioButton` in the same group becomes checked, any indeterminate `RadioButtons` remain in the indeterminate state.

Placing several WPF `RadioButtons` in the same group is very straightforward. By default, any `RadioButtons` that share the same direct logical parent are automatically grouped together. For example, only one of the following `RadioButtons` can be checked at any point in time:

```
<StackPanel>
  <RadioButton>Option 1</RadioButton>
  <RadioButton>Option 2</RadioButton>
  <RadioButton>Option 3</RadioButton>
</StackPanel>
```

If you need to group `RadioButtons` in a custom manner, however, you can use the `GroupName` property, which is a simple string. Any `RadioButtons` with the same `GroupName` value get grouped together (as long as they have the same logical root). Therefore, you can group them across different parents, as shown here:

```
<StackPanel>
  <StackPanel>
    <RadioButton GroupName="A">Option 1</RadioButton>
    <RadioButton GroupName="A">Option 2</RadioButton>
  </StackPanel>
  <StackPanel>
    <RadioButton GroupName="A">Option 3</RadioButton>
  </StackPanel>
</StackPanel>
```

Different parents

Or you can even create subgroups inside the same parent:

```
<StackPanel>
  <RadioButton GroupName="A">Option 1</RadioButton>
  <RadioButton GroupName="A">Option 2</RadioButton>
  <RadioButton GroupName="B">A Different Option 1</RadioButton>
  <RadioButton GroupName="B">A Different Option 2</RadioButton>
</StackPanel>
```

Different groups

Of course, the last example would be a confusing piece of user interface without an extra visual element separating the two subgroups!

Simple Containers

WPF includes several built-in content controls that *don't* have a notion of being clicked like a button. Each has unique features to justify its existence. These content controls are the following:

- `Label`
- `ToolTip`
- `Frame`

`Label`

`Label` is a classic control that, as in previous technologies, can be used to hold some text. Because it is a WPF content control, it can hold arbitrary content in its `Content` property—a `Button`, a `Menu`, and so on—but `Label` is really useful only for text.

You can place text on the screen with WPF in several different ways, such as using a `TextBlock` element. But what makes `Label` unique is its support for access keys. You can designate a letter in a `Label`'s text that gets special treatment when the user presses the access key—the Alt key and the designated letter. You can also specify an arbitrary element that should receive focus when the user presses this access key. To designate the letter (which can appear underlined, depending on the Windows settings), you simply precede it with an underscore. To designate the target element, you set `Label`'s `Target` property (of type `UIElement`).

The classic case of using a `Label`'s access key support with another control is pairing it with a `TextBox`. For example, the following XAML snippet gives focus to the `TextBox` when Alt+U is pressed:

```
<Label Target="userNameBox">_User Name:</Label>
<TextBox x:Name="userNameBox"/>
```

Setting the value of `Target` implicitly leverages the `NameReferenceConverter` type converter described in Chapter 2. In C#, you can simply set the property to the instance of the `TextBox` control as follows (assuming that the `Label` is named `userNameLabel`):

```
userNameLabel.Target = userNameBox;
```

TIP

Controls such as `Label` and `Button` support access keys by treating an underscore before the appropriate letter specially, as in `_Open` or `Save _As`. (Win32 and Windows Forms use an ampersand [&] instead; the underscore is much more XML friendly.) If you really want an underscore to appear in your text, you need to use two consecutive underscores, as in `__Open` or `Save __As`.

ToolTip

The ToolTip control holds its content in a floating box that appears when you hover over an associated control and disappears when you move the mouse away. Figure 9.4 shows a typical ToolTip in action, created from the following XAML:

```
<Button>
  OK
<Button.ToolTip>
  <ToolTip>
    Clicking this will submit your request.
  </ToolTip>
</Button.ToolTip>
</Button>
```

The ToolTip class can never be placed directly in a tree of UIElements. Instead, it must be assigned as the value of a separate element's ToolTip property (defined on both FrameworkElement and FrameworkContentElement).

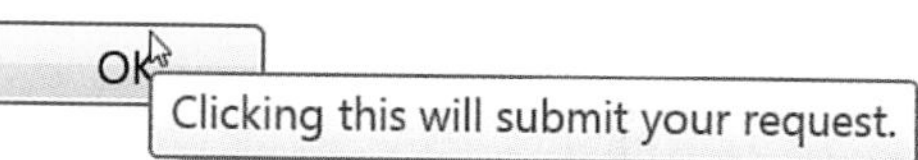

FIGURE 9.4 The WPF ToolTip.

> **TIP**
>
> You don't even need to use the ToolTip class when setting an element's ToolTip property! The property is of type Object, and if you set it to any non-ToolTip object, the property's implementation automatically creates a ToolTip and uses the property value as the ToolTip's content. Therefore, the XAML for Figure 9.4 could be simplified to the following and give the same result:
>
> ```
> <Button>
>   OK
> <Button.ToolTip>
>   Clicking this will submit your request.
> </Button.ToolTip>
> </Button>
> ```
>
> or it could be simplified further, as follows:
>
> ```
> <Button Content="OK" ToolTip="Clicking this will submit your request."/>
> ```

Because of the flexibility of WPF's content controls, a WPF ToolTip can hold anything you want! Listing 9.1 shows how you might construct a Microsoft Office–style ScreenTip. The result is shown in Figure 9.5.

9

LISTING 9.1 A Complex `ToolTip`, Similar to a Microsoft Office ScreenTip

```
<CheckBox>
  CheckBox
<CheckBox.ToolTip>
  <StackPanel>
    <Label FontWeight="Bold" Background="Blue" Foreground="White">
      The CheckBox
    </Label>
    <TextBlock Padding="10" TextWrapping="WrapWithOverflow" Width="200">
      CheckBox is a familiar control. But in WPF, it's not much
      more than a ToggleButton styled differently!
    </TextBlock>
    <Line Stroke="Black" StrokeThickness="1" X2="200"/>
    <StackPanel Orientation="Horizontal">
      <Image Margin="2" Source="help.gif"/>
      <Label FontWeight="Bold">Press F1 for more help.</Label>
    </StackPanel>
  </StackPanel>
</CheckBox.ToolTip>
</CheckBox>
```

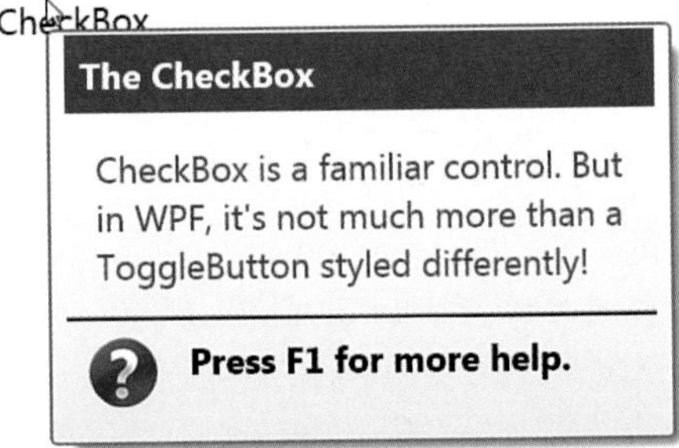

FIGURE 9.5 A tooltip like the ScreenTips in Microsoft Office is easy to create in WPF.

Although a `ToolTip` can contain interactive controls such as `Buttons`, those controls never get focus, and you can't click or otherwise interact with them.

`ToolTip` defines `Open` and `Closed` events in case you want to act on its appearance and disappearance. It also defines several properties for tweaking its behavior, such as its placement, whether it should stay open until explicitly closed, or even whether a drop shadow should be rendered. Sometimes you might want to apply the same `ToolTip` on multiple controls, yet you might want the `ToolTip` to behave differently depending on the control to which it is attached. For such cases, a separate `ToolTipService` static class can meet your needs.

`ToolTipService` defines a handful of attached properties that can be set on any element using the `ToolTip` (rather than on the `ToolTip` itself). It has several of the same properties as `ToolTip` (which have a higher precedence in case the `ToolTip` in question has conflicting values), but it also adds several more. For example, `ShowDuration` controls how long the `ToolTip` should be displayed while the mouse pointer is paused over an element, and `InitialShowDelay` controls the length of time between the pause occurring and the `ToolTip` first being shown. You can add `ShowDuration` to the first `ToolTip` example as follows:

```
<Button ToolTipService.ShowDuration="3000">
  …
</Button>
```

FAQ

How do I get a `ToolTip` to appear when hovering over a disabled element?

Simply use the `ShowOnDisabled` attached property of the `ToolTipService` class. From XAML, this would look as follows on a `Button`:

```
<Button ToolTipService.ShowOnDisabled="True">
  …
</Button>
```

Or from C# code, you can call the static method corresponding to the attached property:

```
ToolTipService.SetShowOnDisabled(myButton, true);
```

`Frame`

The `Frame` control holds arbitrary content, just like all other content controls, but it isolates the content from the rest of the user interface. For example, properties that would normally be inherited down the element tree stop when they reach the `Frame`. In many respects, WPF `Frames` act like frames in HTML.

FAQ

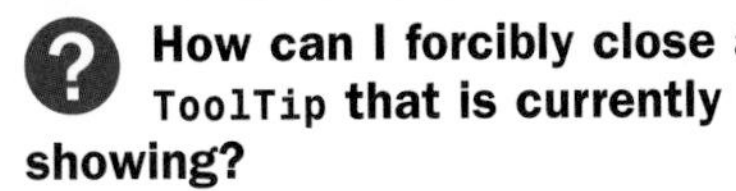

How can I forcibly close a `ToolTip` that is currently showing?

Set its `IsOpen` property to `false`.

Speaking of HTML, `Frame`'s claim to fame is that it can render HTML content in addition to WPF content. `Frame` has a `Source` property of type `System.Uri` that can be set to any HTML (or XAML) page. Here's an example:

```
<Frame Source="http://www.adamnathan.net"/>
```

TIP

When using `Frame` to navigate between web pages, be sure to handle its `NavigationFailed` event to perform any error logic and set `NavigationFailedEventArgs.Handled` to `true`. Otherwise, an unhandled exception (such as a `WebException`) gets raised on a different thread. The `NavigationFailedEventArgs` object passed to the handler provides access to the exception among other details.

As explained in Chapter 7, `Frame` is a navigation container with built-in tracking that applies to both HTML and XAML content. So, you can think of the `Frame` control as a more flexible version of the Microsoft Web Browser ActiveX control or the WPF `WebBrowser` control that wraps this ActiveX control.

Unfortunately, when `Frame` hosts HTML, it has several limitations that don't apply to other WPF controls (due to relying on Win32 for its implementation of HTML rendering). For example, the HTML content is always rendered on top of WPF content, it can't have effects applied to it, its `Opacity` can't be changed, and so on. `Frame` also does not support rendering an arbitrary string or stream of HTML; the content must be a path or URL pointing to a loose file. If you require the ability to display in-memory HTML strings, the best option is to use the WPF `WebBrowser` control instead.

TIP

Compared to using `Frame`, WPF's `WebBrowser` control (introduced in WPF 3.5 SP1) provides a more powerful way to host HTML. It supports rendering HTML supplied from an in-memory string or `Stream`, as well as interactivity with the HTML DOM and its script. It also provides a slick way to host Silverlight content in a WPF application: Just give it a URL that points to a Silverlight `.xap` file. Note that `WebBrowser` is *not* a content control; it cannot directly contain any WPF elements.

DIGGING DEEPER

`Frame`'s `Content` Property

Although `Frame` is a content control and has a property called `Content`, it does not treat `Content` as a content property in the XAML sense. In other words, the `Frame` element in XAML doesn't support a child element. You must explicitly use the `Content` property as follows:

```
<Frame>
<Frame.Content>
  …
</Frame.Content>
</Frame>
```

`Frame` accomplishes this by marking itself with an empty `ContentPropertyAttribute`, overriding the `[ContentProperty("Content")]` marking on the base `ContentControl` class. But why does it bother?

According to the designers of WPF, this was done to deemphasize the use of `Frame`'s `Content` property, as setting its `Source` property to an external file is the typical expected usage of `Frame`. And the only reason `Frame` is a content control is for consistency with `NavigationWindow`, discussed in Chapter 7. Note that if you set both the `Source` and `Content` properties, `Content` takes precedence.

Containers with Headers

All the previous content controls either add very simple default visuals around the content (button chrome, a check box, and so on) or don't add any visuals at all. The following two controls are a little different because they add a customizable *header* to the main content. These controls derive from a subclass of `ContentControl` named `HeaderedContentControl`, which adds a `Header` property of type `Object`.

GroupBox

`GroupBox` is a familiar control for organizing chunks of controls. Figure 9.6 shows a `GroupBox` surrounding `CheckBox`es, created from the following XAML:

Grammar
Check grammar as you type
Hide grammatical errors in this document
Check grammar with spelling

FIGURE 9.6 The WPF `GroupBox`.

```
<GroupBox Header="Grammar">
  <StackPanel>
    <CheckBox>Check grammar as you type</CheckBox>
    <CheckBox>Hide grammatical errors in this document</CheckBox>
    <CheckBox>Check grammar with spelling</CheckBox>
  </StackPanel>
</GroupBox>
```

`GroupBox` is typically used to contain multiple items, but because it is a content control, it can directly contain only a single item. Therefore, you typically need to set `GroupBox`'s content to an intermediate control that can contain multiple children. A `Panel`, such as a `StackPanel`, is perfect for this.

Just like the `Content` property, the `Header` property can be set to an arbitrary object, and if it derives from `UIElement`, it is rendered as expected. For example, changing `Header` to be a `Button` as follows produces the result shown in Figure 9.7:

```
<GroupBox>
<GroupBox.Header>
  <Button>Grammar</Button>
</GroupBox.Header>
  <StackPanel>
    <CheckBox>Check grammar as you type</CheckBox>
    <CheckBox>Hide grammatical errors in this document</CheckBox>
    <CheckBox>Check grammar with spelling</CheckBox>
  </StackPanel>
</GroupBox>
```

In Figure 9.7, the `Button` used in the header is fully functional. It can get focus, it can be clicked, and so on.

Grammar
Check grammar as you type
Hide grammatical errors in this document
Check grammar with spelling

FIGURE 9.7 A `GroupBox` with a `Button` as a header, just to reinforce WPF's flexible content model.

Expander

`Expander` is a bit exciting because it's the only control examined in this chapter that doesn't already exist in Win32-based user interface technologies such as Windows Forms! `Expander` is very much like `GroupBox`, but

9

it contains a button that enables you to expand and collapse the inner content. (By default, the `Expander` starts out collapsed.)

Figure 9.8 displays the `Expander` control in its two states. This `Expander` was created with the same XAML used in Figure 9.6, but with the opening and closing `GroupBox` tags replaced with `Expander` tags:

```
<Expander Header="Grammar">
  <StackPanel>
    <CheckBox>Check grammar as you type</CheckBox>
    <CheckBox>Hide grammatical errors in this document</CheckBox>
    <CheckBox>Check grammar with spelling</CheckBox>
  </StackPanel>
</Expander>
```

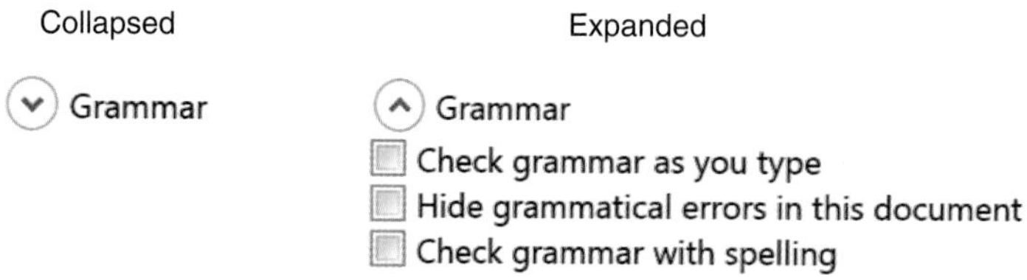

Collapsed

Grammar

Expanded

Grammar

Check grammar as you type

Hide grammatical errors in this document

Check grammar with spelling

FIGURE 9.8 The WPF `Expander`.

`Expander` defines an `IsExpanded` property and `Expanded`/`Collapsed` events. It also enables you to control the direction in which the expansion happens (`Up`, `Down`, `Left`, or `Right`) with an `ExpandDirection` property.

The button inside the `Expander` is actually a restyled `ToggleButton`. Several of the more complicated controls use primitive controls, such as `ToggleButton` and `RepeatButton`, internally.

Summary

Never before has a button been so flexible! In WPF, `Button` and all the other content controls can contain absolutely anything—but they can directly contain only one item. Now, with the tour of content controls complete, it's time to move on to controls that can directly contain more than one item—*items controls*.

CHAPTER 10
Items Controls

IN THIS CHAPTER

- Common Functionality
- Selectors
- Menus
- Other Items Controls

Besides content controls, the other major category of WPF controls is *items controls*, which can contain an unbounded collection of items rather than just a single piece of content. All items controls derive from the abstract `ItemsControl` class, which, like `ContentControl`, is a direct subclass of `Control`.

`ItemsControl` stores its content in an `Items` property (of type `ItemCollection`). Each item can be an arbitrary object that by default gets rendered just as it would inside a content control. In other words, any `UIElement` is rendered as expected, and (ignoring data templates) any other type is rendered as a `TextBlock` containing the string returned by its `ToString` method.

The `ListBox` control used in earlier chapters is an items control. Whereas those chapters always added `ListBoxItems` to the `Items` collection, the following example adds arbitrary objects to `Items`:

```
<ListBox
xmlns="http://schemas.microsoft.com/winfx/2006/xaml/
➥presentation"
  xmlns:sys="clr-namespace:System;assembly=mscorlib">
  <Button>Button</Button>
  <Expander Header="Expander"/>
  <sys:DateTime>1/1/2012</sys:DateTime>
  <sys:DateTime>1/2/2012</sys:DateTime>
  <sys:DateTime>1/3/2012</sys:DateTime>
</ListBox>
```

(This snippet uses `sys:DateTime` instead of `x:DateTime` so it works as both loose XAML and compiled XAML.)

The child elements are implicitly added to the `Items` collection because `Items` is a content property. This `ListBox` is shown in Figure 10.1. The two `UIElements` (`Button` and `Expander`) are rendered normally and are fully interactive. The three `DateTime` objects are rendered according to their `ToString` method.

Button
Expander
1/1/2012
1/2/2012
1/3/2012

FIGURE 10.1 A `ListBox` containing arbitrary objects.

As mentioned in Chapter 2, "XAML Demystified," the `Items` property is read-only. This means that you can add objects to the initially empty collection or remove objects, but you can't point `Items` to an entirely different collection. `ItemsControl` has a separate property—`ItemsSource`—that supports filling its items with an existing arbitrary collection. The use of `ItemsSource` is examined further in Chapter 13, "Data Binding."

TIP

To keep things simple, examples in this chapter fill items controls with visual elements. However, the preferred approach is to give items controls nonvisual items (for example, custom business objects) and use data templates to define how each item gets rendered. Chapter 13 discusses data templates in depth.

Common Functionality

Besides `Items` and `ItemsSource`, `ItemsControl` has a few additional interesting properties, including the following:

- **`HasItems`**—A read-only Boolean property that makes it easy to act on the control's empty state from declarative XAML. From C#, you can either use this property or simply check the value of `Items.Count`.
- **`IsGrouping`**—Another read-only Boolean property that tells if the control's items are divided into top-level groups. This grouping is done directly within the `ItemsCollection` class, which contains several properties for managing and naming groups of items. You'll learn more about grouping in Chapter 13.
- **`AlternationCount` and `AlternationIndex`**—This pair of properties makes it easy to vary the style of items based on their index. For example, an `AlternationCount` of `2` can be used to give even-indexed items one style and odd-indexed items another style. Chapter 14, "Styles, Templates, Skins, and Themes," shows an example of using these properties.
- **`DisplayMemberPath`**—A string property that can be set to the name of a property on each item (or a more complicated expression) that changes how each object is rendered.
- **`ItemsPanel`**—A property that can be used to customize how the control's items are arranged without replacing the entire control template.

The next two sections provide further explanation of the last two properties in this list.

DisplayMemberPath

Figure 10.2 demonstrates what happens when DisplayMemberPath is applied to the preceding ListBox, as follows:

```
<ListBox xmlns="http://schemas.microsoft.com/winfx/2006/xaml/presentation"
  xmlns:sys="clr-namespace:System;assembly=mscorlib" DisplayMemberPath="DayOfWeek">
  <Button>Button</Button>
  <Expander Header="Expander"/>
  <sys:DateTime>1/1/2012</sys:DateTime>
  <sys:DateTime>1/2/2012</sys:DateTime>
  <sys:DateTime>1/3/2012</sys:DateTime>
</ListBox>
```

Setting DisplayMemberPath to DayOfWeek tells WPF to render the value of each item's DayOfWeek property rather than each item itself. That is why the three DateTime objects render as Sunday, Monday, and Tuesday in Figure 10.2. (This is the ToString-based rendering of each DayOfWeek enumeration value returned by the DayOfWeek property.) Because Button and Expander don't have a DayOfWeek property, they are rendered as empty TextBlocks.

Sunday
Monday
Tuesday

FIGURE 10.2 The ListBox from Figure 10.1 with DisplayMemberPath set to DayOfWeek.

DIGGING DEEPER

Property Paths in WPF

DisplayMemberPath supports syntax known as a *property path* that is used in several areas of WPF, such as data binding and animation. The basic idea of a property path is to represent a sequence of one or more properties that you could also use in procedural code to get a desired value. The simplest example of a property path is a single property name, but if the value of that property is a complex object, you can invoke one of its own properties (and so on) by delimiting the property names with periods, as in C#. This syntax even supports indexers and arrays.

For example, imagine an object that defines a FirstButton property of type Button, whose Content property is currently set to an "OK" string. The following property path represents the value of the string ("OK"):

```
FirstButton.Content
```

The following property path represents the length of the string (2):

```
FirstButton.Content.Length
```

And the following property path represents the first character of the string ('O'):

```
FirstButton.Content[0]
```

These expressions match what you would use in C#, except that no casting is required.

ItemsPanel

Like all other WPF controls, the essence of items controls is not their visual appearance but their storage of multiple items and, in many cases, the ways in which their items are logically selected. Although all WPF controls can be visually altered by applying a new control template, items controls have a shortcut for replacing just the piece of the control template responsible for arranging its items. This mini-template, called an *items panel*, enables you to swap out the panel used to arrange items while leaving everything else about the control intact.

You can use any of the panels discussed in Chapter 5, "Layout with Panels" (or any `Panel`-derived custom panel) as an items panel. For example, a `ListBox` stacks its items vertically by default, but the following XAML replaces this arrangement with a `WrapPanel`, as done with Photo Gallery in Chapter 7, "Structuring and Deploying an Application":

```
<ListBox>
<ListBox.ItemsPanel>
  <ItemsPanelTemplate>
    <WrapPanel/>
  </ItemsPanelTemplate>
</ListBox.ItemsPanel>
  …
</ListBox>
```

The translation of this XAML to procedural code is not straightforward, but here's how you can accomplish the same task in C#:

```
FrameworkElementFactory panelFactory = new
  FrameworkElementFactory(typeof(WrapPanel));
myListBox.ItemsPanel = new ItemsPanelTemplate(panelFactory);
```

Here's an example with a custom `FanCanvas` that will be implemented in Chapter 21, "Layout with Custom Panels":

```
<ListBox>
<ListBox.ItemsPanel>
  <ItemsPanelTemplate>
    <custom:FanCanvas/>
  </ItemsPanelTemplate>
</ListBox.ItemsPanel>
  …
</ListBox>
```

Figure 10.3 shows the result of applying this to Photo Gallery (and wrapping the `ListBox` in a `Viewbox`) and selecting one item. The `ListBox` retains all its behaviors with item selection despite the custom inner layout.

FIGURE 10.3 ListBox with a custom FanCanvas used as its ItemsPanel.

FAQ

How can I make ListBox arrange its items horizontally instead of vertically?

By default, ListBox uses a panel called VirtualizingStackPanel to arrange its items vertically. The following code replaces it with a new VirtualizingStackPanel that explicitly sets its Orientation to Horizontal:

```
<ListBox>
<ListBox.ItemsPanel>
  <ItemsPanelTemplate>
    <VirtualizingStackPanel Orientation="Horizontal"/>
  </ItemsPanelTemplate>
</ListBox.ItemsPanel>
  …
</ListBox>
```

TIP

Many items controls use VirtualizingStackPanel as their default ItemsPanel to get good performance. In WPF 4, this panel supports a new mode that improves scrolling performance even further, but you need to turn it on explicitly. To do so, you set the VirtualizingStackPanel.VirtualizationMode attached property to Recycling. When this is done, the panel reuses ("recycles") the containers that hold each onscreen item rather than constructing a new container for each item.

If you look at the default control template for an items control such as `ListBox`, you can see an `ItemsPresenter`, which does the work of picking up the appropriate `ItemsPanel`:

```
<ControlTemplate TargetType="{x:Type ListBox}">
  <Border …>
    <ScrollViewer Padding="{TemplateBinding Padding}" Focusable="false">
      <ItemsPresenter SnapsToDevicePixels="{TemplateBinding SnapsToDevicePixels}"/>
    </ScrollViewer>
  </Border>
<ControlTemplate.Triggers>
  …
</ControlTemplate.Triggers>
</ControlTemplate>
```

The presence of `ScrollViewer` in the default control template explains where the default scrolling behavior comes from. You can control an items control's scrolling behavior with various `ScrollViewer` attached properties.

Controlling Scrolling Behavior

Using `ListBox` as an example, the following properties have the following values by default:

- **`ScrollViewer.HorizontalScrollBarVisibility`**—`Auto`
- **`ScrollViewer.VerticalScrollBarVisibility`**—`Auto`
- **`ScrollViewer.CanContentScroll`**—`true`
- **`ScrollViewer.IsDeferredScrollingEnabled`**—`false`

When `CanContentScroll` is `true`, scrolling is done in item-by-item chunks. When it is `false`, the pixel-by-pixel scrolling is smooth but doesn't do anything to ensure that the first item is "snapped" to the edge.

When `IsDeferredScrollingEnabled` is `false`, scrolling happens in real-time while the scrollbar thumb is dragged. When it is `true`, the `ScrollViewer`'s contents do not update until the scrollbar thumb is released. When an items control is using a virtualizing panel and it contains a large number of complex items, setting `IsDeferredScrollingEnabled` to `true` can result in a significant performance improvement by avoiding the rendering of intermediate states. Applications such as Microsoft Outlook scroll through long lists in this fashion.

Here is an example of a `ListBox` that sets all four of these `ScrollViewer` attached properties to affect the `ScrollViewer`'s behavior in its default control template:

```
<ListBox
  ScrollViewer.HorizontalScrollBarVisibility="Disabled"
  ScrollViewer.VerticalScrollBarVisibility="Disabled"
  ScrollViewer.CanContentScroll="False"
```

```
  ScrollViewer.IsDeferredScrollingEnabled="True"
>
  …
</ListBox>
```

ListBox is not the only items control, of course. Items controls can be divided into three main groups, as discussed in the following sections: selectors, menus, and others.

Selectors

Selectors are items controls whose items can be indexed and, most importantly, selected. The abstract Selector class, which derives from ItemsControl, adds a few properties to handle selection. For example, the following are three similar properties for getting or setting the current selection:

- **SelectedIndex**—A zero-based integer that indicates what item is selected or -1 if nothing is selected. Items are numbered in the order in which they are added to the collection.
- **SelectedItem**—The actual item instance that is currently selected.
- **SelectedValue**—The value of the currently selected item. By default this value is the item itself, making SelectedValue identical to SelectedItem. You can set SelectedValuePath, however, to choose an arbitrary property or expression that should represent each item's value. (SelectedValuePath works just like DisplayMemberPath.)

All three properties are read/write, so you can use them to change the current selection as well as retrieve it.

Selector also supports two attached properties that can be applied to individual items:

- **IsSelected**—A Boolean that can be used to select or unselect an item (or to retrieve its current selection state)
- **IsSelectionActive**—A read-only Boolean that tells whether the selection has focus

Selector also defines an event—SelectionChanged—that makes it possible to listen for changes to the current selection. Chapter 6, "Input Events: Keyboard, Mouse, Stylus, and Multi-Touch," uses this with a ListBox when demonstrating attached events.

WPF ships five Selector-derived controls, described in the following sections:

- ComboBox
- ListBox
- ListView
- TabControl
- DataGrid

ComboBox

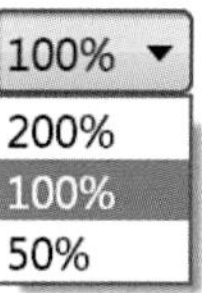

FIGURE 10.4 The WPF ComboBox, with its drop-down showing.

The ComboBox control, shown in Figure 10.4, enables users to select one item from a list. ComboBox is a popular control because it doesn't occupy much space. It displays only the current selection in a *selection box*, with the rest of the list shown on demand in a *drop-down*. The drop-down can be opened and closed by clicking the button or by pressing Alt+up arrow, Alt+down arrow, or F4.

ComboBox defines two events—DropDownOpened and DropDownClosed—and a property—IsDropDownOpen—that enable you to act on the drop-down being opened or closed. For example, you can delay the filling of ComboBox items until the drop-down is opened by handling the DropDownOpened event. Note that IsDropDownOpen is a read/write property, so you can set it directly to change the state of the drop-down.

Customizing the Selection Box

ComboBox supports a mode in which the user can type arbitrary text into the selection box. If the text matches one of the existing items, that item automatically becomes selected. Otherwise, no item gets selected, but the custom text gets stored in ComboBox's Text property so you can act on it appropriately. This mode can be controlled with two poorly named properties, IsEditable and IsReadOnly, which are both false by default. In addition, a StaysOpenOnEdit property can be set to true to keep the drop-down open if the user clicks on the selection box (matching the behavior of drop-downs in Microsoft Office as opposed to normal Win32 drop-downs).

FAQ

What's the difference between ComboBox's IsEditable and IsReadOnly properties?

Setting IsEditable to true turns ComboBox's selection box into a text box. IsReadOnly controls whether that text box can be edited, just like TextBox's IsReadOnly property. This means that IsReadOnly is meaningless unless IsEditable is true, and IsEditable being true doesn't necessarily mean that the selection text can be edited. Table 10.1 sums up the behavior of ComboBox based on the values of these two properties.

TABLE 10.1 The Behavior for All Combinations of IsEditable and IsReadOnly

IsEditable	IsReadOnly	Description
false	false	The selection box displays a visual copy of the selected item, and it doesn't allow the typing of arbitrary text. (This is the default behavior.)
false	true	Same as above.
true	false	The selection box displays a textual representation of the selected item, and it allows the typing of arbitrary text.
true	true	The selection box displays a textual representation of the selected item, but it doesn't allow the typing of arbitrary text.

When the selection box is a text box, the selected item can be displayed only as a simple string. This isn't a problem when items in the `ComboBox` are strings (or content controls containing strings), but when they are more complicated items, you must tell `ComboBox` what to use as the string representation for its items.

Listing 10.1 contains XAML for a `ComboBox` with complex items. Each item displays a PowerPoint design in a way that makes the `ComboBox` look like a Microsoft Office–style gallery, showing a preview and description for each item. A typical gallery in Office restricts the selection box to simple text, however, rather than keeping the full richness of the selected item. Figure 10.5 shows the rendered result of Listing 10.1, as well as what happens by default when this `ComboBox` is marked with `IsEditable` set to `true`.

LISTING 10.1 A `ComboBox` with Complex Items, Such as a Microsoft Office Gallery

```
<ComboBox>
  <!-- Item #1 -->
  <StackPanel Orientation="Horizontal" Margin="5">
    <Image Source="CurtainCall.bmp"/>
    <StackPanel Width="200">
      <TextBlock Margin="5,0" FontSize="14" FontWeight="Bold"
        VerticalAlignment="center">Curtain Call</TextBlock>
      <TextBlock Margin="5" VerticalAlignment="center" TextWrapping="Wrap">
        Whimsical, with a red curtain background that represents a stage.
      </TextBlock>
    </StackPanel>
  </StackPanel>
  <!-- Item #2 -->
  <StackPanel Orientation="Horizontal" Margin="5">
    <Image Source="Fireworks.bmp"/>
    <StackPanel Width="200">
      <TextBlock Margin="5,0" FontSize="14" FontWeight="Bold"
        VerticalAlignment="center">Fireworks</TextBlock>
      <TextBlock Margin="5" VerticalAlignment="center" TextWrapping="Wrap">
        Sleek, with a black sky containing fireworks. When you need to
        celebrate PowerPoint-style, this design is for you!
      </TextBlock>
    </StackPanel>
  </StackPanel>
  …more items…
</ComboBox>
```


Obviously, displaying the type name of `"System.Windows.Controls.StackPanel"` in the selection box is not acceptable, so that's where the `TextSearch` class comes in. `TextSearch` defines two attached properties that provide control over the text that gets displayed in an editable selection box.

`IsEditable=False` (default) `IsEditable=True`

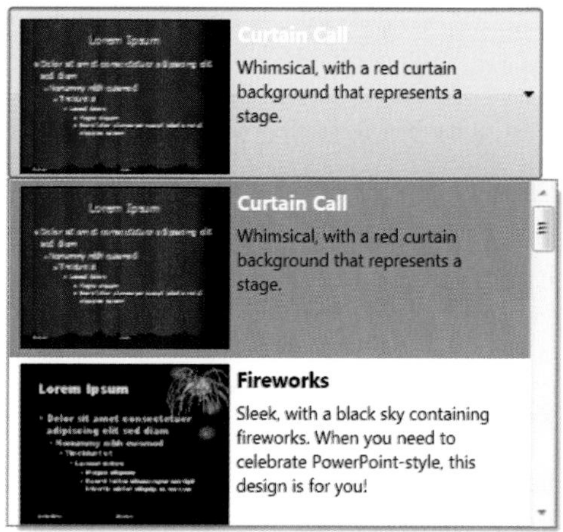

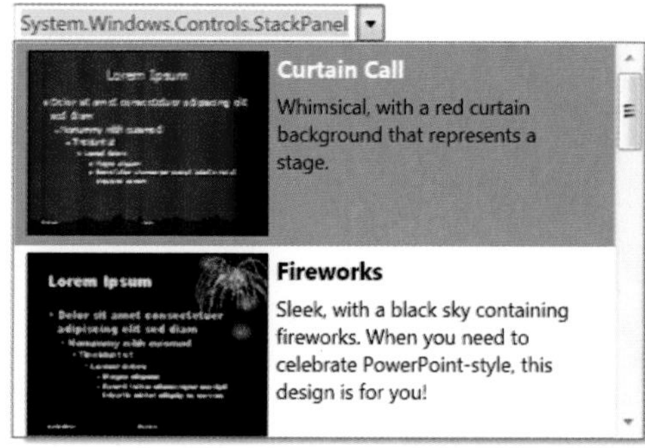

FIGURE 10.5 By default, setting `IsEditable` to `true` causes `ToString`-based rendering in the selection box.

A `TextSearch.TextPath` property can be attached to a `ComboBox` to designate the property (or subproperty) of each item to use as the selection box text. This works just like the `DisplayMemberPath` and `SelectedValuePath` properties; the only difference between these three properties is how the final value is used.

For each item in Listing 10.1, the obvious text to use in the selection box is the content of the first `TextBlock` because it contains the title (such as `"Curtain Call"` or `"Fireworks"`). Because the `TextBlock` is nested within two `StackPanel`s, the desired property path involves referencing the inner `StackPanel` (the second child of each item) before referencing the `TextBlock` (the first child of each inner `StackPanel`). Therefore, the `TextPath` attached property can be applied to Listing 10.1 as follows:

```
<ComboBox IsEditable="True" TextSearch.TextPath="Children[1].Children[0].Text">
  …
</ComboBox>
```

This is a bit fragile, however, because the property path will stop working if the structure of the items is changed. It also doesn't handle heterogeneous items; any item that doesn't match the structure of `TextPath` is displayed as an empty string in the selection box.

`TextSearch`'s other attached property, `Text`, is more flexible but must be applied to individual items in the `ComboBox`. You can set `Text` to the literal text you want to be displayed in the selection box for each item. It could be applied to Listing 10.1 as follows:

```
<ComboBox IsEditable="True">
  <!-- Item #1 -->
  <StackPanel TextSearch.Text="Curtain Call" Orientation="Horizontal" Margin="5">
    …
```

```
  </StackPanel>
  <!-- Item #2 -->
  <StackPanel TextSearch.Text="Fireworks" Orientation="Horizontal" Margin="5">
    …
  </StackPanel>
  …more items…
</ComboBox>
```

You can use TextSearch.TextPath on the ComboBox and TextSearch.Text on individual items simultaneously. In this case, TextPath provides the default selection box representation, and Text overrides this representation for any marked items.

Figure 10.6 shows the result of using either TextSearch.TextPath or TextSearch.Text as in the preceding snippets.

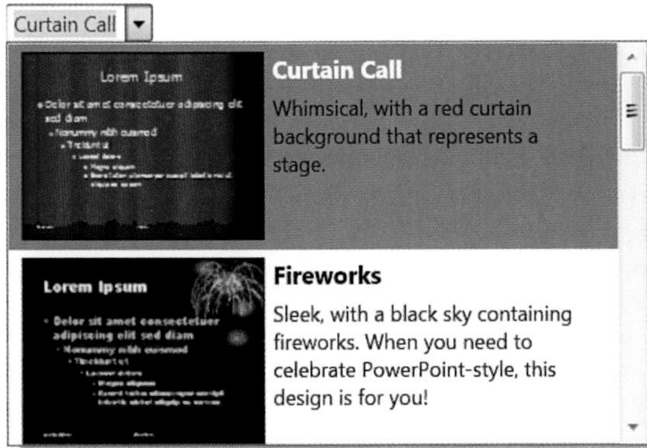

FIGURE 10.6 A proper-looking Office-style gallery, thanks to the use of TextSearch attached properties.

TIP

You can disable TextSearch by setting ItemsControl's IsTextSearchEnabled property to false. ItemsControl's IsTextSearchCaseSensitive property (which is false by default) controls whether the case of typing must match the case of the text.

FAQ

When the SelectionChanged event gets raised, how do I get the new selection?

The SelectionChanged event is designed to handle controls that allow multiple selections, so it can be a little confusing for a single-selection selector such as ComboBox. The SelectionChangedEventArgs type passed to event handlers has two properties of type IList: AddedItems and RemovedItems. AddedItems contains the new selection, and RemovedItems contains the previous selection. You can retrieve a new single selection as follows:

Continued

```
void ComboBox_SelectionChanged(object sender, SelectionChangedEventArgs e)
{
  if (e.AddedItems.Count > 0)
    object newSelection = e.AddedItems[0];
}
```

And, like this code, you should never assume that there's a selected item! Besides the fact that `ComboBox`'s selection can be cleared programmatically, it can get cleared by the user when `IsEditable` is `true` and `IsReadOnly` is `false`. In this case, if the user changes the selection box text to something that doesn't match any item, the `SelectionChanged` event is raised with an empty `AddedItems` collection.

`ComboBoxItem`

`ComboBox` implicitly wraps each of its items in a `ComboBoxItem` object. (You can see this from code if you traverse up the visual tree from any of the items.) But you can explicitly wrap any item in a `ComboBoxItem`, which happens to be a content control. You can apply this to each item in Listing 10.1 as follows:

```
<!-- Item #1 -->
<ComboBoxItem TextSearch.Text="Curtain Call">
  <StackPanel Orientation="Horizontal" Margin="5">
    …
  </StackPanel>
</ComboBoxItem>
<!-- Item #2 -->
<ComboBoxItem TextSearch.Text="Fireworks">
  <StackPanel Orientation="Horizontal" Margin="5">
    …
  </StackPanel>
</ComboBoxItem>
…more items…
```

Notice that if you're using the `TextSearch.Text` attached property, you need to move it to the `ComboBoxItem` element now that `StackPanel` is not the outermost element for each item. Similarly, the `TextSearch.TextPath` value used earlier needs to be changed to `Content.Children[1].Children[0].Text`.

FAQ

Why should I bother wrapping items in a ComboBoxItem?

ComboBoxItem exposes some useful properties—IsSelected and IsHighlighted—and useful events—Selected and Unselected. Using ComboBoxItem also avoids a quirky behavior with showing content controls in the selection box (when IsEditable is false): If an item in a ComboBox is a content control, the entire control doesn't get displayed in the selection box. Instead, the inner content is extracted and shown. By using ComboBoxItem as the outermost content control, the inner content is now the entire control that you probably wanted to be displayed in the first place.

Because ComboBoxItem is a content control, it is also handy for adding simple strings to a ComboBox (rather than using something like TextBlock or Label). Here's an example:

```
<ComboBox>
  <ComboBoxItem>Item 1</ComboBoxItem>
  <ComboBoxItem>Item 2</ComboBoxItem>
</ComboBox>
```

ListBox

The familiar ListBox control is similar to ComboBox, except that all items are displayed directly within the control's bounds (or you can scroll to view additional items if they don't all fit). Figure 10.7 shows a ListBox that contains the same items used in Listing 10.1.

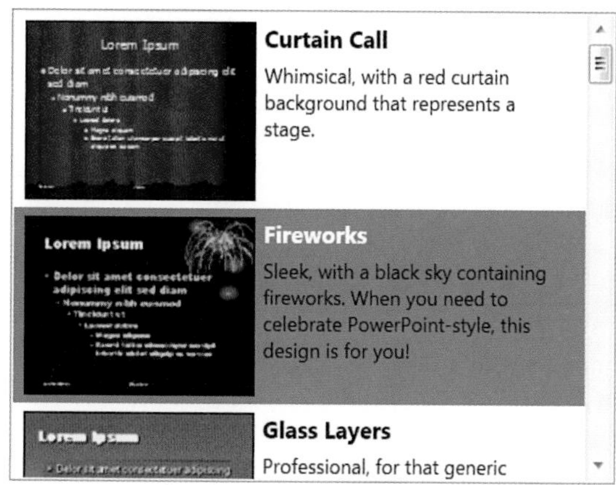

FIGURE 10.7 The WPF ListBox.

Probably the most important feature of `ListBox` is that it can support multiple simultaneous selections. This is controllable via the `SelectionMode` property, which accepts three values (from a `SelectionMode` enumeration):

- **`Single`**—Only one item can be selected at a time, just like with `ComboBox`. This is the default value.
- **`Multiple`**—Any number of items can be selected simultaneously. Clicking an unselected item adds it to `ListBox`'s `SelectedItems` collection, and clicking a selected item removes it from the collection.
- **`Extended`**—Any number of items can be selected simultaneously, but the behavior is optimized for the single selection case. To select multiple items in this mode, you must hold down `Shift` (for contiguous items) or `Ctrl` (for noncontiguous items) while clicking. This matches the behavior of the Win32 `ListBox` control.

DIGGING DEEPER

`ListBox` Properties and Multiple Selection

Although `ListBox` has a `SelectedItems` property that can be used no matter which `SelectionMode` is used, it still inherits the `SelectedIndex`, `SelectedItem`, and `SelectedValue` properties from `Selector` that don't fit in with the multiselect model.

When multiple items are selected, `SelectedItem` simply points to the first item in the `SelectedItems` collection (which is the item selected the earliest by the user), and `SelectedIndex` and `SelectedValue` simply give the index and value for that item. But it's best not to use these properties on a control that supports multiple selections. Note that `ListBox` does *not* define a `SelectedIndices` or `SelectedValues` property, however.

Just as `ComboBox` has its companion `ComboBoxItem` class, `ListBox` has a `ListBoxItem` class, as seen in earlier chapters. In fact, `ComboBoxItem` derives from `ListBoxItem`, which defines the `IsSelected` property and `Selected` and `Unselected` events.

TIP

The `TextSearch` technique shown with `ComboBox` in the preceding section is important for `ListBox`, too. For example, if the items in Figure 10.7 are marked with the appropriate `TextSearch.Text` values, then typing `F` while the `ListBox` has focus makes the selection jump to the Fireworks item. Without the use of `TextSearch`, pressing `S` would cause the items to get focus because that's the first letter in `System.Windows.Controls.StackPanel`. (And that would be a weird user experience!)

FAQ

How can I get `ListBox` to scroll smoothly?

By default, `ListBox` scrolls on an item-by-item basis. Because the scrolling is based on each item's height, it can look quite choppy if you have large items. If you want smooth scrolling, so each scrolling action shifts the items by a small number of pixels regardless of their heights, the easiest solution is to set the `ScrollViewer.CanContentScroll` attached property to `false` on the `ListBox` control, as shown previously in this chapter.

Be aware, however, that by making this change, you lose `ListBox`'s virtualization functionality. *Virtualization* refers to the optimization of creating child elements only when they become visible on the screen. Virtualization is possible only when using data binding to fill the control's items, so setting `CanContentScroll` to `false` can negatively impact the performance of data-bound scenarios only.

FAQ

How can I sort items in a `ListBox` (or any other `ItemsControl`)?

Sorting can be done via a mechanism on the `ItemsCollection` object, so it applies equally to all `ItemsControls`. `ItemsCollection` has a `SortDescriptions` property that can hold any number of `System.ComponentModel.SortDescription` instances. Each `SortDescription` describes which property of the items should be used for sorting and whether the sort is in ascending or descending order. For example, the following code sorts a bunch of `ContentControl` items based on their `Content` property:

```
// Clear any existing sorting first
myItemsControl.Items.SortDescriptions.Clear();
// Sort by the Content property
myItemsControl.Items.SortDescriptions.Add(
  new SortDescription("Content", ListSortDirection.Ascending));
```

FAQ

How do I get the items in my `ItemsControl` to have automation IDs, as seen in tools such as UI Spy?

The easiest way to give any `FrameworkElement` an automation ID is to set its `Name` property, as that is used by default for automation purposes. However, if you want to give an element an ID that is different from its name, simply set the `AutomationProperties.AutomationID` attached property (from the `System.Windows.Automation` namespace) to the desired string.

ListView

The ListView control, which derives from ListBox, looks and acts just like a ListBox, except that it uses the Extended SelectionMode by default. But ListView also adds a property called View that enables you to customize the view in a richer way than choosing a custom ItemsPanel.

The View property is of type ViewBase, an abstract class. WPF ships with one concrete subclass, GridView. Its default experience is much like Windows Explorer's Details view. (In fact, in beta versions of WPF, GridView was even called DetailsView.)

Figure 10.8 displays a simple ListView created from the following XAML, which assumes that the sys prefix corresponds to the System .NET namespace in mscorlib.dll:

```
<ListView>
<ListView.View>
  <GridView>
    <GridViewColumn Header="Date"/>
    <GridViewColumn Header="Day of Week"
      DisplayMemberBinding="{Binding DayOfWeek}"/>
    <GridViewColumn Header="Year" DisplayMemberBinding="{Binding Year}"/>
  </GridView>
</ListView.View>
  <sys:DateTime>1/1/2012</sys:DateTime>
  <sys:DateTime>1/2/2012</sys:DateTime>
  <sys:DateTime>1/3/2012</sys:DateTime>
</ListView>
```

Date	Day of Week	Year
1/1/2012	Sunday	2012
1/2/2012	Monday	2012
1/3/2012	Tuesday	2012

FIGURE 10.8 The WPF ListView, using GridView.

GridView has a Columns content property that holds a collection of GridViewColumn objects, as well as other properties to control the behavior of the column headers. WPF defines a ListViewItem element that derives from ListBoxItem. In this case, the DateTime objects are implicitly wrapped in ListViewItems because they are not used explicitly.

ListView's items are specified as a simple list, as with ListBox, so the key to displaying different data in each column is the DisplayMemberBinding property of GridViewColumn. The idea is that ListView contains a complex object for each row, and the value for every column is a property or subproperty of each object. Unlike ItemsControl's DisplayMemberPath property, however, DisplayMemberBinding requires the use of data binding techniques described in Chapter 13.

What's nice about GridView is that it automatically supports some of the advanced features of Windows Explorer's Details view:

- ▶ You can reorder columns by dragging and dropping them.
- ▶ You can resize columns by dragging the column separators.

- You can cause columns to automatically resize to "just fit" their content by double-clicking their separators.

GridView doesn't, however, support automatic sorting by clicking on a column header, which is an unfortunate gap in functionality. The code to sort items when a header is clicked is not complicated (you simply use the SortDescriptions property mentioned in the previous section), but you also have to manually create the little arrow in the header that typically indicates which column is being used for sorting and whether it's an ascending or descending sort. Basically, ListView with GridView is a poor-man's DataGrid. But now that WPF 4 has a *real* DataGrid control, the usefulness of the GridView control is diminished.

TabControl

The next selector, TabControl, is useful for switching between multiple pages of content. Figure 10.9 shows what a basic TabControl looks like. Tabs in a TabControl are typically placed on the top, but with TabControl's TabStripPlacment property (of type Dock), you can also set their placement to Left, Right, or Bottom.

Tab 1 | Tab 2 | Tab 3
Content for Tab 1.

FIGURE 10.9 The WPF TabControl.

TabControl is pretty easy to use. You simply add items, and each item is placed on a separate tab. Here's an example:

```
<TabControl>
  <TextBlock>Content for Tab 1.</TextBlock>
  <TextBlock>Content for Tab 2.</TextBlock>
  <TextBlock>Content for Tab 3.</TextBlock>
</TabControl>
```

Much like ComboBox with ComboBoxItem, ListBox with ListBoxItem, and so on, TabControl implicitly wraps each item in its companion TabItem type. It's unlikely that you'd add non-TabItem children directly to TabControl, however, because without an explicit TabItem there's no way to label the corresponding tab. For example, the following XAML is the source for Figure 10.9:

```
<TabControl>
  <TabItem Header="Tab 1">Content for Tab 1.</TabItem>
  <TabItem Header="Tab 2">Content for Tab 2.</TabItem>
  <TabItem Header="Tab 3">Content for Tab 3.</TabItem>
</TabControl>
```

TabItem is a headered content control, so Header can be any arbitrary object, just like with GroupBox or Expander.

Unlike with the other selectors, with TabItem, the first item is selected by default. However, you can programmatically unselect all tabs by setting SelectedItem to null or SelectedIndex to -1.

DataGrid

DataGrid is a versatile control for displaying multicolumn rows of data that can be sorted, edited, and much more. It is optimized for easy hook-up to an in-memory database table (such as System.Data.DataTable in ADO.NET). Wizards in Visual Studio and technologies such as LINQ to SQL make this connection especially easy.

Listing 10.2 shows a DataGrid that directly contains a XAML-instantiated collection of two instances of the following custom Record type:

```
public class Record
{
  public string FirstName     { get; set; }
  public string LastName      { get; set; }
  public Uri Website          { get; set; }
  public bool IsBillionaire { get; set; }
  public Gender Gender        { get; set; }
}
```

where the Gender enumeration is defined as follows:

```
public enum Gender
{
  Male,
  Female
}
```

The five columns of data shown in Figure 10.10 (one for each property on the Record object) are defined in the Columns collection.

LISTING 10.2 A DataGrid with Inline Data and a Variety of Column Types

```
<DataGrid IsReadOnly="True"
  xmlns:local="clr-namespace:Listing10_2"
  xmlns:sys="clr-namespace:System;assembly=mscorlib">

  <!-- Support for showing all genders in the DataGridComboBoxColumn: -->
  <DataGrid.Resources>
    <ObjectDataProvider x:Key="genderEnum" MethodName="GetValues"
      ObjectType="{x:Type sys:Enum}">
    <ObjectDataProvider.MethodParameters>
      <x:Type Type="local:Gender"/>
    </ObjectDataProvider.MethodParameters>
    </ObjectDataProvider>
```

LISTING 10.2 Continued

```
  </DataGrid.Resources>

  <!-- The columns: -->
  <DataGrid.Columns>
    <DataGridTextColumn Header="First Name" Binding="{Binding FirstName}"/>
    <DataGridTextColumn Header="Last Name" Binding="{Binding LastName}"/>
    <DataGridHyperlinkColumn Header="Website" Binding="{Binding Website}"/>
    <DataGridCheckBoxColumn Header="Billionaire?"
      Binding="{Binding IsBillionaire}"/>
    <DataGridComboBoxColumn Header="Gender" SelectedItemBinding="{Binding Gender}"
      ItemsSource="{Binding Source={StaticResource genderEnum}}"/>
  </DataGrid.Columns>

  <!-- The data: -->
  <local:Record FirstName="Adam" LastName="Nathan"
    Website="http://adamnathan.net" Gender="Male"/>
  <local:Record FirstName="Bill" LastName="Gates"
    Website="http://twitter.com/billgates" IsBillionaire="True" Gender="Male"/>

</DataGrid>
```

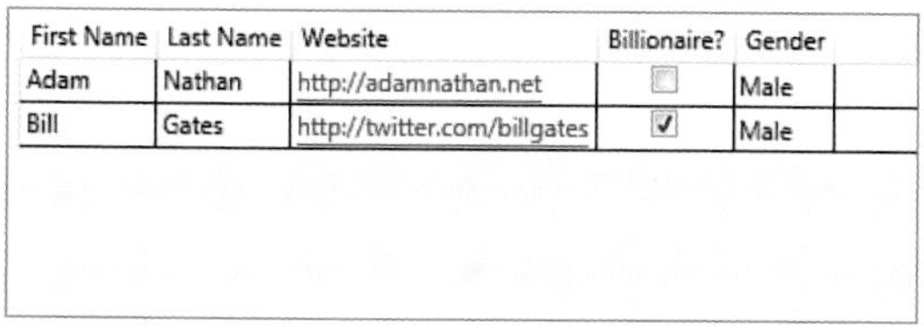

First Name	Last Name	Website	Billionaire?	Gender
Adam	Nathan	http://adamnathan.net	☐	Male
Bill	Gates	http://twitter.com/billgates	☑	Male

FIGURE 10.10 The WPF `DataGrid`, as constructed in Listing 10.2.

The `DataGrid` automatically supports reordering, resizing, and sorting the columns, but any or all of this functionality can be disabled by setting any of the following properties to `false`: `CanUserReorderColumns`, `CanUserResizeColumns`, `CanUserResizeRows`, and `CanUserSortColumns`. The grid lines and headers can be easily disabled via the `GridLinesVisibility` and `HeadersVisibility` properties.

Listing 10.2 highlights the main column types supported by `DataGrid`:

- **`DataGridTextColumn`**—Perfect for strings, this column type displays a `TextBlock` for its normal display and a `TextBox` when the value is being edited.
- **`DataGridHyperlinkColumn`**—Turns what would be plain text into a clickable hyperlink. However, note that there is no default behavior associated with clicking that link (such as opening a web browser). You must explicitly handle such actions.

- **`DataGridCheckBoxColumn`**—Perfect for Boolean values, this column type displays a `CheckBox` to represent a `true` (checked) or `false` (unchecked) value.
- **`DataGridComboBoxColumn`**—Perfect for enumerations, this column type displays a `TextBlock` for its normal display and a `ComboBox` filled with possible values when the value is being edited.

WPF has one more built-in column type:

- **`DataGridTemplateColumn`**—Enables an arbitrary template to be set for a value's normal display as well as its editing display. This is done by setting its `CellTemplate` and `CellEditingTemplate` properties.

Auto-Generated Columns

When `DataGrid`'s items are set via `ItemsSource`, it attempts to automatically generate appropriate columns. When this happens, `DataGridTextColumn` is automatically used for strings, `DataGridHyperlinkColumn` is automatically used for URIs, `DataGridCheckBoxColumn` is automatically used for Booleans, and `DataGridComboBoxColumn` is automatically used for enumerations (with an appropriate items source hooked up automatically).

Therefore, the following empty `DataGrid`:

```
<DataGrid Name="dataGrid" />
```

produces almost exactly the same result as Figure 10.10 when its `ItemsSource` is set as follows in code-behind:

```
dataGrid.ItemsSource = new Record[]
{
  new Record { FirstName="Adam", LastName="Nathan", Website=
    new Uri("http://adamnathan.net"), Gender=Gender.Male },
  new Record { FirstName="Bill", LastName="Gates", Website=
    new Uri("http://twitter.com/billgates"), Gender=Gender.Male,
    IsBillionaire=true }
};
```

The only visual difference is the labels used in the headers, which now match the corresponding property names. Figure 10.11 shows the result.

Besides being much simpler to construct, the `DataGrid` in Figure 10.11 automatically supports editing of the fields in each item, unlike when the items were placed directly in `DataGrid`'s `Items` collection. Cells in the first three columns automatically turn into editable `TextBox`es when clicked, the `CheckBox`es are clickable, and cells in the `Gender` column automatically turn into a `ComboBox` with the appropriate values when clicked. Keyboard gestures such as pressing the spacebar or F2 can also be used on the cell that has keyboard focus. All edits, when committed, are reflected in the underlying `ItemsSource` collection. (Unfortunately, checking the `IsBillionaire` box next to my name did not cause any change to be reflected in my bank account. Perhaps this sample has a bug.)

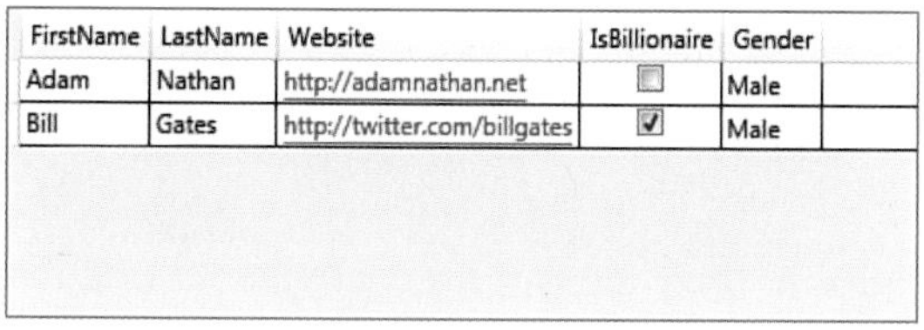

FirstName	LastName	Website	IsBillionaire	Gender
Adam	Nathan	http://adamnathan.net	☐	Male
Bill	Gates	http://twitter.com/billgates	☑	Male

FIGURE 10.11 The WPF `DataGrid`, with autogenerated columns that use `Record`'s property names as the header text.

If a `DataGrid` already has explicit columns defined, any autogenerated columns are placed after them. You can customize or remove individual autogenerated columns by handling the `AutoGeneratingColumn` event, which is raised once for each column. When all the columns have been generated, a single `AutoGeneratedColumns` event is raised. To disable autogenerated columns altogether, simply set `DataGrid`'s `AutoGenerateColumns` property to `false`.

Selecting Rows and/or Cells

`DataGrid` supports multiple selection modes controlled by two properties—`SelectionMode` and `SelectionUnit`. `SelectionMode` can be set to `Single` for single-item selection or `Extended` for multiple-item selection (the default behavior). The definition of "item" depends on the value of `SelectionUnit`. It can be set to any of the following:

- **`Cell`**—Only individual cells can be selected.
- **`FullRow`**—Only full rows can be selected. This is the default.
- **`CellOrRowHeader`**—Either can be selected. (To select a full row, click a row header.)

When multiselection is enabled, the Shift key can be held down to select multiple contiguous items or the Ctrl key can be held down to select multiple noncontiguous items.

When rows are selected, the `Selected` event is raised and the `SelectedItems` property contains the items. For the `DataGrid` in Listing 10.2, these items would be the `Record` instances. When individual cells are selected, the `SelectedCellChanged` event is raised and the `SelectedCells` property contains a list of `DataGridCellInfo` structures that contain information about the relevant columns and data. Instances of `DataGridRow` and `DataGridCell` involved in the selection also raise their own `Selected` event and have an `IsSelected` property set to `true`.

Even if multiple cells or rows are selected, there is at most one cell that has focus at any time. You can get or set that cell with the `CurrentCell` property. In addition, the `CurrentColumn` property reveals the column containing `CurrentCell`, and `CurrentItem` contains the data item corresponding to `CurrentCell`'s row.

A lot of the support for bulk selection and selection transactions comes from the base `MultiSelector` class, which derives from `Selector` and was introduced in WPF 3.5. Other WPF controls support multiple selections, but `DataGrid` is the only one that derives from `MultiSelector`.

Additional Customizations

DataGrid supports a number of customizations easily, such as its interaction with the clipboard, virtualization, the ability to add extra details to rows, and the ability to "freeze" columns.

Clipboard Interaction The data that gets copied to the clipboard from a DataGrid (such as when pressing Ctrl+C on a selection) can be customized with the ClipboardCopyMode property. It can be set to the following values:

- **ExcludeHeader**—Column headers are not included in the copied text. This is the default.
- **IncludeHeader**—Column headers are included in the copied text.
- **None**—Nothing can be copied to the clipboard.

Virtualization By default, DataGrid's rows are virtualized (UIElements are not created for rows offscreen, and the underlying data might even be fetched lazily, depending on the data source), but its columns are not. You can alter this behavior by setting EnableRowVirtualization to false or EnableColumnVirtualization to true. EnableColumnVirtualization is not true by default because it can slow down the frame rate when doing horizontal scrolling.

Extra Row Details DataGrid supports showing extended details on rows by setting the RowDetailsTemplate property. Here's an example:

```
<DataGrid …>
<DataGrid.RowDetailsTemplate>
  <DataTemplate>
    <TextBlock Margin="10" FontWeight="Bold">Details go here.</TextBlock>
  </DataTemplate>
</DataGrid.RowDetailsTemplate>
  …
</DataGrid>
```

Ordinarily, the elements inside RowDetailsTemplate would use data binding to customize the contents for the current row, but this example uses a simple TextBlock. Figure 10.12 shows the result when selecting a row.

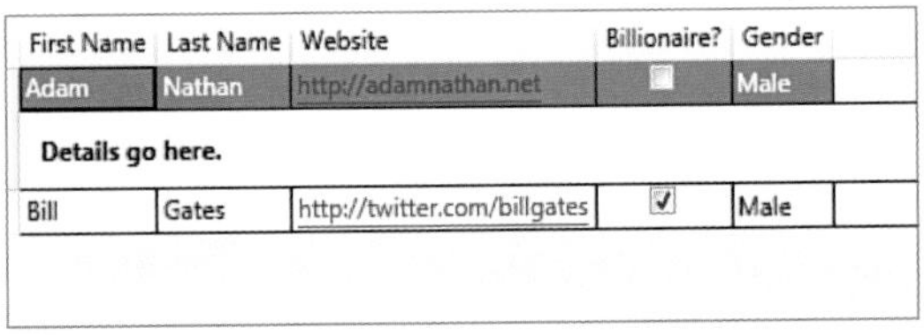

FIGURE 10.12 Showing details on a selected row in a DataGrid.

By default, details are shown only for the selected row(s), but this behavior can be changed with the `RowDetailsVisibilityMode` property. It can be set to one of the following values:

- **`VisibleWhenSelected`**—The row details are shown for only selected rows. This is the default value.
- **`Visible`**—The row details are shown for every row.
- **`Collapsed`**—The row details are not shown for any row.

Column Freezing `DataGrid` supports "freezing" any number of columns, meaning that they never scroll out of view. This is a lot like freezing columns in Microsoft Excel. There are several limitations to this support: They can only be the leftmost columns, and frozen columns cannot be reordered among unfrozen columns (and vice versa).

To freeze one or more columns, you simply set the `FrozenColumnCount` property to a value other than its default value of `0`. Figure 10.13 shows the `DataGrid` from Listing 10.2 but with `FrozenColumnCount` set to `2`. The columns after the first two have been scrolled, which is why you can't see the header text for the third column.

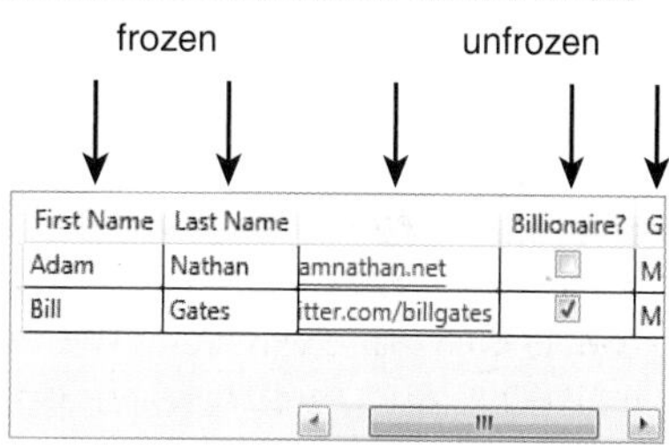

FIGURE 10.13 The `DataGrid` from Listing 10.2 with `FrozenColumnCount="2"`.

Editing, Adding, and Removing Data We've already seen that editing the data in individual items works automatically with `DataGrid`'s `ItemsSource`. If the `ItemsSource` collection supports adding and removing items, then `DataGrid` automatically supports adding and removing items as well. With the previous example, wrapping the array in a `List<Record>` (so the static array is only used to *initialize* the dynamic list) is enough to enable this functionality:

> **FAQ**
>
> **Can I freeze rows in a `DataGrid`?**
>
> No, there is no built-in support for that. The only other things that can be automatically frozen are row *details*. When `AreRowDetailsFrozen` is `true`, any row details that are shown do not scroll horizontally.

```
dataGrid.ItemsSource = new List<Record>(
  new Record[]
  {
    new Record { FirstName="Adam", LastName="Nathan", Website=
      new Uri("http://adamnathan.net"), Gender=Gender.Male },
    new Record { FirstName="Bill", LastName="Gates", Website=
      new Uri("http://twitter.com/billgates"), Gender=Gender.Male,
      IsBillionaire=true }
  }
);
```

This gives the DataGrid an extra blank row at the bottom, so a new entry can be added at any time. DataGrid defines methods and commands for the common actions of beginning an edit (bound to F2), cancelling an edit (bound to Esc), committing an edit (bound to Enter), and deleting a row (bound to Delete).

IsReadOnly can be set to true to prevent editing, and CanUserAddRows/CanUserDeleteRows can be set to false to prevent adding and deleting. Listing 10.2 sets IsReadOnly to true to avoid exceptions, as the inline collection of Record objects does not support editing. Although editing (and switching a cell to editing mode) happens automatically, several events are raised during the process to customize the behavior: PreparingCellForEdit, BeginningEdit, CellEditEnding/RowEditEnding, and InitializeNewItem.

WARNING

CanUserAddRows and CanUserDeleteRows can be automatically changed to false!

Depending on the values of other properties, CanUserAddRows and CanUserDeleteRows can become false even if you explicitly set them to true! For example, if DataGrid's IsReadOnly or IsEnabled properties are set to false, these two previously mentioned properties become false. But even more subtly, if the data source doesn't support adding and removing—ultimately revealed by IEditableCollectionView's CanAddNew and CanRemove properties—then the two properties also become false. See Chapter 13 for more information about collection views such as IEditableCollectionView.

Menus

WPF has both of the familiar menu controls built-in—Menu and ContextMenu. Unlike in Win32-based technologies, WPF menus are not special-cased over other controls to have distinct prominence or limitations. They are just another set of items controls, designed for the hierarchical display of items in a series of cascading popups.

Menu

Menu simply stacks its items horizontally, with the characteristic gray bar (by default) as its background. The only public API that Menu adds to its ItemsControl base class is the IsMainMenu property. When true (which it is by default), the Menu gets focus when the user presses the Alt or F10 key, matching user expectations for Win32 menus.

As with any other items control, Menu's items can be anything, but it's expected that you'll use MenuItem and Separator objects. Figure 10.14 displays a typical menu created from the XAML in Listing 10.3.

LISTING 10.3 A Typical Menu, with MenuItem and Separator Children

```
<Menu>
  <MenuItem Header="_File">
    <MenuItem Header="_New..."/>
```

LISTING 10.3 Continued

```
    <MenuItem Header="_Open..."/>
    <Separator/>
    <MenuItem Header="Sen_d To">
      <MenuItem Header="Mail Recipient"/>
      <MenuItem Header="My Documents"/>
    </MenuItem>
  </MenuItem>
  <MenuItem Header="_Edit">
  …
  </MenuItem>
  <MenuItem Header="_View">
  …
  </MenuItem>
</Menu>
```

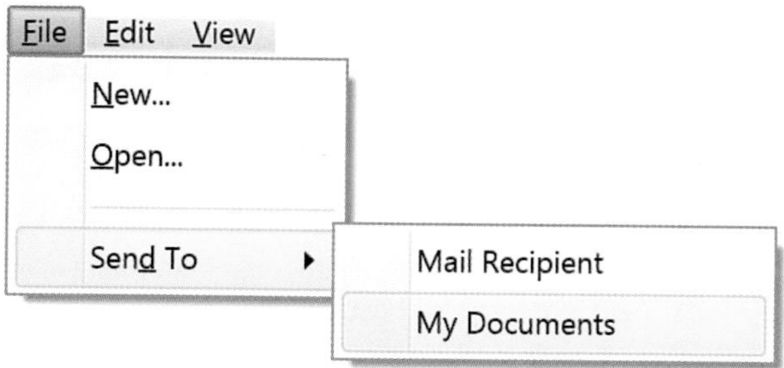

FIGURE 10.14 The WPF Menu.

`MenuItem` is a *headered items control* (derived from `HeaderedItemsControl`), which is much like a headered content control. For `MenuItem`, `Header` is actually the main object (typically text, as in Figure 10.14). The `Items`, if any, are the child elements that get displayed as a submenu. Like `Button` and `Label`, `MenuItem` supports access keys by using the underscore prefix.

`Separator` is a simple control that, when placed in a `MenuItem`, gets rendered as the horizontal line shown in Figure 10.14. `Separator` is also designed for two other items controls discussed later in this chapter: `ToolBar` and `StatusBar`.

Although `Menu` is a simple control, `MenuItem` contains many properties for customizing its behavior. Some of the interesting ones are as follows:

- **`Icon`**—Enables you to add an arbitrary object to be placed alongside the `Header`. The `Icon` object gets rendered just like `Header`, although typically a small image or drawing is used.
- **`IsCheckable`**—Enables you to make a `MenuItem` act like a `CheckBox` control.

- **`InputGestureText`**—Enables you to label an item with an associated gesture (most commonly a keyboard shortcut such as Ctrl+O).

`MenuItem` also defines five events: `Checked`, `Unchecked`, `SubmenuOpened`, `SubmenuClosed`, and `Click`. Although handling a `Click` event is a common way to attach behavior to a `MenuItem`, you can alternatively assign a command to `MenuItem`'s `Command` property.

WARNING

Setting `InputGestureText` doesn't give a `MenuItem` its keyboard shortcut!

In a confusing departure from systems such as Windows Forms and Visual Basic 6, with WPF, setting `MenuItem`'s `InputGestureText` to a string such as `"Ctrl+O"` doesn't automatically invoke the item when Ctrl+O is pressed! Instead, the string just serves as documentation.

To give a `MenuItem` a keyboard shortcut, you should hook it up to a command via its `Command` property. If the command has an associated input gesture, `MenuItem`'s `InputGestureText` property is automatically set to the correct string, so the shortcut is displayed without any explicit action.

TIP

When assigning `MenuItem`'s `Command` property to an instance of `RoutedUICommand`, its `Header` is automatically set to the command's `Text` property. You can override this behavior by explicitly setting `Header`.

FAQ

How can I make `Menu` arrange its items vertically instead of horizontally?

Because `Menu` is just another items control, you can use the same `ItemsPanel` trick shown earlier for `ListBox` but replace the default panel with a `StackPanel`:

```
<Menu>
<Menu.ItemsPanel>
  <ItemsPanelTemplate>
    <StackPanel/>
  </ItemsPanelTemplate>
</Menu.ItemsPanel>
  …
</Menu>
```

The default orientation for `StackPanel` is vertical, so you don't need to set the `Orientation` property in this case. Figure 10.15 shows the result.

FIGURE 10.15 A vertical Menu.

If you want the entire menu to be rotated to the vertical position (with sideways text, like what happens in older Microsoft Office programs when you drag and dock menus to the left or right edge of the window), you should instead use a RotateTransform.

ContextMenu

ContextMenu works just like Menu; it's a simple container designed to hold MenuItems and Separators. You can't embed ContextMenu directly in an element tree, however. You must attach it to a control via an appropriate property, such as the ContextMenu property defined on FrameworkElement and FrameworkContentElement. When a user right-clicks the element (or presses Shift+F10), the context menu is displayed.

Figure 10.16 displays a context menu applied to a ListBox as follows, using exactly the same MenuItems from Listing 10.3:

```
<ListBox>
<ListBox.ContextMenu>
  <ContextMenu>
    …The three MenuItems from Listing 10.3…
  </ContextMenu>
</ListBox.ContextMenu>
  …
</ListBox>
```

FIGURE 10.16 The WPF ContextMenu.

Besides the expected IsOpen property and Opened/Closed events, ContextMenu defines many properties for customizing the placement of the menu. By default, the menu appears with its upper-left corner directly under the mouse pointer. But you can change its Placement to something other than MousePoint (for example, Absolute) and/or set its HorizontalOffset and VerticalOffset to adjust this behavior.

Just as `ToolTip` has a companion `ToolTipService` static class for controlling properties from the `ToolTip`'s target, `ContextMenu` has a `ContextMenuService` static class for the same purpose. It contains several attached properties that correspond to many of the properties defined directly on `ContextMenu`.

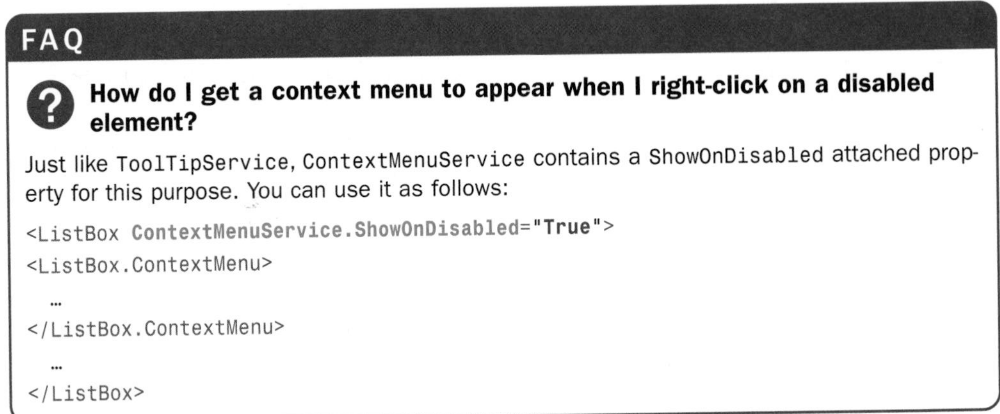

FAQ

How do I get a context menu to appear when I right-click on a disabled element?

Just like `ToolTipService`, `ContextMenuService` contains a `ShowOnDisabled` attached property for this purpose. You can use it as follows:

```
<ListBox ContextMenuService.ShowOnDisabled="True">
<ListBox.ContextMenu>
  …
</ListBox.ContextMenu>
  …
</ListBox>
```

Other Items Controls

The remaining items controls—`TreeView`, `ToolBar` and `StatusBar`—are neither selectors nor menus but can still contain an unbounded number of arbitrary objects.

`TreeView`

`TreeView` is a popular control for displaying hierarchical data with nodes that can be expanded and collapsed, as shown in Figure 10.17. Under the Aero theme, nodes have triangles indicating their expanded/collapsed state, but on the other themes, such as Luna, nodes have the familiar plus and minus indicators.

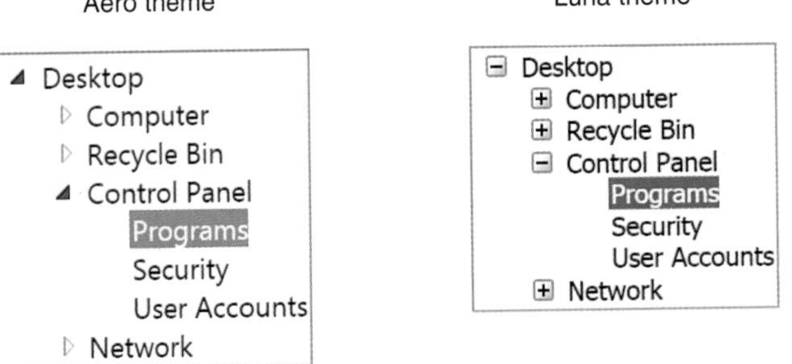

FIGURE 10.17 The WPF `TreeView` control.

DIGGING DEEPER

TreeView Versus Selector

TreeView's APIs make it look a lot like a Selector, but it does not derive from Selector because its hierarchical items can't be naturally indexed with a simple integer. Therefore, the TreeView class defines its own SelectedItem and SelectedValue properties (but not SelectedIndex). It also defines a SelectedItemChanged event that passes simple OldValue and NewValue items to event handlers, as TreeView only handles single selections.

The lack of multiselect support in TreeView is an unfortunate limitation that still exists in WPF 4. If you require such functionality, one option is to use a third-party control, such as Telerik's RadTreeView (http://telerik.com/products/wpf/treeview.aspx). You could try to build your own multiselect TreeView class by deriving from ListBox, but this is not easy.

TreeView, like Menu, is a very simple control. It can contain any items, and it stacks them vertically. But TreeView is pretty pointless unless you fill it with TreeViewItems.

TreeViewItem, just like MenuItem, is a headered items control. TreeViewItem's Header property contains the current item, and its Items collection contains subitems (which, again, are expected to be TreeViewItems).

The TreeView in Figure 10.17 can be created with the following XAML:

```
<TreeView>
  <TreeViewItem Header="Desktop">
    <TreeViewItem Header="Computer">
      …
    </TreeViewItem>
    <TreeViewItem Header="Recycle Bin">
      …
    </TreeViewItem>
    <TreeViewItem Header="Control Panel">
      <TreeViewItem Header="Programs"/>
      <TreeViewItem Header="Security"/>
      <TreeViewItem Header="User Accounts"/>
    </TreeViewItem>
    <TreeViewItem Header="Network">
      …
    </TreeViewItem>
  </TreeViewItem>
</TreeView>
```

TreeViewItem contains handy IsExpanded and IsSelected properties, as well as four events covering all four states from these properties: Expanded, Collapsed, Selected, and Unselected. TreeViewItem also supports rich keyboard navigation, with the plus (+) and minus (-) keys expanding and collapsing an item, and the arrow keys, Page Up, Page Down, Home, and End keys enabling several ways to move focus from one item to another.

TIP

As of WPF 4, TreeView supports virtualization, but you have to turn it on explicitly by setting the VirtualizingStackPanel.IsVirtualizing attached property to true on the TreeView. Doing so can save large amounts of memory and can significantly improve the performance of scrolling when there are lots of items.

WARNING

Always use TreeViewItem to explicitly wrap items in a TreeView!

It might be tempting to use simple TextBlocks as leaf nodes, but when you do so, you can run into a subtle property value inheritance trap that can make the text in such TextBlocks seem to disappear. By default, selecting a parent node changes its Foreground to white, and if TextBlocks are direct logical children, their text turns white as well. (Although the implicit TreeViewItem is the visual parent for each TextBlock, the logical parent takes precedence for inheritance.) Against the default white background, such text cannot be seen. If you make TreeViewItem the explicit (logical) parent of each TextBlock, however, the undesirable inheritance no longer occurs.

ToolBar

The ToolBar control is typically used to group together many small buttons (or other controls) as an enhancement to a traditional menu system. Figure 10.18 displays a ToolBar created from the following XAML:

```
<ToolBar RenderOptions.BitmapScalingMode="NearestNeighbor">
  <Button><Image Source="copy.gif"/></Button>
  <Separator/>
  <ToggleButton><Image Source="bold.gif"/></ToggleButton>
  <ToggleButton><Image Source="italic.gif"/></ToggleButton>
  <ToggleButton><Image Source="underline.gif"/></ToggleButton>
  <Separator/>
  <ToggleButton><Image Source="left.gif"/></ToggleButton>
  <ToggleButton><Image Source="right.gif"/></ToggleButton>
  <ToggleButton><Image Source="justify.gif"/></ToggleButton>
  <Separator/>
  <Label>Zoom</Label>
  <ComboBox>
    …
  </ComboBox>
```

```
    <Separator/>
    <Button><Image Source="superscript.gif"/></Button>
    <Button><Image Source="subscript.gif"/></Button>
    …
</ToolBar>
```

FIGURE 10.18 The WPF ToolBar.

Notice that the Button and ComboBox controls used in the ToolBar look different than they normally do. In addition, Separator now gets rendered as a vertical line instead of the horizontal line seen when it is placed inside a Menu. ToolBar overrides the default styles of its items so that they automatically get the look that most people expect from a ToolBar.

ToolBars can be placed anywhere in an element tree, but they are typically placed inside a FrameworkElement called ToolBarTray. ToolBarTray holds a collection of ToolBars (in its content property called ToolBars) and, unless its IsLocked property is set to true, it enables users to drag and reposition the ToolBars. (ToolBarTray also defines an IsLocked attached property that can be placed on individual ToolBars.) ToolBarTray has an Orientation property that can be set to Vertical to make all its ToolBars arrange its items vertically.

If a ToolBar contains more items than it can fit within its bounds, the extra items move to an overflow area. This overflow area is a popup that can be accessed by clicking the little arrow at the end of the control, as shown in Figure 10.19. By default, the last item is the first to move to the overflow area, but you can control the overflow behavior of individual items with ToolBar's OverflowMode attached property. You can use this property to mark an item to overflow AsNeeded (the default), Always, or Never.

TIP

You can create a Visual Studio–style customizable ToolBar by setting ToolBar.OverflowMode to Never on each item, then adding a Menu with the header "_Add or Remove Buttons" and ToolBar.OverflowMode set to Always (so it always remains in the overflow area). You can then add MenuItems to this Menu that users can check/uncheck to add/remove the corresponding item to/from the ToolBar.

FIGURE 10.19 ToolBar has an overflow area for items that don't fit.

TIP

Whenever elements contain small, iconic images, it's a good idea to set the `RenderOptions.BitmapScalingMode` attached property to `NearestNeighbor`. This makes such images look much crisper than their default rendering. The `ToolBar` in this section takes advantage of this property.

Although the property is placed on the `ToolBar` itself for brevity, it would be better to place it on each `Button` individually. That's because when any of these `Buttons` are moved to the overflow popup, they no longer inherit this value. (The containing `Popup` element is not a child of the `ToolBar`.) The impact is subtle, but this is why the last two icons are blurry in Figure 10.20 compared to Figure 10.19.

DIGGING DEEPER

Customizing Keyboard Navigation

The following `ToolBar` exhibits potentially problematic keyboard behavior:

```
<ToolBar>
  <Button>A</Button>
  <Menu>
    <MenuItem Header="B"/>
    <MenuItem Header="C"/>
  </Menu>
  <Button>D</Button>
</ToolBar>
```

If you give focus to the `ToolBar` and repeatedly press Tab, the focus gets "stuck" in a cycle from A to B to C to D to A to B, and so on. And if you use the left or right-arrow key to focus on either `MenuItem`, the focus gets stuck oscillating between B and C as you keep pressing the arrow key.

The `KeyboardNavigation` class in the `System.Windows.Input` namespace defines a handful of attached properties for customizing this (and other) keyboard behavior. For example, to avoid the cycle when tabbing through a `ToolBar`, you can set `KeyboardNavigation.TabNavigation` to `Continue` (rather than `Cycle`) on the `ToolBar`. To avoid the cycle when navigating through a `Menu` with arrow keys, you can set `KeyboardNavigation.DirectionalNavigation` to `Continue` on the `Menu`.

DIGGING DEEPER

`ToolBar`'s Unused `Header` Property

`ToolBar` is actually a headered items control (like `MenuItem` and `TreeViewItem`). Its `Header` property is never displayed, but it can be useful for implementing extra features for `ToolBarTray`. For example, you could add a context menu that lists all the `ToolBars` (using their `Header`), enabling users to add or remove them. Or, you could implement "tear off" `ToolBars` and show the `Header` on the floating `ToolBar`.

StatusBar

StatusBar behaves just like Menu, but it stacks its items horizontally, as shown in Figure 10.20. It's typically used along the bottom of a Window to display status information.

FIGURE 10.20 The WPF StatusBar.

The StatusBar in Figure 10.20 can be created with the following XAML:

```
<StatusBar RenderOptions.BitmapScalingMode="NearestNeighbor">
  <Label>27 Items</Label>
  <Separator/>
  <Label>Zoom</Label>
  <ComboBox>
    …
  </ComboBox>
  <Separator/>
  <Button><Image Source="justify.gif"/></Button>
</StatusBar>
```

By default, StatusBar gives Separator a control template that renders it as a vertical line, just like when it is within a ToolBar. Items in a StatusBar (other than Separator) are implicitly wrapped in a StatusBarItem, but you can also do this wrapping explicitly. This way, you can customize their position with the layout-related attached properties discussed in Chapter 5.

FAQ

How can I get items in a StatusBar to grow proportionally?

It's common to want StatusBar panes to remain proportionately sized. For example, perhaps you want a left pane that occupies 25% of the StatusBar's width and a right pane that occupies 75% of the width. You can make this happen by overriding StatusBar's ItemsPanel with a Grid and configuring the Grid's columns as follows:

```
<StatusBar>
  <StatusBar.ItemsPanel>
    <ItemsPanelTemplate>
      <Grid>
      <Grid.ColumnDefinitions>
        <ColumnDefinition Width="*"/>
        <ColumnDefinition Width="Auto"/>
        <ColumnDefinition Width="3*"/>
      </Grid.ColumnDefinitions>
      </Grid>
    </ItemsPanelTemplate>
  </StatusBar.ItemsPanel>
```

Continued

```
  <StatusBarItem Grid.Column="0">…</StatusBarItem>
  <Separator     Grid.Column="1"/>
  <StatusBarItem Grid.Column="2">…</StatusBarItem>
</StatusBar>
```

Note that items inside the `StatusBar` need to be explicitly marked with `Grid.Column` (which is meaningful only when `Grid` is the `ItemsPanel`) to avoid all being placed in column zero. Also, be aware that such layout properties work only for children of type `StatusBarItem` or `Separator`. That's because other elements (such as the `Label`, `ComboBox`, and `Button` in the previous `StatusBar` snippet) would get implicitly wrapped with a `StatusBarItem` that would be missing the necessary attached properties. Therefore, you must wrap any such elements explicitly in a `StatusBarItem`.

Summary

Items controls are vital to understand for just about any WPF development. It's hard to imagine a WPF application not using content controls and items controls. But unlike content controls, there's a lot to learn about items controls! A recurring theme throughout this chapter is the importance of data binding if you're working with a sizable or dynamic list of items. However, there are a few more areas of WPF to cover before we get to data binding in depth. The next chapter covers images, text, and other controls.

CHAPTER 11

Images, Text, and Other Controls

IN THIS CHAPTER

- The `Image` Control
- Text and Ink Controls
- Documents
- Range Controls
- Calendar Controls

This chapter looks at a wide range of controls that are neither content controls nor items controls. `Image`, some of the text controls, and controls such as `ProgressBar` and `Slider` should be familiar to you—but with more richness than you might first expect. The `Calendar` and `DatePicker` controls are new to WPF 4. This chapter also covers a number of `FrameworkContentElements` (rather than controls) that enable the creation of *flow documents*, a powerful but lesser-used aspect of WPF.

The `Image` Control

`System.Windows.Controls.Image` enables images (`.BMP`, `.PNG`, `.GIF`, `.JPG`, and so on) to be rendered in a WPF user interface. It has a `Source` property of type `System.Windows.Media.ImageSource`, but thanks to a type converter (`System.Windows.Media.ImageSourceConverter`), you can set the property to a simple string in XAML, as in this example:

```
<Image Source="zoom.gif"/>
```

`ImageSource` can point to images stored at a URL, on the file system, or even embedded in an assembly. (Retrieving and displaying images embedded in assemblies is covered in the next chapter.) `Image` has the same `Stretch` and `StretchDirection` properties seen with `Viewbox` in Chapter 5, “Layout with Panels,” for controlling how it scales.

Although using `Image` is straightforward, some of the advanced options available for image rendering are not. The `RenderOptions.BitmapScalingMode` attached property can be placed on `Image` to optimize rendering for speed versus quality. But its most important setting, `NearestNeighbor`, applies *nearest-neighbor bitmap scaling*, which can help make images look more crisp. This was used on `ToolBar` and `StatusBar` in the preceding chapter and the Photo Gallery application from Chapter 7, "Structuring and Deploying an Application." Here's an example:

```
<Image RenderOptions.BitmapScalingMode="NearestNeighbor" Source="zoom.gif"/>
```

The difference this property makes is subtle when printed in this book, but the improvement in clarity can make a huge difference on the computer screen. Figure 11.1 demonstrates the images from Photo Gallery with and without `NearestNeighbor` applied.

Default rendering

RenderOptions.BitmapScalingMode="NearestNeighbor"

FIGURE 11.1 The `BitmapScalingMode` of `NearestNeighbor` keeps the edges crisp.

TIP

Rather than leveraging the type converter to convert a simple string filename into an `ImageSource`, you can explicitly set `Image`'s `Source` property to any one of several `ImageSource` subclasses to take advantage of advanced functionality. For example, the `BitmapImage` subclass contains a number of properties such as `DecodePixelWidth` and `DecodePixelHeight`, which can be set to values smaller than the natural size of the image to save a potentially-significant amount of memory. The `FormatConvertedBitmap` subclass enables you to change the pixel format of the `Image` to achieve various effects such as making it grayscale. The following XAML leverages `FormatConvertedBitmap` to create the result in Figure 11.2:

```
<StackPanel Orientation="Horizontal">

  <!-- Normal image with the default pixel format of Pbgra32: -->
  <Image Source="photo.jpg" />

  <!-- Grayscale image: -->
  <Image>
  <Image.Source>
    <FormatConvertedBitmap Source="photo.jpg" DestinationFormat="Gray32Float" />
  </Image.Source>
  </Image>

  <!-- Black and white image: -->
  <Image>
  <Image.Source>
    <FormatConvertedBitmap Source="photo.jpg" DestinationFormat="BlackWhite" />
```

Continued

```
    </Image.Source>
  </Image>

</StackPanel>
```

FIGURE 11.2 Displaying an `Image` with three different pixel formats.

The `System.Windows.Media.PixelFormats` enumeration contains a long list of possible formats.

Text and Ink Controls

In addition to `TextBlock` and `Label`, WPF contains a handful of controls for displaying and editing text, whether typed with a keyboard or hand-written with a stylus. This section looks a bit deeper at `TextBlock` and also examines the following controls:

- `TextBox`
- `RichTextBox`
- `PasswordBox`
- `InkCanvas`

But first, it's important to mention an important improvement to WPF 4 that affects all text rendering. From the very beginning, complaints about blurry text have plagued WPF. (I used to claim that I could spot a WPF-based user interface just by looking at the blurriness of its text!) The design of WPF text rendering has been optimized for large text and/or super-high-resolution displays, accurate scaling, and high-fidelity printing. This design has been problematic for the size of fonts used throughout most applications and for the resolutions that most of today's computers support. The polite way to explain this is that WPF text rendering has been ahead of its time.

I'm happy to report that these issues have been fixed with WPF 4. As with many performance improvements in WPF 4, you get some text improvements for free. (For example, WPF will now automatically take advantage of bitmaps embedded in certain East Asian fonts to produce clear text at small sizes.) Other improvements require opting in, to preserve compatibility with existing applications .

The main feature to be aware of is the `TextOptions.TextFormattingMode` attached property. It can be placed on individual text elements or, more likely, on a parent control such as `Window` to affect the text rendering for its entire tree of child elements. By setting `TextFormattingMode` to `Display`, you can opt in to the new WPF 4 text rendering that uses GDI-compatible text metrics. Its key behavior that's important for text clarity is that every glyph is positioned on a pixel boundary (and its width is a whole multiple of pixels).

The default `TextFormattingMode` value—the one that has caused developers and users so much grief—is ironically called `Ideal`. In this case, the text metrics maintain high fidelity with the font definition, even if it means that glyphs don't align nicely with pixel boundaries. In an ideal future world, where screens have a much greater pixel density than they do today, this would indeed give the best results (just like it does for large text today).

The `TextOptions.TextRenderingMode` attached property can be set to `ClearType`, `Grayscale`, `Aliased`, or `Auto` to control WPF's antialiasing behavior. When it is set to `Auto` (the default), `ClearType` is used unless it has been disabled on the current computer, in which case `Grayscale` antialiasing is used.

Figure 11.3 demonstrates the difference between the two `TextFormattingMode` settings and the three non-`Auto` `TextRenderingMode` settings, although it's hard to see the difference on a printed page.

Ideal, ClearType   Display, ClearType
Ideal, Grayscale   Display, Grayscale
Ideal, Aliased   Display, Aliased

FIGURE 11.3 Customizing the rendering of `TextBlocks` with `FontSize=11`.

Furthermore, `TextOptions.TextHintingMode` can be set to `Fixed`, `Animated`, or `Auto` to optimize rendering based on whether the text is stationary or moving.

FAQ

Shouldn't I always set `TextFormattingMode` to `Display` to take advantage of better text rendering?

No. If your text is large enough (a `FontSize` of around 15 or greater), `Ideal` text is just as clear as `Display` text, and its glyphs are arranged better. Even more importantly, if your text is transformed, `Display` text renders more poorly because the pixel alignment no longer applies. `Display` text enlarged by `ScaleTransform` looks the worst of all, because WPF will scale the original text bitmap rather than re-render it at a larger size. (It does this to guarantee that the text is scaled exactly the right amount, which wouldn't happen if pixel alignment happened at the larger size.) For typical small labels, however, `Display` is the clear winner.

TextBlock

TextBlock contains a number of simple properties for modifying its appearance, such as FontFamily, FontSize, FontStyle, FontWeight, and FontStretch. The big secret of TextBlock, however, is that its content property is not its Text property but rather a collection of objects called Inlines. Although the following TextBlock gives the same result as setting the Text property, you're really setting a different property:

```
<!-- TextBlock.Inlines is being set here: -->
<TextBlock>Text in a TextBlock</TextBlock>
```

A type converter makes the value resemble a simple string, but it's really a collection with one element called Run. Therefore, the preceding XAML is equivalent to the following:

```
<TextBlock><Run Text="Text in a TextBlock"/></TextBlock>
```

which is also equivalent to the following XAML because Text is Run's content property:

```
<TextBlock><Run>Text in a TextBlock</Run></TextBlock>
```

A Run is simply a chunk of text with identical formatting. Using a single explicit Run doesn't add value, but things can start to get interesting when you use multiple Runs in the same TextBlock. For example, the preceding TextBlock could be expressed as follows:

```
<TextBlock>
  <Run>Text</Run>
  <Run> in</Run>
  <Run> a</Run>
  <Run> TextBlock</Run>
</TextBlock>
```

This still doesn't change the rendering behavior. Run, however, has several formatting properties that can override the corresponding properties on the parent TextBlock: FontFamily, FontSize, FontStretch, FontStyle, FontWeight, Foreground, and TextDecorations. The following XAML, shown in Figure 11.4, takes advantage of these:

```
<TextBlock>
  <Run FontStyle="Italic" FontFamily="Georgia" Foreground="Red">Rich</Run>
  <Run FontSize="30" FontFamily="Comic Sans MS" Foreground="Blue"> Text </Run>
  <Run FontFamily="Arial Black" Foreground="Orange" FontSize="100">in</Run>
  <Run FontFamily="Courier New" FontWeight="Bold" Foreground="Green"> a </Run>
  <Run FontFamily="Verdana" TextDecorations="Underline">TextBlock</Run>
</TextBlock>
```

Rich Text in a TextBlock

FIGURE 11.4 Several uniquely formatted Runs inside a single TextBlock.

Although this is an extreme example, the same technique can be used for something simple like italicizing or underlining a single word in a paragraph. This is much easier than trying to use multiple TextBlocks and worrying about positioning each one correctly. And by using a single TextBlock, you get one consistent clipping and wrapping behavior across the heterogeneous text. There are many more types of Inline objects besides Run; the "Documents" section later in this chapter examines them.

TIP

When you add content to a TextBlock's Inlines property, the (unformatted) content is appended to its Text property. Therefore, it is still valid to programmatically retrieve the value of the Text property when only Inlines is being explicitly set. For example, the value of Text is the expected "Rich Text in a TextBlock" string for the TextBlock in Figure 11.4.

DIGGING DEEPER

TextBlock and Whitespace

When a TextBlock's content is set via the Text property, any whitespace in the string is preserved. When its content is set via Inlines in XAML, however, whitespace is not preserved. Instead, leading and trailing whitespace is ignored, and any contiguous whitespace is coalesced into a single whitespace character (as in HTML).

DIGGING DEEPER

Explicit Versus Implicit Runs

Although the following TextBlock:

```
<TextBlock>Text in a TextBlock</TextBlock>
```

is equivalent to this:

```
<TextBlock><Run>Text in a TextBlock</Run></TextBlock>
```

the behavior of the type converter is not always straightforward. For example, the following use of another Inline called LineBreak is valid:

```
<TextBlock>Text in<LineBreak/>a TextBlock</TextBlock>
```

whereas the following is not:

```
<TextBlock><Run>Text in<LineBreak/>a TextBlock</Run></TextBlock>
```

The last variation is not valid because Run's content property (Text) is a simple string, and you can't embed a LineBreak element inside a string. The content property of TextBlock (Inlines), however, is converted to one or more Runs via a type converter that specifically handles LineBreak. This type converter makes the following XAML:

```
<TextBlock>Text in<LineBreak/>a TextBlock</TextBlock>
```

equivalent to the following TextBlock containing two Runs, one on each side of the LineBreak:

```
<TextBlock><Run>Text in</Run><LineBreak/><Run>a TextBlock</Run></TextBlock>
```

TextBox

The TextBox control, pictured in Figure 11.5, enables users to type one or more lines of text. Unlike most other controls in WPF, the content of TextBox is not stored as a generic System.Object. Instead, TextBox stores it in a string property called Text.

FIGURE 11.5 A WPF TextBox.

Although it looks like a simple control on the surface, TextBox has built-in support for a variety of features: bindings for Cut, Copy, Paste, Undo, and Redo commands (as discussed in Chapter 6, "Input Events: Keyboard, Mouse, Stylus, and Multi-Touch") and even spell checking!

TextBox contains several methods and properties for grabbing chunks of text (by selection, by line number, and so on) as well as methods for converting between a character index, a line index, and a physical point within the control. It also defines TextChanged and SelectionChanged events.

Unless the size of the TextBox is constrained by its surroundings (or unless it is given an explicit size), it grows as the text inside it grows. But when the TextBox's width is constrained, you can make the text wrap to form additional lines by setting its TextWrapping property to Wrap or WrapWithOverflow. Wrap never allows a line to go beyond the control's bounds, forcing wrapping even if it's in the middle of a word. WrapWithOverflow breaks a line only if there's an opportunity, so long words could get cut off. (TextBlock has the same TextWrapping property.)

FAQ

How can I make TextBox support multiple lines of text?

Setting AcceptsReturn to true allows users to press the Enter key to create a new line of text. Note that TextBox *always* supports multiple lines of text programmatically. If Text is set to a string containing NewLine characters, it displays the multiple lines regardless of the value of AcceptsReturn. Also, the multiline support is completely independent from text wrapping. Text wrapping applies only to individual lines of text that are wider than the TextBox.

DIGGING DEEPER

Spell Checking

To enable spell checking in a TextBox (or RichTextBox), you set the attached SpellCheck.IsEnabled property to true. The result is an experience similar to what you get in Microsoft Word: Misspelled words are underlined in red, and you can right-click to view and apply suggestions. The dictionary that WPF uses matches the one that Microsoft Office uses and is available for multiple languages (along with the corresponding language pack). WPF does not support custom dictionaries, however.

RichTextBox

*Rich*TextBox

FIGURE 11.6 A WPF RichTextBox.

RichTextBox is a more advanced TextBox that can contain formatted text (and arbitrary objects embedded in the text). Figure 11.6 displays a RichTextBox control with simple formatted text.

RichTextBox and TextBox share the same base class (TextBoxBase), so many of the features described with TextBox apply to RichTextBox as well. RichTextBox has more sophisticated versions of various TextBox properties. Whereas TextBox exposes simple integer properties such as CaretIndex, SelectionStart, and SelectionEnd, RichTextBox exposes a CaretPosition property of type TextPointer and a Selection property of type TextSelection. In addition, RichTextBox's content is stored in a Document property of type FlowDocument rather than the simple string Text property. The content can even contain embedded UIElements, and they can be interactive and raise events if RichTextBox's IsDocumentEnabled property is set to true. FlowDocuments are discussed in the upcoming "Documents" section.

PasswordBox

••••••••

FIGURE 11.7 A WPF PasswordBox.

PasswordBox is a simpler TextBox designed for the entry of a password. Rather than display the text typed in, it displays little circles, as shown in Figure 11.7.

PasswordBox does not derive from TextBoxBase like the two previous controls, so it doesn't support Cut, Copy, Undo, and Redo commands (although it does support Paste), and it doesn't support spell checking. This is, of course, quite sensible for a control meant to store passwords!

If you don't like the circle character used to represent each letter of the password, you can choose a new one via the PasswordChar property. (The default character is an asterisk, special-cased to look like a circle.)

PasswordBox's text is stored in a string property called Password. Internally, the password is stored in a System.Security.SecureString object for a little bit of extra protection. The contents of SecureString are encrypted and aggressively cleared, unlike with System.String, whose unencrypted contents can remain in the garbage-collected heap for an indefinite amount of time.

text:TextboxPasswordChanged event. In addition, this event uses the plain RoutedEventHandler delegate, so no information about the old and new passwords is sent with the event. If you must know the current password, you can simply check the Password property within such an event handler.

InkCanvas

The amazing InkCanvas is a versatile element whose primary purpose is to capture handwriting (via a mouse or stylus, but not multi-touch), as pictured in Figure 11.8. InkCanvas is technically not a control, as it derives directly from FrameworkElement, but it acts very much like a control (except for the fact that you can't restyle it with a new template).

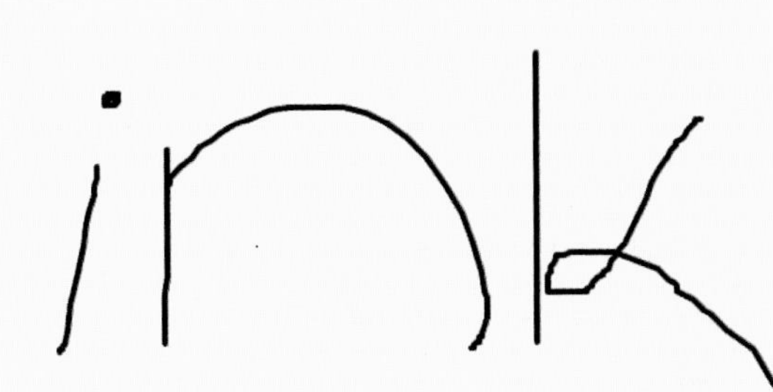

FIGURE 11.8 A WPF InkCanvas.

In its default mode, InkCanvas enables simple writing or drawing on its surface. When you use a stylus, its tip automatically writes, and its back end automatically erases. Each stroke is captured as a System.Windows.Ink.Stroke object and stored in InkCanvas's Strokes collection. But InkCanvas also supports holding any number of arbitrary UIElements in its Children collection (a content property). This makes it easy to annotate just about anything with ink, as shown in Figure 11.9.

FIGURE 11.9 A creative ink annotation on top of an image.

This figure was created by drawing on top of the following Window:

```
<Window xmlns="http://schemas.microsoft.com/winfx/2006/xaml/presentation"
  SizeToContent="WidthAndHeight">
  <Grid>
    <InkCanvas>
      <Image Source="http://adamnathan.net/blog/images/anathan.png"/>
    </InkCanvas>
  </Grid>
</Window>
```

The SizeToContent setting is pretty interesting in this example, because if you draw out of bounds, the Window automatically resizes to fit your ink strokes if you haven't resized it manually!

With InkCanvas's DefaultDrawingAttributes property, you can change the appearance of future strokes (width, color, and so on). Stroke has its own DrawingAttributes property, and appearance can be modified on a stroke-by-stroke basis.

InkCanvas supports several modes, and they can be applied independently to the stylus tip (or mouse) via an EditingMode property and the stylus's back end via an EditingModeInverted property. A read-only ActiveEditingMode property tells you which of the two modes is currently being used. All three of these properties are of type `InkCanvasEditingMode`, which has the following values:

- **`Ink`**—Draws strokes with the mouse or stylus. This is the default for `EditingMode`.
- **`InkAndGesture`**—Like `Ink` but also recognizes gestures made by the user. A list of gestures (such as `Up`, `Down`, `Circle`, `ScratchOut`, or `Tap`) can be found in the `System.Windows.Ink.ApplicationGesture` enumeration.
- **`GestureOnly`**—Only recognizes gestures; does not draw any strokes from user input.
- **`EraseByStroke`**—Erases an entire stroke when it is touched. This is the default for `EditingModeInverted`.
- **`EraseByPoint`**—Erases only the part of a stroke that is directly touched (like a traditional pencil eraser).
- **`Select`**—Selects strokes or any `UIElements` when touched, such that they can be deleted, moved, or resized within the bounds of the `InkCanvas`.
- **`None`**—Does nothing in response to mouse or stylus input.

Using the `Select` mode with normal elements that have nothing to do with ink is pretty interesting, as it automatically gives you a poor-man's runtime design surface for arranging controls. `InkCanvas` also defines 15 events, covering everything from changing the editing mode, to changing, moving, or resizing selections, to collecting or erasing strokes, to performing gestures.

Of course, enabling ink in an application is about more than drawing mustaches on people's faces! Often, you want to apply handwriting recognition to a collection of strokes so you can interpret it as if it were typed text. WPF has built-in gesture recognition but no handwriting recognition engine.

Documents

`TextBlock` and `Label` are made for displaying read-only text, whereas `TextBox` and `RichTextBox` are essential for displaying editable text. But when it comes to text, WPF includes much more functionality than is provided by these simple elements!

WPF contains a rich set of classes for creating, viewing, modifying, packaging, and storing high-quality documents. The focus of this section is what WPF calls *flow documents*. A flow document (represented by the `FlowDocument` element) contains text and other content that can adjust to make optimal use of the space given to the document. For example, on a wide-screen monitor, this could mean automatically adding extra columns.

Creating Flow Documents

`FlowDocument` is a `FrameworkContentElement`, the content-centric parallel to `FrameworkElement`. `FrameworkContentElements`, like `FrameworkElements`, support data binding, animation, and other WPF mechanisms, but they do not participate in WPF's layout mechanism. `FrameworkContentElement`s are ultimately housed in a `FrameworkElement` when displayed on the screen.

Another type of `FrameworkContentElement` is `TextElement`, an abstract class that represents content that can be placed inside a `FlowDocument`. This section examines the various `TextElement`s (from the `System.Windows.Documents` namespace) and demonstrates how to compose them to create rich and flexible documents.

FAQ

How does WPF's flow document support relate to the XML Paper Specification (XPS)?

Unlike the dynamic-layout documents described in this section, XPS documents have a fixed layout and always look the same, whether on screen or on paper. The .NET Framework includes APIs for creating and viewing XPS documents (in the `System.Windows.Xps` and `System.Windows.Documents` namespaces), or you can use tools such as Microsoft Word to create and view them. In WPF applications, XPS documents are typically represented as instances of `FixedDocument` and viewed in a `DocumentViewer` control.

You can think of XPS documents much like Adobe PDF documents; they both have standalone viewers (available on multiple platforms) and can be viewed in a web browser (with the right plug-in installed). One area where XPS is unique is that it's also a native Windows spool file format (starting with Windows Vista). This ensures that XPS documents can be printed without loss of quality or fidelity and without any extra work done by the application initiating the printing.

The specifications for XPS and the Open Packaging Conventions used by XPS (whose APIs are in the `System.IO.Packaging` namespace) can be found at http://microsoft.com/xps.

A Simple `FlowDocument`

The following XAML shows a straightforward `FlowDocument` that is simply a collection of `Paragraph`s (a type of `TextElement`) representing a draft of Chapter 1 from this book:

```
<FlowDocument xmlns="http://schemas.microsoft.com/winfx/2006/xaml/presentation">
  <Paragraph FontSize="22" FontWeight="Bold">Chapter 1</Paragraph>
  <Paragraph FontSize="35" FontWeight="Bold">Why WPF?</Paragraph>
  <Paragraph>
    In movies and on TV, the …
  </Paragraph>
  <Paragraph>…</Paragraph>
  <Paragraph>…</Paragraph>
  …
</FlowDocument>
```

Figure 11.10 shows the rendered result of this XAML. You can use a `FlowDocument` such as this as the root of a XAML file, and it is automatically displayed in an appropriate viewer.

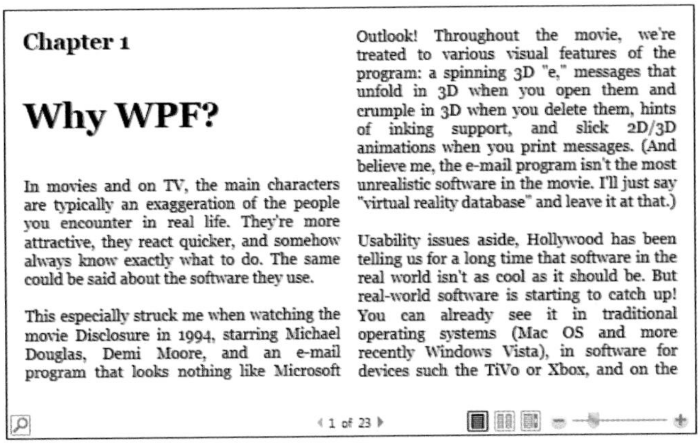

Chapter 1

Why WPF?

In movies and on TV, the main characters are typically an exaggeration of the people you encounter in real life. They're more attractive, they react quicker, and somehow always know exactly what to do. The same could be said about the software they use.

This especially struck me when watching the movie Disclosure in 1994, starring Michael Douglas, Demi Moore, and an e-mail program that looks nothing like Microsoft Outlook! Throughout the movie, we're treated to various visual features of the program: a spinning 3D "e," messages that unfold in 3D when you open them and crumple in 3D when you delete them, hints of inking support, and slick 2D/3D animations when you print messages. (And believe me, the e-mail program isn't the most unrealistic software in the movie. I'll just say "virtual reality database" and leave it at that.)

Usability issues aside, Hollywood has been telling us for a long time that software in the real world isn't as cool as it should be. But real-world software is starting to catch up! You can already see it in traditional operating systems (Mac OS and more recently Windows Vista), in software for devices such the TiVo or Xbox, and on the

1 of 23

FIGURE 11.10 A simple `FlowDocument`.

Two main types of `TextElements` exist—`Blocks` and `Inlines`. (Both of these are abstract classes derived from `TextElement`.) A `Block` is a rectangular region that can't be separated (except when it spans multiple pages), whereas an `Inline` is a region that flows more freely with text, potentially occupying a nonrectangular space (flowing from the end of one line to the beginning of the next). `FlowDocument` supports only `Blocks`, such as `Paragraph`, as its children. (Its content property is called `Blocks`, which is a `BlocksCollection`.) We'll look at the role of `Inlines` after examining `Blocks` more closely.

`Block`

WPF has five different types of `Blocks`:

- **`Paragraph`**—Has a collection of `Inlines`, which typically contain the "meat" of the document. In XAML, you often see `Paragraph`'s content set to simple text, but internally an `Inline` called `Run` is created with that content and added to the `Paragraph`'s `Inlines` collection, just like with `TextBlock`.
- **`Section`**—Groups one or more `Blocks` together without imposing any additional structure. This is handy if you want to set the same property values for multiple `Blocks`, such as a `Background` and `Foreground`.
- **`List`**—Presents a collection of `ListItems` as a bulleted, numbered, or plain list. Each `ListItem` can contain a collection of `Blocks`, so creating a typical text-based `List` involves placing a `Paragraph` inside each `ListItem`. `List`'s `MarkerStyle` property (of type `TextMarkerStyle`) provides plenty of formatting options for bullets—`Box`, `Circle`, `Disc` (the default bullet), and `Square`—and for numbers—`Decimal`, `LowerLatin`, `UpperLatin`, `LowerRoman`, and `UpperRoman`. A plain list can be achieved by setting `MarkerStyle` to `None`.
- **`Table`**—Organizes content into rows and columns, sort of like `Grid` but closer to an HTML `TABLE`. `Table`, unlike `Grid`, can contain only `Blocks` (and elements defining the `Table`'s structure).

- **BlockUIContainer**—Hosts a single `UIElement`. Therefore, `BlockUIContainer` is the key to embedding a wide range of WPF content into a `FlowDocument`, whether it's an `Image`, a `MediaElement`-hosted video, a `Button`, 3D content in a `Viewport3D`, and so on.

Listing 11.1 demonstrates the use of all five types of `Blocks` inside a `FlowDocument`. The resulting document is displayed in Figure 11.11.

LISTING 11.1 The `FlowDocument` in Figure 11.11

```
<FlowDocument xmlns="http://schemas.microsoft.com/winfx/2006/xaml/presentation"
              xmlns:x="http://schemas.microsoft.com/winfx/2006/xaml">
  <Section LineHeight="2" Foreground="White" Background="Black">
    <Paragraph FontSize="18">WPF 4 Unleashed</Paragraph>
    <Paragraph FontSize="30" FontWeight="Bold">Notes from Chapter 1</Paragraph>
  </Section>
  <Paragraph>Here are some highlights of WPF:</Paragraph>
  <List>
    <ListItem>
      <Paragraph>Broad integration</Paragraph>
    </ListItem>
    <ListItem>
      <Paragraph>Resolution independence</Paragraph>
    </ListItem>
    <ListItem>
      <Paragraph>Hardware acceleration</Paragraph>
    </ListItem>
    <ListItem>
      <Paragraph>Declarative programming</Paragraph>
    </ListItem>
    <ListItem>
      <Paragraph>Rich composition and customization</Paragraph>
    </ListItem>
  </List>
  <BlockUIContainer>
    <Viewbox>
      <StackPanel Orientation="Horizontal">
        <Image Source="diagram.jpg" Margin="5"/>
        <TextBlock VerticalAlignment="Center" Width="100" TextWrapping="Wrap">
          The technologies in the .NET Framework.
        </TextBlock>
      </StackPanel>
    </Viewbox>
  </BlockUIContainer>
  <Paragraph>
```

LISTING 11.1 Continued

```
    Here's another version of the diagram, as a Table:
  </Paragraph>
  <Table CellSpacing="5" Padding="15" FontFamily="Segoe UI">
  <Table.Background>
    <LinearGradientBrush>
      <GradientStop Color="Yellow" Offset="0"/>
      <GradientStop Color="Orange" Offset="1"/>
    </LinearGradientBrush>
  </Table.Background>

  <!-- Define four columns: -->
  <Table.Columns>
    <TableColumn/>
    <TableColumn/>
    <TableColumn/>
    <TableColumn/>
  </Table.Columns>

  <!-- Create three rows: -->
    <TableRowGroup>
      <TableRow>
        <TableCell ColumnSpan="4" TextAlignment="Center">
          <Paragraph FontWeight="Bold">.NET Framework</Paragraph>
        </TableCell>
      </TableRow>

      <TableRow>
        <TableCell BorderBrush="Black" BorderThickness="2" Background="LightGray"
          TextAlignment="Center" LineHeight="70">
          <Paragraph FontWeight="Bold">WPF</Paragraph>
        </TableCell>
        <TableCell BorderBrush="Black" BorderThickness="2" Background="LightGray"
          TextAlignment="Center">
          <Paragraph FontWeight="Bold">WCF</Paragraph>
        </TableCell>
        <TableCell BorderBrush="Black" BorderThickness="2" Background="LightGray"
          TextAlignment="Center">
          <Paragraph FontWeight="Bold">WF</Paragraph>
        </TableCell>
        <TableCell BorderBrush="Black" BorderThickness="2" Background="LightGray"
          TextAlignment="Center">
          <Paragraph FontWeight="Bold">WCS</Paragraph>
        </TableCell>
      </TableRow>
```

LISTING 11.1 Continued

```
        <TableRow>
          <TableCell BorderBrush="Black" BorderThickness="2" Background="LightGray"
            TextAlignment="Center">
            <Paragraph FontWeight="Bold">ADO.NET</Paragraph>
          </TableCell>
          <TableCell BorderBrush="Black" BorderThickness="2" Background="LightGray"
            TextAlignment="Center">
            <Paragraph FontWeight="Bold">ASP.NET</Paragraph>
          </TableCell>
          <TableCell BorderBrush="Black" BorderThickness="2" Background="LightGray"
            TextAlignment="Center">
            <Paragraph FontWeight="Bold">Windows Forms</Paragraph>
          </TableCell>
          <TableCell BorderBrush="Black" BorderThickness="2" Background="LightGray"
            TextAlignment="Center">
            <Paragraph FontWeight="Bold">...</Paragraph>
          </TableCell>
        </TableRow>
      </TableRowGroup>
    </Table>
</FlowDocument>
```

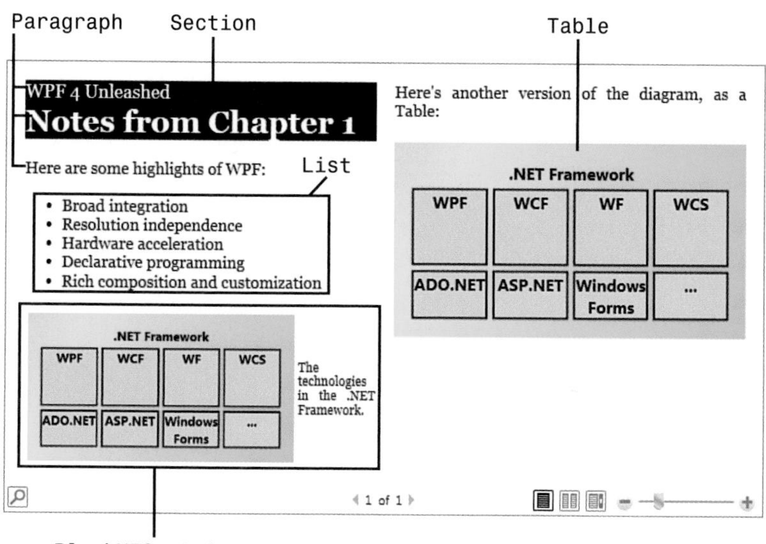

FIGURE 11.11 A `FlowDocument` that uses all five types of `Blocks`.

Paragraphs are used throughout the document, but Section is used at the beginning to give two Paragraphs different Foreground, Background, and LineHeight. List is then used with its default settings for a straightforward bulleted list. BlockUIContainer is used to contain not only an Image, but a corresponding caption in the form of a TextBlock. They are arranged in a StackPanel and then placed inside a Viewbox so both items scale nicely as the width of the document changes.

Finally, for demonstration purposes, the content of the Image is mimicked with a Table. Notice that the APIs exposed by Table (and, therefore, the structure of elements inside Table in XAML) differ considerably from those of Grid. Columns are defined by placing TableColumn elements inside Table's Columns collection (similar to Grid's ColumnDefinitions collection), but the rows are defined directly with the content they contain. Table contains a TableRowGroup with a bunch of TableRows placed in the order in which they appear, from top to bottom. Each TableCell inside a TableRow fills the next available column sequentially, unless ColumnSpan is set to give different behavior. TableCell is the only element that can contain the Blocks that form the content of the Table, which, in this case, are all Paragraphs.

Table can even contain multiple TableRowGroups! The content of each one is placed directly below the previous one.

Figure 11.11 shows that the Table ends up looking pretty similar to the Image embedded in the document. Of course, the two have very different behaviors. The text in the Table is selectable and scales perfectly as you zoom in to the document. But whereas the Image is never split between pages, the Table can be. The inner text content can also wrap when space is tight. Figure 11.12 shows this splitting and wrapping.

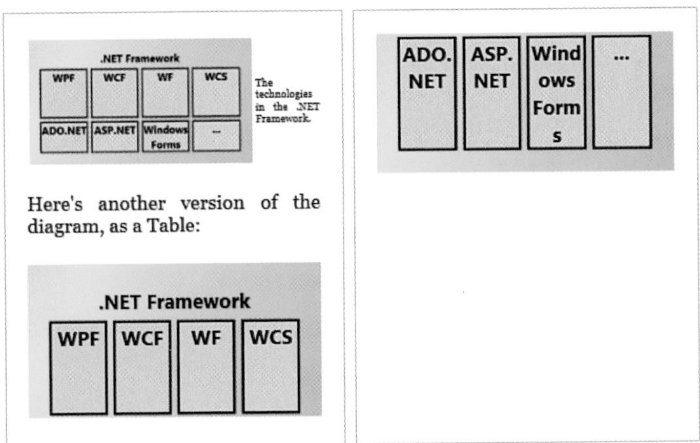

FIGURE 11.12 A different view of the FlowDocument from Figure 11.11, with the Table split between pages 2 and 3.

Inline

Inlines are elements that can be placed inside a Paragraph to make its content more interesting than plain text. As mentioned in the previous section, Paragraphs don't really contain a simple string, but rather a collection of `Inlines`. And when a `Paragraph` defined in XAML appears to contain plain text, it really contains a single `Inline` known as `Run`. `Run` has a simple `Text` string property and a constructor that accepts a string.

Therefore, the following `Paragraph` defined in XAML:

```
<Paragraph>Here are some highlights of WPF:</Paragraph>
```

is equivalent to the following C# code:

```
Paragraph p = new Paragraph(new Run("Here are some highlights of WPF:"));
```

Other `Inlines` for enhancing a paragraph fall into three categories: spans, anchored blocks, and everything else.

Spans The most common spans are `Bold`, `Italic`, `Underline`, and the familiar `Hyperlink` from Chapter 7. They all fittingly derive from `Span`, which can also be used directly in a `Paragraph` for applying additional effects to text. Although `Paragraphs` already support making their text bold, italic, and so on through the setting of properties such as `FontWeight` and `FontStyle`, these spans make it possible to apply these effects to smaller regions within the `Paragraph`.

bold *italic* underline hyperlink superscript subscript ~~strikethrough~~

FIGURE 11.13 Applying different spans to text in a paragraph.

The following `Paragraph`, which is rendered in Figure 11.13, demonstrates all these spans:

```
<Paragraph>
  <Bold>bold</Bold>
  <Italic>italic</Italic>
  <Underline>underline</Underline>
  <Hyperlink>hyperlink</Hyperlink>
  <Span BaselineAlignment="Superscript">superscript</Span>
  <Span BaselineAlignment="Subscript">subscript</Span>
  <Span>
  <Span.TextDecorations>
    <TextDecoration Location="Strikethrough"/>
  </Span.TextDecorations>
    strikethrough
  </Span>
</Paragraph>
```

The `BaselineAlignment` and `TextDecorations` properties used on `Span` are common to all `Inlines`, so they can easily be combined with `Bold`, `Italic`, or other effects. In addition, as with `Paragraph`, the content of any span is actually a collection of `Inlines` rather

TIP

Because `TextBlock` stores its contents as a collection of `Inlines`, you could replace the `Paragraph` tags in the previous XAML snippets with `TextBlock` tags, and they would still work. `Label`, on the other hand, does not directly support such content.

than a simple string. In the previous XAML, this means that there's an implicit Run inside every child of Paragraph. This also means that you can easily embed spans within spans, as in the following Paragraph, rendered in Figure 11.14:

abc*d**e**f*ghi

FIGURE 11.14
Nesting a Hyperlink inside Underline inside Italic inside Bold.

```
<Paragraph>
a<Bold>b<Italic>c<Underline>d<Hyperlink>e</Hyperlink>f</Underline>g</Italic>h
</Bold>i
</Paragraph>
```

Anchored Blocks WPF contains two Inlines that are a bit unusual because they are designed to contain Blocks. They are Figure and Floater, and both derive from the abstract AnchoredBlock class.

Figure is like a mini-FlowDocument that can be embedded in the outer FlowDocument. The inner content is isolated from the outer content, which flows around the Figure. For example, the FlowDocument representing Chapter 1 might want to have its paragraphs flow around images (just like the figures in this book). This could be done as follows:

```
<FlowDocument xmlns="http://schemas.microsoft.com/winfx/2006/xaml/presentation">
  <Paragraph FontSize="22" FontWeight="Bold">Chapter 1</Paragraph>
  <Paragraph FontSize="35" FontWeight="Bold">Why WPF?</Paragraph>
  <Paragraph>
    <Figure Width="130">
      <BlockUIContainer>
        <Image Source="wpf.png"/>
      </BlockUIContainer>
    </Figure>
    In movies and on TV, the …
  </Paragraph>
  <Paragraph>…</Paragraph>
  <Paragraph>…</Paragraph>
  …
</FlowDocument>
```

Because a Figure contains Blocks, you can place a Table, Paragraphs, and so on inside it. But using BlockUIContainer to hold an Image is all we need in this case. The result is shown in Figure 11.15.

You can adjust the placement of a Figure with the HorizontalAnchor and VerticalAnchor properties (of type FigureHorizontalAnchor and FigureVerticalAnchor, respectively). The default value for HorizontalAnchor is ColumnRight, and the default value for `VerticalAnchor` is `ParagraphTop`. Both properties provide many options for placement based on the current column or `Paragraph`, or even relative to the bounds of the entire page. Figure 11.16 demonstrates some alternative placements for the `Figure` in Figure 11.15 by explicitly setting `HorizontalAnchor` and/or `VerticalAnchor`.

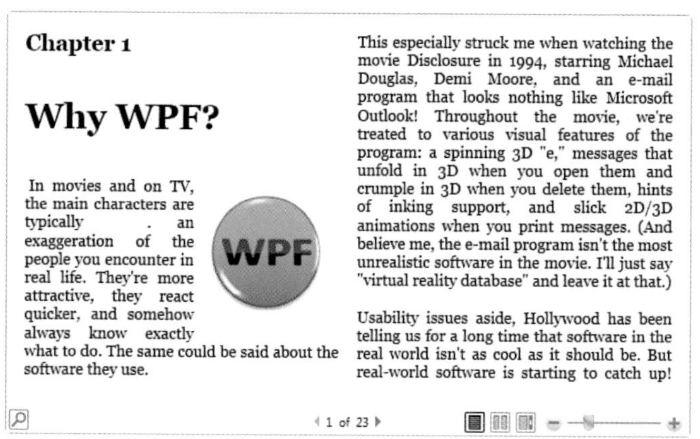

FIGURE 11.15 A `Figure` containing an `Image` inside the third `Paragraph` of the `FlowDocument`.

`Floater` is a simplified form of `Figure`. It can contain arbitrary `Blocks`, but it does not support positioning relative to the page bounds or even spanning columns. Rather than having `HorizontalAnchor` and `VerticalAnchor` properties, it has a simple `HorizontalAlignment` property (of type `HorizontalAlignment`) that can be set to `Left`, `Center`, `Right`, or `Stretch`. If you don't require the full functionality of `Figure`, you might as well use the lighter-weight `Floater` instead.

Other `Inlines` The two remaining `Inlines` don't have anything in common other than the fact that they don't derive from `Span` or `AnchoredBlock`. One of them is `LineBreak`, which functions as a newline. If you simply place an empty `LineBreak` element between any two characters in a paragraph, the second character will start on the following line.

> **TIP**
>
> To place a *page* break rather than a *line* break in a `FlowDocument`, set the `BreakPageBefore` property to `true` on the first `Paragraph` you want after the break. `BreakPageBefore` is defined on `Block`, so this also applies to `Section`, `List`, `BlockUIContainer`, and `Table`.

Chapter 1

Why WPF?

In movies and on TV, the main characters are typically an exaggeration of the people you encounter in real life. They're more attractive, they react quicker, and somehow always know exactly what to do. The same could be said about the software they use.

This especially struck me when watching the movie Disclosure in 1994, starring Michael Douglas, Demi Moore, and an e-mail program that looks nothing like Microsoft Outlook! Throughout the movie, we're treated to various visual features of the program: a spinning 3D "e," messages that unfold in 3D when you open them and crumple in 3D when you delete them, hints of inking support, and slick 2D/3D animations when you print messages. (And believe me, the e-mail program isn't the most unrealistic software in the movie. I'll just say "virtual reality database" and leave it at that.)

Usability issues aside, Hollywood has been telling us for a long time that software in the real world isn't as cool as it should be. But real-world software is starting to catch up!

`HorizontalAnchor="ColumnLeft"`

Chapter 1

Why WPF?

In movies and on TV, the main characters are typically an exaggeration of the people you encounter in real life. They're more attractive, they react quicker, and somehow always know exactly what to do. The same could be said about the software they use.

This especially struck me when watching the movie Disclosure in 1994, starring Michael Douglas, Demi Moore, and an e-mail program that looks nothing like Microsoft Outlook! Throughout the movie, we're treated to various visual features of the program: a spinning 3D "e," messages that unfold in 3D when you open them and crumple in 3D when you delete them, hints of inking support, and slick 2D/3D animations when you print messages. (And believe me, the e-mail program isn't the most unrealistic software in the movie. I'll just say "virtual reality database" and leave it at that.)

Usability issues aside, Hollywood has been telling us for a long time that software in the real world isn't as cool as it should be. But real-world software is

`HorizontalAnchor="PageCenter"`

Chapter 1

Why WPF?

In movies and on TV, the main characters are typically an exaggeration of the people you encounter in real life. They're more attractive, they react quicker, and somehow always know exactly what to do. The same could be said about the software they use.

This especially struck me when watching the movie Disclosure in 1994, starring Michael Douglas, Demi Moore, and an e-mail program that looks nothing like Microsoft Outlook! Throughout the movie, we're treated to various visual features of the program: a spinning 3D "e," messages that unfold in 3D when you open them and crumple in 3D when you delete them, hints of inking support, and slick 2D/3D animations when you print messages. (And believe me, the e-mail program isn't the most unrealistic software in the movie. I'll just say "virtual reality database" and leave it at that.)

Usability issues aside, Hollywood has been telling us for a long time that software in the real world isn't as cool as it should be. But real-world software is starting to catch up! You can already see it in traditional

1 of 23

`HorizontalAnchor="PageRight"` and `VerticalAnchor="PageTop"`

FIGURE 11.16 Controlling the placement of a `Figure` with `HorizontalAnchor` and `VerticalAnchor`.

The last Inline is InlineUIContainer, which is just like BlockUIContainer except with the ability to be inserted into a Paragraph and flow with the rest of the text. As with BlockUIContainer, it can contain a MediaElement-hosted video, a Button, 3D content in a Viewport3D, and so on, but it's often handy simply to include a little inline Image. The following Paragraph, rendered in Figure 11.17, demonstrates this with an inline RSS icon next to a Hyperlink to an RSS feed:

You can read more about this on my blog (subscribe), which I try to update once a month.

FIGURE 11.17 A Paragraph with an inline Image, thanks to InlineUIContainer.

```
<Paragraph>
  You can read more about this on my blog (
  <Hyperlink NavigateUri="http://blogs.msdn.com/adam_nathan/rss.xml">
    subscribe
  </Hyperlink>
  <InlineUIContainer>
    <Image Width="14" Source="rss.gif"/>
  </InlineUIContainer>
  ), which I try to update once a month.
</Paragraph>
```

Displaying Flow Documents

As mentioned earlier, a FlowDocument can be viewed (and edited) inside a RichTextBox. Although you can prevent user edits by setting RichTextBox's IsReadOnly property to true, RichTextBox is not meant to be the typical control that applications use for document reading.

Instead, WPF provides *three* additional controls for displaying flow documents. They can be hard to keep straight at first, but the differences are straightforward:

- **FlowDocumentScrollViewer**—Displays a document as one continuous file with a scrollbar, similar to the Web Layout mode in Microsoft Word (and similar to a read-only RichTextBox inside a ScrollViewer).
- **FlowDocumentPageViewer**—Displays a document as discrete pages, similar to the Full Screen Reading mode in Microsoft Word.
- **FlowDocumentReader**—Combines FlowDocumentScrollViewer and FlowDocumentPageViewer into a single control and exposes additional functionality such as built-in text search. (This is the control you get by default if you use FlowDocument as the root element in your XAML file.)

Figure 11.18 shows the differences between these controls by displaying the FlowDocument containing the Chapter 1 draft. FlowDocumentReader is a rich control (somewhat like the common viewers for XPS or PDF files), but if you don't require switching between scrolling and pagination, you might as well use one of the more lightweight viewers. Both FlowDocumentPageViewer and FlowDocumentReader (in pagination mode) automatically add/remove columns as you zoom out/in to maximize the use of available space.

Chapter 1

Why WPF?

In movies and on TV, the main characters are typically an exaggeration of the people you encounter in real life. They're more attractive, they react quicker, and somehow always know exactly what to do. The same could be said about the software they use.

This especially struck me when watching the movie Disclosure in 1994, starring Michael Douglas, Demi Moore, and an e-mail program that looks nothing like Microsoft Outlook! Throughout the movie, we're treated to various visual features of the program: a spinning 3D "e," messages that unfold in 3D when you open them and crumple in 3D when you delete them, hints of inking support, and slick 2D/3D animations when you print messages. (And believe me, the e-mail program isn't the most unrealistic software in the movie. I'll just say "virtual reality database" and leave it at that.)

Usability issues aside, Hollywood has been telling us for a long time that software in the real world isn't as cool as it should be. But real-world software is starting to catch up! You

`FlowDocumentScrollViewer`

Chapter 1

Why WPF?

In movies and on TV, the main characters are typically an exaggeration of the people you encounter in real life. They're more attractive, they react quicker, and somehow always know exactly what to do. The same could be said about the software they use.

This especially struck me when watching the movie Disclosure in 1994, starring Michael Douglas, Demi Moore, and an e-mail program that looks nothing like Microsoft Outlook! Throughout the movie, we're treated to various visual features of the program: a spinning 3D "e," messages that unfold in 3D when you open them and crumple in 3D when you delete them, hints of inking support, and slick 2D/3D animations when you print messages. (And believe me, the e-mail program isn't the most unrealistic software in the movie. I'll just say "virtual reality database" and leave it at that.)

Usability issues aside, Hollywood has been telling us for a long time that software in the real world isn't as cool as it should be. But real-world software is starting to catch up! You can already see it in traditional operating systems (Mac OS and more recently Windows Vista), in software for devices such the TiVo or Xbox, and on the

`FlowDocumentPageViewer`

Chapter 1

Why WPF?

In movies and on TV, the main characters are typically an exaggeration of the people you encounter in real life. They're more attractive, they react quicker, and somehow always know exactly what to do. The same could be said about the software they use.

This especially struck me when watching the movie Disclosure in 1994, starring Michael Douglas, Demi Moore, and an e-mail program that looks nothing like Microsoft Outlook! Throughout the movie, we're treated to various visual features of the program: a spinning 3D "e," messages that unfold in 3D when you open them and crumple in 3D when you delete them, hints of inking support, and slick 2D/3D animations when you print messages. (And believe me, the e-mail program isn't the most unrealistic software in the movie. I'll just say "virtual reality database" and leave it at that.)

Usability issues aside, Hollywood has been telling us for a long time that software in the real world isn't as cool as it should be. But real-world software is starting to catch up! You can already see it in traditional operating systems (Mac OS and more recently Windows Vista), in software for devices such the TiVo or Xbox, and on the

`FlowDocumentReader`

FIGURE 11.18 Chapter 1 displayed in each of the `FlowDocument` containers.

Notice that FlowDocumentScrollViewer doesn't show the zoom functionality that appears in the other two, but you can enable this by setting its IsToolBarVisible property to true.

Adding Annotations

The three viewers for FlowDocument (plus DocumentViewer, the viewer for FixedDocument) support annotations, which enable users to highlight content or attach notes in the form of text or ink. The strange thing about this support is that you have to define your own user interface for enabling it; there are no default controls to reveal.

Although crafting your own custom user interface for annotations is tedious, it's not very difficult. That's because an AnnotationService class in the System.Windows.Annotations namespace exposes a command for each of the important annotation-controlling features:

- CreateTextStickyNoteCommand attaches a new text-based StickyNoteControl as an annotation on the selected text.
- CreateInkStickyNoteCommand attaches a new ink-based StickyNoteControl as an annotation on the selected text.
- DeleteStickyNotesCommand deletes the currently selected StickyNoteControl(s).
- CreateHighlightCommand highlights the selected text in the color passed as the command's parameter.
- ClearHighlightsCommand removes any highlighting from the currently selected text.

Listing 11.2 defines a Window that adds a few simple Buttons on top of a FlowDocumentReader. Each of these Buttons is assigned to one of the previously described commands.

LISTING 11.2 Window1.xam—The User Interface for an Annotation-Enabled FlowDocumentReader

```
<Window
  xmlns="http://schemas.microsoft.com/winfx/2006/xaml/presentation"
  xmlns:x="http://schemas.microsoft.com/winfx/2006/xaml"
  xmlns:a=
    "clr-namespace:System.Windows.Annotations;assembly=PresentationFramework"
  Title="FlowDocumentReader + Annotations"
  x:Class="Window1" Initialized="OnInitialized" Closed="OnClosed">
  <StackPanel>
    <StackPanel Orientation="Horizontal">
      <Label>Control Annotations:</Label>
      <Button Command="a:AnnotationService.CreateTextStickyNoteCommand"
              CommandTarget="{Binding ElementName=reader}">
        Create Text Note
      </Button>
```

LISTING 11.2 Continued

```
      <Button Command="a:AnnotationService.CreateInkStickyNoteCommand"
              CommandTarget="{Binding ElementName=reader}">
        Create Ink Note
      </Button>
      <Button Command="a:AnnotationService.DeleteStickyNotesCommand"
              CommandTarget="{Binding ElementName=reader}">
        Remove Note
      </Button>
      <Button Command="a:AnnotationService.CreateHighlightCommand"
              CommandParameter="{x:Static Brushes.Yellow}"
              CommandTarget="{Binding ElementName=reader}">
        Create Yellow Highlight
      </Button>
      <Button Command="a:AnnotationService.ClearHighlightsCommand"
              CommandTarget="{Binding ElementName=reader}">
        Remove Highlight
      </Button>
    </StackPanel>

    <FlowDocumentReader x:Name="reader">
      <FlowDocument>
        …
      </FlowDocument>
    </FlowDocumentReader>
  </StackPanel>
</Window>
```

The `System.Windows.Annotations` namespace is given an XML namespace prefix of a, used to refer to each of the commands on `AnnotationService`. Although `AnnotationService` is part of `PresentationFramework`, this namespace happens to not be included in WPF's standard XML namespace. For the commands to work, each of these `Buttons` uses the `FlowDocumentReader` element as the command target. The `Buttons` become enabled and disabled automatically, based on the context in which each command is valid.

The only thing missing is the definition of the `OnInitialized` and `OnClosed` methods referenced in the XAML file. Listing 11.3 contains the code-behind file for Listing 11.2.

LISTING 11.3 `Window1.xaml.cs`—The Logic for an Annotation-Enabled `FlowDocumentReader`

```
using System;
using System.IO;
using System.Windows;
using System.Windows.Annotations;
```

LISTING 11.3 Continued

```
using System.Windows.Annotations.Storage;

public partial class Window1 : Window
{
  FileStream stream;

  public Window1()
  {
    InitializeComponent();
  }

  protected void OnInitialized(object sender, EventArgs e)
  {
    // Enable and load annotations
    AnnotationService service = AnnotationService.GetService(reader);
    if (service == null)
    {
      stream = new FileStream("storage.xml", FileMode.OpenOrCreate);
      service = new AnnotationService(reader);
      AnnotationStore store = new XmlStreamStore(stream);
      store.AutoFlush = true;
      service.Enable(store);
    }
  }

  protected void OnClosed(object sender, EventArgs e)
  {
    // Disable and save annotations
    AnnotationService service = AnnotationService.GetService(reader);
    if (service != null && service.IsEnabled)
    {
      service.Disable();
      stream.Close();
    }
  }
}
```

The main purpose of the `OnInitialized` and `OnClosed` methods is to enable and disable the `AnnotationService` associated with the `FlowDocumentReader`. However, when enabling the service, you must also specify a `Stream` that persists the annotations. Listing 11.3 uses a standalone XML file in the current directory. When the application is closed, any annotations are saved and reappear the next time the application is run (as long as the `storage.xml` file remains untouched).

Figure 11.19 shows an instance of this annotation-enabled `Window` in action.

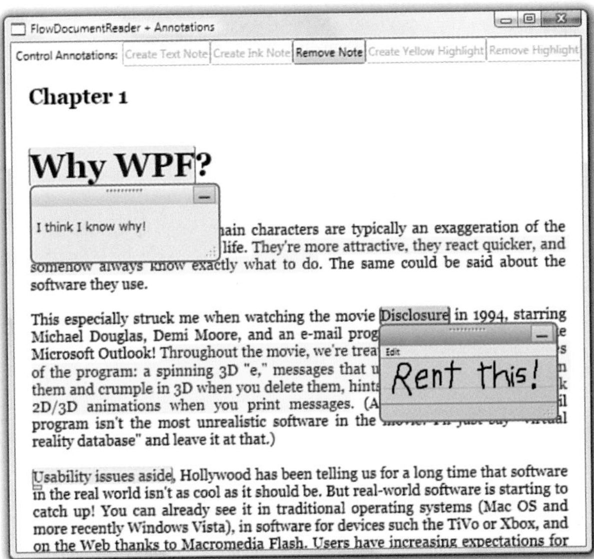

FIGURE 11.19 Annotations on a `FlowDocument`, enabled by the custom `Buttons` at the top of the `Window`.

TIP

The `StickyNoteControls` used by annotations are full-blown WPF controls (in the `System.Windows.Controls` namespace). Therefore, you can restyle them with a completely different control template if you want to customize their look.

Range Controls

Range controls do not render arbitrary content like content controls or items controls. A range control simply stores and displays a numeric value that falls within a specified range.

The core functionality of range controls comes from an abstract class called `RangeBase`. This class defines properties of type `double` that store the current value and the endpoints of the range: `Value`, `Minimum`, and `Maximum`. It also defines a simple `ValueChanged` event.

This section examines the two major built-in range controls—`ProgressBar` and `Slider`. WPF also has a primitive `ScrollBar` control that derives from `RangeBase`, but you're unlikely to want to use it directly. Instead, you would use a `ScrollViewer` object, as described in Chapter 5.

ProgressBar

In an ideal world, you would never need to use a ProgressBar in your software. But when faced with long-running operations, showing users a ProgressBar helps them realize that progress is indeed being made. Therefore, using a ProgressBar in the right places can dramatically improve usability. (Of course, it doesn't improve usability as much as making the slow operation fast enough in the first place!) Figure 11.20 displays the default look for WPF's ProgressBar control.

FIGURE 11.20 The WPF ProgressBar.

ProgressBar has a default Minimum of 0 and a default Maximum of 100. It adds only two public properties to what RangeBase already provides:

- **IsIndeterminate**—When this is set to true, ProgressBar shows a generic animation (so the values of Minimum, Maximum, and Value don't matter). This is a great feature when you have no clue how long something will take or are too lazy to do the work required to show true progress!
- **Orientation**—This is set to Horizontal by default but can be set to Vertical to make progress go from bottom to top rather than left to right. I haven't seen applications use "thermometer-style" vertical progress bars other than the old-fashioned full-screen installation applications, but this property nevertheless makes it easy to achieve such an effect!

> **FAQ**
>
> **How can I give ProgressBar paused or stopped/error states?**
>
> Starting with Windows Vista, the Win32 progress bar can show a paused (yellow) state and a stopped/error (red) state. Unfortunately, the WPF ProgressBar does not have built-in support for this. If you want to achieve a similar effect, you need to create new templates for these states and apply them to the control programmatically, using techniques described in Chapter 14, "Styles, Templates, Skins, and Themes."

Slider

Slider is a bit more complicated than ProgressBar because it enables users to change the current value by moving its *thumb* through any number of optional *ticks*. Slider is shown in Figure 11.21.

FIGURE 11.21 The WPF Slider.

Slider also has a default Minimum of 0, but it has a default Maximum of 10. It also defines an Orientation property (and is Horizontal by default), but it contains several properties for adjusting the placement and frequency of ticks, the placement and precision of ToolTips that can show the current value as the thumb is moved, and whether the thumb snaps to tick values or moves smoothly to any arbitrary value. For keyboard navigation purposes, Slider also contains Delay and Interval properties that work just like RepeatButton's properties of the same names.

Ticks are enabled by setting `TickPlacement` to `TopLeft`, `BottomRight`, or `Both`. The values for `TickPlacement` have odd names, but they cover both orientations of `Slider`. When `TickPlacement` is set to `BottomRight`, the ticks are on the bottom when the `Slider` is horizontal and on the right when the `Slider` is vertical. Similarly, when `TickPlacement` is set to `TopLeft`, the ticks are on the top when the `Slider` is horizontal and on the left when the `Slider` is vertical. When `TickPlacement` is set to `None` (the default value), the thumb is given a simpler look, as shown in Figure 11.22.

FIGURE 11.22 A `Slider` without any ticks.

One interesting feature of `Slider` is its support for displaying a smaller range within the current range, as shown in Figure 11.23. If `IsSelectionRangeEnabled` is set to `true`, `SelectionStart` and `SelectionEnd` can be set to the desired values of this "subrange." There's nothing built in to the control that enables a user to set the subrange via keyboard or mouse, nor does it enforce that the thumb stays within the subrange. With this feature, you could make the `Slider` act like the one in Windows Media Player, where a background bar indicates how much of the current media has been downloaded.

FIGURE 11.23 `Slider` supports a selection range that can be a subset of the main range.

Calendar Controls

WPF 4 introduces two new calendar controls that provide rich visualizations for selecting and displaying dates: `Calendar` and `DatePicker`. These have been sorely missing in prior versions of WPF, so they are a welcome addition to the built-in set of controls.

Calendar

The `Calendar` control, displayed in Figure 11.24, displays a calendar that looks much like the main one in Windows. It supports three different modes with its `DisplayMode` property. The user can initiate upward transitions from `Month` to `Year` to `Decade` by continuing to click the text in the header, and downward transitions by clicking any of the calendar cells. Unlike the Windows calendar, the WPF `Calendar` control doesn't support a century mode, and its built-in style unfortunately doesn't perform the slick animation when transitioning between modes.

`Month` (the default) `Year` `Decade`

FIGURE 11.24 The WPF `Calendar`, displayed with each of its `DisplayMode` values, as it appears on April 20, 2012.

Calendar's DisplayDate (of type DateTime) is initialized to the current day by default (April 20, 2012 in Figure 11.24). Calendar ensures that the DisplayDate is initially visible, although the specific date doesn't appear differently from the other dates in Month mode. The reason April 20 appears in gray in Figure 11.24 is that Calendar highlights today's date independent of DisplayDate's value. To turn this off, you can set Calendar's IsTodayHighlighted property to false.

One or more dates in the calendar can be selected, depending on the value of SelectionMode:

- **SingleDate**—Only one date can be selected at a time, stored in the SelectedDate property. This is the default value.
- **SingleRange**—Multiple dates can be selected, but only if they are in a contiguous range. The selected dates are stored in the SelectedDates property.
- **MultipleRange**—Multiple noncontiguous dates can be selected, stored in the SelectedDates property.
- **None**—No dates can be selected.

You can set the DisplayDateStart and/or DisplayDateEnd properties (also of type DateTime) to restrict the range of available dates displayed inside Calendar. Figure 11.25 shows what this looks like in each of the DisplayModes. The result can look a bit goofy, as the six-week layout of the Month mode and the 4x4 layout of the other two modes never change.

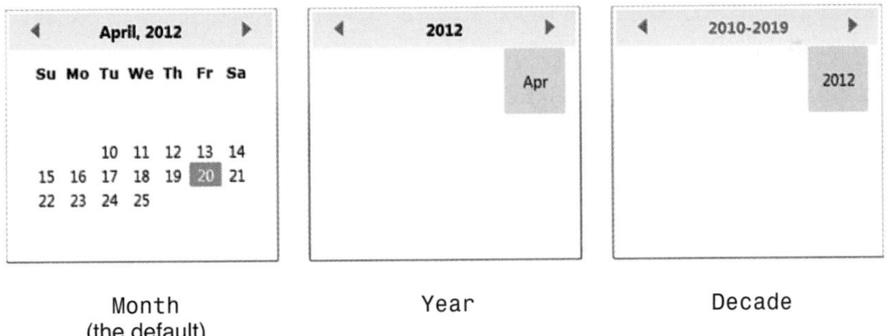

FIGURE 11.25 The impact of setting DisplayDateStart to April 10, 2012 and DisplayDateEnd to April 25, 2010

Alternatively, you can choose ranges of dates to be nonselectable despite being displayed. This is accomplished with Calendar's BlackoutDates property, which is a collection of

CalendarDateRange objects. Figure 11.26 shows the result of setting BlackoutDates to a pair of ranges as follows:

```
<Calendar>
<Calendar.BlackoutDates>
  <CalendarDateRange Start="4/1/2012" End="4/19/2012"/>
  <CalendarDateRange Start="5/1/2012" End="5/5/2012"/>
</Calendar.BlackoutDates>
</Calendar>
```

This only affects the Month mode.

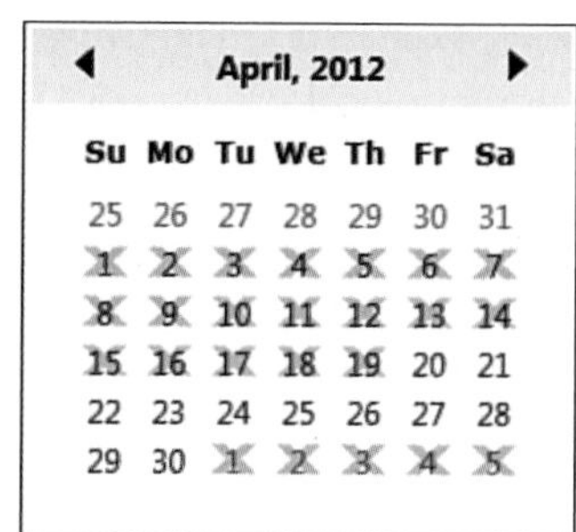

FIGURE 11.26 The impact of setting BlackoutDates to two CalendarDateRanges.

TIP

The type of the BlackoutDates property is CalendarBlackoutDatesCollection, a subclass of ObservableCollection<CalendarDateRange> that has one particularly handy method: AddDatesInPast. By calling this, you can blackout all dates before the current date. However, because calling this method requires procedural code, it might be easier to explicitly use a CalendarDateRange with a Start value of DateTime.MinValue (January 1, 0001) and an End value of DateTime.Today minus one day.

Designed for cultures where Sunday isn't considered to be the first day of the week, Calendar's FirstDayOfWeek property can be set to any value of the System.DayOfWeek enumeration to change its display accordingly. Calendar also has events covering all the major property changes: DisplayDateChanged, DisplayModeChanged, SelectionModeChanged, and SelectedDatesChanged (which handles both single selection and multiselect modes).

DatePicker

The other calendar control—DatePicker—is basically a TextBox for displaying and entering a date with an associated Calendar popup for visually changing the date. It is pictured in Figure 11.27.

FIGURE 11.27 The WPF DatePicker, with its popup showing after clicking the calendar icon.

DatePicker's popup contains an instance of the now-familiar Calendar control, which is responsible for most of DatePicker's interesting functionality. DatePicker contains the same properties and events as Calendar except for DisplayMode, SelectionMode, and the corresponding property change events. Instead, the popup's DisplayMode is always Month and its SelectionMode is always SingleDate. Due to its single selection, DatePicker has a SelectedDateChanged event instead of a

SelectedDatesChanged event. It also lacks Calendar's DisplayDateChanged event, for no particular reason.

DatePicker has a few unique properties and events for controlling the behavior of its TextBox and its interaction with the popup. The Boolean IsDropDownOpen property can be used to programmatically open or close the Calendar popup, or it can be inspected to determine its current state. CalendarOpened and CalendarClosed events are raised when appropriate. SelectedDateFormat controls the format of the string that gets placed in the TextBox when a date is selected in the Calendar. With its default value of Short, it is given a format such as 4/20/2012. It can also be set to Long, which gives a format such as Friday, April 20, 2012. At any time, the string inside the TextBox can be set or retrieved via DatePicker's Text property. If a string is entered that is not a valid date, the DateValidationError event is raised.

DatePicker's TextBox (a TextBox-derived class called DatePickerTextBox) is not the nicest-looking control—it has an odd-looking hover appearance, and the calendar icon that opens the popup when clicked inexplicably always shows "15" as its fake date. The only way to customize its appearance is to completely replace its control template.

Summary

You've now seen the major built-in controls that can be used for creating traditional (and perhaps some not-so-traditional) user interfaces. Although you can radically change the *look* of these controls by using the techniques discussed in Chapter 14, the core *behavior* described in this part of the book remains the same.

PART IV

Features for Professional Developers

IN THIS PART

CHAPTER 12
Resources

IN THIS CHAPTER

- Binary Resources
- Logical Resources

The .NET Framework has generic infrastructure for packaging and accessing *resources*—the noncode pieces of an application or component, such as bitmaps, fonts, audio/video files, and string tables. As with many other parts of WPF, WPF not only leverages the core .NET resources system but adds a little more support. WPF supports two distinct types of resources: binary resources and logical resources.

Binary Resources

The first type—*binary resources*—is exactly what the rest of the .NET Framework considers to be resources. In WPF applications, these are typically traditional items like bitmaps. However, even compiled XAML gets stored as a binary resource behind the scenes. Binary resources can be packaged in three different ways:

- Embedded inside an assembly
- As loose files that are known to the application at compile time
- As loose files that might not be known to the application at compile time

An application's binary resources are often put into two categories: localizable resources that must change depending on the current culture and language-neutral (or nonlocalizable) resources that don't change based on culture. This section looks at the ways in which binary resources are defined, accessed, and localized.

Defining Binary Resources

The typical procedure for defining a binary resource consists of adding the file to a Visual Studio project and selecting the appropriate build action in the property grid, as shown in Figure 12.1 for an image called `logo.jpg`.

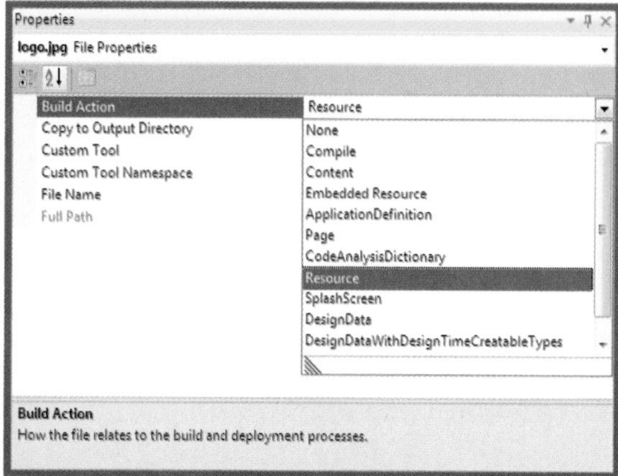

FIGURE 12.1 Marking a file as a binary resource in Visual Studio.

Visual Studio supports several build actions for WPF applications, two of which are relevant for binary resources:

- **`Resource`**—Embeds the resource into the assembly (or a culture-specific satellite assembly).
- **`Content`**—Leaves the resource as a loose file but adds a custom attribute to the assembly (`AssemblyAssociatedContentFile`) that records the existence and relative location of the file.

If you're an MSBuild user editing a project file by hand, you can add such a file with the following syntax:

```
<BuildAction Include="logo.jpg"/>
```

where *`BuildAction`* is the name of the build action. A build action may include child elements that refine its behavior, as in the following example:

```
<Content Include="logo.jpg">
  <CopyToOutputDirectory>Always</CopyToOutputDirectory>
</Content>
```

WARNING

Avoid the `Embedded Resource` build action!

The `Resource` build action is confusingly similar to the `EmbeddedResource` build action (`Embedded Resource` in Visual Studio's property grid). Both embed a binary resource inside an assembly, but the latter should be avoided in WPF projects. Whereas `Resource` was added specifically for WPF, `EmbeddedResource` predates WPF (and is used to embed binary resources in Windows Forms projects).

WPF's APIs that reference resources via uniform resource identifiers (described in the next section) are designed for resources that use the build action `Content` or `Resource` only. This also means that resources embedded with the `Content` or `Resource` build action can be referenced easily from XAML, but resources embedded with the `EmbeddedResource` build action cannot be (unless you write some custom code).

If you want to keep your resources as loose files, adding them to a project with a `Content` build action is not required; you could simply put them at the appropriate location when the application runs and not worry about adding them to the project at all. This is not recommended, however, because it makes accessing the resources a bit less natural (as described in the next section). Still, sometimes using resources that aren't known at compile time is inevitable, such as files that are dynamically generated at runtime.

Resources should be embedded (with the `Resource` build action) if they are localizable, or if you feel the benefits of having a single binary file outweigh the benefits of having a loose file that can be easily replaced independently from the code. If neither of these is true, or if the content needs to be accessible directly from external entities as well (perhaps from HTML pages rendered inside the application), using the `Content` build action is a good choice.

Accessing Binary Resources

Whether binary resources are embedded with the `Resource` build action, linked as loose files with the `Content` build action, or left as loose files with no special treatment at compile time, WPF provides a mechanism for accessing them from code or XAML with a uniform resource identifier (URI). A type converter enables such URIs to be specified in XAML as simple strings with a few built-in shortcuts for common scenarios.

You can see this by examining the source code for the Photo Gallery application introduced in Chapter 7, "Structuring and Deploying an Application." The following XAML snippet from Photo Gallery references several images that are included in the project with the `Resource` build action:

```
<StackPanel Grid.Column="1" Orientation="Horizontal" HorizontalAlignment="Center">
  <Button x:Name="previousButton" ToolTip="Previous (Left Arrow)" …>
    <Image Height="21" Source="previous.gif"/>
  </Button>
  <Button x:Name="slideshowButton" ToolTip="Play Slide Show (F11)" …>
```

```
    <Image Height="21" Source="slideshow.gif"/>
  </Button>
  <Button x:Name="nextButton" ToolTip="Next (Right Arrow)" …>
    <Image Height="21" Source="next.gif"/>
  </Button>
</StackPanel>
```

Note that this same XAML works even if the `.gif` files are given the `Content` build action instead of `Resource` (as long as the loose files are copied to the same directory as the executable when it runs). It does not work, however, if the loose `.gif` files are not added to the project.

WARNING

Compiled XAML can't reference a binary resource in the current directory via its simple filename unless it has been added to the project!

It often surprises people that compiled XAML, unlike loose XAML, can't reference an arbitrary file in the current directory as follows:

```
<Image Height="21" Source="slideshow.gif"/>
```

If you require a resource to be loose and do not want to add it to your project, you have a few easy alternatives. One (unsatisfactory) alternative is to qualify the filename with its full path:

```
<Image Height="21" Source="C:\Users\Adam\Documents\slideshow.gif"/>
```

A better alternative is to use the following odd-looking syntax, described later in the "Accessing Resources at the Site of Origin" section:

```
<Image Height="21" Source="pack://siteOfOrigin:,,,/slideshow.gif"/>
```

The key to accessing binary resources, whether done with the `Image` element or other elements, is understanding what URIs you can use to address a resource that could be embedded or loose. Table 12.1 summarizes the main options for URI strings in XAML. Note that not all of these options are available for partial-trust applications.

TABLE 12.1 URIs for Accessing Binary Resources from XAML

Using `logo.jpg` as the Resource Name	
If the URI Is...	**The Resource Is...**
`logo.jpg`	Embedded in the current assembly, or loose and alongside the current XAML page or assembly (the latter case only if marked as `Content` in the project)

TABLE 12.1 Continued

`A/B/logo.jpg`	Embedded in the current assembly using an internal subfolder (`A\B`) structure defined at compile time, or loose and in an `A\B` subfolder relative to the current XAML page or assembly (the latter case only if marked as `Content` in the project)
`c:\temp\logo.jpg`	Loose in the local `c:\temp` folder
`file://c:/temp/logo.jpg`	Loose in the local `c:\temp` folder
`\\pc1\images\logo.jpg`	Loose on the `\\pc1\images` UNC share
`http://adamnathan.net/logo.jpg`	Loose and hosted at the `adamnathan.net` website
`/MyDll;Component/logo.jpg`	Embedded in a different assembly called `MyDll.dll` or `MyDll.exe`
`/MyDll;Component/A/B/logo.jpg`	Embedded in a different assembly called `MyDll.dll` or `MyDll.exe`, using an internal subfolder structure (`A\B`) defined at compile time
`pack://siteOfOrigin:,,,/logo.jpg`	Loose at the site of origin
`pack://siteOfOrigin:,,,/A/B/logo.jpg`	Loose at the site of origin in an `A\B` subfolder

Note that the first two entries in Table 12.1 can work with both embedded and loose binary resources. This means that you can replace loose resources with embedded ones (or vice versa) without having to change your XAML.

The notion of using subfolders with embedded resources might sound a little odd, but it can be a nice way to organize embedded resources just as you would organize loose ones. For example, say that you put `logo.jpg` in an `images` folder in your Visual Studio project, using either of the following in the project file:

```
<Resource Include="images\logo.jpg"/>
```

or

```
<Content Include="images\logo.jpg"/>
```

Then you can access it as follows, regardless of whether `logo.jpg` physically resides as a loose file in an `images` subfolder at runtime or if it's simply embedded in the assembly:

```
<Image Source="images\logo.jpg"/>
```

FAQ

What happens when attempting to access resources on a slow or unavailable network?

Table 12.1 shows that binary resources can be directly referenced from potentially unreliable sources such as a website or a Universal Naming Convention (UNC) share. This access is done synchronously, so you'll unfortunately see an application "hang" while waiting for all the bits to be retrieved. In addition, failure to retrieve the resource results in an unhandled exception.

The final four rows of Table 12.1 need a bit more explanation. The first two enable you to access binary resources embedded in another assembly, and the second two enable you to access binary resources at a special place known as a site of origin.

Accessing Resources Embedded in Another Assembly

The ability to easily access binary resources embedded in another assembly is very handy (and gives you more options for updating resources without needing to replace the main executable), but the syntax is a little bizarre. As Table 12.1 implies, the syntax is

```
/AssemblyReference;Component/ResourceName
```

where `AssemblyReference` identifies the specific assembly, but `Component` is a keyword and must be used literally. `ResourceName` is the filename (which can include subfolders).

`AssemblyReference` can be the simple assembly display name, or it can optionally include other pieces of a .NET assembly's identity: version number and public key token (if it's a strong-named assembly). So, you have four options for `AssemblyReference`:

- `AssemblyName`
- `AssemblyName;vVersionNumber` (the `v` prefix is required)
- `AssemblyName;PublicKeyToken`
- `AssemblyName;vVersionNumber;PublicKeyToken`

Accessing Resources at the Site of Origin

Although full-trust applications can hard-code a uniform resource locator (URL) or path for loose binary resources, taking advantage of the site of origin notion is a more maintainable approach. (In addition, it is required for partial-trust applications.) The site of origin gets resolved to different places at runtime, depending how the application is deployed:

- For a full-trust application installed with Windows Installer, the site of origin is the application's root folder.
- For a full-trust ClickOnce application, the site of origin is the URL or UNC path from which the application was deployed.
- For a partial-trust XAML Browser Application (XBAP) or ClickOnce application, the site of origin is the URL or UNC path that hosts the application.
- For loose XAML pages viewed in a web browser, there is no site of origin. Attempting to use it throws an exception.

The syntax for taking advantage of the site of origin is even stranger than the syntax to reference resources embedded in another assembly! You must use the `pack://siteOfOrigin:,,,/` prefix, followed by the resource name (which can contain subfolders). Note that `siteOfOrigin` is a keyword to be used literally, not a placeholder for other text.

FAQ

Where does that awful triple-comma syntax come from?

The Pack URI format is part of the XML Paper Specification (XPS), which can be found at http://microsoft.com/whdc/xps/xpsspec.mspx. This is the specified format:

`pack://packageURI/partPath`

packageURI is actually a URI within a URI, so it is encoded by converting its forward slashes into commas. *packageURI* can point to an XPS document, such as `file:///C:/Document.xps` encoded as `file:,,,C:,Document.xps`. Or, in WPF programs, it can be one of two URIs treated specially by the platform:

- `siteOfOrigin:///` (encoded as `siteOfOrigin:,,,`)
- `application:///` (encoded as `application:,,,`)

Therefore, the triple commas are actually encoded forward slashes, not placeholders for optional parameters! (Note that these can also be specified with two slashes/commas rather than three.)

The `application:///` package is implicitly used by all the resource references shown in Table 12.1 that don't use `siteOfOrigin`. (This is thanks to the fact that relevant objects in WPF implement the `IUriContext` interface. `IUriContext` contains a single `BaseUri` property that gives context to relative URIs.) In other words, the following URI used in XAML:

`logo.jpg`

is really just shorthand notation for this:

`pack://application:,,,``/logo.jpg`

and this URI:

`/MyDll;Component/logo.jpg`

is shorthand notation for this:

`pack://application:,,,``/MyDll;Component/logo.jpg`

You can use these longer and more explicit URIs in XAML, but there's no good reason to.

Accessing Resources from Procedural Code

When creating URIs in C# for referencing resources, you aren't able to use the XAML-specific shortcuts from Table 12.1. Instead, such URIs must be constructed with a fully qualified Pack URI or a fully qualified path/URL.

For example, the following code assigns an `Image`'s `Source` property to the contents of `logo.jpg`:

```
Image image = new Image();
image.Source = new BitmapImage(new Uri("pack://application:,,,/logo.jpg"));
```

This instantiates a `System.Windows.Media.Imaging.BitmapImage` object (which works with popular image formats such as JPEG, PNG, GIF, and BMP), which ultimately derives from the abstract `ImageSource` type (the type of the `Source` property). The URI is represented by a `System.Uri` object.

The use of `pack://application:,,,/` works only with resources belonging to the current project marked as `Resource` or `Content`. To reference relative loose files with no relation to the project, the easiest approach is to use a `siteOfOrigin`-based URI.

Localizing Binary Resources

If an application contains some binary resources that are specific to certain cultures, you can partition them into satellite assemblies (one per culture) that get loaded automatically, when appropriate. If you're doing this, then you likely have strings in your user interface that you need to localize as well. LocBaml, a sample tool in the Windows SDK, makes it easy to manage the localization of strings and other items without having to rip them out of XAML and manually apply a level of indirection. This section walks through the basics steps to get started with LocBaml and satellite assemblies.

Preparing a Project for Multiple Cultures

To specify a default culture for resources and automatically build an appropriate satellite assembly, you must add a `UICulture` element to the project file. Visual Studio doesn't have a means to set this within its environment, so you can open the project file in your favorite text editor instead.

> **TIP**
>
> You can open a raw project file without leaving Visual Studio if you right-click and unload it from the current solution first. After it's unloaded, right-click the project again and select Edit from the context menu.

The `UICulture` element should be added under any or all `PropertyGroup` elements corresponding to the build configurations you want to affect (Debug, Release, and so on), or to a property group unrelated to build configuration so it automatically applies to all of them. This setting should look as follows for a default culture of American English:

```
<Project …>
  <PropertyGroup>
    <UICulture>en-US</UICulture>
…
```

If you rebuild your project with this setting in place, you'll find an `en-US` folder alongside your assembly, containing the satellite assembly named *`AssemblyName`*`.resources.dll`.

You should also mark your assembly with the assembly-level `NeutralResourcesLanguage` custom attribute with a value matching your default `UICulture` setting, as follows:

```
[assembly: NeutralResourcesLanguage("en-US",
  UltimateResourceFallbackLocation.Satellite)]
```

Marking a User Interface with Localization IDs

The next step is to apply a `Uid` directive from the XAML language namespace (`x:Uid`) to every object element that needs to be localized. The value of each directive should be a unique identifier.

This would be extremely tedious to do by hand, but it fortunately can be done automatically by invoking MSBuild from a command prompt, as follows:

```
msbuild /t:updateuid ProjectName.csproj
```

Running this gives *every* object element in *every* XAML file in the project an `x:Uid` directive with a unique value. You can add this MSBuild task inside your project before the Build task, although this might produce too much noise if you rebuild often.

Creating a New Satellite Assembly with LocBaml

After compiling a project that has been enhanced with `Uids`, you can run the LocBaml tool from the Windows SDK on a `.resources` file generated by the build process (found in the `obj\debug` directory), as follows:

```
LocBaml /parse ProjectName.g.en-US.resources /out:en-US.csv
```

This generates a simple `.csv` text file containing all the property values you should need to localize. You can edit the contents of this file so it correctly corresponds to a new culture. (There's no magic in this part of localization!) If you save the file, you can then use LocBaml in the reverse direction to generate a new satellite assembly from the `.csv` file! For example, if you changed the contents of the `.csv` file to match the French Canadian culture, you could save the file as `fr-CA.csv` and then run LocBaml as follows:

```
LocBaml /generate ProjectName.resources.dll /trans:fr-CA.csv /cul:fr-CA
```

This new satellite assembly needs to be copied to a folder alongside the main assembly with a name that matches the culture (`fr-CA` in this case).

To test a different culture, you can set `System.Threading.Thread.CurrentThread.CurrentUICulture` (and `System.Threading.Thread.CurrentThread.CurrentCulture`) to an instance of the desired `CultureInfo`.

Logical Resources

The second type of resources is a mechanism first introduced by WPF and supported by both WPF and Silverlight. In this chapter, these resources are called *logical resources* for lack of a better term, but mostly the book refers to them as *resources* in contrast to the *binary resources* just covered. (You might be tempted to call them *XAML resources*, but as with almost everything else in XAML, you can create and use them entirely in procedural code.)

These logical resources are arbitrary .NET objects stored (and named) in an element's `Resources` property, typically meant to be shared by multiple child elements. The `FrameworkElement` and `FrameworkContentElement` base classes both have a `Resources` property (of type `System.Windows.ResourceDictionary`), so most WPF classes you'll encounter have such a property. These logical resources are often styles (covered in Chapter 14, "Styles, Templates, Skins, and Themes") or data providers (covered in Chapter 13, "Data Binding"). But this chapter demonstrates logical resources by storing some simple `Brush`es.

Listing 12.1 contains a simple `Window` with a row of `Button`s along the bottom, similar to ones from the Photo Gallery user interface. It demonstrates a brute-force way to apply a custom `Brush` to each `Button`'s (and the `Window`'s) `Background`, as well as each `Button`'s `BorderBrush`. Figure 12.2 shows the result.

LISTING 12.1 Applying Custom Color `Brush`es Without Using Logical Resources

```
<Window xmlns="http://schemas.microsoft.com/winfx/2006/xaml/presentation"
  Title="Simple Window" Background="Yellow">
  <DockPanel>
    <StackPanel DockPanel.Dock="Bottom" Orientation="Horizontal"
      HorizontalAlignment="Center">
      <Button Background="Yellow" BorderBrush="Red" Margin="5">
        <Image Height="21" Source="zoom.gif"/>
      </Button>
      <Button Background="Yellow" BorderBrush="Red" Margin="5">
        <Image Height="21" Source="defaultThumbnailSize.gif"/>
      </Button>
      <Button Background="Yellow" BorderBrush="Red" Margin="5">
        <Image Height="21" Source="previous.gif"/>
      </Button>
      <Button Background="Yellow" BorderBrush="Red" Margin="5">
        <Image Height="21" Source="slideshow.gif"/>
      </Button>
      <Button Background="Yellow" BorderBrush="Red" Margin="5">
        <Image Height="21" Source="next.gif"/>
      </Button>
      <Button Background="Yellow" BorderBrush="Red" Margin="5">
        <Image Height="21" Source="counterclockwise.gif"/>
      </Button>
      <Button Background="Yellow" BorderBrush="Red" Margin="5">
        <Image Height="21" Source="clockwise.gif"/>
      </Button>
      <Button Background="Yellow" BorderBrush="Red" Margin="5">
        <Image Height="21" Source="delete.gif"/>
      </Button>
    </StackPanel>
```

LISTING 12.1 Continued

```
    <ListBox/>
  </DockPanel>
</Window>
```


Alternatively, you could organize the yellow and red Brushes as logical resources for the Window and apply them to individual elements as resource references. This is a nice way to separate and consolidate the style information, much like using Cascading Style Sheets (CSS) to control colors and styles in a webpage rather than hard-coding them on individual elements. The sharing of objects enabled by the logical resources scheme can also help you consume significantly less memory, depending on the complexity of the objects. Listing 12.2 is an update to Listing 12.1, using logical resources for the two Brushes.

FIGURE 12.2 The rendered Window from Listing 12.1.

LISTING 12.2 Consolidating Color Brushes with Logical Resources

```
<Window xmlns="http://schemas.microsoft.com/winfx/2006/xaml/presentation"
  xmlns:x="http://schemas.microsoft.com/winfx/2006/xaml"
  Title="Simple Window">
<Window.Resources>
  <SolidColorBrush x:Key="backgroundBrush">Yellow</SolidColorBrush>
  <SolidColorBrush x:Key="borderBrush">Red</SolidColorBrush>
</Window.Resources>
<Window.Background>
  <StaticResource ResourceKey="backgroundBrush"/>
</Window.Background>
  <DockPanel>
    <StackPanel DockPanel.Dock="Bottom" Orientation="Horizontal"
      HorizontalAlignment="Center">
      <Button Background="{StaticResource backgroundBrush}"
        BorderBrush="{StaticResource borderBrush}" Margin="5">
        <Image Height="21" Source="zoom.gif"/>
      </Button>
      <Button Background="{StaticResource backgroundBrush}"
        BorderBrush="{StaticResource borderBrush}" Margin="5">
        <Image Height="21" Source="defaultThumbnailSize.gif"/>
      </Button>
      <Button Background="{StaticResource backgroundBrush}"
        BorderBrush="{StaticResource borderBrush}" Margin="5">
        <Image Height="21" Source="previous.gif"/>
      </Button>
```

This forward reference rule is the reason that the `Window` in Listing 12.2 uses property element syntax to set `Background`. By doing so, it ensures that the resource is defined before it is used.

Although `DynamicResource` could be used the same way, you can also use it via property attribute syntax in this case because it doesn't matter that the resource is referenced before it is defined:

```
<Window xmlns="http://schemas.microsoft.com/winfx/2006/xaml/presentation"
  xmlns:x="http://schemas.microsoft.com/winfx/2006/xaml"
  Title="Simple Window" Background="{DynamicResource backgroundBrush}">
<Window.Resources>
  <SolidColorBrush x:Key="backgroundBrush">Yellow</SolidColorBrush>
  <SolidColorBrush x:Key="borderBrush">Red</SolidColorBrush>
</Window.Resources>
  …
</Window>
```

Resources Without Sharing

By default, when a resource is applied in multiple places, the same object instance is used everywhere. This is usually the desired behavior. However, you can mark items in a compiled resource dictionary with `x:Shared="False"` to make each request for that resource produce a distinct instance of the object that can be modified independently of the others.

One case where this behavior can be interesting is the previous example of using an entire `Image` (or any other `Visual`-derived object) as a resource. Such a resource can be applied only once in an element tree because each application is the same instance. But setting `x:Shared="False"` changes this behavior, enabling the resource to be applied multiple times as independent objects. This could be done as follows:

```
<Window xmlns="http://schemas.microsoft.com/winfx/2006/xaml/presentation"
  xmlns:x="http://schemas.microsoft.com/winfx/2006/xaml">
<Window.Resources>
  <Image x:Shared="False" x:Key="zoom" Height="21" Source="zoom.gif"/>
</Window.Resources>
  <StackPanel>
    <!-- Applying the resource multiple times works! -->
    <StaticResource ResourceKey="zoom"/>
    <StaticResource ResourceKey="zoom"/>
    <StaticResource ResourceKey="zoom"/>
  </StackPanel>
</Window>
```

Note that `x:Shared` can be used only in a compiled XAML file. Its use in loose XAML files is not supported.

Defining and Applying Resources in Procedural Code

So far, this chapter has examined how to define and apply logical resources in XAML, but it hasn't yet looked at what it means to do the same things in procedural code. Fortunately, *defining* resources in code is straightforward. The two `SolidColorBrush` resources used in Listing 12.2 can be defined as follows in C#, assuming a `Window` called `window`:

```
window.Resources.Add("backgroundBrush", new SolidColorBrush(Colors.Yellow));
window.Resources.Add("borderBrush", new SolidColorBrush(Colors.Red));
```

Applying resources in code is a different story, however. Because `StaticResource` and `DynamicResource` are markup extensions, the equivalent C# code to find and apply resources is not obvious.

For `StaticResource`, you can get the equivalent behavior by setting an element's property to the result from its `FindResource` method (inherited from `FrameworkElement` or `FrameworkContentElement`).

So, the following `Button` (similar to one declared in Listing 12.2):

```
<Button Background="{StaticResource backgroundBrush}"
        BorderBrush="{StaticResource borderBrush}"/>
```

is equivalent to the following C# code (assuming an appropriate `StackPanel` variable named `stackPanel` for containing the `Button`):

```
Button button = new Button();
// The Button must descend from the Window before looking up resources:
stackPanel.Children.Add(button);
button.Background = (Brush)button.FindResource("backgroundBrush");
button.BorderBrush = (Brush)button.FindResource("borderBrush");
```

`FindResource` throws an exception when the resource cannot be found, but you can alternatively call `TryFindResource`, which returns `null` when the lookup fails.

For `DynamicResource`, a call to an element's `SetResourceReference` (also inherited from `FrameworkElement` or `FrameworkContentElement`) does the trick of setting up the updatable binding with the dependency property.

Therefore, replacing both `StaticResource` references with `DynamicResource`:

```
<Button Background="{DynamicResource backgroundBrush}"
        BorderBrush="{DynamicResource borderBrush}"/>
```

is equivalent to using the following C# code:

```
Button button = new Button();
button.SetResourceReference(Button.BackgroundProperty, "backgroundBrush");
button.SetResourceReference(Button.BorderBrushProperty, "borderBrush");
```

This works as long as the `Button` is eventually added to the element tree as a descendant of the `Window` (where the resources are defined). Unlike the `StaticResource` case, such placement in the tree does not need to happen before referencing each resource.

The forward reference rule with `StaticResource` also applies to procedural code. A call to `FindResource` or `TryFindResource` fails if you call it before adding the resource to an appropriate resource dictionary with the appropriate key. `SetResourceReference`, on the other hand, can be called before the resource has been added.

DIGGING DEEPER

Accessing Resources Directly

Because resource dictionaries are simple collections exposed as public properties, nothing prevents you from accessing a resource dictionary's items directly in source code. For example, you could set a `Button`'s `Background` and `BorderBrush` properties as follows in C# (assuming a `Window` object called `window`):

```
Button button = new Button();
button.Background = (Brush)window.Resources["backgroundBrush"];
button.BorderBrush = (Brush)window.Resources["borderBrush"];
```

This is similar to the use of `StaticResource` in XAML (`FindResource` in code) in that it's a one-time property set. However, it doesn't search the logical tree, application, or system for the named resources. Therefore, this gives you less flexibility and makes the binding between XAML and code more brittle, but it also gives you a minor performance boost by avoiding the lookups. Note that there is no way to use this technique in XAML.

Interaction with System Resources

One obvious place where it's appropriate to use `DynamicResource` is with system settings encapsulated by static properties on three classes in the `System.Windows` namespace: `SystemColors`, `SystemFonts`, and `SystemParameters`. That's because a user can change the settings via Control Panel while your application is running.

The `SystemColors`, `SystemFonts`, and `SystemParameters` classes define their properties in pairs—a property for each actual value and a corresponding property that serves as the resource key to be used for lookups. Each resource key property is given a `Key` suffix by convention. For example, `SystemColors` contains properties of type `Brush` called `WindowBrush` and `WindowTextBrush` along with properties of type `ResourceKey` called `WindowBrush`**`Key`** and `WindowTextBrush`**`Key`**.

Table 12.2 demonstrates the various ways you might try to set a `Button`'s background to the system's currently defined "window color." The second approach is what I see people do most commonly, but only the last approach is completely correct.

TABLE 12.2 Potential Options for Setting a System-Defined Background

The Approach	The Result

XAML:
`<Button Background="SystemColors.WindowBrush"/>`
C#:
`button.Background = (Brush)new`
`  BrushConverter().ConvertFrom("SystemColors.WindowBrush");`
	This doesn't work. `BrushConverter` doesn't support such strings.

XAML:
`<Button Background="{x:Static SystemColors.WindowBrush}"/>`
C#:
`button.Background = SystemColors.WindowBrush;`
	This successfully sets the color once but doesn't respond to the user changing the color while the application runs.

XAML:
`<Button Background=`
`  "{StaticResource SystemColors.WindowBrushKey}"/>`
C#:
`button.Background =`
`  (Brush)FindResource("SystemColors.WindowBrushKey");`
	This doesn't work unless you defined a `Brush` resource with a `"SystemColors.WindowBrushKey"` key, which would have no relation to the static property you probably want to use.

XAML:
`<Button Background=`
`  "{StaticResource {x:Static SystemColors.WindowBrush}}"/>`
C#:
`button.Background =`
`  (Brush)FindResource(SystemColors.WindowBrush);`
	`SystemColors.WindowBrush` is not a valid key, so this code does not find the resource.

XAML:
`<Button Background=`
`  "{StaticResource {x:Static SystemColors.WindowBrushKey}}"/>`
C#:
`button.Background =`
`  (Brush)FindResource(SystemColors.WindowBrushKey);`
	This finds the resource. This is like approach #2 but also allows the application to override the color (during initialization) for simple skinning purposes.

XAML:
`<Button Background=`
`  "{DynamicResource {x:Static SystemColors.WindowBrushKey}}"/>`
C#:
`button.SetResourceReference(`
`  Button.BackgroundProperty, SystemColors.WindowBrushKey);`
	This is the preferred approach. It responds to any user-initiated changes and allows the application to override the values to reskin it at any time.

Summary

Of all the WPF features covered in this part of the book, the support for resources is the one that is practically impossible to live without. It's hard to build a professional-looking application without at least an icon and a few images!

But using resources is about much more than just making an application or a control look (or sound, if you're using audio resources) a little better. It's a fundamental piece of enabling software to be localized into different languages. It also enables higher productivity for developing software because the logical resources support enables you to consolidate information that might otherwise be duplicated, and even factor XAML files into more manageable chunks. The most fun—and perhaps most important—application of logical resources is their use with objects such as styles and templates, covered in Chapter 14.

CHAPTER 13
Data Binding

IN THIS CHAPTER

- Introducing the `Binding` Object
- Controlling Rendering
- Customizing the View of a Collection
- Data Providers
- Advanced Topics
- Putting It All Together: The Pure-XAML Twitter Client

In WPF, the term *data* is generally used to describe an arbitrary .NET object. You can see this naming pattern in terms such as *data binding, data templates,* and *data triggers,* covered in this chapter and the next chapter. A piece of data could be a collection object, an XML file, a web service, a database table, a custom object, or even a WPF element such as a `Button`.

Therefore, data binding is about tying together arbitrary .NET objects. The classic scenario is providing a visual representation (for example, in a `ListBox` or `DataGrid`) of items in an XML file, a database, or an in-memory collection. For example, instead of iterating through a data source and manually adding a `ListBoxItem` to a `ListBox` for each one, it would be nice to just say, "Hey, `ListBox`! Get your items from over here. And keep them up to date, please. Oh yeah, and format them to look like this." Data binding enables this and much more.

Introducing the `Binding` Object

The key to data binding is a `System.Windows.Data.Binding` object that "glues" two properties together and keeps a channel of communication open between them. You can set up a `Binding` once and then have it do all the synchronization work for the remainder of the application's lifetime.

Using `Binding` in Procedural Code

Imagine that you want to add a `TextBlock` to the Photo Gallery application used in earlier chapters that displays the current folder above the `ListBox`:

```
<TextBlock x:Name="currentFolder" DockPanel.Dock="Top"
  Background="AliceBlue" FontSize="16" />
```

You could update this TextBlock's text manually whenever the TreeView's SelectedItem changes:

```
void treeView_SelectedItemChanged(object sender,
  RoutedPropertyChangedEventArgs<object> e)
{
  currentFolder.Text = (treeView.SelectedItem as TreeViewItem).Header.ToString();
  Refresh();
}
```

By using a Binding object, you can remove this line of code and replace it with the following one-time initialization inside MainWindow's constructor:

```
public MainWindow()
{
  InitializeComponent();

  Binding binding = new Binding();
  // Set source object
  binding.Source = treeView;
  // Set source property
  binding.Path = new PropertyPath("SelectedItem.Header");
  // Attach to target property
  currentFolder.SetBinding(TextBlock.TextProperty, binding);
}
```

With this change, currentFolder.Text updates automatically as treeView.SelectedItem.Header changes. If an item in the TreeView is ever selected that doesn't have a Header property (which doesn't happen in Photo Gallery), the data binding silently fails and returns a default value for the property (an empty string in this case). There are ways to get diagnostics, however, discussed later in this chapter.

This code change doesn't appear to be an improvement, because you've exchanged one line of code for four! Keep in mind, however, that this is a very simple use of data binding! In later examples, the use of data binding greatly reduces the amount of code you would have to write to achieve the same results.

Binding has the notion of a *source* property and a *target* property. The source property (treeView.SelectedItem.Header, in this case) is set in two steps—assigning the source object to Source and the name of its relevant property (or chain of property and subproperties) to Path via an instance of PropertyPath. To associate the Binding with the target property (currentFolder.Text, in this case), you can call SetBinding (which is inherited by all FrameworkElements and FrameworkContentElements) with the relevant dependency property and the Binding instance.

TIP

There are actually two ways to set Binding in procedural code. One is to call the SetBinding instance method on the relevant FrameworkElement or FrameworkContentElement, as done previously. The other is to call the SetBinding static method on a class called BindingOperations. You pass this method the same objects you would pass to the instance method, but it has an additional first parameter that represents the target object:

```
BindingOperations.SetBinding(currentFolder, TextBlock.TextProperty, binding);
```

The benefit of the static method is that the first parameter is defined as a DependencyObject, so it enables data binding on objects that don't derive from FrameworkElement or FrameworkContentElement (such as Freezables).

DIGGING DEEPER

Removing a Binding

If you don't want a Binding to exist for the remainder of an application's lifespan, you can "disconnect" it at any time with the static BindingOperations.ClearBinding method. (This is rarely done, however.) You pass it the target object and its dependency property. Here's an example:

```
BindingOperations.ClearBinding(currentFolder, TextBlock.TextProperty);
```

If a target object has more than one Binding attached to it, you can clear them all in one fell swoop by calling BindingOperations.ClearAllBindings, like so:

```
BindingOperations.ClearAllBindings(currentFolder);
```

Another way to clear a Binding is simply to directly set the target property to a new value, as follows:

```
currentFolder.Text = "I am no longer receiving updates.";
```

This only clears one-way Bindings, however. (The different types of Bindings are discussed in the "Customizing the Data Flow" section toward the end of this chapter.) The ClearBinding approach is more flexible anyway, as it still enables the dependency property to receive values from sources with a lower precedence (style triggers, property value inheritance, and so on). Recall the order of precedence for determining a base property value in Chapter 3, "WPF Fundamentals." A Binding set via SetBinding has the same precedence as a local value, and ClearBinding removes the value from the property value equation, just like ClearValue does for *any* local value. (In fact, all ClearBinding does internally is call ClearValue on the target object!)

Using Binding in XAML

Because you can't call an element's SetBinding method from XAML, WPF contains a markup extension to make declarative use of Binding possible. In fact, Binding itself is a markup extension class (despite the nonstandard name without the Extension suffix).

To use `Binding` in XAML, you directly set the target property to a `Binding` instance and then use the standard markup extension syntax to set its properties. Therefore, the preceding `Binding` code could be replaced with the following addition to `currentFolder`'s declaration:

```
<TextBlock x:Name="currentFolder" DockPanel.Dock="Top"
  Text="{Binding ElementName=treeView, Path=SelectedItem.Header}"
  Background="AliceBlue" FontSize="16" />
```

Data binding is now starting to look more attractive than the manual approach! The connection between the source and target properties is not only expressed succinctly, but it's also abstracted away from all procedural code.

TIP

Besides its default constructor, `Binding` has a constructor that accepts `Path` as its single argument. Therefore, you can use alternative markup extension syntax to pass `Path` to the constructor rather than explicitly set the property. In other words, the preceding XAML snippet could also be expressed as follows:

```
<TextBlock x:Name="currentFolder" DockPanel.Dock="Top"
  Text="{Binding SelectedItem.Header, ElementName=treeView}"
  Background="AliceBlue" FontSize="16" />
```

These two approaches are identical except for subtle differences in how namespace prefixes in the property paths are resolved. Explicitly setting the `Path` property is the more reliable approach.

Notice that the XAML snippet uses `Binding`'s `ElementName` property to set the source object rather than `Source`, which was used in the preceding section. Both are valid in either context, but `ElementName` is easier to use from XAML because you only need to give it the source element's name. However, with the introduction of the `x:Reference` markup extension in WPF 4, you could set `Source` as follows:

```
<TextBlock x:Name="currentFolder" DockPanel.Dock="Top"
  Text="{Binding Source={x:Reference TreeView}, Path=SelectedItem.Header}"
  Background="AliceBlue" FontSize="16" />
```

TIP

You can use `Binding`'s `TargetNullValue` property to swap in a pseudo-source value to use for data binding when the real source value is null. For example, this `TextBlock` shows the message "Nothing is selected." rather than an empty string when the source value is `null`:

```
<TextBlock Text="{Binding … TargetNullValue=Nothing is selected.}" …/>
```

Using `TargetNullValue` can also help in more advanced scenarios where objects do not tolerate having their properties set to `null`.

DIGGING DEEPER

Binding's RelativeSource

Another way to specify a data source is by using Binding's RelativeSource property, which refers to an element by its relationship to the target element. The property is of type RelativeSource, which also happens to be a markup extension. Here are some of the ways RelativeSource can be used:

To make the source element equal the target element:

```
{Binding RelativeSource={RelativeSource Self}}
```

To make the source element equal the target element's TemplatedParent (a property discussed in the next chapter):

```
{Binding RelativeSource={RelativeSource TemplatedParent}}
```

To make the source element equal the closest parent of a given type:

```
{Binding RelativeSource={RelativeSource FindAncestor,
  AncestorType={x:Type desiredType}}}
```

To make the source element equal the *n*th closest parent of a given type:

```
{Binding RelativeSource={RelativeSource FindAncestor,
  AncestorLevel=n, AncestorType={x:Type desiredType}}}
```

To make the source element equal the previous data item in a data-bound collection:

```
{Binding RelativeSource={RelativeSource PreviousData}}
```

RelativeSource is especially useful for control templates, discussed in the next chapter. But using RelativeSource with the mode Self is handy for binding one property of an element to another without having to give the element a name. An interesting example is the following Slider, whose ToolTip is bound to its own value:

```
<Slider ToolTip="{Binding RelativeSource={RelativeSource Self}, Path=Value}"/>
```

Binding to Plain .NET Properties

The example with the TreeView and the Label works because both the target and source properties are dependency properties. As discussed in Chapter 3, dependency properties have plumbing for change notification built in. This facility is the key to WPF's ability to keep the target property and source property in sync.

However, WPF supports any .NET property on any .NET object as a data-binding source. For example, imagine that you want to add to the Photo Gallery application a Label that displays the number of photos in the current folder. Rather than manually update the Label with the Count property from the photos collection (of type Photos), you can use data binding to connect the Label's Content with the collection's Count property:

```
<Label x:Name="numItemsLabel"
  Content="{Binding Source={StaticResource photos}, Path=Count}"
  DockPanel.Dock="Bottom"/>
```

13

(Here, the collection is assumed to be defined as a resource so it can be set in XAML via `Source`. `ElementName` is not an option because the collection is not a `FrameworkElement` or `FrameworkContentElement`!) Figure 13.1 shows the result of this addition. Notice that the label says "54" when you really want it to say "54 item(s)." This could be fixed with an adjacent label with a static "item(s)" string as its content or with better approaches, covered later in this chapter.

FIGURE 13.1 Displaying the value of `photos.Count` via data binding in the bottom-left corner of Photo Gallery's main `Window`.

There's a big caveat to using a plain .NET property as a data-binding source, however. Because such properties have no automatic plumbing for change notification, the target is not kept up to date as the source property value changes without doing a little extra work. Therefore, the value displayed in Figure 13.1 does not change as the current folder changes, which is clearly incorrect.

To keep the target and source properties synchronized, the source object must do one of the following:

- Implement the `System.ComponentModel.INotifyPropertyChanged` interface, which has a single `PropertyChanged` event.
- Implement an *`XXX`*`Changed` event, where *`XXX`* is the name of the property whose value changed.

The first technique is recommended, as WPF is optimized for this approach. (WPF only supports *`XXX`*`Changed` events for backward compatibility with older classes.) You could fix Photo Gallery by having the `photos` collection implement `INotifyPropertyChanged`. This would involve intercepting the relevant operations (such as `Add`, `Remove`, `Clear`, and `Insert`) and raising the `PropertyChanged` event. Fortunately, the .NET Framework already has a built-in class that does this work for you! It's called `ObservableCollection`. Therefore, making the binding to `photos.Count` synchronized is a one-line change from this:

```
public class Photos : Collection<Photo>
```

to this:

```
public class Photos : ObservableCollection<Photo>
```

DIGGING DEEPER

How Binding to a Plain .NET Property Works

When retrieving the value of a source property that's a plain .NET property, WPF uses reflection. If the source object implements `ICustomTypeDescriptor`, WPF will leverage it (or more generally, any `TypeDescriptionProvider` registered for the object or its type) to determine which `PropertyDescriptor` to use for the reflection call. Implementing this interface is an advanced technique, but it can be useful for boosting performance or supporting additional scenarios (such as changing the set of properties exposed on the fly).

WARNING

Data sources and data targets aren't treated equally!

Although the source property can be any .NET property on any .NET object, the same is not true for the data-binding target. The target property *must* be a dependency property. Also note that the source member must be a real (and public) property, not just a simple field.

Binding to an Entire Object

Although every example so far has used source objects and source properties, it turns out that the source property (that is, the Path in Binding) is optional! You can bind a target property to the entire source object.

FIGURE 13.2 Displaying the entire photos object via data binding in the bottom-left corner of Photo Gallery's main Window.

But what does it mean to bind to an entire object? Figure 13.2 shows what the Label from Figure 13.1 would look like if the Path were omitted:

```
<Label x:Name="numItemsLabel"
  Content="{Binding Source={StaticResource photos}}"
  DockPanel.Dock="Bottom"/>
```

Because the photos object is not a UIElement, it gets rendered as the string returned from its ToString method. Binding to the whole object is not very useful in this case, but it's essential for elements that can take better advantage of the object, such as the ListBox that we'll examine next.

TIP

Binding to an entire object is a handy technique for setting a property from XAML that requires an instance of an object that can't be obtained via a type converter or markup extension.

For example, Photo Gallery contains a Popup that, when shown, is centered over a Button called zoomButton. Popup enables this with its Placement and PlacementTarget properties, the latter of which must be set to a UIElement. This could easily be done in C# as follows:

```
Button zoomButton = new Button();
...
Popup zoomPopup = new Popup();
zoomPopup.Placement = PlacementMode.Center;
zoomPopup.PlacementTarget = zoomButton;
```

Continued

But instead, Photo Gallery uses the following XAML to accomplish this:

```
<Button x:Name="zoomButton" … >
  …
</Button>
<Popup PlacementTarget="{Binding ElementName=zoomButton}" Placement="Center" …>
  …
</Popup>
```

This technique has been used in previous chapters. Of course, using `x:Reference` in WPF 4 is another way to accomplish this assignment without using `Binding`.

WARNING

Be careful when binding to an entire `UIElement`!

When binding certain target properties to an entire `UIElement`, you might inadvertently be attempting to place the same element in multiple places on the visual tree. For example, the following XAML results in an `InvalidOperationException` explaining, `"Specified element is already the logical child of another element."`

```
<Label x:Name="one" Content="{Binding ElementName=two}"/>
<Label x:Name="two" Content="text"/>
```

However, you get no exception if you change the first `Label` to a `TextBlock` (and, therefore, the `Content` property to `Text`):

```
<TextBlock x:Name="one" Text="{Binding ElementName=two}"/>
<Label x:Name="two" Content="text"/>
```

Whereas `Label.Content` is of type `Object`, `TextBlock.Text` is a string. Therefore, the `Label` undergoes type conversion when assigned to a string and its `ToString` method is called. In this case, the `TextBlock` is rendered with a `"System.Windows.Controls.Label: text"` string, which is still not very useful. To copy the text from one `Label` or `TextBlock` to another, you should really be binding to the specific property (`Label` or `Content`).

Binding to a Collection

Binding a `Label` to `photos.Count` is nice, but it would be even better to bind the `ListBox` (the `Window`'s main piece of user interface) to the `photos` collection. This is the part of the Photo Gallery application that screams the loudest for data binding. The application, as presented in previous chapters, manually maintained the relationship between the collection of photos stored in the `ListBox` and the physical photos. When a new directory is selected, it clears the `ListBox` and creates a new `ListBoxItem` for each photo. If the user decides to delete or rename a photo, the change raises an event on the source collection (because it's internally using `FileSystemWatcher`), and an event handler manually refreshes the `ListBox` contents.

Fortunately, the procedure for replacing such logic with data binding is exactly the same as what we've already seen.

The Raw Binding

It would make sense to create a `Binding` with `ListBox.Items` as the target property, but, alas, `Items` is not a dependency property. But `ListBox` and all other items controls have an `ItemsSource` dependency property that exists specifically for this data-binding scenario. `ItemsSource` is of type `IEnumerable`, so you can use the entire `photos` object as the source and set up the `Binding` as follows:


```
<ListBox x:Name="pictureBox"
  ItemsSource="{Binding Source={StaticResource photos}}" …>
  …
</ListBox>
```

For the target property to stay updated with changes to the source collection (that is, the addition and removal of elements), the source collection must implement an interface called `INotifyCollectionChanged`. Indeed, `ObservableCollection` implements both `INotifyPropertyChanged` and `INotifyCollectionChanged`, so the earlier change to make `Photos` derive from `ObservableCollection<Photo>` is sufficient for making this binding work correctly.

Figure 13.3 shows the result of this data binding.

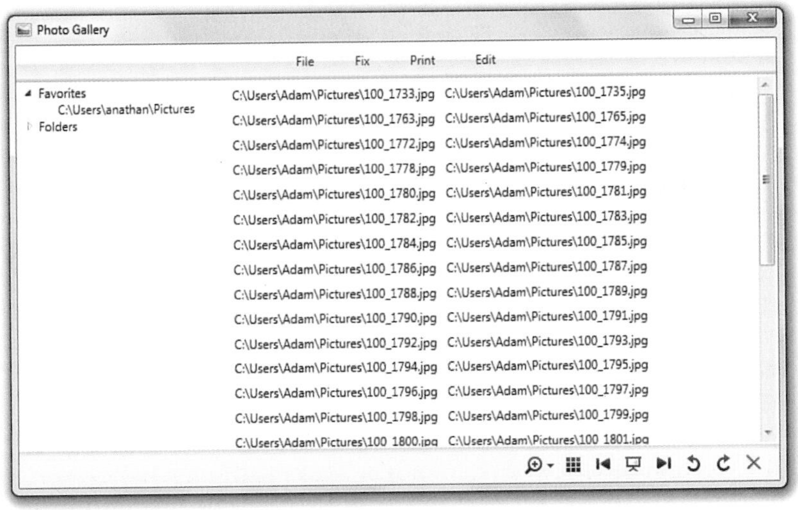

FIGURE 13.3 Binding the `ListBox` to the entire `photos` object shows the data in raw form.

Improving the Display

Clearly, the default display of the `photos` collection—a `ToString` rendering—is not acceptable. One way to improve this is to leverage the `DisplayMemberPath` property present on all items controls, introduced in Chapter 10, "Items Controls." This property works hand in hand with `ItemsSource`. If you set it to an appropriate property path, the corresponding property value gets rendered for each item.

The collection in Photo Gallery consists of application-specific `Photo` objects, which have properties like `Name`, `DateTime`, and `Size`. Therefore, the following XAML produces the results in Figure 13.4, which is a slightly better rendering than Figure 13.3:

```
<ListBox x:Name="pictureBox" DisplayMemberPath="Name"
  ItemsSource="{Binding Source={StaticResource photos}}" …>
  …
</ListBox>
```

However, because we're defining the `Photo` class ourselves, we could have just changed `Photo`'s implementation of `ToString` to return `Name` instead of the full path to get the same results.

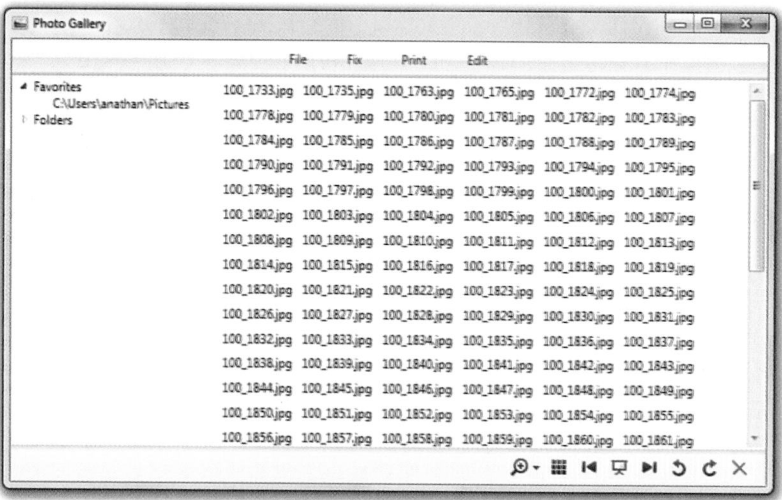

FIGURE 13.4 `DisplayMemberPath` is a simple mechanism for customizing the display of items in a data-bound collection.

For getting the actual images to display in the `ListBox`, you could add an `Image` property to the `Photo` class and use that as the `DisplayMemberPath`. But there are more flexible ways to control the presentation of bound data—ways that don't require changes to the source object. (This is important because you might not be the one defining the source object. Also, don't forget that one of the tenets of WPF is to separate look from logic!) One way (not specific to data binding) is to use a data template, and another way is to use a value converter. The upcoming "Controlling Rendering" section looks at both of these options.

WARNING

ItemsControl's Items and ItemsSource properties can't be modified simultaneously!

You must decide whether you want to populate an items control manually via Items or with data binding via ItemsSource, and you must not mix these techniques. ItemsSource can be set only when the Items collection is empty, and Items can be modified only when ItemsSource is null (otherwise, you'll get an InvalidOperationException). Therefore, if you want to add or remove items to/from a data-bound ListBox, you must do this to the underlying collection (ItemsSource) rather than at the user interface level (Items). Note that regardless of which method is used to *set* items in an items control, you can always *retrieve* items via the Items collection.

Managing the Selected Item

As explained in Chapter 10, Selectors such as ListBox have a notion of a selected item or items. When binding a Selector to a collection (anything that implements IEnumerable), WPF keeps track of the selected item(s) so that other targets binding to the same source can make use of this information without the need for custom logic. This support can be used for creating master/detail user interfaces (as done in the final example in this chapter) or for synchronizing multiple Selectors, which we'll look at now.

To opt in to this support, set the IsSynchronizedWithCurrentItem property (inherited by all Selectors) to true. The following XAML sets this property on three ListBoxes that each displays a single property per item from the same photos collection:

```
<ListBox IsSynchronizedWithCurrentItem="True" DisplayMemberPath="Name"
  ItemsSource="{Binding Source={StaticResource photos}}"></ListBox>
<ListBox IsSynchronizedWithCurrentItem="True" DisplayMemberPath="DateTime"
  ItemsSource="{Binding Source={StaticResource photos}}"></ListBox>
<ListBox IsSynchronizedWithCurrentItem="True" DisplayMemberPath="Size"
  ItemsSource="{Binding Source={StaticResource photos}}"></ListBox>
```

Because each is marked with IsSynchronizedWithCurrentItem="True" and each is pointing to the same source collection, changing the selected item in any of them changes the selected item in the other two to match. (Although note that the scrolling of the ListBoxes is not synchronized automatically!) Figure 13.5 gives an idea of what this looks like. If any one of the ListBoxes omitted IsSynchronizedWithCurrentItem or set it to false, changing its own selected item would not impact the other two ListBoxes, nor would changing the selected item in the other two ListBoxes impact its own selection.

WARNING

IsSynchronizedWithCurrentItem does not support multiple selections!

When a Selector has multiple selected items (as with ListBox's SelectionMode of Multiple or Extended), only the first selected item is seen by other synchronized elements, even if they also support multiple selections!

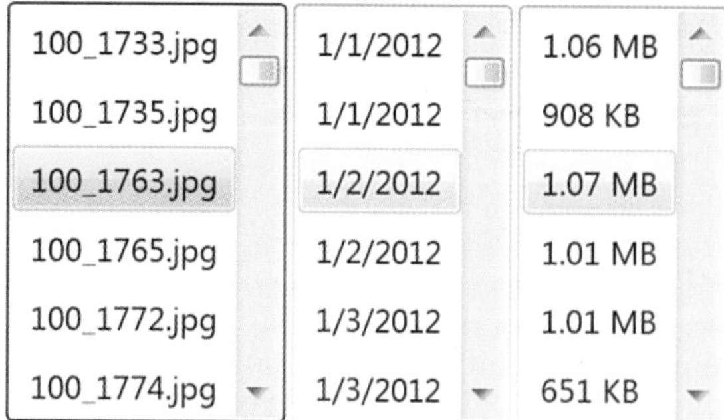

FIGURE 13.5 Three synchronized `ListBox`es, thanks to data binding.

Sharing the Source with `DataContext`

You've now applied data binding to several target properties, and all but one of them used the same source object (the `photos` collection). It's quite common for many elements in the same user interface to bind to the same source object (different source *properties*, but the same source *object*). For this reason, WPF supports specifying an implicit data source rather than explicitly marking every `Binding` with a `Source`, `RelativeSource`, or `ElementName`. This implicit data source is also known as a *data context*.

To designate a source object such as the `photos` collection as a data context, you simply find a common parent element and set its `DataContext` property to the source object. (All `FrameworkElement`s and `FrameworkContentElement`s have this `DataContext` property of type `Object`.) When encountering a `Binding` without an explicit source object, WPF traverses up the logical tree until it finds a non-`null` `DataContext`.

Therefore, you can use `DataContext` as follows to make the `Label` and `ListBox` use it as the source object:

```
<StackPanel DataContext="{StaticResource photos}">
  <Label x:Name="numItemsLabel"
    Content="{Binding Path=Count}" …/>
  …
  <ListBox x:Name="pictureBox" DisplayMemberPath="Name"
    ItemsSource="{Binding}" …>
    …
  </ListBox>
  …
</StackPanel>
```

> **TIP**
>
> Encountering a property set to just `{Binding}` in XAML might look confusing, but it simply means that the source object is specified somewhere up the tree as a data context and that the entire object is being bound rather than a single property on it.

Because `DataContext` is a simple property, it's also really easy to set from procedural code, eliminating the need to store the source object as a resource:

```
parent.DataContext = photos;
```

FAQ

When should I specify a source object using a data context versus specifying it explicitly with Binding?

It's mostly just a matter of personal preference. If a source object is being used by only one target property, using a data context might be a bit of overkill and less readable. But if you are sharing a source object, using a data context to specify the object in only one place makes development less error-prone if you change the source.

One case where the use of a data context is really helpful is when plugging in resources defined elsewhere. Resources can contain Bindings with no explicit source or data context, enabling the binding to be resolved in each *usage context* rather than in the *declaration context*. Each usage context would be the place in the logical tree that the resource is plugged into, which could provide a different data context. (Although using RelativeSource to specify an explicit yet relative source also can provide this kind of flexibility.)

13

Controlling Rendering

Data binding is pretty simple when the source and target properties are compatible data types and the default rendering of the source is all you need to display. But often a bit of customization is required. The need for this in the previous section is obvious, as you want to display Images, not raw strings, in Photo Gallery's ListBox!

These types of customizations would be easy *without* data binding because you're writing all the code to retrieve the data on your own (as done in the original version of Photo Gallery). But WPF provides three mechanisms for customizing how the source value is received and displayed, so you don't need to give up the benefits of data binding to get the desired results in more customized scenarios. These mechanisms are string formatting, data templates, and value converters.

String Formatting

When you want to display a string as a result of data binding, Binding's StringFormat property makes it easy to customize the display. When this is set, WPF will call String.Format with the value of StringFormat as the first parameter (format) and the raw target object as the second parameter (args[0]). Therefore, {0} represents the raw target object, and a variety of format specifiers are supported, such as {0:C} for currency formatting, {0:P} for percent formatting, and {0:X} for hexadecimal formatting.

The Label shown in Figure 13.1 can therefore be changed to say "54 item(s)" instead of just "54" by changing it to a TextBlock and making this simple StringFormat addition to the Binding:

```
<TextBlock x:Name="numItemsLabel"
  Text="{Binding StringFormat={}{0} item(s),
         Source={StaticResource photos}, Path=Count}"
  DockPanel.Dock="Bottom"/>
```

WARNING

Binding's StringFormat only works if the target property is defined as a string!

A major shortcoming of Binding's StringFormat property is that Binding completely ignores it unless the target property is of type string. Attempting to use it with Label's Content property doesn't have any effect because Content is of type Object:

```
<Label x:Name="numItemsLabel"
  Content="{Binding StringFormat={}{0} item(s),
         Source={StaticResource photos}, Path=Count}"
  DockPanel.Dock="Bottom"/>
```

In contrast, TextBlock's Text property is of type string, so the same Binding works just fine when applied to Text. This is why the examples in this section change Label to TextBlock. An alternate workaround is to use Label's ContentStringFormat property, discussed later in this section.

The funky {} at the beginning of the value is there to escape the { at the beginning of the string. Recall from Chapter 2, "XAML Demystified," that without this, the string would be incorrectly interpreted as a markup extension. The {} is not necessary if you use the property element form of Binding:

```
<TextBlock x:Name="numItemsLabel" DockPanel.Dock="Bottom">
<TextBlock.Text>
  <Binding Source="{StaticResource photos}" Path="Count">
  <Binding.StringFormat>{0} item(s)</Binding.StringFormat>
  </Binding>
</TextBlock.Text>
</TextBlock>
```

It is also not necessary if the string doesn't begin with a {:

```
<TextBlock x:Name="numItemsLabel"
  Text="{Binding StringFormat=Number of items: {0},
         Source={StaticResource photos}, Path=Count}"
  DockPanel.Dock="Bottom"/>
```

You could also enhance the formatting with the N0 specifier, which adds thousands-separators without adding any decimal places. So the following Label displays "54 item(s)" when Count is 54 and "1,001 item(s)" when Count is 1,001—at least for the en-US culture:

```
<TextBlock x:Name="numItemsLabel"
  Text="{Binding StringFormat={}{0:N0} item(s),
         Source={StaticResource photos}, Path=Count}"
  DockPanel.Dock="Bottom"/>
```

> **WARNING**
>
> **`System.Xaml` doesn't process the `{}` escape sequence correctly!**
>
> The `System.Xaml` library that is new in WPF 4 has a flaw that breaks the processing of the `{}` escape sequence inside of a markup extension. When processed by `System.Xaml`, the `{}` escape sequence can still be used to escape the *entire* string value of a property (preventing it from being interpreted as a markup extension), but not *within* a markup extension. For example, the following XAML snippet is not correctly parsed by `System.Xaml`:
>
> ```
> <TextBlock Text="{Binding StringFormat={}{0:C}}" />
> ```
>
> Fortunately, `System.Xaml` is not yet used in mainstream scenarios (such as XAML compilation), which limits this bug's impact. The workaround is to use an alternate escape sequence within a markup extension. You can use a backslash to escape individual characters. For example:
>
> ```
> <TextBlock Text="{Binding StringFormat=\{0:C\}}" />
> ```


Many controls have a `XXXStringFormat` property as well, where *XXX* represents the piece that you are formatting. For example, content controls have a `ContentStringFormat` property that applies to the `Content` property, and items controls have an `ItemStringFormat` property that apply to each item in a collection. Table 13.1 lists all the string format properties that are read/write.

TABLE 13.1 String Format Properties Throughout WPF

Property	Classes
`StringFormat`	`BindingBase`
`ContentStringFormat`	`ContentControl`, `ContentPresenter`, `TabControl`
`ItemStringFormat`	`ItemsControl`, `HierarchicalDataTemplate`
`HeaderStringFormat`	`HeaderedContentControl`, `HeaderedItemsControl`, `DataGridColumn`, `GridViewColumn`, `GroupStyle`
`ColumnHeaderStringFormat`	`GridView`, `GridViewHeaderRowPresenter`

Rather than being forced to change `Label` to a `TextBlock` in order to take advantage of `Binding`'s `StringFormat` property, you can instead leverage `Label`'s own `ContentStringFormat` because `Label` is a content control:

```
<Label x:Name="numItemsLabel" ContentStringFormat="{}{0} item(s)"
  Content="{Binding Source={StaticResource photos}, Path=Count}"
  DockPanel.Dock="Bottom"/>
```

You can take advantage of this functionality with or without data binding. Figure 13.6 shows the rendered result of the following `ListBox` for both U.S. English and Korean:

```
<ListBox ItemStringFormat="{}{0:C}"
  xmlns:sys="clr-namespace:System;assembly=mscorlib">
```

```
  <sys:Int32>-9</sys:Int32>
  <sys:Int32>9</sys:Int32>
  <sys:Int32>1234</sys:Int32>
  <sys:Int32>1234567</sys:Int32>
</ListBox>
```

English (United States)	Korean (Korea)
($9.00)	-₩9
$9.00	₩9
$1,234.00	₩1,234
$1,234,567.00	₩1,234,567

FIGURE 13.6 Numbers in a ListBox taking advantage of declarative string formatting.

Using Data Templates

A data template is a piece of user interface that you'd like to apply to an arbitrary .NET object when it is rendered. Many WPF controls have properties (of type `DataTemplate`) for attaching a data template appropriately. For example, `ContentControl` has a `ContentTemplate` property for controlling the rendering of its `Content` object, and `ItemsControl` has an `ItemTemplate` that applies to each of its items. Table 13.2 lists them all. As you can see, WPF defines more *XXX*`Template` properties than *XXX*`StringFormat` properties.

TABLE 13.2 Properties of Type DataTemplate Throughout WPF

Property	Classes
ContentTemplate	ContentControl, ContentPresenter, TabControl
ItemTemplate	ItemsControl, HierarchicalDataTemplate
HeaderTemplate	HeaderedContentControl, HeaderedItemsControl, DataGridRow, DataGridColumn, GridViewColumn, GroupStyle
SelectedContentTemplate	TabControl
DetailsTemplate	DataGridRow
RowDetailsTemplate	DataGrid
RowHeaderTemplate	DataGrid
ColumnHeaderTemplate	GridView, GridViewHeaderRowPresenter
CellTemplate	DataGridTemplateColumn, GridViewColumn
CellEditingTemplate	DataGridTemplateColumn

By setting one of these properties to an instance of a `DataTemplate`, you can swap in a completely new visual tree. `DataTemplate`, like `ItemsPanelTemplate` introduced in Chapter 10, derives from `FrameworkTemplate`. Therefore, it has a `VisualTree` content property that can be set to an arbitrary tree of `FrameworkElement`s. This is easy to set in XAML but cumbersome to set in procedural code.

Let's try using a `DataTemplate` with Photo Gallery's `ListBox`, which in Figure 13.4 shows raw strings rather than `Image`s. The following snippet adds a simple `DataTemplate` by setting `ListBox`'s `ItemTemplate` property inline:

```
<ListBox x:Name="pictureBox"
  ItemsSource="{Binding Source={StaticResource photos}}" …>
<ListBox.ItemTemplate>
```

```
    <DataTemplate>
      <Image Source="placeholder.jpg" Height="35"/>
    </DataTemplate>
  </ListBox.ItemTemplate>
    …
  </ListBox>
```

Figure 13.7 shows that this is a good start. Although a generic `placeholder.jpg` image is shown for each item, at least the items are now `Image`s!

FIGURE 13.7 A simple data template makes each item in the `ListBox` appear as a placeholder `Image`.

With an `Image` data template in place, how do you set its `Source` property to the current `Photo` item's `FullPath` property? With data binding, of course! When you apply a data template, it is implicitly given an appropriate data context (that is, a source object). When applied as an `ItemTemplate`, the data context is implicitly the current item in `ItemsSource`. So, you can simply update the data template as follows to get the result shown in Figure 13.8:

```
<ListBox x:Name="pictureBox"
  ItemsSource="{Binding Source={StaticResource photos}}" …>
<ListBox.ItemTemplate>
  <DataTemplate>
    <Image Source="{Binding Path=FullPath}" Height="35"/>
  </DataTemplate>
</ListBox.ItemTemplate>
  …
</ListBox>
```

FIGURE 13.8 The updated data template gives the desired results—the right photo displayed for each item in the `ListBox`.

Of course, a `DataTemplate` doesn't have to be declared inline. `DataTemplates` are most commonly exposed as resources, so they can be shared by multiple elements. You can even get `DataTemplate` to be automatically applied to a specific type wherever it might appear by setting its `DataType` property to the desired type. If you place such a `DataTemplate` in a `Window`'s `Resources` collection, for example, it automatically gets applied anywhere an item of that data type is rendered inside the `Window`: inside items controls, inside content controls, and so on. If you place such a `DataTemplate` in an `Application`'s `Resources` collection, the same is true for the entire application.

> **TIP**
>
> Although data templates can be used on non-data-bound objects (such as a `ListBox` with a manually constructed set of items), you'll almost always want to use data binding *inside* the template to customize the appearance of the visual tree based on the underlying object(s).

A special subclass of `DataTemplate` exists for working with hierarchical data, such as XML or a file system. This class is called `HierarchicalDataTemplate`. It not only enables you to change the presentation of such data but enables you to directly bind a hierarchy of objects to an element that intrinsically understands hierarchies, such as a `TreeView` or `Menu` control. The "`XmlDataProvider`" section later in this chapter shows an example of using `HierarchicalDataTemplate` with XML data.

DIGGING DEEPER

Template Selectors

Sometimes it can be desirable to heavily customize a data template based on the input data. Although a lot can be done inside a single data template, WPF also provides a mechanism to plug in procedural code that can select any template (or create a new one on-the-fly) at runtime when it is time for the data to be rendered. To do this, you create a class that derives from `DataTemplateSelector` and override its virtual `SelectTemplate` method. You can then associate an instance with the appropriate element by setting that element's *XXX*`TemplateSelector` property. Every *XXX*`Template` property shown in Table 13.2 has a corresponding *XXX*`TemplateSelector` property, as shown in Table 13.3.

TABLE 13.3 Data Template Selector Properties Throughout WPF

Property	Classes
`ContentTemplateSelector`	`ContentControl`, `ContentPresenter`, `TabControl`
`ItemTemplateSelector`	`ItemsControl`, `HierarchicalDataTemplate`
`HeaderTemplateSelector`	`HeaderedContentControl`, `HeaderedItemsControl`, `DataGridRow`, `DataGridColumn`, `GridViewColumn`, `GroupStyle`
`SelectedContentTemplateSelector`	`TabControl`
`DetailsTemplateSelector`	`DataGridRow`
`RowDetailsTemplateSelector`	`DataGrid`
`RowHeaderTemplateSelector`	`DataGrid`
`ColumnHeaderTemplateSelector`	`GridView`, `GridViewHeaderRowPresenter`
`CellTemplateSelector`	`DataGridTemplateColumn`, `GridViewColumn`
`CellEditingTemplateSelector`	`DataGridTemplateColumn`

Using Value Converters

Whereas data templates can customize the way certain target values are rendered, value converters can morph a source value into a completely different target value. They enable you to plug in custom logic without giving up the benefits of data binding.

Value converters are often used to reconcile a source and target that are different data types. For example, you could change the background or foreground color of an element based on the value of some non-`Brush` data source, much like conditional formatting in Microsoft Excel. Or you could use it to simply enhance the information being displayed, without the need for separate elements. The following two sections explore examples of each of these.

Bridging Incompatible Data Types

Imagine that you want to change the `Label`'s `Background` based on the number of items in the `photos` collection (the value of its `Count` property). The following `Binding` makes no sense because it tries to assign `Background` to a number rather than to a `Brush`:

```
<Label Background="{Binding Path=Count, Source={StaticResource photos}}" …/>
```

To fix this, you can plug in a value converter using Binding's Converter property:

```
<Label Background="{Binding Path=Count, Converter={StaticResource myConverter},
  Source={StaticResource photos}}" …/>
```

This assumes that you've written a custom class that can convert an integer into a Brush and defined it as a resource:

```
<Window.Resources>
  <local:CountToBackgroundConverter x:Key="myConverter"/>
</Window.Resources>
```

To create this class called CountToBackgroundConverter, you must implement a simple interface called IValueConverter (in the System.Windows.Data namespace). This interface has two simple methods—Convert, which is passed the source instance that must be converted to the target instance, and ConvertBack, which does the opposite.

Therefore, CountToBackgroundConverter could be implemented in C# as follows:

```
public class CountToBackgroundConverter : IValueConverter
{
  public object Convert(object value, Type targetType, object parameter,
    CultureInfo culture)
  {
    if (targetType != typeof(Brush))
      throw new InvalidOperationException("The target must be a Brush!");

    // Let Parse throw an exception if the input is bad
    int num = int.Parse(value.ToString());

    return (num == 0 ? Brushes.Yellow : Brushes.Transparent);
  }
  public object ConvertBack(object value, Type targetType, object parameter,
    CultureInfo culture)
  {
    return DependencyProperty.UnsetValue;
  }
}
```

The Convert method is called every time the source value changes. It's given the integral value and returns Brushes.Yellow if the value is zero, or Brushes.Transparent otherwise. (The idea is to highlight the Label's background when an empty folder is displayed.) The ConvertBack method is not needed, so CountToBackgroundConverter simply returns a dummy value if it's ever called. Part VI, "Advanced Topics," discusses situations in which ConvertBack is used. Figure 13.9 shows CountToBackgroundConverter in action.

FIGURE 13.9 The value converter makes the Label's Background yellow when there are no items in the photos collection, seen in the bottom-left corner of Photo Gallery's main Window.

TIP

To avoid confusion, it's a good idea to capture the semantics of a value converter in its name. I could have named CountToBackgroundConverter something like IntegerToBrushConverter because technically it can be used anyplace where the source data type is an integer and the target data type is a Brush. But it might make sense only when the source integer represents a count of items and when the Brush represents a Background. (For example, it's unlikely that you'd ever want to set an element's Foreground to Transparent!) You might also want to define additional Integer-to-Brush converters with alternate semantics.

The methods of IValueConverter are passed a parameter and a culture. By default, parameter is set to null and culture is set to the value of the target element's Language property. This Language property (defined on FrameworkElement and FrameworkContentElement, whose value is often inherited from the root element, if set at all) uses "en-US" (U.S. English) as its default value. However, the consumer of Bindings can control these two values via Binding.ConverterParameter and Binding.ConverterCulture. For example, rather than hard-code Brushes.Yellow inside CountToBackgroundConverter.Convert, you could set it to the user-supplied parameter:

```
return (num == 0 ? parameter : Brushes.Transparent);
```

This assumes that parameter is always set as follows:

```
<Label Background="{Binding Path=Count, Converter={StaticResource myConverter},
  ConverterParameter=Yellow, Source={StaticResource photos}}" Content="…" />
```

Setting ConverterParameter to the simple "Yellow" string works, but the reason is subtle. Like all markup extension parameters, "Yellow" undergoes type conversion, but only to the type of the ConverterParameter property (Object). Therefore, Convert receives parameter as the raw "Yellow" string rather than a Brush. Because Convert does nothing with parameter other than return it when num is not zero, it ends up returning a string. At this point, the binding engine does the type conversion in order to make the assignment to Label's Background property work.

ConverterCulture could be set to an Internet Engineering Task Force (IETF) language tag (for example, "ko-KR"), and the converter would receive the appropriate CultureInfo object.

TIP

WPF ships with a handful of value converters to handle a few very common data-binding scenarios. One of these is BooleanToVisibilityConverter, which converts between the three-state Visibility enumeration (which can be Visible, Hidden, or Collapsed) and a Boolean or nullable Boolean. In one direction, true is mapped to Visible, whereas false and null are mapped to Collapsed. In the other direction, Visible is mapped to true, whereas Hidden and Collapsed are mapped to false.

Continued

This is useful for toggling the visibility of elements based on the state of an otherwise unrelated element. For example, the following snippet of XAML implements a Show Status Bar `CheckBox` without requiring any procedural code:

```
<Window.Resources>
  <BooleanToVisibilityConverter x:Key="booltoVis"/>
</Window.Resources>
…
<CheckBox x:Name="checkBox">Show Status Bar</CheckBox>
…
<StatusBar Visibility="{Binding ElementName=checkBox, Path=IsChecked,
  Converter={StaticResource booltoVis}}">…</StatusBar>
```

In this case, the `StatusBar` is visible when (and only when) the `CheckBox`'s `IsChecked` property is `true`.

WARNING

Data-binding errors don't appear as unhandled exceptions!

Instead of throwing exceptions on data-binding errors, WPF dumps explanatory text via debug traces that can be seen only with an attached debugger (or other trace listeners). Therefore, when data binding doesn't work as expected, try running it under a debugger and be sure to check for traces. In Visual Studio, these can be found in the Output window. In Visual Studio 2010 Ultimate, these can also be integrated into the handy IntelliTrace window.

The previous example of a nonsensical binding (hooking up `Background` directly to `photos.Count`) produces the following debug trace:

```
System.Windows.Data Error: 5 : Value produced by BindingExpression is not valid
for target property.; Value='39' BindingExpression:Path=Count; DataItem='Photos'
(HashCode=58961324); target element is 'Label' (Name='numItemsLabel'); target
property is 'Background' (type 'Brush')
```

Even exceptions thrown by the source object (or value converter) get swallowed and displayed as debug traces by default!

Because the tracing is implemented with `System.Diagnostics.TraceSource` objects, there are several standard options for capturing these same traces outside the debugger. Mike Hillberg, a WPF architect, shares details at http://blogs.msdn.com/mikehillberg/archive/2006/09/14/WpfTraceSources.aspx. You can capture traces WPF emits in a number of areas (that aren't even enabled by default under a debugger), such as information about event routing, dependency property registration, resource retrieval, and much more.

You can also use the `PresentationTraceSources.TraceLevel` attached property (from the `System.Diagnostics` namespace in the `WindowsBase` assembly) on any `Binding` to increase or remove the trace information emitted for that specific binding. It can be set to a value from the `PresentationTraceLevel` enumeration: `None`, `Low`, `Medium`, or `High`.

Customizing Data Display

Sometimes, value converters are useful in cases where the source and target data types are already compatible. Earlier, when we set the Content of numItemsLabel to the Count property of the photos collection (shown in Figure 13.1), it displayed just fine but required some additional text for the user to not be confused by what that number means. The use of StringFormat fixed that problem, but we can do better than a static " item(s)" suffix. (I don't know about you, but when I see a user interface report something like "1 item(s)," it just looks lazy to me.)

A value converter enables us to customize the text based on the value, so we can display "1 item" (singular) versus "2 items" (plural). The following RawCountToDescriptionConverter does just that:

```
public class RawCountToDescriptionConverter : IValueConverter
{
  public object Convert(object value, Type targetType, object parameter,
    CultureInfo culture)
  {
    // Let Parse throw an exception if the input is bad
    int num = int.Parse(value.ToString());
    return num + (num == 1 ? " item" : " items");
  }
  public object ConvertBack(object value, Type targetType, object parameter,
    CultureInfo culture)
  {
    return
      DependencyProperty.UnsetValue;
  }
}
```

Note that this uses hard-coded English strings, whereas a production-quality converter would use a localizable resource (or at least make use of the passed-in culture parameter).

TIP

Value converters are the key to plugging in any kind of custom logic into the data-binding process that goes beyond basic formatting. Whether you want to apply some sort of transformation to the source value before displaying it or change how the target gets updated based on the value of the source, you can easily accomplish this with a class that implements IValueConverter.

TIP

You can make a value converter temporarily cancel a data binding by returning the sentinel value Binding.DoNothing. This is different from returning null, as null might be a perfectly valid value for the target property.

Binding.DoNothing effectively means, "I don't want to bind right now; pretend the Binding doesn't exist." In this case, the value of the target property doesn't change from its current value unless there's some other entity that happens to be influencing its value (an animation, a trigger, and so on). This only affects the current call to Convert or ConvertBack, so unless the Binding is cleared (via a call to ClearBinding, for example), the value converter will continue to be called every time the source value changes.

FAQ

How do I use a value converter to perform a conversion on each item when binding to a collection?

You can apply a data template to the ItemsControl's ItemTemplate property and then apply value converters to any Bindings done inside the data template. If you were to apply the value converter to the ItemsControl's Binding instead, an update to the source collection would prompt the Convert method to be called once for the entire collection (not on a per-item basis). You could implement such a converter that accepts a collection and returns a morphed collection, but that would not be a very efficient approach.

Customizing the View of a Collection

In the previous "Binding to a Collection" section, you saw that with the flip of a switch (setting IsSynchronizedWithCurrentItem to true), multiple Selectors pointing to the same source collection can see the same selected item. This behavior seems almost magical, at least when you're watching it in person. (It's hard to capture the synchronized motion in a static screenshot!) The source collection has no notion of a current item, so where is this information coming from, and where is the state being maintained?

It turns out that whenever you bind to a collection (anything that implements IEnumerable), a default *view* is implicitly inserted between the source and target objects. This view (which is an object implementing the ICollectionView interface) stores the notion of a current item, but it also has support for sorting, grouping, filtering, and navigating items. This section digs into these four topics as well as working with multiple views for the same source object.

TIP

Views are automatically associated with each source collection, not with the targets consuming the source. The result is that changes to the view (such as sorting or filtering it) are automatically seen by all targets.

Sorting

ICollectionView has a SortDescriptions property that provides a way to control how the view's items are sorted. The basic idea is that you choose a property on the collection items to sort by (such as Name, DateTime, or Size on the Photo object) and you choose whether you want that property to be sorted in ascending or descending order. This choice is captured by a SortDescription object, which you can construct with a property name and a ListSortDirection. Here's an example:

```
SortDescription sort = new SortDescription("Name", ListSortDirection.Ascending);
```

The SortDescriptions property, however, is a *collection* of SortDescription objects. It was designed this way so you can sort by multiple properties simultaneously. The first SortDescription in the collection represents the most significant property, and the last

SortDescription represents the least significant property. For example, if you add the following two SortDescriptions to the collection, the items get sorted in descending order by DateTime, but if there are any ties, the Name (in ascending order) is used as the tiebreaker:

```
view.SortDescriptions.Add(new SortDescription("DateTime",
  ListSortDirection.Descending));
view.SortDescriptions.Add(new SortDescription("Name",
  ListSortDirection.Ascending));
```

The SortDescriptions collection has a Clear method for returning the view to the default sort. A view's default sort is simply the order in which items are placed in the source collection, which might not be sorted at all!

Listing 13.1 demonstrates how Photo Gallery could implement logic to sort its photos by Name, DateTime, or Size when the user clicks a corresponding Button. As in Windows Explorer, a repeated click toggles the sort between ascending and descending.

LISTING 13.1 Sorting by Three Different Properties

```
// Click event handlers for three different Buttons:
void sortByName_Click(object sender, RoutedEventArgs e)
{
  SortHelper("Name");
}
void sortByDateTime_Click(object sender, RoutedEventArgs e)
{
  SortHelper("DateTime");
}
void sortBySize_Click(object sender, RoutedEventArgs e)
{
  SortHelper("Size");
}

void SortHelper(string propertyName)
{
  // Get the default view
  ICollectionView view = CollectionViewSource.GetDefaultView(
    this.FindResource("photos"));

  // Check if the view is already sorted ascending by the current property
  if (view.SortDescriptions.Count > 0
      && view.SortDescriptions[0].PropertyName == propertyName
      && view.SortDescriptions[0].Direction == ListSortDirection.Ascending)
  {
    // Already sorted ascending, so "toggle" by sorting descending
    view.SortDescriptions.Clear();
```

LISTING 13.1 Continued

```
    view.SortDescriptions.Add(new SortDescription(
      propertyName, ListSortDirection.Descending));
  }
  else
  {
    // Sort ascending
    view.SortDescriptions.Clear();
    view.SortDescriptions.Add(new SortDescription(
      propertyName, ListSortDirection.Ascending));
  }
}
```

Notice that this code has no explicit relationship with the `ListBox` displaying the photos. The view being operated on is associated with the source `photos` collection and is retrieved by a simple call to the static `CollectionViewSource.GetDefaultView` method. Indeed, if additional items controls were bound to the same `photos` collection, they would pick up the same view by default and would all sort together.

DIGGING DEEPER

Custom Sorting

If you want more control over the sorting process than what `ICollectionView.SortDescriptions` gives you (which seems unlikely), you can usually take advantage of custom sorting support. If the underlying collection implements `IList` (as most collections do), the `ICollectionView` returned by `CollectionViewSource.GetDefaultView` is actually an instance of the `ListCollectionView` class. If you can cast the `ICollectionView` to a `ListCollectionView`, you can assign a custom object implementing `IComparer` to its `CustomSort` property. When this is done, your implementation of `IComparer.Compare` will be called to determine the sort order. Inside the `Compare` method, you can use any method you want for sorting the items.

Grouping

`ICollectionView` has a `GroupDescriptions` property that works much like `SortDescriptions`. You can add any number of `PropertyGroupDescription` objects to it to arrange the source collection's items into groups and potential subgroups.

For example, the following code groups items in the `photos` collection by the value of their `DateTime` property:

```
// Get the default view
ICollectionView view = CollectionViewSource.GetDefaultView(
  this.FindResource("photos"));
// Do the grouping
```

```
view.GroupDescriptions.Clear();
view.GroupDescriptions.Add(new PropertyGroupDescription("DateTime"));
```

Unlike with sorting, however, the effects of grouping are not noticeable unless you modify the items control displaying the data. To get grouping to behave properly, you must set the items control's `GroupStyle` property to an instance of a `GroupStyle` object. This object has a `HeaderTemplate` property that should be set to a data template defining the look of the grouping header.

Photo Gallery's `ListBox` could be given the following `GroupStyle` to support the preceding grouping code:

```
<ListBox x:Name="pictureBox"
  ItemsSource="{Binding Source={StaticResource photos}}" …>
<ListBox.GroupStyle>
  <GroupStyle>
    <GroupStyle.HeaderTemplate>
      <DataTemplate>
        <Border BorderBrush="Black" BorderThickness="1">
          <TextBlock Text="{Binding Path=Name}" FontWeight="Bold"/>
        </Border>
      </DataTemplate>
    </GroupStyle.HeaderTemplate>
  </GroupStyle>
</ListBox.GroupStyle>
  …
</ListBox>
```

Notice the use of data binding inside the data template. In this case, the data template is given a data context of a special `CollectionViewGroup` object that's instantiated behind the scenes. The details of this class aren't important aside from the fact that it has a `Name` property representing the value defining each group. Therefore, the data template uses data binding to display this `Name` in the grouping header. Figure 13.10 shows the result of running the preceding code with the updated XAML.

TIP

If you want to group items of an items control but don't care about creating a fancy `GroupStyle`, you can use a built-in `GroupStyle` that ships with WPF. It's exposed as a static `GroupStyle.Default` property. Therefore, you can reference it in XAML as follows:

```
<ListBox x:Name="pictureBox"
  ItemsSource="{Binding Source={StaticResource photos}}" …>
<ListBox.GroupStyle>
  <x:Static Member="GroupStyle.Default"/>
</ListBox.GroupStyle>
  …
</ListBox>
```

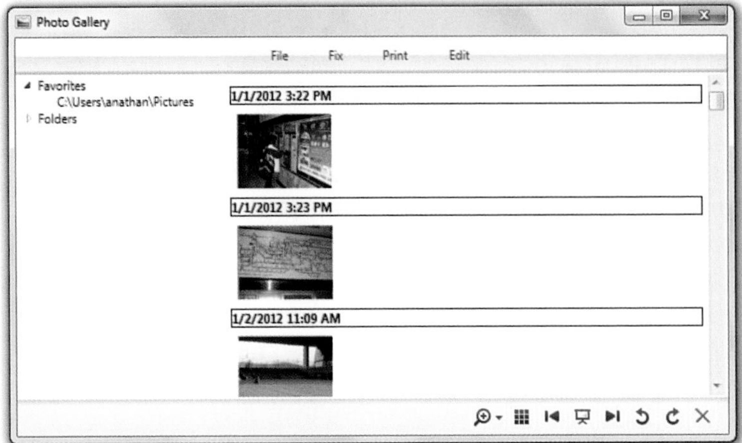

FIGURE 13.10 A first attempt at grouping items in the `ListBox`.

After doing this, you see that perhaps grouping by `Photo.DateTime` is not a great idea. Because `DateTime` includes both a date and a time, each `Photo` tends to have a unique value, leaving many groups of one!

To fix this, you can leverage an overloaded constructor of the `PropertyGroupDescription` class that enables you to tweak the property value before using it as the basis for grouping. To do this, the constructor allows you to pass in a value converter. Therefore, you can write a `DateTimeToDateConverter` class that converts the raw `DateTime` into a string more suitable for grouping:

```
public class DateTimeToDateConverter : IValueConverter
{
  public object Convert(object value, Type targetType, object parameter,
    CultureInfo culture)
  {
    return ((DateTime)value).ToString("MM/dd/yyyy");
  }
  public object ConvertBack(object value, Type targetType, object parameter,
    CultureInfo culture)
  {
    return DependencyProperty.UnsetValue;
  }
}
```

In this case, the returned string simply strips out the time component of the input `DateTime`. Group names don't have to be strings, however, so `Convert` could alternatively strip out the time as follows and return the `DateTime` instance directly:

```
return ((DateTime)value).Date;
```

You could imagine supporting much fancier groupings with this mechanism, such as calculating date ranges and returning strings such as "Last Week", "Last Month", and so on. (Again, you should use the passed-in culture to tweak the formatting of the returned string.)

With this value converter defined, you can use it for grouping as follows:

```
// Get the default view
ICollectionView view = CollectionViewSource.GetDefaultView(
  this.FindResource("photos"));
// Do the grouping
view.GroupDescriptions.Clear();
view.GroupDescriptions.Add(
  new PropertyGroupDescription("DateTime", new DateTimeToDateConverter()));
```


The result of this change is shown in Figure 13.11.

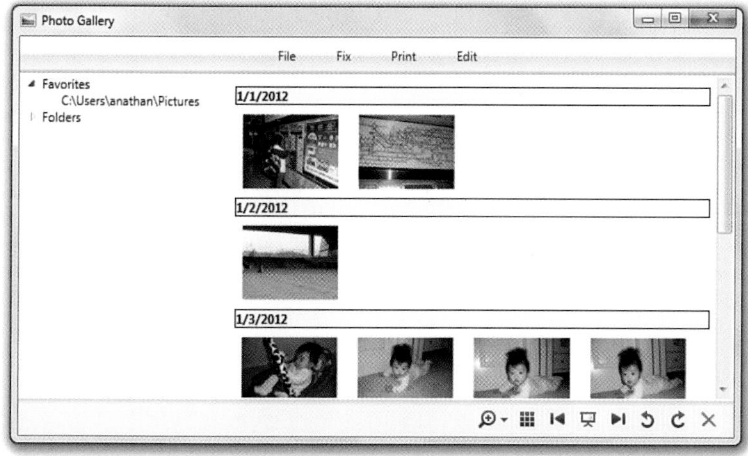

FIGURE 13.11 Improved grouping, based on the date component of `Photo.DateTime`.

To sort groups, you can use the same mechanism described in the preceding section. Sorting is always applied before grouping. The result is that the primary `SortDescription` applies to the groups, and any remaining `SortDescriptions` apply to items within each group. Just make sure that the property (or custom logic) used to do the sorting matches the property (or custom logic) used to do the grouping; otherwise, the resulting arrangement of items is not intuitive.

TIP

Perhaps you want to implement custom grouping based on the values of several properties. You can accomplish this by constructing `PropertyGroupDescription` with a `null` property name. When you do this, the `value` parameter passed to your value converter is the entire source item (a `Photo` object, in the Photo Gallery example) rather than a single property value.

Filtering

As with sorting and grouping, `ICollectionView` has a property that enables *filtering*—selective removal of items based on an arbitrary condition. This property is called `Filter`, and it is a `Predicate<Object>` type (in other words, a delegate that accepts a single `Object` parameter and returns a Boolean).

When `Filter` is `null` (which it is by default), all items in the source collection are shown in the view. But when it's set to a delegate, the delegate is instantly called back for every item in the source collection. The delegate's job is to determine whether each item should be shown (by returning `true`) or hidden (by returning `false`).

By using an anonymous delegate in C#, you can specify a filter pretty compactly. For example, the following code filters out all `Photo` items whose `DateTime` is older than 7 days ago:

```
ICollectionView view = CollectionViewSource.GetDefaultView(this.FindResource
  ("photos"));
view.Filter = delegate(object o) {
  return ((o as Photo).DateTime - DateTime.Now).Days <= 7;
};
```

Although it can be hard for people to parse, you can express this even more compactly with a C# lambda expression:

```
ICollectionView view = CollectionViewSource.GetDefaultView(this.FindResource
  ("photos"));
view.Filter = (o) => { return ((o as Photo).DateTime - DateTime.Now).Days <= 7;};
```

To remove the filter, you simply set `view.Filter` back to `null`.

Navigating

In this context, *navigating* a view refers to managing the current item—not the kind of navigation discussed in Chapter 7, "Structuring and Deploying an Application." `ICollectionView` not only has a `CurrentItem` property (and a corresponding `CurrentPosition` property that exposes the current item's zero-based index), but it also has a handful of methods for programmatically changing the `CurrentItem`. The data-binding version of Photo Gallery uses these methods to implement handlers for the Next Photo/Previous Photo `Button`s, as follows:

```
void previous_Click(object sender, RoutedEventArgs e)
{
  // Get the default view
  ICollectionView view = CollectionViewSource.GetDefaultView(
    this.FindResource("photos"));
  // Move backward
  view.MoveCurrentToPrevious();
  // Wrap around to the end
```

```
  if (view.IsCurrentBeforeFirst) view.MoveCurrentToLast();
}
void next_Click(object sender, RoutedEventArgs e)
{
  // Get the default view
  ICollectionView view = CollectionViewSource.GetDefaultView(
    this.FindResource("photos"));
  // Move forward
  view.MoveCurrentToNext();
  // Wrap around to the beginning
  if (view.IsCurrentAfterLast) view.MoveCurrentToFirst();
}
```


Although a bit wordy, these navigation methods are straightforward to use. These handlers not only update the selected item in the `ListBox` without explicitly referencing it, but any additional elements that wish to display information about the current item can be automatically updated as well, as long as they bind to the same source. Note that until an item is selected on the source collection, `CurrentItem` is `null` and `CurrentPosition` is `-1`. However, this is only true because the `ListBox` made it so. On its own, the collection view initializes `CurrentPosition` to `0` and `CurrentItem` to the first item.

TIP

Property paths used in `Binding`s support referencing a collection's current item with special forward-slash syntax. For example, the following `Binding` binds to the current item, assuming that the data source is a collection:

`"{Binding Path=/}"`

The following binds to the `DateTime` property on the current item:

`"{Binding Path=/DateTime}"`

The following binds to the current item of a collection exposed by a property called `Photos` on a different data source that isn't a collection itself:

`"{Binding Path=Photos/}"`

Finally, the following binds to the `DateTime` property on the current item from the preceding example:

`"{Binding Path=Photos/DateTime}"`

This functionality is incredibly useful for implementing master/detail user interfaces without any procedural code.

> **WARNING**
>
> **Default view navigation isn't exposed automatically!**
>
> Unlike sorting, grouping, and filtering, the effects of navigation on the default view can be seen only on a `Selector` that has `IsSynchronizedWithCurrentItem` set to `true`. Without this setting, `Selector`'s `SelectedItem` and the default view's `CurrentItem` are detached; they can be updated independently without affecting one another. The WPF team wanted synchronization of the selected item to be an explicit choice to expose developers to the concept of a view and avoid potentially confusing behavior. But frankly, I find the inconsistency with the other "automatic" aspects of the default view to be confusing.

Working with Additional Views

The previous examples of sorting, grouping, filtering, and navigating always operated on the default view associated with the source collection. But it's conceivable that you might want elements to have *different* views of the same source collection. It turns out that the `CollectionViewSource` class has more uses than just returning the default view; it can also construct a brand-new view over any source. This view can then be selectively applied to any target, overriding the default view.

To create a new view over Photo Gallery's `photos` collection, you could do the following:

```
CollectionViewSource viewSource = new CollectionViewSource();
viewSource.Source = photos;
// viewSource.View now points to a nondefault ICollectionView implementation
```

`CollectionViewSource` is designed to make it easy to create custom views declaratively, so you can use the following XAML instead:

```
<Window.Resources>
  <local:Photos x:Key="photos"/>
  <CollectionViewSource x:Key="viewSource" Source="{StaticResource photos}"/>
</Window.Resources>
```

To apply the custom view to a target property, simply bind to the `CollectionViewSource` rather than the underlying source object:

```
<ListBox x:Name="pictureBox"
  ItemsSource="{Binding Source={StaticResource photos viewSource}}" …>
  …
</ListBox>
```

Note that although the original source is now wrapped by a `CollectionViewSource`, WPF special-cases the `CollectionViewSource` class so that you don't have to change any `Binding Paths`. Binding to the `Count` property, for example, still refers to the property of the underlying `Photos` object rather than the `CollectionViewSource` object.

Such a ListBox is now exempt from any sorting, grouping, filtering, or navigating being done on the default view. If you want to perform any of these actions on the custom view, you can follow all the same techniques outlined previously using the ICollectionView returned by the CollectionViewSource.View instance property rather than the CollectionViewSource.GetDefaultView static method.

To enable a custom view to be configured with sorting and grouping entirely within XAML, CollectionViewSource has its own SortDescriptions and GroupDescriptions properties that work just like the corresponding properties on ICollectionView. It also has its own Filter member, but it's defined as an event rather than a delegate property so it can also be set inside XAML. (Of course, it must be set to an event handler written in procedural code.) Sorting, grouping, and filtering can, therefore, all be expressed in XAML as follows:


```
<CollectionViewSource x:Key="viewSource" Filter="viewSource_Filter"
  Source="{StaticResource photos}">
<CollectionViewSource.SortDescriptions>
  <componentModel:SortDescription PropertyName="DateTime" Direction="Descending"/>
</CollectionViewSource.SortDescriptions>
<CollectionViewSource.GroupDescriptions>
  <PropertyGroupDescription PropertyName="DateTime"/>
</CollectionViewSource.GroupDescriptions>
</CollectionViewSource>
```

Filtering

Sorting

Grouping

The SortDescription class happens to live in a .NET namespace not included in the standard XML namespace, so the following directive is needed:

```
xmlns:componentModel="clr-namespace:System.ComponentModel;assembly=WindowsBase"
```

The viewSource_Filter method referenced by the XAML could be implemented as follows, which is a translation of the previous filtering delegate that excludes all photos older than seven days from today's date:

```
void viewSource_Filter(object sender, FilterEventArgs e)
{
  e.Accepted = ((e.Item as Photo).DateTime - DateTime.Now).Days <= 7;
}
```

Rather than getting the source item passed in directly, the event handler receives it as e.Item. Rather than *return* a Boolean, it must set the Boolean e.Accepted property to communicate whether the item is in or out.

TIP

Even if you don't require multiple views of the same source collection, you can opt to create and apply a custom view with the explicit CollectionViewSource simply so you can sort and group items without any procedural code!

FAQ

If my application contains a collection, and nobody ever data binds directly to it (but rather to a `CollectionViewSource`), does the default view still exist?

No. For performance reasons, the default view is created on demand. This is unlike a tree falling in a forest, which I'm told still makes a sound even if nobody is around to hear it.

WARNING

Navigation works differently in a custom view!

Changing the current item on a custom view automatically impacts any `Selectors` binding to that view by default; the `Selector`'s `IsSynchronizedWithCurrentItem` property must be explicitly set to `false` in order to opt out of the synchronized navigation. This is opposite the behavior of the default view!

Although the default value for `IsSynchronizedWithCurrentItem` is `false`, WPF automatically sets it to `true` when a `Selector`'s `ItemsSource` is set to a custom view unless it has been given an explicit value (or the `Selector`'s `SelectionMode` isn't `Single`). The idea is that using a custom view is an explicit acknowledgment of the view's existence, so you should get the expected view navigation behavior by default. (These shenanigans are yet another reason I wish that `IsSynchronizedWithCurrentItem` defaulted to `true` for all views.)

Data Providers

Because the source object can be any arbitrary .NET object, you can perform just about any data binding imaginable with enough code. You could bind to a database, the Windows Registry, an Excel spreadsheet, and so on. All you need is an appropriate .NET object that exposes the right set of properties and notifications and handles all the messy implementation details! (That said, the work involved in creating such code might outweigh the benefits of data binding if you're writing everything yourself!)

To cut down on the need for custom code, WPF ships with two classes that provide a generic "data binding–friendly" way to expose common items: `XmlDataProvider` and `ObjectDataProvider`.

TIP

Starting with WPF 3.5 SP1, data binding works really well with Language Integrated Query (LINQ). You can set a `Binding`'s `Source` (or an element's `DataContext`) to a LINQ query, and the enumerable result can be used just like any other collection. Therefore, with the existence of LINQ to SQL, LINQ to XML, and more, using LINQ—rather than WPF's data provider classes—is an easy way to bind to database tables, XML content, and more.

`XmlDataProvider`

The `XmlDataProvider` class provides an easy way to bind data to a chunk of XML, whether it's an in-memory fragment or a complete file. Listing 13.2 shows an example of using `XmlDataProvider` to bind to an embedded data island.

LISTING 13.2 Binding to an Embedded XML Data Island

```
<Window xmlns="http://schemas.microsoft.com/winfx/2006/xaml/presentation"
        xmlns:x="http://schemas.microsoft.com/winfx/2006/xaml"
        Title="XML Data Binding">
  <Window.Resources>
    <XmlDataProvider x:Key="dataProvider" XPath="GameStats">
      <x:XData>
        <GameStats xmlns="">
          <!-- One stat per game type -->
          <GameStat Type="Beginner">
            <HighScore>1203</HighScore>
          </GameStat>
          <GameStat Type="Intermediate">
            <HighScore>1089</HighScore>
          </GameStat>
          <GameStat Type="Advanced">
            <HighScore>541</HighScore>
          </GameStat>
        </GameStats>
      </x:XData>
    </XmlDataProvider>
  </Window.Resources>
  <Grid>
    <ListBox ItemsSource="{Binding Source={StaticResource dataProvider},
     XPath=GameStat/HighScore}" />
  </Grid>
</Window>
```

XML data island

Binding to the XML

The XML data island is set as `XmlDataProvider`'s content property and contained within the `XData` element, which is a requirement to distinguish it from the surrounding XAML. (You get a compiler error if you omit the `XData` tags.) The `XmlDataProvider`'s `XPath` property is set to an `XPath` query that tells it where the relevant data resides inside the XML tree. `XPath`, short for XML Path Language, is a W3C Recommendation published at http://www.w3.org/TR/xpath.

> **TIP**
>
> When embedding an XML data island inside XAML, you should mark its root node with an empty `xmlns` attribute, as done in Listing 13.2. Otherwise, the elements get polluted with the default namespace (`http://schemas.microsoft.com/winfx/2006/xaml/presentation` in this example), preventing XPath queries from working as expected.

The consumption of the `XmlDataProvider` looks like the consumption of any source object, except that `Binding`'s `XPath` property is used rather than `Path` to extract the relevant pieces of the source. This listing uses `XPath` to display the content of each `HighScore` node as an item in the `ListBox`, as shown in Figure 13.12.

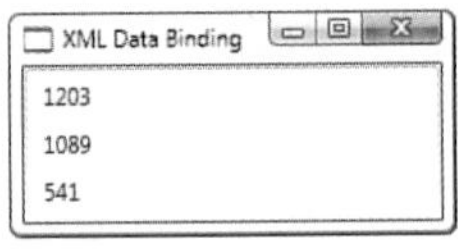

FIGURE 13.12
The result of the XML data binding performed in Listing 13.2.

If the XML resides in a separate file (which is usually the case), you can simply set `XmlDataProvider`'s `Source` property to the appropriate uniform resource identifier (URI) rather than setting its content property. Just like other URIs, this could refer to a local file, a file from the Internet, an embedded resource, and so on. For Listing 13.2, you could replace the `XmlDataProvider` with the following:

```
<XmlDataProvider x:Key="dataProvider" XPath="GameStats" Source="GameStats.xml"/>
```

XPath is a powerful query language—much more powerful than the property paths used in previous bindings. For example, Listing 13.2 could set `XPath` to `"GameStat/@Type"` to fill the `ListBox` with the values of each `GameStat`'s `Type` attribute (Beginner, Intermediate, and Advanced). It could even use the expression `"comment()"` to show the contents of the first XML comment!

DIGGING DEEPER

Interactions Between XPath and Path

You can use `XPath` `XPath` and `Path` simultaneously on the same `Binding`. The XML data provided by `XmlDataProvider` is in the form of objects defined in `System.Xml.dll` (in the `System.Xml` namespace), such as `XmlNode`. This is important to know if you're interacting with the data programmatically, and it also means that you can give `Binding` a `Path` that refers to the current `XmlNode` or `XmlNodeList` instance retrieved. For example, the following `Label` uses `XmlNode`'s `OuterXml` property to display `<HighScore>1203</HighScore>` rather than simply `1203` when used with the previously defined data provider:

```
<Label Content="{Binding Source={StaticResource dataProvider},
                 XPath=GameStat/HighScore, Path=OuterXml}"/>
```

In addition to this support, `ItemsControl`'s `DisplayMemberPath` property supports both `Path` and `XPath` syntax.

If you want to bind the entire set of XML data to an element that understands hierarchies (`TreeView` or `Menu`) without custom code, you must use one or more `HierarchicalDataTemplates`. Listing 13.3 is an update to Listing 13.2 that adds three data templates (two `HierarchicalDataTemplates` and one plain `DataTemplate`) and changes the `ListBox` to a `TreeView` with an updated `XPath` that includes all the XML content.

LISTING 13.3 Binding to a Hierarchy Using HierarchicalDataTemplate

```
<Window xmlns="http://schemas.microsoft.com/winfx/2006/xaml/presentation"
        xmlns:x="http://schemas.microsoft.com/winfx/2006/xaml"
        Title="XML Data Binding">
  <Window.Resources>
    <HierarchicalDataTemplate DataType="GameStats"
      ItemsSource="{Binding XPath=*}">
      <TextBlock FontStyle="Italic" Text="All Game Stats"/>
    </HierarchicalDataTemplate>
    <HierarchicalDataTemplate DataType="GameStat" ItemsSource="{Binding XPath=*}">
      <TextBlock FontWeight="Bold" FontSize="20" Text="{Binding XPath=@Type}"/>
    </HierarchicalDataTemplate>
    <DataTemplate DataType="HighScore">
      <TextBlock Foreground="Blue" Text="{Binding XPath=.}"/>
    </DataTemplate>
    <XmlDataProvider x:Key="dataProvider" XPath="GameStats">
      <x:XData>
        <GameStats xmlns="">
          <!-- One stat per game type -->
          <GameStat Type="Beginner">
            <HighScore>1203</HighScore>
          </GameStat>
          <GameStat Type="Intermediate">
            <HighScore>1089</HighScore>
          </GameStat>
          <GameStat Type="Advanced">
            <HighScore>541</HighScore>
          </GameStat>
        </GameStats>
      </x:XData>
    </XmlDataProvider>
  </Window.Resources>
  <Grid>
    <TreeView ItemsSource="{Binding Source={StaticResource dataProvider},
      XPath=.}" />
  </Grid>
</Window>
```

The idea is to use a HierarchicalDataTemplate for every data type in the hierarchy but then use a simple DataTemplate for any leaf nodes. Each data template gives you the option to customize the rendering of the data type, but HierarchicalDataTemplate also enables you to specify its children in the hierarchy by setting its ItemsSource property. Both HierarchicalDataTemplates in Listing 13.3 bind ItemsSource to the XPath expression * to include all children in the XML data source.

The DataType value on each data template makes each one automatically affect any instances of the specified type within its scope (the Window in this example). When used with XmlDataProvider, the value of DataType corresponds to an XML element name. Note that the three data templates are not given explicit keys, despite being in a ResourceDictionary. This works because internally the value of DataType is used for the template's key.

Figure 13.13 shows the rendered XAML from Listing 13.3. It also shows what happens if you replace the single occurrence of TreeView with Menu and leave the rest of the listing alone.

The TreeView in Listing 13.3

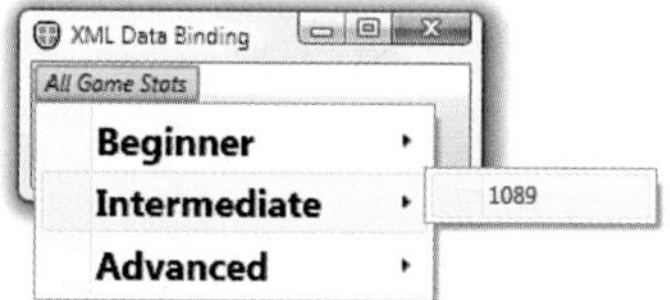

Changing TreeView to Menu

FIGURE 13.13 The use of HierarchicalDataTemplates can automatically fill TreeView and Menu with a hierarchy of data-bound objects.

TIP

Often, XML data defines its own namespace for its elements. For example, Really Simple Syndication (RSS) feeds from Twitter define two:

```
<rss version="2.0" xmlns:atom="http://www.w3.org/2005/Atom"
                   xmlns:georss="http://www.georss.org/georss">
  …
</rss>
```

To reference elements in these namespaces (for example, atom:link) in an XPath, you can set an XmlNamespaceManager property on the XmlDataProvider or on individual Bindings. Here's an example:

```
<XmlDataProvider Source="http://twitter.com/statuses/user_timeline/24326956.rss"
  XmlNamespaceManager="{StaticResource namespaceMapping}"
  XPath="rss/channel" x:Key="dataProvider"/>
```

The typical way to get an instance of an XmlNamespaceManager is to use the derived XmlNamespaceMappingCollection class, which assigns a prefix to each namespace. Here's an example:

```
<XmlNamespaceMappingCollection x:Key="namespaceMapping">
  <XmlNamespaceMapping Uri="http://www.w3.org/2005/Atom" Prefix="atom"/>
  <XmlNamespaceMapping Uri="http://www.georss.org/georss" Prefix="georss"/>
</XmlNamespaceMappingCollection>
```

Continued

Although it's natural to choose prefixes that match the ones in the XML, you can choose any prefixes you want. The prefixes you choose can be used in `XPath` expressions, such as:

```
"{Binding XPath=atom:link}"
```

Whenever an `XPath` value has no prefix, the empty namespace is assumed to be the namespace URI. Therefore, even if your XML source has a default namespace, you must assign an `XmlNamespaceManager` for the queries to work.

ObjectDataProvider

Whereas `XmlDataProvider` exposes XML as a data source, `ObjectDataProvider` exposes a .NET object as a data source. "But that doesn't make any sense," you're probably thinking to yourself! "I can already use any arbitrary .NET object as a data source. What good does `ObjectDataProvider` do?" It opens up a few additional capabilities that you don't get by binding to the raw object. For example, it enables you to do the following:

- Declaratively instantiate the source object with a parameterized constructor
- Bind to a method on the source object
- Have more options for asynchronous data binding

DIGGING DEEPER

Asynchronous Data Binding

Whenever binding to data isn't a quick operation, it should be done asynchronously to avoid freezing the user interface. WPF exposes two independent knobs for making binding happen asynchronously: `Binding` has an `IsAsync` property, and both `XmlDataProvider` and `ObjectDataProvider` have an `IsAsynchronous` property. (Don't you just love the consistency?)

When `IsAsynchronous` is `true`, the data provider creates the source object on a background thread. `IsAsynchronous` is `false` by default for `ObjectDataProvider` but `true` by default for `XmlDataProvider` (because the latter is often used with remote XML files such as RSS feeds that are slow to retrieve). On the other hand, when `IsAsync` (which is always `false` by default) is `true`, the source *property* is invoked on a background thread.

`Binding.IsAsync` exists to enable applications to work around poorly-designed objects. Property getters are supposed to be fast; they're not supposed to invoke expensive calculations, network requests, and so on. If everyone obeyed this guideline, the WPF team wouldn't have created the `IsAsync` property.

If you're tempted to use `IsAsync` with one of your own objects, consider redesigning its slow properties. A nice pattern is to define a method called `Recompute`, for example, that performs the expensive calculation (perhaps on a worker thread) and caches the results. When it finishes, you can raise the relevant `PropertyChanged` events. The property getter should simply retrieve whatever value is in the cache, so it is always fast.

Using a Parameterized Constructor in XAML

Most data sources that you'd use probably have a default constructor, such as the `photos` collection used earlier in the chapter. The following XAML "wraps" this collection in an `ObjectDataProvider`:

```
<Window.Resources>
  <local:Photos x:Key="photos"/>
  <ObjectDataProvider x:Key="dataProvider"
    ObjectInstance="{StaticResource photos}"/>
</Window.Resources>
```

In this case, whether you bind to `photos` or `dataProvider`, you get exactly the same results. Even the `Binding Path` to use is identical because `Binding` automatically "unwraps" objects inside data providers such as `ObjectDataProvider`.

`ObjectDataProvider` also can be given the desired type of its object to wrap (rather than an instance) and construct it on your behalf:

```
<Window.Resources>
  <!-- The collection object is instantiated internally by ObjectDataProvider: -->
  <ObjectDataProvider x:Key="dataProvider" ObjectType="{x:Type local:Photos}"/>
</Window.Resources>
```

When using `ObjectDataProvider` in this fashion, you can get it to instantiate an object via its parameterized constructor by setting its `ConstructorParameters` property to a collection of objects. For example, if the `Photos` constructor required a capacity to be passed in, you could use `ObjectDataProvider` as follows:

```
<ObjectDataProvider x:Key="dataProvider" ObjectType="{x:Type local:Photos}">
<ObjectDataProvider.ConstructorParameters>
  <sys:Int32>23</sys:Int32>
</ObjectDataProvider.ConstructorParameters>
</ObjectDataProvider>
```

This mechanism is just like the `x:Arguments` keyword in XAML2009, except this works in XAML2006 as well. Therefore, this is useful for data sources whose definition you don't control. (If you did control the definition of the data source, presumably you'd add an appropriate default constructor to it.) Of course, if declaring the source in XAML isn't important to you, you could always construct it programmatically and easily set it as a data context for any XAML-defined elements.

Binding to a Method

One scenario that `ObjectDataProvider` enables that you otherwise can't easily achieve declaratively or programmatically is binding to a method. As with support for parameterized constructors, this is mostly useful for existing classes that aren't data binding friendly and can't be changed. For your own types, you might as well expose potential data sources as properties. But imagine that the `photos` collection exposed a method called

GetFolderName that returned a string representing the folder containing all the current items. You could expose this method as a data source as follows:

```
<ObjectDataProvider x:Key="dataProvider" ObjectType="{x:Type local:Photos}"
  MethodName="GetFolderName"/>
```

If parameters need to be passed to the method, you can use ObjectDataProvider's MethodParameters property (which works just like its ConstructorParameters property). To bind to this method, you simply bind to the entire ObjectDataProvider:

```
<TextBlock Text="{Binding Source={StaticResource dataProvider}}"/>
```

Specifying a Path in this case would apply to the instance returned by the method.

DIGGING DEEPER

Suppressing the Automatic Unwrapping of Data Providers

If you want to bind directly to properties of ObjectDataProvider rather than the wrapped data source, you can set Binding's BindsDirectlyToSource property to true to suppress the automatic unwrapping. This works for any DataSourceProvider-derived source (as well as CollectionViewSource), so it includes ObjectDataProvider, XmlDataProvider, and any custom derived classes you might write.

Advanced Topics

The final section of this chapter outlines some of the more esoteric but incredibly useful features of data binding. This includes customizing the flow of data between the source and target, plugging in custom validation logic, and combining disjoint sources into a single bindable entity.

Customizing the Data Flow

In all the data-binding examples you've seen so far, data updates flow from the source to the target. But, in some cases, the target property can be directly changed by users, and it would be useful to support the flowing of such changes back to the source. Indeed, Binding supports this (and more) via its Mode property, which can be set to one of the following values of the BindingMode enumeration:

- **OneWay**—The target is updated whenever the source changes.
- **TwoWay**—A change to either the target or source updates the other.
- **OneWayToSource**—This is the opposite of OneWay. The source is updated whenever the target changes.
- **OneTime**—This works just like OneWay, except changes to the source are not reflected at the target. The target retains a snapshot of the source at the time the Binding is initiated.

TwoWay binding is appropriate for editable DataGrids or other data-bound forms, where you might have TextBoxes that get filled with data that the user is allowed to change. In fact, whereas most dependency properties default to OneWay binding, dependency properties such as TextBox.Text default to TwoWay binding. (Although this section claims to be about relatively esoteric features, TwoWay binding is actually quite common. It's used in almost any application that reacts to user input and properly separates its user interface from its data.)

> **WARNING**
>
> **Watch Out for Different Default BindingModes!**
>
> The fact that different dependency properties have different default BindingModes can easily trip you up. For example, unlike with Label.Content, binding TextBox.Text to a collection's Count property fails unless you explicitly set BindingMode to OneWay (or OneTime) because the Count property is read-only. TwoWay and OneWayToSource require a writable source property.

These different modes are the reason that value converters have both a Convert and a ConvertBack method. Both are called when performing TwoWay binding, and only ConvertBack is called when doing OneWayToSource binding.

> **FAQ**
>
> **Why would I ever use a Binding with a Mode of OneWayToSource? In such a case, it sounds like the target should really be the source, and the source should really be the target.**
>
> One reason could be that you're using multiple Bindings, some with data flowing from the source to the target and others with data flowing from the target to the source. For example, you might want to share a source among many data-bound targets but want one of these target elements to update that source via data binding.
>
> OneWayToSource can also be used as a sneaky way to get around the restriction that a Binding's target property must be a dependency property. If you want to bind a source dependency property to a target property that is *not* a dependency property, OneWayToSource enables you to accomplish this by marking your "real source" as the target and your "real target" as the source!

When using TwoWay or OneWayToSource binding, you might want different behaviors for when and how the source gets updated. For example, if a user types in a TwoWay data-bound TextBox, do you want the source to be updated with each keystroke, or only when the user is done typing? Binding enables you to control such behavior with its UpdateSourceTrigger property.

UpdateSourceTrigger can be set to a member of the UpdateSourceTrigger enumeration, which has the following values:

- **PropertyChanged**—The source is updated whenever the target property value changes.

- **LostFocus**—When the target property value changes, the source is updated only after the target element loses focus.
- **Explicit**—The source is updated only when you make an explicit call to BindingExpression.UpdateSource. You can get an instance of BindingExpression by calling the static BindingOperations.GetBindingExpression method or calling GetBindingExpression on any FrameworkElement or FrameworkContentElement.

DIGGING DEEPER

Dependency Properties and Default Settings

The default settings for dependency properties are stored in a special set of metadata, as shown in Chapter 3. To programmatically check the setting for any dependency property, you can call its GetMetadata method (for example, TextBox.TextProperty.GetMetadata()) and then check the value of properties such as BindsTwoWayByDefault or DefaultUpdateSourceTrigger. The easiest way to discover this information, of course, is with a tool such as .NET Reflector.

Just as different properties have different default Mode settings, they also have different default UpdateSourceTrigger settings. TextBox.Text defaults to LostFocus.

TIP

Although the source and/or target data gets updated automatically when using data binding, you might want to take additional actions when a data update occurs. Perhaps you want to write some data to a log or show a visual effect to indicate the data change.

Fortunately, FrameworkElement and FrameworkContentElement have SourceUpdated and TargetUpdated events that you can handle. But for performance reasons, they only get raised for Bindings that have their NotifyOnSourceUpdated and/or NotifyOnTargetUpdated Boolean properties set to true.

Adding Validation Rules to Binding

When you accept user input, it's a good idea to reject invalid data and give feedback to the user in a timely fashion. The early days of form filling on the Web were accompanied by horror stories of inappropriate validation, such as detecting errors only after everything was submitted and then requiring the user to type in everything again from scratch! Fortunately, data binding has a built-in validation mechanism that makes it relatively easy to create a rich and interactive experience. There are so many different ways to accomplish this and so many different knobs to configure, however, that it's more confusing than it should be.

Imagine that you want the user to type the name of an existing .jpg file into a data-bound TextBox. There are two obvious error conditions here: The user could enter a nonexistent filename or a non-.jpg filename. If the TextBox weren't data bound, you could insert custom validation logic that checks for these two conditions in the code that updates the data source. But when data binding propagates updates automatically, you need a way to inject validation logic into the process. You could write a value converter that performs the logic and throws an exception for bad data. But besides the fact that value converters aren't meant for that purpose, this still doesn't solve the part about displaying the error to the user.

> **TIP**
>
> The techniques described in this section apply only to propagating changes from the target to the source. Therefore, these features work only with a `BindingMode` of `OneWayToSource` or `TwoWay`.

You can handle this situation in a few different ways. One way is to write your own validation rule, and another is to take advantage of exceptions that might already be thrown from attempts to update the source incorrectly.

Writing Your Own Validation Rule

`Binding` has a `ValidationRules` property that can be set to one or more `ValidationRule`-derived objects. Each rule can check for specific conditions and mark the data as invalid. We could write the following `JpgValidationRule` class that enforces our requirements by deriving from `ValidationRule` and overriding its abstract `Validate` method:

```
public class JpgValidationRule : ValidationRule
{
  public override ValidationResult Validate(object value, CultureInfo cultureInfo)
  {
    string filename = value.ToString();

    // Reject nonexistent files:
    if (!File.Exists(filename))
      return new ValidationResult(false, "Value is not a valid file.");

    // Reject files that don't end in .jpg:
    if (!filename.EndsWith(".jpg", StringComparison.InvariantCultureIgnoreCase))
      return new ValidationResult(false, "Value is not a .jpg file.");

    // The input passes the test!
    return new ValidationResult(true, null);
  }
}
```

Invalid data is reported by returning a `false` `ValidationResult`, and valid data is reported by returning a `true` `ValidationResult`. (The check for the `".jpg"` suffix is not a good way to check that the file is a JPEG image, but it still gets the point across.)

With this class in place, it can be applied to a `Binding` as follows:

```
<TextBox>
<TextBox.Text>
  <Binding …>
```

```
  <Binding.ValidationRules>
    <local:JpgValidationRule/>
  </Binding.ValidationRules>
  </Binding>
</TextBox.Text>
</TextBox>
```

The validation check is invoked during any attempt to update the underlying data (which, in this case, is when the `TextBox` loses focus because of the `LostFocus` default for `UpdateSourceTrigger`). This happens before a value converter is called (if present), and only one rule is needed to veto the update and mark the data as invalid.

So, what happens when data is marked as invalid? An error adorner is rendered on top of the element with the target property. By default, this adorner looks like a thin red border. But you can assign a custom control template to be used in such conditions by setting the `Validation.ErrorTemplate` attached property on the target element. (Control templates are covered in the next chapter.) If you use validation, you'll want to assign a custom template because the default one is not very satisfactory.

In addition, when data is marked as invalid, the target element's `Validation.HasError` attached property becomes `true`, and its `Validation.Error` attached event is raised (but only if `Binding`'s `NotifyOnValidationError` property is set to `true`). Therefore, you could implement rich error notification logic with an appropriate trigger or event handler. You can get detailed information about the validation failures, such as the strings returned by the `JpgValidationRule` class, by checking the target element's `Validation.Errors` attached property. These properties are automatically cleared when a subsequent successful bind occurs.

Sending Existing Error Handling Through the Validation System

Writing a custom validation rule might duplicate error-checking logic that is already performed by the data source (or a value converter). If either of these already throws an exception for the same conditions you want to treat as invalid, you can use a built-in `ExceptionValidationRule` object. Here's an example:

```
<TextBox>
<TextBox.Text>
  <Binding …>
  <Binding.ValidationRules>
    <ExceptionValidationRule/>
  </Binding.ValidationRules>
  </Binding>
</TextBox.Text>
</TextBox>
```

`ExceptionValidationRule` simply marks the data as invalid if any exception is thrown when attempting to update the source property. Therefore, this mechanism enables you to react properly to the exception rather than have it swallowed and emitted as a debug trace.

Similarly, if the data source provides error information by implementing System.ComponentModel.IDataErrorInfo, a simple interface used by several data sources (and also consumed by Windows Forms), you can use a built-in DataErrorValidationRule object to mark the corresponding data as invalid. The following TextBox takes advantage of both:

```
<TextBox>
<TextBox.Text>
  <Binding …>
  <Binding.ValidationRules>
    <ExceptionValidationRule/>
    <DataErrorValidationRule/>
  </Binding.ValidationRules>
  </Binding>
</TextBox.Text>
</TextBox>
```

Although it's nice to see built-in validation behavior leverage the same mechanisms as custom code you would write, the WPF team realized that the syntax is pretty verbose and awkward. Therefore, in WPF 3.5 SP1, Binding was given two new Boolean properties—ValidatesOnExceptions and ValidatesOnDataErrors—that provide a shortcut to adding these validation rules to the ValidationRules collection. Therefore, the preceding XAML can be rewritten as follows:

```
<TextBox>
<TextBox.Text>
  <Binding ValidatesOnExceptions="True" ValidatesOnDataErrors="True" …/>
</TextBox.Text>
</TextBox>
```

DIGGING DEEPER

There's More Than One Way to Handle Exceptions

Another way to handle exceptions in source updates is to attach a delegate to Binding's UpdateSourceExceptionFilter property. The delegate gets called whenever an exception occurs from attempting to update the source property, and that Exception object is passed to the delegate. Therefore, you can implement a custom error notification scheme without using any of the ValidationRule features. UpdateSourceExceptionFilter might be simpler to use programmatically, but only the ExceptionValidationRule approach can be used declaratively.

Interestingly, there is still a connection between the UpdateSourceExceptionFilter delegate and the other validation scheme. If you return a ValidationError from your delegate, it will treat your delegate like a custom validation rule, and add the ValidationError to the target element's Validation.Errors collection, set Validation.HasError to true, and potentially raise the Validation.Error event.

To summarize, if the data source or a value converter in use already has logic to throw an exception on bad data, you can do one of the following:

- Use `UpdateSourceExceptionFilter` to plug in custom notification logic
- Set `ValidatesOnExceptions` or use `ExceptionValidationRule`, defining an `ErrorTemplate` and/or plugging in additional notification logic by monitoring `Validation.HasError` or `Validation.Error` (when `NotifyOnValidationError` is `true`)

If the data source uses `IDataErrorInfo`, you can set `ValidatesOnDataErrors` or use `DataErrorValidationRule` instead, and if the data source or value converter doesn't have either kind of error handling, you still use a custom validation rule.

Validation for a Group of Bindings

The validation mechanism described thus far is applied on a `Binding`-by-`Binding` basis, but sometimes it's useful to apply validation in bulk, such as for all cells in a `DataGrid` row or any kind of form in which multiple values are dependent on each other.

This kind of bulk validation is supported by an object known as `BindingGroup`. `BindingGroup`, like `Binding`, can be given a set of `ValidationRules` that are meant to apply to a group of `Bindings`. A `BindingGroup` instance can be assigned to any `FrameworkElement` (or `FrameworkContentElement`) as the value of its `BindingGroup` property. (`ItemsControl` also defines an `ItemBindingGroup` property that applies the `BindingGroup` to each item rather than the `ItemsControl` itself.) This automatically "fills" the `BindingGroup` with all `Bindings` that share the same `DataContext` as the host element. If you give the `BindingGroup` a `Name`, you can then add any other `Bindings` to the group—regardless of their source data—by setting each `Binding`'s `BindingGroupName` to the `Name` of the `BindingGroup`.

When each `BindingGroup`'s `ValidationRule` is invoked, the value passed to `Validate` is the instance of the `BindingGroup`. Because `BindingGroup` contains a number of useful methods and properties, such as an `Items` collection that contains the values for each `Binding` that ended up in the group, the `ValidationRule` can contain arbitrary logic that determines whether the result is valid, based on the entire group of values. `BindingGroup` also enables transactional editing (leveraged by `DataGrid`) when the data source implements the `IEditableObject` interface.

Working with Disjoint Sources

WPF provides a few interesting ways to combine multiple sources of data. The key to these approaches is the following classes:

- `CompositeCollection`
- `MultiBinding`
- `PriorityBinding`

CompositeCollection

The CompositeCollection class provides an easy way to expose separate collections and/or arbitrary items as a single collection. This can be useful when you want to bind to a collection of items that come from more than one source. The following XAML defines a CompositeCollection with all the contents of the photos collection plus two more items:

```
<CompositeCollection>
  <CollectionContainer Collection="{Binding Source={StaticResource photos}}"/>
  <local:Photo …/>
  <local:Photo …/>
</CompositeCollection>
```

The photos collection is wrapped in a CollectionContainer object so that its items are considered part of the CompositeCollection rather than the collection itself. If the photos collection were added directly to the CompositeCollection instead, the CompositeCollection would contain only three items!

MultiBinding

MultiBinding enables you to aggregate multiple Bindings together and spit out a single target value. It requires that you use a value converter because otherwise WPF would have no idea how to combine the multiple input values. The following XAML shows how MultiBinding could be used to calculate a ProgressBar's value by adding together the progress values of three independent data-bound sources, assuming the presence of a value converter and three source objects as resources:

```
<ProgressBar …>
<ProgressBar.Value>
  <MultiBinding Converter="{StaticResource converter}">
    <Binding Source="{StaticResource worker1}"/>
    <Binding Source="{StaticResource worker2}"/>
    <Binding Source="{StaticResource worker3}"/>
  </MultiBinding>
</ProgressBar.Value>
</ProgressBar>
```

Value converters used in MultiBinding are a little different than ones used in Binding, however. They must implement the IMultiValueConverter interface, whose methods accept/return an *array* of values rather than just one. Therefore, the following is an appropriate definition of the value converter used in the previous XAML snippet:

```
public class ProgressConverter : IMultiValueConverter
{
  public object Convert(object[] values, Type targetType, object parameter,
    CultureInfo culture)
  {
    int totalProgress = 0;
```

```
    // Require that each input value is an instance of a Worker
    foreach (Worker worker in values)
      totalProgress += worker.Progress;

    return totalProgress;
  }
  public object[] ConvertBack(object value, Type[] targetTypes, object parameter,
    CultureInfo culture)
  {
    return DependencyProperty.UnsetValue;
  }
}
```

13

TIP

StringFormat can be used with MultiBinding. When it is used this way, {0} represents the first Binding, {1} represents the second Binding, and so on.

PriorityBinding

PriorityBinding looks a lot like MultiBinding, in that it encapsulates multiple Binding objects. But rather than aggregating Bindings together, the idea of PriorityBinding is to let multiple Bindings *compete* for setting the target value!

If you are data binding to a slow data source (and you can't make it faster), you might want to allow faster sources to provide a "rough" version of the data while you wait. This technique can be seen in lots of software. For example, if you open a large document in Microsoft Word, you might first see something like "77,257 characters (an approximate value)" display in the lower-left corner for a few seconds, then something like "Page: 1 of 3," which is still not the correct page count, then finally the expected "Page: 1 of 46." For the Photo Gallery application, this technique could be used to quickly bind to a collection of thumbnail images and then replace that with a collection of full-fidelity images after that slower bind completes.

The following XAML demonstrates a typical declaration of PriorityBinding:

```
<PriorityBinding>
  <Binding Source="HighPri" Path="SlowSpeed" IsAsync="True"/>
  <Binding Source="MediumPri" Path="MediumSpeed" IsAsync="True"/>
  <Binding Source="LowPri" Path="FastSpeed"/>
</PriorityBinding>
```

The Bindings are processed from beginning to end, so the first Binding listed has the highest priority (and, therefore, should be the slowest one to complete), and the last Binding listed has the lowest priority (and should be the quickest one). As different values get returned, higher-priority values overwrite the lower-priority ones.

TIP

When using PriorityBinding, all but the last Bindings should set IsAsync to true so they are processed in the background. Without this setting, the highest-priority Binding would execute synchronously (probably freezing the user interface), and after it returned, there would be no reason to consult the lower-priority Bindings!

Putting It All Together: The Pure-XAML Twitter Client

The canonical example of the power of WPF data binding is a fully functioning RSS reader written without any procedural code. Listing 13.4 provides my version of such an implementation, pointed at my Twitter RSS feed. The result is a decent "Twitter client," shown in Figure 13.14. I pasted the XAML into the wonderful Kaxaml tool (http://kaxaml.com), hence the Kaxaml icon inherited by the `Window`.

LISTING 13.4 The Entire Implementation of an RSS Reader/Twitter Client

```
<Window xmlns="http://schemas.microsoft.com/winfx/2006/xaml/presentation"
        xmlns:x="http://schemas.microsoft.com/winfx/2006/xaml" Title="RSS Reader">
<Window.Resources>
  <XmlDataProvider x:Key="Feed"
    Source="http://twitter.com/statuses/user_timeline/24326956.rss"/>
</Window.Resources>
  <DockPanel
    DataContext="{Binding Source={StaticResource Feed}, XPath=/rss/channel/item}">
    <TextBox DockPanel.Dock="Top" Text="{Binding Source={StaticResource Feed},
      BindsDirectlyToSource=true, Path=Source,
      UpdateSourceTrigger=PropertyChanged}"/>
    <Label DockPanel.Dock="Top" Content="{Binding XPath=/rss/channel/title}"
      FontSize="14" FontWeight="Bold"/>
    <Label DockPanel.Dock="Top"
      Content="{Binding XPath=/rss/channel/description}"/>
    <ListBox DockPanel.Dock="Left" DisplayMemberPath="title"
      ItemsSource="{Binding}" IsSynchronizedWithCurrentItem="True" Width="300"/>
    <Frame Source="{Binding XPath=link}"/>
  </DockPanel>
</Window>
```

As expected, `XmlDataProvider` is used to retrieve the RSS feed.

Here are some of the interesting points about this application:

- The default `TwoWay` binding of `TextBox.Text` is leveraged to initially fill the `TextBox` with the `XmlDataProvider`'s `Source` and also enable the user to change the `Source` at runtime.
- To enable the `XmlDataProvider`'s `Source` to be bound, the `TextBox`'s `Binding` has `BindsDirectlyToSource` set to `true`. Otherwise, its `Path` would incorrectly refer to the RSS feed.

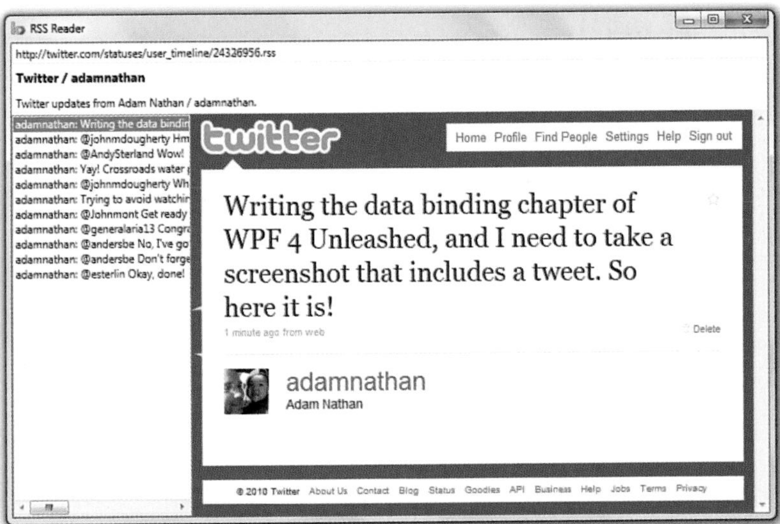

FIGURE 13.14 The all-XAML RSS reader/Twitter client implemented in Listing 13.4.

- The `TextBox`'s `Binding` uses an `UpdateSourceTrigger` of `PropertyChanged`, so an attempt to refresh the data is made with each keystroke. The best solution would probably be to use an `UpdateSourceTrigger` of `Explicit` instead and provide a Go button that can be used to manually refresh the source. But that would require a line of procedural code, which goes against the point of this example!
- The value of `ListBox`'s `DisplayMemberPath` is an XPath expression to extract the `title` element for each item in the XML source.
- The `ListBox` and `Frame` provide a master/detail view simply by sharing the same data source.
- Rather than use `Frame`, the raw content of each RSS item could have been displayed in something like a `TextBlock`. But that would give you raw HTML that would be difficult to read. And there's no declarative way to render HTML properly other than using a `Frame` or `WebBrowser` with a persisted file (which the feed's `link` element conveniently provides).
- As different RSS items (or whole RSS feeds) are selected, `Frame`'s navigation buttons keep track of your actions automatically.

Summary

Data binding is a very powerful feature, although its use is also completely optional. After all, it's not hard to write code that ties two objects together. But writing such code can be tedious, error prone, and a maintenance hassle, especially when managing multiple data sources that might need to be synchronized as items are added, removed, and changed. Such code also tends to tightly couple business logic with the user interface, which makes the software more brittle.

`XmlDataProvider` could be considered a "killer app" for data binding, as it makes retrieving, parsing, navigating, and displaying remote XML data incredibly easy. The ability to get asynchronous behavior on any `Binding` or data provider simply by setting a Boolean property also makes data binding a compelling alternative to performing such work manually.

But there's more to data binding than cutting down on the amount of code you need to write. Much of the appeal of WPF's data binding comes from the fact that the majority of it can be done declaratively. This has some important implications. Design tools such as Expression Blend can (and do) surface data-binding functionality, so nonprogrammers can add sophisticated functionality to any user interface. With this support, Blend also enables designers to specify easily-removable dummy data for testing data-bound user interfaces. Data binding also enables loose XAML pages, which can't use procedural code, to take advantage of functionality that makes them feel less like documents and more like miniature applications.

CHAPTER 14

Styles, Templates, Skins, and Themes

IN THIS CHAPTER

- Styles
- Templates
- Skins
- Themes

Arguably the most celebrated feature in WPF is the ability to give any user interface element a radically different look without having to give up all of the built-in functionality that it provides. Even with Cascading Style Sheets (CSS), HTML lacks this much power, which is the reason most websites use images to represent buttons rather than "real buttons." Of course, it's pretty easy to simulate a button's behavior with an image in HTML, but what if you want to give a completely different look to a `SELECT` element (HTML's version of `ComboBox`)? It's a lot of work if you want to do more than change simple properties (such as its foreground and background colors).

This chapter explains the four main components of WPF's restyling support:

- **Styles**—A simple mechanism for separating property values from user interface elements (similar to the relationship between CSS and HTML). Styles are also the foundation for applying the other mechanisms in this chapter.
- **Templates**—Powerful objects that most people are really referring to when they talk about "restyling" in WPF.
- **Skins**—Application-specific collections of styles and/or templates, typically with the ability to be replaced dynamically.
- **Themes**—Visual characteristics of the host operating system, with potential customizations by the end user.

As you'll see, an important enabler of WPF's restyling support is the semantics of resources.

FAQ

Why does WPF allow people to completely customize the look of standard controls? The inconsistencies from one application to another are going to confuse users!

This "celebrated" feature of WPF also makes many people nervous. Is this power and flexibility going to usher in a new age of beautiful software, or is it going to be abused in ways that annoy and frustrate users (such as the BLINK element in HTML)?

The answer is certainly "both." I, too, was skeptical about WPF back in 2003, when most demos consisted of bouncing buttons and spinning rainbow-filled list boxes. But it's good to know that you *could* create completely insane user interfaces, even if you *shouldn't*. WPF's philosophy is to make an application's experience limited only by the skill of its designers rather than by the underlying platform. It's hard to disagree with that stance.

If you can't hire graphic designers, fortunately the default visual appearance of a WPF application looks consistent with the expectations of Windows users. The same goes for Silverlight, whose controls can easily adapt to different target environments, such as Windows phones. But if you *can* hire designers, WPF makes it easy for them to have an impact across the entire application (not just on icons or a splash screen).

As for inconsistencies between applications, the same could be said about web applications, which tend to infuse their own branding into the entire user experience much more than traditional Windows applications. Despite the lack of consistency (or even *because of* lack of consistency), websites with good user experiences can do very well. Also, people try to create non-standard-looking Windows applications *anyway*. And with lack of platform support, they have to jump through many hoops to get the desired effect, often producing buggy behavior or weird side effects.

Styles

A *style*, represented by the System.Windows.Style class, is a pretty simple entity. Its main function is to group together property values that could otherwise be set individually. The intent is to then share this group of values among multiple elements.

FIGURE 14.1 Three Buttons whose look has been customized.

Take, for example, the three customized Buttons in Figure 14.1. This look is achieved by setting seven properties. Without a Style, you would need to duplicate these identical assignments on all three Buttons, as shown in Listing 14.1.

LISTING 14.1 Copy/Paste Galore!

```
<StackPanel Orientation="Horizontal">
  <Button FontSize="22" Background="Purple" Foreground="White"
    Height="50" Width="50" RenderTransformOrigin=".5,.5">
  <Button.RenderTransform>
    <RotateTransform Angle="10"/>
  </Button.RenderTransform>
    1
```

LISTING 14.1 Continued

```
    </Button>
    <Button FontSize="22" Background="Purple" Foreground="White"
      Height="50" Width="50" RenderTransformOrigin=".5,.5">
    <Button.RenderTransform>
      <RotateTransform Angle="10"/>
    </Button.RenderTransform>
      2
    </Button>
    <Button FontSize="22" Background="Purple" Foreground="White"
      Height="50" Width="50" RenderTransformOrigin=".5,.5">
    <Button.RenderTransform>
      <RotateTransform Angle="10"/>
    </Button.RenderTransform>
      3
    </Button>
</StackPanel>,
```

But with a `Style`, you can add a level of indirection—setting the properties in one place and pointing each `Button` to this new element, as shown in Listing 14.2. `Style` uses a collection of `Setter`s to set the target properties. Creating a `Setter` is just a matter of specifying the name of a dependency property (qualified with its class name) and a desired value for it.

LISTING 14.2 Consolidating Property Assignments Inside a `Style`,

```
<StackPanel Orientation="Horizontal">
<StackPanel.Resources>
  <Style x:Key="buttonStyle">
    <Setter Property="Button.FontSize" Value="22"/>
    <Setter Property="Button.Background" Value="Purple"/>
    <Setter Property="Button.Foreground" Value="White"/>
    <Setter Property="Button.Height" Value="50"/>
    <Setter Property="Button.Width" Value="50"/>
    <Setter Property="Button.RenderTransformOrigin" Value=".5,.5"/>
    <Setter Property="Button.RenderTransform">
    <Setter.Value>
      <RotateTransform Angle="10"/>
    </Setter.Value>
    </Setter>
  </Style>
</StackPanel.Resources>
  <Button Style="{StaticResource buttonStyle}">1</Button>
  <Button Style="{StaticResource buttonStyle}">2</Button>
  <Button Style="{StaticResource buttonStyle}">3</Button>
</StackPanel>,
```

`Style` definition

Applying the `Style`

Using a `Style` is nice for several reasons, such as having only one spot to change if you later have second thoughts about rotating the `Buttons` or if you want to change their `Background`. Defining a `Style` as a resource also gives you all the flexibility that the resource mechanism provides. For example, you could define one version of `buttonStyle` at the application level but override it with a different `Style` (still with a key of `buttonStyle`) in an individual `Window`'s `Resources` collection.

Note that despite its name, there's nothing inherently visual about a `Style`. But it's typically used for setting properties that affect visuals. Indeed, `Style` only enables the setting of dependency properties, which tend to be visual in nature.

TIP

`Styles` can even inherit from one another! The following `Style` adds bold text to the `buttonStyle` defined in Listing 14.2 by using the `BasedOn` property,:

```
<Style x:Key="buttonStyleWithBold" BasedOn="{StaticResource buttonStyle}">
  <!-- The seven properties set by buttonStyle are inherited -->
  <Setter Property="Button.FontWeight" Value="Bold"/>
</Style>
```

Sharing Styles

Although you could set an element's `Style` property directly in its XAML definition (using property element syntax), the whole point of using a `Style` is to share it among multiple elements, as done in Listing 14.2. `Style` supports a few different mechanisms that enable you to control exactly how that sharing occurs.

Sharing Among Heterogeneous Elements

Although the `Style` in Listing 14.2 is shared among three `Buttons`, with some tweaks it can also be shared among heterogeneous elements. Listing 14.3 accomplishes this by changing each `Button.XXX` referenced inside the `Style` to `Control.XXX` and then applying the new style to many elements. The result is shown in Figure 14.2.

FIGURE 14.2 Heterogeneous elements given the same `Style`.

LISTING 14.3 Sharing a Single `Style` with Heterogeneous Elements

```
<StackPanel Orientation="Horizontal">
<StackPanel.Resources>
  <Style x:Key="controlStyle">
    <Setter Property="Control.FontSize" Value="22"/>
```

LISTING 14.3 Continued

```
    <Setter Property="Control.Background" Value="Purple"/>
    <Setter Property="Control.Foreground" Value="White"/>
    <Setter Property="Control.Height" Value="50"/>
    <Setter Property="Control.Width" Value="50"/>
    <Setter Property="Control.RenderTransformOrigin" Value=".5,.5"/>
    <Setter Property="Control.RenderTransform">
    <Setter.Value>
      <RotateTransform Angle="10"/>
    </Setter.Value>
    </Setter>
  </Style>
</StackPanel.Resources>
  <Button Style="{StaticResource controlStyle}">1</Button>
  <ComboBox Style="{StaticResource controlStyle}">
  <ComboBox.Items>2</ComboBox.Items>
  </ComboBox>
  <Expander Style="{StaticResource controlStyle}" Content="3"/>
  <TabControl Style="{StaticResource controlStyle}">
  <TabControl.Items>4</TabControl.Items>
  </TabControl>
  <ToolBar Style="{StaticResource controlStyle}">
  <ToolBar.Items>5</ToolBar.Items>
  </ToolBar>
  <InkCanvas Style="{StaticResource controlStyle}"/>
  <TextBox Style="{StaticResource controlStyle}" Text="7"/>
</StackPanel>
```

You don't need to worry about a `Style` being applied to an element that doesn't have all the listed dependency properties; the properties that exist are set and the ones that don't exist are ignored. For example, `InkCanvas` doesn't have `Foreground` or `FontSize` properties. Yet when the `Style` is applied to it in Listing 14.3, all the relevant properties (`Background`, `Height`, `Width`, and so on) are correctly applied. Similarly, adding the following `Setter` to the `Style` in Listing 14.3 affects the `TextBox` but leaves all the other elements looking as they do in Figure 14.2:

```
<Setter Property="TextBox.TextAlignment" Value="Right"/>
```

DIGGING DEEPER

Strange (but True) `Setter` Behavior

An astute reader might wonder how *any* of the `Setters` in Listing 14.3 are able to affect the `InkCanvas`, given that they are all properties of `Control`, and `InkCanvas` doesn't even derive from `Control`! This happens because of one of the more "magical" aspects of dependency properties (which reinforces how different they are from normal .NET properties).

Continued

Although InkCanvas registers several of its own dependency properties (with DependencyProperty.Register), it also has several—such as Background—whose "ownership" is shared with other types (so it calls DependencyProperty.AddOwner instead). When multiple types own the same dependency property, it doesn't matter which type name you use in Setter.Property, as long as it's one of the owners. Unfortunately, the ownership of dependency properties is an implementation detail that is not well documented.

The implications of this can produce even more baffling results. For example, the Setters in Listing 14.3 didn't even need to change from Listing 14.2. If they reference Button.*XXX* rather than Control.*XXX*, the result is identical. Also, if you add a TextBlock to Listing 14.3, you'd see that setting Button.Foreground successfully changes TextBlock's Foreground property but setting Button.Background *does not* change TextBlock's Background property! That's because TextBlock and all Controls share an implementation of their Foreground dependency property but don't share a Background implementation. (Control shares its Background with types such as Panel and InkCanvas, whereas TextBlock shares its completely independent implementation with TextElement, FlowDocument, and other types.)

My advice is to avoid all this nonsense and create distinct Styles for distinct types.

TIP

Any individual element can override aspects of its Style by directly setting a property to a local value. For example, the Button in Listing 14.3 could do the following to retain the rotation, size, and so on from controlStyle yet have a red Background rather than a purple one:

```
<Button Style="{StaticResource controlStyle}" Background="Red">1</Button>
```

This works because of the order of precedence for dependency property values presented in Chapter 3, "WPF Fundamentals." The local value trumps anything set from a Style.

TIP

To enable sharing of complex property values even *within* a Style, Style has its own Resources property. You can leverage this collection to make your Style self-contained rather than create a potentially brittle dependency to resources defined elsewhere.

Restricting the Use of Styles

If you want to enforce that a Style can be applied only to a particular type, you can set its TargetType property accordingly. For example, the following Style can be applied only to a Button (or a subclass of Button):

```
<Style x:Key="buttonStyle" TargetType="{x:Type Button}">
  <Setter Property="Button.FontSize" Value="22"/>
  <Setter Property="Button.Background" Value="Purple"/>
```

```
  <Setter Property="Button.Foreground" Value="White"/>
  <Setter Property="Button.Height" Value="50"/>
  <Setter Property="Button.Width" Value="50"/>
  <Setter Property="Button.RenderTransformOrigin" Value=".5,.5"/>
  <Setter Property="Button.RenderTransform">
  <Setter.Value>
    <RotateTransform Angle="10"/>
  </Setter.Value>
  </Setter>
</Style>
```

Any attempt to apply this `Style` to a non-`Button` generates a compile-time error. Therefore, `TargetType="{x:Type Control}"` could be applied to the `Style` in Listing 14.3, and it would still work with all the elements except `InkCanvas`.

In addition, when you apply a `TargetType` to a `Style`, you no longer need to prefix the property names inside `Setter`s with the type name. So, the previous XAML snippet could be rewritten as follows and have exactly the same meaning:

```
<Style x:Key="buttonStyle" TargetType="{x:Type Button}">
  <Setter Property="FontSize" Value="22"/>
  <Setter Property="Background" Value="Purple"/>
  <Setter Property="Foreground" Value="White"/>
  <Setter Property="Height" Value="50"/>
  <Setter Property="Width" Value="50"/>
  <Setter Property="RenderTransformOrigin" Value=".5,.5"/>
  <Setter Property="RenderTransform">
  <Setter.Value>
    <RotateTransform Angle="10"/>
  </Setter.Value>
  </Setter>
</Style>
```

Creating Implicit `Style`s

Applying a `TargetType` to a `Style` gives you another feature as well. If you omit its `Key`, the `Style` gets implicitly applied to all elements of that target type within the same scope. This is typically called a *typed style* as opposed to a *named style*, which is the only kind of `Style` you've seen so far.

The scope of a typed `Style` is determined by the location of the `Style` resource. For example, it could implicitly apply to all relevant elements in a `Window` if it's a member of `Window.Resources`. Or, it could apply to an entire application if you define it as an application-level resource, as follows:

```
<Application …>
<Application.Resources>
  <Style TargetType="{x:Type Button}">        No x:Key!
```

```
    <Setter Property="Foreground" Value="Black"/>
  </MultiTrigger>
</Style.Triggers>
```

This means, "if `IsMouseOver` is `true` *and* if `IsFocused` is `true`, apply the rotation and black foreground." `MultiDataTrigger` works the same way as `MultiTrigger` but with support for plain .NET properties.

TIP

If you want to add even more complex event-driven behavior to a `Style`, you can make use of an `EventSetter` (which shares a common base class with `Setter`) to attach an event handler to any element that makes use of the `Style`. `EventSetters` can be added to a `Style` just like `Setters`:

```
<Style x:Key="buttonStyle" TargetType="{x:Type Button}">
  <Setter Property="FontSize" Value="22"/>
  <EventSetter Event="MouseEnter" Handler="Button_MouseEnter"/>
</Style>
```

Although this requires procedural code to handle the event, it is, nevertheless, a handy way to share a common handler among many elements without resorting to copying and pasting.

Templates

`Controls` have many properties you can use to customize their look: `Button` has configurable `Background` and `Foreground` `Brushes` (which can even be fancy gradients), `TabControl`'s tabs can be relocated by setting the `TabStripPlacement` property, and so on. But you can do only so much with such properties.

A template, on the other hand, allows you to completely replace an element's visual tree with anything you can dream up, while keeping all of its functionality intact. And templates (like many other things in WPF) aren't just some add-on mechanism for third parties; the default visuals for every `Control` in WPF are defined in templates (and customized for each Windows theme). The source code for every control is completely separated from its default visual tree representations (or "visual source code").

Templates and the desire to separate visuals from logic are also the reasons that WPF's controls don't expose more simple properties for tweaking their look. For example, it would be nice to change the color of the `Expander`'s arrow back in Figure 14.2, as the gray color doesn't show up nicely against the purple background. This relatively simple change can be accomplished only by defining a new template for `Expander`, however. `Expander` has no `ArrowBrush` or `ArrowColor` property because an `Expander` with a custom template might not even have an arrow!

There are a few different kinds of templates. What has been described so far is the focus of this section: *control templates*. Control templates are represented by the

ControlTemplate class that derives from the abstract FrameworkTemplate class. The other FrameworkTemplate-derived classes are covered in previous chapters: DataTemplate (described in the preceding chapter) and ItemsPanelTemplate (described in Chapter 10). Data templates customize the look of any .NET object, which is especially important for non-UIElements, whose default template is simply a TextBlock containing a string returned by its ToString method. ItemsPanelTemplates can be assigned to an ItemsControl's ItemsPanel as an easy way to alter its layout.

Slick custom visuals undoubtedly involve using 2D (or 3D!) graphics, animation, or other rich media, covered in the next part of the book. This chapter sticks to some simple 2D drawings.

Introducing Control Templates

The important piece of the ControlTemplate class is its VisualTree content property, which contains the tree of elements that define the desired look. After you define a ControlTemplate (undoubtedly in XAML), you can attach it to any Control or Page by setting its Template property. Listing 14.5 defines a simple yet slick control template as a resource and then applies it to a single Button. Figure 14.7 shows the result.

FIGURE 14.7 A fancy round Button, created with a custom ControlTemplate.

LISTING 14.5 A Simple ControlTemplate Applied to a Button

```
<Grid>
<Grid.Resources>
  <ControlTemplate x:Key="buttonTemplate">
    <Grid>
      <Ellipse Width="100" Height="100">
      <Ellipse.Fill>
        <LinearGradientBrush StartPoint="0,0" EndPoint="0,1">
          <GradientStop Offset="0" Color="Blue"/>
          <GradientStop Offset="1" Color="Red"/>
        </LinearGradientBrush>
      </Ellipse.Fill>
      </Ellipse>
      <Ellipse Width="80" Height="80">
      <Ellipse.Fill>
        <LinearGradientBrush StartPoint="0,0" EndPoint="0,1">
          <GradientStop Offset="0" Color="White"/>
          <GradientStop Offset="1" Color="Transparent"/>
        </LinearGradientBrush>
      </Ellipse.Fill>
      </Ellipse>
    </Grid>
```

LISTING 14.5 Continued

```
  </ControlTemplate>
</Grid.Resources>
  <Button Template="{StaticResource buttonTemplate}">OK</Button>
</Grid>
```

To get this look, the template's visual tree uses two circles (created with `Ellipse` elements) placed inside a single-cell `Grid`. Despite the custom look, the resultant `Button` still has a `Click` event, an `IsDefault` property, and all the other functionality you'd expect. After all, it is still an instance of the `Button` class!

> **TIP**
>
> In Listing 14.5, the `Button` is considered the *templated parent* of the elements in the control template's visual tree. `FrameworkElement` and `FrameworkContentElement` both have a `TemplatedParent` property that represents this relationship.

Getting Interactivity with Triggers

As with `Styles`, `Templates` can contain all types of triggers in a `Triggers` collection. Listing 14.6 adds triggers to the preceding `ControlTemplate` to visually respond to a mouse hover and click. A trigger on `Button.IsMouseOver` makes the `Button` orange, and a trigger on `Button.IsPressed` shrinks the button with a `ScaleTransform` to give it a "pushed in" look. Figure 14.8 shows the result.

LISTING 14.6 A `ControlTemplate` Enhanced with Triggers

```
<Grid>
<Grid.Resources>
  <ControlTemplate x:Key="buttonTemplate">
    <Grid>
      <Ellipse x:Name="outerCircle" Width="100" Height="100">
      <Ellipse.Fill>
        <LinearGradientBrush StartPoint="0,0" EndPoint="0,1">
          <GradientStop Offset="0" Color="Blue"/>
          <GradientStop Offset="1" Color="Red"/>
        </LinearGradientBrush>
      </Ellipse.Fill>
      </Ellipse>
      <Ellipse Width="80" Height="80">
      <Ellipse.Fill>
        <LinearGradientBrush StartPoint="0,0" EndPoint="0,1">
          <GradientStop Offset="0" Color="White"/>
          <GradientStop Offset="1" Color="Transparent"/>
        </LinearGradientBrush>
      </Ellipse.Fill>
      </Ellipse>
    </Grid>
```

LISTING 14.6 Continued

```
  <ControlTemplate.Triggers>
    <Trigger Property="Button.IsMouseOver" Value="True">
      <Setter TargetName="outerCircle" Property="Fill" Value="Orange"/>
    </Trigger>
    <Trigger Property="Button.IsPressed" Value="True">
      <Setter Property="RenderTransform">
      <Setter.Value>
        <ScaleTransform ScaleX=".9" ScaleY=".9"/>
      </Setter.Value>
      </Setter>
      <Setter Property="RenderTransformOrigin" Value=".5,.5"/>
    </Trigger>
  </ControlTemplate.Triggers>
  </ControlTemplate>
</Grid.Resources>
  <Button Template="{StaticResource buttonTemplate}">OK</Button>
</Grid>
```

IsMouseOver=True

IsPressed=True
(and IsMouseOver=True)

FIGURE 14.8 The hover and pushed-in effects for the ControlTemplate in Listing 14.6.

Notice that the larger circle in the template's visual tree is given the name outerCircle. This is done so it can be referenced by a trigger. The first trigger uses Setter's TargetName property (which makes sense only inside a template) to make its setting of Fill to Orange apply to only the outerCircle element. Omitting the TargetName would cause an error in this case because the trigger would apply to the entire Button, which doesn't have a Fill property. The capability to target subelements of a template with triggers is essential for sophisticated templates.

TIP

Analogous to Setter's TargetName property, Trigger (as well as EventTrigger and Condition) has a SourceName property that enables you to react to a change on a specific subelement of a template rather than the entire template. For example, you could have triggers for IsMouseOver on individual subelements to get a richly customized hover effect.

The second trigger doesn't need to target a subelement, however. The `ScaleTransform` (applied as a `RenderTransform`) applies to the entire `Button`, as does the setting of `RenderTransformOrigin` to center the scaling. It's hard to convey in Figure 14.8, but a slight centered shrinkage (10% in this case) is a very effective visual effect for a `Button` press.

> **DIGGING DEEPER**
>
> **Named Elements in Templates**
>
> Outside a template, naming an element with `x:Name` generates a field for programmatic access. This is not the case when using `x:Name` inside a template, however. This is because a template can be applied to multiple elements in the same scope. The main purpose of naming elements in a template is for referencing them from triggers (typically defined in XAML). But if you want programmatic access to a named element inside a template, you can use the template's `FindName` method after the template has been applied to a target.

Restricting the Target Type

As with `Style`, `ControlTemplate` has a `TargetType` property that can restrict where the template can be applied. It also enables you to remove the class name qualifications on any property references inside a template (such as the values of `Trigger.Property` and `Setter.Property`). Therefore, the template from Listing 14.6 could be rewritten as follows:

```
<ControlTemplate x:Key="buttonTemplate" TargetType="{x:Type Button}">
  <Grid>
    …
  </Grid>
<ControlTemplate.Triggers>
  <Trigger Property="IsMouseOver" Value="True">
    <Setter TargetName="outerCircle" Property="Fill" Value="Orange"/>
  </Trigger>
  <Trigger Property="IsPressed" Value="True">
    <Setter Property="RenderTransform">
    <Setter.Value>
      <ScaleTransform ScaleX=".9" ScaleY=".9"/>
    </Setter.Value>
    </Setter>
    <Setter Property="RenderTransformOrigin" Value=".5,.5"/>
  </Trigger>
</ControlTemplate.Triggers>
</ControlTemplate>
```

Note that the `Setters` in this example already had unqualified `Property` values in previous listings. That's because the properties are either qualified by the use of `TargetName` or are common to all `Controls`. (Without an explicit `TargetType`, the target type is implicitly `Control`.)

Unlike with a `Style`, the use of `TargetType` does not enable you to remove the template's `x:Key` (when used in a dictionary). There is no such thing as a default control template; you have to set the template inside a typed `Style` to get such behavior.

Respecting the Templated Parent's Properties

There's a bit of a problem with the templates we've created so far. Any `Buttons` they're applied to look exactly the same, no matter what the values of its properties are. For example, in the last two listings, the `Button` has `"OK"` as content, but it never gets displayed. If you're creating a control template that's meant to be broadly reusable, you need to do some work to respect various properties of the target `Control`.

Respecting `ContentControl`'s `Content` Property

The key to inserting property values from the target element inside a control template is data binding. Fortunately, a class called `TemplateBindingExtension` makes this easy.

`TemplateBindingExtension` is a markup extension that is similar to `Binding`, but simpler, more lightweight, and customized for templates. It's often referred to as simply `TemplateBinding` because of the tendency to omit the `Extension` suffix when used in XAML.

The data source for `TemplateBinding` is always the target element, and the path is any of its dependency properties, selected by setting `TemplateBinding`'s `Property` property. Therefore, you could add to the control template in Listing 14.6 a `TextBlock` that contains the target `Button`'s `Content`, as follows:

```
<TextBlock Text="{TemplateBinding Property=Button.Content}"/>
```

Or, because `TemplateBinding` has a constructor that accepts a dependency property, you could simply write this:

```
<TextBlock Text="{TemplateBinding Button.Content}"/>
```

If `TargetType` is used to restrict the template's use for `Buttons` (or other `ContentControls`), you could simplify this even further, like so:

```
<TextBlock Text="{TemplateBinding Content}"/>
```

Of course, a `Button` can contain nontext `Content`, so using a `TextBlock` to display it creates an artificial limitation. To ensure that all types of `Content` get displayed properly in the template, you can use a generic `ContentControl` instead of a `TextBlock`. Listing 14.7 does just that. The `ContentControl` is given a `Margin` and wrapped in a `Viewbox` so it's displayed at a reasonable size relative to the rest of the `Button`.

LISTING 14.7 An Updated ControlTemplate That Displays the Target Button's Content

```
<ControlTemplate x:Key="buttonTemplate" TargetType="{x:Type Button}">
  <Grid>
    <Ellipse x:Name="outerCircle" Width="100" Height="100">
    <Ellipse.Fill>
      <LinearGradientBrush StartPoint="0,0" EndPoint="0,1">
        <GradientStop Offset="0" Color="Blue"/>
        <GradientStop Offset="1" Color="Red"/>
      </LinearGradientBrush>
    </Ellipse.Fill>
    </Ellipse>
    <Ellipse Width="80" Height="80">
    <Ellipse.Fill>
      <LinearGradientBrush StartPoint="0,0" EndPoint="0,1">
        <GradientStop Offset="0" Color="White"/>
        <GradientStop Offset="1" Color="Transparent"/>
      </LinearGradientBrush>
    </Ellipse.Fill>
    </Ellipse>
    <Viewbox>
      <ContentControl Margin="20" Content="{TemplateBinding Content}"/>
    </Viewbox>
  </Grid>
<ControlTemplate.Triggers>
  <Trigger Property="IsMouseOver" Value="True">
    <Setter TargetName="outerCircle" Property="Fill" Value="Orange"/>
  </Trigger>
  <Trigger Property="IsPressed" Value="True">
    <Setter Property="RenderTransform">
    <Setter.Value>
      <ScaleTransform ScaleX=".9" ScaleY=".9"/>
    </Setter.Value>
    </Setter>
    <Setter Property="RenderTransformOrigin" Value=".5,.5"/>
  </Trigger>
</ControlTemplate.Triggers>
</ControlTemplate>
```

Figure 14.9 shows what two Buttons look like with this new control template applied. One Button has simple "OK" text content, and the other has an Image. In both cases, the content is reflected in the new visuals as expected.

FIGURE 14.9 Two different Buttons with the control template defined in Listing 14.7.

TIP

Rather than use a ContentControl inside a control template, you should use the lighter-weight ContentPresenter element. ContentPresenter displays content just like ContentControl, but it was designed specifically for use in control templates. ContentPresenter is a primitive building block, whereas ContentControl is a full-blown control with its own control template (that contains a ContentPresenter)!

In Listing 14.7, you can replace this:

```
<ContentControl Margin="20" Content="{TemplateBinding Content}"/>
```

with this:

```
<ContentPresenter Margin="20" Content="{TemplateBinding Content}"/>
```

ContentPresenter even has a built-in shortcut; if you omit setting its Content to {TemplateBinding Content}, it implicitly assumes that's what you want. So, you can replace the preceding line of code with the following:

```
<ContentPresenter Margin="20"/>
```

This works only when the control template is given an explicit TargetType of ContentControl or a ContentControl-derived class (such as Button).

The remaining templates in this chapter use ContentPresenter instead of ContentControl, as that's what real-world templates use.

WARNING

TemplateBinding works only inside a template's visual tree and doesn't work with properties on Freezables!

TemplateBinding doesn't work outside a template or outside its VisualTree property, so you can't even use TemplateBinding inside a template's trigger. Furthermore, TemplateBinding doesn't work when applied to a Freezable (for mostly artificial reasons). For example, attempting to bind the Color property of any explicit Brush fails.

Continued

However, TemplateBinding is just a less-powerful but convenient shortcut for using a regular Binding. You can get the same effect by using a regular Binding with a RelativeSource equal to {RelativeSource TemplatedParent} and a Path equal to the dependency property whose value you want to retrieve. Such a Binding works in the cases mentioned where TemplateBinding does not.

Respecting Other Properties

No matter what type of control you're creating a control template for, there are undoubtedly other properties on the target control that should be honored if you want the template to be reusable: Height and Width, perhaps Background, Padding, and so on. Some properties (such as Foreground, FontSize, FontWeight, and so on) might automatically inherit their desired values thanks to property value inheritance in the visual tree, but other properties need explicit attention.

Listing 14.8 is an update to Listing 14.7 that respects the Background, Padding, and Content properties of the target Button. It also implicitly respects the size of the target element by *removing* the explicit Height and Width settings and letting the layout system do its job. Listing 14.8 uses a ContentPresenter rather than a ContentControl, although both produce the same result.

LISTING 14.8 Updates to the ControlTemplate That Make It More Reusable

```
<ControlTemplate x:Key="buttonTemplate" TargetType="{x:Type Button}">
  <Grid>
    <Ellipse x:Name="outerCircle">
    <Ellipse.Fill>
      <LinearGradientBrush StartPoint="0,0" EndPoint="0,1">
        <GradientStop Offset="0"
          Color="{Binding RelativeSource={RelativeSource TemplatedParent},
            Path=Background.Color}"/>
        <GradientStop Offset="1" Color="Red"/>
      </LinearGradientBrush>
    </Ellipse.Fill>
    </Ellipse>
    <Ellipse RenderTransformOrigin=".5,.5">
    <Ellipse.RenderTransform>
      <ScaleTransform ScaleX=".8" ScaleY=".8"/>
    </Ellipse.RenderTransform>
    <Ellipse.Fill>
      <LinearGradientBrush StartPoint="0,0" EndPoint="0,1">
        <GradientStop Offset="0" Color="White"/>
        <GradientStop Offset="1" Color="Transparent"/>
      </LinearGradientBrush>
    </Ellipse.Fill>
```

LISTING 14.8 Continued

```
    </Ellipse>
    <Viewbox>
      <ContentPresenter Margin="{TemplateBinding Padding}"/>
    </Viewbox>
  </Grid>
<ControlTemplate.Triggers>
  <Trigger Property="IsMouseOver" Value="True">
    <Setter TargetName="outerCircle" Property="Fill" Value="Orange"/>
  </Trigger>
  <Trigger Property="IsPressed" Value="True">
    <Setter Property="RenderTransform">
    <Setter.Value>
      <ScaleTransform ScaleX=".9" ScaleY=".9"/>
    </Setter.Value>
    </Setter>
    <Setter Property="RenderTransformOrigin" Value=".5,.5"/>
  </Trigger>
</ControlTemplate.Triggers>
</ControlTemplate>
```


The target `Button`'s `Padding` is now used as the `ContentPresenter`'s `Margin`. It's common to use the element's `Padding` in a template as the `Margin` of an inner element. After all, that's basically the definition of `Padding`!

In addition, a few nonintuitive changes have been made to the template's visual tree to accommodate an externally specified size and `Background`. We could have simply used `{TemplateBinding Background}` as the `Fill` for `outerCircle`, giving each `Button` the flexibility to specify a solid color, a gradient, and so on. But perhaps the "red glow" at the bottom is a characteristic that we'd like to keep consistent wherever the template is used. In other words, we want to replace only the blue part of the gradient with the externally specified `Background`. However, `GradientStop.Color` can't be directly set to `{TemplateBinding Background}` because `Color` is of type `Color`, whereas `Background` is of type `Brush` (and because `GradientStop` derives from `Freezable`)! Therefore, the listing uses a normal `Binding` instead, which supports referencing the `Color` subproperty. (Note that this `Binding` works only when `Background` is set to a `SolidColorBrush` because other `Brushes` don't have a `Color` property.)

Both `Ellipses` (or the parent `Grid`) could have been given an explicit `Height` and `Width` matching those of the target `Button` by binding to its `ActualHeight` and `ActualWidth` properties. Instead, these values are omitted altogether because the root element is implicitly given the templated parent's size anyway! This means that an individual target `Button` has the power to make itself look like an ellipse by specifying different values for `Width` and `Height`. If we wanted to preserve the perfect circular look, we could wrap the entire visual tree in a `Viewbox`.

The final trick used by Listing 14.8 is the `ScaleTransform` on the inner circle to make it 80% of the size of the outer circle. In previous listings, this transform is unnecessary because both the outer and inner circles have a hard-coded size. But with a dynamic size, `ScaleTransform` enables us to effectively perform a little math on the size. (If we wanted a fixed-size difference between the circles, a simple `Margin` would do the trick.)

Figure 14.10 shows the rendered result for the following `Button`s that make use of this new control template:

```
<StackPanel Orientation="Horizontal">
  <Button Template="{StaticResource buttonTemplate}"
    Height="100" Width="100" FontSize="80" Background="Black"
    Padding="20" Margin="5">1</Button>
  <Button Template="{StaticResource buttonTemplate}"
    Height="150" Width="250" FontSize="80" Background="Yellow"
    Padding="20" Margin="5">2</Button>
  <Button Template="{StaticResource buttonTemplate}"
    Height="200" Width="200" FontSize="80" Background="White"
    Padding="20" Margin="5">3</Button>
</StackPanel>
```

FIGURE 14.10 `Button`s that tweak the look of their custom template from Listing 14.8.

Each `Button` in Figure 14.10 has values for `Background`, `Padding`, and `Content` that are explicitly used by the control template. Their values for `Height` and `Width` are implicitly respected by the template, and their `FontSize` setting is implicitly picked up by the template's `ContentPresenter`. The size of the font isn't directly reflected in the rendered output because the template wraps the `ContentPresenter` inside a `Viewbox` to keep it within the bounds of the outer circle. The `Margin` specified on each `Button` is not used by the template, but it still affects the `StackPanel` layout as usual, giving a little bit of space between each `Button`.

> **DIGGING DEEPER**
>
> **`TemplateBinding` and Value Converters**
>
> Just like `Binding`, `TemplateBinding` supports a value converter. `TemplateBinding` has `Converter` and `ConverterParameter` properties but, oddly, no `ConverterCulture` property. If you require the use of `ConverterCulture`, you can simply use `Binding` instead.

Hijacking Existing Properties for New Purposes

Sometimes, you might want to parameterize some aspect of a control template, despite there being no corresponding property on the target control. For example, the template in Listing 14.8 has a hard-coded orange `Brush` representing the hover state. What can you do to allow individual `Buttons` to customize this `Brush`? There's no corresponding property already on `Button` to be set!

One option is to define a custom control, using the techniques described in Chapter 20, "User Controls and Custom Controls." It wouldn't be too much work to write a new class that derives from `Button` and adds a single `HoverBrush` property. But that's a bit heavyweight for such a simple task. Another option would be to define several control templates that each uses a different hover `Brush`. But that would be reasonable only if the set of desired `Brushes` were small and known. Yet another option would be to define an appropriate attached property somewhere, perhaps on a utility class that already exists.

Instead, what most people resort to is a devious little hack known as *hijacking* a dependency property. This involves looking at the target control for any dependency properties of the desired type to see if you can leverage them in an unintended way. For example, all `Controls` have three properties of type `Brush`: `Background`, `Foreground`, and `BorderBrush`. Because `Background` and `Foreground` already play important roles in Listing 14.8, neither one would look very good as a hover `Brush`. (There would also be no way to set the hover `Brush` independently of the other two.) But `BorderBrush` is a different story. It's completely unused by the template in Listing 14.8, so why not use that?

There really is no reason not to use it, other than the fact that it makes the usage of the template confusing and less readable. Nevertheless, here's how you could update the `IsMouseOver` trigger from Listing 14.8 to hijack `BorderBrush`:

```
<Trigger Property="IsMouseOver" Value="True">
  <Setter TargetName="outerCircle" Property="Fill"
    Value="{Binding RelativeSource={RelativeSource TemplatedParent},
      Path=BorderBrush}"/>
</Trigger>
```

A `Binding` must be used in this case rather than a `TemplateBinding` because the `Trigger` is outside the visual tree.

If the target control doesn't have an appropriate property, you might even be able to hijack an attached property from a totally unrelated element! When choosing a property, be sure to pay attention to its metadata, such as its default value and what gets triggered when its value changes (such as invalidating layout).

If this hack leaves a bad taste in your mouth, then by all means use an alternative approach. This hack is definitely not recommended by the WPF team! But it's a useful trick to know about if you're looking for a quick fix.

Respecting Visual States with Triggers

When creating a control template for `Buttons`, visually reacting to hover and pressed states with corresponding triggers is a nice touch, but it's purely optional. Imagine using the template from Listing 14.8 on a `CheckBox` or `ToggleButton`, however. (This can be done simply by changing the `TargetType`.) Because the template doesn't show different visuals for the `Checked` versus `Unchecked` versus `Indeterminate` states, it's a pretty lousy template for these controls!

In fact, the template in Listing 14.8 is still incomplete, even for a `Button`! The fact that it doesn't show any different visuals when `IsEnabled` is `false` or `IsDefaulted` is `true` makes it a pretty lousy template!

Therefore, you should consider all the visual states a control should expose when designing a control template for it. This might take the form of triggers on the appropriate properties or events, or it could just be a matter of binding them appropriately.

For example, to be useful, a control template for `ProgressBar` must show the current value. Listing 14.9 contains a control template (defined as an application-level resource) for `ProgressBar` that makes it look like a pie chart. The most important aspect of the template—filling up the pie according to the current `Value`—is accomplished by binding to the templated parent and using value converters to do the necessary trigonometry. In addition to this, triggers on `IsEnabled` and `IsIndeterminate` alter the visuals for these states. Figures 14.11 and 14.12 show the results for `ProgressBars` such as the following:

```
<ProgressBar Foreground="{StaticResource foregroundBrush}" Width="100"
  Height="100" Value="10" Template="{StaticResource progressPie}"/>
```

The `foregroundBrush` resource is defined as a simple green gradient:

```
<LinearGradientBrush x:Key="foregroundBrush" StartPoint="0,0" EndPoint="1,1">
  <GradientStop Offset="0" Color="LightGreen"/>
  <GradientStop Offset="1" Color="DarkGreen"/>
</LinearGradientBrush>
```

LISTING 14.9 The Pie Chart Control Template for `ProgressBar`

```
<Application x:Class="WindowsApplication1.App"
  xmlns="http://schemas.microsoft.com/winfx/2006/xaml/presentation"
  xmlns:x="http://schemas.microsoft.com/winfx/2006/xaml"
  xmlns:local="clr-namespace:WindowsApplication1"
  StartupUri="Window1.xaml">
  <Application.Resources>

    <ControlTemplate x:Key="progressPie" TargetType="{x:Type ProgressBar}">

    <!-- Resources -->
    <ControlTemplate.Resources>
      <local:ValueMinMaxToPointConverter x:Key="converter1"/>
```

LISTING 14.9 Continued

```
    <local:ValueMinMaxToIsLargeArcConverter x:Key="converter2"/>
  </ControlTemplate.Resources>

  <!-- Visual Tree -->
  <Viewbox>
    <Grid Width="20" Height="20">
      <Ellipse x:Name="background" Stroke="{TemplateBinding BorderBrush}"
        StrokeThickness="{TemplateBinding BorderThickness}"
        Width="20" Height="20" Fill="{TemplateBinding Background}"/>
      <Path x:Name="pie" Fill="{TemplateBinding Foreground}">
      <Path.Data>
        <PathGeometry>
          <PathFigure StartPoint="10,10" IsClosed="True">
            <LineSegment Point="10,0"/>
            <ArcSegment Size="10,10" SweepDirection="Clockwise">
            <ArcSegment.Point>
              <MultiBinding Converter="{StaticResource converter1}">
                <Binding RelativeSource="{RelativeSource TemplatedParent}"
                  Path="Value"/>
                <Binding RelativeSource="{RelativeSource TemplatedParent}"
                  Path="Minimum"/>
                <Binding RelativeSource="{RelativeSource TemplatedParent}"
                  Path="Maximum"/>
              </MultiBinding>
            </ArcSegment.Point>
            <ArcSegment.IsLargeArc>
              <MultiBinding Converter="{StaticResource converter2}">
                <Binding RelativeSource="{RelativeSource TemplatedParent}"
                  Path="Value"/>
                <Binding RelativeSource="{RelativeSource TemplatedParent}"
                  Path="Minimum"/>
                <Binding RelativeSource="{RelativeSource TemplatedParent}"
                  Path="Maximum"/>
              </MultiBinding>
            </ArcSegment.IsLargeArc>
            </ArcSegment>
          </PathFigure>
        </PathGeometry>
      </Path.Data>
      </Path>
    </Grid>
  </Viewbox>

  <!-- Triggers -->
```

LISTING 14.9 Continued

```
    <ControlTemplate.Triggers>
      <Trigger Property="IsIndeterminate" Value="True">
        <Setter TargetName="pie" Property="Visibility" Value="Hidden"/>
        <Setter TargetName="background" Property="Fill">
        <Setter.Value>
          <LinearGradientBrush StartPoint="0,0" EndPoint="1,1">
            <GradientStop Offset="0" Color="Yellow"/>
            <GradientStop Offset="1" Color="Brown"/>
          </LinearGradientBrush>
        </Setter.Value>
        </Setter>
      </Trigger>
      <Trigger Property="IsEnabled" Value="False">
        <Setter TargetName="pie" Property="Fill">
        <Setter.Value>
          <LinearGradientBrush StartPoint="0,0" EndPoint="1,1">
            <GradientStop Offset="0" Color="Gray"/>
            <GradientStop Offset="1" Color="White"/>
          </LinearGradientBrush>
        </Setter.Value>
        </Setter>
      </Trigger>
    </ControlTemplate.Triggers>
    </ControlTemplate>

  </Application.Resources>
</Application>
```

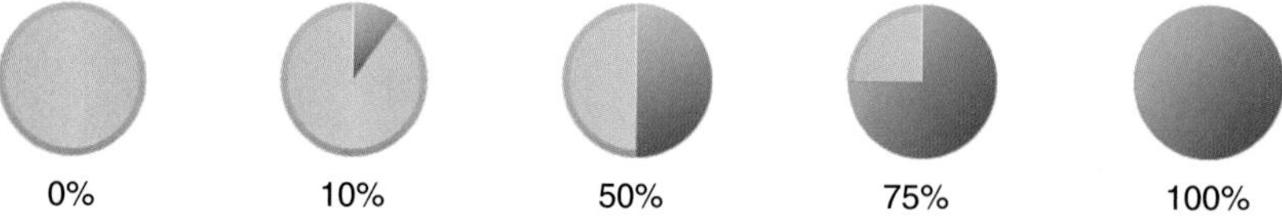

FIGURE 14.11 Customized `ProgressBar` visuals for various stages of progress.

`IsEnabled=false` `IsIndeterminate=true`

FIGURE 14.12 Customized `ProgressBar` visuals for disabled and indeterminate states.

The root of the visual tree is a `Viewbox`, so the 20x20 single-cell `Grid` can scale appropriately. The background circle (which has a radius of 10 prior to scaling) is given the templated parent's `Background`, `BorderBrush`, and `BorderThickness`. The "pie" is a `Path` (an element covered in the next chapter) that is given the templated parent's `Foreground` and relies on two `MultiBinding`s with value converters defined in Listing 14.10 to get the right shape. `MultiBinding` is used rather than a simple `TemplateBinding` or `Binding` so the pie gets updated when any of `ProgressBar`'s three relevant properties change: `Value`, `Minimum`, and `Maximum`. The two triggers create the results in Figure 14.12 by filling an element with a hard-coded `Brush` (and in the case of `IsIndeterminate`, hiding the pie). A more appropriate effect for `IsIndeterminate` is probably an animation that spins the pie around, but at least there's *some* visual distinction as is. Note that not all of `ProgressBar`'s properties are honored by this template. For example, `Orientation` is unused, but there's not a great way to honor it, considering the visual representation.

TIP

Notice that Listing 14.9 defines value converters in `ControlTemplate`'s `Resources` collection. Like `Style`, all `FrameworkTemplate`s have their own `Resources` collection. This collection can be used to keep templates self-contained.

LISTING 14.10 The Value Converters Used in Listing 14.9

```
public class ValueMinMaxToIsLargeArcConverter : IMultiValueConverter
{
  public object Convert(object[] values, Type targetType, object parameter,
    CultureInfo culture)
  {
    double value = (double)values[0];
    double minimum = (double)values[1];
    double maximum = (double)values[2];

    // Only return true if the value is 50% of the range or greater
    return ((value * 2) >= (maximum - minimum));
  }

  public object[] ConvertBack(object value, Type[] targetTypes, object parameter,
    CultureInfo culture)
  {
    throw new NotSupportedException();
  }
}

public class ValueMinMaxToPointConverter : IMultiValueConverter
{
  public object Convert(object[] values, Type targetType, object parameter,
    CultureInfo culture)
  {
```

LISTING 14.10 Continued

```
    double value = (double)values[0];
    double minimum = (double)values[1];
    double maximum = (double)values[2];

    // Convert the value to one between 0 and 360
    double current = (value / (maximum - minimum)) * 360;

    // Adjust the finished state so the ArcSegment gets drawn as a whole circle
    if (current == 360)
      current = 359.999;

    // Shift by 90 degrees so 0 starts at the top of the circle
    current = current - 90;

    // Convert the angle to radians
    current = current * 0.017453292519943295;

    // Calculate the circle's point
    double x = 10 + 10 * Math.Cos(current);
    double y = 10 + 10 * Math.Sin(current);
    return new Point(x, y);
  }

  public object[] ConvertBack(object value, Type[] targetTypes, object parameter,
    CultureInfo culture)
  {
    throw new NotSupportedException();
  }
}
```

The first value converter is pretty simple. `ArcSegment`'s `IsLargeArc` property (from Listing 14.9) must be `true` when the pie is more than half full and `false` otherwise. Therefore, `ValueMinMaxToIsLargeArcConverter` does this simple calculation based on the three values from the target `ProgressBar` and returns the appropriate Boolean value.

The second value converter is much more complicated. Its job is to return the proper `Point` along the circle's circumference, according to the current values. To do this, it converts the `ProgressBar`'s `Value` to an angle (in degrees), makes some adjustments, and then converts it to radians. With this angle, a little trigonometry is used to get the point, based on the fixed radius of 10 and the center point of (10,10).

Respecting Visual States with the Visual State Manager (VSM)

For a control template designer, knowing all the visual states that need to be respected can be difficult. Each control has a large number of properties, and it might not always be clear which ones are visually important or how to manage all the possible states with triggers. Fortunately, WPF 4 makes this task easier with the inclusion of the Visual State Manager (VSM), a feature that first appeared in Silverlight.

The VSM support includes a collection of types and members that make it easy for control authors to formally specify *parts* and *states* for their controls, taking the guesswork out of writing control templates that support them all. Importantly, it enables design tools to provide a decent experience for creating complex templates. Expression Blend takes great advantage of such parts and states.

Control Parts

The "parts" portion of the parts and states model has actually been in WPF from its first release. The idea is that controls can look for specially named elements in the visual tree of the template being applied to them, so that they can apply some logic to those visual pieces. Consider these examples:

- If a `ProgressBar` control template has elements named `PART_Indicator` and `PART_Track`, the control ensures that the `Width` (or `Height`, based on `ProgressBar`'s `Orientation`) of `PART_Indicator` remains the correct percentage of the `Width` (or `Height`) of `PART_Track`, based on `ProgressBar`'s `Value`, `Minimum`, and `Maximum` properties. For the pie chart template from Listing 14.9, this behavior is clearly undesirable. But for a template that more closely matches the standard `ProgressBar` look, taking advantage of this support greatly simplifies it (and removes the need for procedural code to do the math).
- If a `ComboBox` control template has a `Popup` named `PART_Popup`, `ComboBox`'s `DropDownClosed` event is automatically raised when the `Popup` is closed. If it has a `TextBox` named `PART_EditableTextBox`, it integrates automatically with `ComboBox`'s ability to update the selection as the user types.
- Controls such as `TextBox` and `PasswordBox` have most of their functionality tied to an element in the control template called `PART_ContentHost`. If you don't have an element with this name in your control template, you'll have to reimplement the entire editable surface!

In some cases, the named part can be any `FrameworkElement`, but in other cases the type of the named part must be something more specific in order to be respected. Table 14.1 reveals all the named parts leveraged by WPF's built-in controls. Derived classes that automatically inherit the named part logic are not listed, such as `TextBox` and `PasswordBox`, which get their `PART_ContentHost` logic from `TextBoxBase`.

TABLE 14.1 Named Parts Used by WPF's Controls

Control	Part Name	Part Type
Calendar	PART_CalendarItem	CalendarItem
	PART_Root	Panel
CalendarItem	DayTitleTemplate	DataTemplate
	PART_DisabledVisual	FrameworkElement
	PART_HeaderButton	Button
	PART_MonthView	Grid
	PART_NextButton	Button
	PART_PreviousButton	Button
	PART_Root	FrameworkElement
	PART_YearView	Grid
ComboBox	PART_EditableTextBox	TextBox
	PART_Popup	Popup
DataGridColumnFloatingHeader	PART_VisualBrushCanvas	Canvas
DataGridColumnHeader	PART_LeftHeaderGripper	Thumb
	PART_RightHeaderGripper	Thumb
DataGridColumnHeadersPresenter	PART_FillerColumnHeader	DataGridColumnHeader
DataGridRowHeader	PART_BottomHeaderGripper	Thumb
	PART_TopHeaderGripper	Thumb
DatePicker	PART_Button	Button
	PART_Popup	Popup
	PART_Root	Grid
	PART_TextBox	DatePickerTextBox
DatePickerTextBox	PART_Watermark	ContentControl
DocumentViewer	PART_ContentHost	ScrollViewer
	PART_FindToolBarHost	ContentControl
DocumentViewerBase	PART_FindToolBarHost	Decorator
FlowDocumentReader	PART_ContentHost	Decorator
	PART_FindToolBarHost	Decorator
FlowDocumentScrollViewer	PART_ContentHost	ScrollViewer
	PART_FindToolBarHost	Decorator
	PART_ToolBarHost	Decorator
Frame	PART_FrameCP	ContentPresenter
GridViewColumnHeader	PART_FloatingHeaderCanvas	Canvas
	PART_HeaderGripper	Thumb
MenuItem	PART_Popup	Popup
NavigationWindow	PART_NavWinCP	ContentPresenter
ProgressBar	PART_GlowRect	FrameworkElement
	PART_Indicator	FrameworkElement
	PART_Track	FrameworkElement
ScrollBar	PART_Track	Track

TABLE 14.1 Continued

Control	Part Name	Part Type
ScrollViewer	PART_HorizontalScrollBar	ScrollBar
	PART_ScrollContentPresenter	ScrollContentPresenter
	PART_VerticalScrollBar	ScrollBar
Slider	PART_SelectionRange	FrameworkElement
	PART_Track	Track
StickyNoteControl	PART_ClipboardSeparator	Separator
	PART_CloseButton	Button
	PART_ContentControl	ContentControl
	PART_CopyMenuItem	MenuItem
	PART_EraseMenuItem	MenuItem
	PART_IconButton	Button
	PART_InkMenuItem	MenuItem
	PART_PasteMenuItem	MenuItem
	PART_ResizeBottomRightThumb	Thumb
	PART_SelectMenuItem	MenuItem
	PART_TitleThumb	Thumb
TabControl	PART_SelectedContentHost	ContentPresenter
TextBoxBase	PART_ContentHost	FrameworkElement
ToolBar	PART_ToolBarOverflowPanel	ToolBarOverflowPanel
	PART_ToolBarPanel	ToolBarPanel
TreeViewItem	PART_Header	FrameworkElement

Therefore, claims of WPF's controls being "lookless" and having an implementation that's completely independent from their visuals (such as my own claim earlier in this chapter) aren't *entirely* true! However, these "secret handshakes" with magically named parts are optional. This is important, as it means you still have the flexibility to radically change a control's visuals, such as with the pie chart template for `ProgressBar`.

To give design tools the ability to discover every named part available for use, controls document them with a `TemplatePartAttribute` on their class—one for each named part—that reveals the name and expected type of the part. WPF also has a convention of using parts named `PART_`*`XXX`* (a convention broken by one of `CalendarItem`'s parts, seen in Table 14.1), although Silverlight does not have this convention.

On the one hand, named parts are an implementation detail that you don't need to know about. On the other hand, you can sometimes create control templates with much less effort by taking advantage of this built-in logic!

Control States

The "states" portion of the parts and states model is the functionality that is new to WPF 4. As with control parts, controls can have internal logic to transition to named states that they define (by calling a static `VisualStateManager.GoToState` method). Control templates can then use a few new elements to organize visual settings specific to each state rather than use triggers. Writing control templates that take advantage of states is optional, but as of WPF 4, this is the recommended approach. Such templates are not only better supported by tools such as Expression Blend, they are more likely to work for Silverlight controls as well.

The states defined by each control are grouped into mutually exclusive *state groups*. For example, `Button` has four states in a group called `CommonStates`—`Normal`, `MouseOver`, `Pressed`, and `Disabled`—and two states in a group called `FocusStates`—`Unfocused` and `Focused`. At any time, `Button` is in one state from every group, so it is `Normal` and `Unfocused` by default. This grouping mechanism exists to avoid a long list of states meant to cover every combination of independent properties (such as `NormalUnfocused`, `NormalFocused`, `MouseOverUnfocused`, `MouseOverFocused`, and so on).

Table 14.2 lists all the groups and states supported by WPF's built-in controls. Notice the explosion of states for `DataGridRow` and `DataGridRowHeader`; these states really should have been organized into three separate groups. (Someone didn't get the memo.) States inherited from base classes are not listed; you can find `Button`'s states under `ButtonBase`. Similarly, `DataGridColumnHeader` lists only its `SortStates` group, even though it also inherits the two groups from `ButtonBase`. Some controls choose not to respect states defined by its base classes. For example, `ProgressBar` supports two `CommonStates`—`Determinate` and `Indeterminate`—but overrides functionality in the `RangeBase` base class such that its three `CommonStates` and two `FocusStates` never get invoked.

TABLE 14.2 State Groups and States Used by WPF's Controls

Control	State Group	States
ButtonBase	CommonStates	Normal, MouseOver, Pressed, Disabled
	FocusStates	Unfocused, Focused
CalendarButton	SelectionStates	Unselected, Selected
	CalendarButtonFocusStates	CalendarButtonUnfocused, CalendarButtonFocused
	ActiveStates	Inactive, Active
CalendarDayButton	SelectionStates	Unselected, Selected
	CalendarButtonFocusStates	CalendarButtonUnfocused, CalendarButtonFocused
	ActiveStates	Inactive, Active
	DayStates	RegularDay, Today
	BlackoutDayStates	NormalDay, BlackoutDay
CalendarItem	CommonStates	Normal, Disabled
ComboBox	CommonStates	Normal, MouseOver, Disabled
	FocusStates	Unfocused, Focused, FocusedDropDown
	EditStates	Editable, Uneditable

TABLE 14.2 Continued

Control	State Group	States
ComboBoxItem	CommonStates	Normal, MouseOver
	SelectionStates	Unselected, Selected, SelectedUnfocused
	FocusStates	Unfocused, Focused
Control	ValidationStates	Valid, InvalidFocused, InvalidUnfocused
DataGrid	CommonStates	Normal, Disabled
DataGridCell	CommonStates	Normal, MouseOver
	SelectionStates	Unselected, Selected
	FocusStates	Unfocused, Focused
	CurrentStates	Regular, Current
	InteractionStates	Display, Editing
DataGridColumnHeader	SortStates	Unsorted, SortAscending, SortDescending
DataGridRow	CommonStates	Normal, Normal_AlternatingRow, Normal_Editing, Normal_Selected, Unfocused_Editing, Unfocused_Selected, MouseOver, MouseOver_Editing, MouseOver_Selected, MouseOver_Unfocused_Editing, MouseOver_Unfocused_Selected
DataGridRowHeader	CommonStates	Normal, Normal_Selected, Normal_EditingRow, Normal_CurrentRow, Normal_CurrentRow_Selected, Unfocused_Selected, Unfocused_EditingRow, Unfocused_CurrentRow_Selected, MouseOver, MouseOver_Selected, MouseOver_EditingRow, MouseOver_CurrentRow, MouseOver_CurrentRow_Selected, MouseOver_Unfocused_Selected, MouseOver_Unfocused_EditingRow, MouseOver_Unfocused_CurrentRow_Selected
DatePicker	CommonStates	Normal, Disabled
DatePickerTextBox	WatermarkStates	Unwatermarked, Watermarked
Expander	CommonStates	Normal, MouseOver, Disabled
	FocusStates	Unfocused, Focused
	ExpansionStates	Expanded, Collapsed
	ExpandDirectionStates	ExpandDown, ExpandUp, ExpandLeft, ExpandRight

TABLE 14.2 Continued

Control	State Group	States
GridSpliter	CommonStates	Normal, MouseOver, Disabled
ListBoxItem	CommonStates	Normal, MouseOver, Disabled
	SelectionStates	Unselected, Selected, SelectedUnfocused
	FocusStates	Unfocused, Focused
ProgressBar	CommonStates	Determinate, Indeterminate
RangeBase	CommonStates	Normal, MouseOver, Disabled
	FocusStates	Unfocused, Focused
ScrollBar	CommonStates	Normal, MouseOver, Disabled
	FocusStates	Unfocused, Focused
TabControl	CommonStates	Normal, Disabled
TabItem	CommonStates	Normal, MouseOver, Disabled
	SelectionStates	Unselected, Selected
	FocusStates	Unfocused, Focused
TextBox	CommonStates	ReadOnly (and states from TextBoxBase)
TextBoxBase	CommonStates	Normal, MouseOver, Disabled
	FocusStates	Unfocused, Focused
Thumb	CommonStates	Normal, MouseOver, Pressed, Disabled
	FocusStates	Unfocused, Focused
ToggleButton	CheckStates	Checked, Unchecked, Indeterminate
ToolTip	OpenStates	Open, Closed
	FocusStates	Unfocused, Focused
TreeViewItem	CommonStates	Normal, MouseOver, Disabled
	SelectionStates	Unselected, Selected, SelectedInactive
	FocusStates	Unfocused, Focused
	ExpansionStates	Collapsed, Expanded
	HasItemsStates	HasItems, NoItems

To write a control template that takes advantage of states, you set the `VisualStateManager.VisualStateGroups` attached property on the root element in the template's visual tree to a collection of `VisualStateGroup` objects, each of which has a collection of `VisualState` children.

Listing 14.11 updates the pie chart control template from Listing 14.9 to take advantage of `ProgressBar`'s visual states. Because `ProgressBar` only supports states for `Determinate` versus `Indeterminate` and does not have states for `Normal` versus `Disabled`, this template still needs one trigger for the case of `IsEnabled` being `false`. The previous trigger that acted on `IsIndeterminate` being `true` has been replaced by acting on the `Indeterminate` visual state, however.

LISTING 14.11 An Update to the Pie Chart Control Template from Listing 14.9 That Uses the VSM

```
<Application x:Class="WindowsApplication1.App"
  xmlns="http://schemas.microsoft.com/winfx/2006/xaml/presentation"
  xmlns:x="http://schemas.microsoft.com/winfx/2006/xaml"
  xmlns:local="clr-namespace:WindowsApplication1"
  StartupUri="Window1.xaml">
  <Application.Resources>

    <ControlTemplate x:Key="progressPie" TargetType="{x:Type ProgressBar}">

    <!-- Resources -->
    <ControlTemplate.Resources>
      <local:ValueMinMaxToPointConverter x:Key="converter1"/>
      <local:ValueMinMaxToIsLargeArcConverter x:Key="converter2"/>
    </ControlTemplate.Resources>

    <!-- Visual Tree -->
    <Viewbox>
  <!-- Visual State Groups -->
  <VisualStateManager.VisualStateGroups>
    <VisualStateGroup Name="CommonStates">
      <VisualState Name="Determinate"/> <!-- Nothing to do for this state -->
      <VisualState Name="Indeterminate">
        <Storyboard>
          <DoubleAnimation Storyboard.TargetName="pie"
            Storyboard.TargetProperty="Opacity" To="0" Duration="0"/>
          <DoubleAnimation Storyboard.TargetName="backgroundNormal"
            Storyboard.TargetProperty="Opacity" To="0" Duration="0"/>
          <DoubleAnimation Storyboard.TargetName="backgroundIndeterminate"
            Storyboard.TargetProperty="Opacity" To="1" Duration="0"/>
        </Storyboard>
      </VisualState>
    </VisualStateGroup>
  </VisualStateManager.VisualStateGroups>
      <Grid Width="20" Height="20">
        <Ellipse x:Name="backgroundIndeterminate" Opacity="0"
          Stroke="{TemplateBinding BorderBrush}"
          StrokeThickness="{TemplateBinding BorderThickness}" Width="20"
          Height="20">
        <Ellipse.Fill>
```

LISTING 14.11 Continued

```
          <LinearGradientBrush StartPoint="0,0" EndPoint="1,1">
            <GradientStop Offset="0" Color="Yellow"/>
            <GradientStop Offset="1" Color="Brown"/>
          </LinearGradientBrush>
        </Ellipse.Fill>
      </Ellipse>
        <Ellipse x:Name="backgroundNormal" Stroke="{TemplateBinding BorderBrush}"
          StrokeThickness="{TemplateBinding BorderThickness}"
          Width="20" Height="20" Fill="{TemplateBinding Background}"/>
        <Path x:Name="pie" Fill="{TemplateBinding Foreground}">
        <Path.Data>
          <PathGeometry>
            <PathFigure StartPoint="10,10" IsClosed="True">
              <LineSegment Point="10,0"/>
              <ArcSegment Size="10,10" SweepDirection="Clockwise">
              <ArcSegment.Point>
                <MultiBinding Converter="{StaticResource converter1}">
                  <Binding RelativeSource="{RelativeSource TemplatedParent}"
                    Path="Value"/>
                  <Binding RelativeSource="{RelativeSource TemplatedParent}"
                    Path="Minimum"/>
                  <Binding RelativeSource="{RelativeSource TemplatedParent}"
                    Path="Maximum"/>
                </MultiBinding>
              </ArcSegment.Point>
              <ArcSegment.IsLargeArc>
                <MultiBinding Converter="{StaticResource converter2}">
                  <Binding RelativeSource="{RelativeSource TemplatedParent}"
                    Path="Value"/>
                  <Binding RelativeSource="{RelativeSource TemplatedParent}"
                    Path="Minimum"/>
                  <Binding RelativeSource="{RelativeSource TemplatedParent}"
                    Path="Maximum"/>
                </MultiBinding>
              </ArcSegment.IsLargeArc>
              </ArcSegment>
            </PathFigure>
          </PathGeometry>
        </Path.Data>
        </Path>
      </Grid>
    </Viewbox>

    <!-- Only one Trigger -->
```

LISTING 14.11 Continued

```
    <ControlTemplate.Triggers>
      <Trigger Property="IsEnabled" Value="False">
        <Setter TargetName="pie" Property="Fill">
        <Setter.Value>
          <LinearGradientBrush StartPoint="0,0" EndPoint="1,1">
            <GradientStop Offset="0" Color="Gray"/>
            <GradientStop Offset="1" Color="White"/>
          </LinearGradientBrush>
        </Setter.Value>
        </Setter>
      </Trigger>
    </ControlTemplate.Triggers>
    </ControlTemplate>

  </Application.Resources>
</Application>
```


The content of each `VisualState` is a `Storyboard`, a type covered in depth in Chapter 17. It enables you to change certain property values either instantly (as done in Listing 14.11) or with a smooth transition. Changing the arbitrary `background` `Ellipse` `Fill` to a specific `LinearGradientBrush` isn't feasible with a `Storyboard`, so this listing changes the visual tree to contain *two* `Ellipses`—`backgroundNormal` that is visible by default and `backgroundIndeterminate` that is not (due to its `Opacity` being set to `0`). The transition to the `Indeterminate` visual state therefore instantly "animates" the `Opacity` of `backgroundNormal` to `0` and the `Opacity` of `backgroundIndeterminate` to `1`. To make this happen more gradually, you can increase the `Duration` value on the two `DoubleAnimations`. Chapter 17 reveals all the flexibility that the use of these animation objects can give you. It also revisits the `Button` control template created in this chapter (Listing 14.8), to show how it could be rewritten to leverage the VSM.

TIP

`VisualStateGroup` has a `Transitions` property that can be set to one or more `VisualTransitions` that can do automatic animated transitions between any combinations of states. See Chapter 17 for more information.

As with their parts, controls should document their state groups and states by using the `TemplateVisualStateAttribute`. However, the built-in WPF controls do not currently do this.

Mixing Templates with Styles

Although all the control templates thus far are applied directly to elements for simplicity, it's more common to set a Control's Template property inside a Style and then apply that style to the desired elements:

```
<Style TargetType="{x:Type Button}">
  <Setter Property="Template">
  <Setter.Value>
    <ControlTemplate TargetType="{x:Type Button}">
      …
    </ControlTemplate>
  </Setter.Value>
  </Setter>
  …
</Style>
```

Besides the convenience of combining a template with arbitrary property settings, there are important advantages to doing this:

- It gives you the effect of default templates. For example, when a typed Style gets applied to elements by default and that Style contains a custom control template, the control template gets applied without any explicit markings on those elements!
- It enables you to provide default yet overridable property values that control the look of the template. In other words, it enables you to respect the templated parent's properties but still provide your own default values.

The final point is very relevant for the templates examined so far. For the ProgressBar pie chart template, I wanted the pie to be filled with a green gradient by default. If such a Brush is hard-coded inside the template, consumers would have no way to customize the fill. On the other hand, by binding to the templated parent's Foreground (which is what Listing 14.9 does), the onus is on every ProgressBar to set its Foreground appropriately. ProgressBar's default Foreground is a solid green color, not the desired gradient!

By placing the green gradient in a Style's Setter, however, you get the desired default look while still allowing individual ProgressBars to override the fill by explicitly setting their Foreground property locally. And the {TemplateBinding Foreground} expression inside the template doesn't need to change. The Style could look as follows:

```
<Style x:Key="pieStyle" TargetType="{x:Type ProgressBar}">
  <Setter Property="Foreground">
  <Setter.Value>
    <LinearGradientBrush StartPoint="0,0" EndPoint="1,1">
      <GradientStop Offset="0" Color="LightGreen"/>
      <GradientStop Offset="1" Color="DarkGreen"/>
    </LinearGradientBrush>
```

```
    </Setter.Value>
    </Setter>
    <Setter Property="Template">
    <Setter.Value>
      <ControlTemplate TargetType="{x:Type ProgressBar}">
        …
          <Path x:Name="pie" Fill="{TemplateBinding Foreground}">
        …
      </ControlTemplate>
    </Setter.Value>
    </Setter>
</Style>
```

Consumers of the `Style` could do the following:

```
<!-- Use the default gradient fill -->
<ProgressBar Style="{StaticResource pieStyle}"
  Width="100" Height="100" Value="10"/>
<!-- Use a solid red fill instead -->
<ProgressBar Style="{StaticResource pieStyle}" Foreground="Red"
  Width="100" Height="100" Value="10"/>
```

Of course, the same approach can be used for other properties, such as `Width` and `Height`.

14

DIGGING DEEPER

Interactions Between `Styles` and Their Templates

When a `Style` contains a control template, it's possible to see the same property set from several different places: from triggers in the `Style`, from triggers in the `Style`'s template, and from a `Setter` in the `Style`! The order of precedence is the order listed in the preceding sentence. So, `Style` triggers override template triggers, and all triggers override `Style` `Setters`.

FAQ

How do I make small tweaks to an existing control template rather than create a brand-new one from scratch?

There is no mechanism for tweaking existing templates (like `Style`'s `BasedOn`). Instead, you can easily retrieve a XAML representation for any existing `Style` or template, modify it, and then apply it as a brand-new `Style` or template. In fact, even if you want to create a completely different look, the best way to become familiar with how to design robust control templates is to look at the built-in WPF control templates used by their theme styles.

Continued

To obtain the "visual source code" in XAML for any control template, you simply use code such as the following (after the control has undergone layout, so the template gets applied):

```
string xaml = XamlWriter.Save(someControl.Template);
```

Or, you can retrieve the entire `Style` for any element by programmatically grabbing the correct resource. The following code grabs the theme style of an element by using a dependency property called `DefaultStyleKey` (described in the "Themes" section) to identify the `Style` resource:

```
// Get the default style key
object defaultStyleKey = someElement.GetValue(
  FrameworkElement.DefaultStyleKeyProperty);
// Retrieve the resource with that key
Style style = (Style)Application.Current.FindResource(defaultStyleKey);
// Serialize its XAML representation into a string
string xaml = System.Windows.Markup.XamlWriter.Save(style);
```

For other types of `Styles`, you could call `FindResource` with the appropriate key, such as `typeof(Button)` for a typed `Button` style (if it exists).

In addition, there are many alternative approaches that don't involve writing code:

- Consult the Windows SDK, which contains XAML files with all the theme styles used by WPF's controls.
- Use the .NET Reflector tool with its BAML Viewer add-in to view the embedded styles in assemblies such as `PresentationFramework.Aero.dll`.
- Create the appropriate control in Expression Blend and then choose Edit Template, Edit a Copy... to get a copy of its style pasted into your XAML. (You can also find a XAML file for each theme supported by WPF's controls installed with Blend under Program Files.)

The last approach is my personal favorite. Blend also includes "simple styles" for the common controls, which are much easier to tweak and understand. These can be an instructive starting point for creating your own custom templates.

Skins

Skinning refers to the act of changing an application's appearance (or *skin*) on the fly, typically by third parties. WPF doesn't have a distinct concept called a *skin*, nor does it have a formal notion of skinning, but it doesn't need one. You can easily write an application or a component that supports dynamic skinning by using WPF's dynamic resource mechanism (described in Chapter 12, "Resources") combined with `Styles` and/or templates.

To support skinning in an application, one of the first things you need to do is decide on a data format. Whereas it might make sense to invent a format for Win32 or Windows Forms applications, XAML is a no-brainer data format for skins in WPF applications *if* you are okay with loading arbitrary code into your process. (Loading someone's XAML is like loading someone's add-in; it has the power to invoke unrelated code and may therefore do something malicious. See the FAQ at the end of this section for more information.)

But what should such XAML files look like?

Often, the initial instinct is to load an entire `Window` or `Page` dynamically from a loose XAML file and hook it up to the appropriate logic (using the technique shown at the end of Chapter 2, "XAML Demystified"). Loading your entire user interface on the fly gives complete flexibility, but, in most cases, it's probably *too much* flexibility. Authors of such XAML files would need a lot of discipline to include all the right elements with all the right names and all the right event handlers, and so on. (Either that or the code to connect the user interface to the application logic needs to be extremely forgiving.) Visual Studio 2010 follows this approach with its XAML-based Start Page. By loading an arbitrary `Page`, authors can plug in something completely different. If all they want to do is reskin what's there, they need to start by copying the existing `Page` and tweak it from there.

For environments in which you don't want to encourage complete user interface replacement, the best approach is to make `ResourceDictionary` the root of a skin representation. `ResourceDictionary` makes a great extensibility point in general because of the ease with which it can be swapped in and out or merged with others. When defining a skin, it makes sense for the `ResourceDictionary` to contain `Styles` and/or templates.

To demonstrate skinning, the following `Window` is a hypothetical progress dialog, shown in Figure 14.13:

```
<Window x:Class="WindowsApplication1.Window1"
  xmlns="http://schemas.microsoft.com/winfx/2006/xaml/presentation"
  xmlns:x="http://schemas.microsoft.com/winfx/2006/xaml"
  Title="Please Wait" Height="200" Width="300" ResizeMode="NoResize">
  <Grid>
    <StackPanel Style="{DynamicResource DialogStyle}">
      <Label Style="{DynamicResource HeadingStyle}">Loading...</Label>
      <ProgressBar Value="35" MinHeight="20" Margin="20"/>
      <Button Style="{DynamicResource CancelButtonStyle}" Width="70"
        Click="Cancel_Click">Cancel</Button>
    </StackPanel>
  </Grid>
</Window>
```

FIGURE 14.13 A dialog box, shown with its default skin.

Notice that most of the `Window`'s elements are given explicit `Styles`. This is not a requirement for skinning, but it's often a nice touch for giving skin authors more control over the visual experience. For example, suppose you want to give a specific look to a Cancel `Button` that's different from the look you want for all other `Buttons`. Marking all Cancel `Buttons` with an explicit `CancelButtonStyle` allows you to do just that. Referencing the explicit Styles as *dynamic* resources is critical to enable them to be updated at arbitrary times.

> **TIP**
>
> When giving an element a Style that you expect to be reskinned dynamically, don't forget to reference it as a dynamic resource!

So that it will have the look shown in Figure 14.13, the preceding Window is paired with the following App.xaml file that provides a default definition of each Style resource:

```
<Application xmlns="http://schemas.microsoft.com/winfx/2006/xaml/presentation"
    xmlns:x="http://schemas.microsoft.com/winfx/2006/xaml"
    StartupUri="Window1.xaml">
    <Application.Resources>
      <Style x:Key="DialogStyle" TargetType="{x:Type StackPanel}">
        <Setter Property="Margin" Value="20"/>
      </Style>
      <Style x:Key="HeadingStyle" TargetType="{x:Type Label}">
        <Setter Property="FontSize" Value="16"/>
        <Setter Property="FontWeight" Value="Bold"/>
      </Style>
      <Style x:Key="CancelButtonStyle" TargetType="{x:Type Button}"/>
    </Application.Resources>
</Application>
```

Notice that CancelButtonStyle is empty, so applying it to a Button has no effect. This is perfectly valid because the expectation is that a skin might replace this Style with something more meaningful.

With this in place, a skin file could simply look like the following:

```
<ResourceDictionary
  xmlns="http://schemas.microsoft.com/winfx/2006/xaml/presentation"
  xmlns:x="http://schemas.microsoft.com/winfx/2006/xaml">
  <Style x:Key="DialogStyle" TargetType="{x:Type StackPanel}">
    …
  </Style>
  <Style x:Key="HeadingStyle" TargetType="{x:Type Label}">
    …
  </Style>
  <Style x:Key="CancelButtonStyle" TargetType="{x:Type Button}">
    …
  </Style>
  Any additional styles…
</ResourceDictionary>
```

Then all the host application needs to do is dynamically load the skin XAML file and assign it as the new `Application.Resources` dictionary. The following code does this for a `.xaml` file sitting in the current directory:

```
ResourceDictionary resources = null;
using (FileStream fs = new FileStream("CustomSkin.xaml", FileMode.Open,
  FileAccess.Read))
{
  // Get the root element, which must be a ResourceDictionary
  resources = (ResourceDictionary)XamlReader.Load(fs);
}
Application.Current.Resources = resources;
```

You could alternatively use code like the following to retrieve a skin file from the Internet at an arbitrary URL:

```
ResourceDictionary resources = null;
System.Net.WebClient client = new System.Net.WebClient();
using (Stream s = client.OpenRead("http://adamnathan.net/wpf/CustomSkin.xaml"))
{
  // Get the root element, which must be a ResourceDictionary
  resources = (ResourceDictionary)XamlReader.Load(s);
}
Application.Current.Resources = resources;
```

Because assigning a dictionary to `Application.Current.Resources` code wipes out the current dictionary, you should also store the default `ResourceDictionary` if you want to restore it later!

FAQ

What happens if a skin doesn't define a named `Style` expected by the application?

If you take the approach of completely replacing the current `Application.Resources` dictionary with a new `ResourceDictionary`, and if the new dictionary is missing `Styles`, the affected controls will silently revert to their default appearance. This is true of any dynamic resource that gets removed while the application is running. The dynamic resource mechanism does emit a debug trace, however, much like how data binding reports errors. For example, applying a skin missing a `Style` called `CancelButtonStyle` causes the following message to be emitted inside a debugger:

```
System.Windows.ResourceDictionary Warning: 9 : Resource not found;
ResourceKey='CancelButtonStyle'
```

To avoid this, another approach would be to iterate through the new resource dictionary and individually set each key/value pair in the application's resource dictionary.

The progress dialog sample (whose full source code is included with the rest of the book's code at http://informit.com/title/9780672331190) switches the skin when you click the Cancel `Button` for demonstration purposes, but for a real application, this action would likely be taken when a user initiates it from some skin-choosing user interface.

In this book's source code, you'll find two alternative skins for the progress dialog in Figure 14.13. Figure 14.14 shows the dialog with these two skins.

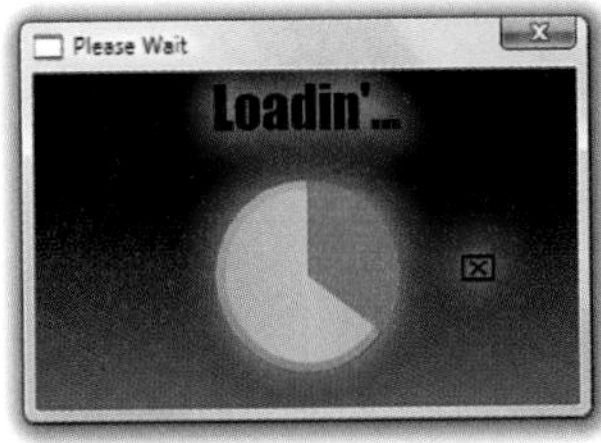

The "Electric" skin

The "Light and Fluffy" skin

FIGURE 14.14 Two alternate skins for the dialog.

Notice that the "electric" skin restyles the `ProgressBar` (using the pie chart template from the previous section) even though the application didn't give it an explicit `Style`. It does this by making it a typed `Style` that applies to all `ProgressBar`s. Fortunately, any additions of, removals of, or changes to typed styles in a `ResourceDictionary` are automatically reflected the same way as explicit dynamic resources. The skin's `CancelButtonStyle` uses a `TranslateTransform` to reposition it next to the `ProgressBar` rather than below it. It also does something quite unique for the `Label`'s `Style`: It uses a template to send the `Label`'s content through a "jive translator" web service. (This, of course, works only if the `Label` contains text.)

DIGGING DEEPER

Skins That Require Procedural Code

The "electric" skin's `ProgressBar` template requires procedural code (as shown in the previous section), so it can't be implemented in a loose XAML file. In such cases, you can compile the `ResourceDictionary` into an assembly and still expose it as a skin. The key is to use `Application.LoadComponent` to retrieve the compiled resource. The resource can be compiled into the same assembly or a different assembly, as explained in Chapter 12.

The progress dialog sample compiles both skins into the same assembly, so it uses code like the following to load them:

```
ResourceDictionary resources = (ResourceDictionary)Application.LoadComponent(
  new Uri("CustomSkin.xaml", UriKind.RelativeOrAbsolute));
Application.Current.Resources = resources;
```

The "light and fluffy" skin has its own set of fairly radical changes. Listing 14.12 shows the complete source for this skin.

LISTING 14.12 The "Light and Fluffy" Skin

```
<ResourceDictionary
  xmlns="http://schemas.microsoft.com/winfx/2006/xaml/presentation"
  xmlns:x="http://schemas.microsoft.com/winfx/2006/xaml">
  <!-- Make the background a simple gradient -->
  <Style x:Key="DialogStyle" TargetType="{x:Type StackPanel}">
    <Setter Property="Margin" Value="0"/>
    <Setter Property="Background">
    <Setter.Value>
      <LinearGradientBrush StartPoint="0,0" EndPoint="1,1">
        <GradientStop Offset="0" Color="LightBlue"/>
        <GradientStop Offset="1" Color="White"/>
      </LinearGradientBrush>
    </Setter.Value>
    </Setter>
  </Style>
  <!-- Rotate and move the main text -->
  <Style x:Key="HeadingStyle" TargetType="{x:Type Label}">
    <Setter Property="Foreground" Value="White"/>
    <Setter Property="FontSize" Value="30"/>
    <Setter Property="FontFamily" Value="Segoe Print"/>
    <Setter Property="RenderTransform">
    <Setter.Value>
      <TransformGroup>
        <RotateTransform Angle="-35"/>
        <TranslateTransform X="-19" Y="55"/>
      </TransformGroup>
    </Setter.Value>
    </Setter>
    <Setter Property="Effect">
    <Setter.Value>
      <DropShadowEffect ShadowDepth="2"/>
    </Setter.Value>
    </Setter>
  </Style>

  <!-- Remove the Cancel button -->
  <Style x:Key="CancelButtonStyle" TargetType="{x:Type Button}">
    <Setter Property="Visibility" Value="Collapsed"/>
  </Style>

  <!-- Wrap the ProgressBar in an Expander -->
```

LISTING 14.12 Continued

```
  <Style TargetType="{x:Type ProgressBar}">
    <Setter Property="Height" Value="100"/>
    <Setter Property="Template">
    <Setter.Value>
      <ControlTemplate TargetType="{x:Type ProgressBar}">
        <Expander Header="More Details" ExpandDirection="Left">
          <ProgressBar Style="{x:Null}"
            Height="30" Value="{TemplateBinding Value}"
            Minimum="{TemplateBinding Minimum}"
            Maximum="{TemplateBinding Maximum}"
            IsEnabled="{TemplateBinding IsEnabled}"
            IsIndeterminate="{TemplateBinding IsIndeterminate}"/>
        </Expander>
      </ControlTemplate>
    </Setter.Value>
    </Setter>
  </Style>
</ResourceDictionary>
```

The customized `DialogStyle` and `HeadingStyle` are pretty straightforward (although the latter uses a slick drop shadow effect introduced in the next chapter). But this skin, to keep a minimalistic user interface, uses `CancelButtonStyle` to *completely hide* the Cancel `Button`! In this case, doing so is appropriate (assuming that closing the `Window` behaves the usual way). In other cases, users might not appreciate a skin that hides pieces of the user interface!

The typed `Style` for `ProgressBar` also performs an interesting trick for the purpose of simplifying the user interface. It defines a custom template to wrap the `ProgressBar` inside an `Expander` (that's collapsed by default)! The wrapped `ProgressBar` has several `TemplateBinding`s to keep its display in sync with the templated parent. Notice that this inner `ProgressBar` is given a `null` `Style`. This is necessary to avoid a nasty recursion problem. Without the explicit `Style`, the inner `ProgressBar` gets the default typed `Style` that it's a part of, making it an `Expander` inside an `Expander` inside an `Expander`, and so on.

FAQ

How can I prevent a user-contributed skin from acting maliciously?

There is no built-in mechanism to do this. It might be tempting to try to write your own logic to examine a user-supplied `ResourceDictionary` and remove things that you consider to be malicious, but this is basically a futile task. For example, if you want to prevent a skin from hiding elements, you can pretty easily remove `Setter`s that operate on `Visibility`. But what about a skin that makes text the same color as the background? Or a skin that gives controls an empty-looking template? There's more than one way to skin a cat! (Pun intended.)

Continued

And making your user interface unusable is the least of your concerns. Imagine a skin that finds a way to send private information displayed by the application back to a web server. There's an inherent risk whenever arbitrary code (or XAML!) is executed inside a full-trust application. Loading the XAML in a separate process is one workaround but is probably too cumbersome for most scenarios.

If you're concerned about this issue, you should probably define your own skin data format that is much more limited in expressiveness. But if you provide an easy way for a user to remove a "malicious skin," then perhaps you don't need to worry about this in the first place.

Themes

Whereas *skins* are application specific, *themes* generally refer to visual characteristics of the operating system that are reflected in user interface elements of all programs. For example, changing your Windows theme to Windows Classic gives buttons and scrollbars a flat and rectangular look. On Windows XP, switching the default theme's color scheme between Blue, Olive Green, and Silver affects the color and sheen of standard controls. To maintain consistency with the user's chosen Windows theme, the built-in WPF controls have a separate control template for each theme, as you saw with `Button` in Chapter 9, "Content Controls."

Consistency with the operating system theme is important for the default control templates. But when somebody creates custom control templates, they typically do so to *avoid* consistency with the rest of the operating system! Nevertheless, it can still be a nice touch to incorporate elements of the user's operating system theme to prevent the customized controls from sticking out like a sore thumb. It's also important to understand how theming works if you create your own custom controls that should blend in with the operating system theme by default.

This section examines how easy it is to create `Style`s and templates (and, therefore, skins) that adapt to the current theme. There are basically two ways to do this. The first is simple but not as powerful, and the second is a bit more work but completely flexible.

Using System Colors, Fonts, and Parameters

The properties exposed by the `SystemColors`, `SystemFonts`, and `SystemParameters` classes automatically get updated when the Windows theme changes. Therefore, incorporating these into your `Style`s and templates is an easy way to blend them in with the user's theme.

The following updated `ProgressBar` pie chart `Style` makes use of the `SystemColors` class to control the colors in its default fill (using the technique explained in Chapter 12):

```
<Style TargetType="{x:Type ProgressBar}">
<Style.Resources>
  <LinearGradientBrush x:Key="foregroundBrush" StartPoint="0,0" EndPoint="1,1">
```

```
    <GradientStop Offset="0"
      Color="{DynamicResource {x:Static SystemColors.InactiveCaptionColorKey}}"/>
    <GradientStop Offset="0.5"
      Color="{DynamicResource {x:Static SystemColors.InactiveCaptionColorKey}}"/>
    <GradientStop Offset="1"
      Color="{DynamicResource {x:Static SystemColors.ActiveCaptionColorKey}}"/>
  </LinearGradientBrush>
</Style.Resources>
<Setter Property="Foreground" Value="{StaticResource foregroundBrush}"/>
<Setter Property="Background"
  Value="{DynamicResource {x:Static SystemColors.ControlBrushKey}}"/>
…
</Style>
```

Figure 14.15 shows how the appearance of this `Style` subtly changes when the user switches Windows themes.

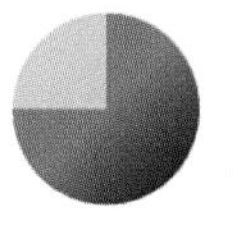

Windows 7 (Aero) Windows Classic

FIGURE 14.15 The same control with the same `Style`, viewed under two different themes.

Per-Theme Styles and Templates

Many of the built-in WPF controls differ from theme to theme in richer ways than just colors, fonts, and simple measurements. For example, they're generally shinier in the Windows 7 Aero theme and dull in Windows Classic. This is accomplished by having a separate control template for each theme.

The ability to define your own styles and templates that differ in interesting ways based on the current theme can be quite useful. For example, it could be argued that the Windows Classic version of `ProgressBar` in Figure 14.15 is *too* pretty! Someone who uses the Windows Classic theme probably isn't going to appreciate fancy gradients and other effects!

If you want to create your own per-theme styles and templates, you could programmatically load and swap them whenever the theme changes (using the techniques discussed in the "Skins" section). WPF doesn't expose a theme-changing event, however, so this would involve intercepting the Win32 `WM_THEMECHANGE` message (the same way `WM_DWMCOMPOSITIONCHANGED` is intercepted in Chapter 8, "Exploiting Windows 7"). Fortunately, WPF does expose a theming mechanism built on top of the low-level Win32 APIs, enabling you to provide per-theme resources with almost no procedural code.

The first step is to organize your theme-specific resources into distinct resource dictionary XAML files (one per theme) that are compiled into your assembly. You can then designate each resource dictionary as a *theme dictionary* by placing it in a `themes` subfolder (which must be in the root of your project!) and naming it *`ThemeName.ThemeColor`*`.xaml` (case-insensitive). A theme dictionary can be loaded and applied automatically by WPF when your application launches and whenever the theme changes. `Style`s inside a theme dictionary are called *theme styles.*

The following are themes that Microsoft has created, along with their corresponding valid theme dictionary URIs:

- The Aero theme (Windows Vista and Windows 7): `themes\Aero.NormalColor.xaml`
- The default Windows XP theme: `themes\Luna.NormalColor.xaml`
- The olive green Windows XP theme: `themes\Luna.Homestead.xaml`
- The silver Windows XP theme: `themes\Luna.Metallic.xaml`
- The Windows XP Media Center Edition 2005 and Windows XP Tablet PC Edition 2005 theme: `themes\Royale.NormalColor.xaml`
- The Windows Classic theme: `themes\Classic.xaml`
- The Zune Windows XP theme: `themes\Zune.NormalColor.xaml`

Note that Windows Classic is a bit special, as it doesn't have the *`ThemeColor`* part of the URI.

Furthermore, you can specify a fallback resource dictionary that gets used if you don't have a dictionary corresponding to the current theme and color. This fallback dictionary, often called the *generic dictionary*, must be named `themes\Generic.xaml`.

> **TIP**
>
> Be sure to provide a generic dictionary whenever you create theme dictionaries. This enables you to provide a consistent experience when encountering an unexpected theme.

With one or more theme dictionaries and/or a generic dictionary in place, you must now opt in to the automatic theming mechanism with an assembly-level `ThemeInfoAttribute`. This attribute's constructor takes two parameters of type `ResourceDictionaryLocation`. The first one specifies where WPF should find the theme dictionaries, and the second one specifies where WPF should find the generic dictionary. Each one can independently be set to the following values:

- **`None`**—Don't look for a resource dictionary. This is the default value.
- **`SourceAssembly`**—Look for them inside the current assembly.
- **`ExternalAssembly`**—Look for them inside a different assembly, which must be named *`AssemblyName`*`.`*`ThemeName`*`.dll` (where *`AssemblyName`* matches the current assembly's name). WPF uses this scheme for its built-in theme dictionaries, found in `PresentationFramework.Aero.dll`, `PresentationFramework.Luna.dll`, and so on. This is a nice way to avoid having extra copies of resources loaded in memory at all times.

Therefore, a typical use of ThemeInfoAttribute looks like the following:

```
// Look for the theme dictionaries and the generic dictionary inside this assembly
[assembly:ThemeInfo(ResourceDictionaryLocation.SourceAssembly,
                    ResourceDictionaryLocation.SourceAssembly)]
```

There's one final catch to the theming support: It's designed to provide the *default styles* for elements. As ThemeInfoAttribute indicates, theme styles must exist in the same assembly defining the target element or a specific companion assembly. Unlike with application-level (or lower) resource dictionaries, you can't define a typed style for externally defined elements such as Button or ProgressBar in a theme dictionary or generic dictionary in your own application and have it override the default style—unless you use an additional mechanism involving ThemeDictionaryExtension.

ThemeDictionaryExtension is a markup extension that enables you to override the theme styles for any elements. It can reference any assembly containing a set of theme dictionaries, even the current application. You can apply ThemeDictionaryExtension as the Source for a ResourceDictionary to affect everything under its scope. Here's an example:

```
<Application …>
<Application.Resources>
  <ResourceDictionary>
  <ResourceDictionary.MergedDictionaries>
    <ResourceDictionary …/>
    <ResourceDictionary Source="{ThemeDictionary MyApplication}"/>
  </ResourceDictionary.MergedDictionaries>
  </ResourceDictionary>
</Application.Resources>
</Application>
```

Imagine that you want to make the pie chart style for ProgressBar vary, based on the Windows theme. If the MyApplication assembly contains per-theme styles with a TargetType of {x:Type ProgressBar}, all ProgressBars in this application get the customized per-theme style by default, thanks to the use of ThemeDictionaryExtension.

Another approach for attaching per-theme styles to existing elements is to define a custom subclass. Creating custom controls is the subject of Chapter 20, but creating a custom control (or another element) solely for the purpose of giving it a theme style is pretty simple. For the per-theme pie chart style example, you could create a custom control called ProgressPie, as follows:

```
public class ProgressPie : ProgressBar
{
  static ProgressPie()
  {
    DefaultStyleKeyProperty.OverrideMetadata(
      typeof(ProgressPie),
```

```
        new FrameworkPropertyMetadata(typeof(ProgressPie)));
  }
}
```

Because `ProgressPie` derives from `ProgressBar`, it automatically has all the necessary functionality. But having a unique type gives you the ability to support a new theme style distinct from `ProgressBar`'s theme style. The only magic incantation is the single line of code in `ProgressPie`'s static constructor that sets the `DefaultStyleKey` dependency property. `DefaultStyleKey` is a protected dependency property on `FrameworkElement` and `FrameworkContentElement` that determines the key to use for its default style. (The terms *default style* and *theme style* are often used interchangeably.)

WPF's built-in elements set this property to their own type, so their corresponding theme dictionaries use typed styles. If the preceding code didn't set a `DefaultStyleKey`, `ProgressPie` would inherit the value from `ProgressBar`, which is `typeof(ProgressBar)`. Therefore, `ProgressPie` makes `typeof(ProgressPie)` its `DefaultStyleKey`.

This book's source code contains a Visual Studio project that contains the preceding definition of `ProgressPie`, the preceding usage of `ThemeInfoAttribute`, and a handful of theme dictionaries that get compiled into the application. Each theme dictionary is a standalone XAML file with the following structure:

```
<ResourceDictionary
  xmlns="http://schemas.microsoft.com/winfx/2006/xaml/presentation"
  xmlns:x="http://schemas.microsoft.com/winfx/2006/xaml"
  xmlns:local="clr-namespace:ThemedProgressPie">
  <Style TargetType="{x:Type local:ProgressPie}">
    …
  </Style>
</ResourceDictionary>
```

Figure 14.16 displays a theme-styled `ProgressPie` under two different themes. Although you can dig into how each `Style` was created, the point is that theme styles give you the flexibility to completely change an element's visuals when the theme changes. Unlike the visuals in Figure 14.15, I think Figure 14.16 succeeds in making the Windows 7 `ProgressPie` extra sexy and the Windows Classic `ProgressPie` extra boring. Kidding aside, making theme styles *too* different from each other will probably confuse your users more than help them.

Windows 7 (Aero)

Windows Classic

FIGURE 14.16 The same control with its theme style, viewed under two different themes.

DIGGING DEEPER

Understanding Windows Themes and Color Schemes

Windows 7 and Windows Vista have a long list of color schemes, found on the advanced Appearance Settings dialog. Whether a user chooses Windows Aero or Windows Basic on either operating system, WPF uses the `Aero.NormalColor` theme dictionary. (This is still true when a user's window color is no longer "normal" because of color customizations made via Control Panel.) And whether a user chooses Windows Standard, Windows Classic, or one of the high-contrast schemes, WPF uses the `Classic` theme dictionary. If you want to distinguish between these color schemes that map to the same theme, your best bet is to incorporate `SystemColors` into your styles and templates.

Summary

The combination of styles, templates, skins, and themes is very powerful and often confusing to someone learning about WPF. Adding to the confusion is the fact that `Styles` can (and often do) contain templates, elements in templates all have `Styles` (whether marked explicitly or inherited implicitly), and theme styles are managed separately from normal `Styles` (so an element like `Button`'s `Style` property is `null` by default, even though it clearly has a theme style applied).

These mechanisms are so powerful, in fact, that often you can restyle an existing control as an alternative to writing your own custom control. This is great news, as restyling an existing control is significantly easier than writing a custom control, and it can perhaps be done entirely by a graphic designer rather than a programmer. If you do find that you need to write a custom control (the topic of Chapter 20), the lessons learned here about creating robust templates and adapting to themes are still very applicable.

TIP

You can play around with alternate skins for many WPF controls by downloading the WPF Themes `.zip` file from http://wpf.codeplex.com. These "themes" are what this chapter calls skins; they are just resource dictionaries that define new typed styles for most of WPF's built-in controls. To use one of them, you can simply reference the resource dictionary as the `Resources` collection in your `Application`, `Window`, or elsewhere:

```
<Application …>
<Application.Resources>
  <ResourceDictionary Source="BureauBlack.xaml"/>
</Application.Resources>
</Application>
```

Unfortunately, at the time of writing, these skins don't include styles for the new controls in WPF 4 such as `DataGrid`, `Calendar`, and `DatePicker`. Figure 14.17 demonstrates the seven included skins applied to several controls.

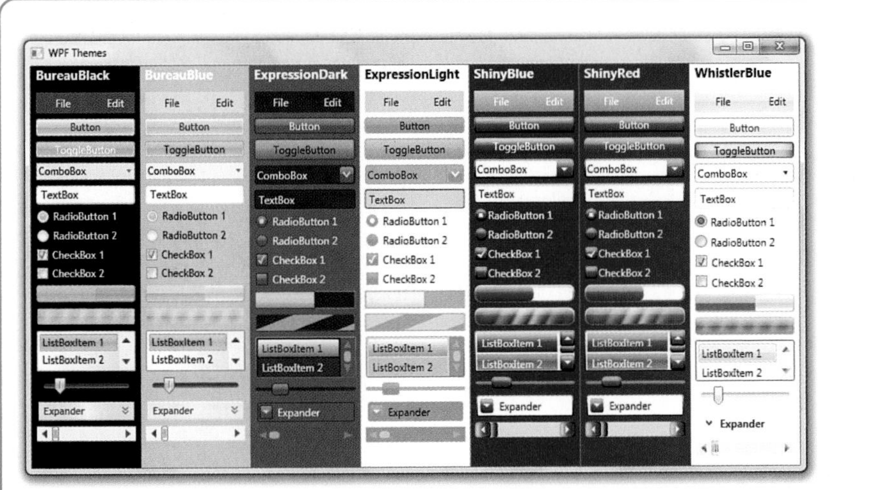

FIGURE 14.17 Applying skins from the “WPF Themes” download.

PART V

Rich Media

IN THIS PART

CHAPTER 15
2D Graphics

IN THIS CHAPTER

- Drawings
- Visuals
- Shapes
- Brushes
- Effects
- Improving Rendering Performance

Applications and components can have many reasons for drawing rectangles, ellipses, lines, or other shapes and paths. Most custom control templates tend to require some drawing to get their custom look, as was done in the previous chapter with `Button` and `ProgressBar` templates. But applications might simply want to provide an experience with custom rendering, regardless of whether it's done in the context of controls. This could be in the form of a product logo or simple curves to separate areas of a `Window`. On the Web, these types of experiences are typically created by embedding images, but with the drawing capabilities of WPF, you can do all this with vector drawings that scale perfectly to any size.

The ability to create and use vector-based 2D graphics is not unique to WPF; even GDI enabled the drawing of paths and shapes. The main difference with drawing in WPF versus GDI or any previous Windows technology is that WPF is a completely *retained-mode* graphics system rather than an *immediate-mode* graphics system.

In an immediate-mode system (GDI, GDI+, DirectX, and so on), you can draw "directly" onto the screen, but you must maintain the state of all visuals. In other words, it's your responsibility to draw the correct pixels when a region of the screen is invalidated. This invalidation can be caused by user actions, such as resizing the window, or by application-specific actions that require updated visuals.

In a retained-mode system, you can describe higher-level concepts such as "place a 10x10 blue square at (0,0)," and the system remembers and maintains the state for you. So, what you're really saying is, "place a 10x10 blue square at (0,0) *and keep it there*." You don't need to worry about invalidation and repainting, so this can save a significant amount of work. It's also the key to WPF's seamless support for overlapping objects, transparency, video, resolution independence, and so on.

As with many other things in WPF, there are multiple ways to create and use two-dimensional graphics. This chapter focuses on three important data types: `Drawing`, `Visual`, and `Shape`. Their relationship to each other is complex. For the most part, `Drawings` are simple descriptions of paths and shapes with associated fill and outline `Brushes`. `Visuals` are one way to draw `Drawings` onto the screen, but `Visuals` also unlock a lower-level and lighter-weight approach for drawing that enable you to ditch `Drawing` objects altogether. Finally, `Shapes` are prebuilt `Visuals` that are the easiest (but most heavyweight) approach for drawing custom artwork onto the screen. `Shapes` also happen to be the only one of these three data types directly exposed by Silverlight. As we examine `Drawings`, `Visuals`, and `Shapes`, we'll look at a simple piece of clip art and see what it means to create and use it in all three contexts.

The end of the chapter covers `Brushes`, special effects, and features for maximizing the performance of graphics-rich applications. `Brushes` are a vital part of all the topics in this chapter, and they have been used throughout the book for mundane tasks such as setting a control's `Foreground` and `Background`. WPF has many different feature-rich `Brushes`, which is why they deserve a dedicated section. Effects such as drop shadows or blurring are not commonly used features, but they can add really slick touches to your user interface that would be difficult to create without them.

Drawings

The abstract `Drawing` class represents a two-dimensional drawing. `Drawing`—specifically its `GeometryDrawing` subclass—was designed to be WPF's version of clip art. It's sufficient for representing any 2D illustration, and, as with all classes deriving from `Animatable`, it even supports animation, data binding, resource references, and more!

WPF includes five concrete subclasses of `Drawing`:

- **`GeometryDrawing`**—Combines a `Geometry` with a `Brush` that fills it and a `Pen` that outlines it. This is the subclass most relevant for this chapter.
- **`ImageDrawing`**—Combines an `ImageSource` with a `Rect` that defines its bounds.
- **`VideoDrawing`**—Combines a `MediaPlayer` (discussed in Chapter 18, "Audio, Video, and Speech") with a bounding `Rect`.
- **`GlyphRunDrawing`**—Combines a `GlyphRun`, a low-level text class, with a `Brush` for its foreground.
- **`DrawingGroup`**—Contains a collection of `Drawings` and has a handful of properties for altering them in bulk (`Opacity`, `Transform`, and so on). `DrawingGroup` is itself a `Drawing` so it can be plugged in wherever a `Drawing` can be used. (This is just like the relationship between `TransformGroup` and `Transform`.)

Here's an example of a `GeometryDrawing` that contains a `Geometry` describing an ellipse (`EllipseGeometry`), an orange `Brush`, and a black `Pen`:

```
<GeometryDrawing Brush="Orange">                                    Brush
<GeometryDrawing.Pen>
  <Pen Brush="Black" Thickness="10"/>                               Pen
</GeometryDrawing.Pen>
<GeometryDrawing.Geometry>
  <EllipseGeometry RadiusX="100" RadiusY="50"/>                     Geometry
</GeometryDrawing.Geometry>
</GeometryDrawing>
```

`Drawings` are not `UIElements`; they don't have any rendering behavior on their own. Therefore, if you try to place the preceding `GeometryDrawing` inside a `Window` or another `ContentControl`, you'll get a simple `TextBlock` containing the string `"System.Windows.Media.GeometryDrawing"` (the fallback `ToString` rendering).

To get `Drawings` rendered appropriately, you can place them inside one of three different host objects:

- **`DrawingImage`**—Derives from `ImageSource`, so it can be used inside an `Image` rather than the typical `BitmapImage`.
- **`DrawingBrush`**—Derives from `Brush`, so it can be applied in many places, such as the `Foreground`, `Background`, or `BorderBrush` on a `Control`.
- **`DrawingVisual`**—Derives from `Visual` and is covered in the "`Visuals`" section, later in this chapter.

Therefore, you can use `DrawingImage` with the preceding `GeometryDrawing` as follows to get it drawn on the screen:

```
<Image>
<Image.Source>
  <DrawingImage>
  <DrawingImage.Drawing>
    <GeometryDrawing Brush="Orange">
    <GeometryDrawing.Pen>
      <Pen Brush="Black" Thickness="10"/>
    </GeometryDrawing.Pen>
    <GeometryDrawing.Geometry>
      <EllipseGeometry RadiusX="100" RadiusY="50"/>
    </GeometryDrawing.Geometry>
    </GeometryDrawing>
  </DrawingImage.Drawing>
  </DrawingImage>
</Image.Source>
</Image>
```

15

`PathFigures` and `PathSegments` Each `PathFigure` in a `PathGeometry` contains one or more connected `PathSegments` in its `Segments` content property. A `PathSegment` is simply a straight or curvy line segment, represented by one of seven derived classes:

- **`LineSegment`**—A class for representing a line segment (of course!)
- **`PolyLineSegment`**—A shortcut for representing a connected sequence of `LineSegments`
- **`ArcSegment`**—A class for representing a segment that curves along the circumference of an imaginary ellipse
- **`BezierSegment`**—A class for representing a cubic Bézier curve
- **`PolyBezierSegment`**—A shortcut for representing a connected sequence of `BezierSegments`
- **`QuadraticBezierSegment`**—A class for representing a quadratic Bézier curve
- **`PolyQuadraticBezierSegment`**—A shortcut for representing a connected sequence of `QuadraticBezierSegments`

DIGGING DEEPER

Bézier Curves

Bézier curves (named after engineer Pierre Bézier) are commonly used in computer graphics for representing smooth curves. Bézier curves are even used by fonts to mathematically describe curves in their glyphs.

The basic idea is that in addition to two endpoints, a Bézier curve has one or more *control points* that give the line segment its curve. These control points are not visible (and not necessarily on the curve itself) but rather are used as input to a formula that dictates where each point on the curve exists. Intuitively, each control point acts like a center of gravity, so the line segment appears to be "pulled" toward these points.

Despite the scarier-sounding name, `QuadraticBezierSegment` is actually simpler than `BezierSegment` and computationally cheaper. A quadratic Bézier curve has only one control point, whereas a cubic Bézier curve has two. Therefore, a quadratic Bézier curve can only form a *U*-like shape (or a straight line), but a cubic Bézier curve can also take the form of an S-like shape.

The following `GeometryDrawing` contains a `PathGeometry` with two simple `LineSegments` that create the *L* shape in Figure 15.3:

```
<GeometryDrawing>
<GeometryDrawing.Pen>
  <Pen Brush="Black" Thickness="10"/>
</GeometryDrawing.Pen>
<GeometryDrawing.Geometry>
  <PathGeometry>
```

```
    <PathFigure>
      <LineSegment Point="0,100"/>
      <LineSegment Point="100,100"/>
    </PathFigure>
  </PathGeometry>
</GeometryDrawing.Geometry>
</GeometryDrawing>
```

FIGURE 15.3 A GeometryDrawing that ultimately contains a pair of LineSegments.

Of course, to produce the visuals in Figure 15.3, the GeometryDrawing must be hosted in something like a DrawingImage, as done previously.

Notice that the definition for each LineSegment includes only a single Point. That's because it implicitly connects the previous point to the current one. The first LineSegment connects the default starting point of (0,0) to (0,100), and the second LineSegment connects (0,100) to (100,100). (The other six PathSegments act the same way.) If you want to provide a custom starting point, you can simply set PathFigure's StartPoint property to a Point other than (0,0).

You might expect that applying a Brush to this GeometryDrawing is meaningless, but Figure 15.4 shows that it actually fills it as a polygon, pretending that a line segment exists to connect the last point back to the starting point. Figure 15.4 was created by adding the following Brush to the preceding XAML:

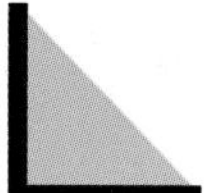

FIGURE 15.4 The GeometryDrawing from Figure 15.3 filled with an orange Brush.

```
<GeometryDrawing Brush="Orange">
  …
</GeometryDrawing>
```

To turn the imaginary line segment into a real one, you could add a third LineSegment to the PathFigure explicitly, or you could simply set PathFigure's IsClosed property to true. The result of doing either is shown in Figure 15.5.

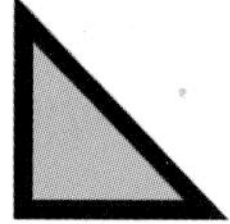

FIGURE 15.5 The GeometryDrawing from Figure 15.4, but with IsClosed="True".

Because all PathSegments within a PathFigure must be connected, you can place multiple PathFigures in a PathGeometry if you want disjoint shapes or paths in the same Geometry. You could also overlap PathFigures to create results that would be complicated to replicate in a single PathFigure. For example, the following XAML overlaps the triangle from Figure 15.5 with a triangle that is given a different StartPoint but is otherwise identical:

```
<GeometryDrawing Brush="Orange">
<GeometryDrawing.Pen>
  <Pen Brush="Black" Thickness="10"/>
</GeometryDrawing.Pen>
```

```
<GeometryDrawing.Geometry>
  <PathGeometry>
    <!-- Triangle #1 -->
    <PathFigure IsClosed="True">
      <LineSegment Point="0,100"/>
      <LineSegment Point="100,100"/>
    </PathFigure>
    <!-- Triangle #2 -->
    <PathFigure StartPoint="70,0" IsClosed="True">
      <LineSegment Point="0,100"/>
      <LineSegment Point="100,100"/>
    </PathFigure>
  </PathGeometry>
</GeometryDrawing.Geometry>
</GeometryDrawing>
```

This dual-`PathFigure` `GeometryDrawing` is displayed in Figure 15.6. If you don't want the sharp point at each corner, you can set each `LineSegment`'s `IsSmoothJoin` property (inherited by all `PathSegments`) to `true`. Figure 15.6 also shows the result of doing this.

From the original XAML

Adding `IsSmoothJoin="True"` on all `LineSegments`

FIGURE 15.6 Overlapping triangles created by using two `PathFigures`.

The behavior of the orange fill might not be what you expected to see. `PathGeometry` enables you to control this fill behavior with its `FillRule` property.

`FillRule` Whenever you have a geometry with intersecting points, whether via multiple overlapping `PathFigures` or overlapping `PathSegments` in a single `PathFigure`, there can be multiple interpretations of which area is *inside* a shape (and can, therefore, be filled) and which area is *outside* a shape.

With `PathGeometry`'s `FillRule` property (which can be set to a `FillRule` enumeration), you have two choices on how filling is done:

- **`EvenOdd`**—Fills a region only if you would cross an odd number of segments to travel from that region to the area outside the entire shape. This is the default.
- **`NonZero`**—Is a more complicated algorithm that takes into consideration the direction of the segments you would have to cross to get outside the entire shape. For many shapes, it is likely to fill all enclosed areas.

The difference between EvenOdd and NonZero is illustrated in Figure 15.7, with the same overlapping triangles from Figure 15.6.

FIGURE 15.7 Overlapping triangles with different values for PathGeometry.FillRule.

Aggregate Geometries

WPF's two classes for aggregating geometries—GeometryGroup and CombinedGeometry—sound similar but behave quite differently. But like TransformGroup's relationship to Transform and DrawingGroup's relationship to Drawing, both aggregate geometry classes derive from Geometry, so they can be used anywhere that a simpler Geometry can be used.

DIGGING DEEPER

StreamGeometry

For complex geometries that don't need to be modified after they are created, you should consider using StreamGeometry rather than PathGeometry as a performance optimization. StreamGeometry works like PathGeometry, except that it can only be directly filled via procedural code. Its odd name refers to an implementation detail: To use less memory (and less of the CPU), its PathFigures and PathSegments are stored as a compact byte stream rather than a graph of .NET objects.

The following code constructs a StreamGeometry with overlapping triangles that is identical to the PathGeometry used to create Figure 15.6:

```
StreamGeometry g = new StreamGeometry();
using (StreamGeometryContext context = g.Open())
{
  // Triangle #1
  context.BeginFigure(new Point(0, 0), true /*isFilled*/, true /*isClosed*/);
  context.LineTo(new Point(0, 100), true /*isStroked*/, true /*isSmoothJoin*/);
  context.LineTo(new Point(100, 100), true /*isStroked*/, true /*isSmoothJoin*/);

  // Triangle #2
  context.BeginFigure(new Point(70, 0), true /*isFilled*/, true /*isClosed*/);
  context.LineTo(new Point(0, 100), true /*isStroked*/, true /*isSmoothJoin*/);
  context.LineTo(new Point(100, 100), true /*isStroked*/, true /*isSmoothJoin*/);
}
// Apply this Geometry to an existing GeometryDrawing:
geometryDrawing.Geometry = g;
```

Rather than create LineSegments, ArcSegments, BezierSegments, and other objects, you call methods such as LineTo, ArcTo, and BezierTo. For performance reasons, WPF internally uses StreamGeometry in a number of situations.

15

GeometryGroup GeometryGroup composes one or more Geometry instances together. For example, the previously shown XAML for creating the overlapping triangles in Figure 15.6 could be rewritten to use two geometries (each with a single PathFigure) rather than one:

```
<GeometryDrawing Brush="Orange">
<GeometryDrawing.Pen>
  <Pen Brush="Black" Thickness="10"/>
</GeometryDrawing.Pen>
<GeometryDrawing.Geometry>
  <GeometryGroup>
    <!-- Triangle #1 -->
    <PathGeometry>
      <PathFigure IsClosed="True">
        <LineSegment Point="0,100"/>
        <LineSegment Point="100,100"/>
      </PathFigure>
    </PathGeometry>
    <!-- Triangle #2 -->
    <PathGeometry>
      <PathFigure StartPoint="70,0" IsClosed="True">
        <LineSegment Point="0,100"/>
        <LineSegment Point="100,100"/>
      </PathFigure>
    </PathGeometry>
  </GeometryGroup>
</GeometryDrawing.Geometry>
</GeometryDrawing>
```

GeometryGroup, like PathGeometry, has a FillRule property that is set to EvenOdd by default. It takes precedence over any FillRule settings of its children.

This, of course, begs the question, "Why would I create a GeometryGroup when I can just as easily create a single PathGeometry with multiple PathFigures?" One minor advantage of doing this is that GeometryGroup enables you to aggregate other geometries such as RectangleGeometry and EllipseGeometry, which can be easier to use. But the major advantage of using GeometryGroup is that you can set various Geometry properties independently on each child.

For example, the following GeometryGroup composes two identical triangles but sets the Transform on one of them to rotate it 25°:

```
<GeometryDrawing Brush="Orange">
<GeometryDrawing.Pen>
  <Pen Brush="Black" Thickness="10"/>
</GeometryDrawing.Pen>
<GeometryDrawing.Geometry>
  <GeometryGroup>
```

```
    <!-- Triangle #1 -->
    <PathGeometry>
      <PathFigure IsClosed="True">
        <LineSegment Point="0,100" IsSmoothJoin="True"/>
        <LineSegment Point="100,100" IsSmoothJoin="True"/>
      </PathFigure>
    </PathGeometry>
    <!-- Triangle #2 -->
    <PathGeometry>
    <PathGeometry.Transform>
      <RotateTransform Angle="25"/>
    </PathGeometry.Transform>
      <PathFigure IsClosed="True">
        <LineSegment Point="0,100" IsSmoothJoin="True"/>
        <LineSegment Point="100,100" IsSmoothJoin="True"/>
      </PathFigure>
    </PathGeometry>
  </GeometryGroup>
</GeometryDrawing.Geometry>
</GeometryDrawing>
```

FIGURE 15.8 A GeometryGroup with two identical triangles, except that one is rotated.

The result of this is shown in Figure 15.8. Creating such a geometry with a single PathGeometry and a single PathFigure would be difficult. Creating it with a single PathGeometry containing two PathFigures would be easier but would still require manually doing the math to perform the rotation. With GeometryGroup, however, creating it is very straightforward.

TIP

Because Brush and Pen are specified at the Drawing level rather than at the Geometry level, GeometryGroup doesn't enable you to combine shapes with different fills or outlines. To achieve this, you can use a DrawingGroup to combine multiple drawings (which might or might not have multiple geometries).

TIP

Unlike UIElements, which can have only a single parent, instances of Geometry, PathFigure, and related classes can be shared. Sharing these objects when possible can result in a major performance improvement, especially for complex geometries. If they aren't going to change, freezing them helps performance even more.

Continued

For the GeometryGroup used for Figure 15.8, there's no need to duplicate the identical PathFigure instances. Instead, with the PathFigure defined as a resource with the key figure, you could rewrite the GeometryGroup as follows:

```
<GeometryGroup>
  <!-- Triangle #1 -->
  <PathGeometry>
    <StaticResource ResourceKey="figure"/>
  </PathGeometry>
  <!-- Triangle #2 -->
  <PathGeometry>
  <PathGeometry.Transform>
    <RotateTransform Angle="25"/>
  </PathGeometry.Transform>
    <StaticResource ResourceKey="figure"/>
  </PathGeometry>
```

CombinedGeometry CombinedGeometry, unlike GeometryGroup, is not a general-purpose aggregator. Instead, it merges two (and only two) geometries using one of the approaches designated by the GeometryCombineMode enumeration:

- **Union**—Gives the combined geometry the entire area of both geometries. This is the default.
- **Intersect**—Gives the combined geometry only the area shared by both geometries.
- **Xor**—Gives the combined geometry only the area that is *not* shared by both geometries.
- **Exclude**—Gives the combined geometry only the area that is unique to the first geometry.

CombinedGeometry defines Geometry1 and Geometry2 properties to hold the two inputs and a GeometryCombineMode property that accepts one of the preceding values. Figure 15.9 demonstrates the result of using each GeometryCombineMode value with the overlapping triangles from Figure 15.8 as follows:

```
<GeometryDrawing Brush="Orange">
<GeometryDrawing.Pen>
  <Pen Brush="Black" Thickness="10"/>
</GeometryDrawing.Pen>
<GeometryDrawing.Geometry>
  <CombinedGeometry GeometryCombineMode="XXX">
  <CombinedGeometry.Geometry1>
    <!-- Triangle #1 -->
```

```
    <PathGeometry>
      ...
    </PathGeometry>
  </CombinedGeometry.Geometry1>
  <CombinedGeometry.Geometry2>
    <!-- Triangle #2 -->
    <PathGeometry>
      ...
    </PathGeometry>
  </CombinedGeometry.Geometry2>
  </CombinedGeometry>
</GeometryDrawing.Geometry>
</GeometryDrawing>
```

FIGURE 15.9 CombinedGeometry with each of the GeometryCombineMode settings, with a surrounding square to provide a frame of reference.

Representing Geometries as Strings

Representing each segment in a Geometry with a separate element is fine for simple shapes and paths, but for complicated artwork, it can get very verbose. Although most people use a design tool to emit XAML-based geometries rather than craft them by hand, it makes sense to keep the resultant file size as small as reasonably possible.

Therefore, WPF has a GeometryConverter type converter that supports a flexible syntax for representing just about any PathGeometry as a string. For programmatic scenarios, Geometry even exposes a static Parse method that accepts the same syntax and returns a Geometry instance. (Although it's an implementation detail, the Geometry returned by the type converter and Geometry.Parse is an instance of the efficient StreamGeometry class.)

For example, the PathGeometry representing the simple triangle displayed in Figure 15.6:

```
<GeometryDrawing>
<GeometryDrawing.Pen>
  <Pen Brush="Black" Thickness="10"/>
</GeometryDrawing.Pen>
<GeometryDrawing.Geometry>
  <PathGeometry>
```

```
    <PathFigure IsClosed="True">
      <LineSegment Point="0,100"/>
      <LineSegment Point="100,100"/>
    </PathFigure>
  </PathGeometry>
</GeometryDrawing.Geometry>
</GeometryDrawing>
```

can be represented with the following compact syntax:

```
<GeometryDrawing Geometry="M 0,0 L 0,100 L 100,100 Z">
<GeometryDrawing.Pen>
  <Pen Brush="Black" Thickness="10"/>
</GeometryDrawing.Pen>
</GeometryDrawing>
```

Representing the overlapping triangles from Figure 15.6 requires a slightly longer string:

```
<GeometryDrawing Geometry="M 0,0 L 0,100 L 100,100 Z M 70,0 L 0,100 L 100,100 Z">
<GeometryDrawing.Pen>
  <Pen Brush="Black" Thickness="10"/>
</GeometryDrawing.Pen>
</GeometryDrawing>
```

These strings contain a series of commands that control properties of `PathGeometry` and its `PathFigures`, plus commands that fill one or more `PathFigures` with `PathSegments`. The syntax is pretty simple but very powerful. Table 15.1 describes all the available commands.

TABLE 15.1 Geometry String Commands

Command	Meaning
`PathGeometry` and `PathFigure` Properties	
`F` *n*	Set `FillRule`, where `0` means `EvenOdd` and `1` means `NonZero`. If you use this, it must be at the beginning of the string.
`M` *x*`,`*y*	Start a new `PathFigure` and set `StartPoint` to (*x*`,`*y*). This must be specified before using any other commands (excluding `F`). The `M` stands for *move*.
`Z`	End the `PathFigure` and set `IsClosed` to `true`. You can begin another disjoint `PathFigure` after this with an `M` command or use a different command to start a new `PathFigure` originating from the current point. If you don't want the `PathFigure` to be closed, you can omit the `Z` command entirely.

TABLE 15.1 Continued

PathSegments	
`L` *x*,*y*	Create a `LineSegment` to (*x*,*y*).
`A` *rx*,*ry* *d* *f1* *f2* *x*,*y*	Create an `ArcSegment` to (*x*,*y*), based on an ellipse with radii *rx* and *yx*, rotated *d* degrees. The *f1* and *f2* flags can be set to `0` (`false`) or `1` (`true`) to control two of `ArcSegment`'s properties: `IsLargeArc` and `Clockwise`, respectively.
`C` *x1*,*y1* *x2*,*y2* *x*,*y*	Create a `BezierSegment` to (*x*,*y*), using control points (*x1*,*y1*) and (*x2*,*y2*). The `C` stands for *cubic* Bézier curve.
`Q` *x1*,*y1* *x*,*y*	Create a `QuadraticBezierSegment` to (*x*,*y*), using control point (*x1*,*y1*).
Additional Shortcuts	
`H` *x*	Create a `LineSegment` to (*x*,*y*), where *y* is taken from the current point. The `H` stands for *horizontal line*.
`V` *y*	Create a `LineSegment` to (*x*,*y*), where *x* is taken from the current point. The `V` stands for *vertical line*.
`S` *x2*,*y2* *x*,*y*	Create a `BezierSegment` to (*x*,*y*), using control points (*x1*,*y1*) and (*x2*,*y2*), where *x1* and *y1* are automatically calculated to guarantee smoothness. (This point is either the second control point of the previous segment or the current point if the previous segment is not a `BezierSegment`.) The `S` stands for *smooth* cubic Bézier curve.
Lowercase commands	Any command can be specified in lowercase to cause its relevant parameters to be interpreted as *relative* to the current point rather than absolute coordinates. This doesn't change the meaning of the `F`, `M`, and `Z` commands, but they can also be specified in lowercase.

DIGGING DEEPER

Spaces and Commas in Geometry Strings

The spaces between commands and parameters are optional, and all commas are optional. But you must have at least one space or comma between parameters. Therefore, the string `M 0,0 L 0,100 L 100,100 Z` is equivalent to the much more confusing `M0 0L0 100L100 100Z`.

Pens

Looking at the three components of `GeometryDrawing`, geometries and `Brush`es are large topics, but `Pen`s are relatively simple. A `Pen` is basically a `Brush` with a `Thickness`. Indeed, the two `Pen` properties used in previous examples are `Brush` (of type `Brush`) and `Thickness` (of type `double`). But `Pen` defines a few more properties for controlling its appearance:

- **`StartLineCap` and `EndLineCap`**—Customize any open segment endpoints with a value from the `PenLineCap` enumeration: `Flat` (the default), `Square`, `Round`, or

Triangle. For any endpoints that join two segments, you can customize their appearance with LineJoin instead.

- **LineJoin**—Affects corners with a value from the PenLineJoin enumeration: Miter (the default), Round, or Bevel. A separate MiterLimit property can be used to limit how far a Miter join extends, which can otherwise be very large for small angles. Its default value is 10.

> **FAQ**
>
> **What's the difference between PenLineCap's Flat and Square values?**
>
> A Flat line cap ends exactly on the endpoint, whereas a Square line cap extends beyond the endpoint. Much like the Round line cap, you can imagine a square with the same dimensions as the Pen's Thickness centered on the endpoint. Therefore, the line ends up extending *half* the length of the Pen's Thickness.

- **DashStyle**—Can make the Pen's stroke a nonsolid line. It can be set to an instance of a DashStyle object. The endpoints of each dash can be customized with Pen's DashCap property, which works just like StartLineCap and EndLineCap, except that its default value is Square instead of Flat.

FIGURE 15.10 Each type of PenLineCap on both ends of a LineSegment.

Figure 15.10 shows each of the PenLineCap values applied to a LineSegment's StartLineCap and EndLineCap. Figure 15.11 demonstrates each of the LineJoin values on the corners of a triangle. Using a LineJoin of Round is like setting IsSmoothJoin to true on all PathSegments. The latter approach enables you to customize each corner individually, whereas setting Pen's LineJoin applies to the entire geometry.

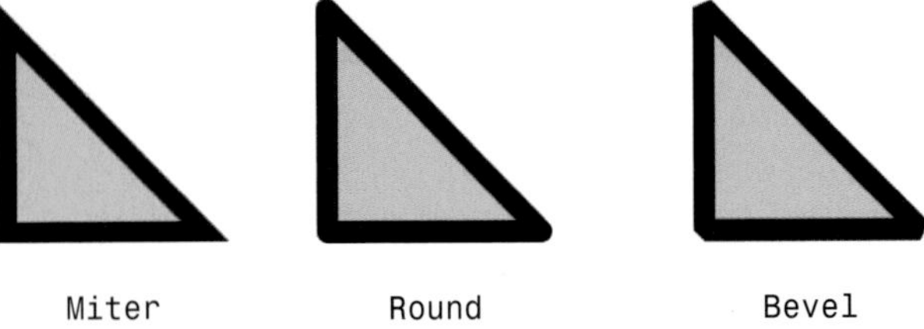

FIGURE 15.11 Each type of LineJoin applied to the familiar triangle.

The DashStyle class defines a Dashes property, which is a simple DoubleCollection that can contain a pattern of numbers that represents the widths of dashes and the spaces between them. The odd values represent the widths (relative to the Pen's Thickness) of dashes, and the even values represent the relative widths of spaces. Whatever pattern you choose is then repeated indefinitely. DashStyle also has a double Offset property that controls where the pattern begins.

The confusing thing about DashStyle is that because DashCap is set to Square by default, each dash is naturally wider when given the same numeric value as a space. Furthermore, giving a dash a width of 0 is common because it simply becomes the DashCap itself. However, a DashStyles class defines a few common patterns in static DashStyle properties. For example, you can use a DashDotDot pattern as follows:

```
<Pen Brush="Black" Thickness="10" DashStyle="{x:Static DashStyles.DashDotDot}"/>
```

Figure 15.12 shows each of the built-in DashStyles, along with the numeric Dashes values they use internally.

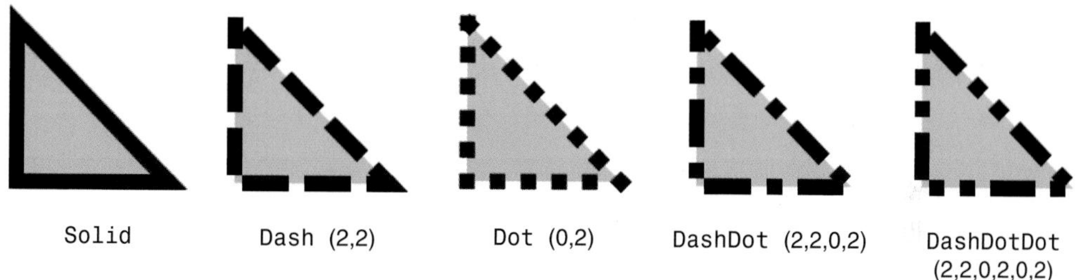

FIGURE 15.12 Each of the built-in DashStyles properties applied to a Pen, with the default Square DashCap and Miter LineJoin.

Clip Art Example

Now that you know everything there is to know about GeometryDrawing, you can create a simple piece of clip art. Listing 15.1 contains an Image-hosted DrawingGroup with three GeometryDrawings to render the ghost shown in Figure 15.13.

LISTING 15.1 The Drawing-Based Implementation of a Ghost, Hosted in an Image

```
<Image>
<Image.Source>
  <DrawingImage>
  <DrawingImage.Drawing>
    <DrawingGroup>

      <!-- The body -->
      <GeometryDrawing Brush="Blue" Geometry="M 240,250
        C 200,375 200,250 175,200
        C 100,400 100,250 100,200
        C 0,350   0,250   30,130
        C 75,0    100,0   150,0
        C 200,0   250,0   250,150 Z"/>

      <!-- The eyes -->
      <GeometryDrawing Brush="Black">
```

LISTING 15.1 Continued

```
      <GeometryDrawing.Pen>
        <Pen Brush="White" Thickness="10"/>
      </GeometryDrawing.Pen>
      <GeometryDrawing.Geometry>
        <GeometryGroup>
          <!-- Left eye -->
          <EllipseGeometry RadiusX="15" RadiusY="15" Center="95,95"/>
          <!-- Right eye -->
          <EllipseGeometry RadiusX="15" RadiusY="15" Center="170,105"/>
        </GeometryGroup>
      </GeometryDrawing.Geometry>
      </GeometryDrawing>

      <!-- The mouth -->
      <GeometryDrawing>
      <GeometryDrawing.Pen>
        <Pen Brush="Black" StartLineCap="Round" EndLineCap="Round"
          Thickness="10"/>
      </GeometryDrawing.Pen>
      <GeometryDrawing.Geometry>
        <LineGeometry StartPoint="75,160" EndPoint="175,150"/>
      </GeometryDrawing.Geometry>
      </GeometryDrawing>

    </DrawingGroup>
  </DrawingImage.Drawing>
  </DrawingImage>
</Image.Source>
</Image>
```

FIGURE 15.13 A ghost created with a `DrawingGroup` that contains three `GeometryDrawings`.

Visuals

Visual, the abstract base class of UIElement (which is the base class of FrameworkElement), contains the low-level infrastructure required to draw anything onto the screen. The previous section uses Image elements as a way to render all Drawings onto the screen. Image ultimately derives from Visual, but its two intermediate base classes, FrameworkElement and UIElement, contain a number of features that often aren't required for drawings—Styles, data binding, resources, participation in layout, support for keyboard/mouse/stylus/touch input and focus, support for routed events, and so on.

Now imagine an application or a component that might want to perform a lot of custom rendering: perhaps a side-scrolling game in the style of Super Mario Bros. or a mapping program like Bing Maps. If implemented with WPF vector graphics, such programs could have hundreds or thousands of Drawings on the screen at any point in time. If they were all hosted in a single Image, you would not be able to support fine-grained interactivity with individual Drawings. But if each one were hosted in a separate Image, there would be an unacceptable amount of overhead for unnecessary features.

Fortunately, a different Visual subclass provides a lightweight mechanism for rendering Drawings onto the screen: DrawingVisual. DrawingVisual has a few handy properties for controlling rendering aspects, such as Opacity and Clip (which DrawingGroup also happens to have). But it also has support for a minimal amount of interaction with input devices. This comes in a form of hit testing called *visual hit testing*.

15

Because DrawingVisual operates at a much lower level than typical WPF features, its use is not very obvious. This section explains how to fill a DrawingVisual with content, how to get that content rendered to the screen, and how to perform visual hit testing.

Filling a DrawingVisual with Content

DrawingVisual does not have a simple Drawing property to which you can attach a Drawing. (It actually *does* have a Drawing property, but it's read-only.) Instead, you must call its RenderOpen method, which returns an instance of a DrawingContext. You can draw into this object and then close it with its Close method.

For example, the following code places the entire ghost Drawing from Listing 15.1 inside a DrawingVisual, assuming that it's defined as a resource with a ghostDrawing key:

```
DrawingGroup ghostDrawing = FindResource("ghostDrawing") as DrawingGroup;
DrawingVisual ghostVisual = new DrawingVisual();
using (DrawingContext dc = ghostVisual.RenderOpen())
{
  dc.DrawDrawing(ghostDrawing);
}
```

This code makes use of the fact that DrawingContext implements IDisposable, mapping its Close method to Dispose (which is implicitly called in a finally block when exiting the using scope).

Listing 15.1 uses a DrawingGroup to combine the three GeometryDrawings defining the ghost simply so it can be set as the single Drawing inside a DrawingImage. With DrawingVisual, however, consolidating the GeometryDrawings in a DrawingGroup is not necessary. The following code adds each of the three GeometryDrawings to the DrawingContext individually, assuming that they are defined as resources with their own keys:

```
GeometryDrawing bodyDrawing = FindResource("bodyDrawing") as GeometryDrawing;
GeometryDrawing eyesDrawing = FindResource("eyesDrawing") as GeometryDrawing;
GeometryDrawing mouthDrawing = FindResource("mouthDrawing") as GeometryDrawing;
DrawingVisual ghostVisual = new DrawingVisual();
using (DrawingContext dc = ghostVisual.RenderOpen())
{
  dc.DrawDrawing(bodyDrawing);
  dc.DrawDrawing(eyesDrawing);
  dc.DrawDrawing(mouthDrawing);
}
```

Later drawings are placed on top of earlier drawings, so this code preserves the proper Z ordering.

Just as you could get rid of the extra DrawingGroup layer and get the same result, you can also get rid of the Drawing objects altogether! Drawings are essentially just wrappers on top of the drawing commands that you can perform directly on DrawingContext. DrawingContext contains several methods for drawing geometries, images, and even video or text. (In other words, these methods cover the functionality provided by the entire list of Drawing types shown earlier in the chapter: GeometryDrawing, ImageDrawing, VideoDrawing, and GlyphRunDrawing.) It also supports pushing and popping a variety of effects. Table 15.2 lists all the DrawingContext methods.

TABLE 15.2 DrawingContext Methods

Task	Methods
Drawing a simple GeometryDrawing without a Geometry or Drawing instance	DrawRectangle, DrawRoundedRectangle, DrawEllipse, DrawLine
Drawing arbitrary Drawings without a Drawing instance	DrawGeometry, DrawImage, DrawVideo, DrawGlyphRun, DrawText
Drawing Arbitrary Drawings with a Drawing instance	DrawDrawing
Applying effects to drawing commands	PushClip, PushEffect, PushGuidelineSet, PushOpacity, PushOpacityMask, PushTransform, Pop
Finishing the sequence of drawing commands	Close

The PushXXX and Pop methods enable you to not only apply the same effect, such as translucency or rotation, to a series of commands but also to nest them. The PushEffect method is obsolete in WPF 4 and has no effect, but the others do what they advertise.

Listing 15.2 contains a new implementation of the ghost clip art from Listing 15.1, entirely in procedural code. In the Window's constructor, the DrawingVisual is created and filled in without the aid of any Drawing instances. Note that the Window in this listing is still completely blank because we actually haven't taken any steps to render the DrawingVisual! That task is saved for the next section.

LISTING 15.2 WindowHostingVisual.cs—The DrawingContext-Based Implementation of the Ghost from Listing 15.1

```
using System;
using System.Windows;
using System.Windows.Media;

public class WindowHostingVisual : Window
{
  public WindowHostingVisual()
  {
    Title = "Hosting DrawingVisuals";
    Width = 300;
    Height = 350;

    DrawingVisual ghostVisual = new DrawingVisual();
    using (DrawingContext dc = ghostVisual.RenderOpen())
    {
      // The body
      dc.DrawGeometry(Brushes.Blue, null, Geometry.Parse(
        @"M 240,250
          C 200,375 200,250 175,200
          C 100,400 100,250 100,200
          C 0,350   0,250   30,130
          C 75,0    100,0   150,0
          C 200,0   250,0   250,150 Z"));
      // Left eye
      dc.DrawEllipse(Brushes.Black, new Pen(Brushes.White, 10),
        new Point(95, 95), 15, 15);
      // Right eye
      dc.DrawEllipse(Brushes.Black, new Pen(Brushes.White, 10),
        new Point(170, 105), 15, 15);
      // The mouth
      Pen p = new Pen(Brushes.Black, 10);
      p.StartLineCap = PenLineCap.Round;
      p.EndLineCap = PenLineCap.Round;
```

15

LISTING 15.2 Continued

```
      dc.DrawLine(p, new Point(75, 160), new Point(175, 150));
    }
  }
}
```

This listing calls `DrawGeometry` to draw the ghost's body, which is the simplest method for drawing a complex shape. Notice that `Geometry.Parse` is used so the path can be described as the same string used in Listing 15.1 rather than an explicit `PathFigure` containing a bunch of `BezierSegment` instances. The drawing of the eyes and mouth doesn't even require using `Geometry` instances; `DrawEllipse` and `DrawLine` are used. A few extra lines of code are needed to initialize the `Pen` for the mouth because `Pen`'s constructor doesn't let you specify advanced features such as the line caps.

Unlike the XAML-based `Drawing` in Listing 15.1, Listing 15.2 is not a particularly great way to share clip art. But it's a valuable technique for drawing-heavy applications. Going back to the mapping program example, `DrawingContext`'s `DrawGeometry` method could be used to draw paths representing roads, lakes, and boundaries, and `DrawText` could be used to add labels on top of this content. Or, if the maps use satellite images, `DrawImage` can be used to position such images without the overhead of an `Image` element for each one. (`DrawImage` accepts an `ImageSource` rather than an `Image`.)

Therefore, the `DrawingContext` class is WPF's closest analog to the Win32 device context or the Windows Forms `Graphics` object. Note that the use of `DrawingContext` doesn't change the fact that you're operating within a retained-mode system. The specified drawing doesn't happen immediately; the commands are persisted by WPF until they are needed.

> **TIP**
>
> Using `DrawingContext` is a lightweight way to perform drawing because it can avoid the overhead of allocating a `Drawing` object on the managed heap for every line, shape, and so on. Therefore, it's the best choice for rendering tens of thousands of items.

Displaying a `Visual` on the Screen

Displaying a `Visual` on the screen that happens to also be a `UIElement` is easy; if you add it as the `Content` of a content control such as `Window`, or a child in a `Panel`, or an item in an items control, and so on, it gets rendered appropriately based on its `OnRender` implementation. But if you have a non-`UIElement` `Visual`, such as the ghostly `DrawingVisual`, all you see rendered if you take one of these actions is the unsatisfactory `ToString` rendering.

To get such a `Visual` properly rendered, you need to manually add it to some `UIElement`'s visual tree. "Now, wait just a minute," you might be saying. "I thought the whole point of using `DrawingVisual` was to avoid the extra overhead of `UIElement`!" Yes, but you still need at least *one* `UIElement`, even if that's simply the top-level `Window`. In the mapping program example, you could host thousands of `Visuals` in a single `Canvas` or `Window` rather than having thousands of `UIElements` in that same host.

The tricky part about adding `Visuals` to an element is that you have to derive your own custom class from an existing `UIElement` and then override two protected virtual members: `VisualChildrenCount` and `GetVisualChild`. Listing 15.3 does this for the `Window` defined in Listing 15.2. This is all the code needed to display the `DrawingVisual`, as shown in Figure 15.14. Notice that the background is black, unlike when hosting a `DrawingImage` inside an `Image` element.

LISTING 15.3 `WindowHostingVisual.cs`—Update for Rendering the Ghost `DrawingVisual`

```
using System;
using System.Windows;
using System.Windows.Media;

public class WindowHostingVisual : Window
{
  DrawingVisual ghostVisual = null;

  public WindowHostingVisual()
  {
    Title = "Hosting DrawingVisuals";
    Width = 300;
    Height = 350;

    ghostVisual = new DrawingVisual();
    using (DrawingContext dc = ghostVisual.RenderOpen())
    {
      The same drawing commands from Listing 15.2…
    }

    // Bookkeeping:
    AddVisualChild(ghostVisual);
    AddLogicalChild(ghostVisual);
  }

  // The two necessary overrides, implemented for the single Visual:
  protected override int VisualChildrenCount
  {
      get { return 1; }
  }
  protected override Visual GetVisualChild(int index)
  {
    if (index != 0)
      throw new ArgumentOutOfRangeException("index");

    return ghostVisual;
  }
}
```

15

VisualChildrenCount must return the number of Visuals contained by the Window. This simple example has only the one DrawingVisual, so this property always returns 1. GetVisualChild must return the actual Visual associated with a zero-based index. Therefore, this method is implemented to return the DrawingVisual when the input is 0 and throw an exception otherwise. If you want to support multiple Visuals, you could maintain a collection of them and update these two members to use that collection. If you want to interact with the layout system, you must override two additional members—MeasureOverride and ArrangeOverride—covered in Chapter 21, "Layout with Custom Panels."

FIGURE 15.14 The ghost DrawingVisual is rendered inside the Window after VisualChildrenCount and GetVisualChild are overridden.

Be aware that the VisualChildrenCount/GetVisualChild implementation in Listing 15.3 causes the Window's Content property to never be rendered, even if it's set. If that's not acceptable, an easy solution is to move this Visual-hosting code to a different UIElement and then place that element in the Window as desired. For the mapping program example, this could mean hosting your custom Visuals in a Canvas-derived class and then placing that in a Window's Grid (or other Panel) so you can overlay Buttons and other controls.

> **WARNING**
>
> **Calling Visual.AddVisualChild is not enough for adding a visual child!**
>
> The name of the AddVisualChild method makes it sound like calling it is all you need to do to add a Visual child to an element. But that is not the case. You must still implement VisualChildrenCount and GetVisualChild to return the appropriate information.

Besides overriding the two members of Visual, Listing 15.3 also passes the DrawingVisual to two protected methods defined on Window's base classes: AddVisualChild (defined on Visual) and AddLogicalChild (defined on FrameworkElement). Calling both of these isn't strictly necessary for rendering the DrawingVisual, but it should be done to "register" the existence of this visual with the appropriate logical and visual trees. That way, features such as event routing, hit testing, and property inheritance work as expected. If you are maintaining a collection of Visual children and ever remove one of these children, you should call RemoveVisualChild and RemoveLogicalChild.

> **DIGGING DEEPER**
>
> **Other Uses for Visuals**
>
> Although non-UIElement Visuals must be hosted in a UIElement to be rendered on the screen, you can do other things with these lightweight Visuals without requiring a UIElement host. For example, any Visual can be sent to a printer with PrintDialog's PrintVisual method, and you can host any Visual in a Win32 application (as described in Chapter 19, "Interoperability with Non-WPF Technologies"). DrawingVisual is also convenient when using RenderTargetBitmap, covered later in this chapter.

> **DIGGING DEEPER**
>
> **Another Option for Performing Custom Rendering**
>
> If an application or a component uses only a single `DrawingVisual`, which means that you don't require its drawings to be independently interactive, you might as well host it in a `UIElement` instead. The extra overhead of `UIElement` compared to `DrawingVisual` is not significant when dealing with a single instance. And working with a custom `UIElement` is easier than working with a `DrawingVisual`: You simply override its `OnRender` method, draw into its `DrawingContext` parameter, and host it anywhere, such as `Content` in a `ContentControl`. That said, hosting a `Drawing` inside an `Image` is easier still, doesn't require any procedural code, and has insignificant overhead over a `UIElement` if you're dealing with only one.

Visual Hit Testing

The term *hit testing* refers to determining whether a point (or set of points) intersects with a given object. Hit testing is typically done in the context of a mouse, stylus, or touch event, where the point in question is the location of the mouse pointer, stylus tip, or finger(s).

In WPF, there are two kinds of hit testing: *visual hit testing*, which is supported by all `Visuals`, and *input hit testing*, which is supported only by `UIElements`. This section describes only visual hit testing; input hit testing is covered in the "`Shapes`" section.

Visual hit testing is crucial for enabling a `Visual` to respond to user actions such as clicks, taps, or hovering because it doesn't have any of the input events that `UIElements` have (`MouseLeftButtonDown`, `MouseEnter`, `MouseLeave`, `MouseMove`, and so on). By handling such events on the host `UIElement` and then using visual hit testing to determine whether relevant child `Visuals` were "hit," you can make any `Visual` respond appropriately to any or all of these events.

Simple Hit Testing

Visual hit testing can be performed with the static `VisualTreeHelper.HitTest` method. The simplest overload of this method accepts a root `Visual` whose visual tree should be searched as well as the coordinate being tested (which must be expressed relative to the passed-in root). It returns a `HitTestResult`, which contains the topmost `Visual` hit by that point.

Therefore, the following method could be added to the `Window` in Listing 15.3 to process clicks on the ghost `DrawingVisual` and respond by rotating it by 1° each time (just for demonstration purposes):

```
protected override void OnMouseLeftButtonDown(MouseButtonEventArgs e)
{
  base.OnMouseLeftButtonDown(e);

  // Retrieve the mouse pointer location relative to the Window
```

```
  Point location = e.GetPosition(this);

  // Perform visual hit testing for the entire Window
  HitTestResult result = VisualTreeHelper.HitTest(this, location);

  // If we hit the ghostVisual, rotate it
  if (result.VisualHit == ghostVisual)
  {
    if (ghostVisual.Transform == null)
      ghostVisual.Transform = new RotateTransform();

    (ghostVisual.Transform as RotateTransform).Angle++;
  }
}
```

Because `Image` is ultimately a `Visual`, you could have implemented the same scheme with the `Image` hosting the `DrawingImage` version of the ghost back in Listing 15.1. (Or you could have simply attached an event handler to `Image`'s `MouseLeftButtonDown` event.) There's an important difference between doing this with an `Image` and doing the visual hit testing with a `DrawingVisual`, however. The preceding code considers the `DrawingVisual` to be hit only for coordinates physically within the ghost's body, whereas an `Image` is considered to be hit for any coordinates within the `Image`'s rectangular bounds.

Hit Testing with Multiple `Visuals`

Having nonrectangular hit testing is nice, but perhaps you want to hit test for individual portions of the ghost, such as the eyes versus the mouth versus the body. To accomplish this, you need to split the single `DrawingVisual` into three `DrawingVisuals`. Listing 15.4 does just that and performs the 1° rotation on any `DrawingVisual` each time it is clicked. Figure 15.15 shows the result of this ability to manipulate visuals independently, with a ghost that is starting to look like a Picasso painting.

LISTING 15.4 `WindowHostingVisual.cs`—Splitting the Ghost into Three `DrawingVisuals` for Independent Hit Testing

```
using System;
using System.Windows;
using System.Windows.Input;
using System.Windows.Media;
using System.Collections.Generic;

public class WindowHostingVisual : Window
{
  List<Visual> visuals = new List<Visual>();

  public WindowHostingVisual()
```

LISTING 15.4 Continued

```
{
  Title = "Hosting DrawingVisuals";
  Width = 300;
  Height = 350;

  DrawingVisual bodyVisual = new DrawingVisual();
  DrawingVisual eyesVisual = new DrawingVisual();
  DrawingVisual mouthVisual = new DrawingVisual();

  using (DrawingContext dc = bodyVisual.RenderOpen())
  {
    // The body
    dc.DrawGeometry(Brushes.Blue, null, Geometry.Parse(
      @"M 240,250
        C 200,375 200,250 175,200
        C 100,400 100,250 100,200
        C 0,350   0,250   30,130
        C 75,0    100,0   150,0
        C 200,0   250,0   250,150 Z"));
  }
  using (DrawingContext dc = eyesVisual.RenderOpen())
  {
    // Left eye
    dc.DrawEllipse(Brushes.Black, new Pen(Brushes.White, 10),
      new Point(95, 95), 15, 15);
    // Right eye
    dc.DrawEllipse(Brushes.Black, new Pen(Brushes.White, 10),
      new Point(170, 105), 15, 15);
  }
  using (DrawingContext dc = mouthVisual.RenderOpen())
  {
    // The mouth
    Pen p = new Pen(Brushes.Black, 10);
    p.StartLineCap = PenLineCap.Round;
    p.EndLineCap = PenLineCap.Round;
    dc.DrawLine(p, new Point(75, 160), new Point(175, 150));
  }

  visuals.Add(bodyVisual);
  visuals.Add(eyesVisual);
  visuals.Add(mouthVisual);

  // Bookkeeping:
  foreach (Visual v in visuals)
```

15

LISTING 15.4 Continued

```
    {
      AddVisualChild(v);
      AddLogicalChild(v);
    }
  }

  // The two necessary overrides, implemented for the single Visual:
  protected override int VisualChildrenCount
  {
    get { return visuals.Count; }
  }
  protected override Visual GetVisualChild(int index)
  {
    if (index < 0 || index >= visuals.Count)
      throw new ArgumentOutOfRangeException("index");

    return visuals[index];
  }

  protected override void OnMouseLeftButtonDown(MouseButtonEventArgs e)
  {
    base.OnMouseLeftButtonDown(e);

    // Retrieve the mouse pointer location relative to the Window
    Point location = e.GetPosition(this);

    // Perform visual hit testing
    HitTestResult result = VisualTreeHelper.HitTest(this, location);

    // If we hit any DrawingVisual, rotate it
    if (result.VisualHit.GetType() == typeof(DrawingVisual))
    {
      DrawingVisual dv = result.VisualHit as DrawingVisual;
      if (dv.Transform == null)
        dv.Transform = new RotateTransform();

      (dv.Transform as RotateTransform).Angle++;
    }
  }
}
```

FIGURE 15.15 The ghost represented by three independent `DrawingVisuals`, after a few clicks on the body and several clicks on the eyes.

Because this `Window` now has three `Visual` children instead of one, it uses a `List<Visual>` collection to store them for the sake of the `VisualChildrenCount` and `GetVisualChild` implementation. Drawing into three `DrawingVisuals` instead of one is a simple change; the `DrawingContext` commands are simply split into three `using` blocks, one per `DrawingVisual`. In the processing of the `HitTestResult`, the code applies the rotation logic to any `Visual` as long as it's a `DrawingVisual`.

DIGGING DEEPER

`DrawingVisuals` as Children of a `DrawingVisual`

`DrawingVisual` derives from `ContainerVisual`, which can contain any number of `Visuals` in its `Children` collection. (`ContainerVisual` really should have been called `VisualGroup`, for consistency with WPF classes such as `TransformGroup`, `DrawingGroup`, and `GeometryGroup`.) Therefore, another way to implement Listing 15.4 would be to add `eyesVisual` and `mouthVisual` as children of `bodyVisual` *instead of* adding them to the `Window`'s `visuals` collection. This also means that the listing could go back to the approach of managing a single `Visual` rather than a collection! Rendering and hit testing automatically work for children of a `DrawingVisual` because `ContainerVisual` overrides and implements `VisualChildrenCount` and `GetVisualChild` similar to how Listing 15.4 implements them. You just need to hook up the `Window` to the root `DrawingVisual` and let the `DrawingVisual` handle the rest!

Hit Testing with Overlapping `Visuals`

Visual hit testing can inform you about *all* `Visuals` that intersect a location, not just the topmost `Visual`. For the three-`Visuals` ghost example, you can set up hit testing such that clicking on the eyes tells you that the eyes were hit *and* the body underneath the eyes was hit. It doesn't matter if a `Visual` is completely obscured; it can still be hit.

To take advantage of this functionality, you must use a more powerful form of the `HitTest` method that accepts a `HitTestResultCallback` delegate. Before this version of

HitTest returns, the delegate is invoked once for each relevant Visual, starting from the topmost and ending at the bottommost.

The following code is an update to the OnMouseLeftButtonDown method from Listing 15.4 that supports hit testing on overlapping Visuals:

```
protected override void OnMouseLeftButtonDown(MouseButtonEventArgs e)
{
  base.OnMouseLeftButtonDown(e);

  // Retrieve the mouse pointer location relative to the Window
  Point location = e.GetPosition(this);

  // Perform visual hit testing
  VisualTreeHelper.HitTest(this, null,
    new HitTestResultCallback(HitTestCallback),
    new PointHitTestParameters(location));
}

public HitTestResultBehavior HitTestCallback(HitTestResult result)
{
  // If we hit any DrawingVisual, rotate it
  if (result.VisualHit.GetType() == typeof(DrawingVisual))
  {
    DrawingVisual dv = result.VisualHit as DrawingVisual;
    if (dv.Transform == null)
      dv.Transform = new RotateTransform();

    (dv.Transform as RotateTransform).Angle++;
  }
  // Keep looking for hits
  return HitTestResultBehavior.Continue;
}
```

There are a few differences here from the earlier code. The most noticeable one is that the logic to process HitTestResult is moved to the callback method because this overload of HitTest doesn't return anything. The callback method must return one of two HitTestResultBehavior values: Continue or Stop. Therefore, you can stop the probing for further Visuals at any time. If the callback *always* returns Stop, only the topmost Visual is processed, just like with the simpler hit-testing approach. The second parameter of this HitTest overload, where null is passed, can be set to a HitTestFilterCallback delegate to skip the processing of certain parts of a visual tree without stopping the processing altogether. You can implement very sophisticated hit-testing schemes with this approach.

Notice that this overload of HitTest isn't given the relevant Point directly but rather is passed a PointHitTestParameters object wrapping the Point. That's because the method accepts an abstract HitTestParameters instance, and WPF has two subclasses:

PointHitTestParameters and GeometryHitTestParameters. The latter can be used to hit test against an arbitrary region. This is useful for supporting more complicated input actions, such as dragging a selection rectangle or drawing a "lasso" to select multiple objects.

FAQ

Why does the more powerful form of visual hit testing involve an awkward callback mechanism instead of simply returning an array of HitTestResults?

The callback scheme was chosen for performance reasons. This way, WPF doesn't have to allocate any extra memory, which is important when dealing with high numbers of Visuals or frequent hit testing. In addition, the callback scheme allows for scenario-specific optimizations by giving callback methods the power to halt processing by returning HitTestResultBehavior.Stop.

TIP

If you want visual hit testing to report a hit anywhere within a Visual's bounding box rather than its precise geometry, you can override Visual's HitTestCore method, which is called whenever the bounding box is hit. (This method enables you to customize hit testing in other ways as well.)

A simpler way to accomplish this is to simply draw a transparent rectangle that matches the size of the bounding box inside the Visual. Visual hit testing doesn't care about the transparency of objects; they get hit just the same, as if they are panes of glass.

WARNING

Don't modify the visual tree in your hit-testing callback methods!

Hit-testing callback methods are called while the visual tree is in the process of being walked, so altering the tree can cause incorrect behavior. If you must modify the visual tree based on certain Visuals being hit, you should store the information you need during the callbacks so that you can act on it after HitTest returns. This is pretty easy to do because HitTest doesn't return until after all callbacks have been called.

Shapes

A Shape, like a GeometryDrawing, is a basic 2D drawing that combines a Geometry with a Pen and Brush. Unlike GeometryDrawing, however, Shape derives from FrameworkElement, so it can be directly placed in a user interface without custom code or a complex hierarchy of objects. For example, Chapter 2, "XAML Demystified," shows how easy it is to embed a square in a `Button` by using `Rectangle` (which derives from `Shape`):

```
<Button MinWidth="75">
  <Rectangle Height="20" Width="20" Fill="Black"/>
</Button>
```

WPF provides six classes that derive from the abstract `System.Windows.Shapes.Shape` class:

- `Rectangle`
- `Ellipse`
- `Line`
- `Polyline`
- `Polygon`
- `Path`

Most of these should look pretty familiar, as they mirror the `Geometry` classes discussed earlier in the chapter. The following sections examine each one individually because they work slightly differently than their `Geometry` counterparts. (In addition, `Polyline` and `Polygon` are `Shape`-specific abstractions over a `PathGeometry`.) `Shape` itself defines many properties for controlling the appearance of its concrete subclasses. The two most important ones are `Fill` and `Stroke`, both of type `Brush`.

FAQ

Why is `Shape.Stroke` a `Brush` rather than a `Pen`?

`Shape`'s `Fill` and `Stroke` properties have the same role as `GeometryDrawing`'s `Brush` and `Pen` properties: `Fill` is for the inner area, and `Stroke` is for the outline. Internally, a `Pen` is indeed used to create the outline of the `Shape`. But rather than exposing the `Pen` directly, `Shape` defines `Stroke` as a `Brush` and exposes eight additional properties to tweak the settings of the internal `Pen` wrapping the `Stroke Brush`: `StrokeStartLineCap`, `StrokeEndLineCap`, `StrokeThickness`, and so on.

This unfortunate inconsistency was created because setting the `Pen`-related properties directly on the `Shape` is simpler than using a separate `Pen` object, especially for the common case in which all you're setting is the `Brush` and the `Thickness`.

WARNING

Overuse of Shapes can lead to performance problems!

It's tempting to use Shapes as the building blocks for any 2D drawings. They are much more discoverable and easier to work with than Drawings, and they work with the content model that WPF developers take for granted. Design tools and XAML exporters also tend to represent artwork as Shapes by default, so Shapes can sneak into your applications without you even realizing it. For example, when you select the XAML Export menu item in Microsoft Expression Design, the resultant .xaml file contains Shapes in a Canvas unless you explicitly change the Document Format option to Resource Dictionary. At this point, you can choose between a DrawingImage and a DrawingBrush. DrawingImage is generally a better choice than DrawingBrush because DrawingImage can usually avoid drawing to an intermediate surface before drawing to the back buffer.

When you have Shape-based artwork, *every single* Shape supports Styles, data binding, resources, layout, input and focus, routed events, and so on. It's nice that you can take advantage of all this without extra work, but as discussed in the "Visuals" section, this is typically unnecessary overhead. Keep this in mind if you find yourself using more than a small number of Shapes.

Rectangle

RectangleGeometry, discussed earlier in this chapter, has a Rect property for defining its dimensions. Rectangle, on the other hand, delegates to WPF's layout system for controlling its size and position. This could involve using its Width and Height properties (among others) inherited from FrameworkElement or controlling its location with Canvas.Left and Canvas.Top, for example.

Just like RectangleGeometry, however, Rectangle defines its own RadiusX and RadiusY properties of type double that enable you to give it rounded corners. Figure 15.16 shows the following Rectangles in a StackPanel with various values of RadiusX and RadiusY:

```
<StackPanel>
  <Rectangle Width="200" Height="100"
    Fill="Orange" Stroke="Black" StrokeThickness="10" Margin="4"/>
  <Rectangle Width="200" Height="100" RadiusX="10" RadiusY="30"
    Fill="Orange" Stroke="Black" StrokeThickness="10" Margin="4"/>
  <Rectangle Width="200" Height="100" RadiusX="30" RadiusY="10"
    Fill="Orange" Stroke="Black" StrokeThickness="10" Margin="4"/>
  <Rectangle Width="200" Height="100" RadiusX="100" RadiusY="50"
    Fill="Orange" Stroke="Black" StrokeThickness="10" Margin="4"/>
</StackPanel>
```

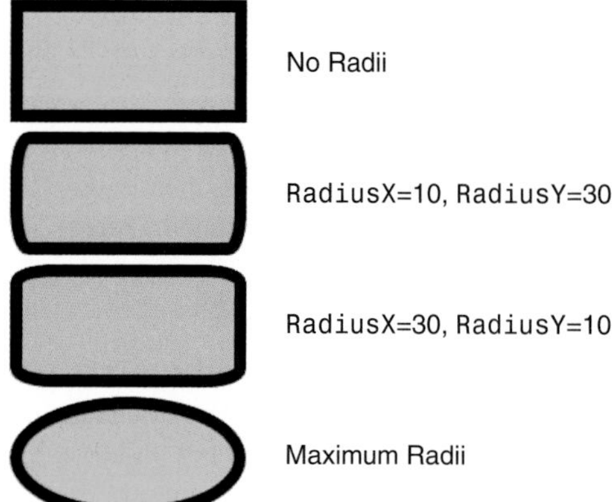

FIGURE 15.16 Four Rectangles with different values for RadiusX and RadiusY.

RadiusX can be at most half the Width of the Rectangle, and RadiusY can be at most half the Height. Setting them any higher makes no difference.

> **WARNING**
>
> **You must explicitly set Stroke or Fill for a Shape to be seen!**
>
> This might sound obvious for someone used to working with GeometryDrawings, but it's a common pitfall for people who think of Shapes the way they think of Buttons and ListBoxes. Although each Shape internally contains the appropriate Geometry, its Stroke and Fill are both set to null by default.

Ellipse

After discovering the flexibility of Rectangle and realizing that it can be made to look like an ellipse (or circle), you'd think that a separate Ellipse class would be redundant. And you'd be right! All Ellipse does is make it easier to get an elliptical shape. It defines no settable properties above and beyond what Shape and its base classes provide. Unlike EllipseGeometry, which exposes RadiusX, RadiusY, and Center properties, Ellipse simply fills its rectangular region with the largest possible elliptical shape.

The following Ellipse could replace the last Rectangle in the previous XAML snippet, and Figure 15.16 would look identical:

```
<Ellipse Width="200" Height="100"
  Fill="Orange" Stroke="Black" StrokeThickness="10" Margin="4"/>
```

The only change is replacing the element name and removing the references to RadiusX and RadiusY.

DIGGING DEEPER

How Shapes Work

Shapes internally override UIElement's OnRender method and use DrawingContext methods to draw the appropriate geometry. For example, Ellipse has an OnRender implementation effectively like the following:

```
protected override void OnRender(DrawingContext drawingContext)
{
  Pen pen = …;    // Fabricate a Pen based on all the StrokeXXX properties
  Rect rect = …; // Layout determines the size of this rectangle
  drawingContext.DrawGeometry(this.Fill, pen, new EllipseGeometry(rect));
}
```

Furthermore, Rectangle has an OnRender implementation effectively like the following:

```
protected override void OnRender(DrawingContext drawingContext)
{
  Pen pen = …;    // Fabricate a Pen based on all the StrokeXXX properties
  Rect rect = …; // Layout determines the size of this rectangle
  drawingContext.DrawRoundedRectangle(this.Fill, pen, rect, this.RadiusX,
    this.RadiusY);
}
```

The bulk of the code inside a Shape is the plumbing needed to interact with the layout system. This plumbing is covered in Chapter 21.

Line

Line defines four double properties to represent a line segment connecting points (*x1*,*y1*) and (*x2*,*y2*). These properties are called X1, Y1, X2, and Y2. These are defined as four properties rather than two Point properties (as in LineGeometry) for ease of use in data-binding scenarios.

The values of Line's properties are not absolute coordinates. They are relative to the space given to the Line element by the layout system. For example, the following StackPanel contains three Lines, rendered in Figure 15.17:

```
<StackPanel>
  <Line X1="0" Y1="0"   X2="100" Y2="100" Stroke="Black" StrokeThickness="10"
    Margin="4"/>
  <Line X1="0" Y1="0"   X2="100" Y2="0"   Stroke="Black" StrokeThickness="10"
    Margin="4"/>
  <Line X1="0" Y1="100" X2="100" Y2="0"   Stroke="Black" StrokeThickness="10"
    Margin="4"/>
</StackPanel>
```

Notice that each `Line` is given the space needed by its bounding box, so the horizontal line gets only 10 units (for the thickness of its `Stroke`) plus the specified `Margin`. `Line` inherits `Shape`'s `Fill` property, but it is meaningless because there is never any area to fill.

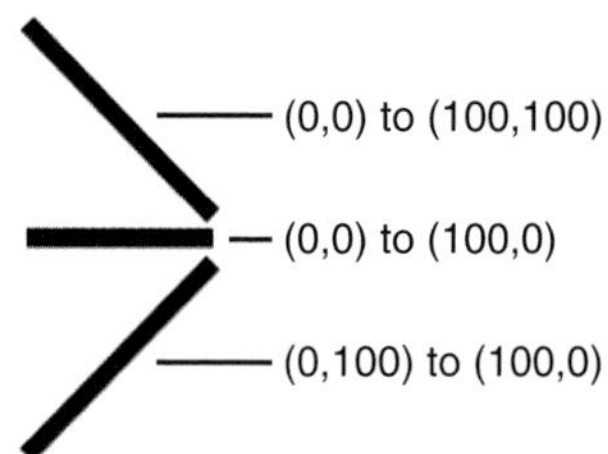

FIGURE 15.17 Three `Lines` in a `StackPanel`, demonstrating that their coordinates are relative.

Polyline

`Polyline` represents a sequence of lines, expressed in its `Points` property (a collection of `Point` objects). The following four `Polylines` are rendered in Figure 15.18:

```
<StackPanel>
<Polyline Points="0,0 100,100" Stroke="Black" StrokeThickness="10" Margin="4"/>
<Polyline Points="0,0 100,100 200,0" Stroke="Black" StrokeThickness="10"
  Margin="4"/>
<Polyline Points="0,0 100,100 200,0 300,100" Stroke="Black" StrokeThickness="10"
  Margin="4"/>
<Polyline Points="0,0 100,100 200,0 300,100 100,100" Stroke="Black"
  StrokeThickness="10" Margin="4"/>
</StackPanel>
```

FIGURE 15.18 Four `Polylines`, ranging from 2 to 5 points.

A type converter enables `Points` to be specified as a simple list of alternating *x* and *y* values. The commas can help with readability but are optional. You can place commas between any two values or use no commas at all.

Figure 15.19 demonstrates that setting `Polyline`'s `Fill` fills it like an open `PathGeometry`, pretending that a line segment exists that connects the first `Point` with the last `Point`. This happens because, internally, `Polyline` *is* using a `PathGeometry`! Figure 15.19 was created simply by taking the `Polylines` from Figure 15.18 and marking them with `Fill="Orange"`.

Polygon

Just as Rectangle makes Ellipse redundant, Polyline makes Polygon redundant. The only difference between Polyline and Polygon is that Polygon automatically adds a line segment connecting the first Point and last Point. (In other words, it sets IsClosed to true in its internal PathGeometry's PathFigure.)

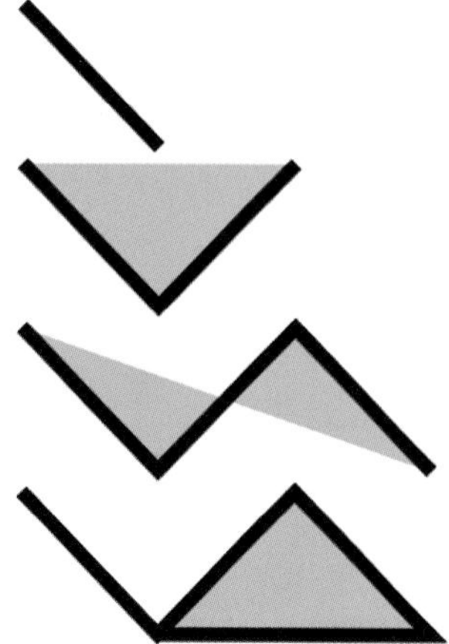

FIGURE 15.19 The same Polylines from Figure 15.18, but with an explicit Fill.

If you take each Polyline from Figure 15.19 and simply change each element name to Polygon, you get the result shown in Figure 15.20. Notice that the initial line segment in the first and last Polygons is noticeably longer than in Figure 15.19. This is because of the Miter corners joining the initial line segment with the final line segment (which happens to share the same coordinates). Because the angle between the two line segments is 0°, the corner would be infinitely long if not for the StrokeMiterLimit property limiting it to 10 units by default.

Both Polygon and Polyline expose the underlying PathGeometry's FillRule with their own FillRule property.

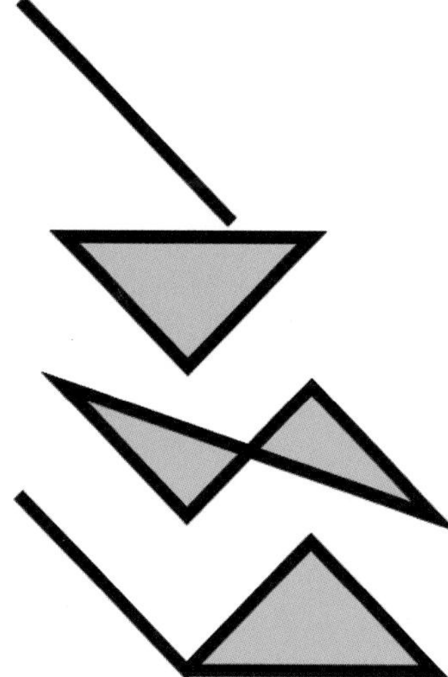

FIGURE 15.20 Polygons are just like Polylines, except that they always form a closed shape.

Path

As you probably expected, just as all basic geometries can be represented as a PathGeometry, all the other Shapes can be alternatively represented with the general-purpose Path. Path only adds a single Data property to Shape, which can be set to an instance of any geometry. Therefore, Path turns out to be the easiest (and most fully featured) way to embed an arbitrary geometry directly into a user interface. There's no need for an explicit Drawing object or low-level DrawingContext techniques; you simply set the Data, Fill, and Stroke-related properties.

The following Path produces the same result as the overlapping triangles from Figure 15.6:

```
<Path Fill="Orange" Stroke="Black"
StrokeThickness="10">
<Path.Data>
  <PathGeometry>
    <!-- Triangle #1 -->
    <PathFigure IsClosed="True">
      <LineSegment Point="0,100"/>
      <LineSegment Point="100,100"/>
```

```
      </PathFigure>
      <!-- Triangle #2 -->
      <PathFigure StartPoint="70,0" IsClosed="True">
        <LineSegment Point="0,100"/>
        <LineSegment Point="100,100"/>
      </PathFigure>
    </PathGeometry>
  </Path.Data>
</Path>
```

Or, you can take advantage of `Geometry`'s type converter and express the whole thing as follows:

```
<Path Fill="Orange" Stroke="Black" StrokeThickness="10"
  Data="M 0,0 L 0,100 L 100,100 Z M 70,0 L 0,100 L 100,100 Z"/>
```

Clip Art Based on Shapes

Let's revisit the ghost clip art that was represented as a `DrawingImage` in Listing 15.1 and as a sequence of `DrawingContext` commands in Listings 15.2 through 15.4. Listing 15.5 places the pieces of the ghost, which are now independent `Shapes`, on a `Canvas`. The result looks identical to hosting the `DrawingImage` in an `Image`, as shown back in Figure 15.13.

LISTING 15.5 The Ghost Represented as Four Independent Shapes

```
<Canvas xmlns="http://schemas.microsoft.com/winfx/2006/xaml/presentation">
  <Path Fill="Blue" Data="M 240,250
    C 200,375 200,250 175,200
    C 100,400 100,250 100,200
    C 0,350   0,250   30,130
    C 75,0    100,0   150,0
    C 200,0   250,0   250,150 Z"/>
  <Ellipse Fill="Black" Stroke="White" StrokeThickness="10"
    Width="40" Height="40" Canvas.Left="75" Canvas.Top="75"/>
  <Ellipse Fill="Black" Stroke="White" StrokeThickness="10"
    Width="40" Height="40" Canvas.Left="150" Canvas.Top="85"/>
  <Line X1="75" Y1="160" X2="175" Y2="150" StrokeStartLineCap="Round"
    StrokeEndLineCap="Round" Stroke="Black" StrokeThickness="10"/>
</Canvas>
```

The numeric data used for the `Path` (body) and the `Line` (mouth) is identical to the data used in the original `DrawingImage`. The property values for both `Ellipses`, however, needed a bit of translation to map from the original `EllipseGeometry` objects to the `Ellipse` objects. The original eyes had a radius of `15` and a `Pen` thickness of `10`. Because the `Pen` outline is centered on any geometry's edge, it only extends the total radius to `20`. That's why the `Ellipses` in Listing 15.5 are given a `Height` and `Width` of `40` (the radius multiplied by 2). In this case, the entire `Shape`, including its outline, fits inside the bounds. As for the values chosen for `Canvas.Left` and `Canvas.Top`, they are the original `EllipseGeometry Center` values minus the total radius of 20.

Unlike previous implementations of the ghost, this one supports *input hit testing* independently on each of its four pieces (each eye is even treated separately!) because they all derive from `UIElement`. Input hit testing differs from visual hit testing in that it more closely represents what a user can physically hit with the mouse pointer, finger, or stylus. It only supports hitting the topmost element at any coordinate, and it allows elements to be hit only if `IsEnabled` and `IsVisible` (properties introduced by `UIElement`) are both `true`. (It also only supports hit testing against a single point rather than a geometry, but that's just an artificial limitation rather than a philosophical difference.)

To perform input hit testing, you simply call `InputHitTest` on an instance of a `UIElement` whose visual tree you want to be tested. You can pass it a `Point`, and it returns an `IInputElement` instance (an interface implemented by `UIElement` and `ContentElement`). But input hit testing is rarely performed directly because all `UIElements` already have a host of events that expose whether they've been pressed, clicked, and so on: `GotKeyboardFocus`, `KeyDown`, `KeyUp`, `GotMouseCapture`, `MouseEnter`, `MouseLeave`, `MouseMove`, `MouseWheel`, `GotStylusCapture`, `StylusEnter`, `StylusLeave`, `StylusInAirMove`, and so on. And if the policy enforced by input hit testing is too restrictive for your needs, you can perform visual hit testing with any `Shape`.

DIGGING DEEPER

Input Hit Testing's Dirty Little Secret

Input hit testing is really just a special case of visual hit testing. In fact, the implementation of `InputHitTest` simply calls `VisualTreeHelper.HitTest` with its own internal callbacks for filtering and results processing! Its filter callback prunes disabled and invisible `UIElements` from the visual tree traversal, and its results callback stops the search after it finds the first match.

15

Brushes

It's not obvious when programming with WPF via XAML, but WPF elements almost never interact directly with colors. Instead, most uses of color are wrapped inside objects known as `Brushes`. This is an extremely powerful indirection because WPF contains seven different kinds of `Brushes` that can do just about everything imaginable. There are three *color brushes*, three *tile brushes*, and one special brush covered at the end of the chapter (`BitmapCacheBrush`). Although this section mostly demonstrates `Brushes` on a `Drawing` or `Window`, keep in mind that `Brushes` can be used as the background, foreground, or outline of just about anything you can put on the screen.

Color Brushes

WPF's three color brushes are `SolidColorBrush`, `LinearGradientBrush`, and `RadialGradientBrush`. You might think you already know everything there is to know about these `Brushes` from their limited use in the book so far, but all of these `Brushes` are more flexible than most people realize.

SolidColorBrush

SolidColorBrush, used implicitly throughout this book, fills the target area with a single color. It has a simple Color property of type System.Windows.Media.Color. Because of the type converter that converts strings such as "Blue" or "#FFFFFF" into SolidColorBrushes, they are indistinguishable from their underlying Color in XAML.

The Color structure has more functionality than you might expect. It natively supports two color spaces:

- **sRGB**—This is the standard RGB color space designed for CRT monitors and familiar to most programmers and web designers. The values for red, green, and blue are each represented as a byte, so there are only 256 possible values.
- **scRGB**—This is an enhanced RGB color space that represents red, green, and blue as floating-point values. This enables a much wider gamut of colors that can be accurately represented. Red, green, and blue values of 0.0 represent black, whereas three values of 1.0 represent white. However, scRGB allows for values outside this range, so information isn't lost if you apply transformations to Colors that temporarily push any channel outside its normal range. scRGB also has increased accuracy because it is a linear color space.

> **TIP**
>
> It is usually more efficient to use colors with translucency coming from their alpha channels than to use the Opacity property to apply translucency to an otherwise-opaque solid color.

Color exposes sets of properties (one per channel) for both color spaces: A, R, G, and B of type Byte for the more familiar sRGB and ScA, ScR, ScG, and ScB of type Single for the more flexible scRGB. (A and ScA represent the alpha channel, for varying the opacity.) Whenever any of these properties are set, Color updates both of its internal representations. Therefore, you can mix and match these properties with the same Color instance, and everything stays in sync. You can also leverage this behavior to easily convert sRGB values to scRGB values and vice versa.

Color defines operators that enable you to add, subtract, and multiply two instances and compare them for equality. However, because scRGB uses floating-point values (which should never be tested for strict equality), Color defines a static AreClose method that accepts two colors and returns true if all their channels are within a very small epsilon of each other.

Color's type converter supports several different string representations:

- A name, like Red, Khaki, or DodgerBlue, matching one of the static properties on the Colors class.
- The sRGB representation #argb, where a, r, g, and b are hexadecimal values for the A, R, G, and B properties. For example, opaque Red is #FFFF0000, or more simply #FF0000 (because A is assumed to be the maximum 255, by default).
- The scRGB representation sc#a r g b, where a, r, g, and b are decimal values for the ScA, ScR, ScG, and ScB properties. In this representation, opaque Red is sc#1.0 1.0 0.0 0.0, or more simply sc#1.0 0.0 0.0. Commas are also allowed between each value.

DIGGING DEEPER

Custom Color Space Profiles

Advanced developers or designers can specify `Colors` based on a custom ICC profile. (ICC is the International Color Consortium, which has defined the cross-platform profile format.) In procedural code, you can construct such a `Color` by calling the static `Color.FromValues` method that accepts an array of `Singles` and a `Uri` pointing to the profile file. In XAML, you can take advantage of `Color`'s type converter that accepts a string of the form `ContextColor` *`Uri Values`*.

For example, the following `SolidColorBrush` gives a `Button` a red `Background` by using the sRGB profile file that you should have in your Windows `system32` directory under `spool\drivers\color`:

```
<Button>
<Button.Background>
  <SolidColorBrush Color="ContextColor
file://C:/WINDOWS/system32/spool/drivers/color/sRGB%20Color%20Space%20Profile.icm
    1.0,1.0,0.0,0.0"/>
</Button.Background>
</Button>
```

Custom profiles can hurt performance because they usually cause color conversions to happen. This is particularly true for bitmaps. To give you some control over this, `BitmapSource` supports an option called `BitmapCreateOptions.IgnoreColorProfile` that can give faster results by ignoring a profile that might otherwise be applied.

`LinearGradientBrush`

`LinearGradientBrush`, which has been used a few times already in this book, fills an area with a gradient defined by colors at specific points along an imaginary line segment, with linear interpolation between those points.

`LinearGradientBrush` contains a collection of `GradientStop` objects in its `GradientStops` content property, each of which contains a `Color` and an `Offset`. The offset is a `double` value relative to the bounding box of the area being filled, where `0` is the beginning and `1` is the end. Therefore, the following `LinearGradientBrush` can be applied to any version of the ghost clip art to create the result in Figure 15.21:

```
<LinearGradientBrush>
  <GradientStop Offset="0" Color="Blue"/>
  <GradientStop Offset="1" Color="Red"/>
</LinearGradientBrush>
```

FIGURE 15.21
A simple blue-to-red `LinearGradientBrush` applied to the ghost.

By default, the gradient starts at the top-left corner of the area's bounding box and ends at the bottom-right corner. You can customize these points, however, with `LinearGradientBrush`'s `StartPoint` and `EndPoint` properties. The values of these points are relative to the bounding box, just like the `Offset` in each `GradientStop`. Therefore, the default values for `StartPoint` and `EndPoint` are `(0,0)` and `(1,1)`, respectively.

If you want to use absolute units instead of relative ones, you can set `MappingMode` to `Absolute` (rather than the default `RelativeToBoundingBox`). Note that this applies only to `StartPoint` and `EndPoint`; the `Offset` values in each `GradientStop` are always relative.

Figure 15.22 shows a few different settings of `StartPoint` and `EndPoint` on the `LinearGradientBrush` used in Figure 15.21 (with the default relative `MappingMode`). Notice that the relative values are not limited to a range of 0 to 1. You can specify smaller or larger numbers to make the gradient logically extend *past* the bounding box. (This applies to `GradientStop` `Offset` values as well.)

The default interpolation of colors is done using the sRGB color space, but you can set `ColorInterpolationMode` to `ScRgbLinearInterpolation` to use the scRGB color space instead. The result is a much smoother gradient, as shown in Figure 15.23.

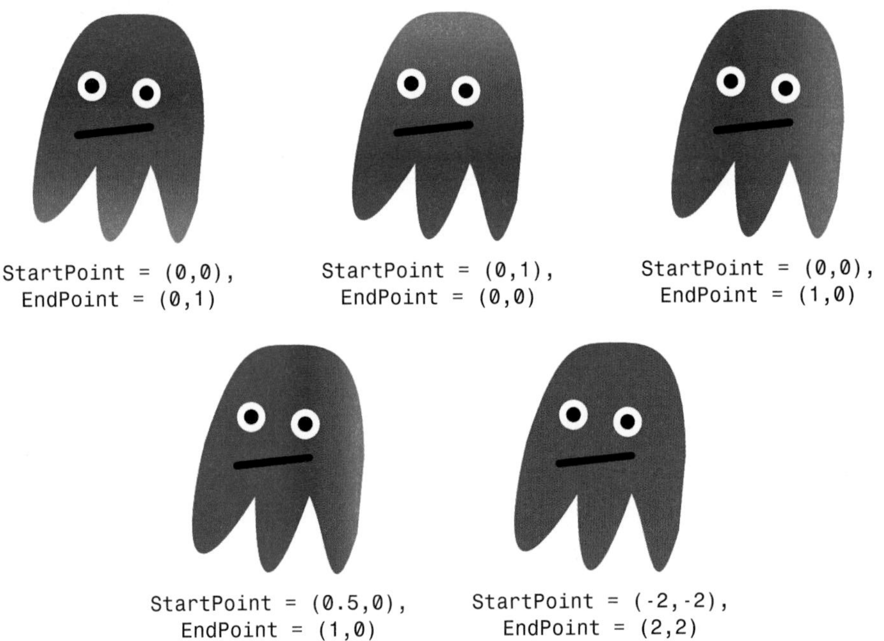

FIGURE 15.22 Various settings of `StartPoint` and `EndPoint`.

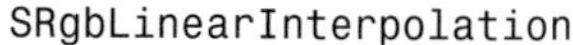

FIGURE 15.23 ColorInterpolationMode affects the appearance of the gradient.

The final property for controlling LinearGradientBrush is SpreadMethod, which determines how any leftover area not covered by the gradient should be filled. This makes sense only when the LinearGradientBrush is explicitly set to *not* cover the entire bounding box. The default value (from the GradientSpreadMethod enumeration) is Pad, meaning that the remaining space should be filled with the color at the endpoint. You could alternatively set it to Repeat or Reflect. Both of these values repeat the gradient in a never-ending pattern, but Reflect reverses every other gradient to maintain a smooth transition. Figure 15.24 demonstrates each of these SpreadMethod values on the following LinearGradientBrush that forces the gradient to cover only the middle 10% of the bounding box:

```
<LinearGradientBrush StartPoint=".45,.45" EndPoint=".55,.55" SpreadMethod="XXX">
  <GradientStop Offset="0" Color="Blue"/>
  <GradientStop Offset="1" Color="Red"/>
</LinearGradientBrush>
```

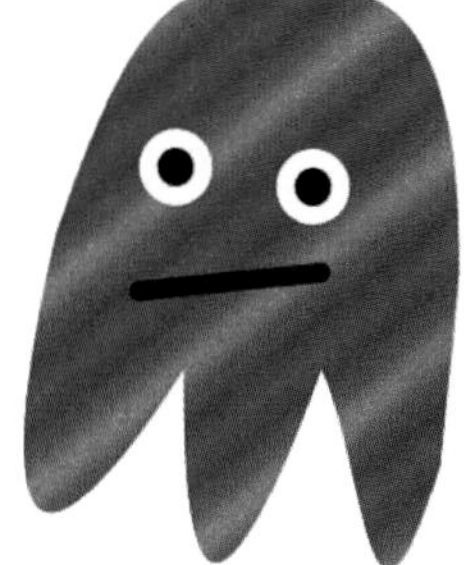

FIGURE 15.24 Different values of SpreadMethod can create vastly different effects.

And don’t forget, because Pens use a Brush rather than a simple Color to fill their area, Drawings, Shapes, Controls, and many other elements in WPF can be outlined with

None

Fill (default)

Uniform

UniformToFill

FIGURE 15.32 Applying different `Stretch` values to a `DrawingBrush`.

Viewport = 0, 0, 0.5, 0.5

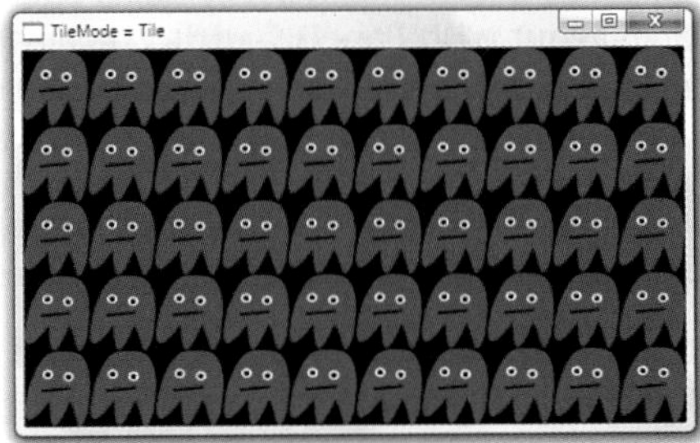

Viewport = 0, 0, 0.1, 0.2

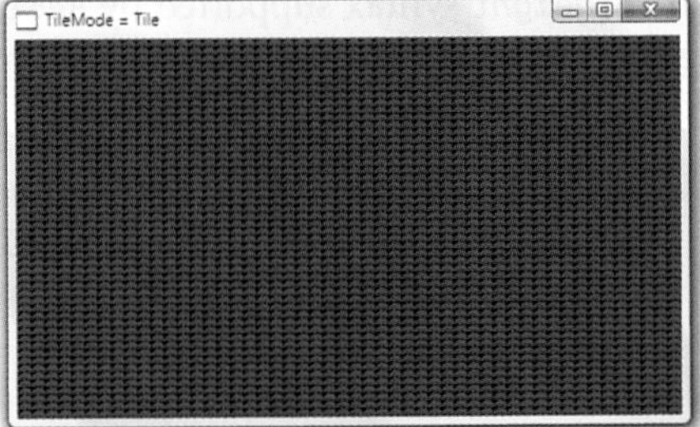

Viewport = 0, 0, 0.02, 0.02

FIGURE 15.33 Different `Viewport` values with `TileMode=Tile` and `Stretch=Fill`.

Just like with some of the gradient brush properties, the units of `Viewport` are relative to the bounding box by default. This enables you to effectively specify how many tiles you want horizontally and how many you want vertically. But you can also switch `Viewport` to use absolute coordinates by changing the value of `ViewportUnits` (a property of the familiar `BrushMappingMode` type).

The `TileMode` enumeration used by the `TileMode` property has more values than just `Tile` and `None`, however. It supports three more values that flip tiles in different ways:

- `FlipX` flips the tiles in every other column horizontally.
- `FlipY` flips the tiles in every other row vertically.
- `FlipXY` does both of the above.

Figure 15.34 demonstrates these three settings. Although these settings might not be very interesting for the ghost `Drawing`, you could use them with certain types of `Drawings` to help create the illusion of a continuous fill.

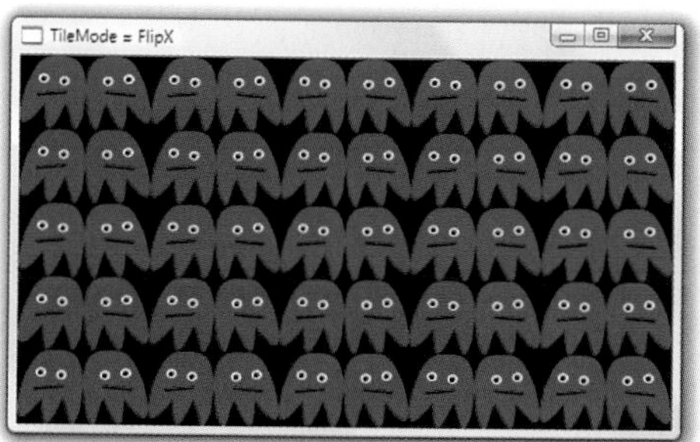

FlipX

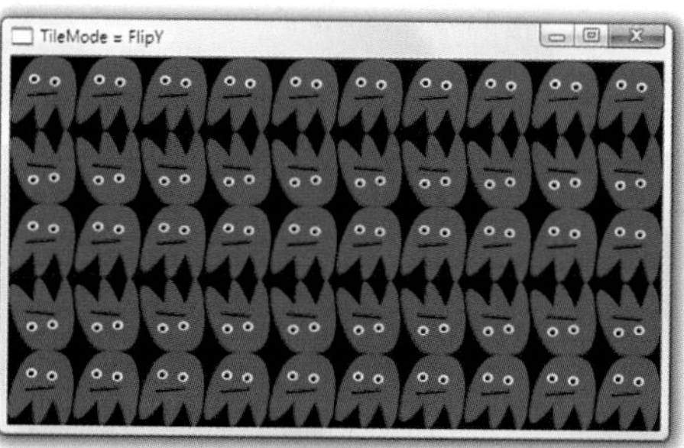

FlipY

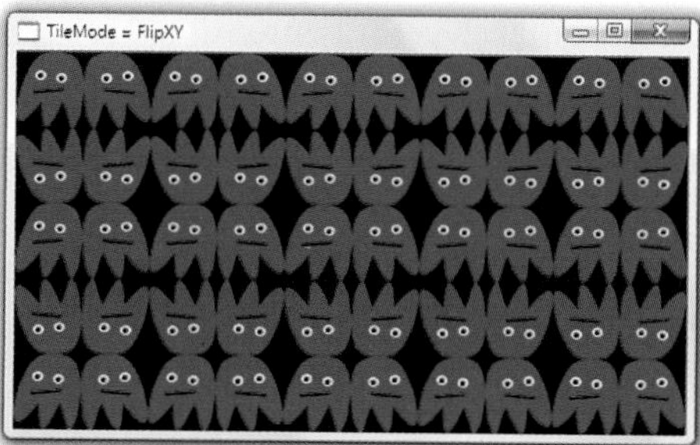

FlipXY

FIGURE 15.34 The three `Flip` settings for `TileMode`.

The final piece of customization is the `Viewbox` property, which enables you to specify a subset of the `Drawing` to use as the source of each tile (or the entire brush, if `TileMode` is set to None). Viewbox is a rectangle specified in bounding-box-relative units by default, just like Viewport. And a separate ViewboxUnits property can be set to make Viewbox use absolute coordinates, independently of the ViewportUnits setting.

Figure 15.35 sets the DrawingBrush's Viewbox property to the top-left quadrant of the ghost Drawing by giving it the Rect value 0, 0, 0.5, 0.5. It then mixes that setting with two different TileModes.

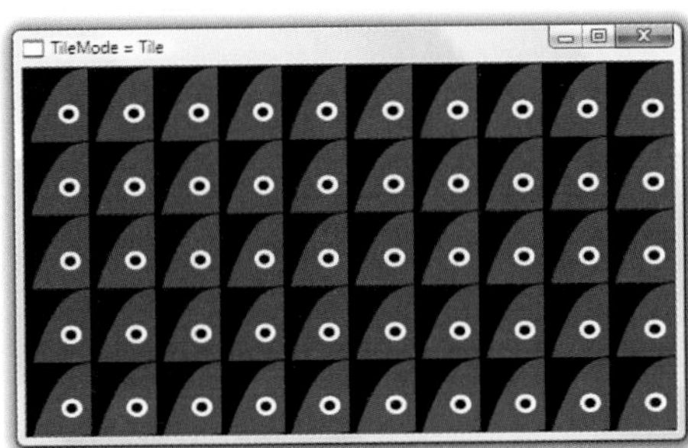

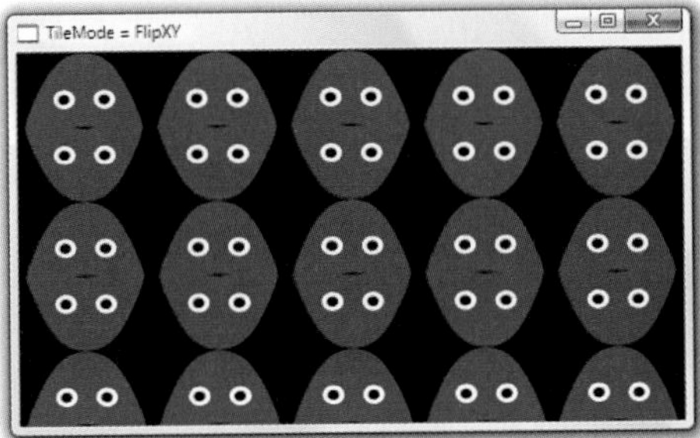

Tile FlipXY

FIGURE 15.35 Setting Viewbox to retrieve only the top-left quadrant of the drawing, used with two different TileModes.

As a final note on DrawingBrush, remember that its Drawing does not have to be a GeometryDrawing. It could be a VideoDrawing, for example!

ImageBrush

ImageBrush is identical to DrawingBrush, except it has an ImageSource property of type ImageSource rather than a Drawing property of type Drawing. It is meant to hold bitmap content rather than vector content. (That said, with the existence of DrawingImage and ImageDrawing, discussed earlier in the chapter, you can make DrawingBrush contain bitmap content and ImageBrush contain vector content!)

The following XAML uses an ImageBrush as the background of a Window. The bitmap content comes from the Winter Leaves.jpg file that ships with Windows Vista:

```
<Window xmlns="http://schemas.microsoft.com/winfx/2006/xaml/presentation"
        Title="ImageBrush with TileMode = FlipXY">
<Window.Background>
  <ImageBrush TileMode="FlipXY" Viewport="0,0,0.1,0.2">
  <ImageBrush.ImageSource>
    <BitmapImage UriSource="C:\Users\Public\Pictures\Sample Pictures\Winter
      Leaves.jpg"/>
  </ImageBrush.ImageSource>
  </ImageBrush>
</Window.Background>
</Window>
```

Figure 15.36 shows the resulting `Window`.

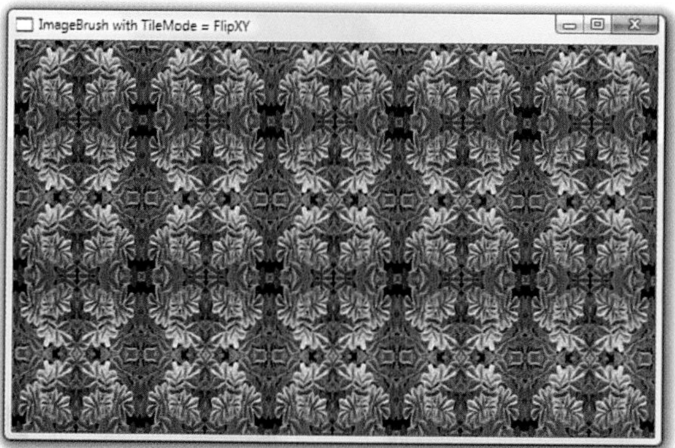

FIGURE 15.36 The `ImageBrush` background, using `TileMode=FlipXY` to create an interesting pattern.

VisualBrush

`VisualBrush` is also identical to `DrawingBrush`, except it has a `Visual` property of type `Visual` instead of a `Drawing` property of type `Drawing`. The power to paint with *any* `Visual`, however, even `FrameworkElements` such as `Button` and `TextBox`, makes `VisualBrush` very unique and powerful.

The following XAML paints a `Window`'s background with a `VisualBrush` containing a simple `Button`. Figure 15.37 shows the rendered result.

```
<Window xmlns="http://schemas.microsoft.com/winfx/2006/xaml/presentation"
        Title="ImageBrush with TileMode = FlipXY">
<Window.Background>
  <VisualBrush TileMode="FlipXY" Viewport="0,0,0.5,0.5">
  <VisualBrush.Visual>
    <Button>OK</Button>
  </VisualBrush.Visual>
  </VisualBrush>
</Window.Background>
</Window>
```

FIGURE 15.37 The `VisualBrush` background based on a `Button`.

Note that the `Button` inside this `VisualBrush` can never be clicked. `VisualBrush` simply paints the appearance of `Visual`s; there is no interactivity within the area that is painted.

Rather than embedding elements directly in a `VisualBrush`, it's more common to set its `Visual` to an instance of a `UIElement` already on the screen and available for user interaction. This could be done with procedural code or a simple `Binding`, as demonstrated with the following `Window`:

```
<Window xmlns="http://schemas.microsoft.com/winfx/2006/xaml/presentation"
  xmlns:x="http://schemas.microsoft.com/winfx/2006/xaml"
  Title="VisualBrush with TileMode = FlipXY">
  <DockPanel>
    <StackPanel Margin="10" x:Name="stackPanel">
      <Button>Button</Button>
      <CheckBox>CheckBox</CheckBox>
    </StackPanel>
    <Rectangle>
    <Rectangle.Fill>
      <VisualBrush TileMode="FlipXY" Viewport="0,0,0.5,0.5"
        Visual="{Binding ElementName=stackPanel}"/>
    </Rectangle.Fill>
    </Rectangle>
  </DockPanel>
</Window>
```

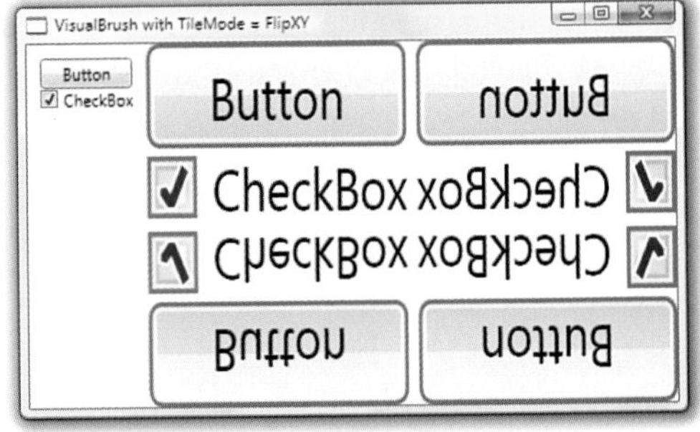

FIGURE 15.38 Copying the appearance of live `Visual`s inside a `VisualBrush`.

Figure 15.38 shows the result that this `Window` produces. The entire `StackPanel` docked on the left is used as the `VisualBrush`'s `Visual`. `VisualBrush` is applied as the `Fill` of a `Rectangle` that occupies the remainder of the `Window`. The "real" instances of the `Button` and `CheckBox` on the left support interactivity, but the visual copies do not. The visual copies do, however, reflect any changes to the `Button` and `CheckBox` visuals as they happen.

These examples may not have done a good job of convincing you that there can actually be a reasonable use for such an unusual `Brush`! But there are some good ones. Applications can leverage `VisualBrush` to provide "live previews" of inner content (perhaps documents) in a smaller, browsable form. Internet Explorer (versions 7 and later) does this with its Quick Tabs view. In addition, Windows leverages the technology underlying `VisualBrush` to create its live preview of each window when you hover over a taskbar item or switch between windows by using Alt+Tab or Windows+Tab.

Another popular use of `VisualBrush` is to create a live reflection effect. The following `Window` creates a simple reflection below a `TextBox`, using essentially the same technique employed in the previous XAML snippet:

```
<Window xmlns="http://schemas.microsoft.com/winfx/2006/xaml/presentation"
  xmlns:x="http://schemas.microsoft.com/winfx/2006/xaml"
  Title="TextBox with Reflection" Width="500" Height="200" Background="DarkGreen">
  <StackPanel Margin="40">
    <TextBox x:Name="textBox" FontSize="30"/>
    <Rectangle Height="{Binding ElementName=textBox, Path=ActualHeight}"
      Width="{Binding ElementName=textBox, Path=ActualWidth}">
    <Rectangle.Fill>
      <VisualBrush Visual="{Binding ElementName=textBox}"/>
    </Rectangle.Fill>
    <Rectangle.LayoutTransform>
      <ScaleTransform ScaleY="-0.75"/>
    </Rectangle.LayoutTransform>
    </Rectangle>
  </StackPanel>
</Window>
```

The `Rectangle` containing the `VisualBrush` reflection is flipped upside down by using a `ScaleTransform`. But rather than setting `ScaleY` to `-1`, the value of `-0.75` is used to give the reflection a little bit of perspective. Figure 15.39 shows the result.

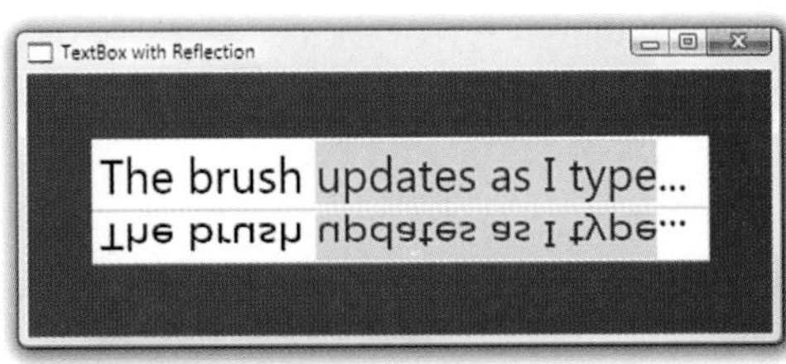

FIGURE 15.39 A simple live reflection effect.

This effect isn't quite satisfactory, however, because the reflection is too crisp and clear. You can improve this with an opacity mask, as discussed in the next section.

Brushes as Opacity Masks

All `Visual` subclasses (and `DrawingGroup`) have an `Opacity` property that affects the entire object evenly, but they also have an `OpacityMask` that can be used to apply custom opacity effects. `OpacityMask` can be set to any `Brush`, and that `Brush`'s alpha channel is used to determine which parts of the object should be opaque, which parts should be transparent, and which parts should be somewhere in between.

The alpha channel used by `OpacityMask` can come from the colors in a color brush, from drawings in a `DrawingBrush`, from images in an `ImageBrush` (for example, PNG transparency), and so on. The following `Window` uses a `LinearGradientBrush` as an `OpacityMask` to create the obnoxious-looking `Button` in Figure 15.40:

```
<Window xmlns="http://schemas.microsoft.com/winfx/2006/xaml/presentation"
  Title="LinearGradientBrush OpacityMask">
<Window.Background>
  <LinearGradientBrush>
    <GradientStop Offset="0" Color="Orange"/>
    <GradientStop Offset="1" Color="Brown"/>
  </LinearGradientBrush>
```

15

```
</Window.Background>
  <Button Margin="40" FontSize="80">OK
  <Button.OpacityMask>
    <LinearGradientBrush EndPoint="0.1,0.1" SpreadMethod="Reflect">
      <GradientStop Offset="0" Color="Blue"/>
      <GradientStop Offset="1" Color="Transparent"/>
    </LinearGradientBrush>
  </Button.OpacityMask>
  </Button>
</Window>
```

FIGURE 15.40 A Button with a striped OpacityMask, courtesy of a LinearGradientBrush.

The LinearGradientBrush used for the OpacityMask defines a repetitive gradient between blue and transparent, but the blue color is immaterial because it is never seen. All that matters is that it's a completely opaque color.

Figure 15.41 shows what this same Button would look like if the OpacityMask were instead set to a DrawingBrush containing the familiar ghost Drawing. On the left, the ghost's body is filled with a completely opaque color. The result is no different from what you could accomplish by clipping the Button to the ghost body's Geometry. On the right, the ghost's body is filled with a translucent color, but its eyes and mouth are still opaque. This gives a result that you could not achieve with clipping alone.

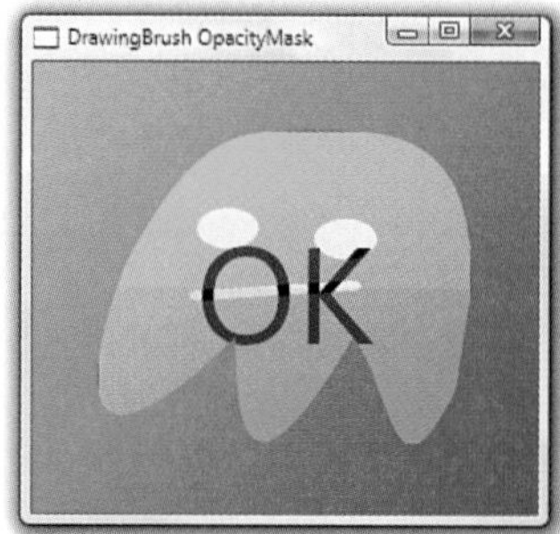

FIGURE 15.41 Using the ghost as DrawingBrush OpacityMask, with two different body fill colors.

With the features for creating a gadget-style application (setting AllowsTransparency to true and so on) described in Chapter 7, "Structuring and Deploying an Application," you can even apply an OpacityMask to the top-level Window!

As promised, here's how you could use OpacityMask to improve the live reflection effect from Figure 15.39:

```
<Window xmlns="http://schemas.microsoft.com/winfx/2006/xaml/presentation"
  xmlns:x="http://schemas.microsoft.com/winfx/2006/xaml"
  Title="TextBox with Reflection" Width="500" Height="200"
```

```
Background="DarkGreen">
  <StackPanel Margin="40">
    <TextBox x:Name="textBox" FontSize="30"/>
    <Rectangle Height="{Binding ElementName=textBox, Path=ActualHeight}"
      Width="{Binding ElementName=textBox, Path=ActualWidth}">
    <Rectangle.Fill>
      <VisualBrush Visual="{Binding ElementName=textBox}"/>
    </Rectangle.Fill>
    <Rectangle.LayoutTransform>
      <ScaleTransform ScaleY="-0.75"/>
    </Rectangle.LayoutTransform>
    <Rectangle.OpacityMask>
      <LinearGradientBrush EndPoint="0,1">
        <GradientStop Offset="0" Color="Transparent"/>
        <GradientStop Offset="1" Color="#77000000"/>
      </LinearGradientBrush>
    </Rectangle.OpacityMask>
    </Rectangle>
  </StackPanel>
</Window>
```

Figure 15.42 shows the result of this change, which is undoubtedly the most tasteful use of OpacityMask in this chapter.

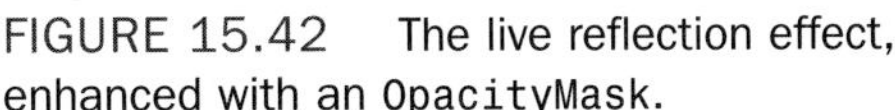

FIGURE 15.42 The live reflection effect, enhanced with an OpacityMask.

Effects

WPF has two special visual effects built in to the System.Windows.Media.Effects namespace that can be applied to any Visual. These effects are DropShadowEffect and BlurEffect, which both derive from the abstract Effect class. Figure 15.43 shows each of them applied to a simple Button. WPF applies these effects to the rendered rasterized output as a postprocessing step.

(BlurEffect)

FIGURE 15.43 The two built-in effects applied to a Button.

Although Visual exposes this functionality via a protected VisualEffect property, all of its subclasses in WPF (such as UIElement) expose it as a public Effect property. To apply an effect to a relevant object, you simply set its Effect property to an instance of one of the Effect-derived classes. For example, the first Button in Figure 15.43 was created as follows:

```
<Button Width="200">
  DropShadowEffect
<Button.Effect>
```

```
    <DropShadowEffect/>
  </Button.Effect>
</Button>
```

WARNING

Don't use the `BitmapEffect` property!

The first version of WPF shipped with a different form of these effect classes derived from a class called `BitmapEffect`. Every class with an `Effect` property also has a `BitmapEffect` property that accepts an instance of a `BitmapEffect`. However, `BitmapEffects` have been deprecated, so setting the property no longer does anything. The biggest difference with the new `Effects` compared to the obsolete `BitmapEffects` is that `Effects` are generally hardware accelerated, whereas `BitmapEffects` never were.

If you have code that uses one of these old `BitmapEffects`, switching to the newer `BlurEffect` or `DropShadowEffect` should be straightforward. Unfortunately, there are three other `BitmapEffects` that have no built-in replacements: `BevelBitmapEffect`, `EmbossBitmapEffect`, and `OuterGlowBitmapEffect`.

Of course, you can still use `BitmapEffect` in code that is running on an older version of WPF. They can easily sabotage an application's performance, but they can be fine when used rarely and appropriately. Furthermore, just because `Effects` are hardware accelerated doesn't mean they can be used with reckless abandon. They should still be used judiciously to avoid impacting performance.

Figure 15.43 uses both effects with their default settings. However, each class provides a handful of properties to customize their appearance. Table 15.3 summarizes these properties and their values.

TABLE 15.3 Properties on the Bitmap Effects

Effect	Properties	Default Value
`DropShadowEffect`	`RenderingBias`: Choose between `Performance` and `Quality`	`Performance`
	`BlurRadius`: A nonnegative `double`	5
	`Color`: Any color (even one with a non-opaque alpha)	`Black`
	`Direction`: A double representing an angle (in degrees)	315
	`Opacity`: A double between `0` (transparent) and `1` (opaque)	1
	`ShadowDepth`: A nonnegative `double`	5
`BlurEffect`	`RenderingBias`: Choose between `Performance` and `Quality`	`Performance`
	`Radius`: A nonnegative `double`	5
	`KernelType`: `Box` or `Gaussian`	`Gaussian`

The exciting part about WPF's effects is not necessarily the two built-in ones but a third `Effect` subclass called `ShaderEffect` that enables you to easily inject your own custom effects. (The obsolete bitmap effects did not allow for this kind of extensibility without writing C++ COM code.) By deriving from the abstract `ShaderEffect` class, you can apply any *pixel shader* to any object with an `Effect` property. This leverages the pixel shader support in DirectX, which means that the shaders themselves must be written in High Level Shader Language (HLSL).

TIP

For a wide range of effects built on `ShaderEffect`, download the WPF Pixel Shader Effects Library from http://wpffx.codeplex.com. It contains the following single-input effects:

`BandedSwirlEffect`	`MagnifyEffect`
`BloomEffect`	`MonochromeEffect`
`BrightExtractEffect`	`PinchEffect`
`ColorKeyAlphaEffect`	`PixelateEffect`
`ColorToneEffect`	`RippleEffect`
`ContrastAdjustEffect`	`SharpenEffect`
`DirectionalBlurEffect`	`SmoothMagnifyEffect`
`EmbossedEffect`	`SwirlEffect`
`GloomEffect`	`ToneEffect`
`GrowablePoissonDiskEffect`	`ToonEffect`
`InvertColorEffect`	`ZoomBlurEffect`
`LightStreakEffect`	

It also contains the following two-input transition effects:

`BandedSwirlTransitionEffect`	`PixelateInTransitionEffect`
`BlindsTransitionEffect`	`PixelateOutTransitionEffect`
`BloodTransitionEffect`	`PixelateTransitionEffect`
`CircleRevealTransitionEffect`	`RadialBlurTransitionEffect`
`CircleStretchTransitionEffect`	`RadialWiggleTransitionEffect`
`CircularBlurTransitionEffect`	`RandomCircleRevealTransitionEffect`
`CloudReveralTransitionEffect`	`RippleTransitionEffect`
`CloudyTransitionEffect`	`RotateTransitionEffect`
`CrumbleTransitionEffect`	`SaturateTransitionEffect`
`DissolveTransitionEffect`	`ShrinkTransitionEffect`
`DropFadeTransitionEffect`	`SlideInTransitionEffect`
`FadeTransitionEffect`	`SmoothSwirlTransitionEffect`
`LeastBrightTransitionEffect`	`SwirlTransitionEffect`
`LineRevealTransitionEffect`	`WaterTransitionEffect`
`MostBrightTransitionEffect`	`WaveTransitionEffect`

This chapter has three purposes. First, it is an introduction to 3D graphics for developers who have no prior experience with 3D. Second, it is a reference for the 3D APIs in WPF. Third, it is a road map for experienced 3D developers familiar with other platforms, such as DirectX, or who need to write tools that interoperate with WPF.

Getting Started with 3D Graphics

The purpose of 3D graphics is to produce 2D images from 3D models suitable for displaying on an output device such as a computer screen. Creating images from 3D models is a different paradigm than most 2D developers are used to. When working in two dimensions, you usually draw the exact shape that you want, using absolute coordinates. If you want a rectangle at (50,75) that is 100 units wide by 30 units tall, you typically create a `Rectangle` element (or a `GeometryDrawing` with a `RectangleGeometry` that has the corresponding bounds). Consider the house drawn in Listing 16.1 using the 2D `Drawing` classes. Figure 16.1 shows the output.

LISTING 16.1 Drawing a House with 2D `Drawings`

```
<Page Background="Black"
  xmlns="http://schemas.microsoft.com/winfx/2006/xaml/presentation"
  xmlns:x="http://schemas.microsoft.com/winfx/2006/xaml">
  <Image>
  <Image.Source>
    <DrawingImage>
    <DrawingImage.Drawing>
      <DrawingGroup x:Name="House">
        <GeometryDrawing x:Name="Front" Brush="Red"
          Geometry="M0,260 L0,600 L110,670 L110,500 L190,550 L190,710 L300,775
            L300,430 L150,175"/>
        <GeometryDrawing x:Name="Side" Brush="Green"
          Geometry="M300,430 L300,775 L600,600 L600,260"/>
        <GeometryDrawing x:Name="Roof" Brush="Blue"
          Geometry="M150,175 L300,430 L600,260 L450,0"/>
      </DrawingGroup>
    </DrawingImage.Drawing>
    </DrawingImage>
  </Image.Source>
  </Image>
</Page>
```

Although the house might have been drawn to look somewhat three-dimensional, the data from which the image was produced is two-dimensional. From the system's point of view, you've drawn some flat 2D polygons. Although you can rotate the polygons within a 2D plane, you cannot turn the house to see the back or generate images of the inside of the house. No information exists for the parts of the house you cannot see. If you want to be able to create images of the house from multiple vantage points (without creating independent 2D drawings for each view), you have to give the system more information.

Listing 16.2 gives a preview of how the same image would be produced using `Model3Ds` instead of 2D `Drawings`. Although Listing 16.2 is longer than its 2D counterpart, it provides a great deal more flexibility in what you can do with your house. Using the 3D model, you can now generate 2D images from any vantage point just by tweaking a few properties, as shown in Figure 16.2.

FIGURE 16.1 A simple house drawn using 2D `Drawings`.

LISTING 16.2 A House Drawn Using `Model3Ds`

```
<Page Background="Black"
  xmlns="http://schemas.microsoft.com/winfx/2006/xaml/presentation"
  xmlns:x="http://schemas.microsoft.com/winfx/2006/xaml">
  <Viewport3D>
  <Viewport3D.Camera>
    <OrthographicCamera Position="5,5,5" LookDirection="-1,-1,-1" Width="5"/>
  </Viewport3D.Camera>
  <Viewport3D.Children>
    <ModelVisual3D x:Name="Light">
    <ModelVisual3D.Content>
      <AmbientLight/>
    </ModelVisual3D.Content>
    </ModelVisual3D>
    <ModelVisual3D>
    <ModelVisual3D.Content>
      <Model3DGroup x:Name="House">


        <GeometryModel3D x:Name="Roof">
        <GeometryModel3D.Material>
          <DiffuseMaterial Brush="Blue"/>
        </GeometryModel3D.Material>
        <GeometryModel3D.Geometry>
          <MeshGeometry3D Positions="-1,1,1 0,2,1 0,2,-1 -1,1,-1 0,2,1 1,1,1
                                     1,1,-1 0,2,-1"
                          TriangleIndices="0 1 2 0 2 3 4 5 6 4 6 7"/>
```

LISTING 16.2 Continued

```
        </GeometryModel3D.Geometry>
        </GeometryModel3D>

        <GeometryModel3D x:Name="Sides">
        <GeometryModel3D.Material>
          <DiffuseMaterial Brush="Green"/>
        </GeometryModel3D.Material>
        <GeometryModel3D.Geometry>
          <MeshGeometry3D Positions="-1,1,1 -1,1,-1 -1,-1,-1 -1,-1,1 1,1,-1
                                     1,1,1 1,-1,1 1,-1,-1"
                          TriangleIndices="0 1 2 0 2 3 4 5 6 4 6 7"/>
        </GeometryModel3D.Geometry>
        </GeometryModel3D>

        <GeometryModel3D x:Name="Ends">
        <GeometryModel3D.Material>
          <DiffuseMaterial Brush="Red"/>
        </GeometryModel3D.Material>
        <GeometryModel3D.Geometry>
          <MeshGeometry3D
            Positions="-0.25,0,1 -1,1,1 -1,-1,1 -0.25,-1,1 -0.25,0,1
              -1,-1,1 0.25,0,1 1,-1,1 1,1,1 0.25,0,1 0.25,-1,1 1,-1,1
              1,1,1 0,2,1 -1,1,1 -1,1,1 -0.25,0,1 0.25,0,1 1,1,1 1,1,-1
              1,-1,-1 -1,-1,-1 -1,1,-1 1,1,-1 -1,1,-1 0,2,-1"
            TriangleIndices="0 1 2 3 4 5 6 7 8 9 10 11 12 13 14 15 16 17 15
             17 18 19 20 21 19 21 22 23 24 25"/>
        </GeometryModel3D.Geometry>
        </GeometryModel3D>

      </Model3DGroup>
    </ModelVisual3D.Content>
    </ModelVisual3D>
  </Viewport3D.Children>
  </Viewport3D>
</Page>
```

Listing 16.2 gives you a peek at most of the objects that are discussed in the remainder of the chapter. While many of the classes in the listing are new, they are straightforward extensions of the 2D types covered in Chapter 15, “2D Graphics.” Table 16.1 shows how some of the 3D types map to their nearest 2D equivalents.

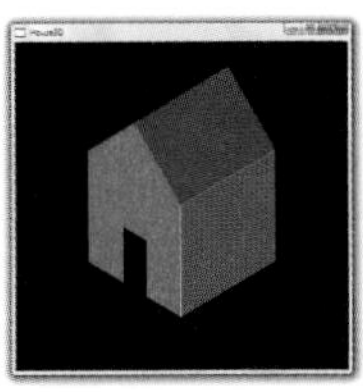    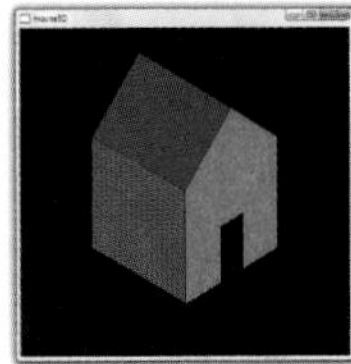

FIGURE 16.2 Several views of the house.

TABLE 16.1 Mapping 2D Types to the Nearest 3D Equivalent

2D Type	3D Type	Description
Drawing	Model3D	Drawings represent pieces of 2D content, such as clip art, which may be rendered by a Visual. Model3Ds represent pieces of 3D models, which may be rendered by a Visual3D.
Geometry	Geometry3D	A Geometry represents a 2D shape. Geometries can answer questions about bounds and intersections. By itself, a Geometry cannot be rendered. A GeometryDrawing combines a Geometry with a Brush to give it an appearance. A Geometry3D represents a 3D surface. To render a Geometry3D, you combine it with a Material using a GeometryModel3D.
Visual	Visual3D	Visual is the base class for elements that render 2D content. This includes DrawingVisual and all FrameworkElements such as Controls and Shapes. Visual3D is the base class for elements that render 3D content. ModelVisual3D is a concrete Visual3D that renders 3D content represented as Model3Ds.
UIElement	UIElement3D	UIElement, a derivative of the Visual class, adds much of the core functionality associated with many of WPF's framework-level concepts. It is often said that the UIElement class introduces LIFE (layout, input, focus, and eventing) to the 2D class hierarchy. UIElement3D, as the 3D analog to the 2D UIElement class, adds IFE (input, focus, and eventing) to the 3D world. It allows 3D objects to directly participate in application behavior rather than act as purely visual representations of 3D content.
Transform	Transform3D	Subclasses of the 2D Transform class are used to position, rotate, and size 2D Drawings and Visuals. There are no Transform3Ds in Listing 16.2, but when you encounter the 3D transform objects later in this chapter, you will see that they perform the same function for Model3Ds and Visual3Ds.

16

While most of the 3D objects are straightforward extensions of the 2D API, there are two concepts that are unique to 3D in WPF and also appear in Listing 16.2:

- **Cameras**—To generate images of 3D models, you place a virtual Camera within the scene. As with a real camera, the position, orientation, and other properties of the Camera determine your view of the scene.
- **Materials and Lights**—In 2D, you use Brushes to specify the appearance of a filled Geometry. In 3D, you also use Brushes, but there is an extra lighting step that influences the appearance of 3D surfaces.

As you will see in the upcoming sections, the Camera, Materials, and Lights all play important roles in enabling you to quickly render views of dynamic 3D scenes.

Cameras and Coordinate Systems

In the real world, what you see depends on where you stand, the direction you look, how you tilt your head, and so on. In WPF, you place a virtual Camera into your 3D scene to control what will appear in the Viewport3D. This is done by positioning and orienting the Camera in the world coordinate system (sometimes called *world space* for short). Figure 16.3 shows the 2D and 3D coordinate systems that WPF uses.

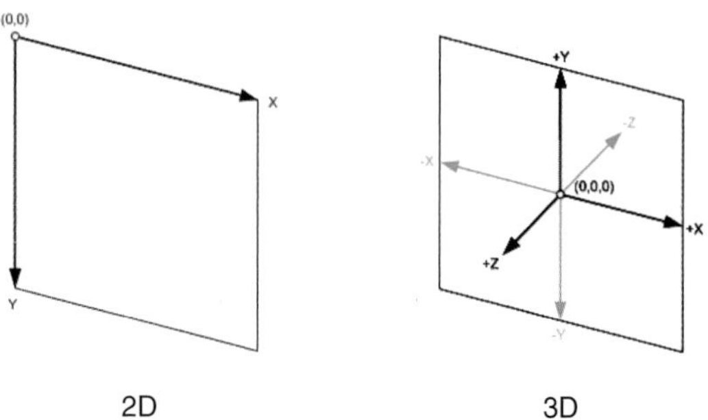

FIGURE 16.3 The 2D and 3D coordinate systems.

Besides the extra z-axis, a couple additional differences exist between the 2D and 3D coordinate systems.

In 3D, the y-axis typically points up instead of down. Also, negative coordinates, which are rarely used in 2D, are quite common in 3D. Because of this, you usually consider the origin to be at the center of space as opposed to the top-left corner, as you do in 2D. Of course, these are merely conventions, and you are free to use transformations to map into whatever system is most convenient for you.

The two common Camera classes you will use, OrthographicCamera and PerspectiveCamera, expose a set of properties to position and orient your Camera in world space. The upcoming sections discuss these properties and how you can use them to control what part of the 3D scene is visible.

Position

The `Position` property controls where the `Camera` is positioned in space. By moving the `Camera`, you can create different views of a scene. The `Position` property is of type `Point3D`. `Point3Ds` contain x, y, and z coordinates and define a location in a coordinate system. When rendering the model of the house, Listing 16.2 used the position `(5,5,5)`:

```
<Viewport3D.Camera>
  <OrthographicCamera Position="5,5,5" LookDirection="-1,-1,-1" Width="5"/>
</Viewport3D.Camera>
```

DIGGING DEEPER

WPF Uses a Right-Handed Coordinate System

The *handedness* of a coordinate system refers to the relationship of the z-axis to the x- and y-axes. If the positive x- and y-axes are arranged as shown in Figure 16.4, there are two directions the z-axis could point. In a left-handed coordinate system, the positive z-axis points away from the viewer, as shown on the left. In a right-handed system, the positive z-axis points toward the viewer, as shown on the right.

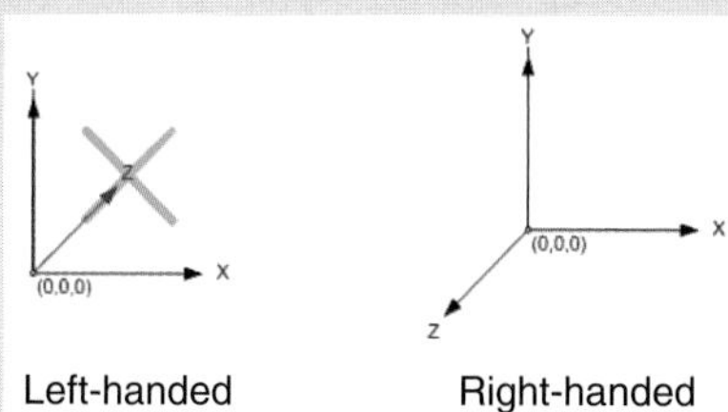

FIGURE 16.4 Left-handed versus right-handed coordinate systems.

WPF standardized on a right-handed coordinate system. The right-handed coordinate system derives its name from the *right-hand rule*: If your index finger points in the direction of the positive x-axis and your middle finger points in the direction of the positive y-axis, your thumb indicates the direction of the positive z-axis, as shown in Figure 16.5.

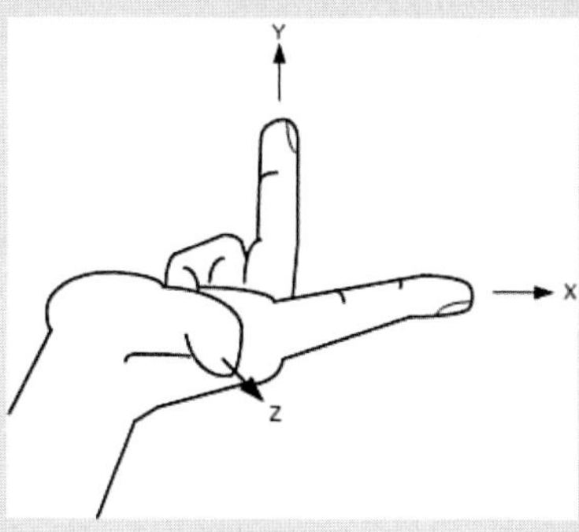

FIGURE 16.5 The right-hand rule.

16

> **Continued**
>
> This is an easy, if not somewhat awkward, way to remember the relationship between the axes. Later in this chapter, you'll discover a different version of the right-hand rule to remember the winding order of triangles in a `MeshGeometry3D`.

This means that the `Camera` is positioned five units to the right on the x-axis, five units up on the y-axis, and five units forward on the z-axis. Looking at Figure 16.6, you can see that this locates the `Camera` above the house, looking at what we will call the southeast side. (There is no standard connection between the axes and the cardinal directions, but you can assign one for your application for convenience.)

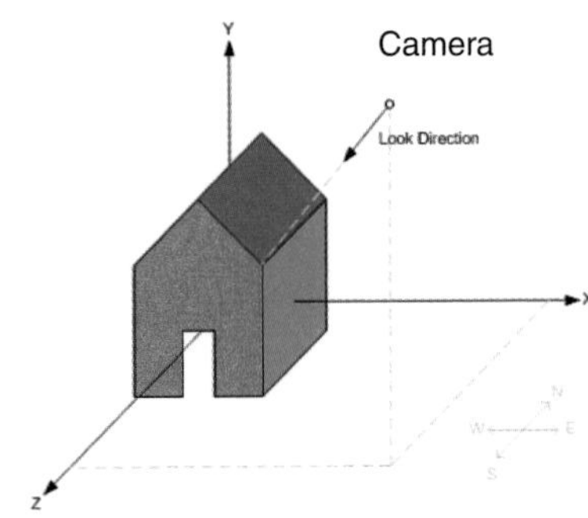

FIGURE 16.6 `Camera` positioned to view the southeast side.

If you wanted to see the southwest side of the house, you would position the `Camera` at `(-5,5,5)`:

```
<Viewport3D.Camera>
  <OrthographicCamera Position="-5,5,5" LookDirection="-1,-1,-1" Width="5"/>
</Viewport3D.Camera>
```

The new position is shown in Figure 16.7.

However, setting the `Camera` to this new position alone would not give you the desired view without adjusting the `LookDirection`. To use a physical analogy, this is like looking at your friend through the viewfinder of a camera and then taking 10 giant steps to the left. Unless you turn to face your friend again, you will now be taking a picture of the wall. You use the `LookDirection` property to control which direction the `Camera` is looking.

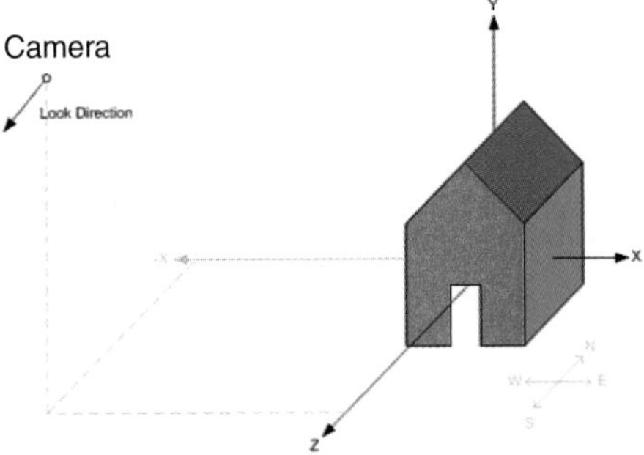

FIGURE 16.7 `Camera` positioned to view the southwest side.

LookDirection

The `LookDirection` property specifies which direction the `Camera` is facing. `LookDirection` is of type `Vector3D`. Like `Point3Ds`, `Vector3Ds` also contain x, y, and z coordinates, but rather than specify a location in space, a `Vector3D` specifies a direction and a magnitude. The magnitude of a `Vector3D` is called its `Length` and is given by

$$\sqrt{x^2 + y^2 + z^2}$$

WARNING

Remember, Cameras have a blind spot!

Surfaces closer than the Camera's NearPlaneDistance will be clipped. When setting the Camera's Position, you need to be careful that any objects you want to see are at least NearPlaneDistance units ahead of the Camera in the LookDirection. Figure 16.8 shows what would happen if you moved the Camera too close to the model of the house.

The purpose of a Camera's NearPlaneDistance is to work around the limited floating-point precision of the GPU's Z buffer. When the precision of the Z buffer is exhausted, a phenomenon known as *Z-fighting* occurs, in which the GPU is unable to determine which surfaces are nearer to the Camera. Figure 16.9 shows an example of the type of rendering artifacts Z-fighting causes. The pattern of the artifacts usually changes with the viewing angle.

Z-fighting is typically caused by attempting to render objects too close to the Camera's Position. The NearPlaneDistance property of the Camera works around Z-fighting by clipping objects closer than a certain distance from the Camera. NearPlaneDistance defaults to 0.125, which is a good setting.

There are other, less common, ways that Z-fighting may occur. One is attempting to render objects that are *really* far away from the Camera. There is a corresponding FarPlaneDistance, which can be used to work around this if it occurs, but because it is rare, this property defaults to positive infinity.

Finally, Z-fighting can occur when you render two surfaces that are nearly, but not quite, on top of each other. The only way to fix this case is to move the surfaces sufficiently far apart, such that one is clearly closer to the Camera than the other. If two surfaces are exactly on top of each other, however, the rendering order is deterministic, and Z-fighting will not occur. In this case, the surface rendered second will always appear on top.

FIGURE 16.8 House clipped by the Camera's near plane.

Continued

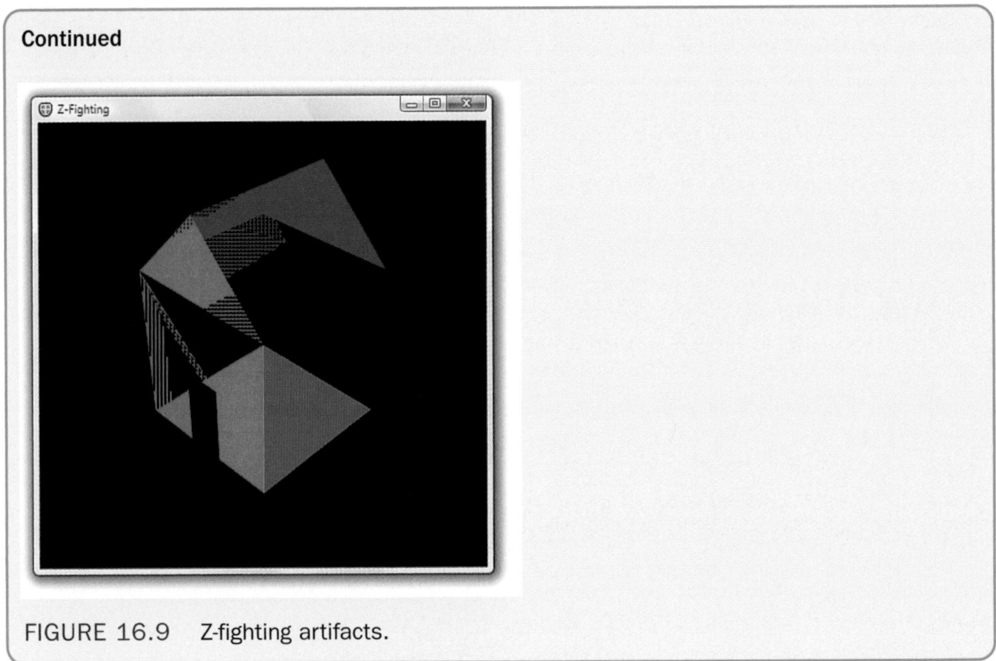

FIGURE 16.9 Z-fighting artifacts.

The `Camera` in Listing 16.2 uses a `LookDirection` of `<-1,-1,-1>`:

```
<Viewport3D.Camera>
  <OrthographicCamera Position="5,5,5" LookDirection="-1,-1,-1" Width="5"/>
</Viewport3D.Camera>
```

The x, y, and z coordinates of this vector tell the camera to look downward, toward the northwest, as shown in Figure 16.10.

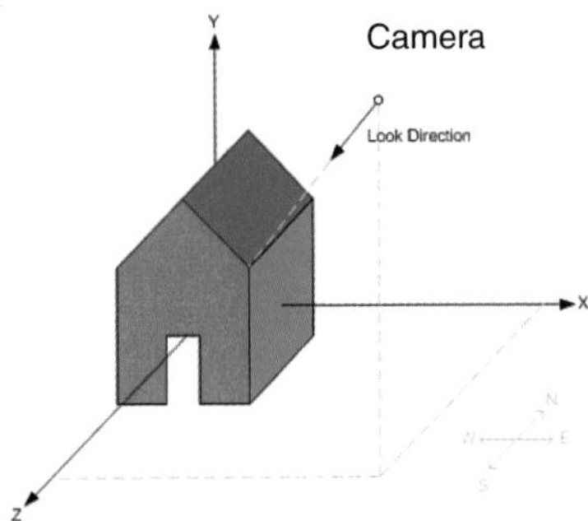

FIGURE 16.10 `Camera` looking downward, toward the northwest.

It was mentioned previously that if you moved the Position of the Camera to (-5,5,5), the house would no longer be visible. Figure 16.11 shows you why. Moving the Camera does not change the LookDirection, so the Camera is no longer facing the house in its new location.

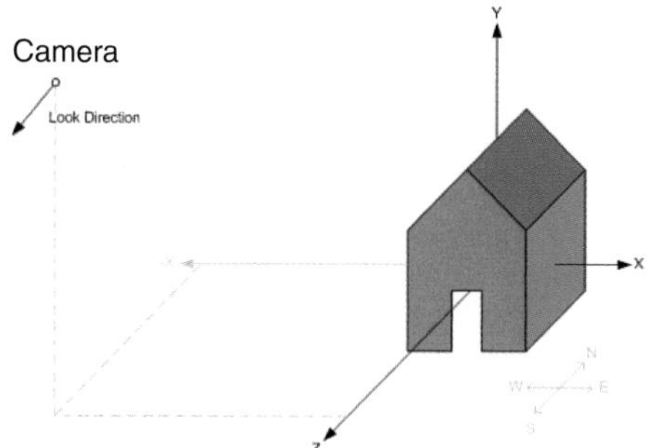

FIGURE 16.11 Moving the Camera does not change the LookDirection.

An easy way to figure out the required LookDirection for the Camera is to find a point in world space that you want to see and subtract it from the Camera's Position. In this case, the model of the house is roughly around the origin (0,0,0). Subtracting (-5,5,5) from (0,0,0) gives a vector in the direction of <5,-5,-5>, as shown in Figure 16.12.

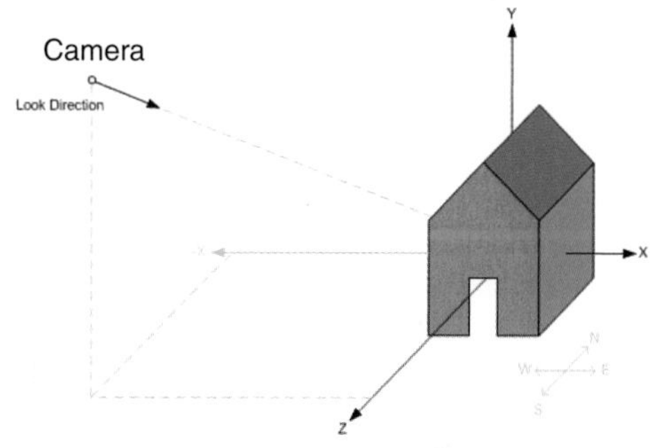

FIGURE 16.12 The new LookDirection.

Using this new LookDirection generates the image in Figure 16.13:

```
<Viewport3D.Camera>
  <OrthographicCamera Position="-5,5,5" LookDirection="5,-5,-5" Width="5"/>
</Viewport3D.Camera>
```

16

TIP

WPF APIs that take a Vector3D to indicate direction are only interested in the direction of the Vector3D, not the Length. A LookDirection of <1,-1,-1> produces an identical image to the one shown in Figure 16.13. If the Length of the Vector3D needs to be normalized for internal calculations, WPF does this for you automatically.

In general, you only need to be concerned that Vector3Ds define a direction (that is, they are not the zero vector <0,0,0>), unless you are using them to calculate Point3Ds. When adding a Vector3D to a Point3D to find a new Point3D, the Length determines how far away the new Point3D will be. You should be aware that the Length of Vector3Ds influences the direction during linear interpolation. Specifically, Vector3DAnimation does not normalize the Vector3Ds first.

FIGURE 16.13 Viewing the other side of the house.

If you are moving the `Camera` a lot, it might make sense to write a small utility method to assign the new `LookDirection` for the `Camera` based on its `Position` and the point you want to look at:

```
private void LookAt(ProjectionCamera camera, Point3D lookAtPoint)
{
  camera.LookDirection = lookAtPoint - camera.Position;
}
```

UpDirection

The `LookDirection` tells which direction the `Camera` is facing, but this does not completely specify the `Camera`'s orientation. You can still twist the `Camera` while keeping the `LookDirection` fixed on the same point in space, as shown in Figure 16.14. This is what you do with a physical camera to go from landscape to portrait orientation. You can use the `UpDirection` property to disambiguate this final component of the `Camera`'s orientation.

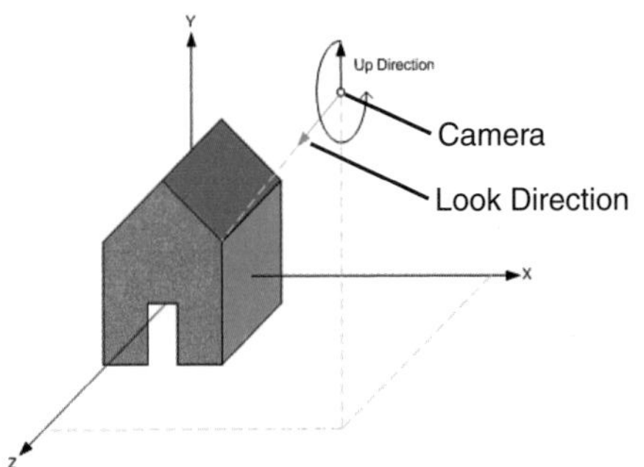

FIGURE 16.14 The `UpDirection` property.

The `UpDirection` property defaults to `<0,1,0>`. By specifying a different direction, such as `<1,0,0>`, you can turn the `Camera` on its side. Figure 16.15 shows the image produced with this `UpDirection`.

```
<Viewport3D.Camera>
  <OrthographicCamera Position="5,5,5" LookDirection="-1,-1,-1"
    UpDirection="1,0,0" Width="5"/>
</Viewport3D.Camera>
```

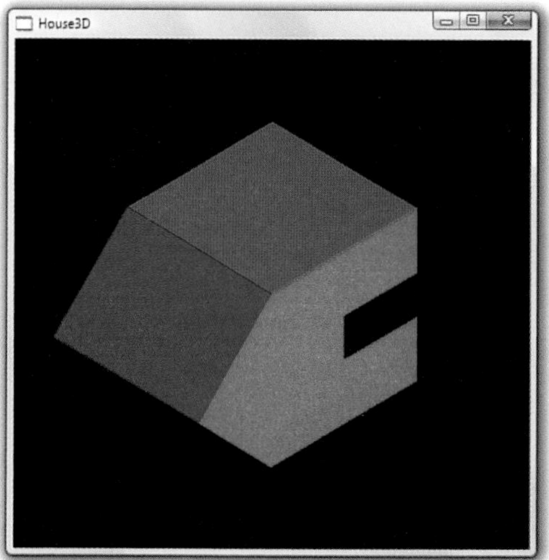

FIGURE 16.15 Specifying the positive x-axis as the `UpDirection`.

In this section, you manipulated the `Camera` in the scene by using the `Position`, `UpDirection`, and `LookDirection` properties. Although this is often the most convenient way to set up a static `Camera` in a scene, most scenarios that involve moving or rotating the `Camera` are more easily accomplished by using the `Camera.Transform` property.

TIP

The `Camera.Transform` property is especially helpful if you want the `Camera` to follow an object moving through the scene because the same `Transform3D` can be applied to both the `Camera` and the object you want to follow.

The key advantage of the `Camera.Transform` property is that it enables the `Camera` to be positioned and animated like other 3D objects in the scene. Keep this in mind when `Transform3D`s are discussed later in this chapter.

WARNING

Don't forget to transform the `UpDirection`!

If you are rotating the `Camera` around an object and the view abruptly flips over as you pass a certain spot, chances are that you forgot to adjust the `UpDirection`. The trouble happens if you move the `LookDirection` past the `UpDirection`, as shown in Figure 16.16.

As the `Camera` approaches the house, the `LookDirection` is adjusted so that you are looking downward. As the `Camera` goes over the roof, you would expect to be looking at the far side of the house upside down. However, because `UpDirection` is still pointing at the positive y-axis, the `Camera` instead spins in place right as you cross the center of the roof. Worse, when you are directly above the roof, the `LookDirection` and `UpDirection` are on the same line and the result is undefined. The correct way to rotate the `Camera` like this is to rotate the `UpDirection` along with the `LookDirection`, as illustrated in Figure 16.17.

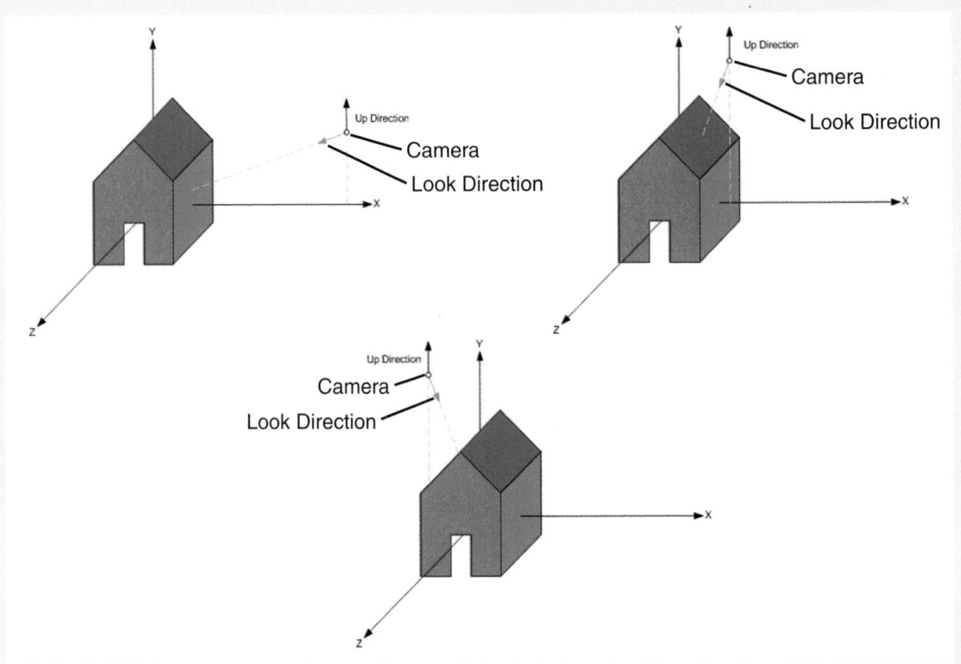

FIGURE 16.16 `Camera` passing over the house incorrectly.

Continued

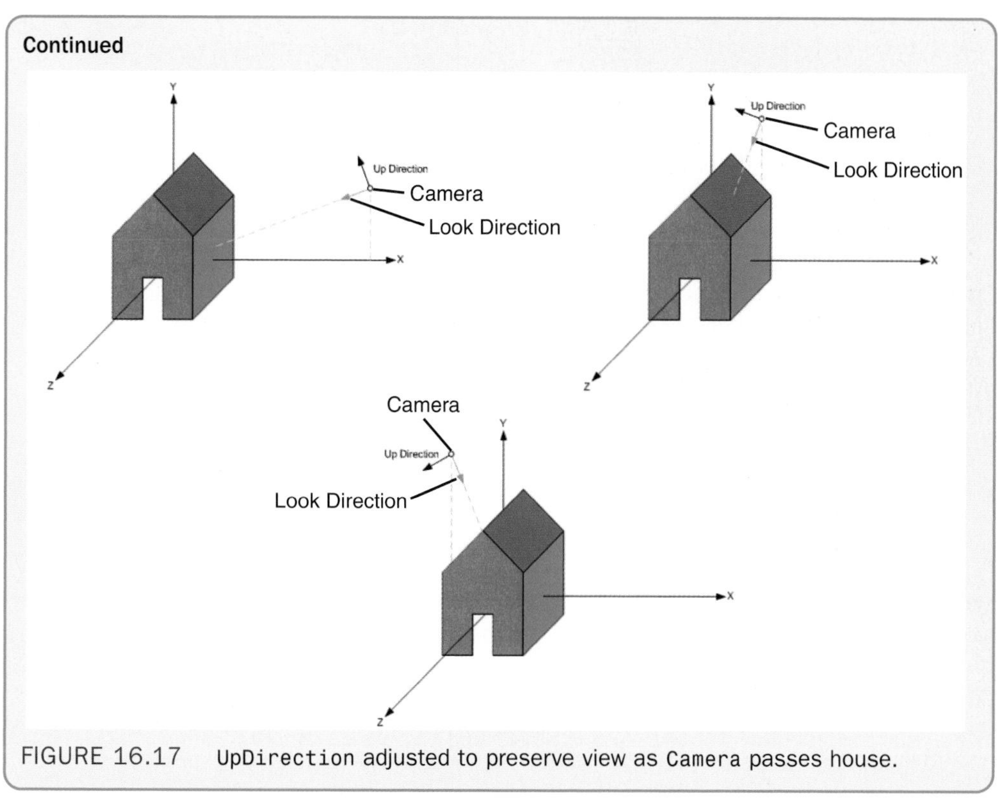

FIGURE 16.17 UpDirection adjusted to preserve view as Camera passes house.

16

OrthographicCamera Versus PerspectiveCamera

WPF has two types of Cameras that most applications choose from. The PerspectiveCamera creates a realistic image in which objects farther from the Camera appear smaller than those closer to the Camera. This models the way humans see things in the real world. The other type of Camera, OrthographicCamera, is more useful for editing tools and some visualizations because objects appear the same size, regardless of their distance from the Camera, allowing for precise measurement and analysis. Technical and manufacturing drawings frequently use OrthographicCameras. Figure 16.18 shows the same model rendered with an OrthographicCamera and a PerspectiveCamera.

All Cameras work by projecting the 3D models in the scene onto an image plane that is then displayed to the user. With an OrthographicCamera, each point on the image plane shows what is straight behind it, as shown in Figure 16.19. This enables you to view a section of space shaped like a rectangular right prism. The width of the viewable space is controlled by the OrthographicCamera.Width property. The height is computed automatically from the Viewport3D's bounding rectangle to preserve an aspect ratio of 1:1. Here is OrthographicCamera in action:

```
<Viewport3D.Camera>
  <OrthographicCamera Position="5,5,5" LookDirection="-1,-1,-1" Width="5"/>
</Viewport3D.Camera>
```

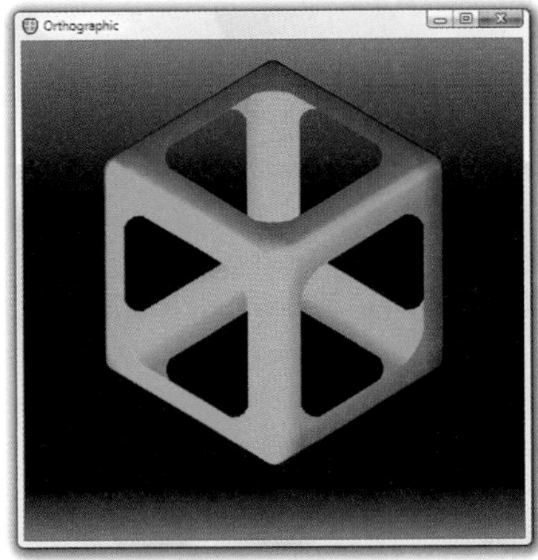

OrthographicCamera example

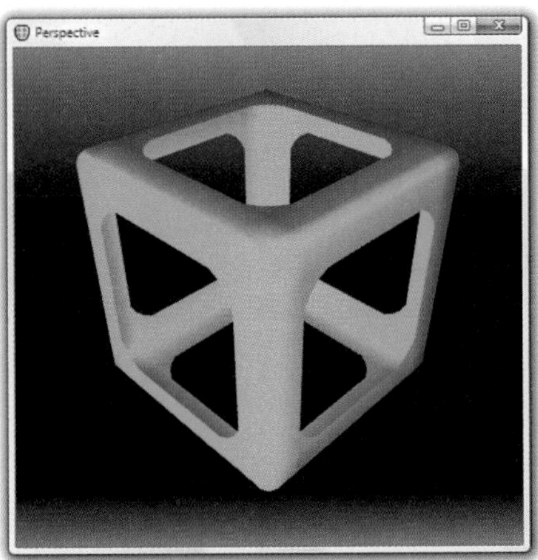

PerspectiveCamera example

FIGURE 16.18 OrthographicCamera and PerspectiveCamera examples.

With a PerspectiveCamera, the width of the viewable area is not constant. As the distance from the Camera increases, more of the 3D world space is visible. This enables you to view a square frustum-shaped region of the scene, as shown in Figure 16.20. Because the viewable area expands as you get farther from the Camera, objects farther away appear smaller in a perspective projection. You control the rate of expansion with the FieldOfView property. In WPF, FieldOfView controls the horizontal angle at which the field of view expands. Here is PerspectiveCamera in action:

```
<Viewport3D.Camera>
  <PerspectiveCamera Position="5,5,5" LookDirection="-1,-1,-1" FieldOfView="45""/>
</Viewport3D.Camera>
```

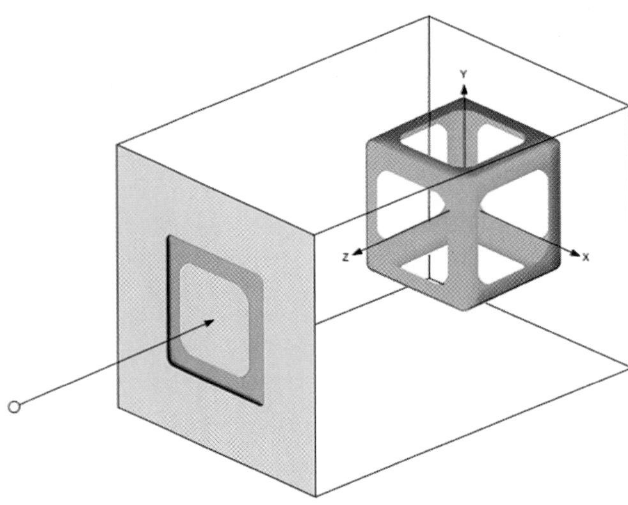

FIGURE 16.19 Orthographic projection.

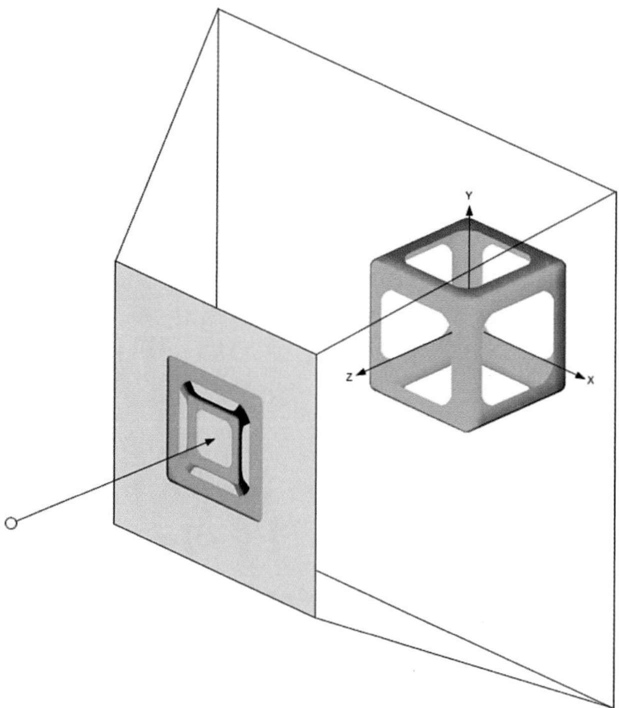

FIGURE 16.20 Perspective projection.

The `FieldOfView` property is comparable to the zoom lens on a physical camera. The `Width` property is the analogous concept for an `OrthographicCamera`. Small values for `Width` and `FieldOfView` "zoom in" on a small part of a 3D object. Larger values of `Width` and `FieldOfView` show more of the scene.

DIGGING DEEPER

`MatrixCamera`

WPF supports a third type of `Camera`, the `MatrixCamera`, which enables you to specify the view and projection transforms as `Matrix3Ds`. The mathematics behind projective transforms is a fascinating topic but beyond the scope of this chapter.

`MatrixCamera` aids with porting code from other platforms, such as Direct3D. An advanced user can use `MatrixCamera` to create `Cameras` not directly supported by the other WPF `Camera` types, such as a frustum `Camera`.

The layout of the matrices used with a `MatrixCamera` is identical to what Direct3D uses. This makes it easy to port methods to construct view and projection matrices from utility libraries such as D3DX. These matrices are well documented in the DirectX SDK.

Transform3D

As with Transforms in 2D, Transform3Ds allow you to position, rotate, and size 3D objects in space. Transform3Ds can be applied to Model3Ds, ModelVisual3Ds, and the Camera. This is done by setting their respective Transform properties. When you set the Transform property on a 3D object, you are mapping your object's coordinate space into a new coordinate space. This is no different than what happens when you position an element in 2D by using the Canvas.Left and Canvas.Top properties.

Figure 16.21 displays the 2D drawing of a ghost from Chapter 15. All the drawing instructions that make up the ghost are relative to the ghost's local coordinate system. Using a 2D TranslateTransform, you can change the ghost's frame of reference so that the point (0,0) in the ghost's coordinate system is no longer the same as point (0,0) in the container's coordinate system. This is shown on the right side of Figure 16.21.

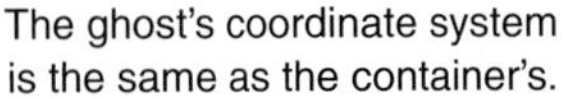

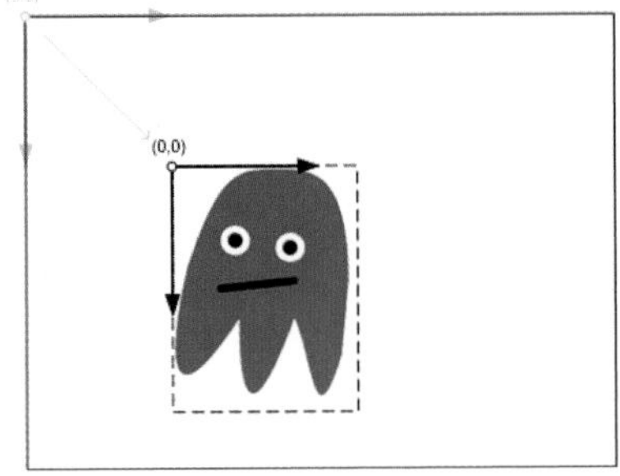

The ghost's coordinate system
is offset relative to the container's.

FIGURE 16.21 The ghost's coordinate system versus the container's coordinate system.

The TranslateTransform causes the ghost and any child Visuals it might contain to move on the screen, but as far as the ghost is concerned, it's business as usual. None of the ghost's drawing instructions are modified, just its frame of reference. This is actually how a Canvas moves elements around—by constructing a TranslateTransform for its contained Visuals behind the scenes.

The same principles apply to 3D transforms. In 3D, there is a top-level world coordinate system. To position, size, and orient 3D objects within the world coordinate system, you use the five subclasses of Transform3D:

- **TranslateTransform3D**—Offsets a 3D object relative to its container.
- **ScaleTransform3D**—Scales a 3D object relative to its container.
- **RotateTransform3D**—Rotates a 3D object relative to its container.
- **MatrixTransform3D**—Transforms a 3D object by a Matrix3D.
- **Transform3DGroup**—Contains a collection of Transform3Ds. The Transform3DGroup is itself a Transform3D and is used to apply multiple transforms to a 3D object.

This section applies these transforms to the simple model of a house shown at the beginning of this chapter. Listing 16.3 presents the same XAML as before, except with two emphasized changes. First, it has an added transform (currently the identity transform which does nothing). Second, it has an increased `Width` for the `Camera` so that you'll be able to see the effect of applying various transforms.

LISTING 16.3 Updates to the House Drawn Using `Model3Ds`

```
<Page Background="Black"
  xmlns="http://schemas.microsoft.com/winfx/2006/xaml/presentation"
  xmlns:x="http://schemas.microsoft.com/winfx/2006/xaml">
  <Viewport3D>
  <Viewport3D.Camera>
    <OrthographicCamera Position="5,5,5" LookDirection="-1,-1,-1" Width="10"/>
  </Viewport3D.Camera>
  <Viewport3D.Children>
    <ModelVisual3D x:Name="Light">
    <ModelVisual3D.Content>
      <AmbientLight/>
    </ModelVisual3D.Content>
    </ModelVisual3D>
    <ModelVisual3D>
    <ModelVisual3D.Transform>
      <x:Static Member="Transform3D.Identity"/>
    </ModelVisual3D.Transform>
    <ModelVisual3D.Content>
      <Model3DGroup x:Name="House">

        <GeometryModel3D x:Name="Roof">
        <GeometryModel3D.Material>
          <DiffuseMaterial Brush="Blue"/>
        </GeometryModel3D.Material>
        <GeometryModel3D.Geometry>
          <MeshGeometry3D Positions="-1,1,1 0,2,1 0,2,-1 -1,1,-1 0,2,1 1,1,1
                                     1,1,-1 0,2,-1"
                          TriangleIndices="0 1 2 0 2 3 4 5 6 4 6 7"/>
        </GeometryModel3D.Geometry>
        </GeometryModel3D>

        <GeometryModel3D x:Name="Sides">
        <GeometryModel3D.Material>
          <DiffuseMaterial Brush="Green"/>
        </GeometryModel3D.Material>
        <GeometryModel3D.Geometry>
```

LISTING 16.3 Continued

```
          <MeshGeometry3D Positions="-1,1,1 -1,1,-1 -1,-1,-1 -1,-1,1 1,1,-1
                          1,1,1 1,-1,1 1,-1,-1"
                          TriangleIndices="0 1 2 0 2 3 4 5 6 4 6 7"/>
        </GeometryModel3D.Geometry>
        </GeometryModel3D>

        <GeometryModel3D x:Name="Ends">
        <GeometryModel3D.Material>
          <DiffuseMaterial Brush="Red"/>
        </GeometryModel3D.Material>
        <GeometryModel3D.Geometry>
          <MeshGeometry3D
            Positions="-0.25,0,1 -1,1,1 -1,-1,1 -0.25,-1,1 -0.25,0,1
              -1,-1,1 0.25,0,1 1,-1,1 1,1,1 0.25,0,1 0.25,-1,1 1,-1,1
              1,1,1 0,2,1 -1,1,1 -1,1,1 -0.25,0,1 0.25,0,1 1,1,1 1,1,-1
              1,-1,-1 -1,-1,-1 -1,1,-1 1,1,-1 -1,1,-1 0,2,-1"
            TriangleIndices="0 1 2 3 4 5 6 7 8 9 10 11 12 13 14 15 16 17 15
             17 18 19 20 21 19 21 22 23 24 25"/>
        </GeometryModel3D.Geometry>
        </GeometryModel3D>

      </Model3DGroup>
    </ModelVisual3D.Content>
    </ModelVisual3D>
  </Viewport3D.Children>
  </Viewport3D>
</Page>
```

TranslateTransform3D

TranslateTransform3D moves an object by an offset relative to its container. The offset is specified by the OffsetX, OffsetY, and OffsetZ properties. For example, setting the OffsetZ property to 3 slides the house forward on the z-axis by three units, as shown in Figure 16.22:

```
<ModelVisual3D.Transform>
  <TranslateTransform3D OffsetZ="3"/>
</ModelVisual3D.Transform>
```

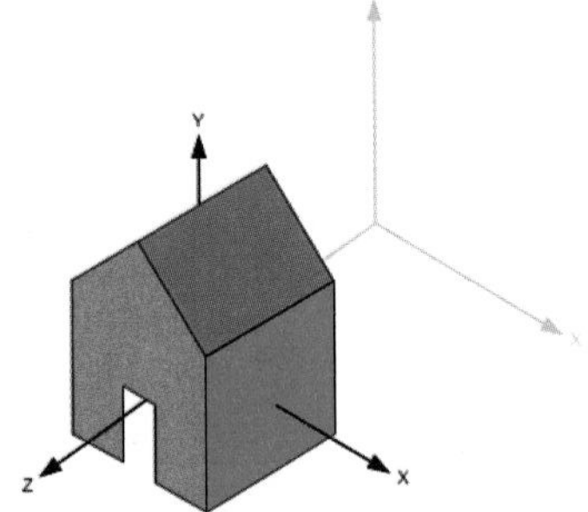

FIGURE 16.22 Translating the house forward three units on the z-axis.

Note that you can position 3D objects more easily by constructing your models such that the origin is at a convenient location. For example, the house model has the origin roughly at the center. To move the house so that the center is at the point (3,2,1), you can translate it as follows:

```
<ModelVisual3D.Transform>
  <TranslateTransform3D OffsetX="3" OffsetY="2" OffsetZ="1"/>
</ModelVisual3D.Transform>
```

ScaleTransform3D

ScaleTransform3Ds are used to change the size of 3D objects. The scale factor is expressed in each dimension by the ScaleX, ScaleY, and ScaleZ properties. Because you can specify different scale factors for each dimension, it is possible to stretch an object using a ScaleTransform3D. For example, the following transform makes the house twice as wide along the x-axis, as shown in Figure 16.23:

```
<ModelVisual3D.Transform>
  <ScaleTransform3D ScaleX="2"/>
</ModelVisual3D.Transform>
```

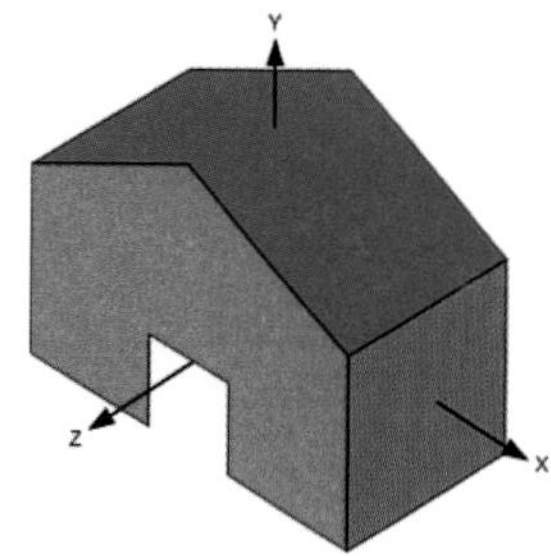

FIGURE 16.23 Scaling the house along the x-axis.

WARNING

Scale by 1, not 0, when you want to keep the original size!

To keep an object at its original size, you want a 1:1 scale—not a 1:0 scale. Setting ScaleX, ScaleY, or ScaleZ to 0 flattens the object in one or more directions. Flattening in one dimension can sometimes be useful—for example, to flatten a sphere into a disk. But flattening in two dimensions collapses the 3D object into an invisible line, and flattening in three dimensions reduces the object to an invisible point!

16

To change the size of a 3D object while maintaining its proportions, set the ScaleX, ScaleY, and ScaleZ properties to the same value. This is called a *uniform scale*. A uniform scale factor of 2 doubles the size of an object. A uniform scale factor of 0.5 halves the size of an object.

When you apply a scale, you are expanding and contracting space. This causes all points to move except for the center of the scale. By default, this center is the origin. In Figure 16.23, the house remained in place because the center of the house is the origin. If you moved the house so that the center is at (0,0,3) and then scaled it to half the size, the center of the house would move to (1.5,0,0) as space contracted toward the origin. This is shown in the following XAML, and the results are shown in Figure 16.24:

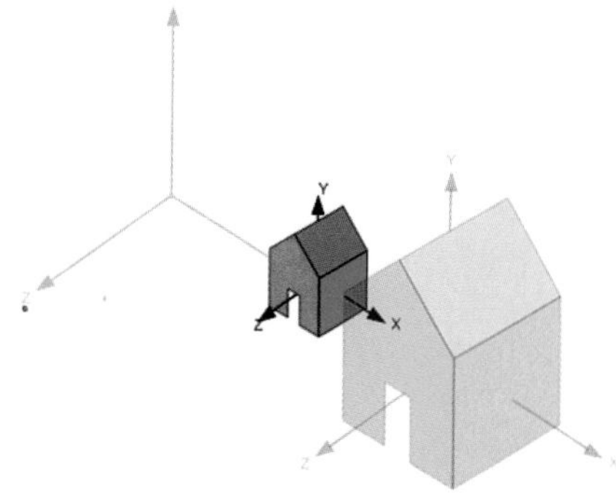

FIGURE 16.24 The house moves as space contracts toward the origin.

```
<ModelVisual3D.Transform>
  <Transform3DGroup>
    <TranslateTransform3D OffsetX="3"/>
    <ScaleTransform3D ScaleX="0.5" ScaleY="0.5" ScaleZ="0.5"/>
  </Transform3DGroup>
</ModelVisual3D.Transform>
```

One way to prevent the house from moving during the scale is to specify a different point in space to be the center of the scale. You do this by setting the `CenterX`, `CenterY`, and `CenterZ` properties. The following XAML illustrates how to do this by choosing the scale center to be the new center of the house:

```
<ModelVisual3D.Transform>
  <Transform3DGroup>
    <TranslateTransform3D OffsetX="3"/>
    <ScaleTransform3D ScaleX="0.5" ScaleY="0.5" ScaleZ="0.5" CenterX="3"/>
  </Transform3DGroup>
</ModelVisual3D.Transform>
```

This causes the house to shrink "in place," as shown in Figure 16.25.

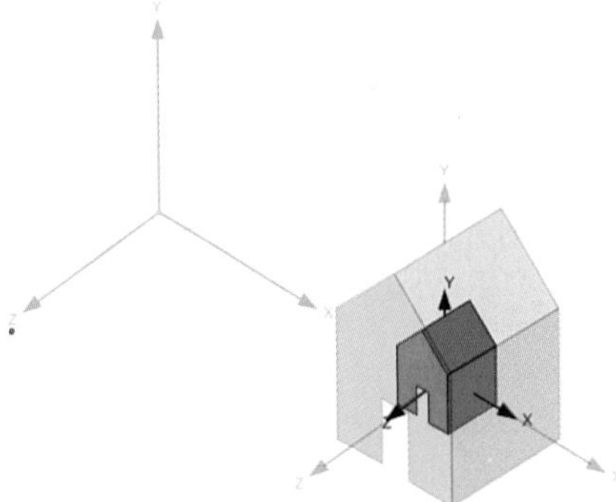

FIGURE 16.25 The scale is centered at the center of the house.

Another way to keep the house from moving is to reorder the translate and scale transforms:

```
<ModelVisual3D.Transform>
  <Transform3DGroup>
    <ScaleTransform3D ScaleX="0.5" ScaleY="0.5" ScaleZ="0.5"/>
    <TranslateTransform3D OffsetX="3"/>
  </Transform3DGroup>
</ModelVisual3D.Transform>
```

If you perform the translation after the scale, the scale does not affect the offset of the translation. This is because the house is first shrunk while it is still at the origin. After the house is the desired size, it is then moved three units on the x-axis.

Looking at Figure 16.24, you might have noticed that as the scale factor approaches zero, the house moves toward the center of the scale. You might wonder what happens if the scale factor goes past zero to negative numbers. This causes the object to be reflected. Figure 16.26 shows how a negative `ScaleZ` causes the house model to be mirrored in the XY plane:

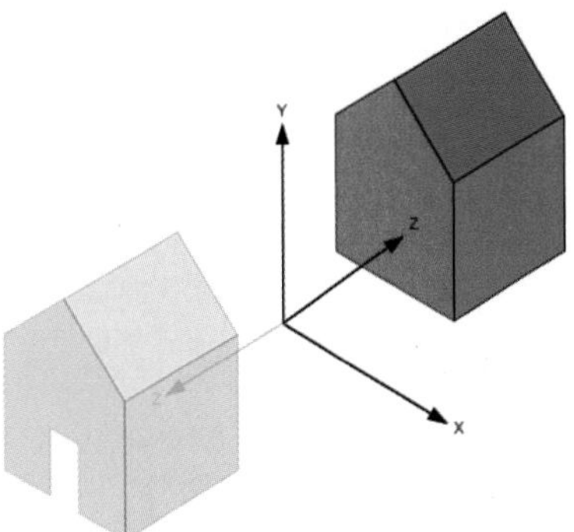

FIGURE 16.26 Reflecting along the z-axis.

```
<ModelVisual3D.Transform>
  <Transform3DGroup>
    <TranslateTransform3D OffsetZ="3"/>
    <ScaleTransform3D ScaleZ="-1"/>
  </Transform3DGroup>
</ModelVisual3D.Transform>
```

Notice that the reflection changes the direction of the z-axis. If you were to apply a translation after the scale, the `OffsetZ` property would now move the object in the opposite direction.

16

DIGGING DEEPER

Scaling About a Nonprinciple Axis

Under the covers, the `CenterX`, `CenterY`, and `CenterZ` properties work by first translating an object so that the specified point is at the origin. The scale is then performed, and the object is translated back so the center point is at its original position.

You can use a similar technique to scale an object along a direction other than the x-, y-, or z-axes. First, you use `RotationTransform3D` to rotate the object so that the desired scale direction rests on one of the x-, y-, or z-axes. After performing the scale, you apply the opposite rotation to restore the newly scaled object back to its original orientation.

RotateTransform3D

`RotateTransform3D`s are used to rotate 3D objects in space. The rotation is described by a `Rotation3D` object. `Rotation3D` is an abstract class with two concrete implementations:

- **`AxisAngleRotation3D`**—Rotates the object around the specified `Axis` by the number of degrees given by the `Angle` property. This is usually the most convenient and human-readable way to describe 3D rotations.
- **`QuaternionRotation3D`**—Specifies the rotation as a `Quaternion`. `Quaternion`s are a clever encoding of an `Axis`/`Angle` rotation with some nice properties that make them popular with many 3D systems and tools.

FAQ

Why doesn't WPF standardize on one way to specify rotations?

Early releases of WPF had support for only Quaternions, but Quaternions turned out to be difficult for 2D developers approaching 3D for the first time. A common mistake was to create a rotation from 0 to 360°, which resulted in no movement during a Rotation3DAnimation because it started and ended in the same orientation. Rotating an object more than 179.9999...° required either cumulative animations or multiple key frames.

Later WPF releases added Axis/Angle rotations to make the trivial spinning-in-place animation easier for developers new to 3D. A simple spin could then be created by animating the Angle property with a DoubleAnimation. However, support for Quaternions was kept as an aid for people writing exporters for modeling packages that often represent rotations as Quaternions.

To support "layout-to-layout" animations where you might have defined one rotational configuration using Axis/Angle and another using Quaternions, WPF derives AxisAngleRotation3D and QuaternionRotation3D from the common Rotation3D base class. You can animate between any two Rotation3Ds using a Rotation3DAnimation, which always takes the shortest path between the two orientations.

One form of rotation not directly supported by WPF is Euler angles. An Euler angle rotation takes the form of three angles that represent rotations about three axes. Which three axes, the order in which the rotations are applied, and the direction of the rotation are not standardized.

There is no EulerAngleRotation3D in WPF, but you can construct an equivalent Transform3D by using a Transform3DGroup containing three RotateTransform3Ds, as in the following XAML:

```
<Transform3DGroup>
  <RotateTransform3D>
  <RotateTransform3D.Rotation>
    <AxisAngleRotation3D x:Name="RotateX" Axis="1,0,0" Angle="0"/>
  </RotateTransform3D.Rotation>
  </RotateTransform3D>
  <RotateTransform3D>
  <RotateTransform3D.Rotation>
    <AxisAngleRotation3D x:Name="RotateY" Axis="0,1,0" Angle="0"/>
  </RotateTransform3D.Rotation>
  </RotateTransform3D>
  <RotateTransform3D>
  <RotateTransform3D.Rotation>
    <AxisAngleRotation3D x:Name="RotateZ" Axis="0,0,1" Angle="0"/>
  </RotateTransform3D.Rotation>
  </RotateTransform3D>
</Transform3DGroup>
```

Note that you might need to tweak the axes to match the ordering you want.

Figure 16.27 shows the result of rotating the house model 45° around the y-axis, as follows:

```
<ModelVisual3D.Transform>
  <RotateTransform3D>
  <RotateTransform3D.Rotation>
    <AxisAngleRotation3D Axis="0,1,0" Angle="45"/>
  </RotateTransform3D.Rotation>
  </RotateTransform3D>
</ModelVisual3D.Transform>
```

In a right-handed coordinate system, a positive angle of rotation rotates the coordinate space counterclockwise.

Note that after the rotation, the x- and z-axes are pointing in new directions. If you had applied a translation prior to the rotation, as follows, you would have encountered behavior similar to what was observed with the ScaleTransform3D:

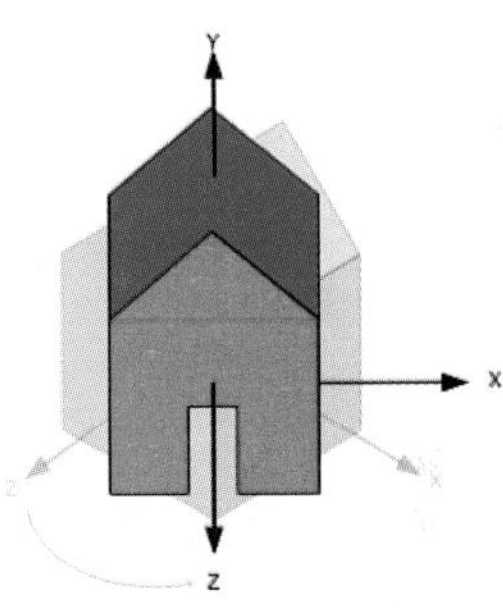

FIGURE 16.27 Rotation of 45° about the positive y-axis.

```
<ModelVisual3D.Transform>
  <Transform3DGroup>
    <TranslateTransform3D OffsetZ="3"/>
    <RotateTransform3D>
    <RotateTransform3D.Rotation>
      <AxisAngleRotation3D Axis="0,1,0" Angle="45"/>
    </RotateTransform3D.Rotation>
    </RotateTransform3D>
  </Transform3DGroup>
</ModelVisual3D.Transform>
```

Rotations rotate space around a point. By default, that point is at the origin. If your model is not centered at the point of rotation, you will find it has moved, as shown in Figure 16.28.

Again, if you want the house to spin "in place," one option is to change the center of rotation, using the CenterX, CenterY, and CenterZ properties:

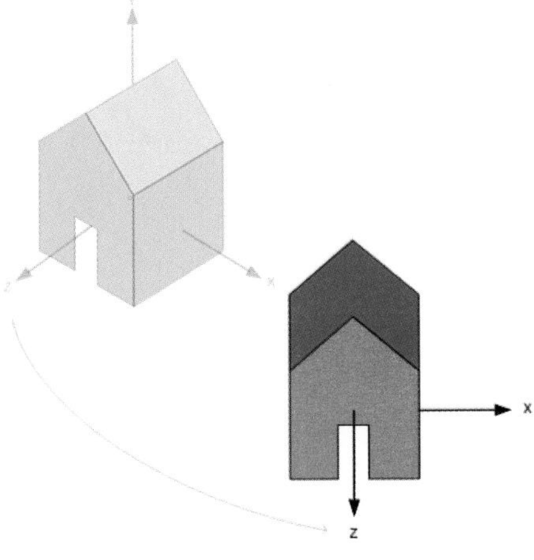

FIGURE 16.28 Side effect of the rotation.

```
<ModelVisual3D.Transform>
  <Transform3DGroup>
    <TranslateTransform3D OffsetZ="3"/>
    <RotateTransform3D CenterZ="3">
    <RotateTransform3D.Rotation>
      <AxisAngleRotation3D Axis="0,1,0" Angle="45"/>
    </RotateTransform3D.Rotation>
    </RotateTransform3D>
```

16

```
  </Transform3DGroup>
</ModelVisual3D.Transform>
```

Another way to work around this is to reorder the translate and rotate transforms. If you perform the translation after the rotation, the rotation does not affect the offset of the translation:

```
<ModelVisual3D.Transform>
  <Transform3DGroup>
    <RotateTransform3D>
    <RotateTransform3D.Rotation>
      <AxisAngleRotation3D Axis="0,1,0" Angle="45"/>
    </RotateTransform3D.Rotation>
    </RotateTransform3D>
    <TranslateTransform3D OffsetZ="3"/>
  </Transform3DGroup>
</ModelVisual3D.Transform>
```

Combining `Transform3D`s

Unlike in 2D, where the common case is to apply just a translation, the common case in 3D is to apply three transforms: scale, rotate, and translate (generally in that order). To apply multiple transforms, use a `Transform3DGroup`. The following XAML shows the typical usage of a `Transform3DGroup`:

```
<Transform3DGroup>
  <ScaleTransform3D x:Name="Size" ScaleX="1" ScaleY="1" ScaleZ="1"/>
  <RotateTransform3D>
  <RotateTransform3D.Rotation>
    <AxisAngleRotation3D x:Name="Orientation" Axis="0,1,0" Angle="0"/>
  </RotateTransform3D.Rotation>
  </RotateTransform3D>
  <TranslateTransform3D x:Name="Position" OffsetX="0" OffsetY="0" OffsetZ="0"/>
</Transform3DGroup>
```

DIGGING DEEPER

`MatrixTransform3D`

WPF supports a fifth type of `Transform3D`: `MatrixTransform3D`. `MatrixTransform3D` enables you to specify a projective 3D transform as a `Matrix3D`. Here *projective* refers to the fact that a `Matrix3D` is a full 4x4 matrix. This does not necessarily mean that you must specify a `Camera`-style projection matrix, although you can. `MatrixTransform3D`s are useful for defining transforms not directly supported by the other `Transform3D` objects and for porting code that calculates transforms as matrices.

It is worth noting that any of the `Transform3D` objects can be converted to a `Matrix3D` via the `Value` property. This includes `Transform3DGroup`s, so it is possible to collapse a graph of `Transform3D`s into a single `MatrixTransform3D`.

Model3D

Model3Ds are the building blocks out of which you build a 3D model for a scene. Multiple Model3Ds are often grouped together to make a single 3D model. The Model3D classes are analogous to the 2D Drawing classes. However, unlike in 2D, where using Drawings is one of many ways to add 2D content to a WPF application, using Model3D is the *only* way to declare 3D content in WPF.

WPF includes three subclasses of Model3D:

- **Light**—Has several subclasses that emit light into the scene. It is often overlooked that Lights are, in fact, Model3Ds, which is very convenient for scenarios such as attaching the headlights to a car with a Model3DGroup.
- **GeometryModel3D**—Renders a surface (described as a Geometry3D) with a given Material. GeometryModel3D is analogous to the 2D GeometryDrawing.
- **Model3DGroup**—Contains a collection of Model3Ds. The Model3DGroup is itself a Model3D and is often used to group multiple GeometryModel3Ds and Lights into a single 3D model.

You have already seen all these classes in use in Listings 16.2 and 16.3, which rendered the simple house.

TIP

Entering XAML by hand is very educational and might be useful for creating simple models or "stand-in" art such as cubes, but it's not a good long-term strategy for creating 3D models.

Just as most bitmaps are created in a paint program, most 3D models are created using modeling software. Those that are not modeled in an application are usually generated procedurally.

When you need shapes more complex than planes and cubes, you should use a 3D modeling program with a XAML exporter. Numerous third-party exporters for the most popular 3D modeling packages exist, including some free packages. There are also 3D modeling programs such as Electric Rain's ZAM 3D, which are explicitly targeted at WPF and use XAML natively.

Lights

Lighting is a concept that is unique to 3D in WPF. In 2D, the colors that appear from the screen usually come directly from the Brush or Pen used. In 3D, there is an extra lighting step, which dynamically calculates the shading of the 3D objects, depending on their proximity to light sources in the scene. Dynamic lighting makes it far easier to create and animate realistic-looking scenes.

There are three components to lighting: Light objects, which emit light into the scene, Materials, which reflect the light back to the Camera, and the Geometry of the model, which determines the angles involved. This section introduces the various `Light` types supported by WPF:

- **`DirectionalLight`**—Casts parallel rays into the scene from an origin at infinity. `DirectionalLight` approximates a far-away light source such as the sun.
- **`PointLight`**—Radiates light uniformly in all directions from a point in the scene. The intensity of the light attenuates as distance from the point increases. `PointLight` approximates unfocused light sources such as light bulbs.
- **`SpotLight`**—Emits a cone of light from a point in the scene. As with `PointLight`, the intensity of the light attenuates as distance from the point increases. `SpotLight` approximates focused light sources such as the beam of a flashlight.
- **`AmbientLight`**—Lights every surface uniformly. A bright `AmbientLight` creates flat-looking images because of lack of shading, but a low-intensity `AmbientLight` approximates the effect of light that has been scattered by reflecting between diffuse surfaces in the scene.

You might have noticed that each of the previous descriptions contains the word *approximates*. It's important to understand that the goal of lighting in real-time graphics systems such as WPF is not to produce an accurate physical simulation of the way light behaves in the real world. To achieve real-time frame rates, graphics systems use clever tricks and rough estimations. Two common approximations are that surfaces do not block light (that is, they do not cast shadows) and lighting is computed only at the vertices of a mesh and then is interpolated across the face. WPF uses both of these approximations.

There is an element of artistry in creating a scene that appears to be realistically lit. To accomplish the desired effect, you might need to do unrealistic things such as add extra light sources, bake lighting effects into your `Materials`, and so on. Don't feel bad about doing these things. Although the lighting and material APIs use real-world metaphors, they are just tools.

`DirectionalLight`

A `DirectionalLight` approximates a light source so far away that the rays have become parallel, such as light from the sun striking the Earth. Figure 16.29 illustrates the effect of the following `DirectionalLight` shining down on a sphere:

```
<DirectionalLight Direction="1,-1,-0.5" Color="White"/>
```

The direction of the light entering the scene is controlled by the `Direction` property. Of course, the `Transform` property inherited from `Model3D` also influences the direction of the light. The color of the `Light` is controlled by the `Color` property.

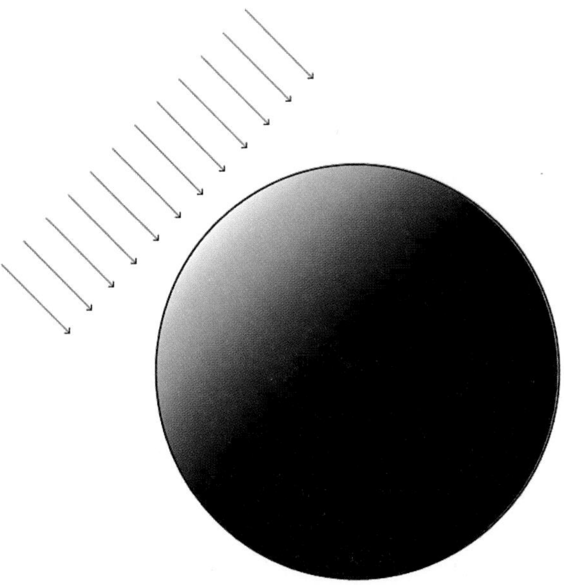

FIGURE 16.29 DirectionalLight shining on a sphere.

TIP

You can control the intensity of lights by using the Color property. For example, #FFFFFF is a full-intensity white light. #808080 is a half-intensity white light. The alpha component of the light color has no effect.

Lights work additively. For example, two identical (same Position, same Direction, and so on) half-intensity lights yield the same effect as one full-intensity light.

Images created with a single DirectionalLight often look somewhat unnatural, and for good reason. In the real world, even when light enters a scene from a single direction (as does sunlight), it generally bounces around between objects in the scene, causing some illumination. One way to approximate this is to add a low-intensity AmbientLight, covered later in this section.

PointLight

A PointLight approximates a light source that radiates light uniformly in all directions from a point in space, such as a naked light bulb. Unlike a DirectionalLight, the intensity of the light from a PointLight diminishes as distance from its position increases. Figure 16.30 illustrates the effect of the following PointLight illuminating a nearby sphere:

```
<PointLight Color="White" Position="2,2,2"
  ConstantAttenuation="0"
```

```
LinearAttenuation="0"
QuadraticAttenuation="0.125"/>
```

The location of a `PointLight` is specified by its `Position` property. The rate at which the light intensity attenuates as distance increases is controlled by a combination of the `ConstantAttenuation`, `LinearAttenuation`, and `QuadraticAttenuation` properties.

The formula for attenuation is

$$Attenuation = \frac{1}{\max(1,\ C + Ld + Qd^2)}$$

where *C*, *L*, and *Q* are `ConstantAttenuation`, `LinearAttenuation`, and `QuadraticAttenuation`, respectively. *d* is the distance between the `Light`'s position and the point being lit. You can derive some useful information from this formula. For example, *C*=1, *L*=0, *Q*=0 gives you a `PointLight` with constant intensity, regardless of distance. However, these properties are usually set by trial and error.

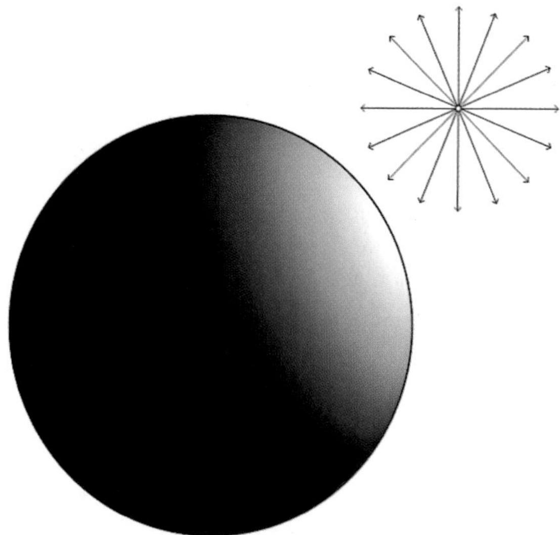

FIGURE 16.30 `PointLight` shining on a sphere.

`PointLight`s also have a `Range` property, which specifies an abrupt cutoff radius outside of which the `PointLight` has no effect. `Range` is unrelated to the attenuation properties in that it does not affect the intensity of the light inside of the cutoff. The default value of `Range` is positive infinity.

`SpotLight`

`SpotLight`s are `PointLight`s that have been focused into a beam. In the real world, light is focused using lenses and reflectors. In real-time computer graphics, this is approximated by limiting the emissions from a `PointLight` to a cone. Figure 16.31 shows how a `SpotLight` is just a `PointLight` whose rays have been constrained to an angular spread.

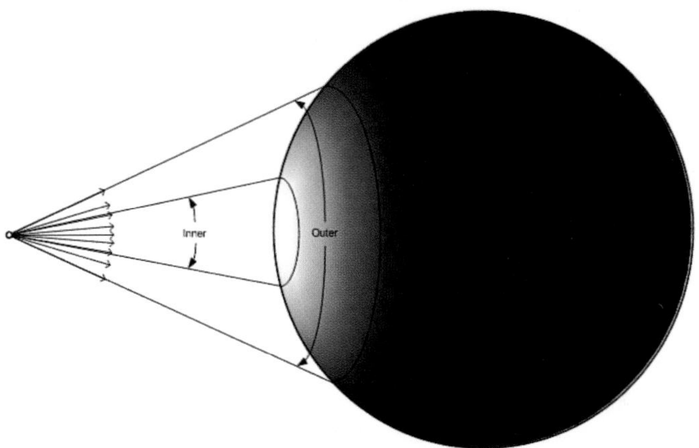

FIGURE 16.31 `SpotLight` shining on a sphere.

FAQ

Why doesn't my `SpotLight` or `PointLight` light my model?

The beginning of this section mentions that real-time lighting uses clever tricks and rough estimations to achieve real-time frame rates. One of the approximations that WPF uses is to compute the intensity of lights only at the vertices.

This approximation can sometimes causes surprising results with `PointLights` and `SpotLights`, as shown in Figure 16.32. The red circle shows where the light intersects the quadrilateral. This could be either the cone of a `SpotLight` or the lit sphere of a `PointLight` with limited `Range`. The surface remains unlit because the light did not extend to the vertices at the corners.

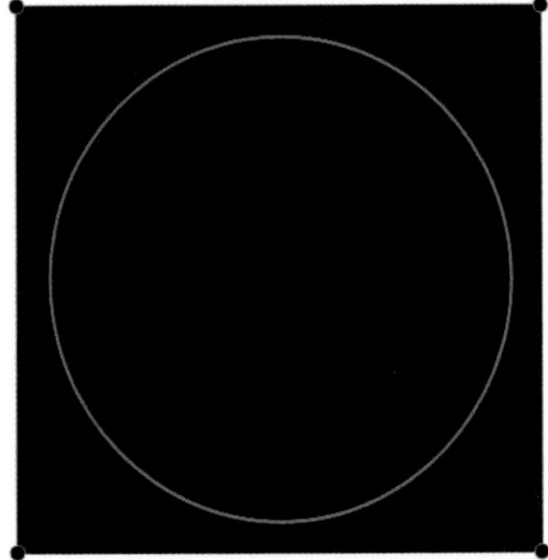

FIGURE 16.32 `Light` inside a quadrilateral.

Continued

To work around this, the surface can be subdivided into a grid of quadrilaterals, as shown in Figure 16.33. Adding vertices increases the number of sample points at which lighting is computed, and you will begin to see the effect of the `SpotLight`.

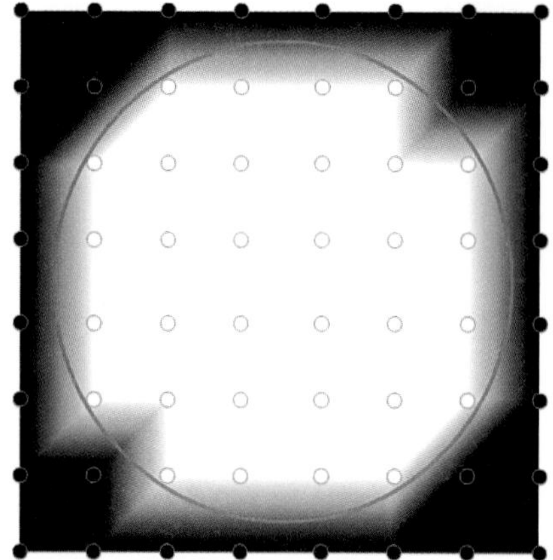

FIGURE 16.33 `Light` inside a subdivided grid.

As you continue to subdivide the mesh, the detail increases. However, to create a perfect circle of light, you need to subdivide until you have about one vertex per pixel.

If you have a reasonably sized falloff area similar to the one shown in Figure 16.31, a small number of subdivisions usually does the trick. If you need a hard boundary between your lit and unlit areas, it might be better to bake the lighting into your `Material`. This can work especially well if the lighting in your scene is static.

The `Direction` property specifies the direction in which the cone is pointing. The shape of the cone is controlled by the `OuterConeAngle` and `InnerConeAngle` properties. Here's an example:

```
<SpotLight Color="White" Position="2,2,2"
  Direction="-1,-1,-1"
  InnerConeAngle="45"
  OuterConeAngle="90"/>
```

The area inside the `InnerConeAngle` receives light that is the color and intensity specified by the `Color` property. The intensity of the light diminishes between the `InnerConeAngle` and `OuterConeAngle`. By adjusting the difference between the `InnerConeAngle` and `OuterConeAngle`, you can vary the size of the falloff area. By setting the `InnerConeAngle` to be equal or greater than the `OuterConeAngle`, you can create a `SpotLight` with no falloff area.

AmbientLight

AmbientLights are typically used to approximate the effect of light that has been scattered by reflecting off multiple diffuse surfaces in a scene. Rays from an AmbientLight strike all surfaces from all directions, as shown in Figure 16.34.

FIGURE 16.34 AmbientLight shining on a sphere.

AmbientLights have only one interesting property, Color, which controls the intensity and the color of the light emitted. The Transform property inherited from Model3D has no effect on AmbientLights.

Adding a full-intensity AmbientLight like the following to the scene usually produces a flat-looking image such as the one shown in Figure 16.35:

```
<AmbientLight Color="White"/>
```

However, a low-intensity AmbientLight added to the scene brightens the unlit areas in the scene to produce a softer image that resembles a scene that receives some natural lighting. Figure 16.36 shows a lit scene with and without the following AmbientLight:

```
<Model3DGroup>
  <DirectionalLight Direction="1,-1,-1" Color="White"/>
  <AmbientLight Color="#FF333333"/>
</Model3DGroup>
```

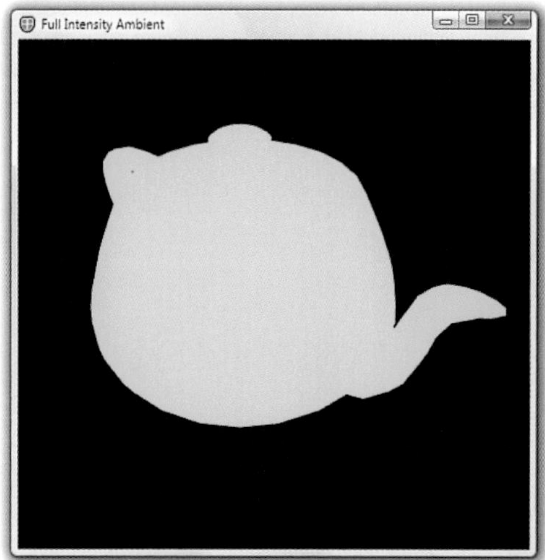

FIGURE 16.35 Full-intensity `AmbientLight`.

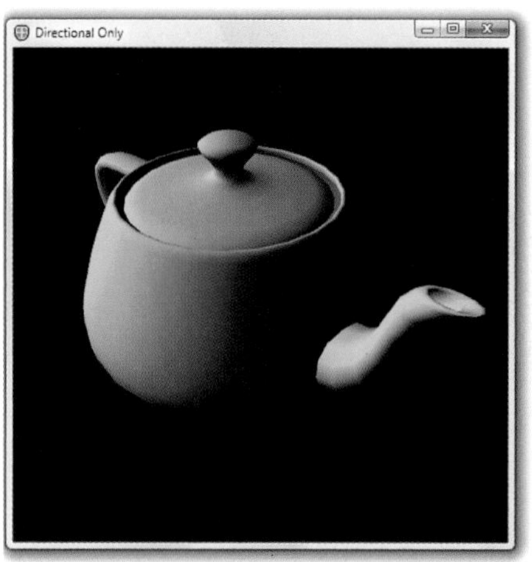

`DirectionalLight` only

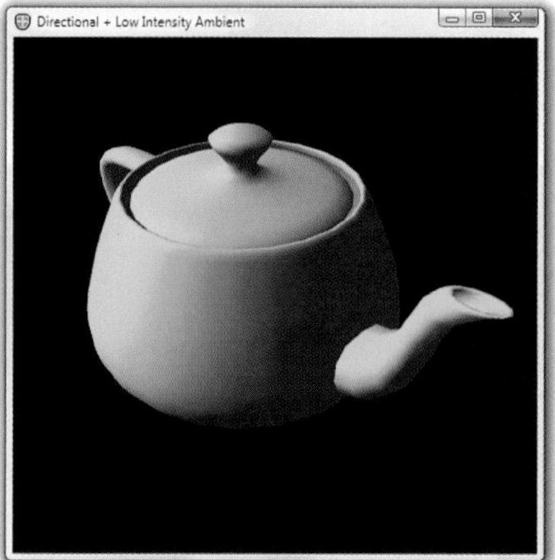

With a low-intensity `AmbientLight`

FIGURE 16.36 Lit scene with and without `AmbientLight`.

TIP

A good rule of thumb to prevent a scene from appearing flat is to only use one `AmbientLight` per scene and keep the intensity at less than one-third white (#555555 *or lower*).

To control how much the `AmbientLight` affects specific objects in a scene, use the `DiffuseMaterial.AmbientColor` property. For example, setting the `AmbientColor` to black prevents models rendered with that `DiffuseMaterial` from being affected by any `AmbientLights` in the scene.

GeometryModel3D

The shape of visible objects in a 3D scene is defined by their geometry. In WPF, you specify 3D geometry by using Geometry3D objects. However, a Geometry3D by itself defines a 3D surface with no appearance. In order to see the 3D surface, you need to combine it with a Material. A GeometryModel3D is a Model3D that combines both, using the Geometry and Material properties.

The following is an example of a GeometryModel3D that renders a square (described as a MeshGeometry3D) using a blue DiffuseMaterial:

```
<GeometryModel3D>
<GeometryModel3D.Material>
  <DiffuseMaterial Brush="Blue"/>
</GeometryModel3D.Material>
<GeometryModel3D.Geometry>
  <MeshGeometry3D Positions="-1,1,0 -1,-1,0 1,-1,0 1,1,0"
                  TriangleIndices="0 1 2, 0 2 3"/>
</GeometryModel3D.Geometry>
</GeometryModel3D>
```

This section first covers the various Material types and then examines MeshGeometry3D.

Material

As discussed earlier, properties of Light objects determine the orientation and color of light rays in a scene. The properties of Materials select which of those rays are reflected back to the viewer to create the image you see. In the real world, materials absorb some wavelengths of light and reflect others. An apple appears red to the human eye because the skin of the fruit reflects red light and absorbs other wavelengths. In WPF, the type and properties of the Material objects determine which colors are reflected back to the Camera to create the image. This section discusses the various Material types supported by WPF:

- **DiffuseMaterial**—Scatters light striking the surface in all directions, producing a flat, matte appearance such as newsprint.
- **SpecularMaterial**—Reflects light at the same angle as the incident ray. SpecularMaterials are used to create glossy highlights present on smooth surfaces such as plastic or metal.
- **EmissiveMaterial**—Approximates a surface that is emitting light. EmissiveMaterials always appear to be lit, regardless of the light objects in the scene; however, they will not cast light onto other objects. Often, EmissiveMaterials are combined with a Light to achieve this effect. EmissiveMaterials are also often used to create objects that are always shown at full intensity and for which no shading is desired, such as in many user interfaces.
- **MaterialGroup**—Applies multiple Materials to a model. Each Material is rendered in order, with the last Material in the group appearing on top.

`DiffuseMaterial` `DiffuseMaterial` is the most commonly used type of `Material`. When light strikes a `DiffuseMaterial`, it is scattered in all directions, producing a matte appearance. Figure 16.37 shows a teapot rendered with a red `DiffuseMaterial`.

FIGURE 16.37 `DiffuseMaterial` on a teapot model.

The scattering is uniform and does not depend on the viewing angle of the `Camera`. However, the angle between the light and the surface does affect the intensity of the reflected light, as shown in Figure 16.38. When the ray strikes the surface directly, it is reflected at maximum intensity. The reflection diminishes as the angle between the light and surface decreases. This is what causes the parts of the teapot facing the light to be illuminated while the parts facing away from the light source remain unlit.

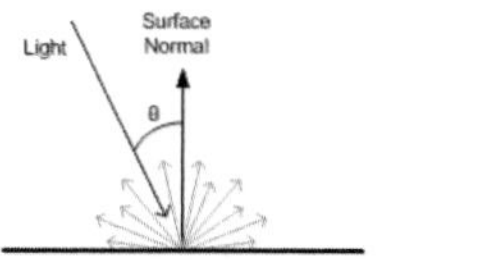

More light is reflected

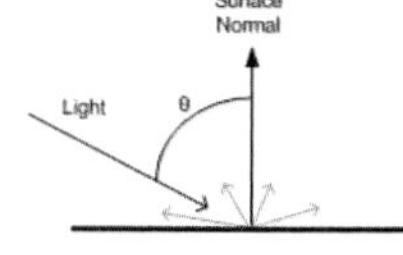

Less light is reflected

FIGURE 16.38 Intensity of reflected light.

The color reflected by the `Material` is controlled by the `Material`'s `Brush` property. The image of the red teapot in Figure 16.37 was created by shining a white light on a `DiffuseMaterial` that reflects only red light:

```
<DiffuseMaterial Brush="Red"/>
```

You can vary which colors are reflected by the `Material` over the object's surface by using one of the nonsolid color `Brushes`. For example, the left side of Figure 16.39 shows the same teapot with zebra stripes applied by an `ImageBrush`:

```
<DiffuseMaterial>
<DiffuseMaterial.Brush>
  <ImageBrush ImageSource="C:\ZebraStripes.png" ViewportUnits="Absolute"/>
```

```
</DiffuseMaterial.Brush>
</DiffuseMaterial>
```

Which part of the Brush appears on which part of the 3D surface is controlled by the texture coordinates (sometimes called UV coordinates) of the Geometry. Texture coordinates are discussed in more detail in the upcoming "TextureCoordinates" section.

ImageBrush with white Material Color

ImageBrush with orange Material Color

FIGURE 16.39 ImageBrush and the ImageBrush tinted orange.

WARNING

If you're not using a SolidColorBrush, you need TextureCoordinates!

If you attempt to use a GradientBrush, ImageBrush, DrawingBrush, or VisualBrush without specifying texture coordinates, your model will not render. Without texture coordinates, there is no mapping between points on the surface to the colors in the Brush. This is not a problem for SolidColorBrushes because all points on the surface map to the same color.

Missing or bad texture coordinates are usually easy to diagnose. If switching your Material to use a SolidColorBrush causes the model to appear, the odds are good that your geometry is missing texture coordinates.

TIP

By allowing you to use Brushes rather than static images as your texture source, texture mapping is made far more expressive in WPF. Not only can the 3D models themselves be data bound and animated, so can the content of their Brushes, which might be animated 2D Drawings, video, or even 2D Controls such as a DocumentViewer!

The right side of Figure 16.39 shows the same `ImageBrush` tinted orange, to look like tiger stripes. There are three ways this effect could be achieved:

- Modify the image used by the `ImageBrush`.
- Change the `Color` of the `Lights` in the scene to orange. White regions of a `DiffuseMaterial` reflect any color of light. If only orange light exists in the scene, orange light is reflected.
- Change the `Color` property on the `Material` to orange. Effectively, this is equivalent to changing the `Light Color` to orange except that it affects only this specific `Material` instead of all the `Materials` in the scene.

Typically, you will want to use the `Color` property on the `Lights` to vary the light intensity in the scene. You might also want to tint the `Lights` to match the ambient light of the environment—for example, green `Lights` for a scene in the forest, blue for underwater, and so on.

The `Color` property on `Materials` is useful when you want to filter the light that is reflected by specific objects. You might use this to tweak the lighting in a scene by darkening specific objects. Another use for this property is to get extra mileage out of an `ImageSource` by tinting it, as in Figure 16.39 to create tiger stripes from the zebra texture:

```
<DiffuseMaterial Color="Orange">
<DiffuseMaterial.Brush>
  <ImageBrush ImageSource="C:\ZebraStripes.png" ViewportUnits="Absolute"/>
</DiffuseMaterial.Brush>
</DiffuseMaterial>
```

This technique can be especially helpful if you want the user to be able to choose a custom color for a 3D model, such as selecting the paint job for a car.

DIGGING DEEPER

Calculating the Final Reflected Color

The final color that is reflected to the user is given by the formula

$$\left(\sum_{i=0}^{n} Lc_i Mc_i\right) Mb$$

where *Lc* is the `Color` property of each `Light`, *Mc* is the `Color` property of the `Material`, and *Mb* is the color sampled from the `Material`'s `Brush`. The alpha components of the `Material`'s `Color` property and the color sampled from the `Brush` are multiplied together. The alpha component of the `Light` is ignored.

FAQ

Why can't you always see through translucent DiffuseMaterials?

There are a number of ways to create a translucent DiffuseMaterial, including using an ImageSource with alpha, using the Brush.Opacity property, or using Alpha in the DiffuseMaterial.Color. If you create a translucent DiffuseMaterial, you might be surprised to find that objects behind it are sometimes not rendered.

This behavior is the result of how WPF handles overlapping surfaces. Rather than sort all the triangles in the scene and render them back-to-front, WPF uses a depth buffer to ensure that the surface nearest the Camera is rendered last (that is, on top). Using depth buffers is much faster than sorting the scene (and potentially subdividing interpenetrating geometry), but it has the side effect that once a surface near the Camera is rendered, surfaces further away are skipped. This is bad news if the nearer surface is intended to be translucent.

In order to ensure that translucent DiffuseMaterials render as intended, you need to take care when constructing a scene. Just as in 2D, objects in a 3D scene are rendered in the order in which they appear in the Children property. By placing translucent objects at the end of the Children collection, you can ensure that the objects behind the translucent objects are rendered first.

Another possibility is to create a translucent-like effect using EmissiveMaterials. EmissiveMaterials are blended additively and therefore do not use the depth buffer. EmissiveMaterials are discussed in the next section.

FAQ

Where is WPF's AmbientMaterial class?

People porting code or importing file formats that are based on the fixed-function lighting from Direct3D or other 3D platforms might wonder why there is no AmbientMaterial class in WPF. Traditional fixed-function lighting allows the user to specify four material colors—ambient, diffuse, emissive, and specular—which are used to calculate the lighting contributions at the vertices.

Ambient and diffuse are similar but are specified separately so that users can limit the contributions of the omnipresent AmbientLight to portions of a scene. For example, you might have an outdoor scene that you want to brighten with an AmbientLight, but you do not want AmbientLight inside the entrance to a cave in a hillside. You would set the ambient color of the Material inside the cave to black to prevent AmbientLights from having an effect.

WPF exposes an AmbientColor property on DiffuseMaterial for this purpose. The normal Color property controls how the DiffuseMaterials reflect light from all Light types in the scene except AmbientLight. The AmbientColor limits the color of the light reflected from AmbientLights only.

Therefore, the diffuse, specular, and emissive materials colors in the traditional pipeline map to the Color properties of DiffuseMaterial, SpecularMaterial, and EmissiveMaterial, respectively. The ambient color maps to the AmbientColor property on DiffuseMaterial.

`EmissiveMaterial` `EmissiveMaterials` always emit light visible to the `Camera`. They do not, however, emit light to other surfaces in the scene the way a `Light` does. The left side of Figure 16.40 shows the effect of the following `EmissiveMaterial` on the teapot model:

```
<EmissiveMaterial Brush="Green"/>
```

EmissiveMaterial

EmissiveMaterial over Black DiffuseMaterial

FIGURE 16.40 `EmissiveMaterial` on a teapot model.

`EmissiveMaterials` are additively blended into the image. Additive blending adds light to the image but does not occlude light from objects behind the material. This is why the checkered background is visible through the teapot on the left side of Figure 16.40. The bright green regions come from overlapping geometry that you wouldn't normally see. (This is the rim of the lid, plus the handle and spout extend a small amount into the body of the teapot.)

To prevent a model from being see-through, you can combine the `EmissiveMaterial` with a `DiffuseMaterial`, using a `MaterialGroup`:

```
<MaterialGroup>
  <DiffuseMaterial Brush="Black"/>
  <SpecularMaterial Brush="Green"/>
</MaterialGroup>
```

The right side of Figure 16.40 shows the result of this change.

In this case, the `EmissiveMaterial` is still additively blended with the image. However, by rendering a black teapot underneath, the end result is black plus the emissive color, resulting in just the emissive color. Also, note that you can no longer see the overlapping geometry inside the teapot. This is because the near side of the black teapot prevents you from seeing through to the overlapping lid, handle, and spout.

SpecularMaterial SpecularMaterials reflect light back to the viewer when the Camera is close to the angle of reflection between the light and the surface. SpecularMaterial is also additively blended and by itself looks glasslike, as demonstrated by the following one shown on the left side of Figure 16.41:

```
<SpecularMaterial Brush="White" SpecularPower="10"/>
```

Often, a SpecularMaterial is combined with a DiffuseMaterial to add a bright highlight characteristic of hard, shiny surfaces, as follows (shown on the right side of Figure 16.41):

```
<MaterialGroup>
  <DiffuseMaterial Brush="Red"/>
  <SpecularMaterial Brush="White" SpecularPower="40"/>
</MaterialGroup>
```

Compare this with the image of the red DiffuseMaterial alone in Figure 16.37.

The "hardness" of the highlight is controlled by the SpecularPower property. The larger the value for this property, the more focused the specular highlight.

SpecularMaterial by itself

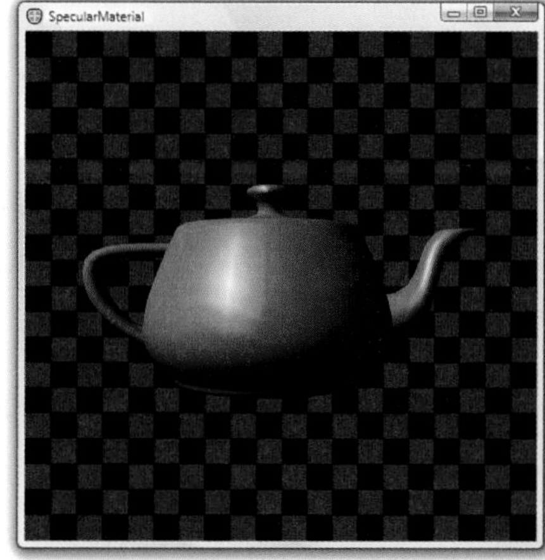

SpecularMaterial over a red DiffuseMaterial

FIGURE 16.41 SpecularMaterial on a teapot model.

TIP

To make plastic-looking surfaces, you can combine a bright DiffuseMaterial with a white SpecularMaterial. To create metal-looking surfaces, you can use a dark DiffuseMaterial with a bright SpecularMaterial of the same hue.

Unlike `DiffuseMaterial`, which scatters light uniformly, `SpecularMaterial` reflects light in the opposite direction of the incident ray. As shown in Figure 16.42, the reflected light bounces off a `SpecularMaterial` like a mirror and is visible only when the `Camera` is close to the reflected ray.

FIGURE 16.42
Light bounces off a `SpecularMaterial`.

Note that because `AmbientLights` are directionless, they have no effect on `SpecularMaterials`.

As with the `DiffuseMaterial`, the final color reflected to the viewer is a combination of the `Color` properties of the `Lights` in the scene, the `Brush` of the `SpecularMaterial`, and the `Material`'s `Color` property. See the "`DiffuseMaterial`" section for more details on how the final color is computed.

TIP

Unlike traditional fixed-function lighting, which only allows you to specify a color for the specular highlight, WPF allows you to use any `Brush`. Using alpha in the image, you can create a `Material` in which specularity varies over the surface. This technique, called *gloss mapping*, can be used to add shininess only to the metallic parts of a texture for a car, fingerprints on glass, and so on.

Combining Materials As you've seen in previous examples, `MaterialGroup` enables you to apply multiple materials to a surface. `Materials` in a `MaterialGroup` are rendered on top of each other in the order specified. Common uses include applying an `EmissiveMaterial` or `SpecularMaterial` over a `DiffuseMaterial`, as was done to create the `Materials` for the teapot in this section.

Geometry3D

Similar to the 2D `Geometry` class, `Geometry3Ds` are used to define the shape of 3D objects. By themselves, `Geometry3Ds` have no appearance. `Geometry3Ds` are combined with `Materials` using a `GeometryModel3D` to create a `Model3D` that can be rendered. There is only one concrete `Geometry3D` class: `MeshGeometry3D`.

A `MeshGeometry3D` represents a set of 3D surfaces specified as a list of triangles. `MeshGeometry3D` is composed of the following properties:

- **`Positions`**—Defines the vertices of the triangles contained in the mesh.
- **`TriangleIndices`**—Describes the connections between the vertices to form triangles. If `TriangleIndices` is not specified, it is implied that the positions should be connected in the order they appear: 0 1 2, then 3 4 5, and so on.
- **`Normals`**—Allows you to optionally tweak the lighting of the mesh.
- **`TextureCoordinates`**—Provides a 3D-to-2D mapping for each position used by the `Materials`.

Each of the `Positions`, `Normals`, and `TextureCoordinates` properties is a collection with one entry for each vertex in the mesh. For example, the position for the 0th vertex comes from the 0th entry in the `Positions` collection, the normal for the 0th vertex comes from the 0th entry in the `Normals` collection, and so on.

`Positions` The triangles in the mesh are defined by specifying the 3D coordinates of their vertices. The coordinates are stored in the `Positions` collection of the `MeshGeometry3D`. By default, each group of three `Point3D`s in the `Positions` collection is drawn as a triangle. The following snippet produces the triangle illustrated in Figure 16.43.

```
<MeshGeometry3D Positions="-1,1,0 -1,-1,0 1,-1,0"/>
```

FIGURE 16.43 A triangle described by a `MeshGeometry3D`.

You can create a square by adding a second triangle, shown in Figure 16.44.

```
<MeshGeometry3D Positions="-1,1,0 -1,-1,0 1,-1,0 -1,1,0 1,-1,0 1,1,0"/>
```

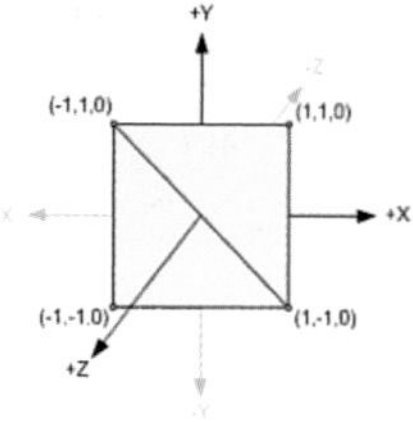

FIGURE 16.44 A square described by a `MeshGeometry3D`.

Front Sides Versus Back Sides One of the things about 3D geometry that often surprises 2D developers is that the triangles in a `MeshGeometry3D` have separate front and back sides. Each side can be rendered using a different material. You also might choose to not render a side by leaving the `Material` property `null`. Which side of a triangle is the front is determined by the winding of the vertices. Figure 16.45 illustrates the winding of the triangles in the square, as viewed from the front and back.

The winding is determined by the order in which the points are connected in the triangle. For example, connecting point 0 to point 1 creates a directed edge starting at 0 and ending at 1. The direction of the edges wind in a counterclockwise direction when viewed from the front, shown on the left of Figure 16.45.

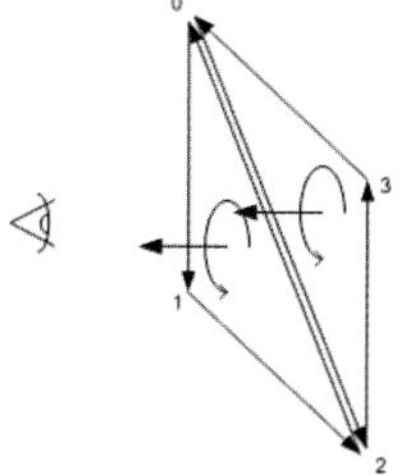

Square from the front

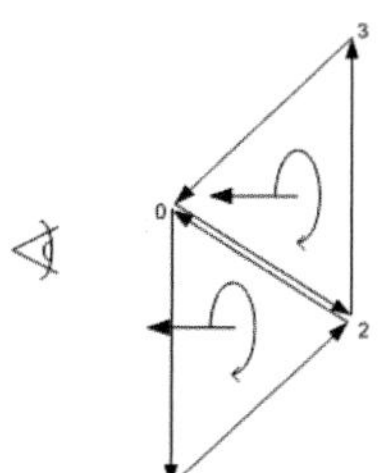

Square from the back

FIGURE 16.45 Viewing the square from two different perspectives.

DIGGING DEEPER

Winding Order and Handedness

The section about `Cameras` introduced a right-hand rule to remember which direction the z-axis points in a right-handed coordinate system. There is a second right-hand rule that tells you which side of a triangle is the front. The direction your fingers curl when looking at your thumb indicates the winding direction. As illustrated in Figure 16.46, this is counterclockwise for a right-handed system.

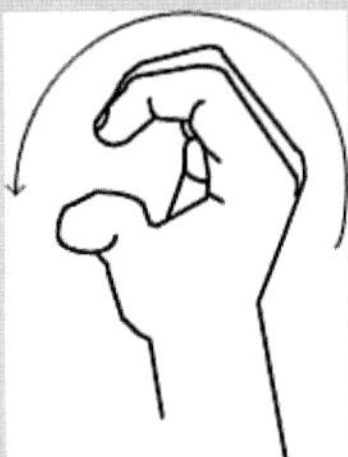

FIGURE 16.46 The other right-hand rule.

The right-hand rule is also useful for remembering the positive direction of rotation in a right-handed coordinate system.

TIP

If you suspect that you have an issue with the winding in a mesh, you can set both the `Material` and `BackMaterial` properties so that the triangle will be visible, regardless of which side you view it from.

If it is acceptable to have the same material on both the front and back, you can ignore the issue of winding. However, it is sometimes useful to be able to specify different `Materials` for the front and the back. It is also faster to avoid rendering the `BackMaterial` if it will not be visible in the scene.

`TriangleIndices` A mesh is built into the desired shape by adding triangles. Even curved surfaces are approximated by lots of little triangles. As the number of triangles in a mesh increases, so does the number of shared edges.

`TriangleIndices` enables you to share positions between triangles. When the `TriangleIndices` collection is empty, it is implied that the points should be connected in the order in which they appear in the `Positions` collection. When `TriangleIndices` exist, the points are connected in groups of three, as specified by the `TriangleIndices`. For example, you can create a square using only four unique points, as illustrated in Figure 16.47:

```
<MeshGeometry3D Positions="-1,1,0 -1,-1,0 1,-1,0 1,1,0"
                TriangleIndices="0 1 2, 0 2 3"/>
```

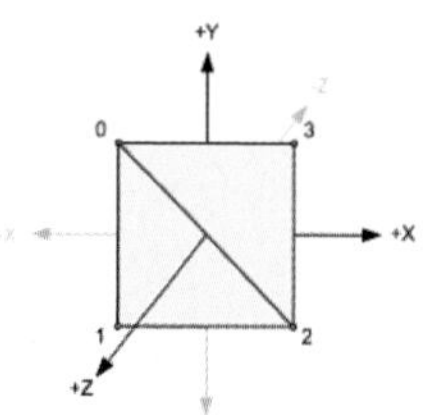

FIGURE 16.47 Indices of the vertices.

Sharing the position between triangles has a slightly different semantic meaning than declaring the same point multiple times. When the position is shared, the triangles are considered to be part of a single continuous surface. When the positions are separate, the triangles are separate abutting surfaces that can have different normals or texture coordinates.

TIP

Regardless of whether you use `TriangleIndices`, you do not need to worry about cracks appearing between triangles within a single `MeshGeometry3D`. WPF has strict rendering rules which guarantee that triangles sharing points are rendered as adjacent, without a seam.

However, you *do* need to be aware that transforms are not always exact. If you are using different transforms on two `MeshGeometry3D`s to make them adjacent, it is possible that floating-point error in the transformations might create small gaps between the meshes.

Sometimes, you can work around this error by fudging the transform to create a small amount of overlap. Other times, you need to construct the `MeshGeometry3D`s with points that are adjacent rather than transform them to be so.

`Normals` A *normal* is a vector that is perpendicular to a surface at a point. You specify normals at vertices to tell the system whether triangles represent flat surfaces or are approximating curved surfaces. Figure 16.48 shows the difference between flat and smooth shading on a tube approximated using 12 quadrilaterals.

TIP

If you do not specify normals, the system generates them for you by averaging the face normals of each triangle that shares each vertex. If vertices are not shared between triangles, the result is the face normals, which gives the flat shaded appearance shown on the left side of Figure 16.48. If the vertices are shaded between adjacent triangles using `TriangleIndices`, the averaging results in the smooth shaded appearance shown on the right side of Figure 16.48.

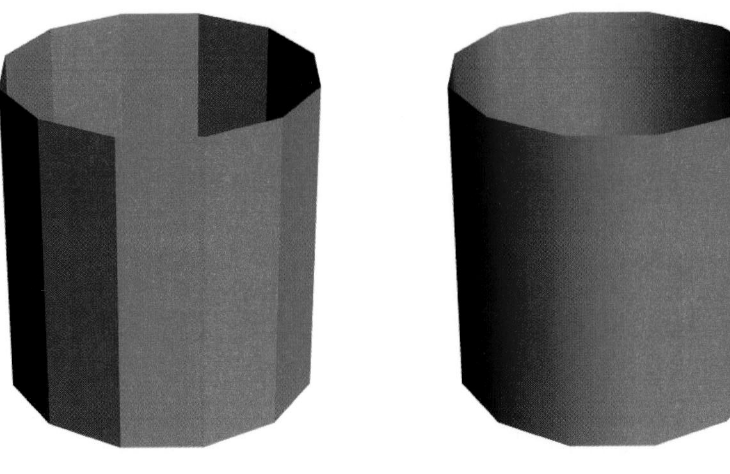

FIGURE 16.48 Two tubes approximated using 12 quadrilaterals.

When the normals for each vertex in a triangle are parallel, as illustrated in the cross section of the tube on the left side of Figure 16.49, the rendered surface appears flat. If the normals point in different directions, the shading is smoothly interpolated across the face of the triangle. To create a smooth surface like that illustrated on the right side of Figure 16.49, the normals of the adjacent triangles should be the same to prevent a crease from appearing.

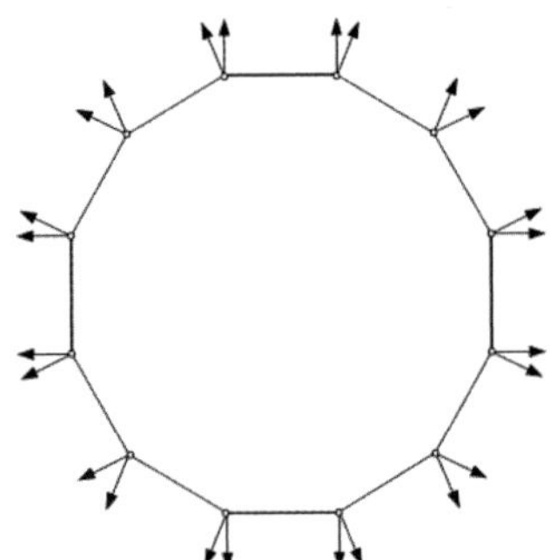

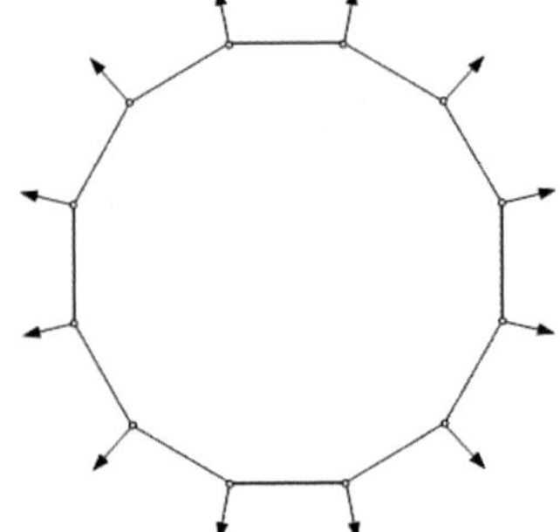

FIGURE 16.49 Cross sections of the tubes from Figure 16.48.

Let's consider the simple square mesh you have been building. If you want the square to appear flat, you specify all the normals perpendicular to the surface, as illustrated on the left side of Figure 16.50:

```
<MeshGeometry3D Positions="-1,1,0 -1,-1,0 1,-1,0 1,1,0"
                TriangleIndices="0 1 2, 0 2 3"
                Normals="0,0,1 0,0,1 0,0,1 0,0,1"/>
```

If you want the square to be lit as if it were an approximation of a slightly curved surface, you specify the normals to match the curvature of the surface, as illustrated on the right side of Figure 16.50:

```
<MeshGeometry3D Positions="-1,1,0 -1,-1,0 1,-1,0 1,1,0"
                TriangleIndices="0 1 2, 0 2 3"
                Normals="-0.25,0.25,1 -0.25,-0.25,1 0.25,-0.25,1 0.25,0.25,1"/>
```

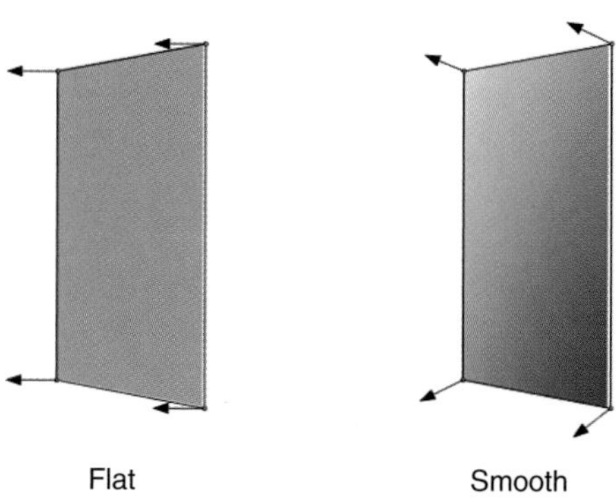

FIGURE 16.50 The result of using two different `Normals` values.

`TextureCoordinates` When you set the `Fill` property on a 2D `Shape`, it is assumed that you want the `Brush` to map to the 2D bounds of the `Shape`. In 3D, you need to provide this mapping yourself. Each entry in the `TextureCoordinates` collection is a 2D point in `Brush` space. These points map triangles in 3D space to triangles in `Brush` space. The triangles in `Brush` space provide the colors for the materials when the surface is rendered. Figure 16.51 illustrates how you would map the vertices in your square to stretch an image across it:

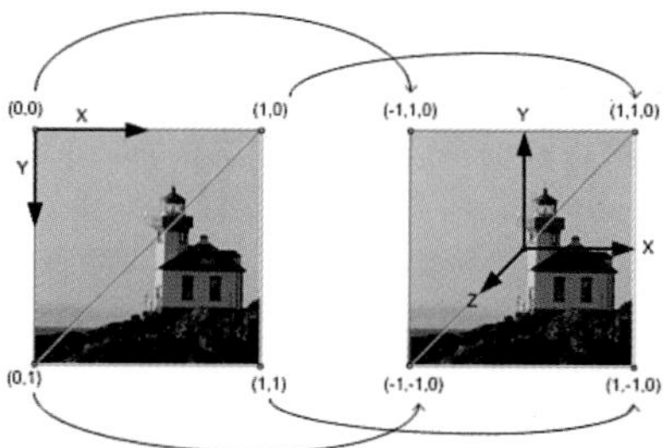

FIGURE 16.51 Mapping between 2D `Brush` space and 3D surface.

```
<MeshGeometry3D Positions="-1,1,0 -1,-1,0 1,-1,0 1,1,0"
                TriangleIndices="0 1 2, 0 2 3"
                TextureCoordinates="0,0 0,1 1,1 1,0"/>
```

Keep in mind that in the 2D coordinate system that WPF uses, the origin is at the top-left corner, and the positive y-axis extends downward. By convention, the source image is usually considered to extend from 0 to 1 in both the X and Y directions.

WARNING

By default, WPF texture coordinates are interpreted differently than you might expect!

You should be aware of a couple quirks with the way WPF handles texture coordinates. The default behavior of WPF texture coordinates closely matches the default behavior of 2D geometry, which is very convenient for 2D/3D integration scenarios. However, when you are attempting to use a mesh containing texture coordinates generated for a different system, there are a few Brush settings you will want to change.

The first is that, by default, Brush space is mapped to the bounds of the texture coordinates. This means that the following does not show the top-left quarter of the Brush as you might expect it to:

```
<MeshGeometry3D Positions="-1,1,0 -1,-1,0 1,-1,0 1,1,0"
                TriangleIndices="0 1 2, 0 2 3"
                TextureCoordinates="0,0 0,0.5 0.5,0.5 0.5,0"/>
```

Instead, the bounds (0,0) – (0.5,0.5) become the relative bounds of the source, and the entire Brush is displayed. To prevent this, you set the ViewportUnits of the Brush to Absolute:

```
<ImageBrush ViewportUnits="Absolute" …/>
```

You will almost always want to do this when applying Brushes to 3D meshes. The default behavior is useful in 2D to map Brush space to the bounds of the 2D geometry being filled. In 3D, it is rarely used.

The second issue to be aware of is that some systems specify their y-axis as pointing upward in 2D instead of downward, as in WPF. If you are using texture coordinates generated for such a system, your Brushes will be applied upside down. You can correct for this with a simple Brush transform:

```
<ImageBrush ViewportUnits="Absolute" Transform="1,0,0,-1,0,1" …/>
```

Finally, if your mesh has texture coordinates that extend outside the 0-to-1 range, it is likely that the intent was to tile. TileMode needs to be turned on explicitly in WPF:

```
<ImageBrush ViewportUnits="Absolute" Transform="1,0,0,-1,0,1" TileMode="Tile" …/>
```

ImageBrush is shown as an example, but these tips apply to all Brushes that use TextureCoordinates.

Model3DGroup

Model3DGroup derives from Model3D. Model3DGroups are used to group together a collection of Model3Ds into a single model. Grouping multiple GeometryModel3Ds together with a Model3DGroup is a way to build a model that uses multiple materials. Listing 16.4 shows how six GeometryModel3Ds can be combined to form a model of a cube. An alternative approach would be to create one MeshGeometry3D that uses a MaterialGroup to achieve the same effect.

TIP

Some 3D systems have an object called a "mesh," which contains not only geometry information but materials as well. Sometimes, even multiple materials are permitted in a mesh. In WPF, this corresponds to a `Model3DGroup` containing multiple `GeometryModel3Ds`, one for each `Material`.

LISTING 16.4 A Cube

```
<Model3DGroup x:Name="Cube">

  <GeometryModel3D x:Name="Front">
  <GeometryModel3D.Material>
    <DiffuseMaterial Brush="Orange"/>
  </GeometryModel3D.Material>
  <GeometryModel3D.Geometry>
    <MeshGeometry3D Positions="1,1,1 -1,1,1 -1,-1,1 1,-1,1"
                    TextureCoordinates="1,1 0,1 0,0 1,0"
                    TriangleIndices="0 1 2 0 2 3"/>
  </GeometryModel3D.Geometry>
  </GeometryModel3D>

  <GeometryModel3D x:Name="Right">
  <GeometryModel3D.Material>
    <DiffuseMaterial Brush="Yellow"/>
  </GeometryModel3D.Material>
  <GeometryModel3D.Geometry>
    <MeshGeometry3D Positions="1,1,-1 -1,1,-1 -1,1,1 1,1,1"
                    TextureCoordinates="0,0 1,0 1,1 0,1"
                    TriangleIndices="0 1 2 0 2 3"/>
  </GeometryModel3D.Geometry>
  </GeometryModel3D>

  <GeometryModel3D x:Name="Back">
  <GeometryModel3D.Material>
    <DiffuseMaterial Brush="Red"/>
  </GeometryModel3D.Material>
  <GeometryModel3D.Geometry>
    <MeshGeometry3D Positions="-1,-1,-1 -1,1,-1 1,1,-1 1,-1,-1"
                    TextureCoordinates="1,0 1,1 0,1 0,0"
                    TriangleIndices="0 1 2 0 2 3"/>
  </GeometryModel3D.Geometry>
  </GeometryModel3D>

  <GeometryModel3D x:Name="Left">
```

LISTING 16.4 Continued

```
<GeometryModel3D.Material>
  <DiffuseMaterial Brush="Blue"/>
</GeometryModel3D.Material>
<GeometryModel3D.Geometry>
  <MeshGeometry3D Positions="-1,1,1 -1,1,-1 -1,-1,-1 -1,-1,1"
                  TextureCoordinates="1,1 0,1 0,0 1,0"
                  TriangleIndices="0 1 2 0 2 3"/>
</GeometryModel3D.Geometry>
</GeometryModel3D>

<GeometryModel3D x:Name="Top">
<GeometryModel3D.Material>
  <DiffuseMaterial Brush="Green"/>
</GeometryModel3D.Material>
<GeometryModel3D.Geometry>
  <MeshGeometry3D Positions="1,-1,1 1,-1,-1 1,1,-1 1,1,1"
                  TextureCoordinates="1,1 0,1 0,0 1,0"
                  TriangleIndices="0 1 2 0 2 3"/>
</GeometryModel3D.Geometry>
</GeometryModel3D>

<GeometryModel3D x:Name="Bottom">
<GeometryModel3D.Material>
  <DiffuseMaterial Brush="Purple"/>
</GeometryModel3D.Material>
<GeometryModel3D.Geometry>
  <MeshGeometry3D Positions="-1,-1,1 -1,-1,-1 1,-1,-1 1,-1,1"
                  TextureCoordinates="0,1 0,0 1,0 1,1"
                  TriangleIndices="0 1 2 0 2 3"/>
</GeometryModel3D.Geometry>
</GeometryModel3D>

</Model3DGroup>
```

Visual3D

All elements that draw 2D content to the screen inherit their ability to render from the `Visual` base class. Similarly, `Visual3D`s are nodes in the visual tree that can display 3D content. The `Visual` services—hit testing, bounding, and so on—extend to `Visual3D`s as well and are accessible via the `VisualTreeHelper` class.

WPF provides three direct subclasses of `Visual3D`: `ModelVisual3D`, `UIElement3D`, and `Viewport2DVisual3D`. This section examines each one.

ModelVisual3D

ModelVisual3D is similar to the 2D DrawingVisual and has been a part of WPF since its first version. To set the content of a ModelVisual3D, you use the Content property:

```
<Viewport3D>
<Viewport3D.Camera>
  <OrthographicCamera Position="5,5,5" LookDirection="-1,-1,-1" Width="5"/>
</Viewport3D.Camera>
<Viewport3D.Children>
  <ModelVisual3D Content="{StaticResource CubeModel}"/>
</Viewport3D.Children>
</Viewport3D>
```

ModelVisual3D also has a Children property. Therefore, you use ModelVisual3Ds to compose multiple models into a scene inside your Viewport3D:

```
<Viewport3D>
<Viewport3D.Camera>
  <OrthographicCamera Position="5,5,5" LookDirection="-1,-1,-1" Width="5"/>
</Viewport3D.Camera>
<Viewport3D.Children>
  <ModelVisual3D Transform="{DynamicResource SquadronTransform}">
    <ModelVisual3D Content="{StaticResource AirplaneModel}"
      Transform="{DynamicResource PlaneTransform1}"/>
    <ModelVisual3D Content="{StaticResource AirplaneModel}"
      Transform="{DynamicResource PlaneTransform2}"/>
  </ModelVisual3D>
</Viewport3D.Children>
</Viewport3D>
```

Children (and not Content!) is designated as ModelVisual3D's content property, so the preceding XAML adds the two children directly to the parent element. Keep in mind that Model3Ds can be reused between ModelVisual3Ds.

16

FAQ

When should I use Model3DGroup versus ModelVisual3D?

Although you can put together an entire scene by using a Model3DGroup displayed under a single ModelVisual3D (or ModelUIElement3D, covered later), you will be missing out on some important performance optimizations if you do this. ModelVisual3D (and ModelUIElement3D) are optimized to be scene nodes. They cache bounds and other information that lightweight Model3DGroups do not.

Going to the other extreme, you could use ModelVisual3Ds for each and every GeometryModel3D in a scene. Doing so is inadvisable because it unnecessarily increases the working set of the application. Model3DGroups are lightweight constructs intended for grouping multiple GeometryModel3Ds into a single model.

Continued

In general, you should use Model3DGroups to combine the various pieces of a single model (for example, the tires, windshield, and body of a car). ModelVisual3Ds (or ModelUIElement3Ds) should be used for displaying instances of 3D models (for example, use a ModelVisual3D for each car you add to the scene).

UIElement3D

Introduced in WPF 3.5, the abstract UIElement3D class and its subclasses take a step beyond the Visual3D class in bringing 2D framework principles to the world of WPF 3D. As mentioned earlier in this chapter, WPF's 2D UIElements are often said to have LIFE (layout, input, focus, and eventing) support. Although there is no 3D layout, UIElement3D does have IFE (input, focus, and eventing). This dramatically simplifies tasks such as attaching mouse event handlers to 3D elements of a scene. Rather than being forced to process every mouse click event on your Viewport3D and then tease out exactly which of your 3D models was hit, you can simply add the event handlers directly to your individual UIElement3Ds.

There are two UIElement3D-derived classes in WPF: ModelUIElement3D and ContainerUIElement3D. If you remember the *FooBar* trick from the preceding chapter, then it shouldn't be a surprise that ModelUIElement3D is a UIElement3D that contains a Model. ContainerUIElement3D is a UIElement3D that acts like a container.

ModelUIElement3D

Listings 16.5 and 16.6 leverage ModelUIElement3D to create a clickable cube that changes color with each click. ModelUIElement3D has its own Model3D but no children. Notice that the MouseDown event handler is on the ModelUIElement3D and not on the Viewport3D.

LISTING 16.5 MainWindow.xaml—A Clickable Cube

```
<Window x:Class="MainWindow"
        xmlns="http://schemas.microsoft.com/winfx/2006/xaml/presentation"
        xmlns:x="http://schemas.microsoft.com/winfx/2006/xaml">
  <Grid>
    <Viewport3D>
    <Viewport3D.Camera>
      <PerspectiveCamera Position="3,3,4" LookDirection="-1,-1,-1"
        FieldOfView="60"/>
    </Viewport3D.Camera>
    <Viewport3D.Children>
      <ModelVisual3D>
      <ModelVisual3D.Content>
        <DirectionalLight Direction="-0.3,-0.4,-0.5" />
      </ModelVisual3D.Content>
      </ModelVisual3D>
```

LISTING 16.5 Continued

```
<ModelUIElement3D MouseDown="Cube_MouseDown">
<ModelUIElement3D.Model>
  <GeometryModel3D>
  <GeometryModel3D.Material>
    <DiffuseMaterial>
    <DiffuseMaterial.Brush>
      <SolidColorBrush Color="Purple" x:Name="CubeBrush"/>
    </DiffuseMaterial.Brush>
    </DiffuseMaterial>
  </GeometryModel3D.Material>
  <GeometryModel3D.Geometry>
    <MeshGeometry3D
     Positions="1,1,-1 1,-1,-1 -1,-1,-1 -1,1,-1 1,1,1 -1,1,1 -1,-1,1 1,-1,1
                1,1,-1 1,1,1 1,-1,1 1,-1,-1 1,-1,-1 1,-1,1 -1,-1,1 -1,-1,-1
               -1,-1,-1 -1,-1,1 -1,1,1 -1,1,-1 1,1,1 1,1,-1 -1,1,-1 -1,1,1"
     TriangleIndices="0 1 2 0 2 3 4 5 6 4 6 7 8 9 10 8 10 11 12 13 14 12 14
                      15 16 17 18 16 18 19 20 21 22 20 22 23"
     TextureCoordinates="0,1 0,0 1,0 1,1 1,1 -0,1 0,-0 1,0 1,1 -0,1 0,-0
                         1,0 1,0 1,1 -0,1 0,-0 -0,0 1,-0 1,1 0,1 1,-0 1,1
                         0,1 -0,0" />
  </GeometryModel3D.Geometry>
  </GeometryModel3D>
</ModelUIElement3D.Model>
</ModelUIElement3D>
</Viewport3D.Children>
</Viewport3D>
</Grid>
</Window>
```

LISTING 16.6 MainWindow.xaml.cs—Code-Behind for the Clickable Cube

```
using System;
using System.Windows;
using System.Windows.Input;
using System.Windows.Media;

public partial class MainWindow : Window
{
  static Random r;

  public MainWindow()
  {
    InitializeComponent();
    r = new Random();
```

LISTING 16.6 Continued

```
  }

  private void Cube_MouseDown(object sender, MouseButtonEventArgs e)
  {
    // Pick a random color
    CubeBrush.Color = Color.FromRgb((byte)r.Next(), (byte)r.Next(),
                                    (byte)r.Next());
  }
}
```

ContainerUIElement3D

ContainerUIElement3D is a simple container for holding one or more ModelUIElement3Ds:

```
<Viewport3D>
<Viewport3D.Children>
  <ContainerUIElement3D>
    <ModelUIElement3D …>
    <ModelUIElement3D …>
  </ContainerUIElement3D>
</Viewport3D.Children>
</Viewport3D>
```

The ContainerUIElement3D class itself does not have its own Model3D, just a Children collection of type Visual3DCollection as its content property. ModelUIElement3DGroup might have been a more appropriate name for this simple class.

Note the difference between ModelVisual3D and the two UIElement3D subclasses. ModelVisual3D has both a Model3D as well as a Visual3DCollection. The UIElement3D classes separate this container and model functionality into the ContainerUIElement3D and ModelUIElement3D classes, respectively.

Viewport2DVisual3D

Introduced in WPF 3.5, the Viewport2DVisual3D class allows live interactive 2D content to be directly mapped to a 3D surface. Previously it was possible to map live 2D content onto 3D surfaces with VisualBrushes and DrawingBrushes. However, because they were just Brushes, they did not allow for interactivity. A Button drawn on a 3D sphere using a VisualBrush could never actually be clicked. Viewport2DVisual3Ds overcome this interactivity barrier: A Button mapped onto a 3D sphere actually responds to mouse clicks in 3D. A TextBox drawn on the face of a cube can be edited with the mouse and keyboard, just as you would expect. Multi-touch can be used to manipulate 2D elements mapped into 3D space. Even context menus for features such as spelling correction on a TextBox work!

The name Viewport2DVisual3D sounds odd, but it basically follows WPF's naming convention. It *is* a Visual3D that *acts like* a 2D viewport. One confusing aspect of this name is that there is no Viewport2D class in WPF.

Listing 16.7 demonstrates how Viewport2DVisual3D is used with a simple Button. You provide the Viewport2DVisual3D with a MeshGeometry3D, a Material, and a target Visual. The interactive Material needs the Viewport2DVisual3D.IsVisualHostMaterial attached property set to true. If a Brush is associated with the interactive Material, it is ignored. The color associated with the host material is modulated with the target Visual's color as usual. Figure 16.52 shows the result.

LISTING 16.7 An Interactive Button in 3D

```
<Window xmlns="http://schemas.microsoft.com/winfx/2006/xaml/presentation">
  <Grid>
    <Viewport3D>
    <Viewport3D.Camera>
      <PerspectiveCamera Position="0.2,0.1,1" LookDirection="-0.2,-.1,-1"
                         FieldOfView="120"/>
    </Viewport3D.Camera>
    <Viewport3D.Children>
      <ModelVisual3D>
      <ModelVisual3D.Content>
        <DirectionalLight Direction="-0.3,-0.4,-0.5" />
      </ModelVisual3D.Content>
      </ModelVisual3D>
      <Viewport2DVisual3D>
      <Viewport2DVisual3D.Geometry>
        <MeshGeometry3D Positions="-1,1,0 -1,-1,0 1,-1,0 1,1,0"
          TextureCoordinates="0,0 0,1 1,1 1,0" TriangleIndices="0 1 2 0 2 3" />
      </Viewport2DVisual3D.Geometry>
      <Viewport2DVisual3D.Material>
        <DiffuseMaterial Viewport2DVisual3D.IsVisualHostMaterial="True" />
      </Viewport2DVisual3D.Material>
        <Button>Hello, 3D</Button>
      </Viewport2DVisual3D>
    </Viewport3D.Children>
    </Viewport3D>
  </Grid>
</Window>
```

TIP

Viewport2DVisual3D supports cached composition. It has a CacheMode property that works the same way as the CacheMode property on UIElement.

FIGURE 16.52 An interactive 2D Button mapped into 3D space.

3D Hit Testing

As mentioned earlier, the simplest way to perform a hit test against a specific 3D model is to create a `ModelUIElement3D` and to give that `ModelUIElement3D` its own `MouseDown` event handler. But `ModelUIElement3Ds` are not a requirement for performing hit testing against 3D models.

Like their 2D `Visual` counterparts, `Visual3Ds` participate in visual hit testing. To perform a hit test against a `Visual3D`, you must first receive a hit test event on some 2D `UIElement` that contains a 3D scene, such as the parent `Viewport3D` element:

```
<Viewport3D MouseDown="MouseDownHandler">
```

When the event handler is called, you can issue a visual hit test at that point:

```
private void MouseDownHandler(object sender, MouseButtonEventArgs e)
{
  base.OnMouseLeftButtonDown(e);

  Viewport3D viewport = (Viewport3D)sender;
  Point location = e.GetPosition(viewport);

  HitTestResult result = VisualTreeHelper.HitTest(viewport, location);

  if (result != null && result.VisualHit is Visual3D)
  {
    MessageBox.Show("Hit Visual3D!");
  }
}
```

Of course, the overload of `VisualTreeHelper.HitTest` shown in Chapter 15, which uses callback delegates to report multiple results, also works with `Visual3Ds`. As in 2D, the results are returned in front-to-back order. To start a hit test from within the 3D scene, you can use the overload of `VisualTreeHelper.HitTest` that takes a `Visual3D` and a `HitTestParameters3D`.

DIGGING DEEPER

Getting Detailed Hit Test Information

`HitTestResult` is the base class for a number of classes, such as `PointHitTestResult` and `GeometryHitTestResult`. The type of `HitTestResult` returned to you depends on the type of hit test you initiated and what the hit test ended up intersecting in the scene. If you issue a point hit test that ends up hitting a 3D mesh, you may cast the `HitTestResult` to a `RayMeshGeometry3DHitTestResult`. `RayMeshGeometry3DHitTestResult` has a wealth of information about the details of the intersection.

Viewport3D

`Viewport3D` provides the opposite functionality of `Viewport2DVisual3D`. Whereas `Viewport2DVisual3D` is a `Visual3D` that enables 2D elements to be embedded inside 3D, `Viewport3D` is the 2D `FrameworkElement` that enables 3D elements to be embedded inside 2D.

The parent of a `Viewport3D` is always a 2D element such as a `Window` or `Grid`. The children of the `Viewport3D` are `Visual3Ds`. The 3D scene described by the `Visual3D` children is rendered inside the rectangular layout bounds of the `Viewport3D`. The `Camera` property on the `Viewport3D` controls the view of the 3D scene you see inside the `Viewport3D`.

TIP

Many container-like elements are normally sized during the layout system's measure pass (described in Chapter 21, "Layout with Custom Panels") to fit their contents. For example, a `Button` is typically sized to accommodate the text or other content inside it. `Viewport3Ds` work the other way around: `Viewport3Ds` adjust the view of the 3D scene to fit whatever its layout bounds turn out to be. By default, `Viewport3D`'s `ClipToBounds` property is set to `false`, meaning that its 3D content can actually *exceed* the layout bounds of the `Viewport3D`. If you'd like the `Viewport3D`'s content to stay within the rectangular region of the layout bounds, you set `Viewport3D.ClipToBounds` to `true`.

For this reason, you need to set the `Width` and `Height` properties of `Viewport3D` elements unless it is already being stretched to fit an area by layout. If you forget to do this, the `Viewport3D` defaults to a size of 0 by 0, and the 3D scene does not appear.

One of the neat things about a `Viewport3D` being a fully featured `FrameworkElement` that participates in layout is that you can easily integrate 3D elements into an application almost anywhere. In fact, it is possible for designers to use features such as `Styles` and `ControlTemplates` to replace the default appearance of controls with interactive 3D content. Figure 16.53 shows the result of applying such a style to the Photo Gallery example introduced in Chapter 7, "Structuring and Deploying an Application." Note that the content and background that appear in the cube faces are data-bound to the templated `Button`. You can update the content and background, and the cubes update in real-time! When you click on the `Button`, the cube spins.

LISTING 16.8 The Cube `Button Style`

```
<!-- This style replaces the appearance of all Buttons with 3D cubes.
     Because the Viewport3D has no "natural size", you need to set
     the Width and Height properties on your Buttons if they are not
     stretched to fit their container. -->
<Style TargetType="{x:Type Button}">
  <Setter Property="Template">
  <Setter.Value>
    <ControlTemplate>
    <ControlTemplate.Triggers>
      <!-- When the button is pressed, spin the cube -->
      <Trigger Property="Button.IsPressed" Value="true">
      <Trigger.EnterActions>
        <BeginStoryboard>
          <Storyboard TargetName="RotateY" TargetProperty="Angle">
            <DoubleAnimation Duration="0:0:1" From="0" To="360"
                             DecelerationRatio="1.0"/>
          </Storyboard>
        </BeginStoryboard>
      </Trigger.EnterActions>
      </Trigger>
    </ControlTemplate.Triggers>
      <Viewport3D>
      <Viewport3D.Camera>
        <PerspectiveCamera Position="2.9,2.65,2.9" LookDirection="-1,-1,-1"/>
      </Viewport3D.Camera>
      <Viewport3D.Children>
        <ModelVisual3D x:Name="Light">
        <ModelVisual3D.Content>
          <DirectionalLight Direction="-0.3,-0.4,-0.5"/>
        </ModelVisual3D.Content>
        </ModelVisual3D>
        <ModelVisual3D x:Name="Cube">
        <ModelVisual3D.Transform>
          <RotateTransform3D>
```

LISTING 16.8 Continued

```
        <RotateTransform3D.Rotation>
          <AxisAngleRotation3D x:Name="RotateY" Axis="0,1,0" Angle="0"/>
        </RotateTransform3D.Rotation>
        </RotateTransform3D>
      </ModelVisual3D.Transform>
      <ModelVisual3D.Content>
        <GeometryModel3D>
        <GeometryModel3D.Material>
          <DiffuseMaterial>
          <DiffuseMaterial.Brush>
            <!-- Use a VisualBrush to display the Button's original
                 Background and Content on the faces of the cube. -->
            <VisualBrush ViewportUnits="Absolute" Transform="1,0,0,-1,0,1">
            <VisualBrush.Visual>
              <Border Background="{Binding Path=Background,
                RelativeSource={RelativeSource TemplatedParent}}">
                <Label Content="{Binding Path=Content,
                  RelativeSource={RelativeSource TemplatedParent}}"/>
              </Border>
            </VisualBrush.Visual>
            </VisualBrush>
          </DiffuseMaterial.Brush>
          </DiffuseMaterial>
        </GeometryModel3D.Material>
        <GeometryModel3D.Geometry>
          <MeshGeometry3D
            Positions="1,1,-1 1,-1,-1 -1,-1,-1 -1,1,-1 1,1,1 -1,1,1 -1,-1,1
              1,-1,1 1,1,-1 1,1,1 1,-1,1 1,-1,-1 1,-1,-1 1,-1,1 -1,-1,1 -1,-1,-1
              -1,-1,-1 -1,-1,1 -1,1,1 -1,1,-1 1,1,1 1,1,-1 -1,1,-1 -1,1,1"
            TriangleIndices="0 1 2 0 2 3 4 5 6 4 6 7 8 9 10 8 10 11 12
              13 14 12 14 15 16 17 18 16 18 19 20 21 22 20 22 23"
            TextureCoordinates="0,1 0,0 1,0 1,1 1,1 0,1 0,-0 1,0 1,1
              0,1 0,-0 1,0 1,0 1,1 0,1 0,-0 0,0 1,-0 1,1 0,1 1,-0
              1,1 0,1 0,0"/>
        </GeometryModel3D.Geometry>
        </GeometryModel3D>
      </ModelVisual3D.Content>
      </ModelVisual3D>
    </Viewport3D.Children>
    </Viewport3D>
  </ControlTemplate>
 </Setter.Value>
 </Setter>
</Style>
```

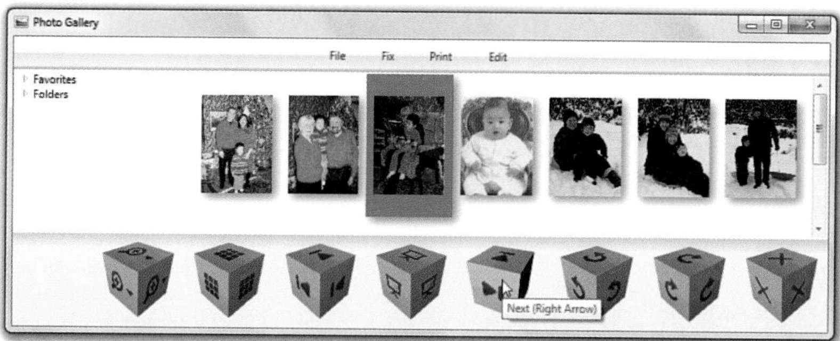

FIGURE 16.53 The cube `Button Style` applied to Photo Gallery.

DIGGING DEEPER

The `Viewport3DVisual`

Under the covers, the `Viewport3D` element uses a `Viewport3DVisual` to bridge the 2D visual tree with the 3D visual tree. The `Viewport3DVisual` is primarily an implementation detail, but if you choose to program at the `Visual` level instead of at the `FrameworkElement` level, `Viewport3DVisual` is the 2D `Visual` you need to connect the `Visual3D` tree. The properties of `Viewport3DVisual` are identical to those of `Viewport3D`, with the addition of the `Viewport` property. `Viewport` is used to set the bounds in which the 3D scene will be displayed because there is no concept of layout at the `Visual` layer.

2D and 3D Coordinate System Transformation

WPF provides a number of services for transforming 3D points into 2D space and vice versa. This can be invaluable when applications require interaction between 2D and 3D content. For example, imagine writing a 3D molecule viewer with 2D text labels for the various atoms comprising the molecule. You'd like the text labels to be drawn as a layer on top of the 3D content, but you want the text to follow the atoms as the model is rotated. With these coordinate space transformation services, you can achieve this. Let's take a look at the 3D transformation APIs provided and how to use them.

`Visual.TransformToAncestor`

`Visual` has a `TransformToAncestor` method that returns a `GeneralTransform2DTo3D`. This is useful when a `Visual` is hosted by a `Viewport2DVisual3D`. The returned object converts the hosted `Visual`'s 2D coordinate space into the 3D coordinate space of the `Visual3D`.

In Listings 16.9 and 16.10, the `Point` (0,0) from the `Viewport2DVisual3D`'s hosted `Button` is mapped into 3D space, and a purple cube is drawn where that `Point3D` lies in 3D space. As the larger cube rotates, the smaller cube follows it because the `GeneralTransform2DTo3D` changes as the larger cube rotates. Figure 16.54 shows the result.

LISTING 16.9 MainWindow.xaml—The Cube of Buttons and the Small Purple Cube

```
<Window x:Class="MainWindow"
        xmlns="http://schemas.microsoft.com/winfx/2006/xaml/presentation"
        xmlns:x="http://schemas.microsoft.com/winfx/2006/xaml">
  <Grid>
    <Viewport3D Panel.ZIndex="0">
    <Viewport3D.Camera>
      <PerspectiveCamera Position="3,3,4" LookDirection="-1,-1,-1"
                         FieldOfView="60" />
    </Viewport3D.Camera>
    <Viewport3D.Children>
      <ModelVisual3D>
      <ModelVisual3D.Content>
        <DirectionalLight Direction="-0.3,-0.4,-0.5" />
      </ModelVisual3D.Content>
      </ModelVisual3D>
      <ModelVisual3D x:Name="Container">
        <Viewport2DVisual3D>
        <Viewport2DVisual3D.Transform>
          <Transform3DGroup>
            <TranslateTransform3D OffsetX="1.5" />
            <RotateTransform3D>
            <RotateTransform3D.Rotation>
              <AxisAngleRotation3D x:Name="rotationY" Axis="0,1,0" Angle="0" />
            </RotateTransform3D.Rotation>
            </RotateTransform3D>
          </Transform3DGroup>
        </Viewport2DVisual3D.Transform>
        <Viewport2DVisual3D.Geometry>
          <MeshGeometry3D Positions="1,1,-1 1,-1,-1 -1,-1,-1 -1,1,-1 1,1,1 -1,1,1
                                     -1,-1,1 1,-1,1 1,1,-1 1,1,1 1,-1,1 1,-1,-1
                                     1,-1,-1 1,-1,1 -1,-1,1 -1,-1,-1 -1,-1,-1
                                     -1,-1,1 -1,1,1 -1,1,-1 1,1,1 1,1,-1 -1,1,-1
                                     -1,1,1"
            TriangleIndices="0 1 2 0 2 3 4 5 6 4 6 7 8 9 10 8 10 11 12 13 14 12
                             14 15 16 17 18 16 18 19 20 21 22 20 22 23"
            TextureCoordinates="0,1 0,0 1,0 1,1 1,1 -0,1 0,-0 1,0 1,1 -0,1 0,-0
                                1,0 1,0 1,1 -0,1 0,-0 -0,0 1,-0 1,1 0,1 1,-0 1,1
                                0,1 -0,0" />
        </Viewport2DVisual3D.Geometry>
        <Viewport2DVisual3D.Material>
          <DiffuseMaterial Viewport2DVisual3D.IsVisualHostMaterial="True" />
        </Viewport2DVisual3D.Material>
          <Button Name="TestButton">
          <Button.RenderTransform>
```

LISTING 16.9 Continued

```
              <ScaleTransform ScaleY="-1" />
            </Button.RenderTransform>
              Hello, 3D
            </Button>
          </Viewport2DVisual3D>
        </ModelVisual3D>
        <ModelUIElement3D>
        <ModelUIElement3D.Transform>
          <Transform3DGroup>
            <ScaleTransform3D ScaleX="0.2" ScaleY="0.2" ScaleZ="0.2" />
            <TranslateTransform3D x:Name="cube_translation" />
          </Transform3DGroup>
        </ModelUIElement3D.Transform>
        <ModelUIElement3D.Model>
          <GeometryModel3D>
          <GeometryModel3D.Material>
            <DiffuseMaterial>
            <DiffuseMaterial.Brush>
              <SolidColorBrush Color="Purple" />
            </DiffuseMaterial.Brush>
            </DiffuseMaterial>
          </GeometryModel3D.Material>
          <GeometryModel3D.Geometry>
            <MeshGeometry3D
              Positions="1,1,-1 1,-1,-1 -1,-1,-1 -1,1,-1 1,1,1 -1,1,1 -1,-1,1
                         1,-1,1 1,1,-1 1,1,1 1,-1,1 1,-1,-1 1,-1,-1 1,-1,1 -1,-1,1
                         -1,-1,-1 -1,-1,-1 -1,-1,1 -1,1,1 -1,1,-1 1,1,1 1,1,-1
                         -1,1,-1 -1,1,1"
              TriangleIndices="0 1 2 0 2 3 4 5 6 4 6 7 8 9 10 8 10 11 12 13 14 12
                               14 15 16 17 18 16 18 19 20 21 22 20 22 23"
              TextureCoordinates="0,1 0,0 1,0 1,1 1,1 -0,1 0,-0 1,0 1,1 -0,1 0,-0
                                  1,0 1,0 1,1 -0,1 0,-0 -0,0 1,-0 1,1 0,1 1,-0 1,1
                                  0,1 -0,0" />
          </GeometryModel3D.Geometry>
          </GeometryModel3D>
        </ModelUIElement3D.Model>
        </ModelUIElement3D>
      </Viewport3D.Children>
      </Viewport3D>
    </Grid>
  <Window.Triggers>
    <EventTrigger RoutedEvent="Window.Loaded">
      <BeginStoryboard>
        <Storyboard>
```

LISTING 16.9 Continued

```
        <DoubleAnimation Storyboard.TargetName="rotationY"
          Storyboard.TargetProperty="Angle"
          From="0" To="360" Duration="0:0:12" RepeatBehavior="Forever" />
      </Storyboard>
    </BeginStoryboard>
  </EventTrigger>
</Window.Triggers>
</Window>
```

LISTING 16.10 MainWindow.xaml.cs—Code-Behind That Keeps the Small Purple Cube in the Correct Location

```
using System;
using System.Windows;
using System.Windows.Media;
using System.Windows.Media.Media3D;

public partial class MainWindow : Window
{
  public MainWindow()
  {
    InitializeComponent();
    CompositionTarget.Rendering += CompositionTarget_Rendering;
  }

  static TimeSpan lastRenderTime = new TimeSpan();

  void CompositionTarget_Rendering(object sender, EventArgs e)
  {
    // Ensure we only do this once per frame
    if (lastRenderTime == ((RenderingEventArgs)e).RenderingTime)
      return;

    lastRenderTime = ((RenderingEventArgs)e).RenderingTime;

    GeneralTransform2DTo3D transform =
      TestButton.TransformToAncestor(Container);
    Point3D point = transform.Transform(new Point(0, 0));

    cube_translation.OffsetX = point.X;
    cube_translation.OffsetY = point.Y;
    cube_translation.OffsetZ = point.Z;
  }
}
```

16

FIGURE 16.54 Mapping (0,0), the `Viewport2DVisual3D`'s origin, into 3D space.

Listing 16.10 uses the `CompositionTarget.Rendering` event to perform the coordinate transformation once per frame. Be careful when using it, as structural changes in the scene can cause the event to be fired more than once within a given frame. This code ensures that the event handler logic runs only once per frame by leveraging the fact that the `EventArgs` instance is actually a `RenderingEventArgs` object that exposes a `RenderingTime` property.

`Visual3D.TransformToAncestor` and `Visual3D.TransformToDescendant`

`Visual3D` contains methods for the opposite scenario of mapping from 3D space into 2D space. The `GeneralTransform3DTo2D` returned by `Visual3D.TransformToAncestor` maps from the `Visual3D`'s 3D coordinate space into some 2D parent's coordinate space. This is especially useful when an application tracks a 3D point on the screen and then draws 2D content whose position must follow that 3D point.

Listings 16.11 and 16.12 use `TransformToAncestor` to make the `TextBlock`s to follow the corners of the rotating cube, as shown in Figure 16.55.

LISTING 16.11 `MainWindow.xaml`—The Cube and `TextBlock`s

```
<Window x:Class="MainWindow"
        xmlns="http://schemas.microsoft.com/winfx/2006/xaml/presentation"
        xmlns:x="http://schemas.microsoft.com/winfx/2006/xaml">
  <Grid Name="myGrid">
    <TextBlock Panel.ZIndex="1" IsHitTestVisible="False">
    <TextBlock.RenderTransform>
```

LISTING 16.11 Continued

```
      <TranslateTransform x:Name="t_000" />
    </TextBlock.RenderTransform>
      (-1,-1,-1)
    </TextBlock>
    <TextBlock Panel.ZIndex="1" IsHitTestVisible="False">
    <TextBlock.RenderTransform>
      <TranslateTransform x:Name="t_001" />
    </TextBlock.RenderTransform>
      (-1,-1,1)
    </TextBlock>
    <TextBlock Panel.ZIndex="1" IsHitTestVisible="False">
    <TextBlock.RenderTransform>
      <TranslateTransform x:Name="t_010" />
    </TextBlock.RenderTransform>
      (-1,1,-1)
    </TextBlock>
    <TextBlock Panel.ZIndex="1" IsHitTestVisible="False">
    <TextBlock.RenderTransform>
      <TranslateTransform x:Name="t_011" />
    </TextBlock.RenderTransform>
      (-1,1,1)
    </TextBlock>
    <TextBlock Panel.ZIndex="1" IsHitTestVisible="False">
    <TextBlock.RenderTransform>
      <TranslateTransform x:Name="t_100" />
    </TextBlock.RenderTransform>
      (1,-1,-1)
    </TextBlock>
    <TextBlock Panel.ZIndex="1" IsHitTestVisible="False">
    <TextBlock.RenderTransform>
      <TranslateTransform x:Name="t_101" />
    </TextBlock.RenderTransform>
      (1,-1,1)
    </TextBlock>
    <TextBlock Panel.ZIndex="1" IsHitTestVisible="False">
    <TextBlock.RenderTransform>
      <TranslateTransform  x:Name="t_110" />
    </TextBlock.RenderTransform>
      (1,1,-1)
    </TextBlock>
    <TextBlock Panel.ZIndex="1" IsHitTestVisible="False">
    <TextBlock.RenderTransform>
      <TranslateTransform  x:Name="t_111" />
```

LISTING 16.11 Continued

```
    </TextBlock.RenderTransform>
      (1,1,1)
    </TextBlock>
    <Viewport3D Panel.ZIndex="0">
    <Viewport3D.Camera>
      <PerspectiveCamera Position="3,3,4" LookDirection="-1,-1,-1"
                         FieldOfView="60"/>
    </Viewport3D.Camera>
    <Viewport3D.Children>
      <ModelVisual3D>
      <ModelVisual3D.Content>
        <DirectionalLight Direction="-0.3,-0.4,-0.5" />
      </ModelVisual3D.Content>
      </ModelVisual3D>
      <ModelUIElement3D x:Name="Cube">
      <ModelUIElement3D.Transform>
        <RotateTransform3D>
        <RotateTransform3D.Rotation>
          <AxisAngleRotation3D x:Name="rotationY" Axis="0,1,0" Angle="0" />
        </RotateTransform3D.Rotation>
        </RotateTransform3D>
      </ModelUIElement3D.Transform>
      <ModelUIElement3D.Model>
        <GeometryModel3D x:Name="OB_Cube">
        <GeometryModel3D.Material>
          <DiffuseMaterial>
            <DiffuseMaterial.Brush>
              <SolidColorBrush Color="Orange" x:Name="CubeBrush" />
            </DiffuseMaterial.Brush>
          </DiffuseMaterial>
        </GeometryModel3D.Material>
        <GeometryModel3D.Geometry>
          <MeshGeometry3D x:Name="ME_Cube2"
            Positions="1,1,-1 1,-1,-1 -1,-1,-1 -1,1,-1 1,1,1 -1,1,1 -1,-1,1
                       1,-1,1 1,1,-1 1,1,1 1,-1,1 1,-1,-1 1,-1,-1 1,-1,1
                       -1,-1,1 -1,-1,-1 -1,-1,-1 -1,-1,1 -1,1,1 -1,1,-1 1,1,1
                       1,1,-1 -1,1,-1 -1,1,1"
            TriangleIndices="0 1 2 0 2 3 4 5 6 4 6 7 8 9 10 8 10 11 12 13 14
                             12 14 15 16 17 18 16 18 19 20 21 22 20 22 23"
            TextureCoordinates="0,1 0,0 1,0 1,1 1,1 -0,1 0,-0 1,0 1,1 -0,1
                                0,-0 1,0 1,0 1,1 -0,1 0,-0 -0,0 1,-0 1,1 0,1
                                1,-0 1,1 0,1 -0,0"/>
        </GeometryModel3D.Geometry>
```

LISTING 16.11 Continued

```
        </GeometryModel3D>
      </ModelUIElement3D.Model>
      </ModelUIElement3D>
    </Viewport3D.Children>
    </Viewport3D>
  </Grid>
<Window.Triggers>
  <EventTrigger RoutedEvent="Window.Loaded">
    <BeginStoryboard>
      <Storyboard>
        <DoubleAnimation Storyboard.TargetName="rotationY"
          Storyboard.TargetProperty="Angle"
          From="0" To="360" Duration="0:0:12" RepeatBehavior="Forever" />
      </Storyboard>
    </BeginStoryboard>
  </EventTrigger>
</Window.Triggers>
</Window>
```


LISTING 16.12 MainWindow.xaml.cs—Code-Behind That Updates the Locations of all TextBlocks

```
using System;
using System.Windows;
using System.Windows.Input;
using System.Windows.Media;
using System.Windows.Media.Media3D;

public partial class MainWindow : Window
{
  public MainWindow()
  {
    InitializeComponent();
    CompositionTarget.Rendering += CompositionTarget_Rendering;
  }

  static TimeSpan lastRenderTime = new TimeSpan();

  void CompositionTarget_Rendering(object sender, EventArgs e)
  {
    // Ensure we only do this once per frame
```

LISTING 16.12 Continued

```
    if (lastRenderTime == ((RenderingEventArgs)e).RenderingTime)
      return;

    lastRenderTime = ((RenderingEventArgs)e).RenderingTime;

    GeneralTransform3DTo2D transform = Cube.TransformToAncestor(myGrid);

    Point p = transform.Transform(new Point3D(-1, -1, -1));
    t_000.X = p.X; t_000.Y = p.Y;

    p = transform.Transform(new Point3D(-1, -1, 1));
    t_001.X = p.X; t_001.Y = p.Y;

    p = transform.Transform(new Point3D(-1, 1, -1));
    t_010.X = p.X; t_010.Y = p.Y;

    p = transform.Transform(new Point3D(-1, 1, 1));
    t_011.X = p.X; t_011.Y = p.Y;

    p = transform.Transform(new Point3D(1, -1, -1));
    t_100.X = p.X; t_100.Y = p.Y;

    p = transform.Transform(new Point3D(1, -1, 1));
    t_101.X = p.X; t_101.Y = p.Y;

    p = transform.Transform(new Point3D(1, 1, -1));
    t_110.X = p.X; t_110.Y = p.Y;

    p = transform.Transform(new Point3D(1, 1, 1));
    t_111.X = p.X; t_111.Y = p.Y;
  }
}
```

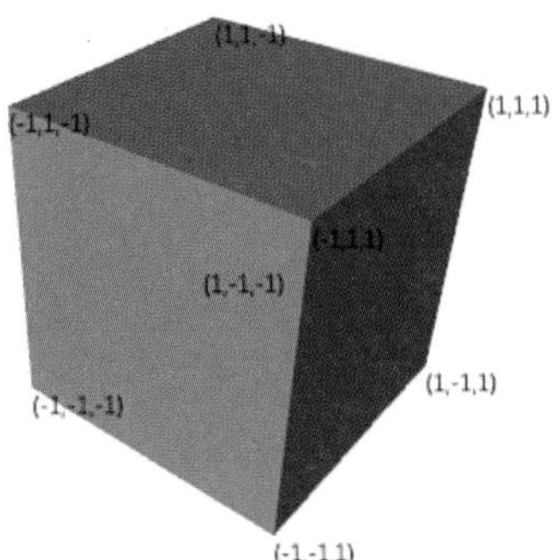

FIGURE 16.55 Mapping the 3D points on the cube's corners into 2D space.

Every frame, the code gets the `GeneralTransform3DTo2D` between the cube and its parent `Grid`. It uses this `GeneralTransform3DTo2D` to transform all eight of the cube's corner positions into screen space. The `TextBlocks` are then transformed in 2D space so that their positions match the transformed corners of the cube. As before, the transformation is done in the `CompositionTarget.Rendering` handler.

The remaining 3D transformation methods on `Visual3D`, `TransformToDescendant`, and another overload of `TransformToAncestor` simply provide `GeneralTransform3Ds` that will allow transformations between different `Visual3Ds` in a 3D object hierarchy.

Summary

You should now understand how the 3D APIs in WPF are a straightforward extension of the 2D APIs you are already familiar with. As shown in Table 16.1 at the beginning of this chapter, most of the 3D types are direct corollaries of the classes discussed in previous chapters. This makes WPF an ideal platform for applications that need to mix 3D graphics with a 2D user interface.

Although the 3D features of WPF might seem basic at a glance, hidden power comes from being a tightly integrated component of the platform. WPF 3D transforms can be data bound. You can display video, `Drawings`, or even 2D `Controls` on the surfaces of a 3D object. Entire 3D scenes can be used as `DataTemplates` and `ControlTemplates`. And all this works when printing, remoting, or running as a partial-trust web application.

This chapter focuses on the 3D-specific APIs, but it tells only part of the story. `D3DImage`, a powerful feature that enables interoperability with `Direct3D`, is covered in Chapter 19, "Interoperability with Non-WPF Technologies." In addition, many of the best 3D features are general features of the platform. As you learn about animation and media in the upcoming chapters, keep in mind that these features can also be applied to 3D objects.

CHAPTER 17
Animation

IN THIS CHAPTER

- Animations in Procedural Code
- Animations in XAML
- Keyframe Animations
- Easing Functions
- Animations and the Visual State Manager

WPF's animation functionality makes it very straightforward to add dynamic effects to applications or components. It's also one of the most obvious features in WPF to abuse! But rather than worry about a future of applications filled with bouncing `Buttons` and spinning `Menus`, think instead of all the ways in which animation can be put to good use. Certainly you've come across an Adobe Flash–enabled website with a slick animation that left a good impression, or watched a baseball game or newscast on TV in which scrolling text or animated transitions enhanced the viewing experience. Subtle animations in user interfaces for iPhone, iPad, Windows phones, Xbox, and Windows 7, to name a few, are used very effectively. Sure, animation might not be appropriate for every piece of software, but many can benefit from its judicious use.

When exposed via design tools such as Microsoft Expression Blend, WPF's animation support provides capabilities much like those of Adobe Flash. But because it's a core part of the WPF platform, with APIs that are fairly simple, you can easily create a wide range of animations without the help of such a tool. Indeed, this chapter demonstrates several different animation techniques with nothing more than short snippets of C# or XAML.

This chapter begins by examining WPF's animation classes and their use from procedural code. After that, we'll look at how to use the same classes from XAML, which involves a few additional concepts. After covering both approaches, the chapter examines more powerful forms of animation that use keyframes and/or easing functions. Finally, we'll take a deeper look at how animations work with the Visual State Manager.

Animations in Procedural Code

When most people think about animation, they think of a cartoon-like mechanism, where movement is simulated by displaying images in rapid succession. In WPF, animation has a more specific definition: varying the value of a property over time. This could be related to motion, such as making an element grow by increasing its `Width`, or it could be something like varying the value of a color.

Such animation can be accomplished without the special support discussed in this chapter, and even without much work—thanks to WPF's retained-mode graphics model. This section begins by examining the options for performing this work manually. It then introduces WPF's many classes that can do almost all the animation work for you.

Performing Animation "By Hand"

The classic way to implement such an animation scheme is to set up a timer and a callback function that is periodically called back based on the frequency of the timer. Inside the callback function, you can manually update the target property (doing a little math to determine the current value based on the elapsed time) until it reaches the final value. At that point, you can stop the timer and/or remove the event handler.

Of course, nothing is stopping you from following this classic approach in WPF. WPF even has its own `DispatcherTimer` class that can be used for implementing such a scheme. You get to choose `DispatcherTimer`'s frequency by setting its `Interval` property, and you can attach an event handler to its `Tick` event.

DIGGING DEEPER

The Difference Between `DispatcherTimer` and Other .NET Timers

The key difference between `DispatcherTimer` and other timers, such as `System.Threading.Timer` or `System.Timers.Timer`, is that handlers for `DispatcherTimer` are invoked on the UI thread. This is important for WPF applications because you can manipulate `UIElements` inside the handler without worrying about threading. If you use one of the other timers, you need to partition your update logic into a different function and use `Dispatcher` to invoke it on the UI thread. Here's an example:

```
void Callback(object sender, EventArgs e)
{
  // Call DoTheRealWork on the UI thread:
  this.Dispatcher.Invoke(DispatcherPriority.Normal,
    new TimerDispatcherDelegate(DoTheRealWork));
}
```

Continued

`Dispatcher.Invoke` performs a synchronous call. You could alternatively call `Dispatcher.BeginInvoke` to perform an asynchronous call. However, when using `DispatcherTimer`, your callback can simply look like the following:

```
void Callback(object sender, EventArgs e)
{
  // Update the property directly in the callback
}
```

By default, `DispatcherTimer` callbacks are handled with the `DispatcherPriority` of `Background`, but you can construct a `DispatcherTimer` with an explicit `DispatcherPriority` if you want the callbacks to be handled differently.

Although this approach may be familiar to Windows programmers, performing animation with a timer is not recommended. The timers are not in sync with the monitor's vertical refresh rate, nor are they in sync with the WPF rendering engine.

Instead of implementing custom timer-based animation, you could perform custom frame-based animation by attaching an event handler to the static `Rendering` event on `System.Windows.Media.CompositionTarget`. Rather than being raised at a customizable interval, this event is raised post-layout and pre-render *once per frame*. (This is like using `enterFrame` when developing Adobe Flash animations, and was used in the two examples at the end of the preceding chapter.)

Using the frame-based `Rendering` event is not only preferred over a timer-based approach, it's even preferred over the animation classes that are the focus of this chapter when dealing with hundreds of objects that require high-fidelity animations. For example, collision detection or other physics-based animations should be done using this approach. Animations that morph a panel's elements from one layout to another are also usually implemented using this approach. The `Rendering` event generally gives the best performance and the most customizations (because you can write arbitrary code in the event handler), although there are tradeoffs. In normal conditions, WPF renders frames only when part of the user interface is invalidated. But as long as any event handler is attached to `Rendering`, WPF renders frames continuously. Therefore, using `Rendering` is best for short-lived animations.

17

Introducing the Animation Classes

Although using the `CompositionTarget.Rendering` event is a reasonable way to implement animations, the designers of WPF wanted animation to be a simpler and more declarative process. So, WPF has many classes in the `System.Windows.Media.Animation` namespace that enable you to describe and apply an animation without doing manual work to perform it. These classes are extremely useful when you know how you want your animation to behave for large amounts of time in advance.

There are two important aspects to these animation classes:

- **They can only vary the value of a *dependency* property.** So, the definition of WPF animation is slightly more constrained than previously stated, unless you use one of the manual approaches with `DispatcherTimer` or the `Rendering` event.
- **They enable animations that are "time resolution independent."** Similar in spirit to the resolution independence of WPF's graphics, animations using the WPF animation classes do not speed up as hardware gets faster; they simply get smoother! WPF can vary the frame rate based on a variety of conditions, and you as the animation developer don't need to care.

`System.Windows.Media.Animation` contains many similar-looking animation classes because distinct data types are animated with a distinct animation class. For example, if you wanted to vary the value of an element's `double` dependency property over time, you could use an instance of `DoubleAnimation`. If you instead wanted to vary the value of an element's `Thickness` dependency property over time, you could use an instance of `ThicknessAnimation`. WPF contains built-in animation classes for 22 different data types, listed in Table 17.1.

TABLE 17.1 Data Types with Built-In Animation Classes

Core .NET Data Types	WPF Data Types
`Boolean`	`Thickness`
`Byte`	`Color`
`Char`	`Size`
`Decimal`	`Rect`
`Int16`	`Point`
`Int32`	`Point3D`
`Int64`	`Vector`
`Single`	`Vector3D`
`Double`	`Rotation3D`
`String`	`Matrix`
`Object`	`Quaternion`

DIGGING DEEPER

Animation Classes and the Lack of Generics

The `System.Windows.Media.Animation` namespace has the following classes:

- 22 *`XXX`*`AnimationBase` classes
- 17 *`XXX`*`Animation` classes
- 22 *`XXX`*`AnimationUsingKeyFrames` classes
- 22 *`XXX`*`KeyFrameCollection` classes

Continued

- 22 *XXX*KeyFrame classes
- 22 Discrete*XXX*KeyFrame classes
- 17 Linear*XXX*KeyFrame classes
- 17 Spline*XXX*KeyFrame classes
- 17 Easing*XXX*KeyFrame classes
- 3 *XXX*AnimationUsingPath classes

(*XXX* represents a data type from Table 17.1.)

The classes within each of these 10 buckets are almost identical to each other, so 10 basic concepts have been exploded into a whopping 181 classes! When people familiar with .NET come across this design, the first reaction is often, "Why didn't the WPF team use generics?" In other words, why isn't there a single `Animation<T>` class that enables `double` to be animated with `Animation<double>`, `Thickness` to be animated with an `Animation<Thickness>`, and so on?

One obvious (but not very satisfactory) reason is the lack of complete support for generics in XAML prior to XAML2009. But even if generics were completely supported, there are aspects of these classes that make them a bad fit for generics. For example, the presence of an `Animation<T>` class implies that you could construct it with any data type, such as `Animation<Window>`. But there is no support for such an animation, nor is there a constraint that can be placed on the generic class that would sufficiently express what it supports.

17

Using an Animation

To understand how the animation classes work, let's look at the `double` data type. Animating a `double` is not only easy to understand, but it's a very common scenario because of the number of useful `double` dependency properties on many elements.

Imagine that we want a `Button`'s `Width` property to grow from `50` to `100`. For demonstration purposes, we can place the `Button` inside a simple `Window` with a `Canvas`:

```
<Window x:Class="Window1" Title="Animation" Width="300" Height="300"
  xmlns="http://schemas.microsoft.com/winfx/2006/xaml/presentation"
  xmlns:x="http://schemas.microsoft.com/winfx/2006/xaml">
  <Canvas>
    <Button x:Name="b">OK</Button>
  </Canvas>
</Window>
```

In the code-behind file, we can use `DoubleAnimation` to very simply express the concept of animating `Width` from `50` to `100`:

```
using System.Windows;
using System.Windows.Controls;
```

```
using System.Windows.Media.Animation;

public partial class Window1 : Window
{
  public Window1()
  {
    InitializeComponent();

    // Define the animation
    DoubleAnimation a = new DoubleAnimation();
    a.From = 50;
    a.To = 100;

    // Start animating
    b.BeginAnimation(Button.WidthProperty, a);
  }
}
```

The instance of `DoubleAnimation` contains the initial and end values for a `double` property—*any* `double` property. The `Button`'s `BeginAnimation` method is then called to associate the animation with its `Width` dependency property *and* to initiate the animation at the point in time. If you were to compile and run this code, you would see the width of the `Button` smoothly grow from `50` to `100` over the course of 1 second.

Animation classes have a number of properties in addition to `From` and `To` that you can use to customize their behavior in interesting ways. We'll be examining these properties throughout this section. Animation classes also have a handful of simple events, such as a `Completed` event that gets raised as soon the target property reaches its final value.

Linear Interpolation

It's important to note that `DoubleAnimation` takes care of smoothly changing the `double` value over time via *linear interpolation*. (Otherwise, the animation would appear to be no different than a simple property set!) In other words, for this 1-second animation, the value of `Width` is `55` when 0.1 seconds have elapsed (5% progress in both the value and time elapsed), `75` when 0.5 seconds have elapsed (50% progress in both the value and time elapsed), and so on. Internally, there is a function being called at regular intervals performing the calculations that you would have to do if performing an animation the "raw" way. This is why most of the data types in Table 17.1 are numeric. (The nonnumeric data types, such as `Boolean` and `String`, are explained further later in this chapter.)

Figuring out how to apply an animation to get the desired results can take a little practice. Here are some examples:

- If you want to make an element fade in, it doesn't make sense to animate its `Visibility` property because there's no middle ground between `Hidden` and `Visible`. Instead, you should animate its `Opacity` property of type `double` from `0` to `1`.

- If you want an element inside a `Grid` to slide across the screen, you *could* animate its `Grid.Column` attached property with an `Int32Animation`, but the transition from column to column would be choppy. Instead, you could give the element a `TranslateTransform` as a `RenderTransform` and then animate its `X` property (of type `double`) with a `DoubleAnimation`.
- Animating the `Width` of a `Grid`'s column (which is useful for the "Creating a Visual Studio–Like Collapsible, Dockable, Resizable Pane" example at the end of Chapter 5, "Layout with Panels") is not straightforward because `ColumnDefinition.Width` is defined as a `GridLength` structure, which has no corresponding animation class built in. Instead, you could animate `ColumnDefinition`'s `MinWidth` and/or `MaxWidth` properties, both of type `double`, or you could set `ColumnDefinition`'s `Width` to `Auto` and then insert an element in that column whose `Width` you animate.

Reusing Animations

The preceding code attached the animation to the `Button` with a `BeginAnimation` call. You can call `BeginAnimation` multiple times to apply exactly the same animation to multiple elements or even multiple properties of the same element. For example, adding the following line of code to the preceding code-behind animates the `Height` of the `Window` in sync with the `Button`'s `Width`:

```
this.BeginAnimation(Window.HeightProperty, a);
```

The result of this addition is shown in Figure 17.1. (Before you sneer at the thought of a `Window` that grows, keep in mind that there could actually be legitimate uses for such a mechanism. For example, you might want to enlarge a dialog when the user expands an inner `Expander`, and a simple animation is more visually pleasing than an abrupt jump to the new size.)

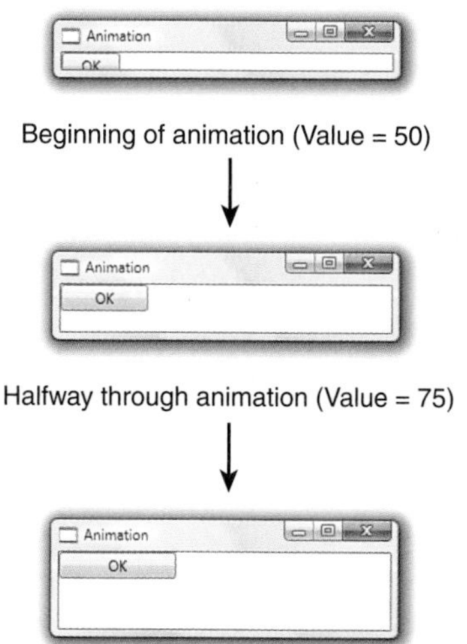

FIGURE 17.1 The same `DoubleAnimation` makes both the `Button`'s `Width` and the `Window`'s `Height` grow from `50` to `100`.

Controlling Duration

The simple `DoubleAnimation` used thus far has the default duration of 1 second, but you can change the duration of an animation by setting its `Duration` property:

```
DoubleAnimation a = new DoubleAnimation();
a.From = 50;
a.To = 100;
a.Duration = new Duration(TimeSpan.Parse("0:0:5"));
```

This makes the animation from Figure 17.1 take 5 seconds rather than one. The typical way to construct a `Duration` instance is with a standard `TimeSpan` object, which is a part of the .NET Framework that predates WPF. By using the static `TimeSpan.Parse` method, you can specify the length of time with a string in the format *`days.hours:minutes:seconds.fraction`*.

WARNING

Be careful when specifying the length of a `Duration` or `TimeSpan` as a string!

`TimeSpan.Parse`, which is also used by a type converter for `Duration` for the benefit of XAML, accepts shortcuts in its syntax so you don't need to specify every piece of *`days.hours:minutes:seconds.fraction`*. However, the behavior is not what you might expect. The string `"2"` means 2 *days*, not 2 seconds! The string `"2.5"` means 2 *days* and 5 *hours*! And the string `"0:2"` means 2 *minutes*. Given that most animations are no more than a few seconds long, the typical syntax used is *`hours:minutes:seconds`* or *`hours:minutes:seconds.fraction`*. So, 2 seconds can be expressed as `"0:0:2"`, and half a second can be expressed as `"0:0:0.5"` or `"0:0:.5"`.

DIGGING DEEPER

The Difference Between `Duration` and `TimeSpan`

The reason WPF defines a `Duration` type rather than just using `TimeSpan` is that `Duration` has two special values that can't be expressed by `TimeSpan`: `Duration.Automatic` and `Duration.Forever`. Both of these values are designed for more complex classes, such as `Storyboard`, described later in this chapter.

`Automatic` is the default value for every animation class's `Duration` property, which is equivalent to a 1-second `TimeSpan`. `Forever` is nonsensical for a simple animation such as `DoubleAnimation` because such a `Duration` would make it stay at its initial value indefinitely. WPF has no way to interpolate values between now and the end of time!

Flexibility with `From` and `To`

Right before the animation used in Figure 17.1 changes the `Button`'s `Width` and the `Window`'s `Height` from `50` to `100`, these properties must jump from their natural values to `50`. This isn't noticeable for animations that begin as soon as the `Window` is shown. But if you were to call `BeginAnimation` in response to an event, the "jump" effect would be jarring.

You could fix this by setting To to the current Width/Height instead of 50, but doing so would require splitting the animation into two distinct objects—one that animates from the Button's ActualWidth to 100 and another that animates from the Window's ActualHeight to 100. Fortunately, there's an alternative. Specifying the From field of the animation can be optional. If you omit it, the animation begins with the current value of the target property, whatever that might be. For example, you might try to update the previous animation as follows:

```
DoubleAnimation a = new DoubleAnimation();
// Comment out: a.From = 50;
a.To = 100;
a.Duration = new Duration(TimeSpan.Parse("0:0:5"));
```

You might expect this to animate the Button's Width from its default value (just wide enough to fit the "OK" content, with a little padding) to 100 over the course of 5 seconds. Instead, this produces an AnimationException that provides the following explanation in its inner exception:

```
'System.Windows.Media.Animation.DoubleAnimation' cannot use default origin value
of 'NaN'.
```

Because Width is unset, it has a value of NaN. And the animation can't interpolate any values between NaN and 100! Furthermore, applying the animation to ActualWidth (which is set to the true width rather than NaN) instead of Width isn't an option because it's read-only and it's not a dependency property. Instead, you must explicitly set the Width of the target Button somewhere for the preceding animation to work. Here's an example:

```
<!-- Now the animation can grow the Button without a From value: -->
<Button x:Name="b" Width="20">OK</Button>
```

The Window from Figure 17.1 works with the From-less animation as is because its Height is already set to 300. But note that the same animation now grows the Button's Width from 20 to 100 yet *shrinks* the Window's Height from 300 to 100! Similarly, if you set the Button's Width to a value larger than 100, the animation would shrink its Width to 100.

TIP

Omitting an explicit From setting is important for getting smooth animations, especially when an animation is initiated in response to a repeatable user action. For example, if the animation to grow a Button's Width from 50 to 100 is started whenever the Button is clicked, rapid clicks would make the Width jump back to 50 each time. By omitting From, however, subsequent clicks make the animation continue from its current animated value, keeping the visual smoothness of the effect. Similarly, if you have an element grow on MouseEnter and shrink on MouseLeave, omitting From on both animations prevents the size of the element from jumping if the mouse pointer leaves the element before it's done growing or if it reenters before it's done shrinking.

In fact, specifying the `To` field can also be optional! If the following animation is applied to the preceding `Button`, its `Width` changes from `50` to `20` (its explicitly marked `Width`) over the course of 5 seconds:

```
DoubleAnimation a = new DoubleAnimation();
a.From = 50;
// Comment out: a.To = 100;
a.Duration = new Duration(TimeSpan.Parse("0:0:5"));
```

Each animation class also has a `By` field that can be set instead of the `To` field. The following animation means "animate the value *by* 100 (to 150)" instead of "animate the value *to* 100":

```
DoubleAnimation a = new DoubleAnimation();
a.From = 50;
a.By = 100; // Equivalent to a.To = 50 + 100;
```

Using `By` without `From` is a flexible way to express "animate the value from its current value to 100 units larger":

```
DoubleAnimation a = new DoubleAnimation();
a.By = 100; // Equivalent to a.To = currentValue + 100;
```

Negative values are supported for shrinking the current value:

```
DoubleAnimation a = new DoubleAnimation();
a.By = -100; // Equivalent to a.To = currentValue - 100;
```

Simple Animation Tweaks

You've seen the core properties of animation classes: `From`, `To`, `Duration`, and `By`. But there are a lot more properties that can alter an animation's behavior in more interesting ways.

As with the `By` property, some of these properties might look like silly tricks that could easily be accomplished manually with a little bit of code. That is true, but the main point of all these properties is to enable a lot of these easy-to-code tweaks purely from XAML.

`BeginTime`

If you don't want an animation to begin immediately when you call `BeginAnimation`, you can insert a delay by setting `BeginTime` to an instance of a `TimeSpan`:

```
DoubleAnimation a = new DoubleAnimation();
// Delay the animation by 5 seconds:
a.BeginTime = TimeSpan.Parse("0:0:5");
a.From = 50;
a.To = 100;
a.Duration = new Duration(TimeSpan.Parse("0:0:5"));
```

Besides being potentially useful in isolation, `BeginTime` can be useful for specifying a sequence of animations that start one after the other. You can even set `BeginTime` to a negative value:

```
DoubleAnimation a = new DoubleAnimation();
// Start the animation half-way through:
a.BeginTime = TimeSpan.Parse("-0:0:2.5");
a.From = 50;
a.To = 100;
a.Duration = new Duration(TimeSpan.Parse("0:0:5"));
```

This starts the animation immediately, but at 2.5 seconds into the timeline (as if the animation really started 2.5 seconds previously). Therefore, the preceding animation is equivalent to one with `From` set to `75`, `To` set to `100`, and `Duration` set to 2.5 seconds.

Note that `BeginTime` is of type `Nullable<TimeSpan>` rather than `Duration` because the extra expressiveness of `Duration` is not needed. (It would be nonsensical to set a `BeginTime` of `Forever`!)

> **TIP**
>
> The code in this section uses `TimeSpan.Parse` because it supports the same syntax used by `TimeSpan`'s type converter (and therefore the same syntax used in XAML). Procedural code can benefit by using other `TimeSpan` methods, however, such as its static `FromSeconds` or `FromMilliseconds` methods.

SpeedRatio

The `SpeedRatio` property is a multiplier applied to `Duration`. It's set to `1` by default, but you can set it to any `double` value greater than `0`:

```
DoubleAnimation a = new DoubleAnimation();
a.BeginTime = TimeSpan.Parse("0:0:5");
// Make the animation twice as fast:
a.SpeedRatio = 2;
a.From = 50;
a.To = 100;
a.Duration = new Duration(TimeSpan.Parse("0:0:5"));
```

A value less than `1` slows down the animation, and a value greater than `1` speeds it up. `SpeedRatio` does not affect `BeginTime`; the preceding animation still has a 5-second delay, but the transition from `50` to `100` takes only 2.5 seconds rather than 5.

AutoReverse

If AutoReverse is set to true, the animation "plays backward" as soon as it completes. The reversal takes the same amount of time as the forward progress. For example, the following animation makes the value go from 50 to 100 in the first 5 seconds, then from 100 back to 50 over the course of 5 more seconds:

```
DoubleAnimation a = new DoubleAnimation();
a.AutoReverse = true;
a.From = 50;
a.To = 100;
a.Duration = new Duration(TimeSpan.Parse("0:0:5"));
```

SpeedRatio affects the speed of *both* the forward animation and backward animation. Therefore, giving the preceding animation a SpeedRatio of 2 would make the entire animation run for 5 seconds and giving it a SpeedRatio of 0.5 would make it run for 20 seconds. Note that any delay specified via BeginTime does *not* delay the reversal; it always happens immediately after the normal part of the animation completes.

RepeatBehavior

By setting RepeatBehavior, you can accomplish one of three different behaviors:

- Making the animation repeat itself a certain number of times, regardless of its duration
- Making the animation repeat itself until a certain amount of time has elapsed
- Cutting off the animation early

To repeat an animation a certain number of times, you can set RepeatBehavior to an instance of a RepeatBehavior class constructed with a double value:

```
DoubleAnimation a = new DoubleAnimation();
// Perform the animation twice in a row:
a.RepeatBehavior = new RepeatBehavior(2);
a.AutoReverse = true;
a.From = 50;
a.To = 100;
a.Duration = new Duration(TimeSpan.Parse("0:0:5"));
```

If AutoReverse is true, the reversal is repeated as well. So, the preceding animation goes from 50 to 100 to 50 to 100 to 50 over the course of 20 seconds. If BeginTime is set to introduce a delay, that delay is *not* repeated. Because RepeatBehavior can be initialized with a double, you can even repeat by a fractional amount.

To repeat the animation until a certain amount of time has elapsed, you can construct RepeatBehavior with a TimeSpan instead of a double. The following animation is equivalent to the preceding one:

```
DoubleAnimation a = new DoubleAnimation();
// Perform the animation twice in a row:
a.RepeatBehavior = new RepeatBehavior(TimeSpan.Parse("0:0:20"));
a.AutoReverse = true;
a.From = 50;
a.To = 100;
a.Duration = new Duration(TimeSpan.Parse("0:0:5"));
```

Twenty seconds is needed to make the animation complete two full cycles because `AutoReverse` is set to `true`. Note that the `TimeSpan`-based `RepeatBehavior` is not scaled by `SpeedRatio`; if you set `SpeedRatio` to `2` in the preceding animation, it performs the full cycle four times rather than two.

TIP

You can make an animation repeat indefinitely by setting `RepeatBehavior` to the static `RepeatBehavior.Forever` field:

```
a.RepeatBehavior = RepeatBehavior.Forever;
```

To use `RepeatBehavior` as a way to cut off an animation early, you simply construct it with a `TimeSpan` value shorter than the natural duration. The following animation makes the value go from `50` to `75` over the course of 2.5 seconds:

```
DoubleAnimation a = new DoubleAnimation();
// Stop the animation halfway through:
a.RepeatBehavior = new RepeatBehavior(TimeSpan.Parse("0:0:2.5"));
a.From = 50;
a.To = 100;
a.Duration = new Duration(TimeSpan.Parse("0:0:5"));
```


DIGGING DEEPER

The Total Timeline Length of an Animation

With all the different adjustments that can be made to an animation by using properties such as `BeginTime`, `SpeedRatio`, `AutoReverse`, and `RepeatBehavior`, it can be hard to keep track of how long it will take an animation to finish after it is initiated. Its `Duration` value certainly isn't adequate for describing the true length of time! Instead, the following formula describes an animation's true duration:

$$\text{Total Timeline Length} = \texttt{BeginTime} + \left(\frac{\texttt{Duration * (AutoReverse ? 2 : 1)}}{\texttt{SpeedRatio}} \texttt{ * RepeatBehavior}\right)$$

This applies if `RepeatBehavior` is specified as a `double` value (or left as its default value of 1). If `RepeatBehavior` is specified as a `TimeSpan`, the total timeline length is simply the value of `RepeatBehavior` plus the value of `BeginTime`.

AccelerationRatio, DecelerationRatio, and EasingFunction

By default, animations update the target value in a linear fashion. When an animation is 25% done, the value is 25% of the way toward the final value, and so on. By changing the values of `AccelerationRatio` and `DecelerationRatio`, however, you can easily make the interpolation nonlinear. This has been a popular technique for causing elements to "spring" to the final value, making the animation more lifelike.

Both properties can be set to a `double` value from `0` to `1` (with `0` being their default value). The `AccelerationRatio` value represents the percentage of time that the target value should accelerate from being stationary. Similarly, the `DecelerationRatio` value represents the percentage of time that the target value should decelerate to being stationary. Therefore, the sum of both properties must be less than or equal to one (100%).

Figure 17.2 illustrates what various values of `AccelerationRatio` and `DecelerationRatio` mean in practice.

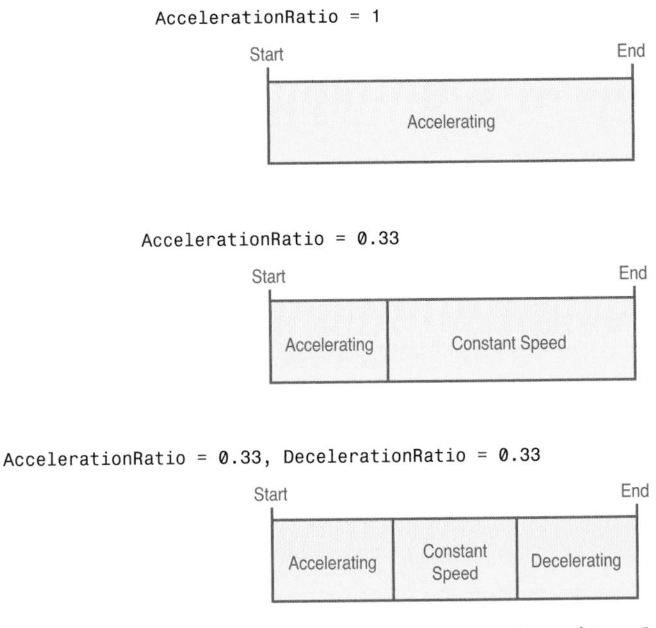

FIGURE 17.2 The effects of `AccelerationRatio` and `DecelerationRatio` as the value changes from start to end.

Starting with WPF 4, animations also have an `EasingFunction` property that can be set to any object implementing the `IEasingFunction` interface. Such objects can control the rate of acceleration and deceleration in arbitrarily complex ways. WPF ships with 11 objects that implement `IEasingFunction`, and writing your own is easy (if you know how to do the math that gives you the desired effect). See the "Easing Functions" section, later in this chapter, for more information.

`IsAdditive` and `IsCumulative`

You can set `IsAdditive` to `true` to implicitly add the target property's current value (post-animation) to the animation's `From` and `To` properties. This doesn't affect repeating an animation with `RepeatBehavior` but rather applies to manually repeating an animation at some later point in time. In essence, this makes an animation operate on a dependency property's post-animation value rather than continue to operate on its pre-animation value.

`IsCumulative` is similar to `IsAdditive`, except that it works with `RepeatBehavior` (and *only* works with `RepeatBehavior`). For example, if you use `RepeatBehavior` to repeat an animation from `50` to `100` three times, the default behavior is to see the value go from `50` to `100`, jump back to `50` then go to `100`, and then jump back to `50` one last time before ending at `100`. With `IsCumulative` set to `true`, the animation instead smoothly changes the value from `50` to `200` over the same amount of time. If you take that same animation and set `AutoReverse` to `true`, you'll see the value go from `50` to `100` to `50`, then jump to `100` and go from `100` to `150` to `100`, then jump to `150` and go from `150` to `200` to `150`.

`FillBehavior`

By default, when an animation completes, the target property remains at the final animated value unless some other mechanism later changes the value. This is typically the desired behavior, but if you want the property to jump back to its pre-animated value after the animation completes, you can set `FillBehavior` to `Stop` (rather than its default value of `HoldEnd`).

Animations in XAML

17

Given that animation classes consist of a bunch of useful properties, it's easy to imagine defining one in XAML. Here's an example:

```
<DoubleAnimation From="50" To="100" Duration="0:0:5" AutoReverse="True"/>
```

But where do you place such an object? One option is to define it as a resource, so that you can retrieve it from procedural code and call `BeginAnimation` at the right time. You could even adjust properties on the animation to get different effects as conditions in the application change.

But, unsurprisingly, WPF supports initiating animations purely in XAML. The key to this support lies in the Visual State Manager as well as triggers, with their ability to contain more than just `Setters` but also *actions*.

All three types of triggers can contain actions, but this chapter focuses on event triggers because actions are the *only* things they can contain. Visual State Manager is covered at the end of the chapter.

`EventTriggers` Containing `Storyboards`

As mentioned in Chapter 3, "WPF Fundamentals," an event trigger (represented by the `EventTrigger` class) is activated when a routed event is raised. The event is specified by the trigger's RoutedEvent property, and it can contain one or more actions (objects deriving from the abstract TriggerAction class) in its Actions collection. Animation classes such as DoubleAnimation are not actions themselves, so you can't add them directly to an EventTrigger's Actions collection. Instead, animations are placed inside an object known as a Storyboard, which is wrapped in an action called BeginStoryboard.

Therefore, placing the preceding DoubleAnimation inside an event trigger that is activated when a Button is clicked can look as follows:

```
<Button>
  OK
<Button.Triggers>
  <EventTrigger RoutedEvent="Button.Click">
  <EventTrigger.Actions>
    <BeginStoryboard>
      <Storyboard TargetProperty="Width">
        <DoubleAnimation From="50" To="100"
          Duration="0:0:5" AutoReverse="True"/>
      </Storyboard>
    </BeginStoryboard>
  </EventTrigger.Actions>
  </EventTrigger>
</Button.Triggers>
</Button>
```

These two extra objects fill the two roles that BeginAnimation plays in procedural code: Storyboard specifies the dependency property that the animation operates on with TargetProperty, and BeginStoryboard specifies when the animation begins by attaching the Storyboard to the trigger.

> **TIP**
>
> An animation can't be initiated in XAML unless it is placed inside a Storyboard.

The BeginStoryboard object might feel superfluous, but WPF ships with other TriggerAction-derived classes. One action is for playing sounds (covered in the next chapter), and several other actions work in concert with BeginStoryboard to declaratively pause a storyboard, seek it, stop it, and so on. (These are called PauseStoryboard, SeekStoryboard, and so on.)

Specifying the Target Property

In the preceding XAML, Storyboard's TargetProperty property is set to the name of a property (Width) directly on the target object. But TargetProperty's type is PropertyPath, which supports more complicated expressions (as seen in previous chapters), such as a property with a chain of subproperties.

The following Button has a LinearGradientBrush with three GradientStops as the Background. It uses a ColorAnimation to make the middle Color repeatedly animate from black to white and back. (The idea of animating a Color might sound strange, but internally it has floating-point values representing the ScA, ScR, ScB, and ScG components, so ColorAnimation can interpolate those values much like DoubleAnimation does for its single value.) To animate the middle Color of the LinearGradientBrush, the Storyboard must have a complex TargetProperty expression:

```
<Button Padding="30">
  OK
<Button.Background>
  <LinearGradientBrush>
    <GradientStop Color="Blue" Offset="0"/>
    <GradientStop Color="Black" Offset="0.5"/>
    <GradientStop Color="Blue" Offset="1"/>
  </LinearGradientBrush>
</Button.Background>
<Button.Triggers>
  <EventTrigger RoutedEvent="Button.Loaded">
  <EventTrigger.Actions>
    <BeginStoryboard>
      <Storyboard TargetProperty="Background.GradientStops[1].Color">
        <ColorAnimation From="Black" To="White" Duration="0:0:2"
          AutoReverse="True" RepeatBehavior="Forever"/>
      </Storyboard>
    </BeginStoryboard>
  </EventTrigger.Actions>
  </EventTrigger>
</Button.Triggers>
</Button>
```


The syntax for TargetProperty mimics what you would have to type to access the property in C#, although without casting. This Storyboard assumes that the Button's Background is set to some object with a GradientStops property that can be indexed, assumes that it has at least two items, and assumes that the second item has a Color property of type Color. If any of these assumptions is incorrect, the animation fails. Of course, in this case these are all correct assumptions, so the Button successfully animates, as shown in Figure 17.3.

FIGURE 17.3 Animating the middle Color in a LinearGradientBrush.

Similarly, you could attach a `DoubleAnimation` to a `TargetProperty` of `Background.GradientStops[1].Offset` and give the `Brush` an animated gleam by making the highlight move from 0 to 1. If you want to animate *both* `Color` and `Offset` in response to the same `Loaded` event, you can add two `BeginStoryboard` actions to the trigger as follows:

```
<EventTrigger RoutedEvent="Button.Loaded">
<EventTrigger.Actions>
  <BeginStoryboard>
    <Storyboard TargetProperty="Background.GradientStops[1].Color">
      <ColorAnimation From="Black" To="White" Duration="0:0:2"
        AutoReverse="True" RepeatBehavior="Forever"/>
    </Storyboard>
  </BeginStoryboard>
  <BeginStoryboard>
    <Storyboard TargetProperty="Background.GradientStops[1].Offset">
      <DoubleAnimation From="0" To="1" Duration="0:0:2"
        AutoReverse="True" RepeatBehavior="Forever"/>
    </Storyboard>
  </BeginStoryboard>
</EventTrigger.Actions>
</EventTrigger>
```

Fortunately, WPF provides a mechanism for animating different properties within the same `Storyboard`. First of all, a `Storyboard` can contain multiple animations. `Storyboard`'s content property is `Children`, a collection of `Timeline` objects (a base class of all animation classes). Second, the `TargetProperty` property is not only a normal dependency property but also an attached property that can be applied to `Storyboard`'s children! Therefore, the previous XAML could be rewritten as follows:

```
<EventTrigger RoutedEvent="Button.Loaded">
<EventTrigger.Actions>
  <BeginStoryboard>
    <Storyboard>
      <ColorAnimation From="Black" To="White" Duration="0:0:2"
        Storyboard.TargetProperty="Background.GradientStops[1].Color"
        AutoReverse="True" RepeatBehavior="Forever"/>
      <DoubleAnimation From="0" To="1" Duration="0:0:2"
        Storyboard.TargetProperty="Background.GradientStops[1].Offset"
        AutoReverse="True" RepeatBehavior="Forever"/>
    </Storyboard>
  </BeginStoryboard>
</EventTrigger.Actions>
</EventTrigger>
```

This single `Storyboard` contains two animations, with each one targeting a different property on the target object. Both animations start simultaneously, but if you want a storyboard to contain animations that begin at different times, you can simply give each animation a different `BeginTime` value.

Specifying the Target Object

In the `Storyboards` shown so far, the target object containing the target property has been implicit. By default, it's the object containing the triggers or, in the case of a `Style`, the templated parent. But you can specify a different target object by using `Storyboard`'s `TargetName` property. And just like `TargetProperty`, `TargetName` can be applied directly to a `Storyboard` or to individual children as an attached property.

Here's a fun example using `TargetName` that morphs one picture to another by animating the opacity of the second picture that sits on top of the first:

```
<Grid xmlns="http://schemas.microsoft.com/winfx/2006/xaml/presentation">
<Grid.Triggers>
  <EventTrigger RoutedEvent="Grid.Loaded">
    <BeginStoryboard>
      <Storyboard TargetName="jim2" TargetProperty="Opacity">
        <DoubleAnimation From="1" To="0" Duration="0:0:4"
          AutoReverse="True" RepeatBehavior="Forever"/>
      </Storyboard>
    </BeginStoryboard>
  </EventTrigger>
</Grid.Triggers>
  <Image Name="jim1" Source="jim1.gif"/>
  <Image Name="jim2" Source="jim2.gif"/>
</Grid>
```


Jim, the subject of these photos, shaved his impressive beard and got a long-overdue haircut, but he took before and after photos that are eerily similar. The result of this animation is shown in Figure 17.4.

FIGURE 17.4 Animating an `Image`'s `Opacity` to morph between two similar photos.

In this example, the use of `TargetName` is a little contrived because the event trigger could have been placed directly on `jim2` rather than the parent `Grid`. But in larger examples (for example, a slide show of `Images`), it can be desirable to accumulate animations in a single location with a single event trigger, perhaps even with a single `Storyboard`, by using `TargetName` as an attached property on each animation.

EventTriggers Inside a Style

Although each XAML snippet in this section adds an event trigger directly to elements, it's more common to see event triggers used inside a `Style`. Listing 17.1 applies a `Style` with built-in animations to eight `Buttons` in a `StackPanel`. The animations make each `Button` grow to twice their size on `MouseEnter` and shrink back to normal size on `MouseLeave`, resulting in a simplified version of a "fisheye" effect. Figure 17.5 shows the result.

LISTING 17.1 Styling `Buttons` with Built-In Animations

```
<Window xmlns="http://schemas.microsoft.com/winfx/2006/xaml/presentation"
  xmlns:x="http://schemas.microsoft.com/winfx/2006/xaml"
  Title="Animation">
<Window.Resources>
  <Style TargetType="{x:Type Button}">
    <Setter Property="VerticalAlignment" Value="Bottom"/>
    <Setter Property="LayoutTransform">
    <Setter.Value>
      <ScaleTransform/>
    </Setter.Value>
    </Setter>
  <Style.Triggers>
    <EventTrigger RoutedEvent="Button.MouseEnter">
    <EventTrigger.Actions>
      <BeginStoryboard>
        <Storyboard>
          <DoubleAnimation Storyboard.TargetProperty="LayoutTransform.ScaleX"
            To="2" Duration="0:0:0.25"/>
          <DoubleAnimation Storyboard.TargetProperty="LayoutTransform.ScaleY"
            To="2" Duration="0:0:0.25"/>
        </Storyboard>
      </BeginStoryboard>
    </EventTrigger.Actions>
    </EventTrigger>
    <EventTrigger RoutedEvent="Button.MouseLeave">
    <EventTrigger.Actions>
      <BeginStoryboard>
        <Storyboard>
          <DoubleAnimation Storyboard.TargetProperty="LayoutTransform.ScaleX"
            To="1" Duration="0:0:0.25"/>
```

LISTING 17.1 Continued

```
        <DoubleAnimation Storyboard.TargetProperty="LayoutTransform.ScaleY"
          To="1" Duration="0:0:0.25"/>
      </Storyboard>
    </BeginStoryboard>
  </EventTrigger.Actions>
  </EventTrigger>
</Style.Triggers>
</Style>
</Window.Resources>
  <StackPanel Orientation="Horizontal">
    <Button>1</Button>
    <Button>2</Button>
    <Button>3</Button>
    <Button>4</Button>
    <Button>5</Button>
    <Button>6</Button>
    <Button>7</Button>
    <Button>8</Button>
  </StackPanel>
</Window>
```

FIGURE 17.5 Each Button is restyled with grow and shrink animations.

This listing leverages TargetProperty as an attached property to animate both ScaleX and ScaleY in the same Storyboard. Both animations assume that LayoutTransform is set to an instance of a ScaleTransform. If LayoutTransform were instead set to a TransformGroup with a ScaleTransform as its first child, these animations could use the expressions LayoutTransform.Children[0].ScaleX and LayoutTransform.Children[0].ScaleY to access the desired properties.

TIP

The best way to animate the size and location of an element is to attach a ScaleTransform and/or TranslateTransform and animate its properties. Animating ScaleTransform's ScaleX and ScaleY is generally more useful than animating Width and Height because it enables you to change the element size by a percentage rather than a fixed number of units. And animating TranslateTransform is better than animating something like Canvas.Left and Canvas.Top because it works regardless of what Panel contains the element.

To animate each `Button` via a `ScaleTransform` without requiring each `Button` to explicitly have `ScaleTransform`, Listing 17.1 sets `LayoutTransform` to an instance of `ScaleTransform` inside the `Style`. (Of course, this scheme breaks down if an individual `Button` has its `LayoutTransform` explicitly set.) `From` is omitted on all animations to keep the effect smooth. `Duration` is set with a simple string, thanks to a type converter that accepts the `TimeSpan.Parse` format (or `"Automatic"` or `"Forever"`).

TIP

Like `Duration`, `RepeatBehavior` has a type converter that makes it easy to use in XAML. A `TimeSpan`-formatted string can be used to set a fixed time, `"Forever"` can be used to indicate `RepeatBehavior.Forever`, and a number followed by `"x"` (for example, `"2x"` or `"3x"`) is treated as a multiplier.

DIGGING DEEPER

Starting Animations from Property Triggers

You can replace the `Style.Triggers` collection from Listing 17.1 with the following equivalent one that uses a single property trigger on `IsMouseOver`:

```
<Style.Triggers>
  <Trigger Property="IsMouseOver" Value="True">
  <Trigger.EnterActions>
    <BeginStoryboard>
      <Storyboard>
        <DoubleAnimation Storyboard.TargetProperty="LayoutTransform.ScaleX"
          To="2" Duration="0:0:0.25"/>
        <DoubleAnimation Storyboard.TargetProperty="LayoutTransform.ScaleY"
          To="2" Duration="0:0:0.25"/>
      </Storyboard>
    </BeginStoryboard>
  </Trigger.EnterActions>
  <Trigger.ExitActions>
    <BeginStoryboard>
      <Storyboard>
        <DoubleAnimation Storyboard.TargetProperty="LayoutTransform.ScaleX"
          To="1" Duration="0:0:0.25"/>
        <DoubleAnimation Storyboard.TargetProperty="LayoutTransform.ScaleY"
          To="1" Duration="0:0:0.25"/>
      </Storyboard>
    </BeginStoryboard>
  </Trigger.ExitActions>
  </Trigger>
</Style.Triggers>
```

Continued

Instead of a simple `Actions` collection, a property trigger has two collections: `EnterActions` and `ExitActions`. Actions inside `EnterActions` are activated when the trigger itself is activated (which is when any `Setters` would be applied). Actions inside `ExitActions` are activated when the trigger is deactivated (which is when any `Setters` would be undone). In this example, because the effect can be accomplished with either event triggers or a property trigger, the choice is one of personal preference.

Using `Storyboard` as a `Timeline`

A `Storyboard` is more than just a simple container that associates one or more animations with one or more target objects and their properties. `Storyboard` derives from `Timeline`, a base class shared with all the animation classes (`DoubleAnimation`, `ColorAnimation`, and so on). This means that `Storyboard` has many of the same properties and events discussed earlier in the chapter: `Duration`, `BeginTime`, `SpeedRatio`, `AutoReverse`, `RepeatBehavior`, `AccelerationRatio`, `DecelerationRatio`, `FillBehavior`, and so on.

Listing 17.2 contains a `Storyboard` that fades one `TextBlock` in and out at a time, for an effect somewhat like that of a movie trailer. The `Storyboard` itself is marked with a `RepeatBehavior` to make the entire sequence of animation repeat indefinitely. Figure 17.6 shows how this listing is rendered at three different spots of the sequence.

LISTING 17.2 A Storyboard Containing Several Animations

```
<Grid xmlns="http://schemas.microsoft.com/winfx/2006/xaml/presentation"
  Background="Black" TextBlock.Foreground="White" TextBlock.FontSize="30">
<Grid.Triggers>
  <EventTrigger RoutedEvent="Grid.Loaded">
    <BeginStoryboard>
      <Storyboard TargetProperty="Opacity" RepeatBehavior="Forever">
        <DoubleAnimation Storyboard.TargetName="title1" BeginTime="0:0:2"
          From="0" To="1" Duration="0:0:2" AutoReverse="True"/>
        <DoubleAnimation Storyboard.TargetName="title2" BeginTime="0:0:6"
          From="0" To="1" Duration="0:0:2" AutoReverse="True"/>
        <DoubleAnimation Storyboard.TargetName="title3" BeginTime="0:0:10"
          From="0" To="1" Duration="0:0:2" AutoReverse="True"/>
        <DoubleAnimation Storyboard.TargetName="title4" BeginTime="0:0:14"
          From="0" To="1" Duration="0:0:2" AutoReverse="True"/>
        <DoubleAnimation Storyboard.TargetName="title5" BeginTime="0:0:18"
          From="0" To="1" Duration="0:0:2" AutoReverse="True"/>
      </Storyboard>
    </BeginStoryboard>
  </EventTrigger>
</Grid.Triggers>
  <TextBlock HorizontalAlignment="Center" VerticalAlignment="Center" Opacity="0"
    Name="title1">In a world</TextBlock>
```

LISTING 17.2 Continued

```
  <TextBlock HorizontalAlignment="Center" VerticalAlignment="Center" Opacity="0"
    Name="title2">where user interfaces need to be created</TextBlock>
  <TextBlock HorizontalAlignment="Center" VerticalAlignment="Center" Opacity="0"
    Name="title3">one book</TextBlock>
  <TextBlock HorizontalAlignment="Center" VerticalAlignment="Center" Opacity="0"
    Name="title4">will explain it all...</TextBlock>
  <TextBlock HorizontalAlignment="Center" VerticalAlignment="Center" Opacity="0"
    Name="title5">WPF 4 Unleashed</TextBlock>
</Grid>
```

FIGURE 17.6 Snapshots of the movie-trailer-like title sequence.

Setting the `Timeline`-inherited properties on `Storyboard` affects the entire set of child animations, although in a slightly different way than setting the same property individually on all children. For example, in Listing 17.2, setting `RepeatBehavior="Forever"` on every child animation rather than on the `Storyboard` itself would wreak havoc. The first title would fade in and out as expected, but then at 6 seconds *both* `title1` and `title2` would fade in and out together. At 10 seconds `title1`, `title2`, and `title3` would fade in and out simultaneously. And so on.

Similarly, setting `SpeedRatio="2"` on each `DoubleAnimation` would make each fade take 1 second rather than 2, but the final animation would still start 18 seconds after the animation starts. On the other hand, setting `SpeedRatio="2"` on the `Storyboard` would speed up the entire animation, including each `BeginTime`, by a factor of two. Therefore, the final animation would start 9 seconds after the animation starts. Setting `AccelerationRatio="1"` on the `Storyboard` would make each animation (and the time between them) faster than the previous one. Setting `Duration` to a time shorter than the natural duration can cut off the entire sequence of animations early.

Keyframe Animations

The normal animation classes only support linear interpolation from one value to another (or limited forms of nonlinear interpolation, thanks to `AccelerationRatio` and `DecelerationRatio`) unless you use an easing function. If you want to specify a custom and more complicated animation declaratively, you can specify *keyframes*, which provide specific values at specific times. The use of keyframes requires a keyframe-enabled animation class. For example, `DoubleAnimation` has a companion class called `DoubleAnimationUsingKeyFrames`, as do all the other *`XXX`*`Animation` classes.

The keyframe animation classes have the same properties and events as their counterparts, except for the `From`, `To`, and `By` properties. Instead, they have a `KeyFrames` collection that can hold keyframe instances specific to the type being animated. WPF has four types of keyframes, which this section examines.

Linear Keyframes

Listing 17.3 uses `DoubleAnimationUsingKeyFrames` to help move an `Image` of a house fly in a zigzag pattern, as illustrated in Figure 17.7. Because the `Image` is inside a `Canvas`, the motion is accomplished by animating the `Canvas.Left` and `Canvas.Top` attached properties rather than using the more versatile `TranslateTransform`.

LISTING 17.3 The Zigzag Animation for Figure 17.7

```
<Window xmlns="http://schemas.microsoft.com/winfx/2006/xaml/presentation"
  Title="Animation Using Keyframes" Height="300" Width="580">
  <Canvas>
    <Image Source="fly.png">
    <Image.Triggers>
      <EventTrigger RoutedEvent="Image.Loaded">
      <EventTrigger.Actions>
        <BeginStoryboard>
          <Storyboard>
            <DoubleAnimation Storyboard.TargetProperty="(Canvas.Left)"
              From="0" To="500" Duration="0:0:3"/>
            <DoubleAnimationUsingKeyFrames Storyboard.TargetProperty="(Canvas.Top)"
              Duration="0:0:3">
              <LinearDoubleKeyFrame Value="0" KeyTime="0:0:0"/>
              <LinearDoubleKeyFrame Value="200" KeyTime="0:0:1"/>
              <LinearDoubleKeyFrame Value="0" KeyTime="0:0:2"/>
              <LinearDoubleKeyFrame Value="200" KeyTime="0:0:3"/>
            </DoubleAnimationUsingKeyFrames>
          </Storyboard>
        </BeginStoryboard>
      </EventTrigger.Actions>
      </EventTrigger>
    </Image.Triggers>
    </Image>
  </Canvas>
</Window>
```

The fly's motion consists of two animations that begin in parallel when the image loads. One is a simple `DoubleAnimation` that increases its horizontal position linearly from `0` to `500`. The other is the keyframe-enabled animation, which oscillates the vertical position from `0` to `200` then back to `0` then back to `200`.

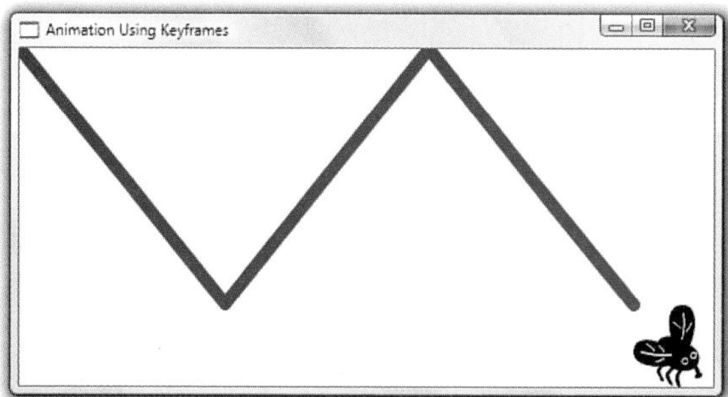

FIGURE 17.7 Zigzag motion is easy to create with a keyframe animation.

DIGGING DEEPER

Animation and Data Binding

To simplify the discussions in this section, Listing 17.3 uses hard-coded values when animating `Canvas.Left` and `Canvas.Top`. Alternatively, you could use data binding to set the various `To` values to match the dimensions of the `Window` or `Canvas`. Here's an example:

```
<DoubleAnimation Storyboard.TargetProperty="(Canvas.Left)" From="0"
  To="{Binding RelativeSource={RelativeSource FindAncestor,
  AncestorType={x:Type Canvas}}, Path=ActualWidth}"
  Duration="0:0:3"/>
```

Unfortunately, such an animation can't be performed in a trigger on `Image.Loaded` because the event is raised before the `Window` or `Canvas` is assigned its `ActualHeight`. (The value is still `NaN`, causing an `AnimationException` to be thrown.) You can perform such binding in animations associated with later events, however.

WARNING

An attached property must be wrapped in parentheses when specified as a `TargetProperty`!

Notice that in Listing 17.3, both `Canvas.Left` and `Canvas.Top` are referenced inside parentheses when used as the value for `Storyboard`'s `TargetProperty` property. This is a requirement for any attached properties used in a property path. Without the parentheses, the animation would look for a property on `Image` called `Canvas` (expecting it to return an object with `Left` and `Top` properties) and throw an exception because it doesn't exist.

Each keyframe instance (`LinearDoubleKeyFrame`) in Listing 17.3 gives a specific value and a time for that value to be applied. Setting `KeyTime` is optional, however. If you omit one, WPF assumes that the keyframe occurs halfway between the surrounding keyframes. If you omit `KeyTime` on all keyframes, they are spaced evenly across the duration of the animation. (This can also be specified explicitly by setting `KeyTime` to `KeyTimeType.Uniform`, or just `"Uniform"` in XAML.)

TIP

`KeyTime` can be specified as a percentage rather than as a `TimeSpan` value. This is handy for expressing the timing of a keyframe independently from the duration of the animation. For example, the `DoubleAnimationUsingKeyFrames` from Listing 17.3 can be replaced with the following to obtain the same result:

```
<DoubleAnimationUsingKeyFrames Storyboard.TargetProperty="(Canvas.Top)"
  Duration="0:0:3">
  <LinearDoubleKeyFrame Value="0" KeyTime="0%"/>
  <LinearDoubleKeyFrame Value="200" KeyTime="33.3%"/>
  <LinearDoubleKeyFrame Value="0" KeyTime="66.6%"/>
  <LinearDoubleKeyFrame Value="200" KeyTime="100%"/>
</DoubleAnimationUsingKeyFrames>
```

`KeyTime` can also be set to `Paced`, which arranges the keyframes in such a way that gives the target property a constant rate of change. In other words, a pair of keyframes that changes the value from `0` to `200` is spaced twice as far apart as a pair of keyframes that changes the value from `0` to `100`.

Although the keyframes in Listing 17.3 specify the exact vertical position of the fly at 0, 1, 2, and 3 seconds, WPF still needs to calculate intermediate values between these "key times." Because each keyframe is represented with an instance of `LinearDoubleKeyFrame`, the intermediate values are derived from simple linear interpolation. For example, at 0.5, 1.5, and 2.5 seconds, the calculated value is 100.

17

But `DoubleAnimationUsingKeyFrames`'s `KeyFrames` property is a collection of abstract `DoubleKeyFrame` objects, so it can be filled with other types of keyframe objects. In addition to `LinearDoubleKeyFrame`, `DoubleKeyFrame` has three other subclasses: `SplineDoubleKeyFrame`, `DiscreteDoubleKeyFrame`, and `EasingDoubleKeyFrame`.

Spline Keyframes

Every `Linear`*`XXX`*`KeyFrame` class has a corresponding `Spline`*`XXX`*`KeyFrame` class. It can be used just like its linear counterpart, so updating `DoubleAnimationUsingKeyFrames` from Listing 17.3 as follows produces exactly the same result:

```
<DoubleAnimationUsingKeyFrames Storyboard.TargetProperty="(Canvas.Top)"
  Duration="0:0:3">
  <SplineDoubleKeyFrame Value="0" KeyTime="0:0:0"/>
  <SplineDoubleKeyFrame Value="200" KeyTime="0:0:1"/>
  <SplineDoubleKeyFrame Value="0" KeyTime="0:0:2"/>
  <SplineDoubleKeyFrame Value="200" KeyTime="0:0:3"/>
</DoubleAnimationUsingKeyFrames>
```

The spline keyframe classes have an additional KeySpline property that differentiates them from the linear classes. KeySpline can be set to an instance of a KeySpline object, which describes the desired motion as a cubic Bézier curve. KeySpline has two properties of type Point that represent the curve's control points. (The start point of the curve is always 0, and the end point is always 1.) A type converter enables you to specify a KeySpline in XAML as a simple list of two points. For example, the following update changes the fly's motion from the simple zigzag in Figure 17.7 to the more complicated motion in Figure 17.8:

```
<DoubleAnimationUsingKeyFrames Storyboard.TargetProperty="(Canvas.Top)"
  Duration="0:0:3">
  <SplineDoubleKeyFrame KeySpline="0,1 1,0" Value="0" KeyTime="0:0:0"/>
  <SplineDoubleKeyFrame KeySpline="0,1 1,0" Value="200" KeyTime="0:0:1"/>
  <SplineDoubleKeyFrame KeySpline="0,1 1,0" Value="0" KeyTime="0:0:2"/>
  <SplineDoubleKeyFrame KeySpline="0,1 1,0" Value="200" KeyTime="0:0:3"/>
</DoubleAnimationUsingKeyFrames>
```

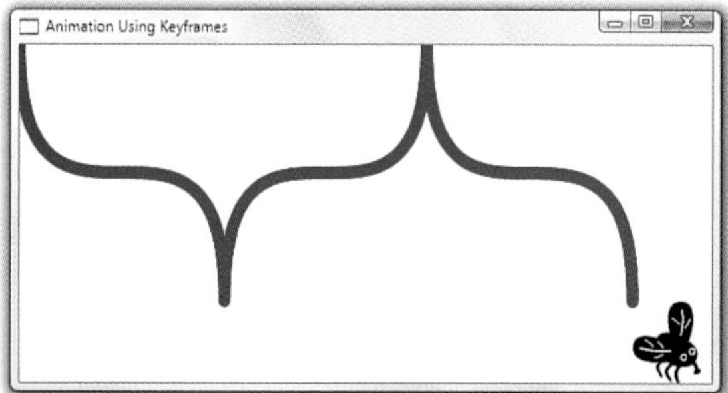

FIGURE 17.8 With KeySpline specified, the interpolation between keyframes is now based on cubic Bézier curves.

Finding the right value for KeySpline that gives the desired effect can be tricky and almost certainly requires the use of a design tool such as Expression Blend. But several free tools can be found online that help you visualize Bézier curves based on the specified control points.

Discrete Keyframes

A discrete keyframe simply indicates that no interpolation should be done from the previous keyframe. Updating DoubleAnimationUsingKeyFrames from Listing 17.3 as follows produces the motion illustrated in Figure 17.9:

```
<DoubleAnimationUsingKeyFrames Storyboard.TargetProperty="(Canvas.Top)"
  Duration="0:0:3">
  <DiscreteDoubleKeyFrame Value="0" KeyTime="0:0:0"/>
  <DiscreteDoubleKeyFrame Value="200" KeyTime="0:0:1"/>
  <DiscreteDoubleKeyFrame Value="0" KeyTime="0:0:2"/>
```

```
  <DiscreteDoubleKeyFrame Value="200" KeyTime="0:0:3"/>
</DoubleAnimationUsingKeyFrames>
```

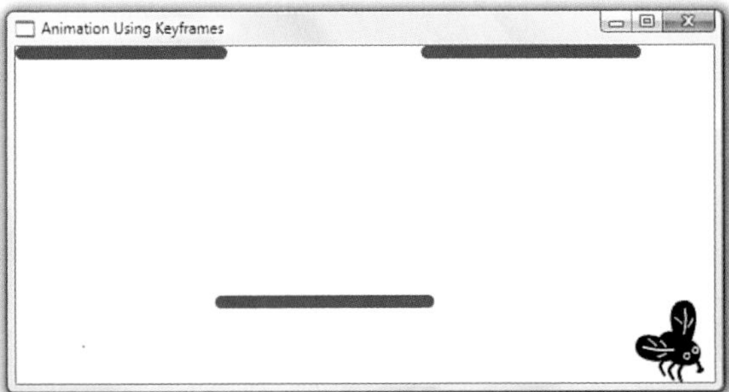

FIGURE 17.9 Discrete keyframes makes the fly's vertical position jump from one key value to the next, with no interpolation.

Of course, different types of keyframes can be mixed into the same animation. The following mixture makes the fly follow the path shown in Figure 17.10:

```
<DoubleAnimationUsingKeyFrames Storyboard.TargetProperty="(Canvas.Top)"
  Duration="0:0:3">
  <DiscreteDoubleKeyFrame Value="0" KeyTime="0:0:0"/>
  <LinearDoubleKeyFrame Value="200" KeyTime="0:0:1"/>
  <DiscreteDoubleKeyFrame Value="0" KeyTime="0:0:2"/>
  <SplineDoubleKeyFrame KeySpline="0,1,1,0" Value="200" KeyTime="0:0:3"/>
</DoubleAnimationUsingKeyFrames>
```

Because the first keyframe's time is at the very beginning, its type is actually irrelevant. That's because each frame only indicates how interpolation is done *before* that frame.

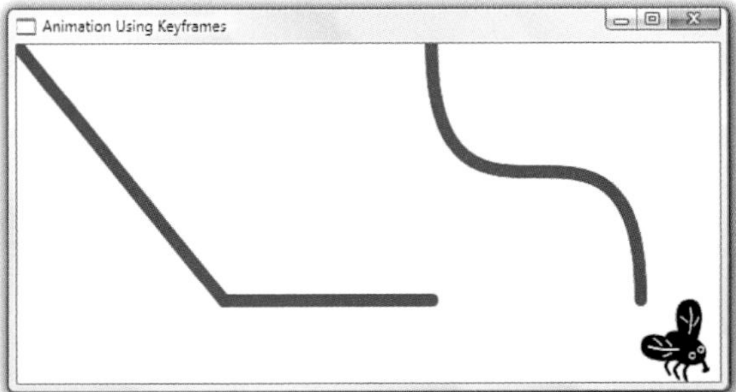

FIGURE 17.10 Mixing three types of keyframes into a single animation.

As with `SplineXXXKeyFrame`, every `LinearXXXKeyFrame` class has a corresponding `DiscreteXXXKeyFrame`. But WPF has five additional discrete keyframe classes that have no linear or spline counterpart. These classes enable you to animate `Boolean`, `Char`, `Matrix`, `Object`, and `String`. WPF supports only discrete keyframe animations with these data types because interpolation would not be meaningful (or even possible, as in the case of `Boolean`).

For example, here's an animation that could be applied to a `TextBlock` to animate its `Text` from a lowercase string to an uppercase string (with each keyframe using the default `KeyTime` of `Uniform`):

```
<StringAnimationUsingKeyFrames Storyboard.TargetProperty="Text" Duration="0:0:.5">
  <DiscreteStringKeyFrame Value="play"/>
  <DiscreteStringKeyFrame Value="Play"/>
  <DiscreteStringKeyFrame Value="PLay"/>
  <DiscreteStringKeyFrame Value="PLAy"/>
  <DiscreteStringKeyFrame Value="PLAY"/>
</StringAnimationUsingKeyFrames>
```

TIP

If you want to simply set a property value inside an event trigger rather than animate it in the traditional sense, you might be able to use a keyframe animation to simulate a `Setter`. For example, the following animation makes the `Button` disappear instantly when clicked by setting `Opacity` to `0` with a keyframe at the beginning of an otherwise empty animation:

```
<Button>
  Click Me Once
<Button.Triggers>
  <EventTrigger RoutedEvent="Button.Click">
  <EventTrigger.Actions>
    <BeginStoryboard>
      <Storyboard>
        <DoubleAnimationUsingKeyFrames Storyboard.TargetProperty="Opacity">
          <DiscreteDoubleKeyFrame Value="0" KeyTime="0"/>
        </DoubleAnimationUsingKeyFrames>
      </Storyboard>
    </BeginStoryboard>
  </EventTrigger.Actions>
  </EventTrigger>
</Button.Triggers>
</Button>
```

Easing Keyframes

Starting with WPF 4, every `Linear`*`XXX`*`KeyFrame` and `Spline`*`XXX`*`KeyFrame` class has a corresponding `Easing`*`XXX`*`KeyFrame` class. The easing keyframe classes have an `EasingFunction` property that can be set to any object implementing `IEasingFunction`. As with the

EasingFunction property on animations, this gives the greatest flexibility in how the interpolation is done. It's now time to see what easing functions are all about.

DIGGING DEEPER

Path-Based Animations

WPF has yet another built-in alternative for animating Double, Point, and Matrix types. The DoubleAnimationUsingPath, PointAnimationUsingPath, and MatrixAnimationUsingPath classes enable you to specify a PathGeometry that dictates how the target value changes (with linear interpolation used between its points). Although these classes can technically be used with any properties of the right type, they are designed for animating the position of an object, using the PathGeometry as the "road" on which the object travels. (In the case of DoubleAnimationUsingPath, you would use a pair of these animations. One can apply the current X value from the PathGeometry to the target X value, whereas the other does the same for the Y value.)

Easing Functions

WPF ships with 11 easing functions—classes implementing IEasingFunction—that can easily be applied to an animation or a keyframe. Each of them supports three different modes with a property called EasingMode. It can be set to EaseIn (the default value), EaseOut, or EaseInOut. Here's how you can apply one of the easing function objects—QuadraticEase—to a basic DoubleAnimation:

```
<DoubleAnimation Storyboard.TargetProperty="(Canvas.Top)" From="200" To="0"
  Duration="0:0:3">
<DoubleAnimation.EasingFunction>
  <QuadraticEase/>
</DoubleAnimation.EasingFunction>
</DoubleAnimation>
```

And here is how you change EasingMode to something other than EaseIn:

```
<DoubleAnimation Storyboard.TargetProperty="(Canvas.Top)" From="200" To="0"
  Duration="0:0:3">
<DoubleAnimation.EasingFunction>
  <QuadraticEase EasingMode="EaseOut"/>
</DoubleAnimation.EasingFunction>
</DoubleAnimation>
```

EaseOut inverts the interpolation done with EaseIn, and EaseInOut produces the EaseIn behavior for the first half of the animation and the EaseOut behavior for the second half.

Built-In Power Easing Functions

Table 17.2 demonstrates how five of the easing functions work in all three modes by showing the path an object takes if its horizontal position animates linearly but its vertical position animates from bottom to top, with each easing function and mode applied.

TABLE 17.2 Five Power Easing Functions

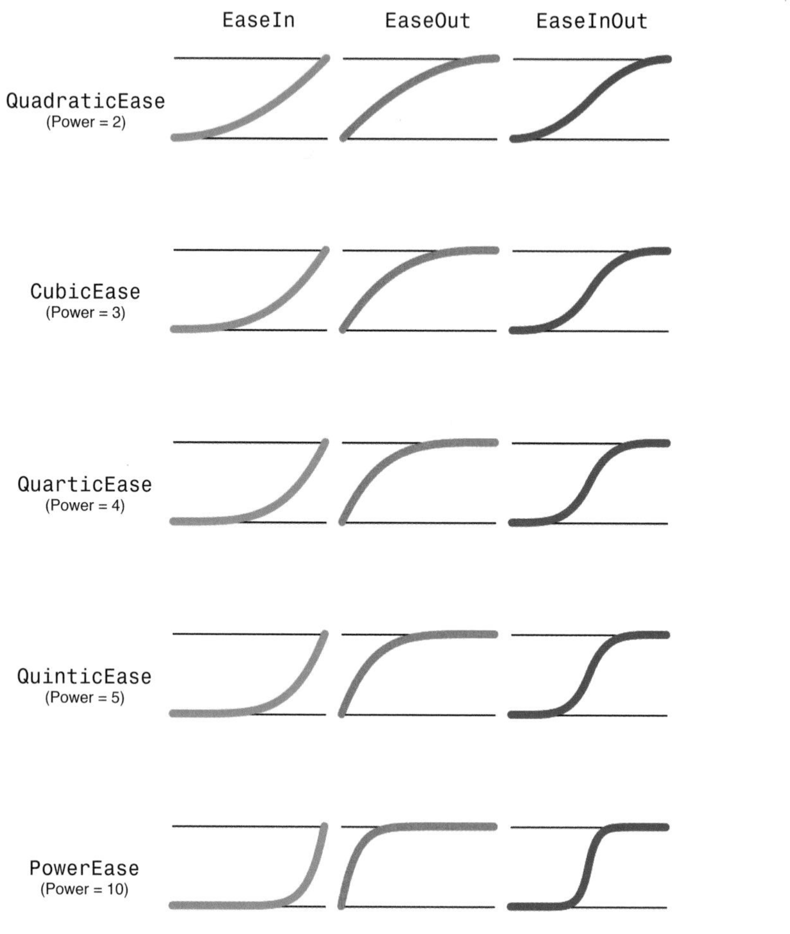

All five functions do interpolation based on a simple power function. With the default linear interpolation, when time has elapsed 50% (.5), the value has changed by 50% (.5). But with quadratic interpolation, the value has changed by 25% (.5 * .5 = .25) when time has elapsed 50%. With cubic interpolation, the value has changed by 12.5% (.5 * .5 * .5 = .125) when time has elapsed 50%. And so on. Although WPF provides four distinct classes for powers 2 through 5, all you really need is the general-purpose `PowerEase` class that performs the interpolation with the value of its `Power` property. The default value of `Power` is `2` (making it the same as `QuadraticEase`) but Table 17.2 demonstrates it with `Power` set to `10`, just to show how the transition keeps getting sharper as `Power` increases. Applying `PowerEase` with `Power` set to `10` can look as follows:

```
<DoubleAnimation Storyboard.TargetProperty="(Canvas.Top)" From="200" To="0"
  Duration="0:0:3">
<DoubleAnimation.EasingFunction>
```

```
  <PowerEase Power="10"/>
</DoubleAnimation.EasingFunction>
</DoubleAnimation>
```

Other Built-In Easing Functions

Table 17.3 demonstrates the remaining six easing functions in all three modes.

TABLE 17.3 The Other Six Built-In Easing Functions

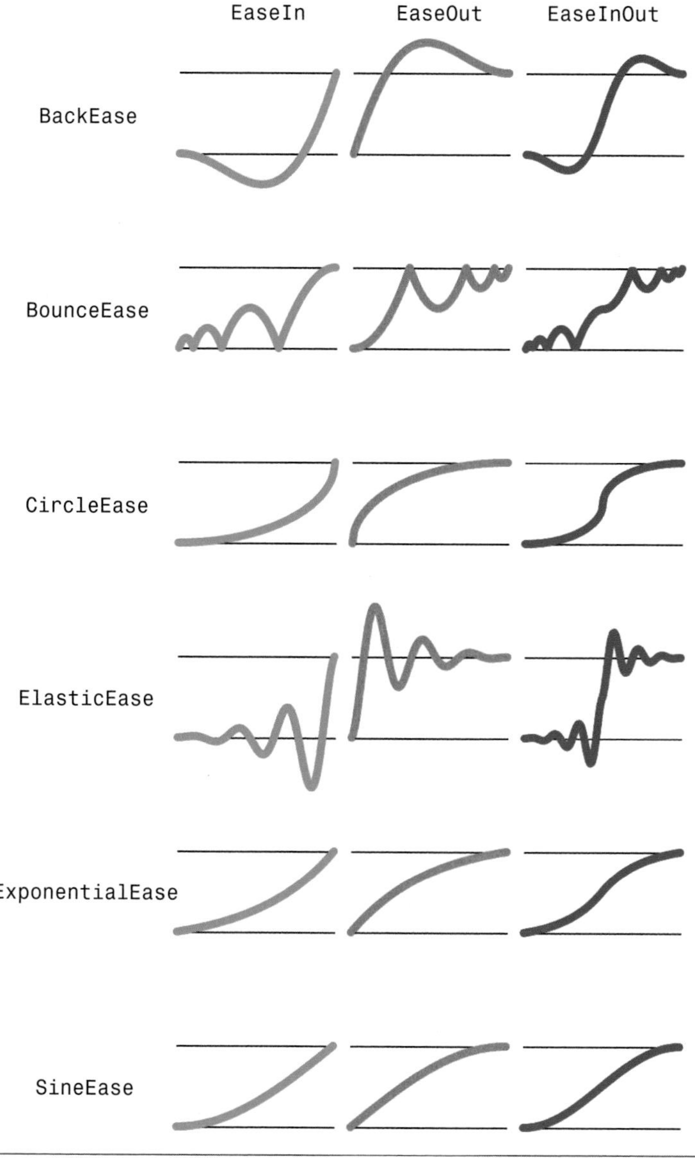

17

Each of these six functions has unique (and sometimes configurable) behavior:

- **BackEase**—Moves the animated value slightly back (away from the target value) before progressing. BackEase has an Amplitude property (default=1) that controls how far back the value goes.
- **BounceEase**—Creates what looks like a bouncing pattern (at least when used to animate position). BounceEase has two properties for controlling its behavior. Bounces (default=3) controls how many bounces occur during the animation, and Bounciness (default=2) controls how much the amplitude of each bounce changes from the previous bounce. For EaseIn, Bounciness=2 doubles the height of each bounce. For EaseOut, Bounciness=2 halves the height of each bounce.
- **CircleEase**—Accelerates (for EaseIn) or decelerates (for EaseOut) the value with a circular function.
- **ElasticEase**—Creates what looks like an oscillating spring pattern (at least when used to animate position). Like BounceEase, it has two properties for controlling its behavior. Oscillations (default=3) controls how many oscillations occur during the animation, and Springiness (default=3) controls the amplitude of oscillations. The behavior of Springiness is subtle: Larger values give smaller oscillations (as if the spring is thicker and more difficult to stretch), and smaller values give larger oscillations (which, in my opinion, seems to make the motion *more* springy rather than *less*.)
- **ExponentialEase**—Interpolates the value with an exponential function, using the value of its Exponent property (default=2).
- **SineEase**—Interpolates the value with a function based on the sine formula.

WARNING

BackEase and ElasticEase can produce unexpected negative values!

Because BackEase and ElasticEase make changes to the value outside the range of From to To, any animation starting at zero (for EaseIn or EaseInOut) or ending at zero (for EaseOut or EaseInOut) will mostly likely veer into negative territory. If such an animation is applied to a value that cannot be negative, such as an element's Width or Height, an exception will be thrown.

Writing Your Own Easing Function

Writing your own easing function is as simple as writing a class that implements IEasingFunction. The IEasingFunction interface has only one function, called Ease:

```
public double Ease(double normalizedTime)
{
  // Return a progress value, normalized from 0 to 1
  …
}
```

Ease is called throughout an animation with a value of time normalized to fall between 0 and 1. For any normalized time value, the implementation of Ease must return a progress value normalized to fall between 0 and 1. (However, the value can go outside this range, as is the case for BackEase and ElasticEase.)

Therefore, the following class successfully (although pointlessly) implements a linear easing function:

```
public class LinearEase : IEasingFunction
{
  public double Ease(double normalizedTime)
  {
    return normalizedTime; // Linear interpolation
  }
}
```

The following class implements a quadratic easing function, similar to the built-in QuadraticEase class:

```
public class SimpleQuadraticEase : IEasingFunction
{
  public double Ease(double normalizedTime)
  {
    // Only covers the EaseIn behavior:
    return normalizedTime * normalizedTime; // Quadratic interpolation
  }
}
```


What makes this SimpleQuadraticEase class different from the built-in QuadraticEase is its lack of support for EasingMode. Fortunately, WPF provides an abstract EasingFunctionBase class (the base class of all 11 built-in easing functions) that gives you EasingMode behavior for free.

EasingFunctionBase defines the EasingMode dependency property and implements IEasingFunction. In its implementation of Ease, it calls an abstract method, EaseInCore, that derived classes must implement the same way as they would implement Ease (if the math considers only the EaseIn case). Based on the value of EasingMode, however, EasingFunctionBase modifies the value of normalizedTime before calling EaseInCore and modifies the value returned by it. These transformations make the same EaseIn logic applicable to all three modes. This is all transparent to the derived class, so implementing an easing function with complete support for EasingMode is as simple as changing the base class and renaming Ease to EaseInCore:

```
public class CompleteQuadraticEase : EasingFunctionBase
{
  protected override double EaseInCore(double normalizedTime)
  {
    return normalizedTime * normalizedTime; // Quadratic interpolation
```

```
  }

  // Required by any subclass of EasingFunctionBase:
  protected override Freezable CreateInstanceCore()
  {
    return new CompleteQuadraticEase();
  }
}
```

The only complication is the need to implement `CreateInstanceCore`, an abstract method defined by `Freezable`, the base class of `EasingFunctionBase`. This `CompleteQuadraticEase` class now behaves exactly like the built-in `QuadraticEase`. You can use this technique to define new and interesting easing functions, such as `SexticEase` (which would come after `QuinticEase`):

```
public class SexticEase : EasingFunctionBase
{
  protected override double EaseInCore(double normalizedTime)
  {
    return normalizedTime * normalizedTime * normalizedTime
         * normalizedTime * normalizedTime * normalizedTime;
  }

  // Required by any subclass of EasingFunctionBase:
  protected override Freezable CreateInstanceCore()
  {
    return new SexticEase();
  }
}
```

DIGGING DEEPER

What `EaseOut` and `EaseInOut` Actually Mean

`EaseIn` is easy to understand because it corresponds exactly to the logic written inside `EaseInCore` implementations and maps to how most people think about an animated value progressing as a function of time. To understand what the `EaseOut` and `EaseInOut` modes actually do, let's examine the transformations made by `EasingFunctionBase.Ease` before and after calling the derived class's `EaseInCore` method.

For `EaseIn`, `EaseInCore` is called repeatedly with values starting at `0` and ending at `1`. For `EaseOut`, however, `EaseInCore` is called repeatedly with values starting at `1` and ending at `0`. (The `normalizedTime` passed to `EaseInCore` is actually `1-normalizedTime`.) The value returned by `EaseInCore` is then inverted in this case; the actual value returned becomes `1-value`.

Continued

For the EaseInOut case, the behavior is different between the first half of the animation (normalizedTime values from 0 up to but not including 0.5) and the second half (normalizedTime values from 0.5 to 1). For the first half, the normalizedTime value passed to EaseInCore is doubled (spanning the full range of 0 to 1 in half the time), but the value returned is halved. For the second half, the normalizedTime value passed to EaseInCore is doubled and inverted (spanning the full range of 1 to 0 in half the time). The value returned from EaseInCore is halved and inverted, then .5 is added to the value (because this is the second half of progress toward the final value). This is why every deterministic EaseInOut animation is symmetrical and hits 50% progress when 50% of the time has elapsed.

Animations and the Visual State Manager

When a control makes use of the Visual State Manager (introduced in Chapter 14, "Styles, Templates, Skins, and Themes"), its template can include any number of VisualStates. Each VisualState is basically just a collection of Storyboards that transition properties that can be animated to their desired values for that state.

Now that you know everything there is to know about animations, you can see how easy and powerful such transitions can be. Listing 17.4 updates the Button control template from Listing 14.8 in Chapter 14, replacing its triggers with VisualStates (and handling some VisualStates that weren't previously handled by the triggers).

LISTING 17.4 A Button ControlTemplate, Using VisualStates

```
<Style TargetType="{x:Type Button}">
  <Setter Property="FocusVisualStyle" Value="{x:Null}"/>
  <Setter Property="Background" Value="Black"/>
  <Setter Property="Template">
  <Setter.Value>
    <ControlTemplate TargetType="{x:Type Button}">
      <Grid RenderTransformOrigin=".5,.5">
      <VisualStateManager.VisualStateGroups>
        <VisualStateGroup Name="CommonStates">
          <VisualState Name="Normal"/>
          <VisualState Name="MouseOver">
            <Storyboard>
              <ColorAnimation Storyboard.TargetName="outerCircle"
                              Storyboard.TargetProperty=
    "(Ellipse.Fill).(LinearGradientBrush.GradientStops)[1].(GradientStop.Color)"
                              To="Orange" Duration="0:0:.4"/>
            </Storyboard>
          </VisualState>
          <VisualState Name="Pressed">
```

17

LISTING 17.4 Continued

```
          <Storyboard>
            <DoubleAnimation Storyboard.TargetName="scaleTransform"
                             Storyboard.TargetProperty="ScaleX" To=".9"
                             Duration="0"/>
            <DoubleAnimation Storyboard.TargetName="scaleTransform"
                             Storyboard.TargetProperty="ScaleY" To=".9"
                             Duration="0"/>
          </Storyboard>
        </VisualState>
        <VisualState Name="Disabled">
          <Storyboard>
            <ColorAnimation Storyboard.TargetName="outerCircle"
                            Storyboard.TargetProperty=
"(Ellipse.Fill).(LinearGradientBrush.GradientStops)[1].(GradientStop.Color)"
                            To="Gray" Duration="0:0:.4"/>
          </Storyboard>
        </VisualState>
      </VisualStateGroup>
      <VisualStateGroup Name="FocusStates">
        <VisualState Name="Unfocused"/>
        <VisualState Name="Focused">
          <Storyboard>
            <DoubleAnimation Storyboard.TargetProperty=
"(Grid.RenderTransform).(TransformGroup.Children)[1].(TranslateTransform.Y)"
                             To="-20" AutoReverse="True"
                             RepeatBehavior="Forever" Duration="0:0:.4">
            <DoubleAnimation.EasingFunction>
              <QuadraticEase/>
            </DoubleAnimation.EasingFunction>
            </DoubleAnimation>
          </Storyboard>
        </VisualState>
      </VisualStateGroup>
    </VisualStateManager.VisualStateGroups>
    <Grid.RenderTransform>
      <TransformGroup>
        <ScaleTransform x:Name="scaleTransform"/>
        <TranslateTransform x:Name="translateTransform"/>
      </TransformGroup>
    </Grid.RenderTransform>
      <Ellipse x:Name="outerCircle">
      <Ellipse.Fill>
        <LinearGradientBrush StartPoint="0,0" EndPoint="0,1">
          <GradientStop Offset="0"
```

LISTING 17.4 Continued

```
            Color="{Binding RelativeSource={RelativeSource TemplatedParent},
                            Path=Background.Color}"/>
          <GradientStop x:Name="highlightGradientStop" Offset="1" Color="Red"/>
        </LinearGradientBrush>
      </Ellipse.Fill>
      </Ellipse>
      <Ellipse RenderTransformOrigin=".5,.5">
      <Ellipse.RenderTransform>
        <ScaleTransform ScaleX=".8" ScaleY=".8"/>
      </Ellipse.RenderTransform>
      <Ellipse.Fill>
        <LinearGradientBrush StartPoint="0,0" EndPoint="0,1">
          <GradientStop Offset="0" Color="White"/>
          <GradientStop Offset="1" Color="Transparent"/>
        </LinearGradientBrush>
      </Ellipse.Fill>
      </Ellipse>
      <Viewbox>
        <ContentPresenter Margin="{TemplateBinding Padding}"/>
      </Viewbox>
    </Grid>
  </ControlTemplate>
</Setter.Value>
</Setter>
</Style>
```


Figure 17.11 shows the results for the various `Button` combinations of states that you encounter in normal user interaction. The `Normal` state in `CommonStates` does nothing; it leaves the default visuals alone. The `MouseOver` state animates the highlight color to orange, the `Pressed` state scales the entire visual tree to 90%, and the `Disabled` state animates the highlight color to `Gray`. In the `FocusStates` state group, the default `Unfocused` state does nothing, but the `Focused` state uses a `QuadraticEase` easing function to give the `Button` a continual bounce, as long as it's in that state. (For this type of auto-reversing repeat-forever animation, `QuadraticEase` actually does a better job of simulating bouncing than `BounceEase`!) The `Style` also sets `FocusVisualStyle` to `null` to avoid the dotted rectangle that would otherwise appear around the bouncing `Button` when it has keyboard focus.

Normal, Unfocused

MouseOver, Unfocused

Pressed, Focused

Disabled, Unfocused

Normal, Focused

FIGURE 17.11 The behavior of Button's VisualStates with the control template in Listing 17.4.

The Focused and Disabled behaviors are new compared to Chapter 14, but you can compare this listing's MouseOver and Pressed states to the IsMouseOver and IsPressed triggers from Chapter 14:

```
<ControlTemplate.Triggers>
  <Trigger Property="IsMouseOver" Value="True">
    <Setter TargetName="outerCircle" Property="Fill" Value="Orange"/>
  </Trigger>
  <Trigger Property="IsPressed" Value="True">
    <Setter Property="RenderTransform">
    <Setter.Value>
      <ScaleTransform ScaleX=".9" ScaleY=".9"/>
    </Setter.Value>
    </Setter>
    <Setter Property="RenderTransformOrigin" Value=".5,.5"/>
  </Trigger>
</ControlTemplate.Triggers>
```

Storyboards can't set properties such as RenderTransform or RenderTransformOrigin, so these two properties are now set directly inside the visual tree. The animations used for the Pressed state simply update the values of ScaleX and ScaleY on the existing ScaleTransform.

Transitions

There's a slight problem with the states as defined in Listing 17.4. The transitions from one state to another are smooth unless the state being transitioned into is `Normal` or `Unfocused`. Because they are left empty, the result is an instant jump to the default visual behavior. This could be solved by adding `Storyboards` with explicit animations to the default values, but one would have to be added for every property animated by any other state in the group, to account for all possible transitions.

Fortunately, `VisualStateGroup` has a much better solution for this. It defines a `Transitions` property that can be set to one or more `VisualTransition` objects that can automatically generate appropriate animations to smooth the transition between any states. `VisualTransition` has `To` and `From` string properties that can be set to the names of the source and target states. You can omit both properties to make it apply to all transitions, specify only a `To` to make it apply to all transitions to that state, and so on. When transitioning from one state to another, the Visual State Manager chooses the most specific `VisualTransition` that matches the transition. The order of precedence is as follows:

1. A `VisualTransition` with matching `To` and `From`
2. A `VisualTransition` with a matching `To` and no explicit `From`
3. A `VisualTransition` with a matching `From` and no explicit `To`
4. The default `VisualTransition`, with no `To` or `From` specified

If `VisualStateGroup`'s `Transitions` property isn't set, the default transition between any states is a zero-duration animation.

To specify the characteristics of a `VisualTransition`, you can set its `GeneratedDuration` property to control the duration of the generated linear animation. You can also set its `GeneratedEasingFunction` property to get a nonlinear animation between states. For the most customization, you can even set its `Storyboard` property to a `Storyboard` with arbitrary custom animations.

17

TIP

The easiest way to manage `VisualStates` and the transitions between them is to give the animations inside each `VisualState` a `Duration` of `0`—making the animations more like `Setters` than real animations—and specify the desired animations between states (with non-zero `Durations`) via `VisualStateGroup`'s `VisualTransitions` property. An exception to this would be states with continual animations, such as the bouncing done in the `Focused` state in Listings 17.4 and 17.5.

Listing 17.5 updates each `VisualStateGroup` from the previous listing to take advantage of `VisualTransitions` to fix the snapping problem when transitioning to the `Normal` and/or `Unfocused` states.

LISTING 17.5 Updated `VisualStateGroups` That Use `Transitions` for Listing 17.4

```
<VisualStateManager.VisualStateGroups>
  <VisualStateGroup Name="CommonStates">
  <VisualStateGroup.Transitions>
    <!-- Apply to all transitions... -->
    <VisualTransition GeneratedDuration="0:0:.4"/>
    <!-- ...but override for transitions to/from Pressed: -->
    <VisualTransition To="Pressed" GeneratedDuration="0"/>
    <VisualTransition From="Pressed" GeneratedDuration="0"/>
  </VisualStateGroup.Transitions>
    <VisualState Name="Normal"/>
    <VisualState Name="MouseOver">
      <Storyboard>
        <ColorAnimation Storyboard.TargetName="outerCircle"
                        Storyboard.TargetProperty=
  "(Ellipse.Fill).(LinearGradientBrush.GradientStops)[1].(GradientStop.Color)"
                        To="Orange" Duration="0"/>
      </Storyboard>
    </VisualState>
    <VisualState Name="Pressed">
      <Storyboard>
        <DoubleAnimation Storyboard.TargetName="scaleTransform"
                         Storyboard.TargetProperty="ScaleX" To=".9"
                         Duration="0"/>
        <DoubleAnimation Storyboard.TargetName="scaleTransform"
                         Storyboard.TargetProperty="ScaleY" To=".9"
                         Duration="0"/>
      </Storyboard>
    </VisualState>
    <VisualState Name="Disabled">
      <Storyboard>
        <ColorAnimation Storyboard.TargetName="outerCircle"
                        Storyboard.TargetProperty=
  "(Ellipse.Fill).(LinearGradientBrush.GradientStops)[1].(GradientStop.Color)"
                        To="Gray" Duration="0"/>
      </Storyboard>
    </VisualState>
  </VisualStateGroup>
```

LISTING 17.5 Continued

```
<VisualStateGroup Name="FocusStates">
<VisualStateGroup.Transitions>
  <!-- Apply only in one direction: -->
  <VisualTransition To="Unfocused" GeneratedDuration="0:0:.4">
  <VisualTransition.GeneratedEasingFunction>
    <QuadraticEase/>
  </VisualTransition.GeneratedEasingFunction>
  </VisualTransition>
</VisualStateGroup.Transitions>
  <VisualState Name="Unfocused"/>
  <VisualState Name="Focused">
    <Storyboard>
      <DoubleAnimation Storyboard.TargetProperty=
  "(Grid.RenderTransform).(TransformGroup.Children)[1].(TranslateTransform.Y)"
                       To="-20" AutoReverse="True"
                       RepeatBehavior="Forever" Duration="0:0:.4">
      <DoubleAnimation.EasingFunction>
        <QuadraticEase/>
      </DoubleAnimation.EasingFunction>
      </DoubleAnimation>
    </Storyboard>
  </VisualState>
</VisualStateGroup>
</VisualStateManager.VisualStateGroups>
```


In the `Transitions` collection for `CommonStates`, a `VisualTransition` lasting 0.4 seconds applies to all state transitions. Two additional `VisualTransitions` override this behavior for transitions to and from the `Pressed` state in order to preserve the instant-press and instant-release behavior. Because the new `VisualTransition` takes care of the smooth animations, the `Durations` of the animations defined for the `MouseOver` and `Disabled` states are changed to `0`.

The `VisualTransition` added to the `FocusStates` group applies only to transitions to the `Unfocused` state to avoid interfering with the continual bouncing animation in the `Focused` sate. In order to not look out of place when transitioning out of the bouncing `Focused` animation, the `VisualTransition` is given a `QuadraticEase` easing function to match the animation it's transitioning from.

WARNING

`VisualTransitions` don't work with animations whose target isn't in the element tree!

You may have noticed the lengthy `Storyboard.TargetProperty` property paths in three of the animations from Listings 17.4 and 17.5:

```
<ColorAnimation Storyboard.TargetName="outerCircle"
                Storyboard.TargetProperty=
     "(Ellipse.Fill).(LinearGradientBrush.GradientStops)[1].(GradientStop.Color)"
                To="Orange" .../>
...
<ColorAnimation Storyboard.TargetName="outerCircle"
                Storyboard.TargetProperty=
     "(Ellipse.Fill).(LinearGradientBrush.GradientStops)[1].(GradientStop.Color)"
                To="Gray" .../>
...
<DoubleAnimation Storyboard.TargetProperty=
     "(Grid.RenderTransform).(TransformGroup.Children)[1].(TranslateTransform.Y)"
                 To="-20" AutoReverse="True"
                 RepeatBehavior="Forever" Duration="0:0:.4">
...
</DoubleAnimation>
```

The draft version of these listings referenced the `GradientStop` (in the first two animations) and the `TranslateTransform` (in the last animation) directly via `Storyboard.TargetName` in order to make the property paths much simpler:

```
<ColorAnimation Storyboard.TargetName="highlightGradientStop"
                Storyboard.TargetProperty="Color"
                To="Orange" .../>
...
<ColorAnimation Storyboard.TargetName="highlightGradientStop"
                Storyboard.TargetProperty="Color"
                To="Gray" .../>
...
<DoubleAnimation Storyboard.TargetName="translateTransform"
                 Storyboard.TargetProperty="Y"
                 To="-20" AutoReverse="True"
                 RepeatBehavior="Forever" Duration="0:0:.4">
...
</DoubleAnimation>
```

Continued

These animations have exactly the same meaning and work the same way as the animations in Listings 17.4 and 17.5, except when you try to use `VisualTransitions`. The generated animations do not work with animations when the target named by `TargetName` isn't in the element tree. The workaround is either to put all behavior inside `VisualStates` rather than using `VisualTransitions`, or to ensure all relevant animations use an element in the tree as their target. Listing 17.5 uses the latter approach. (In the `TranslateTransform` animation, the target is implicitly the root `Grid`.)

Notice that the animations in the `Pressed` state *do* operate directly on the `ScaleTransform`. These were left alone because the transitions into and out of this state are instantaneous anyway. If you want to change Listing 17.5 to produce a smooth transition into and out of `Pressed`, you'll need to change the `Pressed` animations to use the root `Grid` as the target and:

```
"(Grid.RenderTransform).(TransformGroup.Children)[0].(ScaleTransform.ScaleX)"
```

and:

```
"(Grid.RenderTransform).(TransformGroup.Children)[0].(ScaleTransform.ScaleY)"
```

as the `TargetProperty` values.

The property paths in this section use the most explicit syntax normally reserved for attached properties, but they don't have to be quite so long. The various property paths can be shortened as follows:

```
"Fill.GradientStops[1].Color"

"RenderTransform.Children[1].Y"

"RenderTransform.Children[0].ScaleX"

"RenderTransform.Children[0].ScaleY"
```

17

Summary

With animation, you can do something as simple as a subtle rollover effect (which is becoming commonplace for even standard user interfaces) or as complex as an animated cartoon. `Storyboards`, which are a necessary part of performing animations purely in XAML, help to orchestrate complex series of animations.

The same could be said for other areas of WPF, but going overboard with animation can harm the usability and accessibility of an application or a component. Another factor to consider is the performance implication of animation. Too much animation could make an otherwise-useful application become unusable on a less-powerful computer, such as a netbook.

Fortunately, WPF enables you to provide rich animations (or other functionality) on powerful computers while scaling back the experience on less-powerful systems. The key to this is the `RenderCapability` class in the `System.Windows.Media` namespace. It defines a static `Tier` property and a static `TierChanged` event. When you're running on a tier 0 computer, everything is rendered in software. On a tier 1 computer, hardware rendering is sometimes used. And on a tier 2 computer (the top tier), everything that *can be* rendered in hardware is rendered in hardware. Therefore, you should be reluctant to use multiple simultaneous animations (or complicated gradients or 3D) on a tier 0 system. Besides removing animations, another way to adjust to running in the bottom tier is to reduce the natural frame rate (which tends to be 60 fps) with `Storyboard`'s `DesiredFrameRate` attached property. This can decrease CPU utilization on such systems.

TIP

If you find yourself doing a lot of animation (or complicated static graphics, whether 2D or 3D), use `RenderCapability.Tier` to adjust your behavior. Note that although `Tier` is a 32-bit integer, the main value is stored in the high word. Therefore, you need to shift the value by 16 bits to see the true tier:

```
int tier = RenderCapability.Tier >> 16
```

This was done to enable subtiers in the future, but the result is pretty confusing for anyone using the API!

CHAPTER 18
Audio, Video, and Speech

IN THIS CHAPTER

- Audio
- Video
- Speech

This chapter covers the areas of rich media that have been increasingly important to software over the past decade: audio, video, and speech (the latter of which could be considered a very special kind of audio). In all three of these areas, Windows Presentation Foundation significantly lowers the bar of difficulty compared to previous technologies. (Audio, video, and speech are also similar in that it's difficult to demonstrate them in a book with static pictures!) So, although you might not have considered incorporating these feature areas in the past, you might change your mind after reading this chapter!

Audio

The audio support in WPF is simple to use. But unlike most of WPF, it's not revolutionary or next-generation, nor does it exploit the latest advances in hardware. Instead, it's a thin layer over existing functionality in Win32 and Windows Media Player that covers the most common audio needs. You won't be able to build a professional audio application solely using WPF, but you can easily enhance an application with music and sound effects!

As with many other tasks in WPF, you can accomplish playing audio in multiple ways, each with its own pros and cons. The choices for audio are represented by several different classes:

- `SoundPlayer`
- `SoundPlayerAction`
- `MediaPlayer`
- `MediaElement` and `MediaTimeline`

SoundPlayer

The easiest way to play audio files in a WPF application is to use the same mechanism used by non-WPF applications: the `System.Media.SoundPlayer` class. `SoundPlayer`, a part of the .NET Framework since version 2.0, is a simple wrapper for the Win32 `PlaySound` API. This means that it has a bunch of limitations, such as the following:

- It only supports `.wav` audio files.
- It has no support for playing multiple sounds simultaneously. (Any new sound being played interrupts a currently playing sound.)
- It has no support for varying the volume of sounds.

It is, however, the most lightweight approach for playing a sound, so it's very appropriate for simple sound effects. The following code shows how to use `SoundPlayer` to play a sound:

```
SoundPlayer player = new SoundPlayer("tada.wav");
player.Play();
```

The string passed to `SoundPlayer`'s constructor can be any filename or a URL. Starting with version 3.5 of the .NET Framework, you can use any appropriate relative or absolute pack URI, as with controls such as `Image`. Therefore, the sound file can be included your project like other WPF binary resources (with a `Resource` or `Content` build action), or it can be loose at the site of origin.

Calling `Play` plays the sound asynchronously, but you can also call `PlaySync` to play it on the current thread, or `PlayLooping` to make the sound repeat asynchronously until you call `Stop` (or until any other sound is played from any instance of `SoundPlayer`, or even direct calls to the underlying Win32 API).

For performance reasons, the audio file isn't loaded until the first time the sound is played. But this behavior could cause an unwanted pause, especially if you're retrieving a large audio file over the network. Therefore, `SoundPlayer` also defines `Load` and `LoadAsynch` methods for performing the loading at any point prior to the first playing.

If you want to play a familiar system sound without worrying about its filename and path on the target computer, the `System.Media` namespace also contains a `SystemSounds` class with static `Asterisk`, `Beep`, `Exclamation`, `Hand`, and `Question` properties. Each property is of type `SystemSound`, which has its own `Play` method (for asynchronous nonlooping playing only). However, I would use sounds from this class sparingly (if at all) to avoid annoying users with sounds that they expect to come only from Windows itself!

SoundPlayerAction

If you want to use `SoundPlayer` to add simple sound effects to user interface events such as hovering over or clicking a `Button`, you can easily define the appropriate event handlers that use `SoundPlayer` in their implementation. However, WPF defines a

`SoundPlayerAction` class (which derives from `TriggerAction`) that enables you to use `SoundPlayer` without writing any procedural code.

The following XAML snippet adds `EventTriggers` directly to a `Button` that play an audio file when the `Button` is clicked or the mouse pointer enters its bounds:

```
<Button>
<Button.Triggers>
  <EventTrigger RoutedEvent="Button.Click">
  <EventTrigger.Actions>
    <SoundPlayerAction Source="click.wav"/>
  </EventTrigger.Actions>
  </EventTrigger>
  <EventTrigger RoutedEvent="Button.MouseEnter">
  <EventTrigger.Actions>
    <SoundPlayerAction Source="hover.wav"/>
  </EventTrigger.Actions>
  </EventTrigger>
</Button.Triggers>
</Button>
```

`SoundPlayerAction` simply wraps `SoundPlayer` in a trigger-friendly way, so it has all the same limitations. Actually, it has even *more* limitations because you can't customize how it interacts with `SoundPlayer`. `SoundPlayerAction` internally constructs a `SoundPlayer` instance with its `Source` value and calls `Play` whenever the action is invoked. You can't play the sound synchronously (but why would you want to?), make it loop, or preload the audio file.

MediaPlayer

If the limitations of `SoundPlayer` and `SoundPlayerAction` are not acceptable, you can use the WPF-specific `MediaPlayer` class in the `System.Windows.Media` namespace. It is built on top of Windows Media Player, so it supports all of its audio formats (`.wav`, `.wma`, `.mp3`, and so on). Multiple sounds can be played simultaneously (although via different instances of `MediaPlayer`), and the volume can be controlled by setting its `Volume` property to a `double` between `0` and `1` (with `0.5` as the default value).

But `MediaPlayer` has even more features for giving you a lot of control over the audio:

- You can pause the audio with its `Pause` method (if `CanPause` is `true`).
- You can mute the audio by setting its `IsMuted` property to `true`.
- You shift the balance toward the left or right speaker by setting its `Balance` property to a value between `-1` and `1`. `-1` means that all the audio is sent to the left speaker, `0` (the default) means that all the audio is sent to both speakers, and `1` means that all the audio is sent to the right speaker.

- For audio formats that support it, you can speed up or slow down the audio (without affecting its pitch) by setting its `SpeedRatio` property to any nonnegative `double` value. `1.0` is the default value, so a value less than `1.0` slows it down, whereas a value greater than `1.0` speeds it up.
- You can get the length of the audio clip with its `NaturalDuration` property (which is unaffected by `SpeedRatio`) and get the current position with the `Position` property.
- If the audio format supports seeking, you can even *set* the current position with the `Position` property.

Here is the simplest way to use `MediaPlayer` to play an audio file:

```
MediaPlayer player = new MediaPlayer();
player.Open(new Uri("music.wma", UriKind.Relative));
player.Play();
```

A single instance can play multiple audio files, but only one at a time. After you open a file with `Open`, methods such as `Play`, `Pause`, and `Stop` apply to that file. You can also call `Close` to release the file (which also stops the audio if it's currently playing). The file is always played asynchronously, so you would not want to call `Close` immediately after the preceding code because you wouldn't hear anything play!

TIP

For more details and quirks related to `MediaPlayer`, be sure to read the upcoming "Video" section, even if you have no intention of using WPF's video support.

MediaElement and MediaTimeline

`MediaPlayer` gives you a lot more flexibility than `SoundPlayer`, but it is designed for procedural code only. (Its main functionality is exposed through methods, its properties are not dependency properties, and its events are not routed events.) Somewhat like how `SoundPlayerAction` wraps `SoundPlayer` for declarative use, WPF provides a `MediaElement` class that wraps `MediaPlayer` for declarative use.

`MediaElement` is a full-blown `FrameworkElement` in the `System.Windows.Controls` namespace, so it's meant to be embedded in a user interface, it participates in layout, and so on. (This sounds odd until you realize that `MediaElement` is also used for video, as discussed in the next section.) `MediaElement` exposes most of the properties and events of `MediaPlayer` as dependency properties and routed events.

You can set `MediaElement`'s `Source` property to the URI of an audio file, but it would play as soon as the element is loaded. Instead, to declaratively play sounds at arbitrary times, you should set `Source` on the fly using animation with a `MediaTimeline`.

Just like the earlier example that uses `SoundPlayerAction`, the following XAML shows how to use `MediaElement` and `MediaTimeline` to play an audio file when a `Button` is clicked or the mouse pointer enters its bounds:

```
<MediaElement x:Name="audio"/>
…
<Button>
<Button.Triggers>
  <EventTrigger RoutedEvent="Button.Click">
  <EventTrigger.Actions>
    <BeginStoryboard>
      <Storyboard>
        <MediaTimeline Source="click.wma" Storyboard.TargetName="audio"/>
      </Storyboard>
    </BeginStoryboard>
  </EventTrigger.Actions>
  </EventTrigger>
  <EventTrigger RoutedEvent="Button.MouseEnter">
  <EventTrigger.Actions>
    <BeginStoryboard>
      <Storyboard>
        <MediaTimeline Source="hover.wma" Storyboard.TargetName="audio"/>
      </Storyboard>
    </BeginStoryboard>
  </EventTrigger.Actions>
  </EventTrigger>
</Button.Triggers>
</Button>
```

In addition to the `BeginStoryboard` action, you can use the same `Storyboard` with the `PauseStoryboard`, `ResumeStoryboard`, `SeekStoryboard`, and `StopStoryboard` actions to pause, resume, seek, and stop the audio.

TIP

To create continuously looping background audio, you can set `MediaTimeline`'s `RepeatBehavior` to `Forever` and use it in a trigger on `MediaElement`'s `Loaded` event. Here's an example:

```
<MediaElement x:Name="audio">
<MediaElement.Triggers>
  <EventTrigger RoutedEvent="MediaElement.Loaded">
  <EventTrigger.Actions>
    <BeginStoryboard>
      <Storyboard>
        <MediaTimeline Source="music.mp3" Storyboard.TargetName="audio"
          RepeatBehavior="Forever"/>
      </Storyboard>
```

Continued

```
    </BeginStoryboard>
  </EventTrigger.Actions>
  </EventTrigger>
</MediaElement.Triggers>
</MediaElement>
```

Unfortunately, a slight pause might be heard every time the audio reaches the end, before it is played again from the beginning. One (weird) workaround for this is to create a video with the desired audio then replace the `Source` with the video file (and keep the `MediaElement` hidden from view). This works because WPF has tighter integration with video and supports seamless looping in this case.

Video

WPF's video support is built on the same `MediaPlayer` class described in the previous section, and its companion classes, such as `MediaElement` and `MediaTimeline`. Therefore, all file formats supported by Windows Media Player (`.wmv`, `.avi`, `.mpg`, and so on) can be easily used in WPF applications as well. In addition, much of the discussion in this section also applies to playing audio with `MediaPlayer` and/or `MediaElement`.

> **WARNING**
>
> **WPF's audio and video support requires Windows Media Player 10 or higher!**
>
> Without at least Windows Media Player version 10 installed, the use of `MediaPlayer` (and related classes) throws an exception. This only affects versions of Windows prior to Windows Vista.

> **WARNING**
>
> **Prior to Windows Vista, Windows Media Player is 32-bit only!**
>
> The 64-bit versions of Windows prior to Windows Vista contain only a 32-bit version of Windows Media Player. Because WPF's video (and richer audio) support is built on Windows Media Player, you can't use it from a 64-bit application running on these platforms. Instead, you must ensure that your application runs as 32-bit. In this case, your application can automatically use the 32-bit version of the .NET Framework (which is installed alongside the 64-bit version).

Controlling the Visual Aspects of `MediaElement`

Like `Viewbox` and `Image`, `MediaElement` has `Stretch` and `StretchDirection` properties that control how the video fills the space given to it. Figure 18.1 shows the three different `Stretch` values operating on a `MediaElement` placed directly inside a `Window`:

```
<Window xmlns="http://schemas.microsoft.com/winfx/2006/xaml/presentation">
  <MediaElement Source="C:\Users\Public\Videos\Sample Videos\butterfly.wmv"
    Stretch="XXX"/>
</Window>
```

Uniform (default) Fill UniformToFill

FIGURE 18.1 MediaElement in a window with three different Stretch settings.

Of course, the neat thing about MediaElement is that it enables video to be manipulated in richer ways, like most other FrameworkElements. The following XAML, rendered in Figure 18.2, places two instances of a video on top of each other, both half-transparent, both clipped with a circle, and one rotated 180°:

```
<Canvas>
  <MediaElement Source="C:\Users\Public\Videos\Sample Videos\butterfly.wmv"
    Opacity="0.5">
  <MediaElement.Clip>
    <EllipseGeometry Center="220,220" RadiusX="220" RadiusY="220"/>
  </MediaElement.Clip>
  <MediaElement.LayoutTransform>
    <RotateTransform Angle="180"/>
  </MediaElement.LayoutTransform>
  </MediaElement>

  <MediaElement Source="C:\Users\Public\Videos\Sample Videos\butterfly.wmv"
    Opacity="0.5">
  <MediaElement.Clip>
    <EllipseGeometry Center="220,220" RadiusX="220" RadiusY="220"/>
  </MediaElement.Clip>
  </MediaElement>
</Canvas>
```

Furthermore, by placing MediaElement inside a VisualBrush, you can easily use video just about anywhere—as a background for a ListBox, as a material on a 3D surface, and so on. Just be sure to measure the performance implications before going overboard with VisualBrush and video!

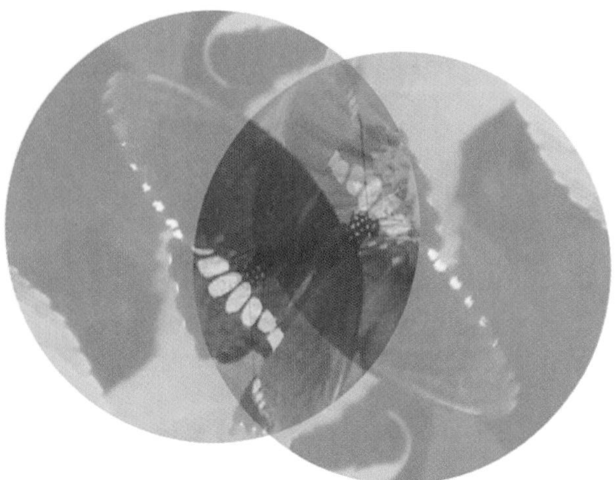

FIGURE 18.2 Clipped, rotated, and half-transparent video inside two MediaElements.

FAQ

How do I take snapshots of individual video frames?

You can set the Position of video to a specific point to "freeze frame" it. But if you want to persist that frame as a separate Image, you render a MediaElement into a RenderTargetBitmap (just like any other Visual). Here's an example:

```
MediaElement mediaElement = …;
Size desiredSize = …;
Size dpi = …;
RenderTargetBitmap bitmap = new RenderTargetBitmap(desiredSize.Width,
  desiredSize.Height, dpi.Width, dpi.Height, PixelFormats.Pbgra32);
bitmap.Render(mediaElement);
Image image = new Image();
image.Source = BitmapFrame.Create(bitmap);
```

If you are working with MediaPlayer rather than MediaElement, you could create a DrawingVisual to pass to RenderTargetBitmap's Render method, as follows:

```
DrawingVisual visual = new DrawingVisual();
MediaPlayer mediaPlayer = …;
Size desiredSize = …;
using (DrawingContext dc = visual.RenderOpen())
{
  dc.DrawVideo(mediaPlayer, new Rect(0, 0, desiredSize.Width,
    desiredSize.Height));
}
```

The key to this code is DrawingContext's DrawVideo method, which accepts an instance of MediaPlayer and a Rect. In fact, MediaElement uses DrawVideo inside its OnRender method to do its own video rendering!

Controlling the Underlying Media

The previous two XAML snippets use the simple approach of setting MediaElement's Source directly. This causes the media to play immediately when the element is loaded. It's more likely that you'll want to play, pause, and stop the video at specific times. As in the "Audio" section, the following XAML accomplishes this with a trigger that uses MediaTimeline. It also contains triggers that use PauseStoryboard and ResumeStoryboard to provide the functionality for a simple media player:

```
<Grid>
<Grid.Triggers>
  <EventTrigger RoutedEvent="Button.Click" SourceName="playButton">
  <EventTrigger.Actions>
    <BeginStoryboard Name="beginStoryboard">
      <Storyboard>
        <MediaTimeline Source="C:\Users\Public\Videos\Sample Videos\butterfly.wmv"
          Storyboard.TargetName="video"/>
      </Storyboard>
    </BeginStoryboard>
  </EventTrigger.Actions>
  </EventTrigger>
  <EventTrigger RoutedEvent="Button.Click" SourceName="pauseButton">
  <EventTrigger.Actions>
    <PauseStoryboard BeginStoryboardName="beginStoryboard"/>
  </EventTrigger.Actions>
  </EventTrigger>
  <EventTrigger RoutedEvent="Button.Click" SourceName="resumeButton">
  <EventTrigger.Actions>
    <ResumeStoryboard BeginStoryboardName="beginStoryboard"/>
  </EventTrigger.Actions>
  </EventTrigger>
</Grid.Triggers>

  <MediaElement x:Name="video"/>
  <StackPanel Orientation="Horizontal" VerticalAlignment="Bottom">
    <Button x:Name="playButton" Background="#55FFFFFF" Height="40">Play</Button>
    <Button x:Name="pauseButton" Background="#55FFFFFF" Height="40">Pause</Button>
    <Button x:Name="resumeButton" Background="#55FFFFFF" Height="40">Resume
    </Button>
  </StackPanel>
</Grid>
```

The user interface includes three translucent Buttons for controlling the video playing underneath them, as shown in Figure 18.3.

18

FIGURE 18.3 A simple video player, with `Buttons` that use storyboards to control the video.

TIP

When combining a `MediaTimeline` with other animations inside the same `Storyboard`, you might want to customize the way in which these animations are synchronized. Playing media often has an initial delay from loading and buffering, causing it to fall behind other animations. And if you give a `Storyboard` a fixed duration, it might cut off the end of the media because of such delays.

To change this behavior, you can set `Storyboard`'s `SlipBehavior` property to `Slip` rather than its default value, `Grow`. This causes all animations to wait until the media is ready before doing anything.

Although the default behavior for media specified as the `Source` of a `MediaElement` is to begin playing when the element is loaded, you can change this behavior with `MediaElement`'s `LoadedBehavior` and `UnloadedBehavior` properties, both of type `MediaState`. `MediaState` is an enumeration with the values `Play` (the default for `LoadedBehavior`), `Pause`, `Stop`, `Close` (the default for `UnloadedBehavior`), and `Manual`.

If you want to control the media from procedural code, `MediaElement` exposes the methods of the `MediaPlayer` it wraps (`Play`, `Stop`, and so on), but you can call these only when `LoadedBehavior` and `UnloadedBehavior` are set to `Manual`. In addition, you can set the `Position` and `SpeedRatio` properties only when the element is in this manual mode.

Note that manual mode is applicable only when you don't have any `MediaTimelines` in triggers attached to the `MediaElement`. When `MediaElement` is an animation target, its behavior is *always* driven by an animation clock (exposed as its `Clock` property of type `MediaClock`) and can't be altered manually unless you interact with the clock.

TIP

To include streaming audio or video in an application, you can simply set `Source` to a streaming URL. Any encoding supported by Windows Media Player works, such as ASF-encoded `.wmv` files. If you want to include a live video feed from a local webcam (which doesn't have a URL you can point to), see Chapter 19, "Interoperability with Non-WPF Technologies," which shows a way to accomplish this.

WARNING

Media files can't be embedded resources!

The URIs given as `Source` values to `MediaPlayer`, `MediaElement`, and `MediaTimeline` are not as general-purpose as the URIs used elsewhere in WPF. They must be paths understood by Windows Media Player, such as absolute or relative file system paths or a URL. This means that there's no built-in support for referencing a media file embedded as a resource. Ironically, the only mechanism discussed in this chapter that supports specifying media as an arbitrary stream is the otherwise very limited `SoundPlayer`/`SoundPlayerAction`!

This also means you can't refer to files at the site of origin using the `pack://siteOfOrigin` syntax. Instead, you can hard-code the appropriate path or URL or programmatically retrieve the site of origin by using `ApplicationDeployment.CurrentDeployment.ActivationUri` (in the `System.Deployment.Application` namespace defined in `System.Deployment.dll`) and then prepend it to a filename to form a fully qualified URI.

TIP

To diagnose any errors when using `MediaPlayer` or `MediaElement`, you should attach an event handler to the `MediaFailed` event defined by both classes. This could look like the following:

```
<MediaElement Source="nonExistentFile.wmv" MediaFailed="OnMediaFailed"/>
```

where the `OnMediaFailed` code-behind method is defined as follows:

```
void OnMediaFailed(object o, ExceptionRoutedEventArgs e)
{
  MessageBox.Show(e.ErrorException.ToString());
}
```

If the `Source` file doesn't exist, you'll now see the following exception rather than silent failure:

```
System.IO.FileNotFoundException: Cannot find the media file. --->
System.Runtime.InteropServices.COMException (0xC00D1197):
Exception from HRESULT: 0xC00D1197
```

Most people are surprised when they learn that you need to opt in to this behavior rather than get such exceptions by default. But because of the asynchronous nature of media processing, a directly thrown exception might not be catchable anywhere outside a global handler.

FAQ

How can I get metadata associated with audio or video, such as artist or genre?

WPF does not expose a way to retrieve such metadata. Instead, you must use unmanaged Windows Media Player APIs to access this information.

18

Speech

The speech APIs in the `System.Speech` namespace make it easy to incorporate both speech recognition and speech synthesis. They are built on top of Microsoft SAPI APIs and use W3C standard formats for synthesis and recognition grammars, so they integrate very well with existing engines.

Although these `System.Speech` APIs were introduced with WPF, they are not *tied to* WPF; you won't find any dependency properties, routed events, the built-in ability to animate voice, and so on. Therefore, you can easily use them in any .NET application, whether WPF based, Windows Forms based, or even console based.

Speech Synthesis

Speech synthesis, also known as *text-to-speech*, is the process of turning text into audio. This requires a "voice" to speak the text. Recent versions of Windows have a great voice installed by default, called Microsoft Anna. Microsoft's SAPI SDK (a free download at http://microsoft.com/speech) includes Microsoft Anna and other voices, such as the more robotic-sounding Microsoft Sam, and can be installed on just about all versions of Windows.

Bringing Text to Life

To get started with speech synthesis, add a reference to `System.Speech.dll` to your project. The relevant APIs are in the `System.Speech.Synthesis` namespace. Getting text to be spoken is as simple as this:

```
SpeechSynthesizer synthesizer = new SpeechSynthesizer();
synthesizer.Speak("I love WPF!");
```

The text is spoken synchronously, using the voice, rate, and volume settings chosen in the Text to Speech area of Control Panel. To have text spoken asynchronously, you can call `SpeakAsync` instead of `Speak`:

```
synthesizer.SpeakAsync("I love WPF!");
```

You can change the rate and volume of the spoken text by setting `SpeechSynthesizer`'s `Rate` and `Volume` properties. They are both integers, but `Rate` has a range of `-10` to `10`, whereas `Volume` has a range of `0` to `100`. You can also cancel pending asynchronous speech by calling `SpeakAsyncCancelAll`.

If you have multiple voices installed, you can change the voice at any time by calling `SelectVoice`:

```
synthesizer.SelectVoice("Microsoft Sam");
```

You can enumerate the voices with `GetInstalledVoices` or even attempt to select a voice with a desired gender and age (which, for some reason, seems a little creepy):

```
synthesizer.SelectVoiceByHints(VoiceGender.Female, VoiceAge.Adult);
```

You can even send its output to a .wav file rather than to speakers with the SetOutputToWaveFile method:

```
synthesizer.SetOutputToWaveFile("c:\Users\Adam\Documents\speech.wav");
```

This affects any subsequent calls to Speak or SpeakAsync. You can point the synthesizer back to the speakers by calling SetOutputToDefaultAudioDevice.

SSML and PromptBuilder

You can do a lot by passing simple strings to SpeechSynthesizer and using its various members to change voices, rate, volume, and so on. But SpeechSynthesizer also supports input in the form of a standard XML-based language known as Speech Synthesis Markup Language (SSML). This enables you to encapsulate complex speech in a single chunk and have more control over the synthesizer's behavior. You can pass SSML content to SpeechSynthesizer directly via its SpeakSsml and SpeakSsmlAsync methods, but SpeechSynthesizer also has overloads of Speak and SpeakAsync that accept an instance of PromptBuilder.

PromptBuilder is a handy class that makes it easy to programmatically build complex speech input. With PromptBuilder, you can express most of what you could accomplish with an SSML file, but it's generally simpler to learn than SSML.

> **TIP**
>
> Speech Synthesis Markup Language (SSML) is a W3C Recommendation published at http://w3.org/TR/speech-synthesis.

The following code builds a simple dialog with PromptBuilder and then speaks it by passing it to SpeakAsync:

```
SpeechSynthesizer synthesizer = new SpeechSynthesizer();
PromptBuilder promptBuilder = new PromptBuilder();

promptBuilder.AppendTextWithHint("WPF", SayAs.SpellOut);
promptBuilder.AppendText("sounds better than WPF.");

// Pause for 2 seconds
promptBuilder.AppendBreak(new TimeSpan(0, 0, 2));

promptBuilder.AppendText("The time is");
promptBuilder.AppendTextWithHint(DateTime.Now.ToString("hh:mm"), SayAs.Time);

// Pause for 2 seconds
promptBuilder.AppendBreak(new TimeSpan(0, 0, 2));

promptBuilder.AppendText("Hey Sam, can you spell queue?");
```

```
promptBuilder.StartVoice("Microsoft Sam");
promptBuilder.AppendTextWithHint("queue", SayAs.SpellOut);
promptBuilder.EndVoice();

promptBuilder.AppendText("Do it faster!");

promptBuilder.StartVoice("Microsoft Sam");
promptBuilder.StartStyle(new PromptStyle(PromptRate.ExtraFast));
promptBuilder.AppendTextWithHint("queue", SayAs.SpellOut);
promptBuilder.EndStyle();
promptBuilder.EndVoice();

// Speak all the content in the PromptBuilder
synthesizer.SpeakAsync(promptBuilder);
```

After you instantiate a `PromptBuilder`, you keep appending different types of content. The preceding code makes use of `AppendTextWithHint` to spell out some words (which produces a better pronunciation of WPF) and to pronounce a string representing time (such as "08:25") more naturally. You can also surround chunks of content with `Start`*XXX*/`End`*XXX* methods that change the voice or style of the surrounding text, and you can denote where paragraphs and sentences begin and end. These chunks can be nested, just like the XML elements you would create if you were writing raw SSML.

DIGGING DEEPER

Converting a `PromptBuilder` to SSML

You can get the SSML representation of a `PromptBuilder` by calling its `ToXml` method (as long as the result is well formed at the time you call it—for example, as long as there are no `Start`*XXX* calls without matching `End`*XXX* calls). Here's the result when calling it on the `PromptBuilder` from the preceding code (at 8:25 p.m.):

```
<speak version="1.0" xmlns="http://www.w3.org/2001/10/synthesis"
  xml:lang="en-US">
  <say-as interpret-as="characters">WPF</say-as>
  sounds better than WPF
  <break time="2000ms"/>
  The time is
  <say-as interpret-as="time">08:25</say-as>
  <break time="2000ms"/>
  Hey Bob, can you spell queue?
  <voice name="Microsoft Sam">
    <say-as interpret-as="characters">queue</say-as>
  </voice>
  Do it faster!
  <voice name="Microsoft Sam">
```

Continued

```
    <prosody rate="x-fast">
      <say-as interpret-as="characters">queue</say-as>
    </prosody>
  </voice>
</speak>
```

This can be a handy way to persist content that you want spoken at a later time.

TIP

SpeechSynthesizer even supports playing .wav audio files! You can do this in two easy ways. One is using PromptBuilder's AppendAudio method:

```
promptBuilder.AppendAudio("sound.wav");
```

(You can also include the equivalent directive in an SSML file and pass it to SpeakSsml or SpeakSsmlAsync.)

Another way is to use an overload of Speak or SpeakAsync that accepts a Prompt instance such as FilePrompt. With FilePrompt, you can speak content of a file, whether it's a plain-text file, an SSML file, or a .wav file:

```
synthesizer.SpeakAsync(new FilePrompt("text.txt", SynthesisMediaType.Text));
synthesizer.SpeakAsync(new FilePrompt("content.ssml", SynthesisMediaType.Ssml));
synthesizer.SpeakAsync(new FilePrompt("sound.wav", SynthesisMediaType.WaveAudio));
```

Speech Recognition

Speech recognition is exactly the opposite of speech synthesis. Recognition is all about extracting speech sounds from an audio input and turning it into text.

TIP

For speech recognition to work, you need to have a speech recognition engine installed and running. Windows Vista or later comes with one, and Office XP or later comes with one as well. You can also install a free one from http://microsoft.com/speech. You can start the built-in Windows engine by selecting Windows Speech Recognition from the Start menu under Accessories, Ease of Access.

Converting Spoken Words into Text

To use speech recognition, you must add a reference to System.Speech.dll to your project (just as with speech synthesis). This time, the relevant APIs are in the System.Speech.Recognition namespace. The simplest form of recognition is demonstrated by the following code, which instantiates a SpeechRecognizer, loads a grammar, and attaches an event handler to its SpeechRecognized event:

```
SpeechRecognizer recognizer = new SpeechRecognizer();
recognizer.LoadGrammar(new DictationGrammar());
recognizer.SpeechRecognized +=
  new EventHandler<SpeechRecognizedEventArgs>(recognizer_SpeechRecognized);
```

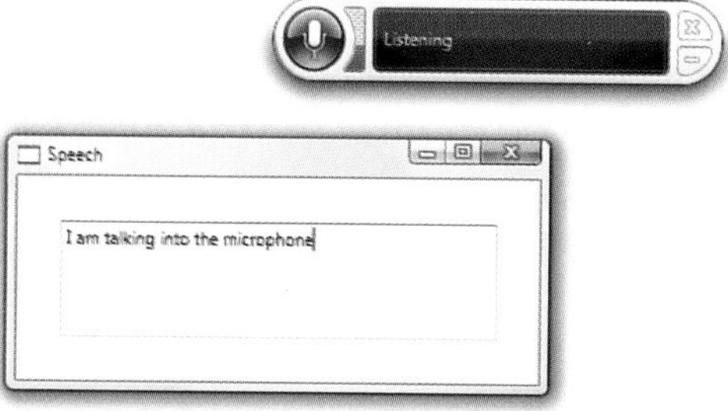

FIGURE 18.6 Dictating content into a WPF `TextBox` using the Windows Speech Recognition program.

Speech recognition is typically used to add custom spoken commands to a program that are more sophisticated than the default functionality exposed through accessibility. Such commands typically consist of a few words or phrases that an application knows in advance. To handle this efficiently, you need to give `SpeechRecognizer` or `SpeechRecognitionEngine` more information about your expectations. That's where SRGS comes in.

Specifying a Grammar with SRGS

If you want to programmatically act on certain words or phrases, writing a `SpeechRecognized` event handler is tricky if you don't constrain the input. You need to ignore irrelevant phrases and possibly pick out relevant words from larger phrases that can't be easily predicted. For example, if one of the words you want to act on is *go*, do you accept words such as *goat*, assuming that the recognizer simply misunderstood the user?

To avoid this kind of grunt work and guesswork, `SpeechRecognizer` and `SpeechRecognitionEngine` support specifying a custom grammar based on the Speech Recognition Grammar Specification (SRGS). With a grammar that captures your possible valid inputs, the recognizer can automatically ignore meaningless results and improve the accuracy of its recognition.

> **TIP**
>
> Speech Recognition Grammar Specification (SRGS) is a W3C Recommendation published at http://w3.org/TR/speech-grammar.

To attach a custom grammar, you can call the same `LoadGrammar` method shown earlier. SRGS-based grammars can be described in XML, so the following code loads a custom grammar from an SRGS XML file in the current directory:

```
SpeechRecognitionEngine engine = new SpeechRecognitionEngine();
SrgsDocument doc = new SrgsDocument("grammar.xml");
engine.LoadGrammar(new Grammar(doc));
```

`SrgsDocument` (and other SRGS-related types) are defined in the `System.Speech.Recognition.SrgsGrammar` namespace.

An SrgsDocument can also be built in-memory using a handful of APIs. The following code builds a grammar that allows only two commands, stop and go:

```
SpeechRecognitionEngine engine = new SpeechRecognitionEngine();
SrgsDocument doc = new SrgsDocument();
SrgsRule command = new SrgsRule("command", new SrgsOneOf("stop", "go"));
doc.Rules.Add(command);
doc.Root = command;
engine.LoadGrammar(new Grammar(doc));
```

You can express much more intricate grammars, however. The following example could be used by a card game, enabling a user to give commands such as *three of hearts* or *ace of spaces* to play those cards:

```
SpeechRecognitionEngine engine = new SpeechRecognitionEngine();
SrgsDocument doc = new SrgsDocument();
SrgsRule command = new SrgsRule("command");
SrgsRule rank = new SrgsRule("rank");
SrgsItem of = new SrgsItem("of");
SrgsRule suit = new SrgsRule("suit");
SrgsItem card = new SrgsItem(new SrgsRuleRef(rank), of, new SrgsRuleRef(suit));
command.Add(card);
rank.Add(new SrgsOneOf("two", "three", "four", "five", "six", "seven",
  "eight", "nine", "ten", "jack", "queen", "king", "ace"));
of.SetRepeat(0, 1);
suit.Add(new SrgsOneOf("clubs", "diamonds", "spades", "hearts"));
doc.Rules.Add(command, rank, suit);
doc.Root = command;
engine.LoadGrammar(new Grammar(doc));
```

This grammar defines the notion of a card as "*rank* of *suit*" where *rank* has 13 possible values, *suit* has 4 possible values, and "of" can be omitted (hence the SetRepeat call that allows it to be said zero or one time).

18

Specifying a Grammar with GrammarBuilder

Specifying grammars with the APIs in System.Speech.Recognition.SrgsGrammar or with an SRGS XML file (whose syntax is not covered here) can be complicated. Therefore, the System.Speech.Recognition namespace also contains a GrammarBuilder class that exposes the most commonly used aspects of recognition grammars via much simpler APIs. Grammar (the type passed to LoadGrammar) has an overloaded constructor that accepts an instance of GrammarBuilder, so it can easily be plugged in wherever you can use an SrgsDocument.

For example, here's the first grammar from the previous section, reimplemented using GrammarBuilder:

```
SpeechRecognitionEngine engine = new SpeechRecognitionEngine();
GrammarBuilder builder = new GrammarBuilder(new Choices("stop", "go"));
engine.LoadGrammar(new Grammar(builder));
```

And here's the reimplemented card game grammar:

```
SpeechRecognitionEngine engine = new SpeechRecognitionEngine();
GrammarBuilder builder = new GrammarBuilder();
builder.Append(new Choices("two", "three", "four", "five", "six", "seven",
  "eight", "nine", "ten", "jack", "queen", "king", "ace"));
builder.Append("of", 0, 1);
builder.Append(new Choices("clubs", "diamonds", "spades", "hearts"));
engine.LoadGrammar(new Grammar(builder));
```

GrammarBuilder doesn't expose all the power and flexibility of SrgsDocument, but it's often all that you need. In the card game example, the user can speak "two clubs" or perhaps something that sounds like "too uh cubs," and the SpeechRecognized event handler should receive the canonical "two of clubs" string. You can get even fancier in your grammars and tag pieces with semantic labels so that the event handler can pick out concepts such as the rank and suit without having to parse even the canonical string.

Summary

WPF's support for audio, video, and speech rounds out its rich media offerings. The audio support is limited but is enough to accomplish the most common tasks. The video support is only a subset of what's provided by the underlying Windows Media Player APIs, but the seamless integration with the rest of WPF (so you can transform or animate video just as you can any other content) makes it extremely compelling. WPF's standards-based speech synthesis and recognition support is state of the art and easy to use, even though it's mainly just a wrapper on top of the unmanaged Microsoft SAPI APIs.

PART VI

Advanced Topics

IN THIS PART

CHAPTER 19

Interoperability with Non-WPF Technologies

IN THIS CHAPTER

- Embedding Win32 Controls in WPF Applications
- Embedding WPF Controls in Win32 Applications
- Embedding Windows Forms Controls in WPF Applications
- Embedding WPF Controls in Windows Forms Applications
- Mixing DirectX Content with WPF Content
- Embedding ActiveX Controls in WPF Applications

Despite the incredible breadth of Windows Presentation Foundation, it lacks some features that other technologies have. When creating a WPF-based user interface, you might want to exploit such features. For example, the fourth release of WPF *still* doesn't include some of the standard controls that Windows Forms has had for almost a decade: `NumericUpDown`, `NotifyIcon`, and more. Windows Forms also has support for multiple-document interface (MDI) window management, wrappers over additional Win32 dialogs and APIs, and various handy APIs, such as `Screen.AllScreens` (which returns an array of screens with information about their bounds). Win32 has controls such as an IP Address text box (`SysIPAddress32`) that have no equivalent in either Windows Forms or WPF. Windows includes many Win32-based user interface pieces that don't have first-class exposure to WPF, such as "glass" effects, task dialogs, and a wizard framework. Tons of ActiveX controls exist for the purpose of embedding rich functionality into your own software. And some technologies cover scenarios that are fundamentally different from what WPF is designed to enable, but it would still be nice to leverage such pieces in a WPF application. Some examples are high-performance immediate-mode DirectX rendering and platform-agnostic HTML-based rendering.

Perhaps you've already put a lot of effort into developing your own pre-WPF user interfaces or controls. If so, you might want to leverage some of your own work that's already in place. Maybe you have developed an application in a non-WPF technology with an extremely complicated main surface (for example, a CAD program) and just want to "WPF-ize" the outer edges of the applications with rich menus, toolbars, and so on. Maybe you've created a web application with tons of HTML content that you want to enhance but not replace.

In earlier chapters, you've seen WPF's HTML interoperability. Given that HTML can be hosted inside a WPF `Frame` or `WebBrowser` and WPF content can be hosted inside HTML (as a XAML Browser Application or a loose XAML page), you can leverage existing HTML content—and any Silverlight, Flash, and other content it contains—alongside new WPF content. Fortunately, WPF's support for interoperability goes much deeper than that. It's fairly easy for WPF applications and controls to leverage all kinds of non-WPF content or APIs, such as all the examples in the previous two paragraphs. Some of these scenarios are possible thanks to the features described in this chapter, some are possible thanks to the .NET Framework's interoperability between managed and unmanaged code, and (in the case of calling miscellaneous Windows Forms APIs from WPF) some are possible simply because the other technology defines managed APIs that just happen to live in non-WPF assemblies.

Figure 19.1 summarizes different user interface technologies and the paths you can take to mix and match them. Win32 is a general bucket that includes any technology that runs on Windows: MFC, WTL, OpenGL, and so on. Notice that there's a direct path between WPF and each technology except for Silverlight and ActiveX. In these cases, you must use another technology as an intermediate layer. Silverlight does provide a mechanism for being directly hosted outside of HTML, leveraged by Visual Studio and Expression Blend. It involves using Silverlight's `HostingRenderTargetBitmap` class to get a bitmap representation of the Silverlight content then feeding that information into a WPF `InteropBitmap` or `WriteableBitmap`. This support is pretty primitive, however, so it is omitted from the figure.

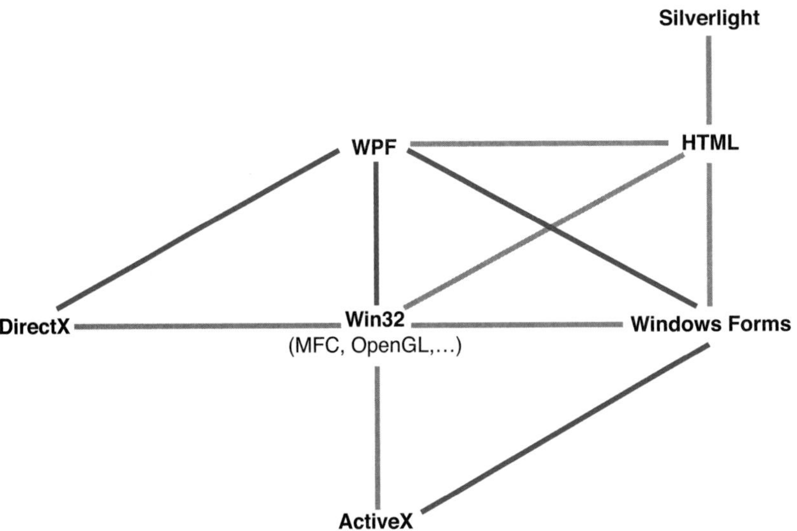

FIGURE 19.1 The relationship between various Windows user interface technologies.

All the blue lines connecting the technologies are discussed in this chapter. The line between Win32 and Windows Forms is enabled by standard .NET Framework interoperability technologies for mixing managed and unmanaged code (and the fact that Windows Forms is based on Win32), and the lines between Win32 and ActiveX/DirectX are somewhat artificial because there are no big barriers separating Win32 and ActiveX or Win32 and DirectX.

This chapter focuses on embedding controls of one type inside applications of another type. It first examines both directions of WPF/Win32 interoperability separately, then both directions of WPF/Windows Forms interoperability separately. WPF/DirectX interoperability is examined in a single section because its seamless mixing can be used to effectively get either direction of interoperability. The chapter ends by examining the options with WPF/ActiveX interoperability. Although the focus is on embedding controls, we'll look at another important scenario at the end of most sections that isn't as straightforward as you might imagine: launching heterogeneous dialogs.

WARNING

You cannot overlap WPF content with non-WPF content (except when using `D3DImage`)!

As with hosting HTML content in `Frame` or `WebBrowser`, any non-WPF content that's hosted in a WPF application has extra limitations that don't apply to native WPF content. For example, you can't apply `Transforms` to non-WPF content. Furthermore, you cannot overlap content from one technology over content from another. You can arbitrarily nest (for example) Win32 inside WPF inside Windows Forms inside WPF, and so on, but every pixel must have one and only one technology responsible for its rendering. DirectX is the only exception to this rule—and only if you use the `D3DImage` feature described later in this chapter—because WPF internally uses DirectX for rendering. Therefore, you can mix WPF and DirectX on the same pixels, and there is still only one technology (DirectX) ultimately responsible for rendering them.

Embedding Win32 Controls in WPF Applications

In Win32, all controls are considered to be "windows," and Win32 APIs interact with them via window handles known as `HWND`s. All Windows-based user interface technologies (such as DirectX and MFC) ultimately use `HWND`s to some degree, so the ability to work with `HWND`s provides the ability to work with all of these technologies.

Although WPF's subsystems (layout, animation, and so on) don't know how to interact directly with `HWND`s, WPF defines a `FrameworkElement` that can host an arbitrary `HWND`. This `FrameworkElement` is `System.Windows.Interop.HwndHost`, and it makes `HWND`-based controls look and act almost exactly like WPF controls.

To demonstrate the use of `HwndHost` in a WPF application, let's look at embedding a custom Win32 control to add webcam functionality to WPF. WPF's video support doesn't include anything for interacting with local video capture devices such as a simple webcam. Microsoft's DirectShow technology has support for this, however, so Win32 interoperability enables you to leverage that webcam support in a WPF application.

A Win32 `Webcam` Control

Listing 19.1 contains the unmanaged C++ definition for a custom Win32 `Webcam` control that wraps a few DirectShow COM objects.

LISTING 19.1 `Webcam.h`—Definition of Some Webcam Win32 APIs

```
#if !defined(WEBCAM_H)
#define WEBCAM_H

#include <wtypes.h>

class Webcam
{
public:
  static HRESULT Initialize(int width, int height);
  static HRESULT AttachToWindow(HWND hwnd);
  static HRESULT Start();
  static HRESULT Pause();
  static HRESULT Stop();
  static HRESULT Repaint();
  static HRESULT Terminate();
  static int GetWidth();
  static int GetHeight();
};
#endif // !defined(WEBCAM_H)
```

The `Webcam` class is designed to work with a computer's default video capture device, so it contains a set of simple static methods for controlling this device. It is initialized with a width and height (which can be later retrieved via `GetWidth` and `GetHeight` methods). Then, after telling `Webcam` (via `AttachToWindow`) what `HWND` to render itself on, the behavior can be controlled with simple `Start`, `Pause`, and `Stop` methods.

Listing 19.2 contains the implementation of the `Webcam` class. The complete implementations of `Webcam::Initialize` and `Webcam::Terminate` are omitted for brevity, but the entire implementation can be found with this book's source code (http://informit.com/title/9780672331190).

LISTING 19.2 `Webcam.cpp`—Implementation of the Webcam APIs

```
LRESULT WINAPI WndProc(HWND hwnd, UINT msg, WPARAM wParam, LPARAM lParam)
{
  switch (msg)
  {
    case WM_ERASEBKGND:
      DefWindowProc(hwnd, msg, wParam, lParam);
      Webcam::Repaint();
      break;
```

LISTING 19.2 Continued

```
    default:
      return DefWindowProc(hwnd, msg, wParam, lParam);
  }
  return 0;
}

HRESULT Webcam::Initialize(int width, int height)
{
  _width = width;
  _height = height;

  // Create and register the Window Class
  WNDCLASS wc;
  wc.style         = CS_VREDRAW | CS_HREDRAW;
  wc.lpfnWndProc   = WndProc;
  wc.cbClsExtra    = 0;
  wc.cbWndExtra    = 0;
  wc.hInstance     = GetModuleHandle(NULL);
  wc.hIcon         = LoadIcon(NULL, IDI_APPLICATION);
  wc.hCursor       = LoadCursor(NULL, IDC_ARROW);
  wc.hbrBackground = (HBRUSH)(COLOR_SCROLLBAR+1);
  wc.lpszMenuName  = 0;
  wc.lpszClassName = L"WebcamClass";
  RegisterClass(&wc);

  HRESULT hr = CoCreateInstance(CLSID_FilterGraph, NULL, CLSCTX_INPROC_SERVER,
    IID_IGraphBuilder, (void **)&_graphBuilder);

  …Create and interact with several COM objects…
  return hr;
}

HRESULT Webcam::AttachToWindow(HWND hwnd)
{
  if (!_initialized || !_windowlessControl)
    return E_FAIL;

  _hwnd = hwnd;

  // Position and size the video
  RECT rcDest;
  rcDest.left = 0;
  rcDest.right = _width;
  rcDest.top = 0;
```

19

LISTING 19.2 Continued

```
  rcDest.bottom = _height;
  _windowlessControl->SetVideoClippingWindow(hwnd);
  return _windowlessControl->SetVideoPosition(NULL, &rcDest);
}

HRESULT Webcam::Start()
{
  if (!_initialized || !_graphBuilder || !_mediaControl)
    return E_FAIL;

  _graphBuilder->Render(_pin);
  return _mediaControl->Run();
}

HRESULT Webcam::Pause()
{
  if (!_initialized || !_mediaControl)
    return E_FAIL;

  return _mediaControl->Pause();
}

HRESULT Webcam::Stop()
{
  if (!_initialized || !_mediaControl)
    return E_FAIL;

  return _mediaControl->Stop();
}

HRESULT Webcam::Repaint()
{
  if (!_initialized || !_windowlessControl)
    return E_FAIL;

  return _windowlessControl->RepaintVideo(_hwnd, GetDC(_hwnd));
}

HRESULT Webcam::Terminate()
{
  HRESULT hr = Webcam::Stop();

  …Release several COM objects…
  return hr;
}
```

LISTING 19.2 Continued

```
int Webcam::GetWidth()
{
  return _width;
}

int Webcam::GetHeight()
{
  return _height;
}
```

The implementation begins with a simple Win32 window procedure, which makes sure to repaint the video whenever a `WM_ERASEBKGND` message is received. Inside `Initialize`, a Win32 window class called `WebcamClass` is defined and registered, and a bunch of DirectShow-specific COM objects are created and initialized. (The `Terminate` method releases all these COM objects.) `AttachToWindow` not only tells DirectShow which window to render on, but it sets the size of the video to match the dimensions passed to `Initialize`. The other methods are simple wrappers for the underlying DirectShow methods.

Using the `Webcam` Control in WPF

The first step in using the `Webcam` control in a WPF application is to create a project that is able to "see" this unmanaged control from the WPF-specific managed code that must be written. Many options exist for integrating managed code into an unmanaged codebase. If you're comfortable with C++, using C++/CLI to seamlessly mix managed and unmanaged code is usually the best approach. This is especially true for the `Webcam` class because it doesn't expose any functionality outside the DLL in which it is compiled.

FAQ

What Is C++/CLI?

C++/CLI is a version of the C++ language that supports managed code. Ignoring the now-deprecated Managed C++ features in earlier versions of Visual C++, C++/CLI is *the way* for C++ developers to consume and produce .NET components. (CLI stands for Common Language Infrastructure, which is the name of the Ecma-standardized pieces of the .NET Framework's common language runtime.) C++/CLI is has been standardized by Ecma (like the CLI and C#).

Just to put some context around these standards: Visual C++ is Microsoft's implementation of C++/CLI, Visual C# is Microsoft's implementation of C#, and the common language runtime (CLR) is Microsoft's implementation of the CLI. Using the managed code features in Visual C++ is often as simple as adding the `/clr` compilation switch to relevant source files or projects, changing incompatible switches, and learning some new bits of syntax specific to managed data types.

LISTING 19.3 Continued

```
};

ref class Window1 : Window
{
public:
  Window1()
  {
    DockPanel^ panel = gcnew DockPanel();
    MyHwndHost^ host = gcnew MyHwndHost();
    Label^ label = gcnew Label();
    label->FontSize = 20;
    label->Content = "The Win32 control is docked to the left.";
    panel->Children->Add(host);
    panel->Children->Add(label);
    this->Content = panel;

    if (FAILED(Webcam::Initialize(640, 480)))
    {
      ::MessageBox(NULL, L"Failed to communicate with a video capture device.",
        L"Error", 0);
    }
    Webcam::Start();
  }

  ~Window1()
  {
    Webcam::Terminate();
  }
};
```

The first thing to notice about Listing 19.3 is that it defines a subclass of `HwndHost` called `MyHwndHost`. This is necessary because `HwndHost` is actually an abstract class. It contains two methods that need to be overridden:

- **`BuildWindowCore`**—In this method, you must return the `HWND` to be hosted. This is typically where initialization is done as well. The parent `HWND` is given to you as a parameter to this method. If you do not return a child `HWND` whose parent matches the passed-in parameter, WPF throws an `InvalidOperationException`.
- **`DestroyWindowCore`**—This method gives you the opportunity to do any cleanup/termination when the `HWND` is no longer needed.

For both methods, `HWND`s are represented as `HandleRef` types. `HandleRef` is a lightweight wrapper (in the `System.Runtime.InteropServices` namespace) that ties the lifetime of the

HWND to a managed object. You'll typically pass this as the managed object when constructing a HandleRef.

> **TIP**
>
> A typical implementation of an HwndHost subclass calls CreateWindow inside BuildWindowCore and DestroyWindow inside DestroyWindowCore. Note, however, that calling DestroyWindow isn't really necessary. That's because a child HWND is automatically destroyed by Win32 when the parent HWND is destroyed. So in Listing 19.3, the implementation of DestroyWindowCore could be left empty.

Listing 19.3 calls the Win32 CreateWindow API inside BuildWindowCore to create an instance of the WebcamClass window that was registered in Listing 19.2, passing the input HWND as the parent. The HWND returned by CreateWindow is not only returned by BuildWindowCore (inside a HandleRef), but it is also passed to the Webcam::AttachToWindow method so the video is rendered appropriately. Inside DestroyWindowCore, the Win32 DestroyWindow API is called to signify the end of the HWND's lifespan.

> **TIP**
>
> For some applications, initialization of the Win32 content might need to wait until all the WPF content has been rendered. In such cases, you can perform this initialization from Window's ContentRendered event.

Inside the Window's constructor, the MyHwndHost is instantiated and added to a DockPanel just like any other FrameworkElement. The Webcam is then initialized, and the video stream is started.

Listing 19.4 contains the final piece needed for the WPF webcam application, which is the main method that creates the Window and runs the Application. It is also compiled with the /clr option. Figure 19.2 shows the running application.

LISTING 19.4 HostingWin32.cpp—The Application's Entry Point

```
#include "Window1.h"

using namespace System;
using namespace System::Windows;
using namespace System::Windows::Media;

[STAThreadAttribute]
int main(array<System::String ^> ^args)
{
  Application^ application = gcnew Application();
  Window^ window = gcnew Window1();
  window->Title = "Hosting Win32 DirectShow Content in WPF";
  window->Background = Brushes::Orange;
  application->Run(window);
  return 0;
}
```

TIP

Because C++/CLI was introduced with Visual C++ 2005, you might find yourself needing to upgrade an older codebase to a later compiler to take advantage of it. This can sometimes be tricky because of increased ISO standard compliance in the compiler and various changes to Windows libraries and headers. Although it might not be an automatic process, there are many benefits to upgrading to the latest Visual C++ compiler, even for your unmanaged code!

FAQ

How do I launch a Win32 modal dialog from a WPF application?

You can still use your favorite Win32 technique for showing the dialog (such as calling the Win32 `DialogBox` function). With C++/CLI, this can be a direct call. With a language such as C#, you can use PInvoke to call the relevant function(s). The only trick is to get the `HWND` of a WPF `Window` to pass as the dialog's parent.

Fortunately, you can get the `HWND` for any WPF `Window` by using the `WindowInteropHelper` class from the `System.Windows.Interop` namespace.

This looks as follows in C++/CLI:

```
WindowInteropHelper^ helper = gcnew WindowInteropHelper(wpfParentWindow);
HWND hwnd = (HWND)helper->Handle.ToPointer();
DialogBox(hinst, MAKEINTRESOURCE(MYDIALOG), hwnd, (DLGPROC)MyDialogProc);
```

Embedding WPF Controls in Win32 Applications

Lots of compelling WPF features can be integrated into a Win32 application: 3D, rich documents support, animation, easy restyling, and so on. Even if you don't require this extra "flashiness," you can still take advantage of important features, such as flexible layout and resolution independence.

WPF's `HWND` interoperability is bidirectional, so WPF controls can be embedded in Win32 applications much like the way Win32 controls are embedded in WPF applications. In this section, you'll see how to embed a built-in WPF control—`DocumentViewer`, the viewer for XPS documents—in a simple Win32 window using a class called `HwndSource`.

Introducing `HwndSource`

`HwndSource` does the opposite of `HwndHost`: It exposes any WPF `Visual` as an `HWND`. Listing 19.6 demonstrates the use of `HwndSource` with the relevant C++ source file from a Win32 project included with this book's source code. It is compiled with `/clr`, so it is managed code that uses both managed and unmanaged data types.

LISTING 19.6 `HostingWPF.cpp`—Embedding a WPF Control in a Win32 Dialog

```
#include "stdafx.h"
#include "HostingWPF.h"
#include "commctrl.h"

#using <PresentationFramework.dll>
#using <PresentationCore.dll>
#using <WindowsBase.dll>

LRESULT CALLBACK DialogFunction(HWND hDlg, UINT message, WPARAM wParam,
  LPARAM lParam)
{
  switch (message)
  {
    case WM_INITDIALOG:
    {
      // Describe the HwndSource
      System::Windows::Interop::HwndSourceParameters p;
      p.WindowStyle = WS_VISIBLE | WS_CHILD;
      p.PositionX = 10;
      p.PositionY = 10;
      p.Width = 500;
      p.Height = 350;
      p.ParentWindow = System::IntPtr(hDlg);

      System::Windows::Interop::HwndSource^ source =
        gcnew System::Windows::Interop::HwndSource(p);

      // Attach a new DocumentViewer to the HwndSource
      source->RootVisual = gcnew System::Windows::Controls::DocumentViewer();

      return TRUE;
    }

    case WM_CLOSE:
      EndDialog(hDlg, LOWORD(wParam));
      return TRUE;
  }
  return FALSE;
}

[System::STAThread]
int APIENTRY _tWinMain(HINSTANCE hInstance, HINSTANCE hPrevInstance,
```

19

Getting the Right Layout

Because you're in the world of Win32 when doing this type of integration, there's no special layout support for the top-level WPF control. In Listing 19.6, the `DocumentViewer` is given an initial placement of `(10,10)` and a size of `(500,350)`. But that placement and size are never going to change without some explicit code to change them. Listing 19.7 makes the `DocumentViewer` occupy the entire space of the window, even as the window is resized. Figure 19.6 shows the result.

LISTING 19.7 `HostingWPF.cpp`—Updating the Size of the WPF Control

```
#include "stdafx.h"
#include "HostingWPF.h"
#include "commctrl.h"

#using <PresentationFramework.dll>
#using <PresentationCore.dll>
#using <WindowsBase.dll>

ref class Globals
{
public:
  static System::Windows::Interop::HwndSource^ source;
};

LRESULT CALLBACK DialogFunction(HWND hDlg, UINT message, WPARAM wParam,
  LPARAM lParam)
{
  switch (message)
  {
    case WM_INITDIALOG:
    {
      System::Windows::Interop::HwndSourceParameters p;
      p.WindowStyle = WS_VISIBLE | WS_CHILD;
      // Initial size and position don't matter due to WM_SIZE handling:
      p.PositionX = 0; p.PositionY = 0;
      p.Width = 100; p.Height = 100;
      p.ParentWindow = System::IntPtr(hDlg);

      Globals::source = gcnew System::Windows::Interop::HwndSource(p);
      Globals::source->RootVisual =
        gcnew System::Windows::Controls::DocumentViewer();
      return TRUE;
    }

    case WM_SIZE:
      RECT r;
```

LISTING 19.7 Continued

```
      GetClientRect(hDlg, &r);
      SetWindowPos((HWND)Globals::source->Handle.ToPointer(), NULL,
        r.left, r.top, r.right - r.left, r.bottom - r.top, 0);
      return TRUE;

    case WM_CLOSE:
      EndDialog(hDlg, LOWORD(wParam));
      return TRUE;
  }
  return FALSE;
}

[System::STAThreadAttribute]
int APIENTRY _tWinMain(HINSTANCE hInstance, HINSTANCE hPrevInstance,
  LPTSTR lpCmdLine, int nCmdShow)
{
  DialogBox(hInstance, (LPCTSTR)IDD_MYDIALOG, NULL, (DLGPROC)DialogFunction);
  return 0;
}
```

FIGURE 19.6 The WPF `DocumentViewer` control hosted and resized in a simple Win32 dialog.

The most important code in Listing 19.7 is the handling of the `WM_SIZE` message. It uses the Win32 `GetClientRect` API to get the current window size, and then it applies it to the `HwndSource` using the Win32 `SetWindowPos` API. There are two interesting points about this new implementation:

- The `HwndSource` variable is now "global," so it can be shared by multiple places in the code. But C++/CLI does not allow a managed variable to be truly global, so the listing uses a common technique of making it a static variable of a managed class.
- To operate on the `HwndSource` with Win32 APIs such as `SetWindowPos`, you need its `HWND`. This is exposed via a `Handle` property of type `IntPtr`. In C++/CLI, you can call its `ToPointer` method (which returns a `void*`) and then cast the result to an `HWND`.

TIP

You don't need to share an HwndSource globally as long as you have its corresponding HWND. HwndSource defines a static FromHwnd method, which returns an HwndSource instance corresponding to any HWND (assuming that the HWND belongs to an HwndSource in the first place). This is very handy when retrofitting Win32 codebases with WPF content because HWNDs are often passed around as parameters. With this technique, you can avoid the need to define a managed Globals class, as was done in Listing 19.7.

TIP

You can use HwndSource with a pure WPF application to respond to obscure Windows messages. In pure WPF applications, you don't need to define a window procedure and respond to Windows messages. But that's not because Windows messages don't exist; the top-level window still has an HWND and still plays by Win32 rules. As mentioned in a previous tip, WPF's Window object actually uses HwndSource to host any content inside the top-level HWND. And internally, WPF has a window procedure that exposes relevant messages in its own way. For example, WPF handles WM_SIZE messages and raises a SizeChanged event.

There are, however, Windows messages that WPF does not expose. But you can use HwndSource with any WPF Window to get exposure to all messages. The key is to use the System.Windows.Interop.WindowInteropHelper class, which exposes the HWND for any WPF Window. After you have this handle, you can get the corresponding HwndSource object (using HwndSource.FromHwnd) and attach a window procedure by calling HwndSource's AddHook method.

In Chapter 8, "Exploiting Windows 7," we performed these actions to discover WM_DWMCOMPOSITIONCHANGED messages. The following Window intercepts WM_TCARD, an obscure message that can be sent by Windows Help when certain directives are selected inside an application's help file:

```
public partial class AdvancedWindow : Window
{
  …
  void AdvancedWindow_Loaded(object sender, RoutedEventArgs e)
  {
    // Get the HWND for the current Window
    IntPtr hwnd = new WindowInteropHelper(this).Handle;
    // Get the HwndSource corresponding to the HWND
    HwndSource source = HwndSource.FromHwnd(hwnd);
    // Add a window procedure to the HwndSource
    source.AddHook(new HwndSourceHook(WndProc));
  }

  private static IntPtr WndProc(
    IntPtr hwnd, int msg, IntPtr wParam, IntPtr lParam, ref bool handled)
  {
```

Continued

```
    // Handle any Win32 message
    if (msg == WM_TCARD)
    {
      ...
      handled = true;
    }
    return IntPtr.Zero;
  }

  // Define any Win32 message constants
  private const int WM_TCARD = 0x0052;
}
```

FAQ

How do I launch a WPF modal dialog from a Win32 application?

To launch a WPF `Window`, whether from Win32 code or WPF code, you can instantiate it and call its `ShowDialog` method. The trick, as with the reverse direction, is assigning the proper parent to the WPF `Window`. Correctly setting the parent of a modal dialog is important to get the desired behavior—ensuring that it remains on top of the parent window at all times, that both windows minimize together, and so on.

The problem is that `Window`'s `Owner` property is of type `Window`, and it has no other property or method that enables its parent to be set to an arbitrary `HWND`. Furthermore, you can't fabricate a `Window` object from an arbitrary `HWND`.

The solution to this dilemma is to use the `WindowInteropHelper` class in the `System.Windows.Interop` namespace. This class not only exposes the `HWND` for any WPF `Window` but enables you to set its owner to an arbitrary `HWND`. This looks as follows in C++/CLI:

```
Nullable<bool> LaunchWpfDialogFromWin32Window(Window^ dialog, HWND parent)
{
  WindowInteropHelper^ helper = gcnew WindowInteropHelper(dialog);
  helper->Owner = parent;
  return dialog->ShowDialog();
}
```

19

Embedding Windows Forms Controls in WPF Applications

You've seen that WPF can host Win32 controls by wrapping any `HWND` inside an `HwndHost`. And Windows Forms controls can easily be exposed as Win32 controls. (Unlike WPF controls, they are all `HWND` based, so `System.Windows.Forms.Control` directly defines a

Handle property exposing the HWND.) Therefore, you could use the same techniques previously discussed to host Windows Forms controls inside WPF.

However, there is an opportunity for much richer integration between Windows Forms and WPF, without delving into the underlying HWND-based plumbing. Sure, they have different rendering engines and different controls. But they both have rich .NET-based object models with similar properties and events, and both have services (such as layout and data binding) that go above and beyond their Win32 common denominator.

Indeed, WPF takes advantage of this opportunity and also has built-in functionality for direct interoperability with Windows Forms. This support is still built on top of the Win32 HWND interoperability described in the preceding two sections, but with many features to make the integration much simpler. The hard work is done for you, so you can communicate more directly between the technologies, usually without needing to write any unmanaged code.

As with Win32 interoperability, WPF defines a pair of classes to cover both directions of communication. The analog to HwndHost is called WindowsFormsHost, and it appears in the System.Windows.Forms.Integration namespace (in the WindowsFormsIntegration.dll assembly).

Embedding a PropertyGrid with Procedural Code

This chapter's introduction mentions that Windows Forms has several interesting built-in controls that WPF lacks. One such control—the powerful PropertyGrid—helps to highlight the deep integration between Windows Forms and WPF, so let's use that inside a WPF Window. (Of course, you can also create custom Windows Forms controls and embed them in WPF Windows as well.)

The first step is to add a reference to System.Windows.Forms.dll and WindowsFormsIntegration.dll to your WPF-based project. After you've done this, your Window's Loaded event is an appropriate place to create and attach a hosted Windows Forms control. For example, consider this simple Window containing a Grid called grid:

```
<Window x:Class="HostingWindowsFormsControl.Window1"
  xmlns="http://schemas.microsoft.com/winfx/2006/xaml/presentation"
  xmlns:x="http://schemas.microsoft.com/winfx/2006/xaml"
  Title="Hosting a Windows Forms Property Grid in WPF"
  Loaded="Window_Loaded">
    <Grid Name="grid"/>
</Window>
```

The following handler of the Loaded event adds the PropertyGrid to the Grid, using WindowsFormsHost as the intermediate element:

```
private void Window_Loaded(object sender, RoutedEventArgs e)
{
  // Create the host and the PropertyGrid control
  System.Windows.Forms.Integration.WindowsFormsHost host =
```

```
    new System.Windows.Forms.Integration.WindowsFormsHost();
  System.Windows.Forms.PropertyGrid propertyGrid =
    new System.Windows.Forms.PropertyGrid();

  // Add the PropertyGrid to the host, and the host to the WPF Grid
  host.Child = propertyGrid;
  grid.Children.Add(host);

  // Set a PropertyGrid-specific property
  propertyGrid.SelectedObject = this;
}
```

The integration-specific code is as simple as instantiating `WindowsFormsHost` and setting its `Child` property to the desired object. `WindowsFormsHost`'s `Child` property can be set to any object that derives from `System.Windows.Forms.Control`.

The last line, which sets `PropertyGrid`'s `SelectedObject` property to the instance of the current WPF `Window`, enables a pretty amazing scenario. `PropertyGrid` displays the properties of any .NET object, and, in some cases, enables the editing of the object's values. It does this via .NET reflection. Because WPF objects are .NET objects, `PropertyGrid` provides a fairly rich way to edit the current `Window`'s properties on the fly, without writing any extra code. Figure 19.7 shows the previously defined `Window` in action. When running this application, you can see values change as you resize the `Window`, you can type in new property values to resize the `Window`, you can change its background color or border style, and so on.

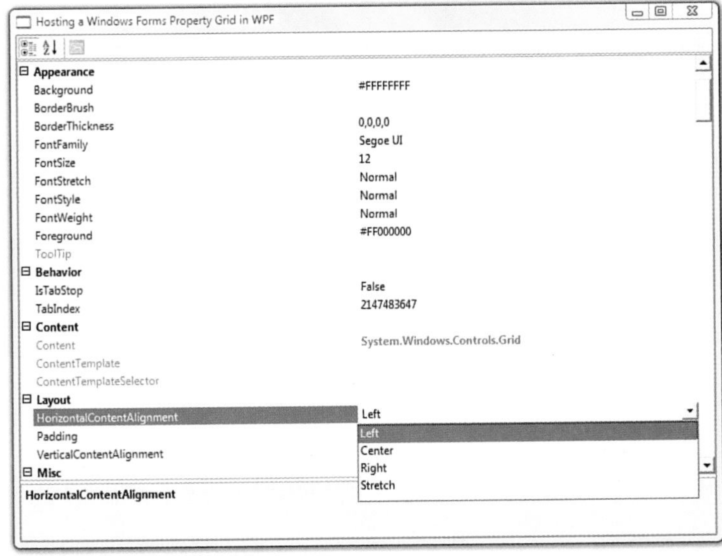

FIGURE 19.7 The hosted Windows Forms `PropertyGrid` enables you to change properties of the WPF `Window` on the fly.

Notice that the enumeration values for properties such as `HorizontalContentAlignment` are automatically populated in a drop-down list, thanks to the standard treatment of .NET enums. But Figure 19.7 highlights some additional similarities between Windows Forms and WPF, aside from being .NET-based. Notice that `Window`'s properties are grouped into categories such as "Behavior," "Content," and "Layout." This comes from `CategoryAttribute` markings that are used by both Windows Forms and WPF. The type converters that WPF uses are also compatible with Windows Forms, so you can type in "red" as a color, for example, and it gets automatically converted to the hexadecimal ARGB representation (#FFFF0000). Another neat thing about the `PropertyGrid` used in this manner is that you can see attached properties that could be applied to the object, with the syntax you would expect.

> **TIP**
>
> The `WindowsFormsHost` class actually derives from `HwndHost`, so it supports the same HWND interoperability features described earlier, just in case you want to dig into lower-level mechanics, such as overriding its `WndProc` method.

Embedding a `PropertyGrid` with XAML

There's no reason that you have to instantiate a `WindowsFormsHost` instance in procedural code; you could instead define it right inside your XAML file. Furthermore, there's nothing to stop you from using Windows Forms controls inside XAML, except for limitations of the expressiveness of XAML. (The controls must have a default constructor, useful instance properties to set, and so on, unless you're in an environment in which you can use XAML2009.)

Not all Windows Forms controls work well within XAML, but `PropertyGrid` works reasonably well. For example, the previous XAML can be replaced with the following XAML:

```
<Window x:Class="HostingWindowsFormsControl.Window1"
  xmlns="http://schemas.microsoft.com/winfx/2006/xaml/presentation"
  xmlns:x="http://schemas.microsoft.com/winfx/2006/xaml"
  xmlns:swf="clr-namespace:System.Windows.Forms;assembly=System.Windows.Forms"
  Title="Hosting a Windows Forms Property Grid in WPF"
  Loaded="Window_Loaded" x:Name="rootWindow">
  <Grid>
    <WindowsFormsHost>
      <swf:PropertyGrid x:Name="propertyGrid"
                        SelectedObject="{x:Reference rootWindow}"/>
    </WindowsFormsHost>
  </Grid>
</Window>
```

The `System.Windows.Forms.Integration` .NET namespace is already included as part of WPF's standard XML namespace, so `WindowsFormsHost` can be used without any additional work, as long as your project has a reference to `WindowsFormsIntegration.dll`. And with the `System.Windows.Forms` .NET namespace given the prefix `swf`, the `PropertyGrid` object can be instantiated directly in the XAML file. Notice that the `PropertyGrid` can be added as a child element to `WindowsFormsHost` because its `Child` property is marked as a content property. `PropertyGrid`'s properties can generally be set in XAML rather than C#. Thanks to `x:Reference`, `SelectedObject` can be set to the current `Window` instance (now named `rootWindow`), replicating the entire example without any procedural code needed!

TIP

The `x:Reference` markup extension is often mistakenly associated with the XAML2009 features that can only be used from loose XAML at the time of this writing. Although `x:Reference` is a new feature in WPF 4, it can be used from XAML2006 just fine as long as your project is targeting version 4 or later of the .NET Framework. One glitch is that the XAML designer in Visual Studio 2010 doesn't properly handle `x:Reference`, so it gives the following design-time error that you can safely ignore:

```
Service provider is missing the INameResolver service
```

TIP

By default, Windows Forms controls hosted in WPF applications might look old-fashioned. That's because they use the "classic" Win32 Common Controls library unless you explicitly enable the Windows XP–era visual styles. You can do this by embedding a special manifest file in an application, but it's easiest to just call the `System.Windows.Forms.Application.EnableVisualStyles` method before any of the Windows Forms controls are instantiated. The Visual Studio template for Windows Forms projects automatically inserts this method call, but the template for WPF projects does not.

FAQ

How do I launch a Windows Forms modal dialog from a WPF application?

The answer to this question seems like it should be simple: Instantiate your `Form`-derived class and call its `ShowDialog` method. But for it to behave like a correct modal dialog, you should call the overload of `ShowDialog` that accepts an owner. This owner, however, must be in the form of an `IWin32Window`, a type that's incompatible with a WPF `Window`.

As explained in the previous section, you can get the `HWND` for a WPF `Window` by using the `WindowInteropHelper` class from the `System.Windows.Interop` namespace, but how do you get an `IWin32Window`? You actually have to define a custom class that implements it. Fortunately, this is pretty easy because `IWin32Window` defines only a single `Handle` property. The following code defines an `OwnerWindow` class that can be used in this situation:

```
class OwnerWindow : IWin32Window
{
  private IntPtr handle;
```

Continued

```
  public IntPtr Handle
  {
    get { return handle; }
    set { handle = value; }
  }
}
```

With this class in place, you can write code like the following that launches a modal Windows Forms dialog, using a WPF `Window` as its parent:

```
DialogResult LaunchWindowsFormsDialogFromWpfWindow(Form dialog, Window parent)
{
  WindowInteropHelper helper = new WindowInteropHelper(parent);
  OwnerWindow owner = new OwnerWindow();
  owner.Handle = helper.Handle;
  return dialog.ShowDialog(owner);
}
```

Embedding WPF Controls in Windows Forms Applications

WPF controls can be embedded inside a Windows Forms application, thanks to a companion class of `WindowsFormsHost` called `ElementHost`. `ElementHost` is like `HwndSource` but it is customized for hosting WPF elements inside a Windows Forms `Form` rather than inside an arbitrary `HWND`. `ElementHost` is a Windows Forms control (deriving from `System.Windows.Forms.Control`) and internally knows how to display WPF content.

To demonstrate the use of `ElementHost`, we'll create a simple Windows Forms application that hosts a WPF `Expander` control. After creating a standard Windows Forms project in Visual Studio, the first step is to add `ElementHost` to the Toolbox using the Tools, Choose Toolbox Items menu item. This presents the dialog shown in Figure 19.8.

With `ElementHost` in the Toolbox, you can drag it onto a Windows Forms `Form` just like any other Windows Forms control. Doing this automatically adds references to the necessary WPF assemblies (`PresentationFramework.dll`, `PresentationCore.dll`, and so on). Listing 19.8 shows the main source file for a Windows Forms project whose `Form` contains an `ElementHost` called `elementHost` docked to the left and a `Label` on the right.

LISTING 19.8 `Form1.cs`—Embedding a WPF `Expander` in a Windows Forms `Form`

```
using System.Windows.Forms;
using System.Windows.Controls;

namespace WindowsFormsHostingWPF
{
```

LISTING 19.8 Continued

```
  public partial class Form1 : Form
  {
    public Form1()
    {
      InitializeComponent();

      // Create a WPF Expander
      Expander expander = new Expander();
      expander.Header = "WPF Expander";
      expander.Content = "Content";

      // Add it to the ElementHost
      elementHost.Child = expander;
    }
  }
}
```

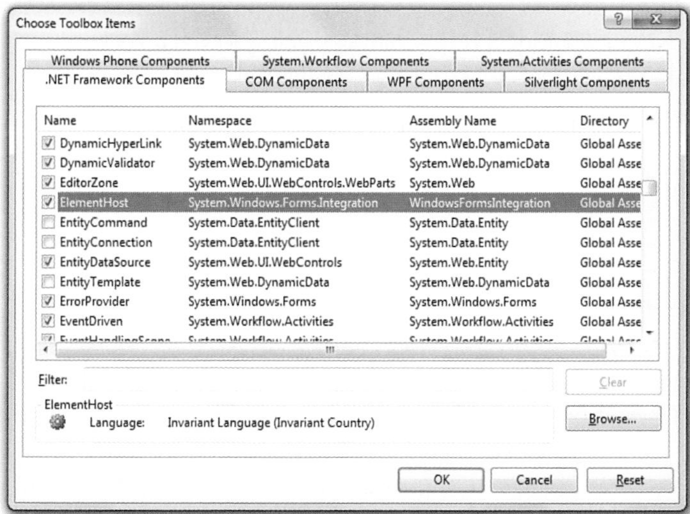

FIGURE 19.8 Adding `ElementHost` to the Toolbox in a Windows Forms project.

This code uses the `System.Windows.Controls` namespace for `Expander`, which it simply instantiates and initializes inside the `Form`'s constructor. `ElementHost`, like `WindowsFormsHost`, has a simple `Child` property that can be set to any `UIElement`. This property must be set in source code rather than in the Windows Forms designer, so here it is set to the `Expander` instance. Figure 19.9 shows the result. Notice that, by default, the `Expander` occupies all the space given to the `ElementHost`.

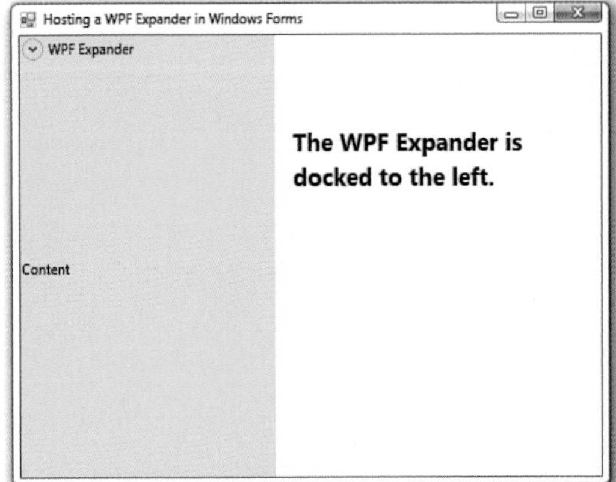

FIGURE 19.9 A Windows Forms application containing a WPF `Expander` control.

Taking this example one step further, you can use a combination of `ElementHost` and `WindowsFormsHost` to have a Windows Forms control embedded in a WPF control embedded in a Windows Forms application! All you need to do is set the `Content` of the WPF `Expander` to a `WindowsFormsHost`, which can contain an arbitrary Windows Forms control. Listing 19.9 does just that, placing a Windows Forms `MonthCalendar` inside a WPF `Expander`, all on the same Windows Forms `Form`. Figure 19.10 shows the result.

LISTING 19.9 `Form1.cs`—Using Both Directions of Windows Forms and WPF Integration

```
using System.Windows.Forms;
using System.Windows.Controls;
using System.Windows.Forms.Integration;

namespace WindowsFormsHostingWPF
{
  public partial class Form1 : Form
  {
    public Form1()
    {
      InitializeComponent();

      // Create a WPF Expander
      Expander expander = new Expander();
      expander.Header = "WPF Expander";

      // Create a MonthCalendar and wrap it in a WindowsFormsHost
      WindowsFormsHost host = new WindowsFormsHost();
      host.Child = new MonthCalendar();
```

LISTING 19.9 Continued

```
      // Place the WindowsFormsHost in the Expander
      expander.Content = host;

      // Add the Expander to the ElementHost
      elementHost.Child = expander;
    }
  }
}
```

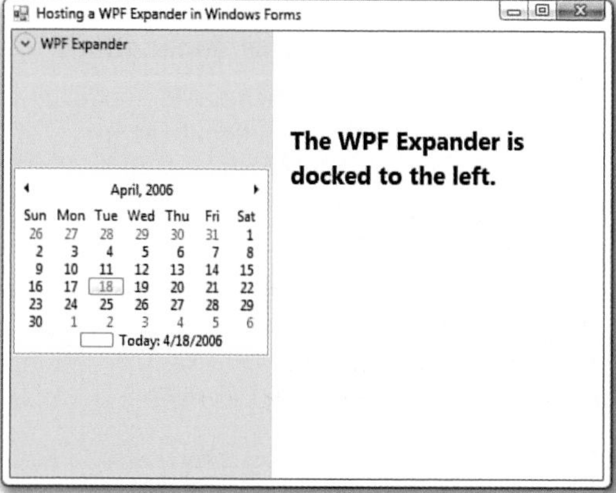

FIGURE 19.10 The Windows Forms `MonthCalendar` is inside the WPF `Expander`, which is on a Windows Forms `Form`.

DIGGING DEEPER

Converting Between Two Representations

One of the headaches of working with a hybrid Windows Forms/WPF application is dealing with the separate managed data types defined for the same concepts. For example, WPF has its own `Color`, `Cursor`, `Size`, `Rect`, and `Point` types that are different from the Windows Forms `Color`, `Cursor`, `Size`, `Rectangle`, and `Point` types. In most cases, however, converting between the two types is fairly simple. For example:

- Both `Color` types have a `FromArgb` static method, so you can create one `Color` from the other by passing this method the `A`, `R`, `G`, and `B` values from the source `Color`.
- To get a Windows Forms font size from a WPF font size, multiply the value by 0.75. To get a WPF font size from a Windows Forms font size, divide the value by 0.75.

In other cases, doing the conversion requires more work. In the case of converting from a `System.Drawing.Bitmap` to a `System.Windows.Media.Imaging.BitmapSource`, you need to work with a representation that both technologies understand—a Win32 `HBITMAP`.

Continued

The Windows Forms `Bitmap` object is based on an `HBITMAP`, so it has a simple `GetHbitmap` function that returns the handle (as an `IntPtr`). On the WPF side, `BitmapSource` has nothing to do with `HBITMAP`s, but fortunately the `System.Windows.Interop.Imaging` class defines three static helper methods for creating `BitmapSource`s from three different origins—a memory section, an `HICON`, and an `HBITMAP`. That last method, called `CreateBitmapSourceFromHBitmap`, can be given the handle and dimensions from the Windows Forms `Bitmap`, and it returns the desired WPF object.

FAQ

How do I launch a WPF modal dialog from a Windows Forms application?

The technique for doing this is almost identical to the way you launch a WPF modal dialog from Win32. You can instantiate a `Window`-derived class and call its `ShowDialog` method. But you also need to set the `Window`'s `Owner` property for it to behave correctly. `Owner` must be set to a `Window`, whereas in a Windows Forms application, the owner is undoubtedly a `System.Windows.Forms.Form`.

Once again, you can use the `WindowInteropHelper` class to set its owner to an arbitrary `HWND`. Therefore, you can set it to the value returned by `Form`'s `Handle` property. The following code does just that:

```
bool? LaunchWpfDialogFromWindowsForm(Window dialog, Form parent)
{
  WindowInteropHelper helper = new WindowInteropHelper(dialog);
  helper.Owner = parent.Handle;
  return dialog.ShowDialog();
}
```

Mixing DirectX Content with WPF Content

As with Windows Forms content, DirectX content can be hosted in WPF applications using `HwndHost`, and WPF content can be hosted in DirectX applications using `HwndSource`. In the first version of WPF, using such `HWND` interoperability mechanisms was the only way to mix WPF and DirectX. Given that WPF is built on top of DirectX, however, there was again the opportunity for much richer integration between the two technologies, without being forced through a largely orthogonal `HWND` mechanism.

Starting with WPF 3.5 SP1 (and WPF 3.0 SP2), direct mixing of WPF and DirectX is now possible, no matter which direction you want to achieve interoperability. This feature—an `ImageSource` called `D3DImage`—doesn't make interoperability significantly easier, but it does remove the inability to overlap that is unavoidable in the other interoperability scenarios. This means that you can blend, layer, and transform the two types of content with the same seamlessness that you get with any two WPF elements. The `D3DImage` functionality is not layered on top of `HWND` interoperability; it is a distinct and more powerful mechanism.

D3DImage is a container that can host an arbitrary DirectX surface. (Despite the name, this surface can contain 2D as well as 3D content.) Because D3DImage is an ImageSource, it can be used in a number of places, such as an Image, ImageBrush, or ImageDrawing.

For the example that demonstrates D3DImage, we'll use a slightly different approach than the previous examples. This section's example uses a simple unmanaged C++ application from the DirectX SDK. (The details of the example are unimportant for this chapter, but the full source code is available with this book's source code on the website, http://informit.com/title/9780672331190.) This DirectX SDK example will remain completely unmanaged, but it will be turned into a DLL instead of an EXE. Then, a WPF C# application will access the functionality of the DirectX sample by using PInvoke to call three unmanaged APIs that it exposes.

The resulting sample is a hypothetical order form for tigers, where the background is a 3D spinning tiger provided by the DirectX DLL, and the foreground contains a bunch of standard WPF controls directly on top of the spinning tiger. Figure 19.11 shows the result.

FIGURE 19.11 A WPF Window containing a DirectX-based spinning 3D tiger underneath basic WPF controls.

Listing 19.10 contains the XAML for this WPF Window. It uses a D3DImage as its background, thanks to ImageBrush. It then places several WPF controls inside the Window at 70% opacity, to help demonstrate the blending of these controls with the DirectX background.

LISTING 19.10 MainWindow.xaml—A WPF Window Control with DirectX Background Content

```
<Window x:Class="WpfDirectX.MainWindow"
  xmlns="http://schemas.microsoft.com/winfx/2006/xaml/presentation"
  xmlns:x="http://schemas.microsoft.com/winfx/2006/xaml"
  xmlns:interop="clr-namespace:System.Windows.Interop;assembly=PresentationCore"
  Title="Mixing DirectX with WPF" Height="350" Width="400">
<Window.Background>
  <ImageBrush>
  <ImageBrush.ImageSource>
    <interop:D3DImage x:Name="d3dImage"
      IsFrontBufferAvailableChanged="d3dImage_IsFrontBufferAvailableChanged"/>
  </ImageBrush.ImageSource>
  </ImageBrush>
</Window.Background>
  <Grid Margin="20" Opacity=".7" TextBlock.Foreground="White">
```

19

LISTING 19.10 Continued

```
    …
  </Grid>
</Window>
```

The IsFrontBufferAvailableChanged event on D3DImage is important to handle. Throughout the application's lifetime, WPF's DirectX surface might occasionally become unavailable. (This can happen in a number of situations, such as when the user presses Ctrl+Alt+Delete to bring up Winlogon or when the video driver changes.) Therefore, this event can trigger the initialization (or reinitialization) of the custom DirectX content as well as its cleanup, based on the value of D3DImage's IsFrontBufferAvailable property.

The work of connecting the empty D3DImage to the actual DirectX content happens in the code-behind file, shown in its entirety in Listing 19.11.

LISTING 19.11 MainWindow.xaml.cs—Making D3DImage Work with DirectX Content from an Unmanaged C++ DLL

```
using System;
using System.Runtime.InteropServices;
using System.Windows;
using System.Windows.Interop;
using System.Windows.Media;

namespace WpfDirectX
{
  // Three PInvoke signatures for communicating
  // with the unmanaged C++ DirectX Sample DLL
  class Sample
  {
    [DllImport("DirectXSample.dll")]
    internal static extern IntPtr Initialize(IntPtr hwnd, int width, int height);

    [DllImport("DirectXSample.dll")]
    internal static extern void Render();

    [DllImport("DirectXSample.dll")]
    internal static extern void Cleanup();
  }

  public partial class MainWindow : Window
  {
    public MainWindow()
    {
```

LISTING 19.11 Continued

```
    InitializeComponent();
  }

  protected override void OnSourceInitialized(EventArgs e)
  {
    base.OnSourceInitialized(e);
    // Now that we can get an HWND for the Window, force the initialization
    // that is otherwise done when the front buffer becomes available:
    d3dImage_IsFrontBufferAvailableChanged(this,
      new DependencyPropertyChangedEventArgs());
  }

  private void d3dImage_IsFrontBufferAvailableChanged(object sender,
    DependencyPropertyChangedEventArgs e)
  {
    if (d3dImage.IsFrontBufferAvailable)
    {
      // (Re)initialization:
      IntPtr surface = Sample.Initialize(new WindowInteropHelper(this).Handle,
        (int)this.Width, (int)this.Height);

      if (surface != IntPtr.Zero)
      {
        d3dImage.Lock();
        d3dImage.SetBackBuffer(D3DResourceType.IDirect3DSurface9, surface);
        d3dImage.Unlock();

        CompositionTarget.Rendering += CompositionTarget_Rendering;
      }
    }
    else
    {
      // Cleanup:
      CompositionTarget.Rendering -= CompositionTarget_Rendering;
      Sample.Cleanup();
    }
  }

  // Render the DirectX scene when WPF itself is ready to render
  private void CompositionTarget_Rendering(object sender, EventArgs e)
  {
    if (d3dImage.IsFrontBufferAvailable)
    {
      d3dImage.Lock();
```

LISTING 19.11 Continued

```
        Sample.Render();
        // Invalidate the whole area:
        d3dImage.AddDirtyRect(new Int32Rect(0, 0,
          d3dImage.PixelWidth, d3dImage.PixelHeight));
        d3dImage.Unlock();
      }
    }
  }
}
```

The listing begins by defining three simple PInvoke signatures for the three unmanaged APIs exported from `DirectXSample.dll`. Although the source code for `DirectXSample.dll` is not shown here, it is included in this book's source code. (To build it yourself, you must first download and install a recent DirectX SDK from http://microsoft.com.) Regardless of the actual work done by the DirectX code, the pattern of `Initialize`, `Render`, and `Cleanup` is pretty universal. `Initialize` requires an `HWND`, because the underlying DirectX API—creating a Direct3D device—requires an `HWND`.

Because `Initialize` needs an `HWND`, you can't call it from `MainWindow`'s constructor (unless you give it an `HWND` for a different window). Therefore, `Window`'s `OnSourceInitialized` method is overridden so initialization can be done from there. At this point, `WindowInteropHelper` is able to give you a valid `HWND` for the WPF `Window`. But rather than duplicate the initialization code from the `d3dImage_IsFrontBufferAvailableChanged` event handler, the code in `OnSourceInitialized` just calls it.

TIP

If you want to obtain an `HWND` for a WPF `Window` before it is shown, `WindowInteropHelper`'s `EnsureHandle` method enables you to do so. `EnsureHandle` creates the underlying Win32 window (and raises the `SourceInitialized` event) if it hasn't been created yet then returns the appropriate `HWND`. After calling this method, you could even decide *never* to show the `Window`! For example, Visual Studio 2010 does exactly that when it is invoked during a command-line build.

Inside `d3dImage_IsFrontBufferAvailableChanged`, the initialization path calls `Initialize` with the `Window`'s `HWND`, width, and height and gets back a reference to an `IDirect3DSurface9` interface pointer disguised as an `IntPtr` (a common trick to avoid the need to create a managed definition of the interface). This `IntPtr` can then be passed to `D3DImage.SetBackBuffer` (while the `D3DImage` is locked) to associate the content. The unmanaged `Render` method needs to be called once per frame, so `CompositionTarget`'s static `Rendering` event is perfect for this purpose. The cleanup path of `d3dImage_IsFrontBufferAvailableChanged`—when `IsFrontBufferAvailable` is `false`—simply detaches the `Rendering` event handler and calls the unmanaged `Cleanup` method so the C++ code has a chance to release its resources.

WARNING

Remember that WPF has a reference to the Direct3D surface!

Memory management can be tricky in hybrid managed/unmanaged applications. It's easy to forget about reference counting when you're primarily using managed code, but be aware that WPF is referencing the surface passed to `SetBackBuffer` until `IsFrontBufferAvailable` becomes `false` or until `SetBackBuffer` is called again. Therefore, if you want to break that reference, you can call `SetBackBuffer` with `IntPtr.Zero` as the second parameter.

WARNING

`D3DImage` must be locked before any modifications are done to the back buffer!

Locking is necessary to avoid WPF presenting an incomplete frame. (If you're in the midst of drawing to it when WPF wants to present it, it won't look right.) Operations that require locking include method calls on `D3DImage`—`SetBackBuffer` and `AddDirtyRect`—as well as any rendering done by the custom DirectX code that is using the `IDirect3DSurface9` pointer. This locking can be accomplished by either calling `D3DImage.Lock`, which blocks when WPF is busy reading the back buffer, or `D3DImage.TryLock`, which will wait only as long as a user-specified timeout. Regardless of which you use, be sure to call `D3DImage.Unlock` when you are done modifying the back buffer!

WARNING

Allow WPF to present the back buffer!

If you're modifying existing DirectX code to be used with WPF (as in this example), you need to make sure it no longer calls `Present` on the Direct3D device. That's because WPF presents its own back buffer, based on internal contents and the contents of the surface you passed to `SetBackBuffer`. Doing your own presenting of the back buffer would interfere with the proper operation of the rendering system.

Finally, the `CompositionTarget_Rendering` event handler calls the unmanaged `Render` method (while the `D3DImage` is locked) and also invalidates the entire area of the `D3DImage` by calling `AddDirtyRect` with the dimensions of the `D3DImage`. WPF composes any dirty regions from the `D3DImage` with its own internal surface and then renders the result. In some applications, this could be optimized by reducing invalidation to one or more smaller regions. In addition, some applications might not require the DirectX rendering and `D3DImage` invalidation to happen *every* frame.

DIGGING DEEPER

Ensuring That DirectX Usage Is Compatible with `D3DImage`

There are a number of small details to be aware of for the code that is directly using the DirectX APIs (the unmanaged C++ code inside `DirectXSample.dll` in this case) to ensure that it works or that it gets the best performance.

First and foremost, only DirectX 9 and later are supported, as evidenced by the fact that the only value of the `D3DResourceType` enumeration used by `D3DImage.SetBackBuffer` is `IDirect3DSurface9`! (You can exploit later versions of Direct3D and use an intermediate `IDirect3DDevice9Ex` device to still work inside this scheme.)

When running on Windows XP, `Direct3DCreate9` must be used, and then you can create an `IDirect3DDevice9` device. This surface must use D3DPOOL_DEFAULT , D3DUSAGE_RENDERTARGET, and D3DFMT_X8R8G8B8 (RGB) or D3DFMT_A8R8G8B8 (ARGB). On Windows Vista or later, however, using `Direct3DCreate9Ex` (and an `IDirect3DDevice9Ex` device) provides better performance, assuming that the display is using the Windows Display Driver Model (WDDM) and the video card supports the right capabilities.

You can get better performance (from hardware acceleration) on Windows XP when the Direct3D surface is created as lockable, but lockable surfaces generally perform worse when running on Windows Vista or later. Details like these hopefully help you appreciate how much easier WPF makes programming compared to its DirectX underpinnings!

WARNING

`D3DImage` doesn't work under software rendering!

When the WPF render thread is doing software rendering (for less powerful hardware, remote desktop, and similar situations), the content inside `D3DImage` simply doesn't get rendered. `D3DImage` does work when printing or using `RenderTargetBitmap`, however. Despite the fact that these mechanisms use software rendering, they operate on the UI thread and therefore don't run into this limitation.

Embedding ActiveX Controls in WPF Applications

There must thousands of ActiveX controls in existence, and they can be easily embedded in WPF applications. But that's not because of any hard work done by the WPF team. Ever since version 1.0, Windows Forms has had a bunch of plumbing built in for interoperability with ActiveX controls. Rather than duplicate all that plumbing natively inside WPF, the team decided to simply depend on Windows Forms for this scenario. WPF gets the functionality "for free" just by working well with Windows Forms.

Using Windows Forms as an intermediate layer between ActiveX and WPF might sound suboptimal, but the development experience is just about as pleasant as can be expected. To demonstrate how to embed an ActiveX control in a WPF application, this section uses the Microsoft Terminal Services control that ships with Windows. This control contains basically all the functionality of Remote Desktop, but it is controllable via a few simple APIs.

The first step for using an ActiveX control is to get a managed and Windows Forms–compatible definition of the relevant types. This can be done in two different ways:

- Run the ActiveX Importer (`AXIMP.EXE`) on the ActiveX DLL. This utility is included in the .NET Framework component of the Windows SDK.
- In any Windows Forms project in Visual Studio, add the component to the Toolbox using the COM Components tab from the dialog shown by choosing the Tools, Choose Toolbox Items menu item. Then drag the control from the Toolbox onto any `Form`. This process causes Visual Studio to invoke the ActiveX Importer behind the scenes.

No matter which approach you use, two DLLs are generated. You should add references to these in your WPF-based project (along with `System.Windows.Forms.dll` and `WindowsFormsIntegration.dll`). One is an interop assembly that contains "raw" managed definitions of the unmanaged interfaces, classes, enums, and structures defined in the type library contained inside the ActiveX DLL. The other is an assembly that contains a Windows Forms control that corresponds to each ActiveX class. The first DLL is named with the library name from the original type library, and the second DLL is named the same but with an `Ax` prefix.

For the Microsoft Terminal Services control, the original ActiveX DLL is called `mstscax.dll` and is found in the Windows `system32` directory. (In the Choose Toolbox Items dialog, it shows up as Microsoft Terminal Services Client Control.) Running the ActiveX Importer generates `MSTSCLib.dll` and `AxMSTSCLib.dll`.

With the four relevant assemblies added to a project (`MSTSCLib.dll`, `AxMSTSCLib.dll`, `System.Windows.Forms.dll`, and `WindowsFormsIntegration.dll`), Listings 19.12 and 19.13 contain the XAML and C# code to host the control and get the resulting application shown in Figure 19.12.

LISTING 19.12 `Window1.xaml`—XAML for the Terminal Services WPF Application

```
<Window x:Class="HostingActiveX.Window1"
  xmlns="http://schemas.microsoft.com/winfx/2006/xaml/presentation"
  xmlns:x="http://schemas.microsoft.com/winfx/2006/xaml"
  Title="Hosting the Terminal Services ActiveX Control">
  <DockPanel Name="panel" Margin="10">
    <StackPanel Margin="0,0,0,10" DockPanel.Dock="Top" Orientation="Horizontal">
      <TextBox x:Name="serverBox" Width="180" Margin="0,0,10,0"/>
      <Button x:Name="connectButton" Click="connectButton_Click">Connect</Button>
    </StackPanel>
  </DockPanel>
</Window>
```

19

LISTING 19.13 Window1.xaml.cs—C# Code for Hosting the Terminal Services ActiveX Control

```
using System;
using System.Windows;
using System.Windows.Forms.Integration;

namespace HostingActiveX
{
  public partial class Window1 : Window
  {
    AxMSTSCLib.AxMsTscAxNotSafeForScripting termServ;

    public Window1()
    {
      InitializeComponent();

      // Create the host and the ActiveX control
      WindowsFormsHost host = new WindowsFormsHost();
      termServ = new AxMSTSCLib.AxMsTscAxNotSafeForScripting();

      // Add the ActiveX control to the host, and the host to the WPF panel
      host.Child = termServ;
      panel.Children.Add(host);
    }

    void connectButton_Click(object sender, RoutedEventArgs e)
    {
      termServ.Server = serverBox.Text;
      termServ.Connect();
    }
  }
}
```

There's nothing special about the XAML in Listing 19.12; it simply contains a `DockPanel` with a `TextBox` and `Button` for choosing a server and connecting to it. In Listing 19.13, a `WindowsFormsHost` is added to the `DockPanel`, and the Windows Forms representation of the ActiveX control is added to the `WindowsFormsHost`. This control is called `AxMsTscAxNotSafeForScripting`. (In versions of Windows prior to Windows Vista, it has the somewhat simpler name `AxMsTscAx`.) The interaction with the complicated-sounding `AxMsTscAxNotSafeForScripting` control is quite simple. Its `Server` property can be set to a simple string, and you can connect to the server by calling `Connect`.

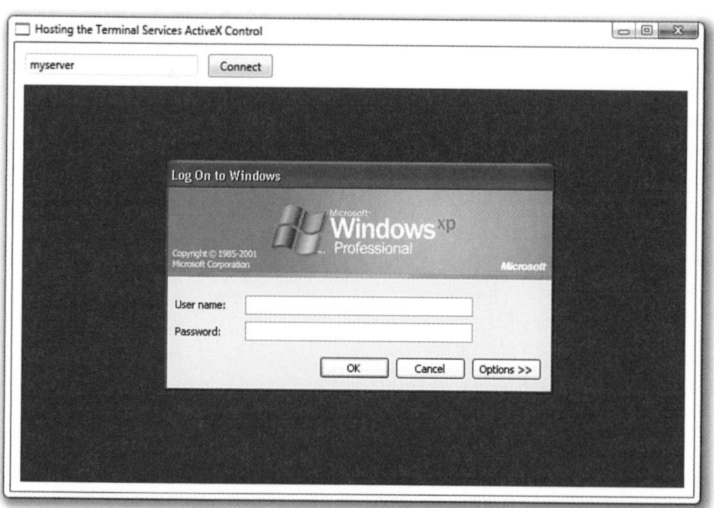

FIGURE 19.12 Hosting the Terminal Services ActiveX control in a WPF `Window`.

Of course, the instantiation of the `WindowsFormsHost` *and* the `AxMsTscAxNotSafeForScripting` control can be done directly in XAML, replacing the boldface code in Listing 19.13. This is shown in Listing 19.14. You could go a step further and use data binding to replace the first line in `connectButton_Click`, but you would still need the event handler for calling the `Connect` method.

LISTING 19.14 `Window1.xaml`—Updated XAML for the Terminal Services WPF Application

```
<Window x:Class="HostingActiveX.Window1"
  xmlns="http://schemas.microsoft.com/winfx/2006/xaml/presentation"
  xmlns:x="http://schemas.microsoft.com/winfx/2006/xaml"
  xmlns:ax="clr-namespace:AxMSTSCLib;assembly=AxMSTSCLib"
  Title="Hosting the Terminal Services ActiveX Control">
  <DockPanel Name="panel" Margin="10">
    <StackPanel Margin="0,0,0,10" DockPanel.Dock="Top" Orientation="Horizontal">
      <TextBox x:Name="serverBox" Margin="0,0,10,0"/>
      <Button x:Name="connectButton" Click="connectButton_Click">Connect</Button>
    </StackPanel>
    <WindowsFormsHost>
      <ax:AxMsTscAxNotSafeForScripting x:Name="termServ"/>
    </WindowsFormsHost>
  </DockPanel>
</Window>
```

TIP

It's possible to host ActiveX controls in a partial-trust XAML Browser Application or loose XAML page, but you can't use Windows Forms interoperability to do so (because this feature requires a higher level of trust). Instead, you can use a `Frame` or `WebBrowser` control that hosts a webpage containing the ActiveX control. For example:

```
<Frame Source="pack://siteoforigin:,,,/webpage.html"/>
```

where `webpage.html` contains the following:

```
<html>
  <body>
    <object Width="100%" Height="100%" ClassId="clsid:…"/>
  </body>
</html>
```

As far as security goes, you will see the same behavior as if you navigated to `webpage.html` directly in Internet Explorer. You might get security prompts, determined by the user's settings and the current zone. But you can avoid prompts in some cases by using a signed, safe-for-scripting ActiveX control.

FAQ

What about the reverse direction—exposing WPF controls as ActiveX controls?

There is no built-in support for this above and beyond HWND interoperability, so your best bet is to use your favorite means of creating a non-WPF ActiveX control (using Active Template Library [ATL], for example) and inject WPF content inside it.

Summary

Most developers understand that it's possible to build really powerful applications with WPF. But with the `HWND`, Windows Forms, DirectX, and ActiveX interoperability features discussed in this chapter, there's essentially no limit to the power. That's because you can tap into decades of effort that has been poured into controls and functionality that have already been developed, tested, and deployed. For organizations with huge investments in existing code, this is a critical feature.

The main scenarios discussed in this chapter boil down to five classes. Their names are a bit confusing and inconsistent, so Table 19.1 provides a summary that you can flip back to if you ever forget which class is which.

TABLE 19.1 The Five Main Interoperability Classes

Class Name	Usage
`HwndHost`	Hosting an `HWND` in WPF
`WindowsFormsHost`	Hosting Windows Forms in WPF
`D3DImage`	Hosting DirectX in WPF without an `HWND`
`HwndSource`	Hosting WPF in an `HWND`
`ElementHost`	Hosting WPF in Windows Forms

The benefits of interoperability are broader than the features discussed in this chapter, however. You could completely overhaul an application's user interface with WPF but hook it up to back-end logic already in place—even if that logic is unmanaged code. This could be done using a number of techniques, such as using C++/CLI, PInvoke, or COM interoperability.

Despite the ease and power of the features described in this chapter, there are still clear benefits to having an all-WPF user interface rather than a hybrid one. For example, in a pure WPF user interface, all the elements can be scaled, styled, and restyled in a similar fashion. They can be seamlessly overlaid on top of each other. Keyboard navigation and focus works naturally without much extra effort. In addition, you don't have to worry about mixing resolution-independent elements with resolution-dependent elements. A pure WPF user interface also opens the door to being able to run in a partial-trust environment (depending on how you separate your back-end logic)—perhaps even buildable for Silverlight as well.

Even complex applications with years of user-interface investment can easily benefit from WPF if they are well factored. For example, I once came across an MFC-based program that showed street maps across the United States. The application used various MFC (therefore GDI-based) primitives to draw each line and shape in the current scene. By swapping in a WPF surface and performing the same drawing actions using the drawing APIs discussed in Chapter 15, "2D Graphics," the map could be replaced with a WPF version with relatively small code changes. After making the leap to WPF, the application could now easily support features that would have been difficult otherwise: crisp zooming, tilting the map in 3D, and so on.

Therefore, if you have developed a pre-WPF application, there are many ways to improve its look or functionality by using interoperability to incrementally add WPF features. If you've developed pre-WPF *controls*, there's another nice use of interoperability that doesn't necessarily involve updating end-user functionality: Simply wrap such controls in a WPF object model so consumers can treat it like a first-class WPF control without having to learn about WPF's interoperability features. Creating custom controls (whether pure WPF or not) is the topic of the next chapter.

CHAPTER 20

User Controls and Custom Controls

IN THIS CHAPTER

- Creating a User Control
- Creating a Custom Control

Chapter 9, "Content Controls," claims that no modern presentation framework would be complete without a standard set of controls that enable you to quickly assemble traditional user interfaces. I think it's also safe to say that no modern presentation framework would be complete without the ability to create your own reusable controls. You might want to create a control because your own applications have custom needs, or because there's money to be made by selling unique controls to other software developers! This chapter is about two WPF mechanisms for writing your own controls: *user controls* (the easier of the two) and *custom controls* (the more complicated but also more flexible variety).

The role that user controls and custom controls play in WPF is quite different than in other technologies. In other technologies, custom controls are often created simply to get a nonstandard look. But WPF has many options for achieving nonstandard-looking controls without creating brand-new controls. You can completely restyle built-in controls with WPF's style and template mechanisms, demonstrated in Chapter 14, "Styles, Templates, Skins, and Themes." Or you can sometimes simply embed complex content inside built-in controls to get the look you want. In other technologies, a `Button` containing an `Image` or a `TreeView` containing `ComboBox`es might necessitate a custom control, but not in WPF! (That's not to say that there are fewer opportunities for selling reusable components. It just means you have more implementation options.)

The decision to create a new control should be based on the APIs you want to expose rather than the look you want to achieve. If no existing control has a *programmatic* interface that naturally represents your concept, go ahead and create a user control or custom control. The biggest mistake people make with user controls and custom controls is creating one from scratch when an existing control can suffice!

FAQ

I've concluded that I need to write my own control. But should I write a user control or a custom control?

You should create a user control if its reuse will be limited and you don't care about exposing rich styling and theming support. You should create a custom control if you want it to be a robust first-class control (like WPF's built-in controls). A user control tends to contain a logical tree defining its look and tends to have logic that directly interacts with these child elements. A custom control, on the other hand, tends to get its look from a visual tree defined in a separate control template and generally has logic that works even if a consumer changes its visual tree completely (using the techniques from Chapter 14).

This distinction is mostly imposed by the default development experience provided by Visual Studio, however. Visual Studio pushes you in a certain direction based on the type of control you add to a project. When you add a user control, you get a XAML file with a corresponding code-behind file, so you can easily build your user control much as you would build a `Window` or `Page`. But when you add a custom control to a project, you get a normal `.cs` (or `.vb`) code file plus a theme style with a simple control template injected into the project's generic dictionary (`themes\generic.xaml`).

Therefore, to answer this question with less hand-waving, let's look at the precise differences between user controls and custom controls. A custom control can derive from `Control` or any of its subclasses. The definition of a user control, on the other hand, is a class that derives from `UserControl`, which itself derives from `ContentControl`, which derives from `Control`. So, user controls are technically a type of custom control, but this chapter uses the term *custom control* to mean any `Control`-derived class that isn't a user control.

If the control you want to create would benefit from taking advantage of functionality already present in a non-`ContentControl` (such as `RangeBase` or `Selector`) or a `ContentControl`-derived class (such as `HeaderedContentControl` or `Button`), it's logical to derive your class from it. If your control doesn't need any of the extra functionality that classes such as `ContentControl` add on top of `Control`, deriving directly from `Control` makes sense. Both of these choices mean that you're writing a custom control rather than a user control.

But if neither of these conditions is true, the choice between deriving directly from `ContentControl` (which means you're writing a custom control) versus deriving from `UserControl` (which means you're writing a user control) is fairly insignificant if you ignore the development experience. That's because `UserControl` differs very little from its `ContentControl` base class; it has a different default control template, it has a default content alignment of `Stretch` in both directions (rather than `Left` and `Top`), it sets `IsTabStop` and `Focusable` to `false` by default, and it changes the source of any events raised from inner content to be the `UserControl` itself. And that's all. WPF does no special-casing of `UserControl` at runtime. Therefore, in this case, it makes sense to choose based on your intention to create a "lookless" control (which would be a custom control) versus a "look-filled" control (which would be a user control).

Creating a User Control

There's no better way to understand the process of creating a user control than actually creating one. So in this section, we'll create a user control called `FileInputBox`.

`FileInputBox` combines a `TextBox` with a Browse `Button`. The intention is that a user could type a raw filename in the `TextBox` or click the `Button` to get a standard `OpenFileDialog`. If the user chooses a file in this dialog box, its fully qualified name is automatically pasted into the `TextBox`. This control works exactly like `<INPUT TYPE="FILE"/>` in HTML.

Creating the User Interface of the User Control

Listing 20.1 contains the user control's XAML file that defines the user interface, and Figure 20.1 shows the rendered result.

LISTING 20.1 `FileInputBox.xaml`—The User Interface for `FileInputBox`

```
<UserControl x:Class="Chapter20.FileInputBox"
    xmlns="http://schemas.microsoft.com/winfx/2006/xaml/presentation"
    xmlns:x="http://schemas.microsoft.com/winfx/2006/xaml">
  <DockPanel>
    <Button x:Name="theButton" DockPanel.Dock="Right" Click="theButton_Click">
      Browse...</Button>
    <TextBox x:Name="theTextBox"
      MinWidth="{Binding ActualWidth, ElementName=theButton}" Margin="0,0,2,0"/>
  </DockPanel>
</UserControl>
```

FIGURE 20.1 The `FileInputBox` user control combines a simple `TextBox` with a simple `Button`.

The `Button` is docked on the right and has an event handler for the `Click` event (covered in the next section). The `TextBox` fills the remaining space except for a two-unit margin on the right to give some space between itself and the `Button`. The XAML definition is very simple, but it handles every layout situation flawlessly. The setting of `MinWidth` on `TextBox` isn't necessary, but it's a slick way to ensure that the `TextBox` doesn't look too small in certain layout conditions. And by making its minimum width match the width of the `Button` (which is always just big enough to fit its content, thanks to the right-docking), a hard-coded size is avoided.

Figure 20.2 shows what happens when an application uses an instance of `FileInputBox` and sets various properties inherited from `ContentControl` and `Control`, as follows:

```
<local:FileInputBox BorderBrush="Orange" BorderThickness="4" Background="Blue"
  HorizontalContentAlignment="Right"/>
```

FIGURE 20.2 FileInputBox automatically respects visual properties from its base classes.

The fact that setting these properties works correctly seems like a no-brainer, but it's actually not as automatic as you might think. The appearance of FileInputBox depends on its control template, which it inherits from UserControl. Fortunately, UserControl's default control template respects properties such as the ones used in Figure 20.2:

```
<ControlTemplate TargetType="{x:Type UserControl}">
  <Border Background="{TemplateBinding Background}"
    BorderBrush="{TemplateBinding BorderBrush}"
    BorderThickness="{TemplateBinding BorderThickness}"
    Padding="{TemplateBinding Padding}">
    <ContentPresenter
      HorizontalAlignment="{TemplateBinding HorizontalContentAlignment}"
      VerticalAlignment="{TemplateBinding VerticalContentAlignment}"/>
  </Border>
</ControlTemplate>
```

If FileInputBox derived directly from ContentControl (UserControl's base class) instead, these properties would *not* be respected unless FileInputBox were given a custom template. As is, FileInputBox can be restyled by its consumers, and individual elements (the TextBox, Button, and/or DockPanel) can even be restyled if the consumer creates typed styles for them!

TIP

If you want to prevent an application's typed styles from impacting elements inside your control, your best bet is to give them an explicit Style (which can be null to get the default look).

From a visual perspective, consuming a FileInputBox as follows:

```
<Window xmlns="http://schemas.microsoft.com/winfx/2006/xaml/presentation"
  xmlns:x="http://schemas.microsoft.com/winfx/2006/xaml"
  xmlns:local="clr-namespace:Chapter20">
  <StackPanel Margin="20">
    <local:FileInputBox/>
  </StackPanel>
</Window>
```

is just a shortcut for plopping the logical tree of elements from FileInputBox.xaml into your user interface:

```
<Window xmlns="http://schemas.microsoft.com/winfx/2006/xaml/presentation"
  xmlns:x="http://schemas.microsoft.com/winfx/2006/xaml"
  xmlns:local="clr-namespace:Chapter20">
  <StackPanel Margin="20">
```

```
    <UserControl>
      <DockPanel>
        <Button DockPanel.Dock="Right">Browse...</Button>
        <TextBox MinWidth="{Binding ActualWidth, ElementName=theButton}"
          Margin="0,0,2,0"/>
      </DockPanel>
    </UserControl>
  </StackPanel>
</Window>
```

This alone can be handy, but it is also achievable by giving an arbitrary existing control an explicit control template containing the `DockPanel`, `Button`, and `TextBox` (ignoring the subtle differences from the elements being in a visual tree rather than the logical tree). However, user controls typically add value by encapsulating custom behavior.

Creating the Behavior of the User Control

Listing 20.2 contains the entire code-behind file for Listing 20.1. This gives `FileInputBox` the appropriate behavior when the `Button` is clicked, exposes the text from the `TextBox` as a read/write property, and exposes a simple `FileNameChanged` event corresponding to the `TextChanged` event exposed by the `TextBox`. The event handler for `TextChanged` marks the event as handled (to stop its bubbling) and raises the `FileNameChanged` event instead.

LISTING 20.2 `FileInputBox.xaml.cs`—The Logic for `FileInputBox`

```
using System;
using System.Windows;
using System.Windows.Controls;
using Microsoft.Win32;

namespace Chapter20
{
  public partial class FileInputBox : UserControl
  {
    public FileInputBox()
    {
      InitializeComponent();
      theTextBox.TextChanged += new TextChangedEventHandler(OnTextChanged);
    }

    private void theButton_Click(object sender, RoutedEventArgs e)
    {
      OpenFileDialog d = new OpenFileDialog();
      if (d.ShowDialog() == true) // Result could be true, false, or null
        this.FileName = d.FileName;
```

LISTING 20.2 Continued

```
    }

    public string FileName
    {
      get { return theTextBox.Text; }
      set { theTextBox.Text = value; }
    }

    void OnTextChanged(object sender, TextChangedEventArgs e)
    {
      e.Handled = true;
      if (FileNameChanged != null)
        FileNameChanged(this, EventArgs.Empty);
    }

    public event EventHandler<EventArgs> FileNameChanged;
  }
}
```

That's all there is to it! If you don't care about broadly sharing your user control or maximizing the integration with WPF's subsystems, you can often expose plain .NET methods, properties, and events and have a control that's "good enough." Figure 20.3 shows the control in action.

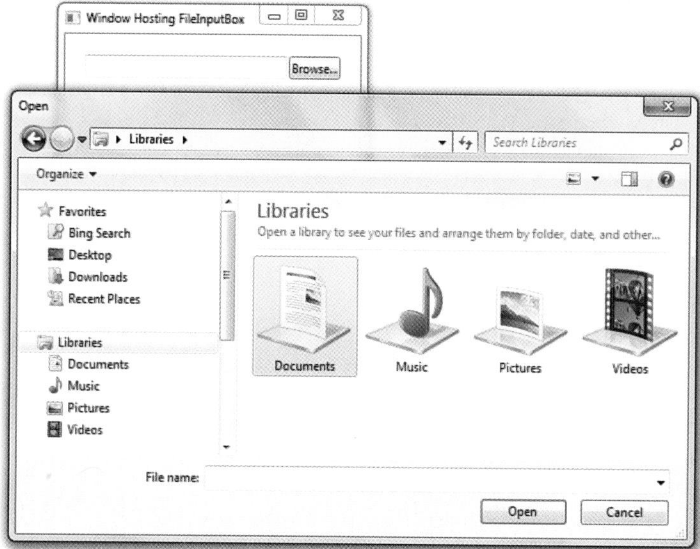

FIGURE 20.3 `FileInputBox` spawns a standard `OpenFileDialog` when its `Button` is clicked.

Consuming a user control is very straightforward. If you want to use it from a Window or Page in the same assembly, you simply reference the appropriate namespace, which, in this case, is Chapter20:

```
<Window xmlns="http://schemas.microsoft.com/winfx/2006/xaml/presentation"
  xmlns:x="http://schemas.microsoft.com/winfx/2006/xaml"
  xmlns:local="clr-namespace:Chapter20">
  <StackPanel Margin="20">
    <local:FileInputBox/>
  </StackPanel>
</Window>
```

If you want to use it from a separate assembly, the clr-namespace directive simply needs to include the assembly information along with the namespace:

```
xmlns:local="clr-namespace:Chapter20;assembly=Chapter20Controls"
```

DIGGING DEEPER

Protecting User Controls from Accidental Usage

The following is a valid way to initialize FileInputBox, giving its TextBox an initial FileName value of c:\Lindsay.htm:

```
<local:FileInputBox FileName="c:\Lindsay.htm"/>
```

But because FileInputBox ultimately derives from ContentControl, here are two other ways a consumer might attempt to use FileInputBox:

```
<local:FileInputBox Content="c:\Lindsay.htm"/>
```

or:

```
<local:FileInputBox>c:\Lindsay.htm</local:FileInputBox>
```

Can you guess what happens in these cases? The default value of Content (the DockPanel containing the Button and TextBox) gets completely replaced with this string! This is clearly not what the consumer intended; otherwise, they should have just used a TextBlock element!

Fortunately, you can take some actions to prevent such mistakes. For FileInputBox, you can designate FileName to be the content property instead of Content, as follows:

```
[ContentProperty("FileName")]
public partial class FileInputBox : UserControl
{
  …
}
```

This simple change makes this:

```
<local:FileInputBox>c:\Lindsay.htm</local:FileInputBox>
```

equivalent to this:

```
<local:FileInputBox FileName="c:\Lindsay.htm"/>
```

Continued

But how can you change the explicit setting of `Content` from being disastrous? One way is to add the following method to `FileInputBox`:

```
protected override void OnContentChanged(object oldContent, object newContent)
{
  if (oldContent != null)
    throw new InvalidOperationException("You can't change Content!");
}
```

Another solution is to place your control's user interface inside a control template (rather than `Content`) and bind `TextBox.Text` to the `Content` property. But if you do that, you might as well write a custom control rather than a user control!

Adding Dependency Properties to the User Control

One possible enhancement to `FileInputBox` is to change `FileName` from a plain .NET property to a dependency property. That way, consumers of the control can use it as a data-binding target, more easily use the value in a custom control template, and so on.

To turn `FileName` into a dependency property, you can add a `DependencyProperty` field to the class, initialize it appropriately, and change the implementation of the `FileName` property to use the dependency property mechanism:

```
public static readonly DependencyProperty FileNameProperty =
  DependencyProperty.Register("FileName", typeof(string), typeof(FileInputBox));

public string FileName
{
  get { return (string)GetValue(FileNameProperty); }
  set { SetValue(FileNameProperty, value); }
}
```

By convention, WPF's built-in objects give the field the name *`PropertyName`*`Property`. You should follow this convention with your own controls to avoid confusion.

The preceding implementation of `FileName` as a dependency property is flawed, however. It's no longer associated with the `Text` property of the control's inner `TextBox`! To update `FileName` when `Text` changes, you could add a line of code inside `OnTextChanged`:

```
void OnTextChanged(object sender, TextChangedEventArgs e)
{
  this.FileName = theTextBox.Text;
  e.Handled = true;
  if (FileNameChanged != null)
    FileNameChanged(this, EventArgs.Empty);
}
```

And to update Text when FileName changes, it's tempting to add a line of code to the FileName property's set accessor as follows:

```
set { theTextBox.Text = value; SetValue(FileNameProperty, value); }
```

But this isn't a good idea because, as explained in Chapter 3, "WPF Fundamentals," the set accessor never gets called unless someone sets the .NET property in procedural code. When setting the property in XAML, data binding to it, and so on, WPF calls SetValue directly.

To respond properly to any value change in the FileName dependency property, you could register for a notification provided by the dependency property system. But the easiest way to keep Text and FileName in sync is to use data binding. Listing 20.3 contains the entire C# implementation of FileInputBox, updated with FileName as a dependency property. This assumes that the XAML for FileInputBox has been updated to take advantage of data binding as follows:

```
<UserControl x:Class="Chapter20.FileInputBox"
    xmlns="http://schemas.microsoft.com/winfx/2006/xaml/presentation"
    xmlns:x="http://schemas.microsoft.com/winfx/2006/xaml"
    x:Name="root">
  <DockPanel>
    <Button x:Name="theButton" DockPanel.Dock="Right" Click="theButton_Click">
      Browse...</Button>
    <TextBox x:Name="theTextBox"
      MinWidth="{Binding ActualWidth, ElementName=theButton}"
      Text="{Binding FileName, ElementName=root}" Margin="0,0,2,0"/>
  </DockPanel>
</UserControl>
```

LISTING 20.3 FileInputBox.xaml.cs—An Alternate Version of Listing 20.2, in Which FileName Is a Dependency Property

```
using System;
using System.Windows;
using System.Windows.Controls;
using Microsoft.Win32;

namespace Chapter20
{
  public partial class FileInputBox : UserControl
  {
    public FileInputBox()
    {
      InitializeComponent();
      theTextBox.TextChanged += new TextChangedEventHandler(OnTextChanged);
```

LISTING 20.3 Continued

```
    }

    private void theButton_Click(object sender, RoutedEventArgs e)
    {
      OpenFileDialog d = new OpenFileDialog();
      if (d.ShowDialog() == true) // Result could be true, false, or null
        this.FileName = d.FileName;
    }

    public string FileName
    {
      get { return (string)GetValue(FileNameProperty); }
      set { SetValue(FileNameProperty, value); }
    }

    private void OnTextChanged(object sender, TextChangedEventArgs e)
    {
      e.Handled = true;
      if (FileNameChanged != null)
        FileNameChanged(this, EventArgs.Empty);
    }

    public static readonly DependencyProperty FileNameProperty =
    DependencyProperty.Register("FileName", typeof(string), typeof(FileInputBox));

    public event EventHandler<EventArgs> FileNameChanged;
  }
}
```

With the data binding in place on `TextBox.Text` (which is two-way by default), the standard dependency property implementation works with no extra code, despite the fact that the value for `FileName` is stored separately from the `TextBox`.

WARNING

Avoid implementing logic in a dependency property's property wrapper other than calling `GetValue` and `SetValue`!

If you deviate from the standard implementation, you'll introduce semantics that apply only when the property is directly set from procedural code. To react to calls to `SetValue`, regardless of the source, you should register for a dependency property changed notification and place your logic in the callback method instead. Or you can find another mechanism to respond to property value changes with the help of data binding, as done in Listing 20.3.

TIP

FrameworkPropertyMetadata, an instance of which can be passed to DependencyProperty.Register, contains several properties for customizing the behavior of the dependency property. Besides attaching a property changed handler, you can set a default value, control whether the property is inherited by child elements, set the default data flow for data binding, control whether a value change should refresh the control's layout or rendering, and so on.

Adding Routed Events to the User Control

If you go to the effort of giving a user control appropriate dependency properties, you should probably make the same effort to transform appropriate events into routed events. Consumers can write triggers based on a routed event you expose, but they can't directly do that for normal .NET events. For FileInputBox, it makes sense for its FileNameChanged event to be a bubbling routed event, especially because the TextChanged event it's wrapping is itself a bubbling routed event!

As discussed in Chapter 6, "Input Events: Keyboard, Mouse, Stylus, and Multi-Touch," defining a routed event is much like defining a dependency property: You define a RoutedEvent field (with an Event suffix by convention), register it, and optionally provide a .NET event that wraps the AddHandler and RemoveHandler APIs. Listing 20.4 shows what it looks like to update the FileNameChanged event from the previous two listings to be a bubbling routed event. In addition to the routed event implementation, the private OnTextChanged method is updated to raise the routed event with the RaiseEvent method inherited from UIElement.

LISTING 20.4 FileInputBox.xaml.cs—An Update to Listing 20.3, Making FileNameChanged a Routed Event

```
using System;
using System.Windows;
using System.Windows.Controls;
using Microsoft.Win32;

namespace Chapter20
{
  public partial class FileInputBox : UserControl
  {
    public FileInputBox()
    {
      InitializeComponent();
      theTextBox.TextChanged += new TextChangedEventHandler(OnTextChanged);
    }

    private void theButton_Click(object sender, RoutedEventArgs e)
```

LISTING 20.4 Continued

```
    {
      OpenFileDialog d = new OpenFileDialog();
      if (d.ShowDialog() == true) // Result could be true, false, or null
        this.FileName = d.FileName;
    }

    public string FileName
    {
      get { return (string)GetValue(FileNameProperty); }
      set { SetValue(FileNameProperty, value); }
    }

    private void OnTextChanged(object sender, TextChangedEventArgs e)
    {
      e.Handled = true;
      RoutedEventArgs args = new RoutedEventArgs(FileNameChangedEvent);
      RaiseEvent(args);
    }

    public event RoutedEventHandler FileNameChanged
    {
      add { AddHandler(FileNameChangedEvent, value); }
      remove { RemoveHandler(FileNameChangedEvent, value); }
    }

    public static readonly DependencyProperty FileNameProperty =
    DependencyProperty.Register("FileName", typeof(string), typeof(FileInputBox));

    public static readonly RoutedEvent FileNameChangedEvent =
      EventManager.RegisterRoutedEvent("FileNameChanged",
      RoutingStrategy.Bubble, typeof(RoutedEventHandler), typeof(FileInputBox));
  }
}
```

Creating a Custom Control

Just as the previous section uses `FileInputBox` to illustrate creating a user control, this section uses a `PlayingCard` control to illustrate the process of creating a custom control. Whereas the tendency for designing a user control is to start with the user interface and then later add behavior, it usually makes more sense to start with the behavior when designing a custom control. That's because a good custom control has a pluggable user interface.

Creating the Behavior of the Custom Control

The PlayingCard control should have a notion of a *face*, which can be set to one of 52 possible values. It should be clickable. It could also have a notion of being *selected*, for which each click toggles its state between selected and unselected.

Before implementing the control, it helps to think about the similarities between the control and any of the built-in WPF controls. That way, you can choose a base class more specific than just Control and leverage as much built-in support as possible.

For PlayingCard, the notion of a face is sort of like the Foreground property that all controls have. But Foreground is a Brush, and I want to enable setting the control's face to a simple string such as "H2" for two of hearts or "SQ" for queen of spades. We could hijack some control's existing property of type string (for example, TextBlock.Text), as described in Chapter 14, but such a hack would be a poor experience for consumers of the control. Therefore, it feels logical to implement a distinct Face property.

The notion of being clickable is what defines a Button, so it seems obvious that Button should be the base class we choose. But what about the notion of being *selected*? ToggleButton already provides that in the form of an IsChecked property, as well as the notion of being clickable! So ToggleButton sounds like an ideal base class.

A First Attempt

Listing 20.5 contains an implementation of a ToggleButton-derived PlayingCard control.

LISTING 20.5 PlayingCard.cs—Logic for the PlayingCard Custom Control

```
using System.Windows.Media;
using System.Windows.Controls.Primitives;

namespace Chapter20
{
  public class PlayingCard : ToggleButton
  {
    public string Face
    {
      get { return face; }
      set { face = value; Foreground = (Brush)TryFindResource(face); }
    }
    private string face;
  }
}
```


With the Click, Checked, and Unchecked events and the IsChecked property inherited from ToggleButton, all PlayingCard needs to do is implement a Face property. Listing 20.5 uses the input string as the key to a resource used for the control's Foreground. By using TryFindResource, any invalid strings result in the Foreground being set to null, which is reasonable behavior. But this also implies that we need to store valid resources somewhere with the keys "HA", "H2", "H3", and so on. That's not a problem; we could store them in PlayingCard's Resources collection, and the TryFindResource call will find them.

To create the visuals for PlayingCard, I designed 52 drawings in Adobe Illustrator—one for each possible face—and then exported them to XAML, using the exporter from http://mikeswanson.com/xamlexport. Each of the 52 resources is a DrawingBrush with a number of GeometryDrawing objects. These are the resources to add to PlayingCard's Resources collection. It would be ridiculous to attempt to convert such a large chunk of XAML to C# code, so one approach we could take is to split the definition of PlayingCard between a XAML file and a C# file, making the code in Listing 20.5 the code-behind file. Listings 20.6 and 20.7 show what this would look like.

LISTING 20.6 PlayingCard.xaml.cs—The Code from Listing 20.5, Now as a Code-Behind File

```
using System.Windows.Media;
using System.Windows.Controls.Primitives;

namespace Chapter20
{
  public partial class PlayingCard : ToggleButton
  {
    public PlayingCard()
    {
      InitializeComponent();
    }

    public string Face
    {
      get { return face; }
      set { face = value; Foreground = (Brush)TryFindResource(face); }
    }
    private string face;
  }
}
```

LISTING 20.7 PlayingCard.xaml—Resources for the PlayingCard Custom Control

```
<ToggleButton x:Class="Chapter20.PlayingCard"
  xmlns="http://schemas.microsoft.com/winfx/2006/xaml/presentation"
  xmlns:x="http://schemas.microsoft.com/winfx/2006/xaml"
  xmlns:local="clr-namespace:Chapter20">
<ToggleButton.Resources>
```

LISTING 20.7 Continued

```
<DrawingBrush x:Key="HA" Stretch="Uniform">
<DrawingBrush.Drawing>
  ...
</DrawingBrush.Drawing>
</DrawingBrush>
<DrawingBrush x:Key="H2" Stretch="Uniform">
<DrawingBrush.Drawing>
  ...
</DrawingBrush.Drawing>
</DrawingBrush>
...
<Style TargetType="{x:Type local:PlayingCard}">
  ...
  <Setter Property="Template">
  <Setter.Value>
    <ControlTemplate TargetType="{x:Type local:PlayingCard}">
      ...
      <Rectangle Fill="{TemplateBinding Foreground}"/>
      ...
    </ControlTemplate>
  </Setter.Value>
  </Setter>
</Style>
</ToggleButton.Resources>
</ToggleButton>
```

The changes to the C# code are straightforward additions needed to support the compilation of `PlayingCard` across both files. Listing 20.7 fills the `Resources` collection with all 52 `DrawingBrushes`, plus a typed `Style` with a template that improves the visual appearance (so `PlayingCard` looks even less like a `Button`). The `Style` contains triggers that start animations based on the `Checked`, `Unchecked`, `MouseEnter`, and `MouseLeave` events (not shown in this listing). Alternatively, it could leverage the Visual State Manager because `ToggleButton` defines `Checked` and `Unchecked` states in its `CheckStates` group, plus it respects the `Normal` and `MouseOver` states from `ButtonBase`'s `CommonStates` group.

The key to the template is that the control's `Foreground`, which is assigned to one of the `DrawingBrush` resources whenever `Face` is assigned a value, fills a `Rectangle`. Showing the entire contents of Listing 20.7 would occupy *over 100 pages* (I kid you not!) because of the size and number of `DrawingBrushes`. Therefore, the whole listing isn't provided here, but this book's source code includes it in its entirety (on the website, http://informit.com/title/9780672331190).

Figure 20.4 shows instances of `PlayingCard` in action, using the following `Window` that assigns a unique `Face` to each instance and rotates them in a "fan" formation:

```
<Window xmlns="http://schemas.microsoft.com/winfx/2006/xaml/presentation"
  xmlns:x="http://schemas.microsoft.com/winfx/2006/xaml"
  xmlns:local="clr-namespace:Chapter20"
  Title="Window Hosting PlayingCards">
<Window.Background>
  …
</Window.Background>
  <Viewbox>
    <Canvas Width="220" Height="400">
      <local:PlayingCard Face="C3" Width="100" Height="140" Canvas.Left="0"
        Canvas.Top="100">
      <local:PlayingCard.RenderTransform>
        <RotateTransform CenterX="50" CenterY="140" Angle="300"/>
      </local:PlayingCard.RenderTransform>
      </local:PlayingCard>
      <local:PlayingCard Face="CQ" Width="100" Height="140" Canvas.Left="10"
        Canvas.Top="100">
      <local:PlayingCard.RenderTransform>
        <RotateTransform CenterX="50" CenterY="140" Angle="310"/>
      </local:PlayingCard.RenderTransform>
      </local:PlayingCard>
      …
    </Canvas>
  </Viewbox>
</Window>
```

This approach to implementing `PlayingCard` works, and the output looks just fine on paper. But if you run the application shown in Figure 20.4, you'll probably notice that the performance is sluggish. It also consumes a lot of memory. And both of these issues get worse for every additional `PlayingCard` you place in the `Window`. The problem is that the 52 `DrawingBrush` resources are stored inside the control, so every instance has its own copy of all of them! (100 book pages of resources x 13 instances = a lot of memory!)

This approach also suffers from unexpected behavior for consumers of the control. For example, if the preceding `Window` attempts to set an individual `PlayingCard`'s `Resources` property in XAML, an exception is thrown, explaining that the `ResourceDictionary` can't be reinitialized.

There was a warning sign that indicated that we were heading down the wrong path (in addition to the title of this section being "A First Attempt"): The logic in Listings 20.5 and 20.6 does not purely focus on the behavior of the `PlayingCard` control. Instead, it dictates a visual implementation detail by requiring resources with specific keys and by assigning them to `Foreground`.

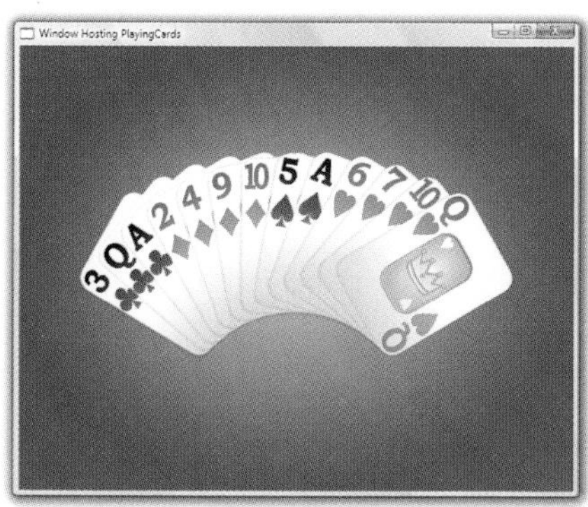

`PlayingCard` "springs out" at you when you hover over it.

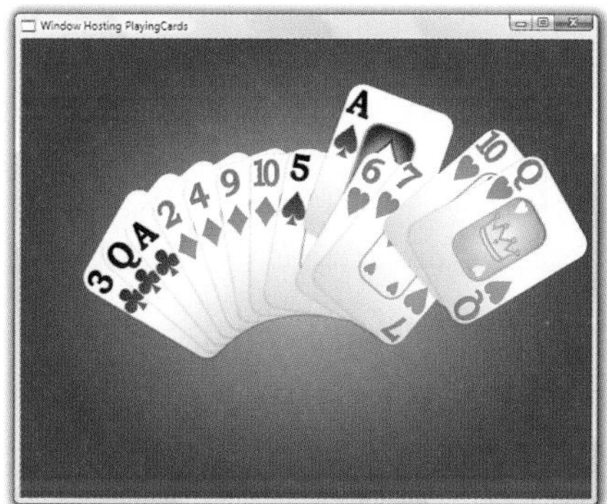

`PlayingCard` jumps up or down when you click to select or unselect it.

FIGURE 20.4 A hand of `PlayingCard` instances that individually react to hover and selection.

A quick fix is to take the contents of `PlayingCard.Resources` and slap them into any consumer's `Application.Resources` instead. This avoids the performance and memory problems, but it breaks the encapsulation of the control. If the application pictured in Figure 20.4 accidentally omitted these resources, it would look like Figure 20.5.

The bottom line is that when creating this version of `PlayingCard`, we were still thinking in terms of the user control model, in which the control "owns" its user interface. We need to break free of that thinking and reorganize the code.

The Recommended Approach

Looking back at Listing 20.5, we should remove the resource retrieval and setting of `Foreground`, leaving that detail to the `Style` applied to `PlayingCard`:

```
public string Face
{
  get { return face; }
  set { face = value; Foreground = (Brush)TryFindResource(face); }
}
```

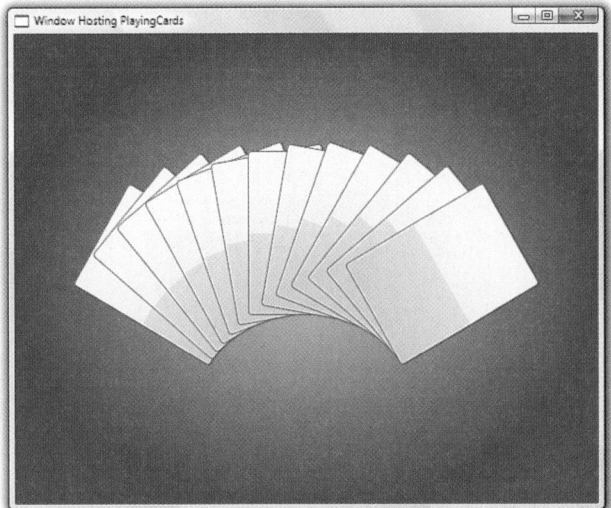

FIGURE 20.5 A hand of PlayingCard instances looks no different than ToggleButtons when the necessary resources aren't present.

The reasonable place to put PlayingCard's Style is inside the assembly's generic dictionary (themes\generic.xaml, covered in Chapter 14). Therefore, to apply the custom Style to PlayingCard (and avoid having it look as it does in Figure 20.5), we should place the following line of code in PlayingCard's static constructor:

```
DefaultStyleKeyProperty.OverrideMetadata(typeof(PlayingCard),
  new FrameworkPropertyMetadata(typeof(PlayingCard)));
```

Also, to facilitate the use of Face with WPF subsystems, we should turn it into a dependency property. Listing 20.8 contains all three of these changes, giving the final implementation of PlayingCard.

LISTING 20.8 PlayingCard.cs—The Final Logic for the PlayingCard Custom Control

```
using System.Windows;
using System.Windows.Media;
using System.Windows.Controls.Primitives;

namespace Chapter20
{
  public class PlayingCard : ToggleButton
  {
    static PlayingCard()
    {
      // Override style
      DefaultStyleKeyProperty.OverrideMetadata(typeof(PlayingCard),
```

LISTING 20.8 Continued

```
        new FrameworkPropertyMetadata(typeof(PlayingCard)));
      // Register Face dependency property
      FaceProperty = DependencyProperty.Register("Face",
        typeof(string), typeof(PlayingCard));
    }

    public string Face
    {
      get { return (string)GetValue(FaceProperty); }
      set { SetValue(FaceProperty, value); }
    }
    public static DependencyProperty FaceProperty;
  }
}
```

It almost seems too simple, but this is all the logic you need. The code captures the essence of `PlayingCard`: The only way it's unique from `ToggleButton` is that it has a string `Face` property. The rest is just a difference in default visuals.

TIP

When you create a WPF Custom Control Library project in Visual Studio or use Add, New Item to add a WPF custom control to an existing project, Visual Studio automatically creates a code file with the correct `DefaultStyleKeyProperty.OverrideMetadata` call and a placeholder `Style` inside the generic dictionary (generating the file if it doesn't already exist). It does *not* give you a XAML file that shares the class definition. Therefore, if you use these mechanisms, you're unlikely to fall into implementation traps such as the first attempt at implementing `PlayingCard` shown in this section.

Creating the User Interface of the Custom Control

To give the final implementation of `PlayingCard` an appropriate user interface, we need to fill the assembly's generic dictionary with the appropriate `Style` and supporting resources. (You should also fill one or more theme dictionaries if you care about customizing the visuals for specific Windows themes.) To get the same visual results achieved in Figure 20.4, we should move all the resources that we originally defined *inside* `PlayingCard` (in Listing 20.7) into the generic dictionary.

The following line of the control template from Listing 20.7 also needs to be modified:

```
<Rectangle Fill="{TemplateBinding Foreground}"/>
```

Filling the main `Rectangle` with `Foreground`'s value isn't appropriate anymore because `PlayingCard` itself doesn't set its value, and it would be too much of a burden to require consumers of the control to set this `Brush`.

20

What we want to do instead is set `Fill` to the appropriate `DrawingBrush` resource in the generic dictionary, based on the current value of `Face`. We should use `StaticResource` to do this because the `DynamicResource` mechanism won't find resources inside a generic or theme dictionary. Because `Face` is a dependency property, your first instinct might be to change the value of `Fill` as follows:

```
<Rectangle>
<Rectangle.Fill>
  <StaticResource ResourceKey="{TemplateBinding Face}"/>
</Rectangle.Fill>
</Rectangle>
```

Unfortunately, this produces an exception at runtime with the following horribly confusing message:

```
Cannot convert the value in attribute 'ResourceKey' to object of type ''.
```

If you replace `TemplateBinding` with the equivalent `Binding`:

```
<Rectangle>
<Rectangle.Fill>
  <StaticResource ResourceKey=
    "{Binding Face, RelativeSource={RelativeSource TemplatedParent}}"/>
</Rectangle.Fill>
</Rectangle>
```

you'll still get an exception, but at least its message makes sense:

```
'Binding' cannot be set on the 'ResourceKey' property of type
'StaticResourceExtension'. A 'Binding' can only be set on a DependencyProperty
of a DependencyObject.
```

`ResourceKey` isn't a dependency property (and couldn't possibly be because `StaticResourceExtension` doesn't even derive from `DependencyObject`), so you can't use it as the target of data binding.

If we define the key to each `DrawingBrush` as a `ComponentResourceKey` (with the `PlayingCard` type as its `TypeInTargetAssembly` and the face name as its `ResourceId`) rather than a simple string, we could restore the C# code that programmatically sets `Foreground` by calling `TryFindResource` and leave the `TemplateBinding` to `Foreground` intact. (The use of the `ComponentResourceKey` class is important because otherwise `FindResource` and `TryFindResource` can't find resources inside a generic or theme dictionary.) There's another option, however, that enables us to keep the C# code as shown in Listing 20.8 and keep the resource keys as simple strings: Define 52 property triggers (one per valid `Face` value) that assign `Fill` to a resource specified at compile time. Although this is verbose, it's also simple. Listing 20.9 shows 13 of these 52 triggers.

LISTING 20.9 Generic.xaml—The Generic Dictionary Containing PlayingCard's Default Style and Control Template

```
<ResourceDictionary
  xmlns="http://schemas.microsoft.com/winfx/2006/xaml/presentation"
  xmlns:x="http://schemas.microsoft.com/winfx/2006/xaml"
  xmlns:local="clr-namespace:Chapter20">
  …
  <Style TargetType="{x:Type local:PlayingCard}">
   …
   <Setter Property="Template">
   <Setter.Value>
    <ControlTemplate TargetType="{x:Type local:PlayingCard}">
     …
     <Rectangle Name="faceRect"/>
     …
    <ControlTemplate.Triggers>
     <Trigger Property="Face" Value="HA">
      <Setter TargetName="faceRect" Property="Fill" Value="{StaticResource HA}"/>
     </Trigger>
     <Trigger Property="Face" Value="H2">
      <Setter TargetName="faceRect" Property="Fill" Value="{StaticResource H2}"/>
     </Trigger>
     <Trigger Property="Face" Value="H3">
      <Setter TargetName="faceRect" Property="Fill" Value="{StaticResource H3}"/>
     </Trigger>
     <Trigger Property="Face" Value="H4">
      <Setter TargetName="faceRect" Property="Fill" Value="{StaticResource H4}"/>
     </Trigger>
     <Trigger Property="Face" Value="H5">
      <Setter TargetName="faceRect" Property="Fill" Value="{StaticResource H5}"/>
     </Trigger>
     <Trigger Property="Face" Value="H6">
      <Setter TargetName="faceRect" Property="Fill" Value="{StaticResource H6}"/>
     </Trigger>
     <Trigger Property="Face" Value="H7">
      <Setter TargetName="faceRect" Property="Fill" Value="{StaticResource H7}"/>
     </Trigger>
     <Trigger Property="Face" Value="H8">
      <Setter TargetName="faceRect" Property="Fill" Value="{StaticResource H8}"/>
     </Trigger>
     <Trigger Property="Face" Value="H9">
      <Setter TargetName="faceRect" Property="Fill" Value="{StaticResource H9}"/>
     </Trigger>
     <Trigger Property="Face" Value="H10">
      <Setter TargetName="faceRect" Property="Fill" Value="{StaticResource H10}"/>
```

LISTING 20.9 Continued

```
      </Trigger>
      <Trigger Property="Face" Value="HJ">
       <Setter TargetName="faceRect" Property="Fill" Value="{StaticResource HJ}"/>
      </Trigger>
      <Trigger Property="Face" Value="HQ">
       <Setter TargetName="faceRect" Property="Fill" Value="{StaticResource HQ}"/>
      </Trigger>
      <Trigger Property="Face" Value="HK">
       <Setter TargetName="faceRect" Property="Fill" Value="{StaticResource HK}"/>
      </Trigger>
      …
     </ControlTemplate.Triggers>
    </Setter.Value>
    </Setter>
  </Style>
</ResourceDictionary>
```

Of course, as long as we are manually mapping values of `Face` to resource keys, we might as well redefine `Face` as an integer from 0 to 51, to be friendlier to typical algorithms that operate on playing cards. We could then add properties such as `Suit` and `Rank` to make working with the information easier.

This approach fixes the performance problems of the first attempt because the generic resources are shared among all instances of `PlayingCard`. (And if you don't want to share a certain resource, you can mark it with `x:Shared="False"`.) But more than that, the complete separation of user interface and logic enables `PlayingCard` to be restyled with maximum flexibility. Unlike the first version of the code, it doesn't require a `Brush` for each face, so you could even plug in a control template that represents each card as a simple `TextBlock`. If you want to advertise the customizable resources from a control such as `PlayingCard` and encourage them to be overridden by others, you could define 52 static properties that return an appropriate `ComponentResourceKey` for each resource.

DIGGING DEEPER

Other Approaches for Designing `PlayingCard`

Rather than embed the notion of being selected into `PlayingCard` itself, you could place `PlayingCards` into a `ListBox` and rely on its selection behavior. You could then change its `SelectionMode` to automatically switch between allowing single selections or multiple selections.

If you host the items in a `ListBox`, however, you won't get the nice "fan" layout shown in Figures 20.4 and 20.5 by default. But you could write a custom "fan" panel and plug it into the `ListBox` as its `ItemsPanel` template. The next chapter creates such a panel, and calls it `FanCanvas`.

Continued

You could also rewrite `PlayingCard` as a simple object rather than a custom control and use a data template to give it the appropriate visuals. You could even use simple strings, as long as a data template is in place to treat the strings like card faces!

TIP

The "Creating the Behavior of the Custom Control" section discusses reusing as much existing logic as possible by choosing an appropriate base class for a custom control. On the user interface side of things, WPF also has many built-in elements that you should try to leverage in your control template.

For the nontraditional user interface inside `PlayingCard`, it makes sense to start from scratch. But for other controls, you might find a lot of unfamiliar reusable components to leverage in the `System.Windows.Controls.Primitives` namespace, such as `BulletDecorator`, `ResizeGrip`, `ScrollBar`, `Thumb`, `Track`, and so on.

Considerations for More Sophisticated Controls

The `PlayingCard` control has minimal interactivity that could be handled in the control template with some simple triggers or visual states. But controls with more interactivity need to use other techniques. For example, imagine that you want to change `FileInputBox` from the beginning of this chapter from a user control to a custom control. This implies that you'll move its user interface (repeated in the following XAML) into a control template:

```
<DockPanel>
  <Button x:Name="theButton" DockPanel.Dock="Right" Click="theButton_Click">
    Browse...</Button>
  <TextBox x:Name="theTextBox"
    MinWidth="{Binding ActualWidth, ElementName=theButton}"
    Text="{Binding FileName, ElementName=root}" Margin="0,0,2,0"/>
</DockPanel>
```

But how should you attach the clicking of the `Button` to `FileInputBox`'s `theButton_Click` event handler? You can't set the `Click` event the same way inside the control template. (Well, you could if you redefined `theButton_Click` in a code-behind file for the generic dictionary. But that would effectively reimplement all the control's logic, and it would mean that anyone overriding the default template with his or her own would have to do the same thing!)

20

You can handle this kind of interactivity using two reasonable approaches, both of which are employed by WPF's built-in controls in different situations:

- Using control parts
- Using commands

This section also examines the technique of defining and using new control states, using the PlayingCard control as an example.

Using Control Parts

As mentioned in Chapter 14, a *control part* is a loose contract between a control and its template. A control can retrieve an element in its template with a given name and then do whatever it desires with that element.

After you decide on elements to designate as control parts, you should choose a name for each one. The general naming convention is PART_*XXX*, where *XXX* is the name of the control. You should then document each part's existence by marking your class with TemplatePartAttribute (one for each part). This looks as follows for a version of FileInputBox that expects a Browse Button in its control template:

```
[TemplatePart(Name="PART_Browse", Type=typeof(Button))]
public class FileInputBox : Control
{
  …
}
```

WPF doesn't do anything with TemplatePartAttribute, but it serves as documentation that design tools can leverage.

To process your specially designated control parts, you should override the OnApplyTemplate method inherited from FrameworkElement. This method is called any time a template is applied, so it gives you the opportunity to handle dynamic template changes gracefully. To retrieve the instances of any elements inside your control template, you can call GetTemplateChild, also inherited from FrameworkElement. The following implementation retrieves the designated Browse Button and attaches the necessary logic to its Click event:

```
public override void OnApplyTemplate()
{
  base.OnApplyTemplate();

  // Retrieve the Button from the current template
  Button browseButton = base.GetTemplateChild("PART_Browse") as Button;

  // Hook up the event handler
  if (browseButton != null)
    browseButton.Click += new RoutedEventHandler(theButton_Click);
}
```

Note that this implementation gracefully handles templates that omit PART_Browse, causing the Button variable to be null. This is the recommended approach, making your control handle any control template with varying degrees of functionality. After all, it's quite reasonable to imagine someone wanting to restyle FileInputBox such that it doesn't have a Browse Button. If you want to go against recommendations and be stricter, you could always throw an exception in OnApplyTemplate if the template doesn't contain the parts you require. But such a control likely won't work well inside graphic design tools such as Expression Blend.

Using Commands

A more flexible way to attach logic to pieces of a template is to define and use commands. With a command on FileInputBox representing the notion of browsing, a control template could associate a subelement with it as follows:

```
<Button Command="{x:Static local:FileInputBox.BrowseCommand}">Browse...</Button>
```

Not only does this avoid the need for magical names, but the element triggering this command no longer has to be a Button!

To implement this command, FileInputBox needs a static .NET property of type RoutedCommand or RoutedUICommand (with a static backing field that can be private):

```
private static RoutedUICommand browseCommand = new
  RoutedUICommand("Browse...", "BrowseCommand", typeof(FileInputBox));

public static RoutedUICommand BrowseCommand
{
  get { return browseCommand; }
}
```

The control should bind this command to the desired custom logic (theButton_Click in this case) in its static constructor:

```
static FileInputBox()
{
  // Specify the gesture that triggers the command:
  CommandManager.RegisterClassInputBinding(typeof(FileInputBox),
    new MouseGesture(MouseAction.LeftClick));

  // Attach the command to custom logic:
  CommandManager.RegisterClassCommandBinding(typeof(FileInputBox),
    new CommandBinding(browseCommand, theButton_Click));
}
```

Using Control States

As explained in Chapter 14, WPF 4 adds the ability for controls to define *control states* in order to provide an optimal experience inside design tools such as Expression Blend. Both user controls and custom controls can—and do—support states. Any class that derives from Control already supports three states from the ValidationStates group: Valid, InvalidFocused, and InvalidUnfocused. The PlayingCard control automatically supports the CheckStates group (with Checked, Unchecked, and Indeterminate states) from its

ToggleButton base class and the CommonStates group (with Normal, MouseOver, Pressed, and Disabled states) from its ButtonBase base class.

Thanks to the richness of PlayingCard's base classes, defining additional states is not necessary. Still, it might be nice to define the notion of a PlayingCard being flipped on its back rather than always showing its face. That way, a graphic designer could easily plug in a beautiful design for a card back without worrying about what events or properties might cause the card to be flipped over.

For this scenario, it makes sense to have two states—Front and Back—and assign them to a new state group called FlipStates. (Every new state group should include one state that acts as the default state.) You should document the existence of these states by marking the PlayingCard class with two TemplateVisualState custom attributes:

```
[TemplateVisualState(Name="Front", GroupName="FlipStates")]
[TemplateVisualState(Name="Back", GroupName="FlipStates")]
public class PlayingCard : ToggleButton
{
  …
}
```

WARNING

Controls should not add any states to state groups already defined by a base class!

New states should be added to new state group(s). Because each state group works independently, new transitions among states in a new state group cannot interfere with base class logic. If you add new states to an existing state group, however, there's no guarantee that the base class logic to transition among states will continue operate correctly.

WARNING

Every state must have a unique name, even across different state groups!

Despite any partitioning into multiple state groups, a control must not have two states with the same name. This limitation can be surprising until you've implemented state transitions and realize that VisualStateManager's GoToState method doesn't have the concept of state groups. State groups are really just a documentation tool for understanding the behavior of a control's states and the possible transitions.

This limitation is why state names tend to be very specific. For example, the default set of states for CalendarDayButton include Normal (from the CommonStates group), NormalDay (from the BlackoutDayStates group), RegularDay (from the DayStates group), Unfocused (from the FocusStates group), CalendarButtonUnfocused (from the CalendarButtonFocusStates group), and more. They could not all simply be called Default or Normal.

Once you have chosen and documented your states, the only other thing to do is transition to the appropriate states at the appropriate times by calling VisualStateManager's static GoToState method. This is usually done from a helper method such as the following:

```
internal void ChangeState(bool useTransitions)
{
  // Assume that IsShowingFace is the property that determines the state:
  if (this.IsShowingFace)
    VisualStateManager.GoToState(this, "Front", useTransitions);
  else
    VisualStateManager.GoToState(this, "Back", useTransitions);
}
```

Controls typically call such a method in the following situations:

- Inside OnApplyTemplate (with useTransitions=false)
- When the control first loads (with useTransitions=false)
- Inside appropriate event handlers (for this example, it should be called inside a PropertyChanged handler for the IsShowingFace property)

There is no harm in calling GoToState when the destination state is the same as the current state. (When this is done, the call does nothing.) Therefore, helper methods such as ChangeState typically set the current state for *every* state group without worrying about which property just changed.

WARNING

When a control loads, it must explicitly transition to the default state in every state group!

If a control does not explicitly transition to the default state(s), it introduces a subtle bug for consumers of the control. Before the initial transition for any state group, the control is not yet in *any* of those states. That means that the first transition to a non-default state will not invoke any transition from the default state that consumers may have defined.

When you perform this initial transition, you should pass false for VisualStateManager.GoToState's useTransitions parameter to make it happen instantaneously.

Control defines a similar helper method called ChangeVisualState that is effectively implemented as follows:

```
internal virtual void ChangeVisualState(bool useTransitions)
{
  // Handle the states in the ValidationStates group:
  if (Validation.GetHasError(this))
```

```
  {
    if (this.IsKeyboardFocused)
      VisualStateManager.GoToState(this, "InvalidFocused", useTransitions);
    else
      VisualStateManager.GoToState(this, "InvalidUnfocused", useTransitions);
  }
  else
  {
    VisualStateManager.GoToState(this, "Valid", useTransitions);
  }
}
```

ChangeVisualState is a virtual method, and other controls in WPF override it. ButtonBase effectively overrides it as follows:

```
internal override void ChangeVisualState(bool useTransitions)
{
  // Handle the base states in the ValidationStates group:
  base.ChangeVisualState(useTransitions);

  // Independently handle states in the CommonStates group:
  if (!this.IsEnabled)
    VisualStateManager.GoToState(this, "Disabled", useTransitions);
  else if (this.IsPressed)
    VisualStateManager.GoToState(this, "Pressed", useTransitions);
  else if (this.IsMouseOver)
    VisualStateManager.GoToState(this, "MouseOver", useTransitions);
  else
    VisualStateManager.GoToState(this, "Normal", useTransitions);

  // Independently handle states in the FocusStates group:
  if (this.IsKeyboardFocused)
    VisualStateManager.GoToState(this, "Focused", useTransitions);
  else
    VisualStateManager.GoToState(this, "Unfocused", useTransitions);
}
```

ToggleButton effectively overrides ButtonBase's implementation as follows:

```
internal override void ChangeVisualState(bool useTransitions)
{
  // Handle the base states in the ValidationStates,
  // CommonStates, and FocusStates groups:
  base.ChangeVisualState(useTransitions);

  // Independently handle states in the CheckStates group:
  if (this.IsChecked == true)
```

```
    VisualStateManager.GoToState(this, "Checked", useTransitions);
  else if (this.IsChecked == false)
    VisualStateManager.GoToState(this, "Unchecked", useTransitions);
  else // this.isChecked == null
  {
    // Try to transition to the Indeterminate state. If one isn't defined,
    // fall back to the Unchecked state
    if (!VisualStateManager.GoToState(this, "Indeterminate", useTransitions))
      VisualStateManager.GoToState(this, "Unchecked", useTransitions);
  }
}
```

`GoToState` returns `false` if it is unable to transition to a state. This happens if a template has been applied that simply doesn't include a corresponding `VisualState` definition. Controls should be resilient to this condition, and normally they are by simply ignoring the return value from `GoToState`. `ToggleButton`, however, attempts to transition to the `Unchecked` state if an `Indeterminate` state doesn't exist. (Note that this condition does not affect the value of `IsChecked`; the `ToggleButton` is still logically indeterminate even if visually it looks unchecked.)

Although `PlayingCard` is unable to override `ToggleButton`'s `ChangeVisualState` method (because it is internal to the WPF assembly), it still inherits all of its behavior as a consequence of deriving from `ToggleButton`. The code from `PlayingCard`'s `ChangeState` method defined earlier happily runs independently of the existing `ChangeVisualState` logic, and the resulting control supports all the expected states from all five state groups.

DIGGING DEEPER

Supporting UI Automation

For a custom control to be truly first class, it should support UI Automation. The pattern for doing this is to create a companion class that derives from `FrameworkElementAutomationPeer`, named *`ControlName`*`AutomationPeer`, that describes the control to the automation system. You should then override `OnCreateAutomationPeer` (inherited from `UIElement`) in the custom control, making it return an instance of the companion class:

```
protected override AutomationPeer OnCreateAutomationPeer()
{
  return new FileInputBoxAutomationPeer(this);
}
```

Whenever an event occurs that should be communicated to the automation system, you can retrieve the companion class and raise an automation-specific event, as follows:

```
FileInputBoxAutomationPeer peer =
  UIElementAutomationPeer.FromElement(myControl) as FileInputBoxAutomationPeer;
if (peer != null)
  peer.RaiseAutomationEvent(AutomationEvents.StructureChanged);
```

TIP

A sophisticated control might want to determine whether it is running in *design mode* (for example, being displayed in the Visual Studio or Expression Blend designer). The static `System.ComponentModel.DesignerProperties` class exposes an `IsInDesignMode` attached property that gives you this information. Design tools change the default value when appropriate, so a custom control can call the static `GetIsInDesignMode` method with a reference to itself to obtain the value.

Summary

If you're reading this book in order, you should be familiar enough with WPF to find the process of creating a custom control fairly understandable. For WPF beginners, however, creating a custom control—even when guided by Visual Studio—involves many unorthodox concepts. And if such a user doesn't care about restyling and theming but rather just wants to build simple applications and controls as with Windows Forms, all that extra complication doesn't even add much value! That's why WPF takes a bifurcated view of custom controls versus user controls.

Of course, even these two approaches are not the only options for plugging reusable pieces into WPF applications. For example, you could create a custom lower-level element that derives directly from `FrameworkElement`. A common non-`Control` to derive from is `Panel`, for creating custom layout schemes. That's the topic of the next (and final) chapter.

CHAPTER 21

Layout with Custom Panels

IN THIS CHAPTER

- Communication Between Parents and Children
- Creating a `SimpleCanvas`
- Creating a `SimpleStackPanel`
- Creating an `OverlapPanel`
- Creating a `FanCanvas`

Chapter 5, "Layout with Panels," examines the variety of panels included with WPF. If none of the built-in panels do exactly what you want, you have the option of writing your own panel. Of course, with all the flexibility of the built-in panels, the layout properties on child elements (discussed in Chapter 4, "Sizing, Positioning, and Transforming Elements"), plus the ability to embed panels within other panels to create arbitrarily complex layout, it's unlikely that you're going to need a custom panel. Actually, you never *need* a custom panel; with enough procedural code, you can achieve any layout with just a `Canvas`. It's just a matter of how easy and automatic you want to be able to repetitively apply certain types of layout.

For example, perhaps you want to create a version of `WrapPanel` that stacks or wraps in a different direction than the two built-in directions. Or perhaps you want to create a version of `StackPanel` that stacks from the bottom up, although you could alternatively get this effect pretty easily with a `DockPanel` by giving each element a `Dock` value of `Bottom`. User interface virtualization might be a good incentive for creating a custom panel, such as creating a `VirtualizingWrapPanel` much like the `VirtualizingStackPanel` that already exists. You could also create a custom panel that incorporates automatic drag and drop, similar to `ToolBarTray`.

Although writing a custom panel can often be avoided by combining more primitive panels, creating a new panel can be useful when you want to repetitively arrange controls in a unique way. Encapsulating the custom logic in a panel can make the arrangement of a user interface less error prone and help to enforce consistency. Panels that are made for very limited scenarios can also perform much better than the super-flexible WPF panels, especially if you replace multiple nestings of generic panels with a single, limited one.

To understand the steps involved in creating a custom panel, we'll first create two panels in this chapter that replicate the functionality of existing panels in WPF. After that, we'll create two unique panels. The good news is that there is no special mechanism for creating a custom panel; you use exactly the same approach used by the built-in panels. But this also means we should take a closer look at how panels and their children communicate, which was glossed over in Chapters 4 and 5.

Communication Between Parents and Children

Chapters 4 and 5 explain that parent panels and their children work together to determine their final sizes and positions. To strike a reasonable balance between the needs of the parent and its children, layout is a recursive two-pass process. The first pass is called *measure*, and the second pass is called *arrange*.

The Measure Step

In the measure step, parents ask their children how big they want to be, given the amount of space available. Panels (and children, when appropriate) do this by overriding the `MeasureOverride` method from `FrameworkElement`. Here's an example:

```
protected override Size MeasureOverride(Size availableSize)
{
  …
  // Ask each child how big it would like to be, given a certain amount space
  foreach (UIElement child in this.Children)
  {
    child.Measure(new Size(…));
    // The child's answer is now in child.DesiredSize
    …
  }
  …
  // Tell my parent how big I would like to be given the passed-in availableSize
  return new Size(…);
}
```

All children can be accessed via the panel's `Children` collection (a `UIElementCollection`), and asking each child for its desired size is done by simply calling its `Measure` method (inherited from `UIElement`). `Measure` doesn't return a value, but after the call, the child's `DesiredSize` property contains its answer. As the parent, you can decide if you want to alter your behavior based on the desired sizes of any of your children.

WARNING

In MeasureOverride, panels must always call Measure on each child!

You might want to implement a panel that doesn't have any use for checking its children's DesiredSize values simply because it doesn't care how big its children want to be. Still, all panels *must* ask their children anyway (by calling Measure) because some elements don't work correctly if their Measure method never gets called. This is somewhat like asking your spouse "How was your day?" when you really don't care about the answer but want to avoid the repercussions. (Or so I'm told. Personally, I always care about the answer!)

The preceding snippet of C# code, like all MeasureOverride implementations, uses two important Size values, discussed in the following sections.

The Size Passed to Each Child's Measure Method

This value should represent the amount of space you're planning to give the child. It could be all the space given to you (captured in MeasureOverride's availableSize parameter), some fraction of your space, or some absolute value, depending on your desires.

In addition, you can use Double.PositiveInfinity for either or both of Size's dimensions to find out how large the child wants to be in an ideal situation. In other words, this line of code means, "How big do you want to be given all the space in the world?":

```
child.Measure(new Size(Double.PositiveInfinity, Double.PositiveInfinity));
```

The layout system automatically handles the child layout properties discussed in Chapter 4, such as Margin, so the size ultimately passed to the child's implementation of MeasureOverride is the size you passed to Measure minus any margins. This also means that the availableSize parameter passed to your own MeasureOverride implementation represents whatever *your* parent allocated for you minus your own margins.

The Size Returned by MeasureOverride

The Size you return represents how big you want to be (answering your parent's request, just as your children have already answered it for you). You could return an absolute size, but that would ignore the requests from your children. More likely, you'd pick a value that enables you to "size to content," being big enough to fit all your children in their ideal sizes but no bigger.

WARNING

You can't simply return availableSize from MeasureOverride!

Whether because of its simplicity or because of your own greediness, it's tempting to use the passed-in availableSize parameter as the return value for MeasureOverride. This basically means, "Give me all the space you've got."

Continued

However, whereas a `Size` with `Double.PositiveInfinity` in both dimensions is a legal value for `availableSize`, it is not a valid value for `DesiredSize`. Even when given unlimited space, you must choose a concrete size. If you ever end up returning an infinite size, `UIElement`'s `Measure` implementation throws an `InvalidOperationException` with a helpful message: "`Layout measurement override of element 'XXX' should not return PositiveInfinity as its DesiredSize, even if Infinity is passed in as available size.`"

If you have only one child, sizing to your content is as simple as returning that child's `DesiredSize` as your own desired size. For multiple children, you would need to combine the widths and heights of your children according to how you plan to arrange them.

The Arrange Step

After measurement has been completed all the way through the element tree, it's time for the physical arranging of elements. In the arrange step, parents *tell* their children where they are getting placed and how much space they are given (which might be a different `Size` than the one given earlier). Panels (and children, when appropriate) do this by overriding the `ArrangeOverride` method from `FrameworkElement`. Here's an example:

```
protected override Size ArrangeOverride(Size finalSize)
{
  …
  // Tell each child how much space it is getting
  foreach (UIElement child in this.Children)
  {
    child.Arrange(new Rect(…));
    // The child's size is now in child.ActualHeight & child.ActualWidth
    …
  }
  …
  // Set my own actual size (ActualHeight & ActualWidth)
  return new Size(…);
}
```

You tell each child its location and size by passing a `Rect` and a `Size` to its `Arrange` method (inherited from `UIElement`). For example, you can give each child its desired size simply by passing the value of its `DesiredSize` property to `Arrange`. You can be certain that this size is set appropriately because all measuring is done before any arranging begins.

Unlike with `Measure`, you cannot pass an infinite size to `Arrange` (and the `finalSize` passed to you will never be infinite). The child can choose to occupy a different amount of space than what you've specified, such as a subset of the space. Parents can determine what actions (if any) they want to take if this happens. The actual size chosen by each child can be obtained from its `ActualHeight` and `ActualWidth` properties after the call to `Arrange`.

As with your children, the size you return from `ArrangeOverride` becomes the value of your `RenderSize` and `ActualHeight`/`ActualWidth` properties. The size must not be infinite, but unlike with `MeasureOverride`, it's valid to simply return the passed-in `Size` if you want to take up all the available space because `finalSize` can never be infinite.

As with the measure step, in the arrange step, properties such as `Margin` are handled automatically, so the information getting passed to children (and the `finalSize` passed to you) has any margins subtracted. In addition, alignment is automatically handled by the arrange step. When a child is given exactly the amount of space it needs (for example, passing its `DesiredSize` to its `Arrange` method), alignment appears to have no effect because there's no extra space for the element to align within. But when you give a child more space than it occupies, the results of its `HorizontalAlignment` and/or `VerticalAlignment` settings are seen.

WARNING

Don't do anything in `MeasureOverride` or `ArrangeOverride` that invalidates layout!

You can do some exotic things in `MeasureOverride` or `ArrangeOverride`, such as apply additional transforms to children (either as `LayoutTransforms` or `RenderTransforms`). But be sure that you don't invoke any code that invalidates layout; otherwise, you could wind up in an infinite loop!

Any method or property invalidates layout if it calls `UIElement.InvalidateMeasure` or `UIElement.InvalidateArrange`. These are public methods, however, so it can be difficult to know what code calls them. Within WPF, dependency properties that use these methods document this fact with one or more metadata flags from the `FrameworkPropertyMetadataOptions` enumeration: `AffectsMeasure`, `AffectsArrange`, `AffectsParentArrange`, and/or `AffectsParentMeasure`.

If you feel that you must execute some code that invalidates layout, and you have a plan for avoiding a never-ending cycle, you can factor that logic into a separate method then use `Dispatcher.BeginInvoke` to schedule its execution after the current layout pass completes. To do this, be sure to use a `DispatcherPriority` value no higher than `Loaded`.

Creating a `SimpleCanvas`

Before creating some unique panels, let's see how to replicate the behavior of existing panels. The first one we'll create is a simplified version of `Canvas` called `SimpleCanvas`. `SimpleCanvas` behaves exactly like `Canvas`, except that it only respects `Left` and `Top` attached properties on its children rather than `Left`, `Top`, `Right`, and `Bottom`. This is done only to reduce the amount of repetitive code, as supporting `Right` and `Bottom` looks almost identical to supporting `Left` and `Top`. (As a result, the arrange pass in `SimpleCanvas` is negligibly faster than in `Canvas`, but only for children not already marked with `Left` and `Top`.)

Implementing `SimpleCanvas` (or any other custom panel) consists of the following four steps:

1. Create a class that derives from `Panel`.
2. Define any properties that would be useful for customizing layout, potentially including attached properties for the children.
3. Override `MeasureOverride` and measure each child.
4. Override `ArrangeOverride` and arrange each child.

Listing 21.1 contains the entire implementation of `SimpleCanvas`.

LISTING 21.1 `SimpleCanvas.cs`—The Implementation of `SimpleCanvas`

```
using System;
using System.ComponentModel;
using System.Windows;
using System.Windows.Controls;
using System.Windows.Media;

namespace CustomPanels
{
  public class SimpleCanvas : Panel
  {
    public static readonly DependencyProperty LeftProperty =
      DependencyProperty.RegisterAttached("Left", typeof(double),
      typeof(SimpleCanvas), new FrameworkPropertyMetadata(Double.NaN,
      FrameworkPropertyMetadataOptions.AffectsParentArrange));

    public static readonly DependencyProperty TopProperty =
      DependencyProperty.RegisterAttached("Top", typeof(double),
      typeof(SimpleCanvas), new FrameworkPropertyMetadata(Double.NaN,
      FrameworkPropertyMetadataOptions.AffectsParentArrange));

    [TypeConverter(typeof(LengthConverter)),AttachedPropertyBrowsableForChildren]
    public static double GetLeft(UIElement element)
    {
      if (element == null) { throw new ArgumentNullException("element"); }
      return (double)element.GetValue(LeftProperty);
    }

    [TypeConverter(typeof(LengthConverter)),AttachedPropertyBrowsableForChildren]
    public static void SetLeft(UIElement element, double length)
    {
      if (element == null) { throw new ArgumentNullException("element"); }
```

LISTING 21.1 Continued

```
      element.SetValue(LeftProperty, length);
    }

    [TypeConverter(typeof(LengthConverter)),AttachedPropertyBrowsableForChildren]
    public static double GetTop(UIElement element)
    {
      if (element == null) { throw new ArgumentNullException("element"); }
      return (double)element.GetValue(TopProperty);
    }

    [TypeConverter(typeof(LengthConverter)),AttachedPropertyBrowsableForChildren]
    public static void SetTop(UIElement element, double length)
    {
      if (element == null) { throw new ArgumentNullException("element"); }
      element.SetValue(TopProperty, length);
    }

    protected override Size MeasureOverride(Size availableSize)
    {
      foreach (UIElement child in this.Children)
      {
        // Give each child all the space it wants
        if (child != null)
          child.Measure(new Size(Double.PositiveInfinity,
                                 Double.PositiveInfinity));
      }

      // The SimpleCanvas itself needs no space
      return new Size(0, 0);
    }

    protected override Size ArrangeOverride(Size finalSize)
    {
      foreach (UIElement child in this.Children)
      {
        if (child != null)
        {
          double x = 0;
          double y = 0;

          // Respect any Left and Top attached properties,
          // otherwise the child is placed at (0,0)
          double left = GetLeft(child);
          double top = GetTop(child);
```

LISTING 21.1 Continued

```
          if (!Double.IsNaN(left)) x = left;
          if (!Double.IsNaN(top)) y = top;

          // Place at the chosen (x,y) location with the child's DesiredSize
          child.Arrange(new Rect(new Point(x, y), child.DesiredSize));
        }
      }

      // Whatever size you gave me is fine
      return finalSize;
    }
  }
}
```

Listing 21.1 begins by defining the `Left` and `Top` attached properties, which each consist of the `DependencyProperty` field with the pair of static `Get`/`Set` methods. As with `Canvas`'s `Left` and `Top` attached properties, their default value is `Double.NaN`, which serves as the not-set-to-anything value. The registration passes `FrameworkPropertyMetadataOptions.AffectsParentArrange` to the `FrameworkPropertyMetadataOptions` constructor to tell WPF that when the values of these properties change on child elements, the parent `SimpleCanvas` needs to redo its arrange layout pass so it can place the element in its new location.

The static `Get`/`Set` methods are a standard implementation of the two attached properties. Notice the association with the `LengthConverter` type converter, which allows these properties to be set to a variety of strings in XAML, such as `"Auto"` (mapped to `Double.NaN`) or numbers with explicit units (`"px"`, `"in"`, `"cm"`, or `"pt"`). The `AttachedPropertyBrowsableForChildren` attribute helps with design-time support by requesting that designers show these two properties in the list of available properties that can be set on children.

The implementation of `MeasureOverride` couldn't be simpler, which makes sense considering the desired behavior of `SimpleCanvas`. It just tells each child to take all the space it wants, and then it tells its parent that it doesn't require any space for itself (because its children do not get clipped to its bounds unless `ClipToBounds` is set to `true`, thanks to behavior inherited from `FrameworkElement`).

`ArrangeOverride` is where the interesting work is done. Each child is placed at `(0,0)` with its `DesiredSize` unless it is marked with a `Left` and/or `Top` attached property. To check for this, `ArrangeOverride` simply calls `GetLeft` and `GetTop` and looks for values other than `Double.NaN`.

You can see that the panel doesn't need to care about any of the children's layout properties (`Height`, `MinHeight`, `MaxHeight`, `Width`, `MinWidth`, `MaxWidth`, `Margin`, `Padding`, `Visibility`, `HorizontalAlignment`, `VerticalAlignment`, `LayoutTransform`, and so on). In addition, tabbing between child elements is handled automatically. The tab order is defined by the order in which children are added to the parent.

The project included with this book's source code consumes SimpleCanvas as follows:

```
<Window x:Class="CustomPanels.SimpleCanvasWindow"
        xmlns="http://schemas.microsoft.com/winfx/2006/xaml/presentation"
        xmlns:x="http://schemas.microsoft.com/winfx/2006/xaml"
        xmlns:local="clr-namespace:CustomPanels"
        Title="Four Buttons in a SimpleCanvas">
  <local:SimpleCanvas>
    <Button Content="1" Background="Red"/>
    <Button local:SimpleCanvas.Left="40" local:SimpleCanvas.Top="40"
            Content="2" Background="Orange"/>
    <Button local:SimpleCanvas.Left="80" local:SimpleCanvas.Top="80"
            Content="3" Background="Yellow"/>
    <Button local:SimpleCanvas.Left="120" local:SimpleCanvas.Top="120"
            Content="4" Background="Lime"/>
  </local:SimpleCanvas>
</Window>
```

The XAML for the `Window` maps the `CustomPanels` .NET namespace to a `local` prefix, so `SimpleCanvas` and its attached properties can be used with the `local:` prefix. Because `SimpleCanvas.cs` is compiled into the same assembly, no `Assembly` value needs to be set with the `clr-namespace` directive.

Note that the `SimpleCanvas` implementation could reuse `Canvas`'s existing `Left` and `Top` attached properties by getting rid of its own and changing two lines of code inside `ArrangeOverride`:

```
double left = Canvas.GetLeft(child);
double top = Canvas.GetTop(child);
```

Then the panel could be used as follows:

```
<Window x:Class="CustomPanels.SimpleCanvasWindow"
        xmlns="http://schemas.microsoft.com/winfx/2006/xaml/presentation"
        xmlns:x="http://schemas.microsoft.com/winfx/2006/xaml"
        xmlns:local="clr-namespace:CustomPanels"
        Title="Four Buttons in a SimpleCanvas">
  <local:SimpleCanvas>
    <Button Content="1" Background="Red"/>
    <Button Canvas.Left="40" Canvas.Top="40"
            Content="2" Background="Orange"/>
    <Button Canvas.Left="80" Canvas.Top="80"
            Content="3" Background="Yellow"/>
```

```
    <Button Canvas.Left="120" Canvas.Top="120"
            Content="4" Background="Lime"/>
  </local:SimpleCanvas>
</Window>
```

It's pretty nonstandard, however, for one panel to require the use of a different panel's attached properties.

Creating a `SimpleStackPanel`

Let's look at replicating one more existing panel, but one that does a bit more work while measuring and arranging. We'll create a `SimpleStackPanel` that acts just like `StackPanel`. The only major difference between `SimpleStackPanel` and `StackPanel` is that our version is missing some performance optimizations. Listing 21.2 contains the entire implementation.

LISTING 21.2 `SimpleStackPanel.cs`—The Implementation of `SimpleStackPanel`

```
using System;
using System.Windows;
using System.Windows.Controls;

namespace CustomPanels
{
  public class SimpleStackPanel : Panel
  {
    // The direction of stacking
    public static readonly DependencyProperty OrientationProperty =
      DependencyProperty.Register("Orientation", typeof(Orientation),
      typeof(SimpleStackPanel), new FrameworkPropertyMetadata(
      Orientation.Vertical, FrameworkPropertyMetadataOptions.AffectsMeasure));

    public Orientation Orientation
    {
      get { return (Orientation)GetValue(OrientationProperty); }
      set { SetValue(OrientationProperty, value); }
    }

    protected override Size MeasureOverride(Size availableSize)
    {
      Size desiredSize = new Size();

      // Let children grow indefinitely in the direction of stacking,
      // overwriting what was passed in
      if (Orientation == Orientation.Vertical)
        availableSize.Height = Double.PositiveInfinity;
```

LISTING 21.2 Continued

```
    else
      availableSize.Width = Double.PositiveInfinity;

    foreach (UIElement child in this.Children)
    {
      if (child != null)
      {
        // Ask the first child for its desired size, given unlimited space in
        // the direction of stacking and all our available space (whatever was
        // passed in) in the other direction
        child.Measure(availableSize);

        // Our desired size is the sum of child sizes in the direction of
        // stacking, and the size of the largest child in the other direction
        if (Orientation == Orientation.Vertical)
        {
          desiredSize.Width = Math.Max(desiredSize.Width,
                                       child.DesiredSize.Width);
          desiredSize.Height += child.DesiredSize.Height;
        }
        else
        {
          desiredSize.Height = Math.Max(desiredSize.Height,
                                        child.DesiredSize.Height);
          desiredSize.Width += child.DesiredSize.Width;
        }
      }
    }

    return desiredSize;
  }

  protected override Size ArrangeOverride(Size finalSize)
  {
    double offset = 0;

    foreach (UIElement child in this.Children)
    {
      if (child != null)
      {
        if (Orientation == Orientation.Vertical)
        {
          // The offset moves the child down the stack.
          // Give the child all our width, but as much height as it desires.
```

LISTING 21.2 Continued

```
            child.Arrange(new Rect(0, offset, finalSize.Width,
                                              child.DesiredSize.Height));

            // Update the offset for the next child
            offset += child.DesiredSize.Height;
          }
          else
          {
            // The offset moves the child down the stack.
            // Give the child all our height, but as much width as it desires.
            child.Arrange(new Rect(offset, 0, child.DesiredSize.Width,
                                              finalSize.Height));

            // Update the offset for the next child
            offset += child.DesiredSize.Width;
          }
        }
      }

      // Fill all the space given
      return finalSize;
    }
  }
}
```

Similar to Listing 21.1, this listing begins with the definition of a dependency property—`Orientation`. Its default value is `Vertical`, and its `FrameworkPropertyMetadataOptions` reveals that a change in its value requires its measure layout pass to be re-invoked. (This also re-invokes the arrange pass, after the measure pass.)

In `MeasureOverride`, each child is given the panel's available size in the non-stacking direction (which may or may not be infinite) but is given infinite size in the stacking direction. As each child's desired size is revealed, `SimpleStackPanel` keeps track of the results and updates its own desired size accordingly. In the stacking dimension, its desired length is the sum of all its children's desired lengths. In the non-stacking dimension, its length is the length of its longest child.

In ArrangeOverride, an offset ("stack pointer," if you will) keeps track of the position to place the next child as the stack grows. Each child is given the entire panel's length in the stacking direction and its desired length in the non-stacking direction. Finally, SimpleStackPanel consumes all the space given to it by returning the input finalSize. With that, SimpleStackPanel behaves just like the real StackPanel.

Creating an OverlapPanel

The OverlapPanel is truly a custom panel. It builds on the work we did to create SimpleStackPanel but adds a few tweaks that make its behavior unique. Like SimpleStackPanel, it sequentially stacks its children based on the value of its Orientation property. But, as its name suggests, rather than allow its children to be arranged beyond its bounds, it overlaps its children when the available space is less than the desired space. In this case, children are still given the same size as they are given in SimpleStackPanel, but their locations are evenly "compressed" to completely fill the width or height (depending on Orientation) of the panel. When OverlapPanel is given more space than needed to stack its children, it stretches its children to (again) completely fill the dimension of stacking. Figure 21.1 shows OverlapPanel in action, used in the following Window:

```
<Window x:Class="CustomPanels.OverlapPanelWindow"
        xmlns="http://schemas.microsoft.com/winfx/2006/xaml/presentation"
        xmlns:x="http://schemas.microsoft.com/winfx/2006/xaml"
        xmlns:local="clr-namespace:CustomPanels"
        Title="Four Buttons in an OverlapPanel">
  <local:OverlapPanel>
    <Button FontSize="40" Content="1" Background="Red"/>
    <Button FontSize="40" Content="2" Background="Orange"/>
    <Button FontSize="40" Content="3" Background="Yellow"/>
    <Button FontSize="40" Content="4" Background="Lime"/>
  </local:OverlapPanel>
</Window>
```

With its evenly distributed overlapping and stretching behavior, OverlapPanel behaves somewhat like a single-column (or single-row) Grid, where each child is in its own *-sized cell. The main difference is that it allows each child to render outside its effective "cell," which doesn't happen in a Grid cell unless each child is wrapped in a Canvas. But when you wrap an element in a Canvas, you lose the stretching behavior. In Figure 21.1, you can't tell whether the Buttons are truly overlapping or just cropped, but you can tell the difference with nonrectangular elements or, in the case of Figure 21.2, translucent elements.

Overlapping when space is less than desired

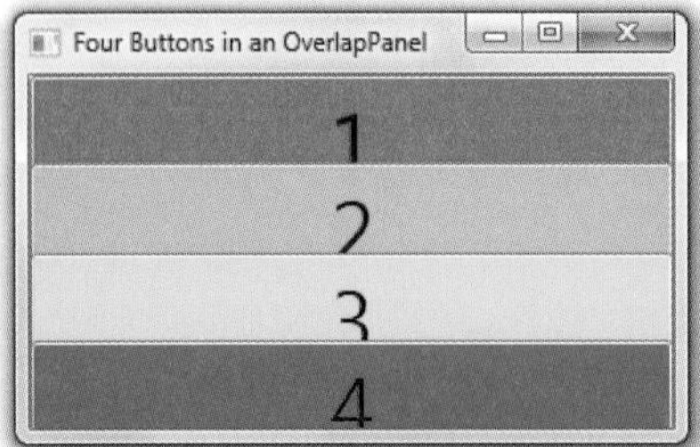

Stretching when space is more than desired

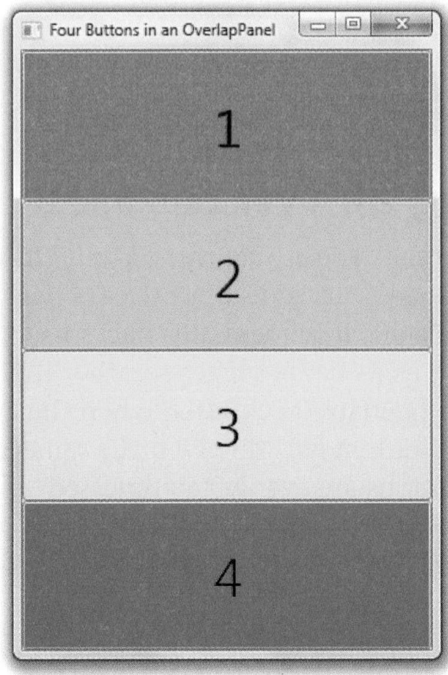

FIGURE 21.1 `OverlapPanel` containing four `Buttons` inside a `Window` at different sizes.

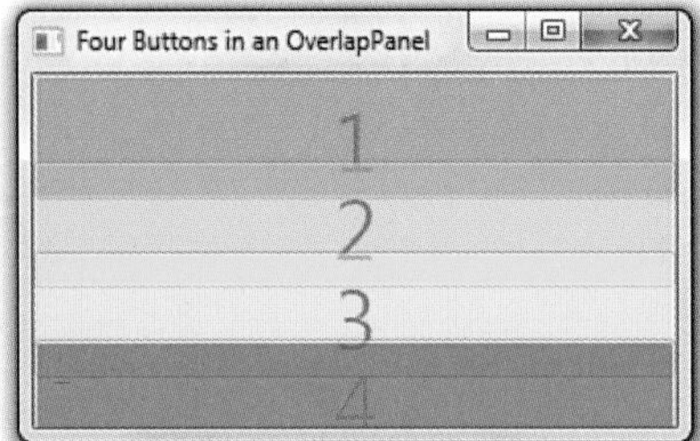

FIGURE 21.2 Giving the `Buttons` in Figure 21.1 an `Opacity` of `.5` reveals that they are truly overlapping and not simply cropped.

Listing 21.3 contains the entire implementation of `OverlapPanel` and uses boldface for the code that differs from `SimpleStackPanel` from Listing 21.2.

LISTING 21.3 `OverlapPanel.cs`—An Updated `SimpleStackPanel` That Either Overlaps or Stretches Children

```
using System;
using System.Windows;
using System.Windows.Controls;

namespace CustomPanels
{
```

LISTING 21.3 Continued

```
public class OverlapPanel : Panel
{
  double _totalChildrenSize = 0;

  // The direction of stacking
  public static readonly DependencyProperty OrientationProperty =
    DependencyProperty.Register("Orientation", typeof(Orientation),
    typeof(OverlapPanel), new FrameworkPropertyMetadata(Orientation.Vertical,
    FrameworkPropertyMetadataOptions.AffectsMeasure));

  public Orientation Orientation
  {
    get { return (Orientation)GetValue(OrientationProperty); }
    set { SetValue(OrientationProperty, value); }
  }

  protected override Size MeasureOverride(Size availableSize)
  {
    Size desiredSize = new Size();

    foreach (UIElement child in this.Children)
    {
      if (child != null)
      {
        // See how big each child wants to be given all our available space
        child.Measure(availableSize);

        // Our desired size is the sum of child sizes in the direction of
        // stacking, and the size of the largest child in the other direction
        if (Orientation == Orientation.Vertical)
        {
          desiredSize.Width = Math.Max(desiredSize.Width,
                                       child.DesiredSize.Width);
          desiredSize.Height += child.DesiredSize.Height;
        }
        else
        {
          desiredSize.Height = Math.Max(desiredSize.Height,
                                        child.DesiredSize.Height);
          desiredSize.Width += child.DesiredSize.Width;
        }
      }
    }
```

LISTING 21.3 Continued

```
      _totalChildrenSize = (Orientation == Orientation.Vertical ?
                            desiredSize.Height : desiredSize.Width);

      return desiredSize;
    }

    protected override Size ArrangeOverride(Size finalSize)
    {
      double offset = 0;
      double overlap = 0;

      // Figure out the amount of overlap by seeing how much less space
      // we got than desired, and divide it equally among children.
      if (Orientation == Orientation.Vertical)
      {
        if (finalSize.Height > _totalChildrenSize)
          // If we're given more than _totalChildrenSize, the negative overlap
          // represents how much the layout should stretch
          overlap = (_totalChildrenSize - finalSize.Height) /
                    this.Children.Count;
        else
          // In this case, this.DesiredSize gives us the actual smaller size
          overlap = (_totalChildrenSize - this.DesiredSize.Height) /
                    this.Children.Count;
      }
      else
      {
        if (finalSize.Width > _totalChildrenSize)
          // If we're given more than _totalChildrenSize, the negative overlap
          // represents how much the layout should stretch
          overlap = (_totalChildrenSize - finalSize.Width) /
                    this.Children.Count;
        else
          // In this case, this.DesiredSize gives us the actual smaller size
          overlap = (_totalChildrenSize - this.DesiredSize.Width) /
                    this.Children.Count;
      }

      foreach (UIElement child in this.Children)
      {
        if (child != null)
        {
          if (Orientation == Orientation.Vertical)
          {
```

LISTING 21.3 Continued

```
            // The offset moves the child down the stack.
            // Give the child all our width, but as much height as it desires
            // or more if there is negative overlap.
            child.Arrange(new Rect(0, offset, finalSize.Width,
              child.DesiredSize.Height + (overlap > 0 ? 0 : -overlap)));

            // Update the offset for the next child
            offset += (child.DesiredSize.Height - overlap);
          }
          else
          {
            // The offset moves the child down the stack.
            // Give the child all our height, but as much width as it desires
            // or more if there is negative overlap.
            child.Arrange(new Rect(offset, 0,
              child.DesiredSize.Width + (overlap > 0 ? 0 : -overlap),
              finalSize.Height));

            // Update the offset for the next child
            offset += (child.DesiredSize.Width - overlap);
          }
        }
      }

      // Fill all the space given
      return finalSize;
    }
  }
}
```

The only difference between OverlapPanel's MeasureOverride and SimpleStackPanel's MeasureOverride is that OverlapPanel doesn't give each child infinite space in the direction of stacking; instead, it gives the availableSize in both dimensions. That's because this panel tries to compress its children to fit in its bounds when they are too big. It also captures the total length of its children in the dimension of stacking (which is also its desired size in that dimension) in a separate _totalChildrenSize variable to be used by ArrangeOverride.

In ArrangeOverride, the difference between the available space and desired space is determined in order to calculate a proper overlap value that can be subtracted from the offset when each child is arranged. A positive overlap value indicates how many logical pixels of overlap there are between each child, and a negative overlap indicates how many logical pixels of additional space each child is given.

Notice the odd-looking expression added to the stacking dimension length in each call to `child.Arrange`:

```
(overlap > 0 ? 0 : -overlap)
```

This adds the absolute value of `overlap` to the size of the child, but only when `overlap` is negative. This is necessary to enable the children to stretch when they are spaced out further than their natural lengths, as seen in Figure 21.1. Without adding this value, the stretched `Buttons` would appear as they do in Figure 21.3.

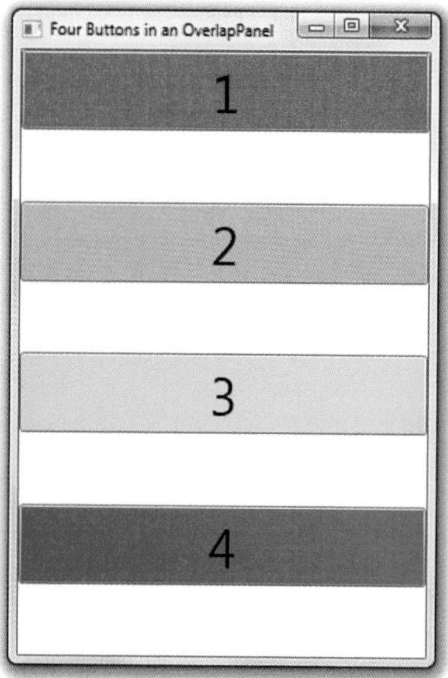

FIGURE 21.3 How `OverflowPanel` would behave if it didn't give its children the gift of extra space in the direction of stacking.

Note that the stretching in Figure 21.1 happens only because of `Button`'s default `VerticalAlignment` of `Stretch`. If each `Button` were marked with a `VerticalAlignment` of `Top`, then the correct implementation of `OverlapPanel` would still give the result shown in Figure 21.3. But that's fine; it's the panel's job to indicate how much space each child is really given, and it's each child's decision whether it wants to stretch to fill that space or align with certain edges of it.

Creating a `FanCanvas`

The final custom panel is a bit unusual and special purpose. `FanCanvas` arranges its children in a fan shape. The killer application for such a panel is to arrange playing cards like the ones from the previous chapter. It could also be interesting for other purposes. `FanCanvas` made an appearance in Chapter 10, "Items Controls," as the items panel for a `ListBox` that displays photos. Listing 21.4 contains the entire implementation of `FanCanvas`.

LISTING 21.4 FanCanvas.cs—The Implementation of FanCanvas

```
using System;
using System.Windows;
using System.Windows.Controls;
using System.Windows.Media;

namespace CustomPanels
{
  public class FanCanvas : Panel
  {
    public static readonly DependencyProperty OrientationProperty =
      DependencyProperty.Register("Orientation", typeof(Orientation),
      typeof(FanCanvas), new FrameworkPropertyMetadata(Orientation.Horizontal,
      FrameworkPropertyMetadataOptions.AffectsArrange));


    public static readonly DependencyProperty SpacingProperty =
      DependencyProperty.Register("Spacing", typeof(double),
      typeof(FanCanvas), new FrameworkPropertyMetadata(10d,
      FrameworkPropertyMetadataOptions.AffectsArrange));

    public static readonly DependencyProperty AngleIncrementProperty =
      DependencyProperty.Register("AngleIncrement", typeof(double),
      typeof(FanCanvas), new FrameworkPropertyMetadata(10d,
      FrameworkPropertyMetadataOptions.AffectsArrange));

    public Orientation Orientation
    {
      get { return (Orientation)GetValue(OrientationProperty); }
      set { SetValue(OrientationProperty, value); }
    }

    public double Spacing
    {
      get { return (double)GetValue(SpacingProperty); }
      set { SetValue(SpacingProperty, value); }
    }


    public double AngleIncrement
    {
      get { return (double)GetValue(AngleIncrementProperty); }
      set { SetValue(AngleIncrementProperty, value); }
    }

    protected override Size MeasureOverride(Size availableSize)
```

LISTING 21.4 Continued

```
  {
    foreach (UIElement child in this.Children)
    {
      // Give each child all the space it wants
      if (child != null)
        child.Measure(new Size(Double.PositiveInfinity,
                               Double.PositiveInfinity));
    }

    // The FanCanvas itself needs no space, just like SimpleCanvas
    return new Size(0, 0);
  }

  protected override Size ArrangeOverride(Size finalSize)
  {
    // Center the children
    Point location = new Point(0,0);
    double angle = GetStartingAngle();

    foreach (UIElement child in this.Children)
    {
      if (child != null)
      {
        // Give the child its desired size
        child.Arrange(new Rect(location, child.DesiredSize));

        // WARNING: Overwrite any RenderTransform with one that
        //          arranges children in the fan shape
        child.RenderTransform = new RotateTransform(angle,
          child.RenderSize.Width / 2, child.RenderSize.Height);

        // Update the offset and angle for the next child
        if (Orientation == Orientation.Vertical)
          location.Y += Spacing;
        else
          location.X += Spacing;

        angle += AngleIncrement;
      }
    }

    // Fill all the space given
    return finalSize;
  }
```

LISTING 21.4 Continued

```
    double GetStartingAngle()
    {
      double angle;

      if (this.Children.Count % 2 != 0)
        // Odd, so the middle child will have angle == 0
        angle = -AngleIncrement * (this.Children.Count / 2);
      else
        // Even, so the middle two children will be half of
        // the AngleIncrement on either side of 0
        angle = -AngleIncrement * (this.Children.Count / 2) + AngleIncrement / 2;

      // Rotate 90 degrees if vertical
      if (Orientation == Orientation.Vertical)
        angle += 90;

      return angle;
    }
  }
}
```

FanCanvas shares some similarities with each of the three previous panels. FanCanvas is similar to SimpleStackPanel and OverflowPanel in that children are basically stacked in one dimension. FanCanvas defines an Orientation dependency property like the others, although it defaults to Horizontal and is marked AffectsArrange instead of AffectsMeasure. Changes to Orientation don't affect the measure pass because of a difference in FanCanvas's MeasureOverride implementation that makes it agnostic to Orientation.

FanCanvas defines two more dependency properties that control the amount of fanning done. Spacing controls how far children are spread apart in terms of logical pixels. It's like the overlap variable in OverlapPanel, except that it's the amount of *non*overlap. AngleIncrement controls how much each child is rotated compared to the previous child. It is expressed in terms of degrees. Both Spacing and AngleIncrement have a default value of 10 and, like Orientation, affect only the arrange pass. The fact that these are dependency properties opens the door to performing some cool animations with this panel.

FanCanvas is called a "Canvas" mainly because its MeasureOverride implementation is identical to Canvas (and SimpleCanvas earlier in this chapter). It tells each child to take all the space it wants, and then it tells its parent that it doesn't require any space for itself (again because its children do not get clipped to its bounds unless ClipToBounds is set to true). That's why measurement is Orientation agnostic; the logic doesn't care in which direction the stacking is performed. The "Canvas" designation also helps to justify its relatively simplistic layout support! A better implementation would account for the exact angles and spacing of the children to figure out an appropriate bounding box for its own desired size. Instead, the consumer of `FanCanvas` likely needs to give it an explicit size and appropriate `Margin` in order to get the exact results desired.

The logic in `ArrangeOverride` is pretty close to `ArrangeOverride` in `SimpleStackPanel`, aside from the fact that it rotates each child with a `RenderTransform` that uses an ever-increasing angle. The starting angle is determined by `GetStartingAngle`, which ensures that the middle child is unrotated or, if there are an even number of children, the middle two children evenly straddle the unrotated angle (0° when `Horizontal` or 90° when `Vertical`).

Changing properties on the children (such as `RenderTransform`) is generally not a good thing for a panel to do. It can cause confusion when child properties that were already set by the consumer don't end up working, and it can break programmatic assumptions made by the consuming code. Another approach would be to define and use a `FanCanvasItem` content control that implicitly contains each child so you can apply the transforms to these instead. This is normally done for items controls, however, rather than panels. Despite its limitations, this version of `FanCanvas` works perfectly well for limited reuse.

Figure 21.4 shows `FanCanvas` in action with instances of the `PlayingCard` custom control from the previous chapter. Lots of interesting patterns can be created by adjusting the `Spacing` and `AngleIncrement` properties!

`Spacing=10, AngleIncrement=10` (default)

`Spacing=30, AngleIncrement=10`

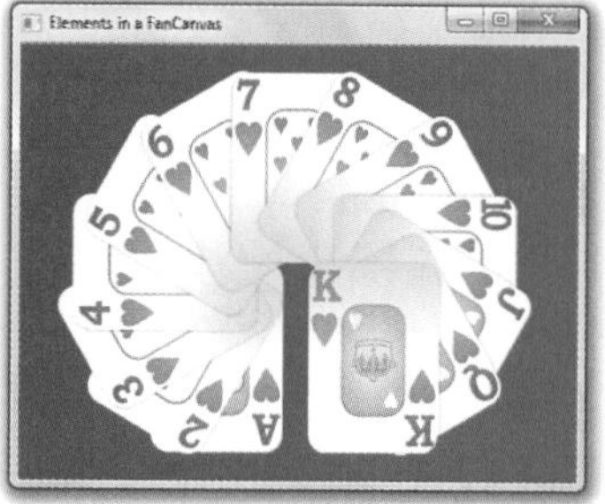

`Spacing=10, AngleIncrement=30`

`Spacing=0, AngleIncrement=30`

FIGURE 21.4 Using `FanCanvas` with the previous chapter's `PlayingCard` control.

Summary

This chapter digs into the mechanism used by child elements and parent panels—how they compromise to give great results in a wide variety of situations. Implementing your own custom panels is considered an advanced topic only because it's rare that you would need to do so. As you've seen, custom panels are pretty easy to write. Because of the measure/arrange protocol and all the work automatically handled by WPF, existing controls can be placed inside brand-new custom panels, and they still behave very reasonably.

As with creating a custom control, you should spend a little time determining the appropriate base class for a custom panel. The choices for panels are easy, however. Most of the time, as with the panels in this chapter, it makes sense to simply derive from `Panel`. If you plan on supporting user interface virtualization, you should derive from `VirtualizingPanel`, the abstract base class of `VirtualizingStackPanel`. Otherwise, it could be handy to derive from a different `Panel` subclass (such as `Canvas` or `DockPanel`), especially if you plan on supporting the same set of attached properties that these classes define.

Symbols/Numbers

A

B

How can we make this index more useful? Email us at indexes@samspublishing.com

C

D

How can we make this index more useful? Email us at indexes@samspublishing.com

E

G

H

I

J

How can we make this index more useful? Email us at indexes@samspublishing.com

K

L

M

N

P

Q

R

S

U

V

W

X

Y-Z

How can we make this index more useful? Email us at indexes@samspublishing.com